Introduction to the [illegible]ian and Serbian Language

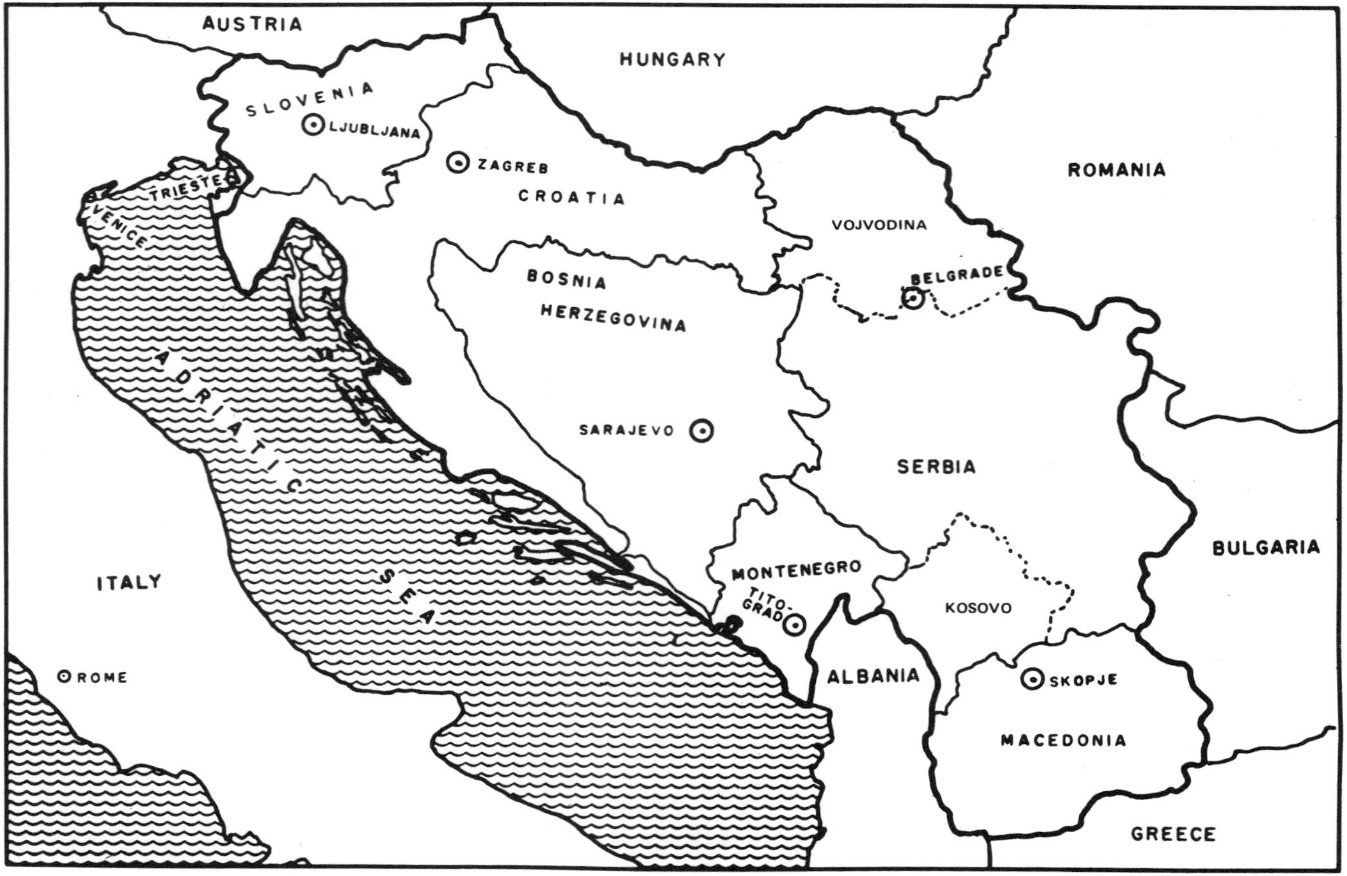
AUSTRIA
HUNGARY
ROMANIA
SLOVENIA
LJUBLJANA
ZAGREB
CROATIA
TRIESTE
VENICE
VOJVODINA
BOSNIA
HERZEGOVINA
BELGRADE
ADRIATIC
SARAJEVO
SERBIA
BULGARIA
MONTENEGRO
TITO-GRAD
ITALY
SEA
KOSOVO
ROME
ALBANIA
SKOPJE
MACEDONIA
GREECE

Introduction to the Croatian and Serbian Language

Revised Edition

Thomas F. Magner

The Pennsylvania State University Press
University Park, Pennsylvania

Library of Congress Cataloging-in-Publication Data

Magner, Thomas F.

Introduction to the Croatian and Serbian language /
Thomas F. Magner. — Rev. ed.
p. cm.

ISBN 0-271-00685-4 (cloth)
ISBN 0-271-01536-5 (paper)
1. Serbo-Croatian language—Grammar—1950– I. Title.
PG1231.M26 1991
491.8'282421—dc20 89–37132

It is the policy of The Pennsylvania State University Press to use acid-free paper for the first printing of all clothbound books. Publications on uncoated stock satisfy the minimum requirements of American National Standard for Information Sciences—Permanence of Paper for Printed Library Materials, ANSI Z39.48–1984.

First paperback, 1991
Tenth printing, 2004

CONTENTS

ADVICE TO STUDENTS

Do not be discouraged by the seeming complexity of the Croatian and Serbian language (Cr&S) or by the amount of material in this textbook. If you absorb all the book's material in a year, I would be the first to say *Bravo*! But it is unrealistic to expect such a feat. Unlike the situation for languages like French, German, Russian, and Spanish, there are not enough students of Cr&S to justify the publication of graded readers, reference manuals, and the like. So, think of this book as a resource for study over a number of years and thereafter as a reference grammar and dictionary.

There are grammatical explanations in the first several lessons, but the bulk of the grammar is contained in a separate section. That is not ideal for lesson-by-lesson study, but it is an advantage in later study, since, with the help of the Index, you can easily locate explanations for specific points. The Glossary, or small dictionary, is at the end of the book, just before the Index. When you are studying a particular reading text, I recommend that you make a photocopy of that text so that you can then use the Glossary with text in hand, saving you from having to move back and forth in the book.

On the last page of this book you will find information about acquiring tape recordings of the various lessons. If you have access to a tape recorder and also to a native, educated Croat or Serb, you may simply wish to record that person articulating the various conversations or reading texts. Ask the native speaker to speak slowly at first so that you will become familiar with nuances of pronunciation, then request the speaker to read other lessons in a normal, colloquial tempo. It would also be helpful to have the native speaker articulate the examples given for various Cr&S sounds in the "Pronunciation" section of the grammar (see Index).

If you have previously studied Russian, your knowledge of that language will be helpful in approaching Cr&S. For one thing, it will be easier for you to master Serbian Cyrillic, once you have learned the small differences between Serbian Cyrillic and Russian Cyrillic. But be careful: Similarities are not identities. Both Russian and Cr&S have the words **sestra**, "sister," and **mikroskop**, "microscope," but in Russian the stress accent is on the final syllable, that is, **sestrá** and **mikroskóp**, while in Cr&S, which as a general rule *never* has an accent on a final syllable, the accentuation would be **sèstra** and **mikròskop**. And what language scholars call "false friends," that is, words that look alike but have quite different meanings, can cause confusion and sometimes embarrassment. For example, in Russian **urók** and **ponós** mean "lesson" and "diarrhea," respectively; in Cr&S, however, **ùrok** means "a spell" or "a charm," while **pònos** means "pride."

Unlike Russian and English, Cr&S has no reduced vowels; every vowel in Cr&S **gòvorite**, "you speak," is pronounced as spelled, while in Russian **vi govoríte** only the accented vowel is pronounced as spelled. You will notice that it is not necessary to use the pronoun in Cr&S, since pronouns are used only for emphasis: **vi govorite**, "*you* speak." So while a knowledge of Russian can be helpful, don't lean on it too heavily; Cr&S and Russian are distinct languages.

To all students, regardless of background or previous foreign-language study, I wish you success and enjoyment in your study of the fascinating Croatian and Serbian language.

Dr. Thomas F. Magner

PRVA LEKCIJA

Ràzgovor

Croatian

1. Dòbar dán.
2. Kàko ste?
3. Hvála, dòbro. A ví?
4. I já sam dòbro.
5. Já sam Péro Stánić.
6. Kàko se ví zòvete?
7. Zòvem se Dùnja Pàvlović.
8. Tkò je tá djèvojka, Péro?
9. Tó je mòja sèstra.
10. Òna se zòve Vèsna.
11. Òna je lijèpa djèvojka.
12. Jè li ùdata?
13. Jèst. Òna je sàda gòspođa Reilly.
14. Do viđénja, Péro.
15. Do viđénja, Dùnja.

Serbian

1. Dòbar dán.
2. Kàko ste?
3. Hvála, dòbro. A ví?
4. I já sam dòbro.
5. Já sam Péro Stánić.
6. Kàko se ví zòvete?
7. Zòvem se Dùnja Pàvlović.
8. Kò je tá dèvojka, Péro?
9. Tó je mòja sèstra.
10. Òna se zòve Vèsna.
11. Òna je lèpa dèvojka.
12. Dà li je ùdata?
13. Jèste. Òna je sàda gòspođa Rajli.
14. Do viđénja, Péro.
15. Do viđénja, Dùnja.

SVÀKI POČÉTAK JE TÉŽAK.

CONVERSATION—1. Good day. 2. How are you? 3. Fine, thanks. And you? 4. I'm fine, too. 5. My name is Pero Stanić (literally: I am Pero Stanić). 6. What's your name? 7. My name is Dunja Pavlović. 8. Who is that girl, Pero? 9. That's my sister. 10. Her name is Vesna. 11. She's a good-looking girl. 12. Is she married? 13. Yes. Now she's Mrs. Reilly. 14. Goodbye, Pero. 15. Goodbye, Dunja.

Sayings and Proverbs. Quite a few Yugoslav sayings and proverbs are scattered throughout this book. For some of them a literal translation is sufficient to render the point of the saying; for example, the saying presented above is quite clear in a literal rendition: "Every beginning is difficult." Others make little or no sense when translated literally but may be represented by an equivalent expression in English; **U làži su kràtke nòge** means literally "In a lie there are short legs" but is used by Croats and Serbs in situations where the English-speaker might say "The truth will out." Sufficient information about meaning will be provided in the various word lists and the general glossary so that the reader will be able to determine the point of these sayings and then to render the general meaning by an English expression.

Máli rjèčnik/rèčnik	**Vocabulary**
a	and, but
dán	day
dèvojka (S.)	girl, young woman
djèvojka (Cr.)	girl, young woman
dòbar, dȍbro, dòbra *adj.**	good
dòbro *adv.*	well, fine
gòspođa	Mrs., lady, madam
hvála	thanks
ìme	name
já	I
já sam	I am
je	is [unemphatic]
jèst (Cr.)	yes, is [emphatic, contrasting with unemphatic *je*]
jèste (S.)	yes, is [emphatic; unemphatic *je*]
kàko	how
kò (S.)	who
lèkcija	lesson
lép, lépo, lépa (S.)	beautiful, good-looking
li	[indicates a question]
lìjep, lijèpo, lijèpa (Cr.)	beautiful, good-looking
mlád, mládo, mláda	young
mój, mòje, mòja	my
nìje	is not, isn't
ón, òno, òna	he, it, she
počétak	beginning
pŕvi, pŕvo, pŕva	first
ràzgovor	conversation
Rajli	[Serbian phonetic spelling for Reilly]
sàda	now
sam	am [unemphatic]
se	-self (myself, himself, herself, etc.)
sèstra	sister
ste	you are [unemphatic]
svàki	every, each
táj, tó, tá	that, that one
tó je	that's
téžak, téško, téška	difficult, heavy

***dobar** is masculine singular, **dobro** is neuter singular, while **dobra** is feminine singular. The neuter form will usually be given after the masculine because in most of the other cases the masculine and neuter forms are identical.

tkò (Cr.)	who
ùdata *fem. adj.*	married [for women; òženjen for men]
vèžba (S.)	exercise
vjèžba (Cr.)	exercise
ví	you
ví se zòvete	you are named
ví ste	you are
viđénje	meeting, seeing
do *prep.*	until, up to
do viđénja	goodbye
zòve se	he/she is named
zòvem se	my name is, I am named/called
žèna	woman, wife

Working with the Sentences. Each of the thirty lessons begins with a series of related sentences in the Croatian and Serbian language. A more or less literal translation of the sentences into English then follows. This material can be used in a variety of ways. For example, two or more students may use the Cr&S sentences as material for a dialogue, putting themselves into the particular situation and articulating the model sentences. In the beginning students will probably not be able to change the sentences very much, but later on, as their knowledge of the grammar increases, they will be able to adjust the model sentence to their own needs. Another use would be to utilize the sentences for translation exercises, going either from the Cr&S sentences to English or from the English sentences to their Cr&S equivalents.

Grammar. In this textbook explanations of various features of Cr&S grammar are presented in one part of this book. The student is advised to spend some time browsing through this section in order to get an idea of the contents and their locations. The Index will also be helpful in providing the location of a particular item. In the first several lessons the student will be asked to study relevant grammatical explanations; in later lessons it is hoped that the student will be able to search out necessary explanations.

Grammar for Lesson I. Read and study the following items: letters and sounds, pronunciation, accent, case, nouns and gender, nominative case, the present tense of the verb "to be."

vjèžba/vèžba* I (exercise I)

Translate the following conversation into Cr&S.

*The form to the left of the slash mark is the standard Croatian form; the one to the right is the standard Serbian form.

1. Good day.
2. My name is ________ ________. (Use your name.)
3. What's your name?
4. My name is ________ ________. (Name of a friend.)
5. That's my brother.
6. His name is Peter. (Pètar is Peter)
7. Who is that young girl?
8. That's Miss Petrović. (gòspođica for Miss)
9. She's a good-looking girl.
10. Goodbye. Goodbye.

vjèžba/vèžba II

The following patterns may be extended by using the nouns given below.

Tkò/Kò je òvo?	Who is this?
Òvo je nástavnik.	This is a teacher.
Òvo nìje nástavnik.	This is not a teacher.
Òvo je mój nástavnik.	This is my teacher.
Tkò/Kò je tó?	Who is that?
Tȍ je bràt.	That's the brother.
Tȍ je mój bràt.	That's my brother.
Tȍ nìje mój bràt.	That's not my brother.

Nouns:

bràt	brother	sèstra	sister
mòmak	young man, lad	djèvojka/ dèvojka	girl, young woman
muškárac	man, male		
nástavnik	teacher	žèna	woman, wife
òtac	father	nástavnica	teacher (female)
sín	son	májka	mother
stùdent	student	kćérka, ćérka	daughter
ùčenik	pupil	stùdentica/ stùdentkinja	student (female)
čòvjek/čòvek	man, person		
		ùčenica	pupil (female)

vjèžba/vèžba III

Odgovòrite na slijèdeća/slédeća pítanja. (Answer the following questions.)

1. Kàko se zòvete?
2. (Cr.) Tkò je tá djèvojka?
   (S.) Kò je tá dèvojka?
3. Kàko se zòve?

4. Jè li ùdata?
5. Kàko se sàda zòve?

Personal Pronouns. Cr&S uses personal pronouns for emphasis or where (in the third person, for example) there might be some ambiguity. Thus, English "I am speaking," but Cr&S **gòvorim**; the addition of the personal pronoun, as in **já gòvorim**, would mean "*I* am the one speaking." If the reference is clear in the third person, one would say, for example, **Kako se zove?** instead of **Kako se on zove?** or **Kako se ona zove?** In sentence 4 below, "she" is being emphasized.

vjèžba/vèžba IV

Pòpunite izòstavljene rìječi/réči. (Put in the missing words.)
1. Dùnja ________djèvojka/dèvojka.
2. (Cr.) ________je lijèpa djèvojka.
   (S.) ________je lépa dèvojka.
3. Jè li ________ùdata? (use woman's name)
4. ________se òna sàda zòve?
5. Svàki ________je téžak.

Collateral Reading. The student who is not familiar with Yugoslavia, the land where Cr&S is spoken, will profit from reading about the country in any of the encyclopedias available in the local library. Subject headings for relevant texts would include Yugoslavia, Serbo-Croatian Language,* Bosnia and Herzegovina,† Croatia, Dalmatia, Montenegro, and Serbia.

Svakòdnevni ìzrazi	**Everyday Expressions**
zdràvo	greetings, hello, goodbye
dòbar dán	good day
dòbro jùtro	good morning

*The term "Serbo-Croatian" or "Serbocroatian" is the usual designation in English for this language. This textbook separates the two parts of that term (Serbian, Croatian) and puts them in alphabetical order to indicate that equal treatment will be given to both variants of the language; thus Cr&S or the Croatian and Serbian language. In Yugoslavia the language is referred to as **hr̀vatski ili sr̀pski jèzik**, that is, Croatian or Serbian language, or as **sr̀pski ili hr̀vatski jèzik**, the Serbian or Croatian language. In practice, however, speakers of the language simply refer to it as **hr̀vatski** or **sr̀pski**, depending on their ethnic affiliation.

† Also spelled Hercegovina.

dòbar vèče* (S.)	good evening
dòbar vèčer* (Cr.)	good evening
dòbro dòšli	welcome
làku nóć	good night
do viđénja	goodbye
zbògom	goodbye [literally, with God]
mòje poštovánje	my respects, regards [formal greeting or departure formula]
srètan (Cr.) pút	Bon voyage! Have a good trip!
srèćan (S.) pút	Bon voyage! Have a good trip!

*Also possible are **dòbro vèče** and **dòbra vèčer**.

DRUGA LEKCIJA

Ràzgovor (hȑvatski)

1. Štò rádite, Péro?
2. Ùčim hȑvatski, Dùnja.
3. Zàšto? Pa ví vèć gòvorite hȑvatski.
4. Dà. Gòvorim màlo hȑvatski, ali bih htìo takóđer písati i čìtati hȑvatski.
5. Jè li tó vàša knjìga?
6. Dà. Ȍvo je mòja knjìga za hȑvatski.
7. A tàmo je mój rjèčnik.
8. Tȍ je neòbična abecéda, Péro.
9. Mòže bìti, ali hȑvatska abecéda vȑlo je sistèmatska.
10. Svàki glás ìma sàmo jèdno slòvo.
11. Zbog tóga nìje téško písati hȑvatski.
12. Dà. Nìje téško, ako vèć znáte govòriti hȑvatski.
13. Tàko je, Dùnja.

Ràzgovor (sȑpski)

1. Štà rádite, Péro?
2. Ùčim sȑpski, Dùnja.
3. Zàšto? Pa ví vèć gòvorite sȑpski.
4. Dà. Gòvorim màlo sȑpski, ali bih htèo takóđe da pìšem i čìtam sȑpski.
5. Dà li je tó vàša knjìga?
6. Dà. Ȍvo je mòja knjìga za sȑpski.
7. A tàmo je mój rèčnik.
8. Tȍ je neòbična àzbuka, Péro.
9. Mòže bìti, ali sȑpska àzbuka vȑlo je sistèmatska.
10. Svàki glás ìma sàmo jèdno slòvo.
11. Zbog tóga nìje téško písati sȑpski.
12. Dà. Nìje téško, ako vèć znáte da gòvorite sȑpski.
13. Tàko je, Dùnja.

ČÌTANJE JE PÚT DO ZNÁNJA.

CONVERSATION—1. What are you doing, Pero? 2. I'm studying Croatian/Serbian, Dunja. 3. Why? You already speak Croatian/Serbian. 4. Yes, I speak a little Croatian/Serbian, but I'd also like to write and read Croatian/Serbian. 5. Is that your book? 6. Yes. This is my Croatian/Serbian book. 7. And there's my dictionary. 8. That's an unusual alphabet, Pero. 9. Perhaps, but the Croatian/Serbian alphabet is very systematic. 10. Every sound has only one letter. 11. Because of that, it's not difficult to write Croatian/Serbian. 12. Yes. It's not difficult, if you already know how to speak Croatian/Serbian. 13. That's right, Dunja.

Pòslovica ("proverb, saying"). What is its literal meaning? Is there an equivalent saying in English?

Máli rjèčnik/rèčnik	**Vocabulary**
abecéda (Cr.)	alphabet
àko	if
àli	but
àzbuka (S.)	alphabet
bih	I would
bìti	to be
čìtanje	reading
čìtati	to read
čìtam	I read, am reading
čìtate	you read, are reading
dà	yes
glás	sound, voice
govòriti	to speak
gòvorim	I speak, am speaking
gòvorite	you speak, are speaking
hȑvatski *adj.*	Croatian
hȑvatski *adv.*	in Croatian
hrvatskosȑpski	Serbo-Croatian [lit. Croato-Serbian]
htèo bih (S.)	I would like
htìo bih (Cr.)	I would like
i	and
jè li	is . . . [?]
jèdan, jèdno, jèdna	one
jèzik	language, tongue
knjìga	book
máli *adj.*	small
màlo *adv.*	a little
mòže bìti	maybe, perhaps
neòbičan, -čno, -čna	unusual
òvo je	this is
pa	and, also
Pávle, Pàvao	Paul
písati	to write
píšem	I write, am writing
píšete	you write, are writing
pút	road, time
ráditi	to work, to do
rádim	I work, am working
rádite	you work, are working
sàmo *adv.*	only
sistèmatski *adj.*	systematic
slòvo	letter (of alphabet)

sȑpski *adj.*	Serbian
sȑpski *adv.*	in Serbian
srpskohȑvatski	Serbo-Croatian
Stánko	Stan
svàki	each, every
štà (S.)	what
štò (Cr.)	what
tàko	thus, so
takóđe (S.)	also
takóđer (Cr.)	also
téško *adv.*	difficult
toga (G of to)	of that
tvój, tvòje, tvòja	your
ùčiti	to study
ùčim	I study, am studying
ùčite	you study, are studying
vèć	already
vȑlo	very
za *prep.*	for
zàšto	why
zbog *prep.*	because (of)
znánje	knowledge
znàti	to know
znám	I know
znáte	you know

Pronunciation

The native speaker of English must be careful to pronounce each syllable of Cr&S distinctly and not slur unaccented syllables. In a sentence such as **Dòbro gòvorite èngleski**, "You speak English well," the student must take pains to maintain the proper vowel quality in all syllables. Thus, the final **e** in **govorite** should be pronounced like the vowel in English *bet* and not like the vowel sound in English *bee*. Here are some Cr&S words for pronunciation practice.

dòista	indeed	žèni	to a woman
ròsa	dew	žèno	woman!
pòlje	field	jède	he eats
pòlja	fields	jèdi	eat
pòezija	poetry	jèdemo	we eat
legitimácija	identity card	jèdimo	let us eat
žèna	woman	mjèriti/mèriti	to measure
žène	women	mjèrite/mèrite	you measure

Grammar for Lesson II. Read and study the following: Differences between Croatian and Serbian, gender and agreement, "you" and "you," adjectives, possessive adjectives, present tense of verbs, questions.

vježba/vežba I

Prevèdite na hȑvatski ili sȑpski. (Translate into Croatian or Serbian)

1. What's Pero doing?
2. He's studying Croatian/Serbian.
3. I speak Croatian/Serbian.
4. But I'd also like to read and write Croatian/Serbian.
5. Where is your dictionary, Pero?
6. It's not difficult to read and write Croatian/Serbian.
7. Every beginning is difficult.
8. Who is your teacher?
9. Her name is Dunja Dùplančić.
10. Do you know where Yugoslavia is?

vježba/vežba II

Slijèdeća/Slédeća pítanja i òdgovori mògu se prošíriti dátim ìmenicama. (The following question and answer patterns may be extended by using the nouns given below.)

Štò/Štà je òvo?	What is this?
Òvo je knjìga.	This is a book.
Jè li òvo knjìga?	Is this a book?
Dà li je òvo knjìga?	Is this a book?
Dà, òvo je knjìga.	Yes, it's a book.
Nè, òvo nìje knjìga.	No, this isn't a book.
Nè, òvo nìje knjìga, òvo je kárta.	No, this isn't a book, this is a map.
Što/Štà je tó?	What is that?
Tó je knjìga.	That is a book.
Jè li tó prózor?	Is that a window?
Dà li je tó prózor?	Is that a window?
Dà, tó je prózor.	Yes, that's a window.
Nè, tó nìje prózor	No, that's not a window.
Nè, tó nìje prózor, tó je radìjator.	No, that's not a window, that's a radiator.

Some examples:

Jè li òvo vàša òlovka?	Jè li tó vàš ùdžbenik?
Dà li je òvo vàša òlovka?	Dà li je tó vàš ùdžbenik?
Dà, òvo je mòja òlovka.	Dà, tó je mój ùdžbenik.
Nè, òvo nìje mòja òlovka.	Nè, tó nìje mój ùdžbenik.

a	and, but
Amerikánac	American (male)
Amerikánka	American (female)
Beògrad	Belgrade, capital city of Serbia and Yugoslavia
dèda (S.)	grandfather
djèd (Cr.)	grandfather
Hȑvat	Croat (male)
Hrvàtica	Croat (female)
Hȑvatska	Croatia
i	also, too
iz (prep. with G)	from
Jugoslávija	Yugoslavia
kàko	how
kòd (prep. with G)	at
kòd kuće	at home
Králjevo	a city S of Belgrade
kȑv (fem. noun)	blood
kùća	house
màgarac	donkey
májka	mother
màma	mom
nà žalost	unfortunately
nìje	isn't
Nòvi Sád	a large city NW of Belgrade
òdakle	from where, whence
Òsijek	a city in Slavonia
òtac, G òca	father
rázlika	difference
razùmeti (S.)	to understand
razùmem (S.)	I understand
razùmete (S.)	you understand
razùmjeti (Cr.)	to understand
razùmijem (Cr.)	I understand
razùmijete (Cr.)	you understand
réč (fem. noun–S.)	word
rìječ (fem. noun–Cr.)	word
ròditelj	parent
ròditelji (pl.)	parents
Splìt	a large city on the Adriatic
Sȑbija	Serbia
Sȑbin	Serb (male)
Sȑpkinja	Serb (female)
svi	all, everyone

tàta	dad
tvòji (pl.)	your
ustvári, u stvári *adv.*	actually, in fact
vòda	water
Zágreb	the capital city of Croatia
západni	western
zàpravo	actually, more precisely
zar nè	isn't that so

Pronunciation Practice: s : z, š : ž **ìzgovor**

sín	son	šèšir	hat
súh/súv	dry	súša	drought
pàs	dog	nàš	our
kòsa	hair	šìšmiš	bat
zíma	winter	žìvot	life
zúb	tooth	žàba	frog
mràz	frost	nóž	knife
kòza	goat	kòža	skin

Grammar for Lesson III. Read and study the following: accusative case of nouns, genitive case with prepositions, nominative plural of nouns, negated forms of the verb "to be" (i.e. **nisam** . . .).

vježba/vežba I

Odgovòrite na slijèdeća/slédeća pítanja. (Answer the following questions.)

1. Dà li je Péro Amerikánac?
2. Jè li njègova májka iz Splìta/Nòvog Sáda?
3. Kàko òna gòvori?
4. Òdakle je njègov òtac?
5. Kàko ón gòvori?
6. Òdakle ste ví?
7. (Cr.) Gòvorite li hr̀vatski?
   (S.) Dà li gòvorite sr̀pski?

vježba/vežba II

Slijèdeće/Slédeće rečènice mògu se dòpuniti odgovárajućim ìmenicama u àkuzativu. (The following sentences may be completed by adding relevant nouns in the accusative case.)

1. Čùješ li ________ ? Do you hear ________ ?
   (**glás** voice, **šúm** noise, **pàs (ps-)** dog, **mùzika** music, **zvòno** bell, **nástavnik** teacher, **nástavnica** woman teacher, **kòlo** kolo)

2. Dà li pòznajete ________? Do you know (acquainted with) ________?
(**májka** mother, **Sàrajevo, ròman** novel, **prìjatelj** friend, **prijatèljica** woman friend, **ròđak** relative, **žèna** woman, wife)
3. Sàda ìdemo u ________. Now we're going into ________.
(**škóla** school, **sèlo** village, **Opàtija, Zágreb, gìmnazija** secondary school, **Ljùbljana, Beògrad, Skòplje, Cŕna Gòra** Montenegro)

vježba/vežba III

Prevèdite na hr̀vatski/sr̀pski. (Translate into Croatian/Serbian.)
1. I am American.
2. Your parents are from Yugoslavia.
3. Do you speak Croatian/Serbian?
4. No. I don't speak Croatian/Serbian.
5. Do you understand Croatian/Serbian?
6. Yes, I understand a little.

vježba/vežba IV

Stàvite odogovárujući òblik prídjeva/prídeva ispred ìmenica. (Put the appropriate form of the adjective in front of the nouns.)
________knjiga
__nova__knjiga

adjectives:
stàr, stàro, stàra old
dòbar, dòbro, dòbra good
skúp, skúpo, skúpa expensive
nòv, nòvo, nòva new
cŕn, cŕno, cŕna black
jèftin, jèftino, jèftina cheap
jèvtin, jèvtino, jèvtina cheap

nouns:
1. ________ škóla (school)
2. ________ pàs (dog)
3. ________ sèlo (village)
4. ________ hàljina (dress)
5. ________ òlovka (pencil)
6. ________ kùća (house)
7. ________ pèro (pen)
8. ________ tórba (briefcase)
9. ________ màgarac (donkey)
10. ________ odijèlo/odélo (suit)

vježba/vežba V

Stàvite glàgole u sàdašnje vrijème/vréme. (Put the verbs into the present tense.)
Já ________(písati)
Já píšem.

1. Štò/Štà ________(ráditi)

2. ________hr̀vatski/sr̀pski. (ùčiti)
3. Mój òtac ________iz Hr̀vatske. (bìti)
4. Mòja májka ________sr̀pski. (govòriti)
5. Dà li tí ________hr̀vatski/sr̀pski. (razùmjeti/razùmeti)

Children's Chant

En-ten-tini, sava-raka-tini
Sava-raka-tika-taka
Bija-baja-buf
Bistra voda iz lavora–tuf!

Svakòdnevni ìzrazi	**Everyday Expressions**
kàda	when
ùvijek/ùvek	always
nìkada	never
kàtkada	sometimes
pònekad	sometimes
sàda, sàd	now
òdmah	immediately
màlo prìje/pré	little while ago
dávno	long ago
nèdavno	recently
gdjè/gdè	where
svùgdje/svùgde	everywhere
svùda	everywhere
nìgdje/nìgde	nowhere
nàokolo	around
óvdje/óvde	here
tú	here
tàmo	there
tú ì tamo	here and there
ámo-tàmo	to and fro

PETA LEKCIJA

Hàjde da razgòvaramo o vrèmenu (hr̀vatski)

1. Kàkvo je dànas vrijème?
2. Vrijème je lijèpo.
3. Vrijème je fíno.
4. Vrijème je dívno.
5. Vrijème je rđavo.
6. Vrijème je strášno.
7. Kìša pàda.
8. Kìša je prèstala.
9. Kišòvito je.
10. Pàda snìjeg.
11. Snìjeg pàda pòmalo.
12. Snìjeg je prèstao pàdati.
13. Súnce sìja.
14. Èno dúge!
15. Vjètar jòš púše.
16. Sàda púše ùgodan povjetárac.
17. Maglòvito je.
18. Spárno je.
19. Vàni je vrúće.
20. Vàni je tòplo.
21. Vàni je svjèže.
22. Vàni je hládno.
23. Vàni je mràz.
24. Vàni je sùsnježica.

Hàjde da razgòvaramo o vrèmenu (sr̀pski)

1. Kàkvo je dànas vréme?
2. Vréme je lépo.
3. Vréme je fíno.
4. Vréme je dívno.
5. Vréme je r̀đavo.
6. Vréme je strášno.
7. Kìša pàda.
8. Kìša je prèstala.
9. Kišòvito je.
10. Pàda snég.
11. Snég pàda pòmalo.
12. Snég je prèstao pàdati.
13. Súnce sìja.
14. Èno dúge!
15. Vètar jòš dúva.
16. Sàda dúva ùgodan povetárac.
17. Maglòvito je.
18. Spárno je.
19. Nàpolju je vrúće.
20. Nàpolju je tòplo.
21. Nàpolju je svèže.
22. Nàpolju je hládno.
23. Nàpolju je mràz.
24. Nàpolju je sùsnežica.

KÌŠA PÀDA,
TRÁVA RÁSTE.

LET'S TALK ABOUT THE WEATHER!—1. How's the weather today? 2. The weather is good. 3. The weather is fine. 4. The weather is wonderful. 5. The weather is bad. 6. The weather is frightful. 7. It's raining. 8. It's stopped raining. 9. It's rainy (weather). 10. It's snowing. 11. A light snow is falling. 12. The snow has stopped falling. 13. The sun is shining. 14. There's a rainbow! 15. The wind is still blowing. 16. Now a pleasant breeze is blowing. 17. It's foggy. 18. It's steamy. 19. It's hot outside. 20. It's warm outside. 21. It's cool outside. 22. It's cold outside. 23. It's freezing outside. 24. It's sleeting outside.

Pòslovica—?

Máli rjèčnik/rèčnik	**Vocabulary**
dànas	today
dívan, dívno, dívna	wonderful
dúga	rainbow
dúvati (S.)	to blow
èno (with G)	there is!, see there!
fín, fíno, fína	fine
gràd	hail
[grád	city]
hàjde da	let's
hládan, hládno, hládna	cold
hládno *adv.*	cold
kàkav, kàkvo, kàkva	what kind of
kìša	rain
kišòvit, kišòvito, kišòvita	rainy
lòš, lòše, lòša	bad
maglòvit, maglòvito, maglòvita	foggy
mràz	frost
nàpolju (S.)	outside
o (prep. with D)	about, concerning
pàdati	to fall
pòmalo	slowly, bit by bit
povetárac (S.)	breeze
povjetárac (Cr.)	breeze
prèstati	to stop
púhati [púše] (Cr.)	to blow
rásti [ráste]	to grow
razgovárati	to talk, to converse
r̀đav. r̀đavo, r̀đava	bad
sìjati	to shine
snég (S.)	snow
snìjeg (Cr.)	snow
spáran, spárno, spárna	steamy
strášan, strášno, strášna	frightful
súnce (neut. noun)	sun
sùsnežica (S.)	sleet
sùsnježica (Cr.)	sleet
svèž, svèže, svèža (S.)	cool, fresh
svèže *adv.*	cool, fresh
svjèž, svjèže, svjèža (Cr.)	cool, fresh
svjèže *adv.*	cool, fresh
tòpao, tòplo, tòpla	warm
tòplo *adv.*	warm

tráva	grass
tùča	hail
ùgodan, ùgodno, ùgodna	pleasant
váni (Cr.)	outside
vètar (S.)	wind
vjètar (Cr.)	wind
vréme, G vrèmena (S.)	weather, time
vrijème, G vrèmena (Cr.)	weather, time
vrúć, vrúće, vrúća	hot
vrúće *adv.*	hot

Grammar for Lesson V. Read and study the following: adverbs, indefinite and definite adjectives, ekavian, ijekavian, neuter nouns in **-men-** (e.g. **ime**), present tense of **imati, nemati, moći**, past tense.

vježba/vežba I

Proširite slijèdeći/slédeći ùzorak dátim ìmenicama i prídjevima/pridevima. (Extend the following pattern by using the nouns and adjectives below.)

Kàkve je bòje knjìga?	What color is the book?
Knjìga je zelèna.	The book is green.
Kàkve je bòje pèro?	What color is the pen?
Pèro je cr̀no.	The pen is black.

Nouns:

kàput	coat	hàljina	dress
stól (Cr.)	table	òlovka	pencil
stó (S.)	table	kravàta (Cr.)	tie
zid	wall	màšna (S.)	tie
pèro	pen	sòba	room
nèbo	sky		

Adjectives:

bìjel (Cr.)	bijèlo	bijèla	white
ƀeo (S.)	bélo	béla	white
cr̀n	cr̀no	cr̀na	black
cr̀ven	crvèno	crvèna	red
pláv	plávo	pláva	blue
smèđ	smèđe	smèđa	brown
zèlen	zelèno	zelèna	green
žút	žúto	žúta	yellow

vježba/vežba II

Pòpunite slijèdeće/slédeće rečènice prema dátim prímjerima/prímerima.

(Complete the following sentences below according to the models provided.)

1. Gdjè/Gdè je vàš stàriji bràt? [**bràt,** brother]
   Gdjè/Gdè je ________ ________sèstra?
2. Tkò/Kò je tàj mládi gospòdin? [**gospòdin,** gentleman, sir]
   Tkò/Kò je ________ ________žèna?
3. Čìji je òvaj máli krèvet? [**krèvet,** bed]
   Čìja je ________ ________sòba?
   Čìje je ________ ________dȑvo? [**dȑvo,** tree]
4. Kàko se zòve njìhova mála kćérka? [**kćérka,** daughter]
   Kàko se zòve ________ ________sín? [**sín,** son]
5. Òvaj tvój kàput je smèđ.
   ________ ________hàljina je pláva.
   ________ ________kravàta/màšna je cȑna.

vježba/vežba III

Sàstavite pítanja za slijèdece/slédeće òdgovore. (Make questions for the following answers.)

1. Zòvem se Péro Stánić.
2. Tȍ je mòja sèstra.
3. Zòve se Vèsna.
4. Ùdata je.
5. Njézin sùprug gòvori hȑvatski/sȑpski [**sùprug**, husband]

Yugoslavia: Physical Characteristics. Yugoslavia is a relatively small country of 23 million inhabitants living on a land surface of 98,766 square miles. That figure has significance only when we consider that Oregon, with about the same land surface, has a population of less than 3 million. A comparison with Canada is even more dramatic: Canada, with its 3,851,790 square miles, is the second largest country in the world but has a population of about 25 million people. Though Yugoslavia has some rich plains in the north, most of the country is mountainous: its topography is like a crumpled-up handkerchief. Since it is difficult for humans to live on jagged peaks and precipitous slopes, Yugoslavia's 23 million are crowded into the available lowlands and valleys.

Yugoslavia's location in the Balkans shows quite clearly other types of problems: Yugoslavia is bordered by seven distinct countries, Italy, Austria, Hungary, Romania, Bulgaria, Greece, and Albania. The American homeowner who feels happy when he or she is on good terms with two immediate neighbors can well imagine the possibilities for tension and conflict for a country with seven neighbors. It must also be remembered that America's history of friendly relations with its two neighbors, Canada and Mexico, is not typical, either for the Balkans or for the rest of the globe.

Yugoslavia's location requires that it invest more money in border patrols, customs officials, and a military establishment than a small country would ordinarily spend. One great asset is Yugoslavia's Dalmatian coast with fishing and ship-building industries and, above all, that most modern of industries, tourism. Travel literature about this beautiful coast usually understates the charm and attraction of the coastal cities and islands.

Children's Chant

Ìde pàtka
prèko Sáve,
nòsi písmo
nàvrh gláve.
Ù tom písmu
píše:
"Nè volim te
vìše."

Dialect Choice. Since most Yugoslavs speak either **ijekavski** (also called **jekavski**) or **ekavski**, and since practically all printed matter appears in one or the other form, the student must decide which of these slightly differing varieties of Cr&S to learn. Students of Croatian descent who have the opportunity to converse with Americans who have come here from Croatia or from another area where **ijekavski** is spoken and written will probably decide for **ijekavski** speech. However, if they prefer to follow the standard Serbian practice, they should adopt **ekavski** speech. Yugoslavs will understand a foreigner whether he or she speaks **ekavski** or **ijekavski**, but they may be annoyed if forms from both varieties of Cr&S speech are mixed together.

Svakòdnevni ìzrazi	**Everyday Expressions**
Kàko ste?	How are you?
Kàko si?	How are you? [informal]
Dòbro.	Good
Já sam dòbro.	I'm fine.
Vȑlo dòbro	Very fine.
Já sam vȑlo dòbro.	I'm very fine.
Kojekàko.	So-so. Getting along.
Já nísam dòbro.	I'm not good.
Mèni je zlò.	I feel bad.
Kàko je vàša obítelj/pòrodica?	How is your family?
Hvála, dòbro je.	They're fine, thanks.
Kàko je vàš òtac?	How is your father?

Kàko je vàša májka?	How is your mother?
Kàko je vàš bràt?	How is your brother?
Kàko je vàša sèstra?	How is your sister?
Kàko je vàš sùprug?	How is your husband?
Kàko je vàša sùpruga?	How is your wife?
Kàko je njègov sín?	How is his son?
Kàko je njègova kćérka?	How is his daughter?
Kàko su vàša djèca/dèca?	How are your children?
Hvála, dòbro su.	They're fine, thanks.

ùred *m*/kancelàrija *f*	office
vìdjeti/vìdeti [vìdi] I/P	to see
zár *adv.*	really, do you mean to say that . . .
žào *adv.*	sorry
žào mi je	I'm sorry
žèljeti/žèleti [žèli]	to wish, desire

Svakòdnevni ìzrazi	**Everyday Expressions**
Štò/Štà ìma nòvog?	What's new?
Nìšta.	Nothing.
Tó je svè.	That's all.
Svè zàjedno.	All together
Jè li u rédu?	Is it all right?
U rédu.	All right, O.K.
Nìje u rédu.	It's not all right.
Bùdite tàko dòbri!	Be so kind. Please.
Žào mi je.	I'm sorry.
Kàko vam se svíđa/dòpada škóla?	How do you like school?
Mèni se veòma svíđa/dòpada škóla?	I like school very much.
Žívio/Žíveo nàš pròfesor!	Long live our professor!
Žívjeli/Žíveli!	Your health!
Srètno/Srèćno!	Good luck!

SEDMA LEKCIJA

Dáni u tjèdnu

1. Kòji je dànas dán?
2. Dànas je nèdjelja.
3. A pòslije nèdjelje dòlazi ponèdjeljak.
4. Pa ònda ùtorak.
5. Srèdnji dán je srijèda.
6. Čètvrti dán u tjèdnu zòve se četvŕtak.
7. A péti dán u sèdmici je pétak.
8. Sùbota je stári sàbat.
9. U ùtorak pòslije pódne ìći ću kod zubára.
10. Nèdjeljom òbično ìdem u cŕkvu.
11. Mòji sàtovi pòčinju u ponèdjeljak ùjutro.
12. U srijèdu ùvečer ìgrat ću šàh sa svòjim prìjateljem.
13. A u četvŕtak ìći ću sa svòjom djèvojkom u kíno.
14. Mórat ću prìsustvovati sàstanku nàšeg stùdentskog klúba u pétak pòslije pódne.
15. Sùbotom ùjutro òbično vòzim májku na tŕg.
16. Za tjèdan dána bìt ću u Nèw Yorku.

LIJÈPA RÌJEČ I ŽÈLJEZNA VRÁTA ÒTVARA.

Dáni u nèdelji

1. Kòji je dànas dán?
2. Dànas je nèdelja.
3. A pòsle nèdelje dòlazi ponèdeljak.
4. Pa ònda ùtorak.
5. Srèdnji dán je srèda.
6. Čètvrti dán u nèdelji zòve se četvŕtak.
7. A péti dán u sèdmici je pétak.
8. Sùbota je stári sàbat.
9. U ùtorak pòsle pódne ìći ću kod zubára.
10. Nèdeljom òbično ìdem u cŕkvu.
11. Mòji čàsovi pòčinju u ponèdeljak ìzjutra.
12. U srédu ùveče ìgraću šàh sa svòjim prìjateljem.
13. A u četvŕtak ću da ìdem sa svòjom dèvojkom u bìoskop.
14. Móraću da prìsustvujem sàstanku nàšeg stùdentskog klúba u pétak pòsle pódne.
15. Sùbotom ùjutro òbično vòzim májku na pìjacu.
16. Za nèdelju dána bìću u Njùjorku.

LÉPA RÉČ I ŽÈLEZNA VRÁTA ÒTVARA.

DAYS OF THE WEEK—1. What day is it today? 2. Today is Sunday. 3. And after Sunday comes Monday. 4. And then Tuesday. 5. The middle day is Wednesday. 6. The fourth day of the week is Thursday. 7. And the fifth day of the week is Friday. 8. Saturday is the old Sabbath. 9. I'll go to the dentist Tuesday afternoon. 10. I usually go to church on Sundays. 11. My classes begin Monday morning. 12. Wednesday evening I'll be playing chess with my friend. 13. And on Thursday I'll

CAROLYN E GOODSTEIN MD FAAA

180 N Dean St	**235 Prospect Ave**
Englewood, NJ 07631	**Hackensack, NJ 07601**
201-871-4755	**201-487-7677**

Please note our office is connected to our answering service if the office is closed. Please hit 0 as soon as the announcement comes on to get through to an operator.

Welcome new and old. Information to share regarding Dr. Goodstein's practice

Information regarding office hours. After your first visit, patients are seen on a first come first serve basis.

Dr. Goodstein is in her Englewood office every day but Wednesday with the following hours

Monday 9:15 AM to 11:45 AM
1:00 PM to 5:45 PM
6:30 PM-8:45 PM

If a major Holiday falls on Monday, i.e. Memorial Day, July 4, Labor Day, the above hours will be held on Tuesday. (We are also closed for Thanksgiving Day only.). We are open the Friday after Thanksgiving with regular hours, We are open all other holidays, i.e. Presidents Day, Columbus Day. If unsure please check with us.

Vacation is usually sometime during the end of July and first week or two week of August. Please check with office in May-June for details. We are also closed between Christmas and New Years. Please check for start and end dates.

Tuesday 1:00-5:45 PM
Thursday 9:15-11:45 AM
1:00-5:45 PM
6:30-8:45 PM
Friday 2-:45 -4:45 PM

Hackensack office only on
Wednesday 9:30-12:15
1:30-5:15

Please note that testing patients require a minimum of 1 hour for regular skin testing (i.e.) Inhalant allergies) For Insect, Penicillin, and Caine testing could need as much as 2 hours
Please call us if unable to keep your appointment or if you wish to change the date so that if for some reason, Dr. Goodstein will not be here on the date you are scheduled. If the weather is inclement, please call to make sure the office is open.

Donna is in the office every Tuesday and Friday AM, in addition to the above hours if you would like to come in for the immunizations we give or for blood tests. Please also call just in case I am not in for some reason. We offer the following immunizations Flu, Pneumonia, Tetanus, Diphtheria, Pertussis (TDAP), Zostavax (shingles)

We can also get upon request, Hepatitis A and B, and other injections if readily available.

be going to the movie with my girlfriend. 14. I'll have to attend a meeting of our student club on Friday afternoon. 15. On Saturday morning I usually drive my mother to the market. 16. In a week I'll be in New York.

Pòslovica—?

Pronunciation Practice: ć : č **ìzgovor**

ćèmer	belt	čèmer	poison
ćórda	saber	čórda	herd
bùća	ball	bùča	pumpkin
jahàćica	saddle mule	jahàčica	rider (fem.)
spavàćica	nightshirt	spavàčica	sleeper (fem.)
vràćanje	returning	vráčanje	fortune-telling
glùhać	deaf person	glùhač	type of plant
mràvić	little ant	mràvič	type of grass
Ràdić	[family name]	Ràdič	[first name]
ríbić	muscle	rìbič	fisherman
vràtić	little neck	vràtič	tansy (herb)
já ću čùti	I will hear	čùt ću/čùću	I will hear

Many speakers of Cr&S do not make a pronunciation distinction between **ć** and **č**. Residents of Zagreb and of cities along the Dalmatian coast generally cannot hear a difference and so do not produce one.

Grammar for Lesson VII. Read and study the following: imperative, reinforced negation, reflexive verbs, verbal aspect, and sequence of tenses.

vježba I (Croatian version)

Odgovòrite na slijèdeća pítanja.
(Answer the following questions.)

1. Kòji je dànas dán?
2. Kàda ìdete u škólu?
3. Ìdete li u škólu sùbotom?
4. Kàda ćete ìći u kíno?
5. Štò rádite u sùbotu?
6. Gdje ìdete nèdjeljom?
7. Gdjè ćete bìti za tjèdan dána?
8. Kòji je péti dán u sèdmici?
9. Kàda vam pòčinju sàtovi?
10. Ìmate li dànas sàstanak stùdentskog klúba?

vežba I (Serbian version)

Odgovòrite na slédeća pítanja.
(Answer the following questions.)

1. Kòji je dànas dán?
2. Kàda ìdéte u škólu?
3. Dà li idéte u škólu sùbotom?
4. Kàda ćete ìći u bìoskop?
5. Štà rádite u sùbotu?
6. Gdè idéte nèdeljom?
7. Gdè ćete bìti za nèdelju dána?
8. Kòji je péti dán u nèdelji?
9. Kàda vam pòčinju čàsovi?
10. Dà li dànas ìmate sàstanak stùdentskog klúba?

vježba II

Pòpunite òve rečènice odgovárajućim òblikom ìmenice. (Complete these sentences with the correct form of the noun.)

_________òbično ìdem u cŕkvu. (nèdjelja)
Nèdjeljom òbično ìdem u cŕkvu.

1. _________dòlazi pòslije nèdjelje. (ponèdjeljak)
2. _________ìdem u Nèw York. (ùtorak)
3. _________ùvečer òbično ìdem u kíno. (srijèda)
4. Štò ví rádite _________? (srijèda)
5. Htìo bih da dóđeš u _________. (pétak)
6. _________ìmam sàstanak u klúbu. (četvŕtak)
7. Ìdeš li u škólu _________? (sùbota)
8. Spávaš li dùgo _________ ùjutro? (nèdjelja)
9. _________ùvečer òbično glèdam televíziju. (ponèdjeljak)
10. Gdjè ìdete u òvu _________? (nèdjelja)

vežba II

Pòpunite òve rečènice odgovárajućim òblikom imenice. (Complete these sentences with the correct form of the noun.)

_________òbično ìdem u cŕkvu. (nèdelja)
Nèdeljom òbično ìdem u cŕkvu.

1. _________dòlazi pòsle nèdelje. (ponèdeljak)
2. _________ìdem u Njùjork. (ùtorak)
3. _________ùveče òbično ìdem u bìoskop. (sréda)
4. Štà ví rádite _________? (sréda)
5. Htèo bih da dóđeš u _________. (pétak)
6. _________ìmam sàstanak u klúbu. (četvŕtak)
7. Dà li ìdeš u škólu _________? (sùbota)
8. Dà li dùgo spávaš _________ ìzjutra? (nèdelja)
9. _________ùveče òbično glèdam televíziju. (ponèdeljak)
10. Gdè idéte u òvu _________? (nèdelja)

vježba/vežba III

Pòpunite prázna mjèsta/mèsta odgovárajućim òblikom glàgola u prèzentu. (Fill in the blank spaces with the relevant present tense form of the verb; the first person singular form will be given as a point of departure.)

1. Stùdenti _________. (pjèvam/pèvam)
2. Zàšto ví _________hr̀vatski/sr̀pski jèzik? (ùčim)
3. Mílka _________bràta. (čèkam)
4. _________li tí pèro u džèpu? (ìmam)
5. Òni _________písma. (píšem)

6. ________li móga òca? (pòznajem)
7. Mòji ròditelji ________da je tàko. (mìslim)
8. Mòja májka ________vèčeru. (sprémam)
9. Dà li ví ________u sudbìnu? (vjèrujem/vèrujem)
10. Kàko se ________tvòja sèstra? (zòvem se)

vježba/vežba IV

Pòpunite òve rečènice odgovárajućim bùdućim vrèmenom. (Complete these sentences with the appropriate future tense.)

Já ________sùtra. (ùčiti)
Já ću ùčiti sùtra.

1. Nástavnik ________nòvu pjèsmu/pèsmu. (čìtati)
2. Òni ________u Londónu. (žívjeti/žíveti)
3. Pètar ________u nèdjelju/nèdelju. (ožèniti se)
4. Mí ________u cŕkvi svètoga Màrka. (bìti)
5. Mój òtac ________takóđer/takóđe. (dóći)
6. Májka ________na sèlo. (otíći)
7. Tȍ ________mòja kùća jèdnog dána. (bìti)
8. ________televíziju pòslije/pòsle vèčere. (glèdati)
9. Òna ________sùtra ________rano. (ùstati)
10. (Cr.) Snìjeg ________pàdati. (prèstati)
    (S.) Snég ________da pàda. (prèstati)

Divisions of the Day

day	dán	night	nóć
today	dànas	tonight	nòćas
good day	dòbar dán	last night	sìnoć
		good night	làku nóć
dawn	zòra		
at dawn	ù zoru	midnight	pónoć
		before midnight	prìje/pré pónoći
morning	jùtro	at midnight	u pónoć
this morning	jùtros	after midnight	pòslije/pòsle pónoći
in the morning	ìzjutra, ùjutro		
good morning	dòbro jùtro	yesterday	jùčer/jùče
		day before yesterday	prèkjučer/prèkjuče
noon	pódne		
before noon	prìje/pré pódne	tomorrow	sùtra
at noon	u pódne	day after tomorrow	prèkosutra
afternoon	pòslije/pòsle pódne		

evening	vèčer/vèče
this evening	večèras
in the evening	ùvečer/ùveče
good evening	dòbar [or] dòbro vèče (S.)
	dòbar [or] dòbra vèčer (Cr.)

Days of the Week

In answer to the question: **Kòji je dán dànas?** "What day is today?," one might say: **Dànas je sùbota,** "Today is Saturday," or whatever day it happened to be. In this type of statement the name of the day appears in the nominative case. However, to say that something will happen or has happened on a particular day, one would use the preposition **u** and the accusative case of the appropriate name, e.g. **u sùbotu.** If this event usually takes place on a particular day, then the name of the day appears in the instrumental case, e.g. **sùbotom.** Here are all the days of the weeks in the three situations just described.

Sunday	nèdjelja/nèdelja
on Sunday	u nèdjelju/nèdelju
on Sundays	nèdjeljom/ nèdeljom
Monday	ponèdjeljak/ ponèdeljak
[also used:	ponèdjeljnik/ ponèdeljnik]*
on Monday	u ponèdjeljak/ ponèdeljak
on Mondays	ponèdjeljkom/ ponèdeljkom
Tuesday	ùtorak
[also used:	ùtornik]
on Tuesday	u ùtorak
on Tuesdays	ùtorkom
Wednesday	srijèda/sréda
on Wednesday	u srijèdu/u srédu
on Wednesdays	srijèdom/srédom
Thursday	četvŕtak
on Thursday	u četvŕtak
on Thursdays	četvŕtkom
Friday	pétak
on Friday	u pétak
on Fridays	pétkom
Saturday	sùbota
on Saturday	u sùbotu
on Saturdays	sùbotom

*Serbian also uses **ponèdeonik, u ponèdeonik, ponèdeonikom.**

Ùčeni sín

Dòšao je sín iz gráda k òcu na sèlo. Òtac mu je rèkao:

—Sàd je kòsidba, ùzmi gràblje, pa hàjde, pomòzi mi.

A sín nìje vòlio ráditi, pa je rèkao:—Já sam nàuke ùčio, a sèljačke sam rìječi svè zabòravio: štò su tó gràblje?* *

I jèdva da je pòšao dvòrištem, stào je na gràblje, a òne su ga ùdarile po čèlu. Ònda se sjètio, štò su tó gràblje, pa se ùhvatio za čèlo i víknuo:

—A kàkva je tó budàla òstavila óvdje gràblje!

* The verb is plural because the noun **grablje,** "rake," is feminine plural in Cr&S.

OSMA LEKCIJA

Mòja sòba

1. Mòja je sòba malèna ali ùdobna.
2. U jèdnom kútu nàlazi se mój krèvet.
3. Krèvet je nàmješten kad ìma posteljìnu, t.j. màdrac, plàhte, pokriváče, jàstuk i prekrìvač.
4. Blízu prózora kòji glèda na ùlicu nàlaze se pìsaći stól i stòlica.
5. Na pìsaćem stòlu je mála stólna svjètiljka.
6. Između ùličnog prózora i pìsaćeg stòla nàlazi se vìsok òrmar za mòje knjìge.
7. Uza zíd nasùprot vràtima nàlazi se òrmar za odijèla.
8. Između òvoga ormára i stràžnjeg prózora nàlaze se naslònjač i vìsoka svjètiljka.
9. Zìdovi su òbojeni svjetlò-smeđom bòjom, a stròp bìjelom bòjom.
10. Na pòdu je lìjep ság, a na òba prózora su bìjele závjese.
11. Ako stòjim kraj ùličnog prózora, ispred kùće vìdim trávu, nàš vèliki hrást i plòčnik.
12. S drùgog prózora vìdim kùću nàšega sùsjeda, njègovu garážu i njègov cvjètnjak.
13. Ùvečer sjèdim za pìsaćim stòlom i izràđujem svòje zadátke.

Mòja sòba

1. Mòja je sòba malèna ali ùdobna.
2. U jèdnom ùglu nàlazi se mój krèvet.
3. Krèvet je nàmešten kad ìma posteljìnu, t.j. dùšek, čàršave, pokriváče, jàstuk i prekrìvač.
4. Blízu prózora kòji glèda na ùlicu nàlaze se pìsaći stó i stòlica.
5. Na pìsaćem stòlu je mála stóna lámpa.
6. Između ùličnog prózora i pìsaćeg stòla nàlazi se vìsok òrman za mòje knjìge.
7. Uza zíd nasùprot vràtima nàlazi se òrman za odéla.
8. Između òvoga ormána i zàdnjeg prózora nàlaze se naslònjača i vìsoka lámpa.
9. Zìdovi su òbojeni svetlò-smeđom bòjom, a tavànica bélom bòjom.
10. Na pòdu je lép tèpih, a na òba prózora su béle závese.
11. Ako stòjim kraj ùličnog prózora, ispred kùće vìdim trávu, nàš vèliki hrást i trotòar.
12. S drùgog prózora vìdim kùću nàšeg sùseda, njègovu garážu i njègov cvèćnjak.
13. Ùveče sèdim za pìsaćim stòlom i izràđujem svòje zadátke.

14. Pònekad sjèdim u naslonjáču i čìtam čàsopis.
15. Kàd mi se ne spáva, lèžim u krèvetu i čìtam detèktivsku prìpovijest.

14. Pònekad sèdim u naslònjáči i čìtam čàsopis.
15. Kàd mi se ne spáva, lèžim u krèvetu i čìtam detèktivsku prìpovetku.

ÀKO JE KRÀTAK DÁN, DÙGA JE GÒDINA.

MY ROOM—1. My room is small but comfortable. 2. My bed is in one corner. 3. A bed is complete when it has bedding, that is, a mattress, sheets, blankets, a pillow and a bedspread. 4. There is a desk and a chair near the street-window (the window which looks at the street). 5. There's a small lamp on the desk. 6. Between the street-window and the desk there's a large bookcase (cabinet for my books). 7. Along the wall opposite the door there's a clothes closet (cabinet for clothes). 8. Between this closet and the rear window there's an armchair and a floor lamp (large lamp). 9. The walls are painted light brown (with a light-brown color) and the ceiling white. 10. There's a pretty rug on the floor, and there are white curtains on both windows. 11. If I stand near the street-window, I can see the grass in front of the house, our large oak tree, and the sidewalk. 12. From the other window I see my neighbor's house, his garage, and his flower garden. 13. In the evening I sit at the desk and do my assignments. 14. Sometimes I sit in the armchair and read a magazine. 15. When I can't sleep (to me it does not sleep), I lie in bed and read a detective story.

Pronunciation Practice: đ : dž **ìzgovor**

đak	student	džak	sack	Đórđe	George	Džórdž	George
đèm	bridle bit	džèm	jam	vòđa	leader	hòdža	Moslem priest
đída	hero	džìda	spear	rìđ	reddish-brown	brìdž	bridge (game)
đòn	sole	Džón	John				

As in the case of **ć : č,** many speakers of Cr&S (e.g. in Zagreb) do not distinguish between đ and **dž** and would pronounce **đak** in the same way as **džak.**

Grammar for Lesson VIII. Read and study the following: dative case, prepositions (especially those with genitive case), special uses of **na**, past passive participles, the categories of the Croatian and Serbian verb in diagram form.

vježba I

Odgovòrite na slijèdeća pítanja.
1. Vàša sòba je malèna?
2. Kàda je krèvet nàmješten?

vežba I

Odgovòrite na slédeća pítanja.
1. Vàša sòba je malèna?
2. Kàda je krèvet nàmešten?

3. Štò se nàlazi blízu prózora kòji glèda na ùlicu?
4. Kàkve su bòje zìdovi?
5. Štò se nàlazi na pòdu?
6. Štò vìdite ispred kùće?
7. Ìma li vàš sùsjed garážu?
8. Kàda píšete svòje zadátke?
9. Vòlite li čìtati čàsopise?
10. Štò čìtate u krèvetu?

3. Štà se nàlazi blízu prózora kòji glèda na ùlicu?
4. Kàkve su bòje zìdovi?
5. Štà se nàlazi na pòdu?
6. Štà vìdite ispred kùće?
7. Dà li vàš sùsed ìma garážu?
8. Kàda píšete svòje zadátke?
9. Dà li vòlite da čìtate čàsopise?
10. Štà čìtate u krèvetu?

vježba/vežba II

Svè òve rečènice mògu se dòpuniti odgovárajućim ìmenicama u dàtivu. (All of the sentences below may be completed by the addition of an appropriate noun in the dative case.)

1. Òva knjìga prìpada ________. (ùčenik, ùčenica, nástavnica, nástavnik, sùprug, sùpruga)
2. Ìdem k ________. (sèlo, zgràda, prìjatelj, stól/stó, škóla, jèzero)
3. Govòrili smo o ________. (pèro, pút, sòbarica, činòvnik, rúka, pàs)
4. Tȏ se nàlazi u ________. (Zágreb, Ljùbljana, Líka, Sàrajevo, Cètinje, Beògrad)
5. Prìjatno mi je na ________. (bród, móre, tráva, vóda)

vježba III

Pòpunite òve rečènice odgovárajućim pádežom: àkuzativom, gènetivom ili dàtivom. (Complete these sentences with the appropriate case: accusative, genitive, or dative.)

1. Pètar je jùčer òtišao za ________(Rijèka).
2. Tȏ su òčale ________ ________ ________(mój stàriji bràt).
3. Žèlite li sjèditi u ________ ________ ________(òvaj ùdobni naslònjač) ili na ________ ________ (táj krèvet)?
4. Lìjep ság nàlazi se ispod ________ ________ ________(òvaj máli stól).
5. Pètar je kúpio ________ ________ ________ (lijèpa crvèna kravàta).
6. U pétak ìdem k ________ ________(mládi zùbar).

vežba III

1. Pètar je jùče òtišao za ________(Rijèka).
2. Tȏ su nàočare ________ ________ ________(mój stàriji bràt).
3. Dà li žèlite da sèdite u ________ ________ (òva ùdobna naslònjača) ili na ________ ________ (táj krèvet)?
4. Lép tèpih nàlazi se ispod ________ ________ (òvaj máli stó).
5. Pètar je kúpio ________ ________ ________(lépa crvèna màšna).
6. U pétak ìdem k ________ ________(mlàdi zùbar).

7. Náda ùvijek gòvori o ________ ________ ________(svòja vèlika sòba).	7. Náda ùvek gòvori o ________ ________ ________(svòja vèlika sòba).
8. Bez ________(šèšir) i ________(rukàvice) ne mòžeš ìći vàn.	8. Bez ________(šèšir) i ________(rukàvice) ne mòžeš ìći nàpolje.
9. Tkò tó ìzlazi iz ________ ________(zèleni àutobus)?	9. Kò tó ìzlazi iz ________ ________(zèleni àutobus)?
10. Vìdim trávu ispred ________ ________ ________(vàša nòva kùća).	10. Vìdim trávu ispred________ ________ ________(vàša nòva kùća).

vježba/vežba IV

Napíšite kràtki sástav na tému "Mòja sòba." (Write a short composition on the topic "My Room.")

Tongue-Twister

I cvŕči, cvŕči cvŕčak
na čvòru cŕne smȑče.

The two lines by the poet Vladimir Nazor provide Yugoslavs with a tongue-twister. Literally, they mean "And the cricket chirps, chirps on a knot of the black juniper tree."

Expressions of Endearment	**Ìzrazi drágosti**
1. You're a great guy.	Tí si sjájan mòmak. Ví ste sjájan mòmak.
2. You're a fine girl.	Tí si dòbra cùra. Tí si dòbra djèvojka. (Cr.) Ví ste dòbra cùra. Ví ste dòbra djèvojka. Tí si dòbra dèvojka. (S.) Ví ste dòbra dèvojka.
3. How are you, dear?	Kàko si, drága? [to a girl] Kàko si, drági? [to a boy]
4. I like you.	Svíđaš mi se. (Cr.) Svíđate mi se. Dòpadaš mi se. (S.) Dòpadate mi se.
5. I love you.	Vòlim te.
6. I'm in love with you.	Zàljubljen(a) sam u tèbe.

7. I'm madly in love with you.	Lúdo sam u tèbe zàljubljen(a).
8. I'm head over heels in love with you.	Zàljubljen(a) sam u tèbe do ùšiju.
9. By the way, what's your name?	Nego, kàko se zòveš?

Smiljaniću

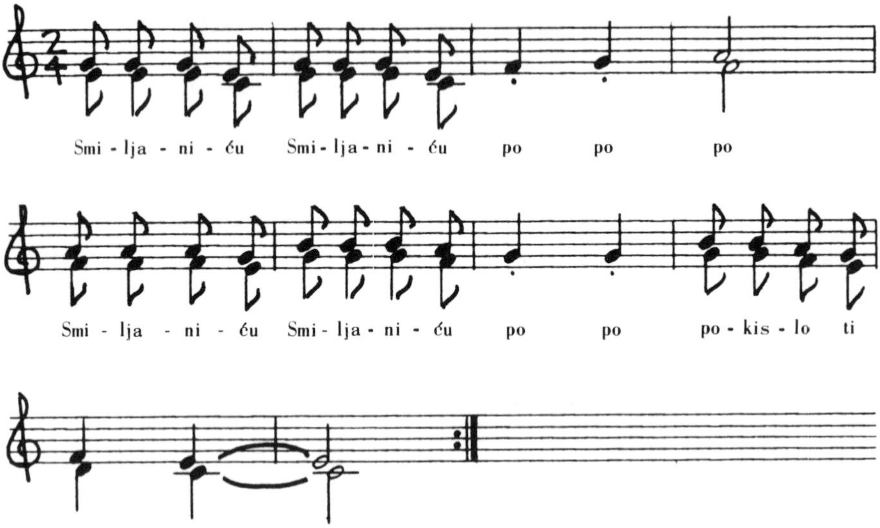
Smi - lja - ni - ću Smi - lja - ni - ću po po po
Smi - lja - ni - ću Smi - lja - ni - ću po po po - kis - lo ti
pe - rje

Smiljaniću

Smiljaniću, Smiljaniću po, po, po
Smiljaniću, Smiljaniću po, po, pòkislo ti pérje.

Nèka kìsne, neka kisne po, po, po
Neka kisne, neka kisne po, po, pòkisnuti néće.

Nìje mèni, nije meni do, do, do
Nije meni, nije meni do, do, do mòjega pérja.

Vèć je mèni, već je meni do, do, do
Već je meni, već je meni do, do, do mòje mlàdosti.

Sìnoć me je, sinoć me je o, o, o
Sinoć me je, sinoć me je o, o, o, ožènila májka.

A jùtros mi, a jutros mi po, po, po
A jutros mi, a jutros mi po, po, pòbegla dèvojka.

The song above tells the sad tale of a young man named Smiljanić, whose friends asks why he is so depressed (why his feathers [**pérje**] are soaking wet [**pòkislo** from **pòkisnuti P**]). Smiljanić says: "Let them get wet, they won't get completely soaked. I'm not worried about my feathers, but rather about my youth. Last night my mother married me off, but this morning the girl (bride) ran away." The ijekavian version of the last two words would be **pòbjegla djèvojka,** the ikavian **pòbigla dìvojka.**

DEVETA LEKCIJA

Sàstanak

1. Kòliko je sàda sáti, Péro?
2. Mój sát ìde dànas nàprijed, ìako òbično kàsni.
3. Sàd je tòčno čètiri sáta, Ána.
4. Ó, já ìmam sàstanak u čètiri sáta i pètnaest minúta.
5. Pa jòš ìmaš pètnaest minúta do sàstanka.
6. Tvój sàstanak tràjat će vjèrojatno do déset minúta do pét.
7. Ònda ću te čèkati óvdje u pét sáti.
8. Bòlje će bìti da me óvdje čèkaš u pét i trídeset, jer mògu na sàstanku òstati nèšto dùže.
9. Dòbro. Nèmoj zàkasniti.
10. Bùdi bez brìge. Bìt ću óvdje na vrijème. Do viđénja, Péro. [Kàsnije, u pét i četrdèset]
11. Zànima me, štò se dogòdilo Áni.
12. Kàsni vèć dèset minúta.
13. Péro, veòma mi je žào, štò sam zàkasnila.
14. Sàstanak je tràjao dùže, nego štò sam mìslila da će tràjati.

Sàstanak

1. Kòliko je sàda sáti, Péro?
2. Mój sát ìde dànas nàpred, ìako òbično kàsni.
3. Sàd je tàčno čètiri sáta, Ána.
4. Ó, já ìmam sàstanak u čètiri sáta i pètnaest minúta.
5. Pa jòš ìmaš pètnaest minúta do sàstanka.
6. Tvój sàstanak tràjaće vèrovatno do déset minúta do pét.
7. Ònda ću te čèkati óvde u pét sáti.
8. Bòlje će bìti da me óvde čèkaš u pét i trídeset, jer mògu na sàstanku da òstanem nèšto dùže.
9. Dòbro. Nèmoj da zàdocniš.
10. Bùdi bez brìge. Bìću óvde na vrème. Do viđénja, Péro. [Dòcnije, u pét i četrdèset]
11. Zànima me, štà se dèsilo Áni.
12. Kàsni vèć dèset minúta.
13. Péro, mnògo mi je žào, štò sam zadòcnila.
14. Sàstanak je tràjao dùže, nego štò sam mìslila da će tràjati.

ŠTÒ MÒŽEŠ UČÌNITI DÀNAS, NE ÒSTAVLJAJ ZA SÙTRA.

THE APPOINTMENT—1. What time is it now, Pero? 2. My watch is running fast today, although usually it runs slow. 3. It's exactly four o'clock now, Ann. 4. Oh, I have an appointment (meeting) at four-fifteen. 5. Well, you still have fifteen minutes until the meeting. 6. Your appointment will probably last until ten minutes till five. 7. Then I'll wait for you here at five o'clock. 8. It'll be better if you wait for me here at five-thirty, because I may stay there (at the meeting) somewhat longer. 9.

O.K. Don't be late. 10. Don't worry. I'll be here on time. So long, Pero. [Later, at five-forty] 11. I wonder (it interests me) what happened to Ann. 12. She's already ten minutes late. 13. Pero, I'm terribly sorry that I'm late. 14. The appointment lasted longer than I had expected.

Pòslovica—?

Pronunciation Practice: h : k **ìzgovor**

hàps	custody	káp	drop
hèroj	hero	kèrov	hound
hìtro	quickly	kìtno	neatly
hòtel	hotel	kòtar	district
hȑpa	heap	kȑpa	rag
húmor	humor	kúmov	godfather's
dùh	spirit	lùk	onion
hvála	thanks	kváran	damaged
dàhnuti	to breathe	tàknuti	to touch
shvàćati	to grasp	skvàčen	clutched
hrákati	to clear one's throat	krákati	to step out
tȑbuh	belly	múk	stillness
mùha (Cr.)	fly	mùka	torture
hȑt	greyhound	kȑt	mole

The sound **h** does not occur in some dialects of Cr&S, while in other dialects it is omitted in colloquial speech, e.g. **oću** for **hoću.** In the speech of Serbia the sound **v** occurs with regularity in words that in Croatian have **h** after the vowel **u,** e.g. Cr. **kùhati:** S. **kùvati,** "to cook"; Cr. **ùho:** S. **ùvo,** "ear"; Cr. **glúh:** S. **glúv,** "deaf"; Cr. **mùha:** S. **mùva,** "fly"; etc. Another substitution made by many speakers of Cr&S is that of **f** for the cluster **hv,** e.g. **fála** for **hvála,** "thanks."

Grammar for Lesson IX. Read and study the following: instrumental case, demonstrative adjectives, cardinal numbers, aorist, verbal adverbs.

Kazívanje vrèmena	**Telling Time**
1. Kòliko je sàd sáti?	1. What time is it now?
2. Sàd je jèdan sát.	2. It's one o'clock now.
3. Sad je dvá sáta.	3. It's two o'clock now.
4. Sad je trí sata.	4. It's three o'clock now.
5. Sad je čètiri sata.	5. It's four o'clock now.
6. Sad je pét sáti.	6. It's five o'clock now.
7. Sad je šést sati.	7. It's six o'clock now.
8. Sad je sèdam sati.	8. It's seven o'clock now.
9. Sad je òsam sati.	9. It's eight o'clock now.
10. Sad je dèvet sati.	10. It's nine o'clock now.

11. Sad je dèset sati.	11. It's ten o'clock now.
12. Sad je jedànaest sati.	12. It's eleven o'clock now.
13. Sad je dvánaest sati.	13. It's twelve o'clock now.
14. Sad je dva sata pòslije/pòsle pónoći.	14. It's two o'clock in the morning (2 A.M.).
15. Sad je dva sata poslije/posle pódne.	15. It's two o'clock in the afternoon (2 P.M.).
16. Sad je devet sati prìje/pré pódne.	16. It's nine o'clock in the morning (9 A.M.).
17. Sad je devet sati ùvečer/ ùveče.	17. It's nine o'clock in the evening (9 P.M.).

Sát i mìnut **Hour and Minute**

8:01	Sàd je òsam (sáti) i jèdan mìnut.*	
8:02	osam (sati) i dvá minúta	
8:03	osam (sati) i trí minuta	
8:04	osam (sati) i čètiri minuta	
8:05	osam (sati) i pét (minúta)	
8:10	osam (sati) i dèset (minuta)	
8:15	osam (sati) i pètnaest (minuta)	
	osam (sati) i čètvrt	(eight and a quarter)
8:30	osam i trídeset	
	osam i pól/pó	(eight and a half)
	pòla dèvet	(a half of nine)
8:35	osam i trídeset pét	
	dvádeset pet do devet	(twenty-five to/until nine)
8:45	osam i četrdèset pet	
	četvrt do devet	
	petnaest do devet	
	tri četvrt(i) devet	(three quarters of nine)
8:59	jedan minut do devet	

vježba/vežba I

Pòpunite slijèdeće/slédeće rečènice ìmenicom u ìnstrumentalu. (Complete the following sentences with a noun in the instrumental case.)

1. Tkò/Kò će ìći s[or]sa ________? (**májka** mother, **student** student, **ùjak** uncle, **Amerikánka** American [female])
2. Pàs lèži pod ________. (**stòlica** chair, **krèvet** bed, **klúpa** bench)
3. Kríž/Kȑst vìsi nad ________. (**òltar** altar, **kòlijevka/kòlevka** cradle, **prózor** window)

*Also **minúta,** e.g. **òsam sáti i jèdna minúta.**

4. Pùtujemo ________. (**vlák/vóz** train, **tràmvaj** trolley, **avìon** plane, **láđa** boat)
5. Sijèčem/Séčem dȉva ________. (**sjèkira/sèkira** axe, **nóž** knife, **píla** saw, **dlijèto/dléto** chisel)

vježba II

Pòpunite slijèdeće rečènice odgovárajućim pádežom: dàtivom ili ìnstrumentalom. (Complete the following sentences with the appropriate case: dative or instrumental.)

1. Večèras ìdem s ________u kíno. (prȉjatelj)
2. Gdjè je Pètar? Ón je u ________. (škóla)
3. Svàkog dána pùtujem ________do mjèsta gdjè rádim. (àutobus)
4. Na sàstanku stùdentskog klúba govòrili smo o ________stùdenata. (problémi)
5. Òlovke i knjìge nàlaze se na ________ ________. (pìsaći stól)
6. Píšeš li ________ili ________? (òlovka, pèro)
7. Dóći ću s ________u òsam i trídeset. (djèvojka)
8. U ________ìma mnògo džámija. (Sàrajevo)
9. Putòvat ćemo ________i bìt ćemo u ________ popódne. (avìon, Sàrajevo)
10. Nèmoj zàkasniti. Móramo ìći k ________. (pròfesor)

vežba II

Pòpunite slédeće rečènice odgovárajućim pádežom: dàtivom ili instrumentalom. (Complete the following sentences with the appropriate case: dative or instrumental.)

1. Večèras ìdem s ________u bìoskop. (prȉjatelj)
2. Gdè je Petar? Ón je u ________. (škóla)
3. Svàkog dána pùtujem ________do mèsta gdè rádim. (àutobus)
4. Na sàstanku stùdentskog klúba govòrili smo o ________stùdenata. (problémi)
5. Òlovke i knjìge nàlaze se na ________ ________. (pìsaći stó)
6. Dà li píšeš ________ili ________? (òlovka, pèro)
7. Dóći ću s ________u òsam i trídeset. (dèvojka)
8. U ________ìma mnògo džámija. (Sàrajevo)
9. Putòvaćem ________i bìćemo u ________ popódne. (avìon, Sàrajevo)
10. Nèmoj da zàdocniš. Móramo da idémo k ________. (pròfesor)

vježba/vežba III

Čìtajte òve bròjeve hȑvatski/sȑpski (Read these numbers in Croatian/ Serbian)

1, 5, 13, 7, 40, 32, 55, 3, 11, 64, 12, 10, 61, 41, 65, 27, 8, 19, 29, 37, 50.

vježba/vežba IV

Kòliko je sáti? (What time is it?)
5:00; 6:30; 7:45; 2:50; 7:05; 9:43; 11:20; 12:00; 8:05; 12:10; 4:22; 3:12; 1:01; 6:58; 8:27; 9:45

vježba/vežba V

Pòstavite pítanja na slijèdeće/slédeće òdgovore. (Make questions for the following answers.)

1. Sàda je dèvet i trídeset.
2. Popódne ìmam sàstanak.
3. Dà, dóći ću u pét.
4. (Cr.) Zàkasnila sam dèset minúta.
   (S.) Zadòcnila sam dèset minúta.
5. Sàstanak je tràjao dùgo.
6. Pùtujemo aviónom.
7. Trí sáta i dèset minúta.
8. Mój sát ìde nàprijed/nàpred.
9. (Cr.) Pètar ne vòli ùčiti.
   (S.) Pètar ne vòli da ùči.
10. Òna píše pjèsme/pèsme.

Protective Expressions	**Ìzrazi za òbranu/òdbranu**
Leave me alone!	Òstavi me na míru! Òstavite me na míru!
Don't bother me!	Ne gnjávi me! Ne gnjávite me!
I'll call a policeman.	Zvàt ću/Zvàću milicájca.
You jerk!	Màngupe jèdan!
Get lost!	Gùbi se! Gùbite se!
Why are you bugging me?	Štò/Štà si se mene ùhvatio! Štò/Štà ste se mene ùhvatili!
I hate you.	Mŕzim te. Mŕzim vas.
I loathe you.	Gàdiš mi se. Gàdite mi se.
Go to hell!	Póđi k vrágu! (Cr.) Póđite k vrágu! Ìdi do đàvola! (S.) Ìdite do đàvola!
Help!	U pòmoć!

Mále Šále

—Ùhvatio sam pét múha:
dvìje žénke i trí mužjáka.
—Kàko tó znáš?
—Dvìje su bíle na zr̀calu a trí
na bòci s vínom.

—Glè, kàkva kìša pàda vàni!
A dànas je bílo nàjavljeno
na rádiju lijèpo vrijème.
—Ùvijek gòvorim da móramo nàbaviti nòvi rádio.

Little Jokes

—Mój je sín izvànredan spòrtaš. Tr̀či dèset kìlometara a zàtim skáče preko prèpreka vìsokih dvá mètra.
—Nije ni čùdo pri tàkvom zàletu.

Bòbić: Tàta, zàšto se Zèmlja
stálno òkreće?
Bòbi: Kàko òkreće? Dà tí nísi
nègde nàšao mòju flàšu sa
ràkijom?

DESETA LEKCIJA

Zanímanja i zvánja

1. Štò rádi tvój òtac, Pávle?
2. Ón je stròjar u tvórnici, Márko.
3. Mój je òtac tèsar u gràđevinskom poduzéću.
4. Mój bràt ùči za lìječnika.
5. Ali já žèlim bìti ùčitelj.
6. Pa èto, já bih vòlio bìti inžènjer.
7. Tèhnika je zanìmljiva, a pláća je dòbra.
8. Ali trèba vȑlo dòbro znàti matemàtiku, a tó je prédmet u kòjem sam nájslabiji.
9. Zàto ću mòžda studírati právo i bìti advòkat.
10. Ònda ràdije pòčni ùčiti jèr ćeš ìnače òstati sàmo sànjar.

Zanímanja i zvánja

1. Štà rádi tvój òtac, Pávle?
2. Ón je mašìnista u fàbrici, Márko.
3. Mój òtac je tèsar u gràđevinskom preduzéću.
4. Mój bràt ùči za lekára.
5. Ali já žèlim da bùdem ùčitelj.
6. Pa èto, já bih vòleo da bùdem inžènjer.
7. Tèhnika je zanìmljiva, a plàta je dòbra.
8. Ali trèba da se vȑlo dòbro zná matemàtika, a tó je prédmet u kòjem sam nájslabiji.
9. Zàto ću možda da stùdiram práva i da bùdem advòkat.
10. Ònda ràdije pòčni da ùčiš jèr ćeš ìnače da òstaneš sàmo sánjalica.

ÙČIŠ SE DOK ŽÍVIŠ

OCCUPATIONS AND PROFESSIONS—1. What does your father do, Paul? 2. He's a machinist in a factory, Mark. 3. My father is a carpenter in a construction firm. 4. My brother is studying to be a doctor. 5. But I want to be a schoolteacher. 6. Well, I'd like to be an engineer. 7. Engineering is interesting and the pay is good. 8. But one must know mathematics very well and that's my weakest subject (the subject in which I am weakest). 9. So perhaps I'll study law and be a lawyer. 10. Then you better start studying or otherwise you'll just be (remain) a dreamer.

Some Occupations and Professions. For those occupations and professions that are engaged in by women as well as men, there are specific words indicating whether a man or a woman is being referred to; usually the word for the female is derived by means of the suffixes **-ka, -ica,** or **-kinja,** e.g. **učitelj,** "teacher, male teacher," **učiteljica,** "female teacher." Where variants occur in the listing below the first form will be Croatian, while the second form (after the slash mark) will be Serbian, e.g. **pjevač/pevač,** "singer"; **konobar/kelner,** "waiter."

However, some words are peculiar to one or the other variant, e.g. **kasapin** (S.), "butcher," while **mesar** is common to both variants; the few special words will have (S.) or (Cr.) indicated.

accountant	računòvođa *m*
actor	glúmac *m*, G glúmca
actress	glùmica *f*
announcer	spìker *m*; spìkerica/spìkerka *f*
apprentice	nàučnik/ùčenik
architect	arhìtekt/arhìtekta *m*
artist	ùmjetnik/ùmetnik *m*; ùmjetnica/ùmetnica *f*
athlete	atlètičar *m*; atlètičarka *f*; spòrtaš/spòrtista *m*
baker	pèkar *m*; pèkarica/pèkarka *f*
ballad singer	gùslar *m*
bank teller	blàgajnik *m*; blàgajnica *f*
banker	bànkar *m*
barber	brìjač/bèrberin *m*
bureaucrat	biròkrat/biròkrata *m*
butcher	mèsar *m*; kàsapin (S.) *m*
carpenter	stòlar *m*; tèsar *m*
cashier	blàgajnik *m*; blàgajnica *f*
chauffeur, driver	šòfer *m*
chief, head, boss	šèf *m*
clerk	pìsar *m*; činòvnik *m*; činòvnica *f*
conductor	kondùkter *m*; kondùkterka *f*
conductor (musical)	dirigènt *m*
cook	kùhar/kùvar *m*; kùharica/kùvarica *f*
craftsman	òbrtnik/zanàtlija *m*
criminal	prèstupnik *m*; kriminálac *m*; krìminalka *f*
dancer	plèsač/ìgrač *m*; plesàčica/igràčica *f*
dentist	zùbar *m*; zùbarica/zùbarka *f*
dictator	dìktator *m*
diplomat	diplòmat/diplòmata *m*
director	dìrektor *m*; dìrektorica *f*; dìrektorka *f*
doctor (medical)	lìječnik/lèkar *m*; lìječnica/lèkarka *f*
driver	šòfer *m*
electrician	elèktričar *m*
elevator operator	lìftboj *m*
engineer	inžènjer *m*; inžènjerka *f*
factory worker	tvórnički rádnik/fàbrički rádnik *m*; tvórnička rádnica/fàbrička rádnica *f*
farmer	ràtar *m*; zemjlòradnik *m*
grocer	prodàvač/prodávac *m*
helper	pomòćnik *m*; pomòćnica *f*

housewife	domàćica *f*
interpreter	tùmač *m*
journalist	nòvinar *m*; nòvinarka *f*
king	kràlj *m*
lawyer	advòkat *m*; právnik *m*; òdvjetnik *m* (Cr.)
librarian	knjìžničar/bibliotèkar *m*; knjìžničarka/bibliotèkarka *f*
locomotive engineer	stròjovođa/mašinòvođa *m*
maid	sòbarica *f*; slùžavka *f*; slùškinja *f*
mailman	pòštar *m*; pòštarica *f*
manager	upràvitelj *m*; upràviteljica *f*
mechanic	mehàničar *m*; mehàničarka *f*
merchant	tr̀govac *m*, G tr̀govca
minister (government)	mìnistar *m*; mìnistarka *f*
minister (religious)	pàstor *m*
musician (light)	muzìkant *m*
musician (serious)	mùzičar *m*
nurse	bólničarka *f*
office worker	činòvnik *m*; činòvnica *f*
officer	ofìcir *m*
painter (artistic)	slìkar *m*; slìkarica/slìkarka *f*
painter (house)	lìčilac/mòler *m*
party member	partíjac *m*, G partíjca; pàrtijka *f*
pharmacist	apotèkar *m*; apotèkarka *f*
pickpocket	džèpar *m*; džèparoš *m*
pilot	pìlot *m*
plumber	vodoinstalàter *m*
policeman	miliciònar *m*; miliciòner *m*; milicájac *m*, G milicájca
politician	polìtičar *m*; polìtičarka *f*
porter	nòsač *m*
president	prèdsjednik/prèdsednik *m*; prèdsjednica/prèdsednica *f*
priest	svèćenik/svèštenik *m*
printer	štàmpar *m*
professor	pròfesor *m*; pròfesorka *f*
railroad worker	žèljezničar/žèlezničar *m*
representative	prèdstavnik *m*; prèdstavnica *f*
sailor	mòrnar *m*
salesman	prodàvač/prodávac *m*; prodaváčica *f*
scientist	učènjak/nàučnik *m*
seamstress	krojàčica *f*
secretary	sekrètar *m*; sekretàrica *f*

servant	slúga *m*; slùškinja *f*
shoemaker	òbućar *m*; pòstolar *m* (Cr.)
singer	pjèvač/pèvač *m*; pjevàčica/pevàčica *f*
soldier	vòjnik *m*
specialist	strùčnjak *m*
student	đák *m*; ùčenik *m*; ùčenica *f*
student (university)	stùdent *m*; stùdentica/stùdentkinja *f*
tailor	kròjač *m*; šnàjder *m*
teacher	ùčitelj *m*; učitèljica *f* nástavnik *m*; nástavnica *f*
thief	tát *m*; lópov *m*
tourist	tùrist/tùrista *m*; tùristkinja *f*
typist	daktilògraf *m*; daktilògrafkinja *f*
veterinarian	veterìnar *m*; veterìnarka *f*
waiter	kònobar/kèlner *m*; kònobarica/kèlnerica *f*
worker	rádnik *m*; rádnica *f*
writer	písac *m*; spìsateljica *f*; knjìževnik *m*; knjìževnica *f*

vježba I

Odgovorite na slijedeća pitanja.

1. Štò rádi Pávlov òtac?
2. Štò rádi vàš òtac?
3. Ùči li vàš bràt za lìječnika?
4. Štò biste vòljeli bìti?
5. Štò stùdirate?
6. Dà li ćete ìmati dòbru pláću?
7. Vòlite li matemàtiku?
8. Kòji prédmet nájviše vòlite?
9. U kòjem prédmetu ste nájslabiji?
10. Kòju pòslovicu o znánju znáte?

vežba I

Odgovorite na sledeća pitanja.

1. Štà rádi Pávlov òtac?
2. Štà rádi vàš òtac?
3. Dà li vàš bràt ùči za lekára?
4. Štà biste vòleli da bùdete?
5. Štà stùdirate?
6. Dà li ćete ìmati dòbru plátu?
7. Dà li vòlite matemàtiku?
8. Kòji prédmet nàjviše vólite?
9. U kòjem prédmetu ste nájslabiji?
10. Kòju pòslovicu o znánju znáte?

vježba/vežba II

Ùmjesto/Ùmesto zàmjenice/zàmenice stàvite ìmenicu kòja oznàčava odgovárajuću pròfesiju. (Instead of the pronoun use a noun that indicates the appropriate profession.)

Ón je ùkrao pedèset dòlara.
Džèparoš je ùkrao pedèset dòlara.

1. Òna će dànas sprémiti dòbar rúčak.
2. Ón rádi u bibliotéci.
3. Òna se brìne o bolesnícima.

4. Ón vòzi àuto.
5. Òn pópravlja zúbe.
6. Ón je čìtao nòvu lékciju.
7. Òn nòsi písma ùjutro i popódne.
8. Òn je pòpravio mój àuto.
9. Òna šìje vrlo lijèpe/lépe hàljine.
10. Òn je svírao stáru sȑpsku pjèsmu/pèsmu.

vježba/vežba III

Pòpunite slijèdeće/slédeće rečènice odgovárajućim pròšlim vrèmenom. (Complete the following sentences by supplying the appropriate past tense form.)

1. Žèna je ________pìsmo. (**písati,** to write)
2. ________smo knjìge. (**vrátiti,** to return)
3. Mí (= 2 girls) smo ________knjìge. (vrátiti)
4. ________sam kòd kuće. (**bìti,** to be)
5. Já sam ________kòd kuće. (bìti; Ja = Náda)
6. Sèlo je ________mírno. (bìti)
7. Sèla su ________pod snìjegom/snégom. (bìti)
8. Ví ________ ________nàgradu. (**dòbiti,** to get, to receive)
9. Dà li ________òni ________táj prédmet? (**znàti,** to know)
10. Dà li ________tí ________pjèsmu/pèsmu? (**zabòraviti,** to forget, **ti = Mílka**)

vježba/vežba IV

Stàvite òve rečènice u òdrečni òblik. (Put these sentences into the negative form.)

1. Mój òtac je rádio u tvórnici/fàbrici.
2. Òni su studírali matemàtiku.
3. Pávle je mnògo putòvao mórem.
4. Rìbar se utòpio u móru.
5. Pròšlog ljèta/lèta bílo je mnògo tùrista u Splìtu.

vježba/vežba V

Pòpunite slijèdeće/slédeće rečènice odgovárajućim òblikom pròšlog vrèmena, a zàtim ih stàvite u òdrečni i ùpitni òblik. (Complete the following sentences by supplying the appropriate past tense form and then put them into the negative and interrogative form.)

Òn ________ ________lìftboj. (bìti)
Ón je bìo lìftboj.
Ón nìje bìo lìftboj.
Jè li ón bìo lìftboj? [or] Dà li je ón bìo lìftboj?

1. Ví _________ _________tóg pjeváča/peváča. (čùti)
2. Òni _________ _________príču o tȑgovcu i mornáru. (znàti)
3. Tȑgovac _________ _________mornáru da se bòji móra. (rèći)
4. Mój djèd/dèda _________ _________rìbar. (bìti)
5. Dùnja _________ _________rùski. (studìrati)

Historical Background. When the Kingdom of the Serbs, Croats, and Slovenes came into existence in 1918 (the name was changed to Yugoslavia in 1929), it brought together a variety of nationalities that had had long histories of separate development. For centuries two empires, the Austro-Hungarian and the Ottoman Turkish, held sway in these regions and bequeathed to their subject peoples distinct heritages of tradition and outlook. The Moslem heritage is still strong in Bosnia and Herzegovina, and even the casual visitor will be startled by the cultural contrast between the people in this republic with their eastern way of life and those in Croatia and Slovenia, who were formed in a western mold through their centuries-long contact with the Austro-Hungarian Empire. During the 19th century Serbia freed itself from the Turks and established its own kingdom with a population base of peasantry and a thin layer of officialdom and aristocracy. One of the more picturesque constituent elements of this new country of Yugoslavia is the former Kingdom of Montenegro, which contributed its heroic history along with its bleak landscapes and meager resources. In Dalmatia the long influence of the Venetians and Italians had made itself felt, producing that appealing Dalmatian type, with its combination of languor and effervescence. The latest entry into the state is Macedonia, which even into the first years of this century was under Turkish rule; Macedonia has been, throughout its history, such a conglomerate of nationality types (Macedonian Slavs, Greeks, Albanians, Turks, Bulgarians, Vlachs, Gypsies, etc.) that it has given its name to a fruit salad called *la macédoine*.

World War II visited a series of disasters on this young state with its variegated inhabitants, among which the worst misfortunes were the invasion by Germans and Italians and a civil war of dreadful ferocity. In the postwar period, political power was in the hands of Yugoslavia's League of Communists and Marshal Tito (Josip Broz), who was president-for-life until his death in 1980. In recent years the monopoly on power exercised by the Communists was loosened and a multiparty system began to flourish in Slovenia and Croatia. Ethnic tensions continue to threaten the stability of the country.

Tȑgovac i mòrnar

Tȑgovac je upítao mornára: -Kàkvom je smȓću ùmro tvój òtac?
— Utòpio se u móru. — odgovòrio je mòrnar.
— A tvój djèd?

— I ón se utòpio.

— Pa kàko da se ne bòjiš putòvati mórem? — upìtao ga je tȑgovac. Na tó mòrnar nìje odgovòrio tȑgovcu, àli ga je upítao:

— A káži mi tí sàd, mòlim te, gdjè je ùmro tvój òtac, djèd i pràdjed?

— Ùmrli su mírno u svòjim pòsteljama. — odgovòrio je tȑgovac.

— É, bràte, -mòrnar je rèkao tȑgovcu, -pa kàko da se tí ònda ne bòjiš svàki dán lèći u pòstelju spávati?

LEKCIJA

Godišnja doba

1. Godina se dijeli na četiri godišnja doba.
2. To su: proljeće, ljeto, jesen i zima.
3. Zima službeno počinje dvadeset prvog prosinca, proljeće dvadeset prvog ožujka, ljeto dvadeset prvog lipnja, a jesen dvadeset prvog rujna.
4. Ako volite snijeg, uživat ćete u Minnesoti za vrijeme zime.
5. Ako volite toplo sunčano vrijeme i oceanski povjetarac, uživat ćete u Floridi.
6. Naša je država velika i u naših pedeset država možete naći sve vrste klime.
7. Ali mi se navikavamo na klimu države u kojoj smo se rodili i u kojoj živimo.
8. Kad pada snijeg, možemo ići na skijanje po obližnjim brdima.
9. Ako je vrijeme hladno, možemo ići na klizanje po jezeru ili rijeci.
10. Kad pada kiša, možemo čitati ili raditi u sobi.
11. Kad je vruće, možemo se rashladiti kupanjem u jezeru ili rijeci.

ЛЕКЦИЈА

Ѓодишња доба

1. Ѓодина се дели на четири годишња доба.
2. То су: пролеће, лето, јесен и зима.
3. Зима званично почиње двадесет првог децембра, пролеће двадесет првог марта, лето двадесет првог јуна, а јесен двадесет првог септембра.
4. Ако волите снег, уживаћете у Минесоти за време зиме.
5. Ако волите топло сунчано време и океански поветарац, уживаћете у Флориди.
6. Наша је држава велика и у наших педесет држава можете да нађете све врсте климе.
7. Али ми се навикавамо на климу државе у којој смо се родили и у којој живимо.
8. Кад пада снег, можемо да идемо на скијање по оближњим брдима.
9. Ако је време хладно, можемо да идемо на клизање по језеру или реци.
10. Кад пада киша, можемо да читамо или да радимо у соби.
11. Кад је врућина, можемо да се расхладимо купањем у језеру или реци.

KORIJEN NAUKE JE GORAK, ALI PLOD JE SLADAK.	КОРЕН НАУКЕ ЈЕ ЃОРАК, АЛИ ПЛОД ЈЕ СЛАДАК.

SEASONS OF THE YEAR—1. This year is divided into four seasons (four yearly times). 2. They are: spring, summer, fall, and winter. 3. Winter begins officially on the 21st of December, spring on the 21st of March, summer on the 21st of June, and fall on the 21st of September. 4. If you like snow, you will enjoy Minnesota in the wintertime. 5. If you like warm sunshine (warm sunny weather) and the ocean breeze, you will enjoy Florida. 6. Our country is large and you can find all varieties of climate in our fifty states. 7. But we get used to the climate of the state in which we were born and in which we live. 8. When it's snowing, we can go skiing on nearby hills. 9. If the weather is cold, we may go ice-skating on the lake or the river. 10. When it's raining, we can read or work indoors. 11. When it's hot, we can cool off by swimming in the lake or the river.

Ćiril i Metod su bili slavenski apostoli.	Ћирило и Методије су били словенски апостоли.

This lesson introduces the Cyrillic alphabet, one of the two official alphabets of the Croatian and Serbian language. If you wish, you may ignore it completely and rely on the Latin alphabet. However, even if you have no intention of using the Cyrillic alphabet actively, it would be useful to acquire a passive knowledge of it.

The Cyrillic alphabet is so named because it was long thought that it had been invented by Saint Cyril. As the title sentence above states, Cyril and his brother Methodius were apostles to the Slavs, bringing Christianity in the Slavic tongue to Moravia (in present-day Czechoslovakia) in A.D. 863.

Cyril is also referred to as Constantine, which actually was his name up until 869, when, in accepting monastic vows in Rome, he took the name Cyril. Constantine and his brother Methodius were two Slavic-speaking missionaries from Salonika (NE Greece), sent by the Patriarch Photius of Byzantium to the Slavic state of Moravia at the request of Prince Rostislav. In order to provide a written translation of the New Testament for the Slavs, Constantine (Cyril) devised a special alphabet, called the *Glagolitic*. This was displaced by another alphabet, one based on the Greek and called, mistakenly, Cyrillic. Glagolitic disappeared from general use at an early date, though in a few areas (parts of Dalmatia) it survived into this century.

The Cyrillic alphabet has, since the time of Cyril, been used principally in those Slavic countries or areas where the principal religious denomination was the Orthodox. Thus the new alphabet in this lesson is actually *Serbian Cyrillic*, since there are distinctive forms of Cyrillic in use for the Russian, Ukrainian, Belorussian, Bulgarian, and Macedonian languages.

vježba/vežba I

Za bolje upoznavanje s ćirilicom, napišite štampanim slovima slijedeća/sledeća imena mjesta/mesta. (For familiarization with Cyrillic, print the following place names in Cyrillic letters.)

Amerika	Beograd	Šestine	Sraćinec
Jugoslavija	Zagreb	Đakovo	Šćepanje
Hrvatska	Sarajevo	Vrnjačka Banja	Brečevići
Srbija	Skoplje	Ulcinj	Frkljevci
Makedonija	Ljubljana	Slunj	Džigolj
Slovenija	Cetinje	Peć	Ičići
Bosna	Orebić	Rijeka	Ptuj
Hercegovina	Ilidža	Posušje	Split
Crna Gora	Požega	Škofja Loka	Pučišće

vježba II

Odgovorite na slijedeća pitanja.

1. Na koliko se godišnjih doba dijeli godina?
2. Koja su to godišnja doba?
3. Kada službeno počinje zima?
4. Volite li zimu i snijeg?
5. Idete li na klizanje zimi?
6. Koje je vaše najdraže godišnje doba?
7. Gdje idete ljeti?
8. Volite li se kupati u moru?
9. Što radite kad pada kiša?
10. Kakva je klima u vašoj domovini?

vežba II

Odgovorite na sledeća pitanja.

1. Na koliko se godišnjih doba deli godina?
2. Koja su to godišnja doba?
3. Kada službeno počinje zima?
4. Da li volite zimu i sneg?
5. Da li idete na klizanje zimi?
6. Koje je vaše najdraže godišnje doba?
7. Gde idete leti?
8. Da li volite da se kupate u moru?
9. Šta radite kad pada kiša?
10. Kakva je klima u vašoj otadžbini?

Exercises in Cyrillic. Though the exercises in this and subsequent lessons will be in the Latin alphabet, you may easily convert them into Cyrillic versions. For example, **vežba II** above would appear as:

вежба **II**

1. На колико се годишњих доба дели година?
2. Која су то годишња доба?
3. Када службено почиње зима?

4. Да ли волите зиму и снег?
5. Да ли идете на клизање зими?
6. Које је ваше најдраже годишње доба?
7. Где идете лети?
8. Да ли волите да се купате у мору?
9. Шта радите кад пада киша?
10. Каква је клима у вашој отаџбини?

vježba/vežba III

Popunite ove rečenice odgovarajućim glagolskim vremenom: prezentom, futurom ili prošlim vremenom. (Complete these sentences with the correct tense: present, future, or past tense. The personal pronouns in parentheses are simply to indicate which form of the verb is called for; it is not necessary to use them unless for emphasis.)

Godina ________ ________ na četiri godišnja doba. (dijeliti se/deliti se)

Godina se dijeli/deli na četiri godišnja doba.

1. Svake godine (ja) ________ na Floridu. (ići)
2. Što/Šta ________ (vi) ________ idućeg petka? (raditi)
3. Prošlog petka (mi) ________ ________ na klizanju. (biti)
4. Dogodine (ja) ________ se ________ u moru. (kupati se)
5. (Cr.) Idućeg tjedna ________ ________ snijeg. (padati)
   (Sr.) Iduće nedelje ________ ________ sneg. (padati)
6. (Cr.) Oni ________ se ________ sa skijanja prošlog tjedna. (vratiti se)
   (S.) Oni ________ se ________ sa skijanja prošle nedelje. (vratiti se)
7. Tjedan/Nedelja ________ sedam dana. (imati)
8. Mi ________ ________ za Jugoslaviju iduće godine. (putovati)
9. Ovog ljeta/leta (ja) ________ ________ kod kuće. (ostati)
10. Jesen službeno ________ dvadeset prvog rujna/septembra. (počinjati)

vježba/vežba IV

Popunite slijedeće/sledeće rečenice odgovarajućim oblikom budućeg vremena. (Complete the sentences below with the appropriate future tense form.)

1. Moj brat ________ sutra ________. (raditi)
2. Ja ________________ hrvatski/srpski. (govoriti)
3. Da li ________ Jovo ________ novu pjesmu/pesmu? (pjevati/pevati)
4. Mi ________ se brzo ________. (obući se)

5. Tako ________vi ________našu lijepu/lepu zemlju. (upoznati)
6. Gdje/Gde ________oni ________preksutra. (biti)
7. "________________se kući", rekao je mali Bogdan. (vratiti se)
8. Petre! Kada ________ ________svoj posao? (svršiti)
9. Kada vi ________ ________moje pismo? (čitati)
10. Mi ________ ________u kino/bioskop. (ići)

Weeks, Months, Years **sèdmice, mjèseci/mèseci, gòdine**

week	sèdmica tjèdan (Cr.) nèdelja dána (S.)
weekly	sèdmično tjèdno nèdeljno
every week	svàke sèdmice svàkog tjèdna svàke nèdelje*
this week	òve sèdmice òvog tjèdna òve nèdelje
next week	ìduće sèdmice ìdućeg tjèdna ìduće nèdelje
last week	pròšle sèdmice pròšlog tjèdna pròšle nèdelje
Which week?	Kòje sèdmice? Kòjega tjèdna? Kòje nèdelje?
month	mjèsec, mjèsec dána (Cr.) mèsec, mèsec dána (S.)

monthly	mjèsečno/mèsečno
every month	svàkog mjèseca/mèseca
this month	òvog mjèseca/mèseca
next month	ìdućeg mjèseca/mèseca
last month	pròšlog mjèseca/mèseca
Which month?	Kòjega mjèseca/mèseca?
year	gòdina
yearly	gòdišnje
every year	svàke gòdine
this year	òve gòdine
last year	pròšle gòdine, láni/láne
next year	ìduće gòdine, dògodine
Which year?	Kòje gòdine?

Seasons

Gòdišnja dòba	**Seasons of the Year**
pròljeće/pròleće	spring

*This expression could also mean "every Sunday"; the context will indicate whether "Sunday" or "week" is being specified.

ljèto/lèto	summer
jèsen, G jèseni	fall, autumn
zíma	winter
početkom zíme	at the beginning of winter
sredìnom zíme	in the middle of winter
kràjem zíme	at the end of winter

ДВА МЕРИЛА

Једном је неки дипломата признао Лојду Џорџу да је био помало разочаран кад је видео да је један тако славан човек тако малог раста.

-То зависи од начина, -одговори Лојд Џорџ, -на који ви мерите људе. Не треба их мерити од браде наниже, већ од браде навише.

DVANAESTA LEKCIJA

Školovanje

1. Kamo ideš sada, Jim?
2. Idem u školu, Miroslave.
3. U koju školu ideš?
4. Idem u koledž. Jesi li ti student?
5. Ne, još sam učenik srednje škole.
6. A moja mlađa sestra, Nada, učenica je osnovne škole.
7. Je li u Jugoslaviji sličan sistem školovanja?
8. Nije sasvim sličan.
9. U Jugoslaviji osnovna škola ima obično osam razreda.
10. A njihova gimnazija ima četiri razreda.
11. Tada se maturant može upisati u jedno od dvadesetak sveučilišta u Jugoslaviji.
12. Zar tamo nema koledža?
13. Struktura njihova sveučilišta malo je drugačija.
14. Njihova sveučilišta se dijele na razne fakultete, kao na primjer na pravni fakultet, medicinski fakultet, filozofski fakultet i tako dalje.
15. A zasebno od sveučilišta imaju Više pedagoške škole
16. Pretpostavljam da bi njihov filozofski fakultet otprilike

ДВАНАЕСТА ЛЕКЦИЈА

Школовање

1. Куда идеш сада, Џим?
2. Идем у школу, Мирославе.
3. У коју школу идеш?
4. Идем у колеџ. Да ли си ти студент?
5. Не, још сам ученик средње школе.
6. А моја млађа сестра, Нада, ученица је основне школе.
7. Да ли је у Југославији сличан систем школовања?
8. Није сасвим сличан.
9. У Југославији основна школа има обично осам разреда.
10. А њихова гимназија има четири разреда.
11. Тада матурант може да се упише у један од двадесетак универзитета у Југославији.
12. Зар тамо нема колеџа?
13. Структура њиховог универзитета мало је другачија.
14. Њихови универзитети се деле на разне факултете, као на пример на правни факултет, медицински факултет, филозофски факултет и тако даље.
15. А засебно од универзитета имају Више педагошке школе.
16. Претпостављам да би њихов филозофски факул-

odgovarao našem "liberal arts" koledžu.

тет отприлике одговарао нашем "либерал артс" колеџу.

17. Gdje se ta sveučilišta nalaze?

17. Ѓде се ти универзитети налазе?

18. Ima ih dvadesetak i ona se nalaze u Zagrebu, Beogradu, Ljubljani, Sarajevu, Rijeci, Novom Sadu, Zadru, Splitu, Skoplju, Nišu, Prištini, Osijeku, Banjaluci, Tuzli, Mostaru itd.

18. Има их двадесетак и они се налазе у Загребу, Београду, Љубљани, Сарајеву, Ријеци, Новом Саду, Задру, Скопљу, Сплиту, Нишу, Приштини, Осијеку, Бањалуци, Тузли, Мостару итд.

19. Sveučilišta Zagreba i Beograda poznata su širom svijeta.

19. Универзитети Загреба и Београда познати су широм света.

DOBAR GLAS DALEKO SE ČUJE, A LOŠ JOŠ DALJE.

РЂАВО СЕ ЧУЈЕ ДАЉЕ ОД ДОБРОЃА.

SCHOOLING—1. Where are you going now, Jim? 2. I'm going to school, Miroslav. 3. What school do you go to? 4. I go to college. Are you a college student? 5. No, I'm still in high school (still a student of high school). 6. And my younger sister, Nada, is a pupil in (of) the elementary school. 7. Is there a similar system of education in Yugoslavia? 8. Not exactly similar. 9. In Yugoslavia the elementary (basic) school usually has eight grades. 10. And their secondary school has four grades. 11. Then a student may enroll in one of some twenty universities in Yugoslavia. 12. Don't they have colleges there? 13. The makeup of their university is somewhat different. 14. Their universities are divided into various "faculties," as for example, a law "faculty," a medical "faculty," a philosophical "faculty," and so forth. 15. And they have separate Teachers' Colleges. 16. I suppose that their "faculty of philosophy" would correspond roughly to our liberal arts college. 17. Where are those universities located? 18. There are some twenty of them and they are located in Zagreb, Belgrade, Ljubljana, Sarajevo, Rijeka, Novi Sad, Zadar, Split, Skoplje, Niš, Priština, Osijek, Banjaluka, Tuzla, Mostar, and so on. 19. The universities of Zagreb and Belgrade are world-famous (famous throughout the world.)

vježba I

Odgovorite na slijedeća pitanja.

1. Jeste li vi učenik?
2. Jeste li student?

vežba I

Odgovorite na sledeća pitanja.

1. Da li ste vi učenik?
2. Da li ste student?

3. Je li u Jugoslaviji isti sistem školovanja kao u Americi?
4. Koliko razreda ima osnovna škola?
5. Koliko razreda ima gimnazija?
6. Ima li koledža u Jugoslaviji?
7. Kako se dijele sveučilišta?
8. Jesu li Više pedagoške škole odijeljene od sveučilišta?
9. Koliko sveučilišta ima u Jugoslaviji?
10. Gdje se ta sveučilišta nalaze?

3. Da li je u Jugoslaviji isti sistem školovanja kao u Americi?
4. Koliko razreda ima osnovna škola?
5. Koliko razreda ima gimnazija?
6. Da li ima koledža u Jugosla viji?
7. Kako se dele univerziteti?
8. Da li su Više pedagoške škole odeljene od univerziteta?
9. Koliko univerziteta ima u Jugoslaviji?
10. Gde se ti univerziteti nalaze?

vježba/vežba II

Prepišite i popunite slijedeće/sledeće rečenice pravilnim oblikom riječi/reči u zagradama. (Copy down and complete the following sentences, using the correct forms of the words in parentheses.)

1. Primio sam pismo od ________ ________. (mladi Hrvat/Srbin)
2. Sada pišem pismo ________________ ________. (lijepa/lepa mlada glumica)
3. Bio sam u svim ________ ________Evrope. (velike države)
4. Stari profesor je ušao u ________ ________. (stara zgrada)
5. Pas leži na ________ ________. (novi ćilim)
6. Prijatno je govoriti s ________ ________. (pametni studenti)
7. Vojnik je izašao iz ________ ________. (siromašno selo)
8. Tko/Ko stanuje u ________ ________ ________? (ta stara kuća)
9. Između ________ ________ ________(ova glavna ulica) i ________ ________(velika katedrala) je park.
10. Od ________ ________(naša kuča) do ________ ________(glavni trg) nije daleko.

vježba/vežba III

Stavite ove rečenice u množinu. (Put these sentences into the plural.)

Ja sam u školi.
Mi smo u školi.

1. On je student.
2. Što/Šta ćeš studirati?
3. Moj prijatelj je završio pravni fakultet.
4. Kupat ću/Kupaću se u moru.

5. Ribar je ulovio veliku ribu.
6. Ide li on s nama?
7. Bio sam student filozofskog fakulteta.
8. Sjećam se/Sećam se svoga profesora.
9. On je putovao po Evropi.
10. Da li ćeš biti u New Yorku/Njujorku u petak?

vježba/vežba IV

Dovršite rečenice. (Complete the sentences.)

Nada ________dva ________. (imati, brat)
Nada ima dva brata.

1. Jim/Džim ________u ________. (ići, škola)
2. Miroslav ________ ________ ________iduće godine. (studirati, medicina)
3. Sveučilišta/Univerziteti ________na ________. (dijeliti se/deliti se, fakultet)
4. Ona ________u ________. (sjediti/sediti, klupa)
5. Učenik ________ ________ispred ________. (stajati, ploča/tabla)
6. On ________tri ________. (imati, sin)
7. Jedan sin ________ ________deset ________idućeg mjeseca/meseca. (imati, godina)
8. Jučer/Juče ________ ________Pavla s ________. (vidjeti/videti, prijatelj)
9. ________ ________kod ________popodne. (ići, zubar)
10. Ivan ________student ________u ________. (biti, matematika, Zagreb.)

vježba/vežba V

Prevedite na hrvatski/srpski.

1. I shall come when I finish this letter.
2. If the weather is nice, we shall go out.
3. When I buy a car, we'll go to New York sometimes.
4. If your son is six, he'll go to school next year.
5. If it is cold outside, I shall wear my brown coat.

vježba/vežba VI

Sastavite pitanja za slijedeće/sledeće odgovore. (Make questions for the following answers.)

1. Idem kući.
2. Imam sestru.
3. Studiram u Splitu.
4. Split ima Pravni fakultet.
5. Doći ću kad se vrati majka.

6. Jim/Džim je sa prijateljem.
7. Ovaj auto je moj.
8. U koledžu.
9. To je kolo iz Srbije.
10. Ja plešem/igram kolo.

MLADOST–LUDOST. МЛАДОСТ–ЛУДОСТ.

Months of the Year There are two sets of names for the months in Cr&S.: a Serbian set, which is similar to the English terms, and a Croatian set of Slavic names. In order to show the oblique (non-N) forms of these names, examples are given that could appear in the following types of statement.

Ovaj mjesec je *ožujak* [N sg.]./ Ovaj mesec je *mart* [N sg.]	This month is March.
To se desilo osmoga *ožujka* [G sg.]. / To se desilo osmoga *marta* [G sg.].	That happened on the eighth of March.
Rođen sam u *ožujku* [D sg.]. / Rođen sam u *martu* [D sg.]	I was born in March.

Serbian	*Croatian*	*Serbian*	*Croatian*
jànuar	sìječanj	àvgust [or]	kòlovoz
ósmoga jànuara	òsmog sìječnja	àugust	
u jànuaru	u sìječnju	ósmog àvgusta,	ósmog kòlovoza
		àugusta	
fèbruar	vèljača	u àvgustu,	u kòlovozu
òsmog fèbruara	ósmog vèljače	àugustu	
u fèbruaru	u vèljači		
		sèptembar	rújan
màrt	òžujak	ósmog	ósmog rújna
ósmog màrta	ósmog òžujka	sèptembra	
u màrtu	u òžujku	u sèptembru	u rújnu
àpril	trávanj	òktobar	lìstopad
ósmog apríla	ósmog trávnja	ósmog òktobra	ósmog lìstopada
u aprílu	u trávnju	u òktobru	u lìstopadu
máj	svíbanj	nòvembar	stùdeni [adj. in
ósmog màja	ósmog svíbnja		form]
u màju	u svíbnju	ósmog nòvembra	òsmog stùdenog(a)
jún [or] jȕni	lípanj	u nòvembru	u stùdenom(e)
ósmog júna	ósmog lípnja		
u júnu	u lípnju	dècembar	pròsinac

		ósmog dècembra	ósmog pròsinca
júl [or] júli	sŕpanj	u dècembru	u pròsincu
ósmog júla	ósmog sŕpnja		
u júlu	u sŕpnju		

Male Šale

Kod advokata.
—Susjed me uvrijedio.
—A što vam je rekao?
—Poslao me je k vragu.
—A vi?
—Došao sam k vama.

Rudi: A zna li tvoja zaručnica držati tajnu?
Bobi: Kako ne. Mi smo bili zaručeni mjesec dana prije nego što sam ja to doznao.

Profesor sjedne u gostionici, dođe konobar i upita ga:
—Što želite, profesore?
—Ovaj, ako nisam jeo, donesite mi objed, a ako sam jeo, dajte mi račun.

МАЛЕ ШАЛЕ

Путник у бродском ресторану:
—Келнер, молим вас, ако је ово што сте донели кафа, дајте ми чај; али ако је чај, боље ми донесите кафу!

—Постоје пси који су интелигентнији од својих господара.
—То је истина! Ја имам једног таквог пса.

Два лопова стоје пред кућом познатог тврдице, иначе великог богаташа, и одлучују да покушају срећу као просјаци. Први уђе, али се врати већ после неколико минута.
—Но, како је било? —упита га други.
—Избацио ме напоље!
—Баш је немилосрдан. Али казниће га Бог!
—Већ га је казнио.
—Како?
—Ево овако, —одговори први лопов и показа сребрну кашику.

TRINAESTA LEKCIJA

Dva Amerikanca

1. Koje si ti narodnosti, Jack?
2. Ja sam stopostotni Amerikanac, Rade.
3. O, to znači da si ti Indijanac, potomak "otmjenih crvenokožaca."
4. Nemoj zadirkivati. Hoću reći da sam se rodio u Americi.
5. U Sjevernoj ili u Južnoj Americi?
6. Ti danas zacijelo tražiš dlaku u jajetu. Rođen sam u Minneapolisu, u državi Minnesoti, u Sjedinjenim Američkim Državama.
7. Jesu li se tvoji roditelji rodili ovdje?
8. Tata se rodio ovdje, ali njegovi su roditelji ovamo došli iz Norveške; a mama je kao djevojčica došla iz Irske.
9. Onda si ti irsko-norveškog porijekla.
10. Da . . . Reci, a nisi li ti prije nekoliko godina došao iz Jugoslavije?
11. Imaš pravo! Rođen sam u Bosni, u Jugoslaviji, a u Sjedinjene Američke Države došao sam prije pet godina kao raseljeno lice.
12. Jesi li sad državljanin?
13. Ponosan sam što mogu reći da

ТРИНАЕСТА ЛЕКЦИЈА

Два Американца

1. Које си ти народности, џек?
2. Ја сам стопроцентни Американац, Раде.
3. О, то значи да си ти Индијанац, потомак "отмених рвенокожаца."
4. Немој да ме задиркујеш. Хоћу рећи да сам се родио у Америци.
5. У Северној или у Јужној Америци?
6. Ти данас зацело тражиш длаку у јајету. Рођен сам у Минеаполису, у држави Минесоти, у Сједињеним Америчким Државама.
7. Да ли су се твоји родитељи родили овде?
8. Тата се родио овде, али његови су родитељи овамо дошли из Норвешке; а мама је као девојчица дошла из Ирске.
9. Онда си ти ирско-норвешког порекла.
10. Да . . . Реци, а ниси ли ти пре неколико година дошао из Југославије?
11. Имаш право! Рођен сам у Босни, у Југославији, а у Сједињене Америчке Државе дошао сам пре пет година као расељено лице.
12. Јеси ли сад држављанин?
13. Поносан сам што могу рећи

sam jučer dobio američko državljanstvo.	да сам јуче добио америчко држављанство.
14. Čestitam! Dobro došao u "zemlju slobodnih i u dom hrabrih!"	14. Честитам! Добро дошао у "земљу слободних и у дом храбрих!"
S KIM SI, ONAKAV SI.	С КИМ СИ, ОНАКАВ СИ.

TWO AMERICANS—1. What's your nationality, Jack? 2. I'm a hundred percent American, Rade. 3. Oh, that means you're an Indian, a descendant of the "noble redskins." 4. Stop your kidding! I mean I was born in America. 5. In North or in South America? 6. You're certainly splitting hairs today (looking for the hair in the egg). I was born in Minneapolis, in the state of Minnesota, in the United States of America. 7. Were your parents born here? 8. Dad was born here, but his parents came here from Norway; and mom came from Ireland as a little girl. 9. Then you're of Irish-Norwegian descent. 10. Yes . . . Say, didn't you come from Yugoslavia a few years back? 11. You're right! I was born in Bosnia, in Yugoslavia, and I came to the United (American) States as a displaced person five years ago. 12. Are you a citizen now? 13. I am proud to be able to say that I received American citizenship yesterday. 14. Congratulations (I congratulate)! Welcome to the "land of the free and the home of the brave.!"

vježba/vežba I

Popunite rečenice množinom riječi/reči u zagradama.

1. Poznajete li _________ _________? (moj prijatelj)
2. _________rade u poljima. (žena)
3. Imate li mnogo _________? (prijatelj)
4. Prijatno je govoriti o _________. (praznik)
5. Čujemo _________. (zvono)
6. Govorili smo o _________. (žena)
7. _________ _________ _________idu u osnovnu školu. (moja mlađa sestra)
8. Napisali su _________ _________o moru. (nova pjesma/pesma)
9. Ovo su _________ _________. (veliko stablo)
10. Tu ima mnogo _________ _________. (mala kuća)

vježba/vežba II

Stavite u odgovarajući padež.

1. Solun je grad u _________. (Grčka)
2. Stigao je iz _________. (Lenjingrad)

3. Letjeli/Leteli smo preko ________. (Engleska)
4. Moj brat živi u ________. (Madžarska/Mađarska)
5. Kroz ________ smo putovali avionom. (Čehoslovačka)
6. Volim ________. (Danska)
7. Živio/Živeo je dugo godina u ________. (Japan)
8. Do ________ idemo avionom. (Moskva)
9. Da li ste bili u ________? (Albanija)
10. Mnogo smo putovali po ________. (Evropa)

vježba III

Popunite ove rečenice odgovarajućim glagolskim vremenom.

Kad ________ (ja), ne ________. (raditi, pjevati)
Kad radim, ne pjevam.

1. Ako (vi) ________ kod prozora, ________ ________ veliki hrast, (stajati, vidjeti)
2. Kad ________ kiša, ja ________. (padati, spavati)
3. Kad ________ vruće, mi se ________. (biti, kupati se)
4. Ako (ti) ________, ________ ________ ti istinu. (doći, reći)
5. Ako (vi) ________ ljeto, ________ ________ u Dalmaciji. (voljeti, uživati)
6. Ako ________ hladno, mi ne ________ ići vani. (biti, morati)
7. Ako (ti) ________, (mi) ________ u kino. (htjeti, ići)
8. Ako (vi) ________ glazbu, (mi) ________ ________ na koncert. (voljeti, poći)
9. Kada ________ moj prijatelj, ________ ________ o nogometu. (doći, pričati)
10. Ako (ti) ________ more, ________ ________ zajedno brodom. (voljeti, putovati)

vježba/vežba IV

Napišite kratki sastav na temu "Moja narodnost."

Countries and Continents **dȑžave i kontìnentí**

English name	Cr&S name	Inhabitant	Relevant adjective
Africa	Àfrika	Afrikánac	afrìkanski, àfrički
Albania	Àlbanija	Albánac	àlbanski
America	Amèrika	Amerikánac	amerìkanski, amèrički
Antarctic	Antàrktik	pìngvin	antàrktični
Arctic	Àrktik	bìjeli mèdvjed/béli mèdved	àrktični
Asia	Àzija	Azìjat	azìjatski, àzijski
Australia	Àustralija	Austrálac	àustralski

Austria	Àustrija	Austrijánac	àustrijski
Belgium	Bèlgija	Belgijánac	bèlgijski
Bulgaria	Bùgarska*	Bùgarin	bùgarski
Canada	Kanáda	Kanáđanin	kànadski
China	Kína	Kìnez	kìneski
Cuba	Kúba	Kubánac	kùbanski
Czechoslovakia	Čehoslòvačka*	Čehoslòvak, Čèh, Slòvak	čehoslòvački, čèški, slòvački
Denmark	Dánska*	Dánac	dánski
Egypt	Ègipat	Ègipćanin	ègipatski
England	Èngleska*	Ènglez	èngleski
Estonia	Èstonija	Estónac	èstonski
Europe	Evrópa	Evrópljanin	èvropski
Finland	Fínska*	Fínac	fìnski
France	Fràncuska*	Fràncuz	fràncuski
Germany	Njèmačka*/ Nèmačka*	Nijèmac/Némac	njèmački/nèmački
Great Britain	Vèlika Brìtanija	Británac	brìtanski
Greece	Gȑčka*	Gȑk	gȑčki
Holland	Holàndija	Holànđanin	hòlandski
Hungary	Màdžarska*/ Màđarska*	Màdžar/Màđar	màdžarski/ màđarski
India	Ìndija	Indíjac	ìndijski
Iran	Ìran	Iránac	ìranski
Iraq	Ìrak	Iráčanin	ìrački
Ireland	Írska*	Írac	írski
Israel	Ìzrael	Izsraélac	izràelski
Italy	Ìtalija	Italìjan, Talìjan	italìjanski, talìjanski
Japan	Jàpan	Japánac	jàpanski
Latvia	Lètonija	Letónac	lètonski
Lebanon	Lìban	Libánac	lìbanski
Lithuania	Lìtva, Lìtvanija	Litvánac	lìtvanski
Norway	Nòrveška*	Norvéžanin	nòrveški
Poland	Pòljska*	Pòljak	pòljski
Portugal	Portùgalija	Portugálac	portùgalski
Rumania	Rùmunjska*/ Rùmunija	Rùmun	rùmunjski/ rùmunski
Russia	Rùsija	Rùs	rùski
Scotland	Škòtska*	Škotlànđanin	škòtski

*These names have an adjectival declension, e.g. **u Bugarskoj, u Grčkoj**; the other country names have a regular nominal declension, e.g. **u Africi, u Kanadi**.

Slovakia	Slòvačka*	Slòvak	slòvački
Spain	Špànjolska*/ Špánija	Španjólac/Špánac	špànjolski/špánski
Sweden	Švèdska*	Švéđanin	švèdski
Switzerland	Švìcarska*/ Svàjcarska*	Švìcarac/Švajcárac	švìcarski/švàjcarski
Turkey	Tùrska*	Tùrčin (pl. Túrci)	tùrski
U.S.A.	SAD = Sjèdinjene Amèričke Dr̀žave	Amerikánac	amerìkanski, amèrički
U.S.S.R.	SSSR = Sávez Sóvjetskih Socijalìstičkih Repùblika	Rùs itd.	sòvjetski, rùski itd.
Yugoslavia	Jugoslávija	Jugoslàven/ Jugoslòven	jugoslàvenski/ jugoslòvenski

Yugoslavia's Structure. The official name of Yugoslavia is **Socijalìstička Fèderativna Repùblika Jugoslávija (SFRJ)** or, in English, the Socialist Federal Republic of Yugoslavia. The country is divided into six constituent republics, which are:

repùblika	*republic*	*glávni grád*	*capital city*
Bòsna i Hèrcegovina	Bosnia and Herzegovina	Sàrajevo	Sarajevo
Cŕna Gòra	Montenegro	Tìtograd	Titograd
Hr̀vatska	Croatia	Zágreb	Zagreb
Makèdonija	Macedonia	Skòpje	Skopje
Slòvenija	Slovenia	Ljùbljana	Ljubljana
Sr̀bija	Serbia	Beògrad	Belgrade

In addition, there are two autonomous regions, both located in Serbia: **Vòjvodina** in the north, with the principal city, **Nòvi Sád**; and **Kòsovo** in the south, with the principal city, **Príština**. In Vojvodina, Hungarians make up about 20 percent of the population; in Kosovo, Albanians number over 77 percent. Belgrade is not only the capital city of Serbia, but it is also the capital of the entire country.

In 1990 political forces in Croatia and Slovenia demanded a looser national structure in the form of a confederation or, failing that, separate status as independent nations.

*These names have an adjectival declension, e.g. **u Bugarskoj, u Grčkoj**; the other country names have a regular nominal declension, e.g. **u Africi, u Kanadi**.

Најкраћи новински извештај

Новинарско друштво у Филаделфији доделило је репортеру Хари Тејлору награду за најкраћу новинску вест. Тејлор је награду заиста и заслужио, јер је једну несрећу описао тако кратко, а опет потпуно јасно, да у његовом тексту стварно ниједна реч није била сувишна. Тај текст Хари Тејлора гласи:

> Вилијам Хардер је запалио
> шибицу да види има ли још
> бензина у резервоару. Стар
> педесет шест година.

ČETRNAESTA LEKCIJA

Čovječje tijelo

1. Čovječje tijelo ima mnogo dijelova.
2. Na vrhu tijela nalazi se glava.
3. Na glavi je obično kosa.
4. Ako nema kose, čovjek je ćelav.
5. Muškarci češljaju kosu na jedan način, žene na drugi.
6. Onda dolazi zatiljak, po kojem se češemo kad mislimo.
7. Na svakoj strani glave nalazi se po jedno uho.
8. Prednji dio glave zove se lice.
9. Na licu su dva oka, nos, čelo, dva obraza, usta, usne, brada i gdjekad brkovi i brada.
10. Dakle, lice je važan dio glave.
11. Vrat spaja glavu s trupom.
12. Kad promatramo trup, možemo vidjeti grudni koš i trbuh sprijeda, a leđa su otraga.
13. Dvije strane tijela počinju s ramenima i spuštaju se do kukova, gdje se postepeno sužavaju u noge.
14. Svaka noga ima gornji i donji dio; dijelovi su spojeni koljenom.
15. Najniži dio noge zove se stopalo.

ЧЕТРНАЕСТА ЛЕКЦИЈА

Човечје тело

1. Човечје тело има много делова.
2. На врху тела налази се глава.
3. На глави је обично коса.
4. Ако нема косе, човек је ћелав.
5. Мушкарци чешљају косу на један начин, жене на други.
6. Онда долази потиљак, по коме се чешемо кад мислимо.
7. На свакој страни главе налази се по једно уво.
8. Предњи део главе зове се лице.
9. На лицу су два ока, нос, чело, два образа, уста, усне, брада и понекад бркови и брада.
10. Дакле, лице је важан део главе.
11. Врат спаја главу са трупом.
12. Кад проматрамо труп, можемо да видимо грудни кош и стомак спреда, а леђа су позади.
13. Две стране тела почињу с раменима и спуштају се до кукова, где се постепено сужавају у ноге.
14. Свака нога има горњи и доњи део; делови су спојени коленом.
15. Најнижи део ноге зове се стопало.

16. S donjim dijelom noge stopalo je spojeno gležnjem.
17. Svako stopalo ima pet prstiju koji nisu jednaki.
18. Ruke su spojene s trupom u ramenima.
19. Ruka ima dva glavna dijela. Oba se dijela spajaju u laktu.
20. Donji dio ruke završava se šakom koja je s rukom vezana u zglobu

16. С доњим делом ноге стопало је спојено чланком.
17. Свако стопало има пет прстију који нису једнаки.
18. Руке су спојене с трупом у раменима.
19. Рука има два главна дела. Оба се дела спајају у лакту.
20. Доњи део руке завршава се шаком која је с руком везана у зглобу.

RUKA RUKU MIJE,
OBRAZ OBADVIJE.

РУКА РУКУ МИЈЕ,
ОБРАЗ ОБАДВИЈЕ.

THE HUMAN BODY—1. The human body has many parts. 2. At the top of the body there is the head. 3. On the head there is usually hair. 4. If there is no hair, the person is bald. 5. Men comb their hair in one fashion, women in another. 6. Then comes the back of the head, which we scratch while we're thinking. 7. On each side of the head there is one ear. 8. The front part of the head is called the face. 9. On the face there are two eyes, a nose, a forehead, two cheeks, a mouth, lips, a chin, and sometimes moustaches and a beard. 10. The face is thus an important part of the head. 11. The neck connects the head with the body. 12. When we consider the trunk, we can see the chest and stomach in front, while the back is in the back. 13. The two sides of the body begin with (from) the shoulders and descend to the hips, where they taper into the legs. 14. Each leg has an upper and a lower part; the parts are joined by the knee. 15. The lowest part of the leg is called the foot. 16. The foot is joined to (with) the lower part of the leg by the ankle. 17. Each foot has five toes, which are of unequal size (are unequal). 18. The arms are joined to (with) the trunk at the shoulders. 19. The arm has two main parts. Both parts join at the elbow. 20. The lower part of the arm ends in the hand, which is connected with the arm at the wrist.

vježba/vežba I

Prevedite slijedeće/sledeće rečenice na hrvatski/srpski.

1. He wrote me a letter, [**napísati,** to write]
2. I gave him a new dictionary. [**dàti,** to give]
3. Did he tell you his name? [**kázati,** to tell]
4. I saw him yesterday. [**vìdjeti/vìdeti,** to see]
5. I was born in a village. [**ròditi se,** to be born]

6. I bought her a present. [**kúpiti,** to buy]
7. We watched them for a while. [**glèdati,** to watch]
8. I'll tell her the truth. [**rèći,** to tell]
9. I played with them. [**ìgrati se,** to play]
10. He invited her to dinner. [**pòzvati,** to invite]

vježba II

Odgovorite na slijedeća pitanja.

1. Koji su dijelovi tijela?
2. Koji su dijelovi ruke?
3. Koji su dijelovi noge?
4. Koliko prstiju imate?
5. Koliko nogu imaju zdravi ljudi?
6. Što ima u grudnom košu?
7. Kako se zove najniži dio noge?
8. Što se nalazi u žilama?
9. Što imamo na prstima?
10. Opišite lice.

vežba II

Odgovorite na sledeća pitanja.

1. Koji su delovi tela?
2. Koji su delovi ruke?
3. Koji su delovi noge?
4. Koliko prstiju imate?
5. Koliko nogu imaju zdravi ljudi?
6. Šta ima u grudnom košu?
7. Kako se zove najniži deo noge?
8. Šta se nalazi u žilama?
9. Šta imamo na prstima?
10. Opišite lice.

vježba/vežba III

Popunite rečenice odgovarajućim redom riječi/reči.

1. Vratili ________ ________iz Splita. (se, smo)
2. Reći ________ ________da dođe. (ću, joj)
3. Da li ________ ________dao knjigu? (mu, si)
4. Prošetali ________ ________gradom. (se, smo)
5. Da li ________ ________razumjeli/razumeli? (ga, ste)
6. Susreo ________ ________jučer/juče popodne. (sam, je)
7. Dao ________ ________rječnik/rečnik. (je, joj)
8. Napisala ________ ________nekoliko riječi/reči. (im, sam)
9. Oni ________ ________ ________dali sinoć. (nam, su, ga)
10. Da li ________________vratili? (im, ste, ga)

ŠTO DALJE OD OČIJU,
DALJE I OD SRCA!

ШТО ДАЉЕ ОД ОЧИЈУ,
ДАЉЕ И ОД СРЦА!

Parts of the Body **dijèlovi tìjela/délovi téla**

ankle	glèžanj, člának na nòzi
arm	rúka; G pl. rúka, rȕku
back	léđa (neut. pl.)
beard	bráda

blood	kŕv, G kr̀vi
breast(s)	grúdi, G grúdi
brain	mòzak, G mòzga
cheek	òbraz
chest	grúdni kòš
chin	bráda
elbow	lákat, G lákta; N pl. làktovi, lákti
ear	ùho/ùvo; N pl. ùši, G ùšiju
eye	òko; N pl. òči, G òčiju
finger	pr̀st (na rúci); G pl. pr̀sti, pŕsta, pr̀stiju
fingernail	nòkat, G nòkta; G pl. nokáta, nòktiju
foot	stòpalo, nòga
forearm	pòdlaktica
forehead	čèlo
groin	prèpona
hair	kòsa
hand	šàka
head	gláva
heart	sr̀ce; G pl. srdáca, sŕca
heel	péta
hip	kùk; N pl. kùkovi
jaw	čèljust, G čèljusti; vìlica
kidney	bùbreg; N pl. bùbrezi
knee	kòljeno/kòleno
leg	nòga; G pl. nóga, nògu
lip	ùsna
lungs	plúća (N pl.)
mouth	ústa (neut. pl.)
navel	pùpak, G pùpka
neck	vrát; N pl. vràtovi
nose	nós; N pl. nòsovi
palm	dlàn
posterior	zàdnjica, túr
rib	rèbro
sexual organs	spólni/pólni orgáni
shoulder	ràme, G ràmena
side	bók; N pl. bókovi
skin	kòža
stomach	stòmak, žèludac, tr̀buh
thumb	pàlac, G pálca
tongue	jèzik

toe	pȑst na nòzi
big toe	pàlac na nòzi
tooth	zúb
waist	pòjas, pás, strúk
wrist	zglòb; N pl. zglòbovi

(**górnji,** upper, and **dónji,** lower, may be used for specification, e.g. **dónja vilica,** lower jaw, **górnja ùsna,** upper lip.)

Ako svaki čovjek ima uši, da li to znači da svaki čovjek ima i uši?*

Male Šale

Kod okulista.
—Vidite li dobro na ove naočale?
—Pa, tako . . .
—A na ove druge?
—Nešto bolje.
—Čekajte, sad ću vam dati najjače. Tako. Kako sad vidite?
—Izvrsno, gospođice.

Na školskom izletu nađu se nekako sami profesor i učenica koja je potajno bila u njega zaljubljena.
—Što mislite — upita ona profesora
—Što bi rekao ovaj stari hrast, da zna govoriti?
—Rekao bi—odvrati profesor—oprostite, drugarice, ali ja nisam hrast nego bukva.

—Zdravo, Pero, već se davno nismo vidjeli. Čini mi se da si se jako promijenio.
—Oprostite, ali ja nisam Pero, nego Mato.
—Gle, bogati, i ime si čak promijenio!

Мале Шале

—Зашто плачеш, мали?
—Моја браћа имају распуст, а ја немам!
—А зашто ти немаш распуста?
—Ја још не идем у школу.

—Радиш ли гимнастику ујутру кад устанеш? Знаш то је веома здраво!
—Како да не! Свако јутро прескачем доручак.

Два сељака села су на воз по први пут и купили су неколико банана. Пошто никад нису видели банане, пажљиво су их прегледавали и један од сапутника показао им је како да скину кору. Један од сељака сакупи снагу и загризе банану. У том тренутку воз је ушао у дуги тунел а сељак викне своме пријатељу:
—Немој бре да једеш ово пошто ево ја губим вид, слеп сам!

*This is word-play based on the homonyms (i.e. same pronunciation) **ùši,** "ears" (N, A pl. of **ùho**), and **ùši,** "lice" (N, A pl. of **úš**). **úš,** "louse," is usually Croatian and **váš** Serbian.

PETNAESTA LEKCIJA

Zanimljiv doživljaj

1. Jučer sam doživio nešto zanimljivo.
2. Išao sam ulicom u pravcu knjižnice, kad ugledam jednog mladića kako ide prema meni.
3. Stao je preda mnom i započeo razgovor.
4. Slabo je govorio engleski i nisam mogao razumjeti što želi.
5. Slučajno je upotrebio riječ knjižnica.
6. Onda sam s njim počeo govoriti hrvatski.
7. Ja ponešto govorim hrvatski jer su moji roditelji došli u Ameriku iz Hrvatske.
8. Mladić je bio Slovenac koji je nedavno došao u našu zemlju.
9. Iako je njegov materinski jezik slovenski, on razumije hrvatski.
10. Bio je oduševljen kad je saznao da ja govorim hrvatski.
11. Još je rekao da vrlo dobro govorim hrvatski.
12. To je bio lijep kompliment, ali mu nisam potpuno vjerovao, jer moja mama kaže da gutam nastavke riječi kad govorim hrvatski.
13. I mnogo miješam engleske i hrvatske riječi.
14. Ali ako budem učio hrvatski, možda će mi uspjeti da svladam jezik svojih predaka.

ПЕТНАЕСТА ЛЕКЦИЈА

Интересантан доживљај

1. Јуче сам доживео нешто интересантно.
2. Ишао сам улицом у правцу библиотеке кад угледам једног младића како иде према мени.
3. Стао је преда мном и започео разговор.
4. Слабо је говорио енглески и нисам могао разумети шта жели.
5. Случајно је употребио реч библиотека.
6. Онда сам с њим почео да говорим српски.
7. Ја помало говорим српски јер су моји родитељи дошли у Америку из Србије.
8. Младић је био Словенац који је недавно дошао у нашу земљу.
9. Иако је његов матерњи језик словеначки, он разуме српски.
10. Био је одушевљен кад је сазнао да ја говорим српски.
11. Још је рекао да врло добро говорим српски.
12. То је био леп комплимент, али му нисам потпуно веровао, јер моја мама каже да гутам наставке речи кад говорим српски.
13. И много мешам енглеске и српске речи.
14. Али ако будем учио српски, можда ће ми успети да савладам језик својих предака.

NITKO SE NIJE NAUČEN RODIO.	НИКО СЕ НИЈЕ НАУЧЕН РОДИО.

AN INTERESTING EXPERIENCE—1. Yesterday I had an interesting experience. 2. I was walking along the street in the direction of the library, when I caught sight of (I catch sight of [hist. present] a young man coming toward me. 3. He stopped in front of me and began a conversation. 4. He spoke English poorly and I wasn't able to understand what he wanted (what he wants). 5. It happened that he used the word **knjižnica/biblioteka.** 6. Then I began to talk with him in Croatian/ Serbian. 7. I speak a little Croatian/Serbian because my parents came to America from Croatia/Serbia. 8. The young man was a Slovene who had recently arrived in our country. 9. Although his native language is Slovenian, he understands Croatian/Serbian. 11. Furthermore, he said that I speak Croatian/Serbian very well. 12. That was a nice compliment, but I didn't believe him completely, because my mom says that I swallow the endings of the words when I speak Croatian/Serbian. 13. And I mix a lot of English words with the Croatian/Serbian words. 14. But, if I study Croatian/Serbian, perhaps I will succeed (to me it will succeed) in mastering the language of my ancestors.

vježba/vežba I

Postavite pitanja na slijedeće/sledeće odgovore.

1. Mladić je bio pokraj knjižnice/pored biblioteke.
2. On je počeo razgovor.
3. Nisam ga razumio/ razumeo.
4. Znao je hrvatski/srpski.
5. Moji roditelji su iz Hrvatske/Srbije.
6. Ja sam Slovenac.
7. Oni govore slovenski/slovenački.
8. Rekao je da dobro govorim hrvatski/srpski.
9. Ja mu nisam potpuno vjerovao/verovao.
10. To je jezik mojih predaka.

vježba/vežba II

Prevedite slijedeće/sledeće rečenice na hrvatski/srpski.

1. That street is wider than this one.
2. My house is bigger than yours.
3. Your brother is stronger than Peter [**Pètar, G Petra**]
4. The Danube is longer than the Sava. [**Dùnav, Sáva**]
5. My mother is more gentle than my father. [**njèžan/nèžan, -žni,** gentle]

vježba/vežba III

Stavite pridjeve/prideve u komparativ.

Pavle je ________od Nade. (star)
Pavle je stariji od Nade.

1. Nada je ________od Pavla. (lijepa/lepa)
2. Ja sam hrabar, ali ti si ________. (hrabar)
3. U sobi je ________nego vani/napolju. (topao)
4. Njegovi roditelji su ________od tvojih. (bogat)
5. (Cr.) Danas je ________vrijeme nego jučer. (ružan)
   (S.) Danas je ________vreme nego juče. (ružan)
6. Moj pas je ________od tvoga. (velik)
7. Otac je mnogo ________od majke. (visok)
8. Naš auto je ________od vašega. (dobar)
9. Vaša hrana je ________i ________od naše. (dobar, ukusan)
10. Ja sam ________i ________od njega. (gladan, žedan)

vježba/vežba IV

Napišite kratko pismo prijatelju.

KNJIGA JE NAJBOLJI PRIJATELJ	КЊИГА ЈЕ НАЈБОЉИ ПРИЈАТЕЉ

Letter-Writing Formulas

Formal beginnings:

Poštovani gospodine Popoviću!	Dear Mr. Popović:
Poštovani druže Skorojeviću!	Dear Comrade Skorojević:
Mnogopoštovani kolega!	My dear colleague:
Cijenjeni/Cenjeni gospodine direktore!	Dear Director:
Uvaženi gospodine profesore!	My dear professor:
Poštovana gospođo ministarko!	Dear Madame Minister:
Mnogopoštovana gospođice Jovanović!	Dear Miss Jovanović:
Poštovana drugarice Skorojević!	Dear Comrade [fem.] Skorojević:

Informal beginnings:

Dragi prijatelju,	Dear friend,
Dragi Jovo,	Dear Jovo
Voljeni sine,	Dearest [Beloved] son,
Draga sestro,	Dear sister,
Voljena Nado,	Dearest Nada,
Draga moja,	Darling, [to a female]

Dragi moj,	Darling, [to a male]
Mili moji,	Dear ones,
Formal endings:	
s poštovanjem Skorojević Sretan	Respectfully, Sretan Skorojević
s osobitim poštovanjem Popović Bogdan	Very respectfully, Bogdan Popović
Vaš odani Miodrag Ranković	Faithfully yours, Miodrag Ranković
Informal endings:	
Primi puno pozdrava od Ane	Many greetings from Ann
Voli vas vaš Pero	With love, Pero
Toplo [ili] Srdačno Te pozdravlja Vlado	Warm greetings from Vlado
U mislima s tobom Jovo	Thinking of you, Jovo

Cursive forms of Latin and Cyrillic. These two letters* illustrate the hand-

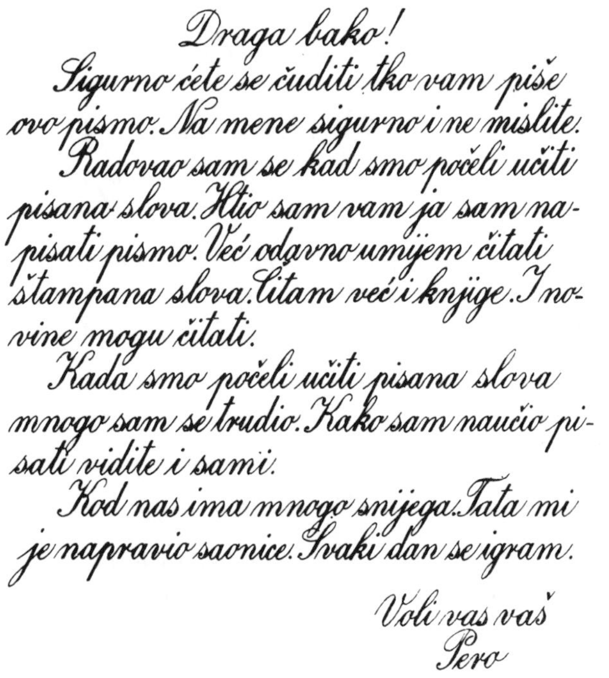
Draga bako!
Sigurno ćete se čuditi tko vam piše ovo pismo. Na mene sigurno i ne mislite.
Radovao sam se kad smo počeli učiti pisana slova. Htio sam vam ja sam napisati pismo. Već odavno umijem čitati štampana slova. Čitam već i knjige. I novine mogu čitati.
Kada smo počeli učiti pisana slova mnogo sam se trudio. Kako sam naučio pisati vidite i sami.
Kod nas ima mnogo snijega. Tata mi je napravio saonice. Svaki dan se igram.
Voli vas vaš
Pero

*Taken with permission from **Početnica** by Krešo Mihaljević and Antun Kolarević (Zagreb, 1961) and from Буквар by the same authors (Zagreb, 1957).

Драга бако!
Сигурно ћете се чудити, тко вам
пише ово писмо. На мене сигурно и
не мислите. Радовао сам се, кад смо
почели учити писана слова.
Хтио сам вам ја сам написати
писмо. Већ одавно умијем читати
штампана слова. Читам већ и
књиге. И новине могу читати.
Када смо почели учити писана
слова, много сам се трудио. Како сам
научио писати, видите и сами.
Код нас има много снијега. Тата
ми је направио саонице. Сваки дан се
играм.
Воли вас ваш
Перо

written forms of letters in the Latin and Cyrillic alphabets.
The two versions were written by a Croatian boy, Pero, to his grandmother. In the Cyrillic version, a Serbian boy would use the following variants: ко, Хтео, умем, снега.

Dva susjeda

U nekom su selu živjela dva susjeda. Jedan je bio jako siromašan, te nije imao ni jednog komada marve. Drugi je bio bogat i imao je uz drugo blago i magarca.

Nestalo je siromahu brašna. Napunio je on vreću kukuruza, no nije imao na čemu odvesti je u vodenicu, a na leđima nije mogao odnijeti.

—Otići ću, —rekao je on, —svom susjedu i zamolit ću ga, da mi posajmi magarca.

To je rekao i odmah je otišao. Čim je susjedu saopćio, zašto je došao, počeo se ovaj tužiti:

—Ah, susjede, kako mi je žao, što ti ne mogu poslužiti! Jučer sam bio u gradu i prodao magarca. Samo da sam znao, da ćeš ga trebati, ne bih ga prodao.

U isti čas se počeo magarac u štali derati, jer ga još nisu nahranili.

—Zašto veliš, susjede, da si prodao magarca? —rekao je siromah. —Čuj ga, kako ti viče: Lažeš, lažeš!

—Ah, susjede! —odgovorio je postiđeni bogataš, ti magarcu vjeruješ, a meni ne vjeruješ!

(Narodna priča)

ŠESNAESTA LEKCIJA

Ispit iz biologije

1. Zašto plačeš, Ana?*
2. Ah, Pero! Pala sam na posljednjem ispitu iz biologije
3. Nastavnik je bio vrlo nepravičan.
4. Ne vjerujem ti, Ana.
5. Ti jednostavno nisi znala odgovoriti na njegovo pitanje.
6. Ne, znala sam. Pitanje je bilo jednostavno.
7. Nastavnik je želio da mu kažem: "Koja su temeljna osjetila u čovjeka?"
8. Kao odgovor sam na papiru napisala: glad, ljubav, hladnoća, ponos i zdrav razum.
9. To zna svaka luda.
10. Možda to zna svaka luda, ali ja bih odgovorio: vid, sluh, njuh, opip i okus.
11. Objasni mi svoj odgovor, doktore!
12. To je jednostavno, Ana. Ja vidim tvoje žalosno lice svojim plavim očima.
13. To je osjetilo vida.

ШЕСНАЕСТА ЛЕКЦИЈА

Испит из биологије

1. Зашто плачеш, Ана?*
2. Ах, Перо! Пала сам на последњем испиту из биологије.
3. Наставник је био врло неправедан.
4. Не верујем ти, Ана.
5. Ти једноставно ниси знала да одговориш на његово питање.
6. Не, знала сам. Питање је било једноставно.
7. Наставник је желео да му кажем: "Која су основна чула у човека?"
8. Као одговор сам на хартији написала: глад, љубав, хладноћа, понос и здрав разум.
9. То зна свака луда.
10. Можда то зна свака луда, али ја бих одговорио: вид, слух, мирис, пипање и укус.
11. Објасни ми свој одговор, докторе!
12. То је једноставно, Ана. Ја видим твоје жалосно лице својим плавим очима.
13. То је чуло вида.

*This is a V usage, but the form is N; the V form would be **Ano**. Some speakers of Cr&S only use N forms in such situations; other speakers tend to use the V form for masculine nouns, but the N form for feminine nouns, e.g. **Petre!** (N **Petar**), but **Ana**! (N **Ana**).

14. Ja čujem tvoj tužni glas svojim velikim ušima.	14. Ја чујем твој тужни глас својим великим ушима.
15. To je osjetilo sluha.	15. То је чуло слуха.
16. Ja mirišem cvijeće, koje je na stolu, svojim prćastim nosom.	16. Ја миришем цвеће, које је на столу, својим прћастим носом.
17. To je osjetilo njuha.	17. То је чуло мириса.
18. Ja opipavam ovaj bijeli zid svojom lijevom rukom.	18. Ја опипавам овај бели зид својом левом руком.
19. To je osjetilo opipa.	19. То је чуло пипања.
20. I na kraju, ja probam ovu crvenu jabuku svojim jezikom i ustima.	20. И на крају, ја пробам ову црвену јабуку својим језиком и устима.
21. To je osjetilo okusa.	21. То је чуло укуса.
22. A kako je sa šestim osjetilom, Pero?	22. А како је са шестим чулом, Перо?
23. Šestog osjetila nema, Ana.	23. Шестог чула нема, Ана.
24. Ima! Ima! To je osjetilo pomoću kojega sam dala odgovor na to pitanje na ispitu—moje šesto osjetilo!	24. Има! Има! То је чуло помоћу кога сам дала одговор на то питање на испиту—моје шесто чуло.
SVAKA JE PTICA U SVOM GNIJEZDU JAKA.	СВАКА ЈЕ ПТИЦА У СВОМ ЃНЕЗДУ ЈАКА.

THE BIOLOGY EXAM—1. Why are you crying, Ann? 2. O, Peter! I failed my last exam in biology. 3. The teacher was very unfair. 4. I don't believe you, Ann. 5. You simply didn't know the answer (to answer) to this question. 6. No, I knew it. The question was very simple. 7. The teacher wanted to know (wanted that I tell him): "What are the basic senses of a human being." 8. In answer to that (as an answer) I wrote on the paper: hunger, love, cold, pride, and common sense. 9. Any simpleton knows that. 10. Maybe any simpleton knows that, but I would have answered: sight, hearing, smell, touch, and taste. 11. Explain your answer to me, Doctor! 12. That's easy, Ann. I see your sad face with my blue eyes. 13. That's the sense of sight. 14. I hear your tearful voice with my big ears. 15. That's the sense of hearing. 16. I smell the flowers on the table (which are on . . .) with my turned-up nose. 17. That's the sense of smell. 18. I feel this white wall with my left hand. 19. That's the sense of touch. 20. And, finally, I'm tasting this red apple with my tongue and mouth. 21. That's the sense of taste. 22. And what about the sixth sense, Peter? 23. There is no sixth sense, Ann. 24. There is! That's the sense that helped me to give (with the help of which I gave) the answer to that question on the exam—my sixth sense!

vježba I

Odgovorite na slijedeća pitanja.

1. Koja su temeljna osjetila kod čovjeka?
2. Koliko osjetila ima čovjek?
3. Čemu služi osjetilo vida?
4. Čemu služi osjetilo sluha?
5. Kada mirišite ružu, kojim se osjetilom služite?
6. Čemu služi osjetilo opipa?
7. Koje je peto osjetilo?
8. Imate li šesto osjetilo?

vežba I

Odgovorite na sledeća pitanja.

1. Koja su osnova čula kod čoveka?
2. Koliko čula ima čovek?
3. Čemu služi čulo vida?
4. Čemu služi čulo sluha?
5. Kada mirišite ružu, kojim se čulom služite?
6. Čemu služi čulo opipa?
7. Koje je peto čulo?
8. Imate li šesto čulo?

vježba/vežba II

Prevedite na hrvatski/srpski.

1. She bought ten new books.
2. Mr. Delić has three small daughters.
3. Give me two apples.
4. Four soldiers arrived.
5. Six Dalmatian fishermen were singing.

vježba/vežba III

Popunite ove rečenice pridjevima/pridevima u superlativu.

Ana je moja ________ prijateljica. (dobra)
Ana je moja najbolja prijateljica.

1. Fizika je moj ________ predmet. (drag)
2. Moj ________ predmet je biologija. (loš)
3. Nada je ________ djevojka/devojka u razredu. (velika)
4. Tko/Ko je ________ u vašem društvu? (hrabar)
5. Koji je ________ vrh na svijetu/svetu? (visok)
6. Moj ________ brat živi u Beogradu. (mlad)
7. Koja je ________ rijeka/reka u Jugoslaviji? (duga)
8. ________ otok/ostrvo Dalmacije je Brač. (velik)
9. ________ vjetar/vetar u Srbiji zove se košava. (hladan)
10. Njegova ________ sestra je ________ . (stara, marljiva)

vježba/vežba IV

Postavite pitanja s imenicom u vokativu.

Nada uči biologiju.
Što/Šta učiš, Nado?

1. Marka šije haljinu.
2. Prijatelj dolazi popodne.
3. Otac čita knjigu.
4. Ribar pjeva/peva o moru.
5. Sestra sprema ručak.
6. Bogdan jede kolač.

vježba/vežba V

Prevedite na hrvatski/srpski.

1. Ann failed her exam in biology.
2. The question was difficult.
3. She didn't know what the basic senses of a human being are.
4. I answered that question with my sixth sense.
5. The teacher was strict, but he was just, too.

vježba/vežba VI

Popunite slijedeće/sledeće rečenice odgovarajućim glagolskim vremenom povratnih glagola.

Sinoć ________ Pero ________ iz Južne Amerike. (vratiti se)
Sinoć se Pero vratio iz Južne Amerike.

1. Obećao je da ________ ________ ________ svakog jutra. (brijati se)
2. Jednom ________ ________ oni ________ za prvu nagradu. (takmičiti se).
3. Djevojke/Devojke ________ ________ ________ sutra. (vratiti se)
4. Sutra ________ ________ studenti ________ što nema profesora, (čuditi se)
5. Kad napišeš zadatak, ________ ________ ________ s prijateljima. (igrati se)
6. Igrači ________ uvijek/uvek ________ pobjedi/pobedi. (nadati se)
7. Mi ________ obično ________ dobroj šali. (smijati se/smejati se)
8. Kad dobijemo sina, ________ ________ ________ Marko. (zvati se)

BOLJE DOBAR GLAS NEGO ZLATNI PAS.

БОЉЕ ДОБАР ГЛАС НЕГО ЗЛАТНИ ПАС.

Oj Violo

Oj Vi- o- lo oj Vi- o- lo kraj vo-de stu- de- ne
dra- ga du- šo dra-ga du-šo spo-men' se od me- ne.

Oj, Violo, oj, Violo, kraj vode studene, [dva
Draga dušo, draga dušo, spomen' se od mene. puta]

I od mene, i od mene, i od mog imena, [2]
Goj se za me, goj se za me još malo vrimena.

I još malo, i još malo, nek te goji mati. [2]
Ufajući, ufajući, moja ćeš se zvati.

Doći ću ti, doći ću ti, kad proliće sine. [2]
Od ljubavi, dušo moja, za te srce gine.

Vapor trubi, vapor trubi, prid rivu pristaje. [2]
Meni draga, meni draga desnu ruku daje.

Zbogom, draga, zbogom, draga, i nemoj me kleti, [2]
Moje riči, moje riči drži na pameti.

Na to se je, na to se je mala smilovala. [2]
Ljubit' lice, ljubit' lice ona mi je dala.

The Dalmatian song "Oj Violo" is popular throughout Yugoslavia. It is about a sailor saying farewell to his young sweetheart, Viola (Violet), as his ship prepares to leave. Its text shows ikavian variants and has, in addition, a few regional words.

prid [=**pred**] "before, in front of, at"
pròliće [=**pròljeće/pròleće**] "Spring"
rìč [=**rìječ/réč**] "word"
rìva [reg. for **òbala**] "shore, wharf"
smìlovati se P "to have pity on"
spòmen' se [=**spomèni se** imper.] "remember"
trúbiti [trúbi] I "to blow, to sound"
ùfajući [reg. for **nádajući se**] "hoping"

vàpor [reg. for **bród**] "steamer, boat"
Viòlo [V of Viola] "Violet"
vríme, G **vrìmena** [=**vrijème/vréme**, **G vrèmena**] "time"

ПТИЦА—ЧОВЕК

Једног је дана видео сељак папагаја у вароши, па се стао да га загледа. Одједном је папагај викнуо на сељака: —Шта је, шта је?

Сељак се уплашио, скинуо шешир с главе и рекао: —Извините, молим вас, ја сам мислио да сте ви птица.

SEDAMNAESTA LEKCIJA

Moj dan

1. Radnim danom obično ustajem u sedam sati.
2. Tada se idem u kupaonicu tuširati i brijati.
3. Onda idem dolje u kuhinju gdje mama sprema doručak.
4. Kava je obično gotova i ja sebi naspem šalicu.
5. U to vrijeme moj otac već odlazi u tvornicu, jer on mora biti tamo u sedam i četrdeset pet.
6. Kao mnogi mladi Amerikanci jedem dosta za doručak.
7. Pijem sok od naranče, jedem dva pržena jajeta, prepečen kruh sa džemom, a onda pijem još jednu šalicu kave.
8. Tada opet idem u svoju sobu, skidam pidžamu i oblačim majicu, gaćice, hlače, košulju, čarape i cipele.
9. Odabiram kravatu koja se slaže s mojim čarapama, oblačim kaput i onda silazim.
10. Ako je zimsko doba, oblačim zimski kaput i navlačim kaljače.
11. Pošto se obučem, uzimam svoje knjige i zadatke, onda se pozdravljam s majkom i idem u garažu.
12. Tamo palim motor svoga sta-

СЕДАМНАЕСТА ЛЕКЦИЈА

Мој дан

1. Радним даном обично устајем у седам сати.
2. Тада идем у купатило, туширам се и бријем се.
3. Онда идем доле у кухињу где мама спрема доручак.
4. Кафа је обично готова и ја себи наспем шољу.
5. У то време мој отац већ одлази у фабрику, јер он мора да буде тамо у седам и четрдесет пет.
6. Као многи Американци једем доста за доручак.
7. Пијем сок од поморанџе, једем два пржена јајета, препечен хлеб са џемом, а онда пијем још једну шољу кафе.
8. Тада опет идем у своју собу, скидам пиџаму и облачим мајицу, гаћице, панталоне, кошуљу, чарапе и ципеле.
9. Одабирам машну која се слаже с мојим чарапама, облачим капут и онда силазим.
10. Ако је зимско доба, облачим зимски капут и навлачим каљаче.
11. Пошто се обучем, узимам своје књиге и задатке, онда се поздрављам са мајком и идем у гаражу.
12. Тамо палим мотор свога ста-

rog auta, puštam ga da se malo zagrije, i onda se vozim do sveučilišta, kamo stižem oko osam sati.

13. Moj prvi sat počinje u osam i trideset, pa ako nađem mjesto za parkiranje, tada sam u učionici na vrijeme.
14. Ja se specijaliziram u matematici, te moji predmeti nisu laki.
15. Ručam obično u dvanaest i petnaest.
16. Često idem s nekoliko prijatelja u obližnji restoran i tamo pojedem sendvič i popijem kavu.
17. Poslije popodnevnih satova idem u knjižnicu čitati knjige i naučne časopise.
18. Član sam nekoliko studentskih klubova, a klubovi ponekad imaju sastanke kasno poslije podne.
19. Moja djevojka studira filozofiju i obično se s njom sastajem poslije njenog posljednjeg sata.
20. Vraćam se kući, parkiram auto, čistim snijeg s pločnika, a onda idem u kuću.
21. Svaki dan večeram u šest sati.
22. Budući da moja majka odlično kuha, moj otac i ja uživamo u tom obroku.
23. Poslije večere pomažem svojoj majci oko suda.
24. Moja mama i tata vole gledati televiziju.
25. Mama želi na televiziji gledati kazališne predstave, a tata jednostavno želi vidjeti sve

рог аута, пуштам га да се мало загреје, и онда се возим до универзитета, где стижем око осам сати.

13. Мој први час почиње у осам и тридесет, па ако нађем место за паркирање, тада сам у учионици на време.
14. Ја се специјализујем у математици, те моји предмети нису лаки.
15. Ручам обично у дванаест и петнаест.
16. Често идем с неколико пријатеља у оближњи ресторан, и тамо поједем сендвич и попијем кафу.
17. После поподневних часова идем у библиотеку да читам књиге и научне часописе.
18. Члан сам неколико студентских клубова, а клубови имају понекад састанке касно после подне.
19. Моја девојка студира филозофију и обично се с њом састајем после њеног последњег часа.
20. Враћам се кући, паркирам ауто, чистим снег са тротоара, а онда идем у кућу.
21. Сваки дан вечерам у шест сати.
22. Пошто моја мајка одлично кува, мој отац и ја уживамо у том оброку.
23. После вечере помажем својој мајци око судова.
24. Моја мама и тата воле да гледају телевизију.
25. Мама жели да на телевизији гледа позоришне представе, а тата једноставно

vrste sportskih borbi.

26. Zato često dolazi do žive diskusije oko izbora programa.

27. Ja lično mislim da je televizija dosadna.

28. Kad imam slobodnog vremena, obično idem na sastanak sa svojom djevojkom.

29. To je zanimljivije.

30. Obično idem spavati oko ponoći i spavam kao top do jutra.

JEDNA LASTA NE ČINI PROLJEĆE.

жели да види све врсте спортских борби.

26. Зато често долази до живе дискусије око избора програма.

27. Ја лично мислим да је телевизија досадна.

28. Кад имам слободног времена, обично идем на састанак са својом девојком.

29. То је интересантније.

30. Обично идем да спавам око поноћи и спавам као топ до јутра.

ЈЕДНА ЛАСТА НЕ ЧИНИ ПРОЛЕЋЕ.

MY DAY—1. On a school day I usually get up at seven o'clock. 2. Then I go to the bathroom, take a shower, and shave. 3. Then I go downstairs to the kitchen, where mom is preparing breakfast. 4. The coffee is usually ready and I pour myself a cup. 5. At that time my father is already leaving for the factory, because he has to be there at seven forty-five. 6. Like most young Americans I eat a heavy breakfast. 7. I drink orange juice, eat two fried eggs, toast and (with) jam, and then drink another cup of coffee. 8. Then I go to my room again, take off my pajamas and put on a T-shirt, shorts, trousers, shirt, socks, and shoes. 9. I pick out a tie to match my socks (which agrees with my socks), put on my coat and then go downstairs. 10. If it's wintertime, I put on my overcoat (winter coat) and pull on my rubbers. 11. After I'm dressed, I get my books and assignments, then I say goodbye to my mother and go to the garage. 12. There I start the motor of my old car, let it warm up a bit, and then drive to the university, where I arrive about eight o'clock. 13. My first class starts at eight-thirty, and if I find a parking place, then I'm in class on time. 14. I'm majoring in mathematics and so my subjects aren't easy. 15. I have lunch usually at twelve-fifteen. 16. Often I go with a few friends to a nearby restaurant and there I have (eat) a sandwich and drink coffee. 17. After my afternoon classes I go to the library to read books and scientific journals. 18. I'm a member of a few student clubs and the clubs sometimes hold meetings in the late afternoon. 19. My girlfriend is majoring in (studies) philosophy and I usually meet her after her last class. 20. I return home, park the car, clean the snow off the sidewalk, and then go inside the house. 21. I eat supper at six o'clock every day. 22. Since my mother is an excellent cook (cooks excellently), my father and I enjoy that meal. 23. After supper I help my mother with (around) the dishes. 24. My mom and dad like to watch television. 25. Mom wants to watch plays on television, but dad simply has to see all (kinds of) sporting events. 26. So often there's a lively discussion (it comes to a lively . . .) about the selection of a program. 27. Personally I think that television is boring. 28. When I have free time, I usually go on dates with my girlfriend. 29. That's more interesting. 30. Usually I go to sleep around midnight and sleep like a log until morning.

vježba I

Odgovorite na slijedeća pitanja.

1. Kada obično ustajete?
2. Što jedete za doručak?
3. Kako idete do sveučilišta?
4. Kada ručate?
5. Kako provodite popodne?
6. U koliko sati je večera?
7. Pomažete li majci oko suda?
8. Volite li gledati televiziju?
9. Izlazite li poslije večere?
10. Kad obično idete na spavanje?

vežba I

Odgovorite na sledeća pitanja.

1. Kad obično ustajete?
2. Šta jedete za doručak?
3. Kako idete do univerziteta?
4. Kada ručate?
5. Kako provodite poslepodne?
6. U koliko sati je večera?
7. Da li pomažete majci oko sudova?
8. Da li volite da gledate televiziju?
9. Da li izlazite posle večere?
10. Kada obično idete na spavanje?

vježba/vežba II

Prevedite slijedeće/sledeće rečenice na hrvatski/srpski.

1. Although I read the book, I forgot how the hero died.
2. As soon as you finish, go into the other room.
3. They lost the war because there weren't enough soldiers.
4. I'll read the newspaper until the doctor returns.
5. After Peter had left, we began to work.

vježba/vežba III

Popunite ove rečenice odgovarajućim veznicima [véznik, "conjunction, clause connective"].

1. ________smo se žurili, nismo stigli na vrijeme/vreme.
2. Telefoniraj mi ________stigneš.
3. ________sam došla, on nije bio kod kuće.
4. Čovjek/Čovek se uči ________živi.
5. Nisu znali ________sam bio.
6. Nisu večerali ________su se žurili.

7. Išli smo na izlet ________je bilo toplo.
8. Ne mogu kupiti auto ________nemam novaca.
9. Ana ide na spavanje u deset sati ________ja u ponoć.
10. ________sam primila vaše pismo, dočekala bih vas.

vježba/vežba IV

Stavite ove rečenice u prošlo vrijeme/vreme.

1. On redovito uči.
2. Vraćamo se u pet sati popodne.
3. (Cr.) Ne moraš gledati televiziju.
   (S.) Ne moraš da gledaš televiziju.
4. Oni stanuju u Zagrebu.
5. Čekamo vas pred kućom.
6. Studiramo matematiku i fiziku.
7. Idem s prijateljem na ručak.
8. Mi kupujemo novine.
9. Ne spremam večeru.
10. Uzimam knjige pošto imam predavanje.

vježba/vežba V

Napišite sastav na temu "Moj radni dan."

Pronunciation: Consonant Clusters **izgovor**

Cr&S has many combinations of consonants that normally do not occur in English. The following words exhibit possible consonant clusters in initial position, that is, at the beginning of a word.

bdijènje/ bdénje	vigil	čmávati	to doze.
		čvórak	starling
cmòk	hearty kiss	dlàn	palm of hand
crèpar	tile-maker	dnévni	daily
cvìjet/cvét	flower	džbún	bush
čkálj	thistle	gmìzati	to crawl
člán	member	gnját	shin bone
gvòzd	wedge	špìnat (Cr.)	spinach
hládno	chilly	štàla	stable
hmèlj	hops	štràjk	strike
hrást	oak	Švèđanka	Swede (f.)
htjèti/htèti	to be willing	tkàti	to weave
hvála	thanks	tlò	ground
kmèt	headman	tmìna	darkness
knèz	prince	tvòr	skunk
kvár	damage	tvŕd	hard

mlád	young	vlás	hair
mnògo	many, much	vráta	door
mràz	frost	zbòg	on account of
pčèla	bee	zdénac	a well
psèto	cur	zdràv	healthy
pšènica	wheat	zgòdan	opportune
ptìca	bird	zláto	gold
shlàpljen	evaporated	zgráda	building
shvàćen	grasped	zmìja	snake
skvàčen	gripped	znój	sweat
smrád	stench	zrák	air (Cr.), ray (S.)
srám	shame	zvàti	to call
svét	holy	zvŕk	top (toy)
svráb	itch	žbùka	mortar
ščèpati	to seize	ždèrati	to devour
šćućúriti se	to crouch	ždrál	crane
škàre (Cr.)	scissors	žgànica	brandy
škljóca	pocketknife	žlìca (Cr.)	spoon
škràbica	cash box	žmíriti	to blink
škvórac	starling	žnjèti	to reap
šljèm/šlèm	helmet	žvákati	to chew
šmŕk	hose		

Clothing and Footwear	**òdjeća/òdeća i òbuća**
bathing suit	kùpaći kòstim (for women), kùpaće gàćice (for men)
belt	pòjas, pás, opàsač
blouse	blúza
bobby pin	ùkosnica, šnálica
brassiere	grùdnjak, pr̀slučić
cap	kàpa
cloth	štòf, súkno, tkànina
clothing	òdjeća/òdeća, odijèlo/ odélo
coat	kàput
winter coat	zímski kàput
rain coat	kìšni kàput
costume	nòšnja
folk costume	národna nòšnja
dress	hàljina
earring	nàušnica, mìnđuša
glasses	òčale,* očáli, nàočari, nàočare,* nàočale,* nàočali

*These forms are feminine plural.

sunglasses	támne òčale, òčale za súnce
glove	rukàvica
girdle	pòjas, míder
hairpin	ùkosnica, šnálica
handkerchief	màramica, džèpni rùpčić
hat	šèšir
jacket	(kràtki) kàput, sàko
kerchief	màrama; rúbac, G rúpca
lipstick	kàrmin, rúž, crvènilo za ùsne
nightgown	spavàćica
pajamas	pidžáma
pants	hlàče*/pantalóne*
petticoat	pòdsuknja
powder	púder
sandals	sandále*
scarf	šál
shirt	kòšulja
shorts	gàće*
shoe	cìpela
pair of shoes	pár cìpela
shoelaces	vr̀pce* za cìpele, ùzice* za cìpele, pèrtle* za cìpele
skirt	sùknja
slip	kombinèzon
slipper	pàpuča
sock	čàrapa, sòkna
pair of socks	pár čàrapa
stocking	dùga čàrapa, žènska čàrapa
suit	odijèlo/odélo
man's suit	mùško odijèlo/odélo
sweater	pulòver, džèmper
suspenders	nàramenice*
T-shirt	màja, màjica
tie	kravàta/màšna
trousers	hlàče/pantalóne
undershirt	pòtkošulja
undershorts	gàće,* gàćice*
underwear	dónje rúblje, dónji vèš
vest	pr̀sluk

BLIŽA JE KOŠULJA
NEGO HALJINA.

БЛИЖА ЈЕ КОШУЉА
НЕГО ХАЉИНА.

*These forms are feminine plural.

Relevant verbs for the vocabulary items above are the following:

nòsiti [3rd sg. pres. **nòsi**]	to wear
Zašto Dunja ne nosi svoju novu haljinu?	Why isn't Dunja wearing her new dress?
obláčiti [òblači] I, obúći [obúče] P	to put on (clothing)
Sada òblačim drugo odijelo/odelo.	I'm putting on another suit now.
Obúcite zelenu košulju!	Put on the green shirt
obláčiti se I, obúći se P	to dress oneself
Obúci se brzo, gosti su došli.	Get dressed quickly, the guests have arrived.
svláčiti [svláči] I, svúći [svúče] P	to take off (clothing)
Svúkla je mokru suknju.	She took off the wet skirt.
svláčiti se I, svúći se P	to undress oneself
Dijete/Dete se sporo svláči.	The child is slowly undressing.

There are two more transitive verbs meaning "to put on" and "to take off" respectively; these verbs (**stàvljati** I, **stàviti** P, and **skídati** I, **skìnuti** P) have a broader range of usage than **obláčiti-obúći** and **svláčiti-svúći.** For example,

Òblačim kaput [or] Stàvljam kaput na sebe.	I'm putting on my coat.
Obúci košulju [or] Stàvi košulju na sebe!	Put on your shirt!
Svúkao je kaput [or] Skìnuo je kaput.	He took off his shirt.
Zašto svláčiš kaput [or] Zašto skídaš kaput?	Why are you taking off your coat?
Svúci mokru suknju [or] Skìni mokru suknju!	Take off the wet skirt!

[but only]

Mama skída šal.	Mom is taking off her scarf.
Skìni pojas!	Take off the belt!
Sada stàvljam puder na lice.	I'm powdering my face now.
Stàvila je naušnice.	She put on the earrings.

Economic Factors. Yugoslavia is potentially a rich country, but actually a poor one. Its rugged terrain contains large deposits of many important ores and minerals. In Europe Yugoslavia is first in the production of bauxite, lead, and antimony and second in the production of quicksilver, copper, and zinc. It has extensive forests and a wealth of animal life. Before World War II foreign capital dominated in the development and exploitation of Yugoslavia's natural resources. The war itself brought widespread destruction to Yugoslavia, leveling its plants and mines, destroying 50 percent of its railways, large percentages of its livestock and orchards, and killing 1,700,000 people. After the war the fledgling Communist state embarked on the path of textbook Marxism in order to rebuild and reinvigorate the Yugoslav economy. The results of such efforts have not been successful and by the late 1980s Yugoslavia found itself burdened by a large foreign debt and soaring inflation. This severe economic situation will undoubtedly lead to major changes in Yugoslavia's economy and perhaps even in its governmental structure.

At present, almost a million Yugoslavs work outside the country, in Western Europe for the most part. These migrants contribute to the economy because they earn "hard" currency that they bring back to Yugoslavia. They also bring back work habits better attuned to industrial society than those traditionally associated with the more leisurely tempo of Balkan life.

One great economic resource Yugoslavia has is its 1,300-mile coastline on the Adriatic with its many islands. The salubrious climate and the abundance of historical monuments draw foreign tourists by the hundreds of thousands. This is Yugoslavia's "natural industry," one that produces impressive economic returns.

SVAKOG GOSTA TRI DANA DOSTA.	СВАКОЃ ЃОСТА ТРИ ДАНА ДОСТА.

НА ЃРОБУ ЛЕКАРА ИСАКА

Овде лежи лекар Исак
пореклом из Сенте.
Спустио се у земљицу
да походи пацијенте.

OSAMNAESTA LEKCIJA

Praznici

1. Kako ćeš provesti praznike, Pero?
2. Ići ću na nekoliko dana na farmu svoje bake i djeda na sjeveru Minnesote.
3. Tamo ću do mile volje loviti ribu i divljač.
4. Hoćeš li što učiti dok budeš tamo?
5. Nemoj biti smiješan, Ranko! Pročitat ću koji roman, napisat ću nekoliko pisama, ali apsolutno ništa neću učiti.
6. Ima li tamo dobrih mjesta za ribolov?
7. Najbolje na svijetu!
8. Vjerojatno ću biti na jezeru svaki dan u zoru.
9. Kamo ćeš ti ići o praznicima?
10. Ostat ću ovdje u gradu i naći ću štogod zanimljivo da radim.
11. Kao na primjer što?
12. O, mogao bih pogledati koji film, poći na koji ples ili sjedjeti i gledati televiziju.
13. To nije odmor. Zašto ne bi pošao sa mnom?
14. Dobro, u redu, ako si siguran da će tamo biti mjesta za mene.
15. Mjesta ima dosta. Moja će nas baka smjestiti u veliku gostinsku sobu.

ОСАМНАЕСТА ЛЕКЦИЈА

Празници

1. Како ћеш провести празнике, Перо?
2. Ићи ћу на неколико дана на фарму своје бабе и деде на северу Минесоте.
3. Тамо ћу до миле воље да ловим рибу и дивљач.
4. Хоћеш ли нешто да учиш док будеш тамо?
5. Немој да будеш смешан, Ранко! Прочитаћу који роман, написаћу неколико писама, али апсолутно ништа нећу учити.
6. Има ли тамо добрих места за риболов?
7. Најбоље на свету!
8. Вероватно ћу бити на језеру сваки дан у зору.
9. Где ћеш ти да идеш о празницима?
10. Остаћу овде у граду и наћи ћу штогод занимљиво да радим.
11. Као на пример шта?
12. О, могао бих да погледам који филм, да одем на коју игранку или да седим и гледам телевизију.
13. То није одмор. Зашто не би пошао са мном?
14. Добро, у реду, ако си сигуран да ће тамо бити места за мене.
15. Места има доста. Моја ће нас баба сместити у велику гостинску собу.

16. Što bi trebalo da ponesem sa sobom?
17. Ništa osim toaletnog pribora.
18. U koliko sati da budem gotov?
19. Poći ćemo vlakom sutra rano, oko pet sati.
20. Doručkovat ćemo u vlaku, a tamo ćemo stići oko podne.
21. Dobro. Doći ću autom do tvoje kuće oko pola pet.

TKO VISOKO LETI,
NISKO PADA.

16. Шта би требало да понесем са собом?
17. Ништа сем тоалетног прибора.
18. У колико сати да будем готов?
19. Поћи ћемо возом сутра рано, око пет сати.
20. Доручковаћемо у возу, а тамо ћемо стићи око подне.
21. Добро. Доћи ћу аутом до твоје куће око пола пет.

КО ВИСОКО ЛЕТИ,
НИСКО ПАДА.

HOLIDAYS—1. How will you spend the holidays, Pero? 2. I'll go to my grandparents' farm in northern Minnesota for a few days. 3. There I can fish (catch fish) and hunt (catch game) to my heart's content. 4. Will you do any studying while you're there? 5. Don't be silly, Ranko! I'll read a few novels and write some letters but absolutely no studying. 6. Is the fishing good up there (are there good places for fishing there)? 7. The best [place] in the world! 8. I'll probably be out on the lake every day at dawn. 9. Where are you going for the holidays? 10. I'll stay here in the city and find something interesting to do. 11. What, for example? 12. Oh, I might see a few movies, go to a dance, or sit around and watch TV. 13. That's no vacation. Why don't you come along with me? 14. Well, OK, if you're sure that there'll be room for me. 15. There's plenty of room. My grandmother will put us in the large guest room. 16. What should I bring with me? 17. Nothing besides your toilet articles. 18. What time should I be ready? 19. We'll leave by train early, around five o'clock. 20. We'll have breakfast on the train and we'll arrive there about noon. 21. Fine. I'll drive (come by auto) over to your house about four-thirty.

vježba/vežba I

Stavite pitanja na slijedeće/sledeće odgovore.

1. Praznike ćemo provesti u planini.
2. Tamo ćemo loviti ribu.
3. Čitam samo jedan roman.
4. Neću učiti.
5. Ja ostajem u gradu.
6. Volim televiziju.

7. Doći ću s vama ako imate veliki auto.
8. Mi ćemo spavati u gostinskoj sobi.
9. Putujemo rano ujutro/izjutra.
10. Doći ću po vas oko četiri sata.

vježba/vežba II

Stavite u ženski rod imenice u muškom rodu.

Ovo je moj prijatelj.
Ovo je moja prijateljica.

1. Vaš muž je Jugoslaven/Jugosloven.
2. Moj učenik je marljiv.
3. Imao sam dobre nastavnike.
4. On je plemenit čovjek/čovek.
5. Da li znate onog starca?
6. On je moj drug iz škole.
7. Ovaj radnik je vrlo pošten.
8. To je naš najbolji glumac.
9. Vaš krojač šije dobro.
10. Tvoj stariji brat je dobar mladić.

TRESLA SE BRDA,
RODIO SE MIŠ.

ТРЕСЛА СЕ БРДА,
РОДИО СЕ МИШ.

Kàko gòvore ptìce i živòtinje!		How Birds and Animals Talk!	
Ptìca pjèva/pèva	ćiu-ćiu-ćiu	A bird sings	tweet-tweet
Gàvran gràkće	graa-graa*	A crow croaks	caw-caw
Pàs làje	av-av	A dog barks	bow-wow
Màčka mjàuče	mijao	A cat meows	meow
Kràva múče	muu	A cow moos	moo
Óvca bléji	beee-beee	A sheep bleats	baa-baa
Svínja gròkće	grrok-grrok	A pig grunts	oink-oink
Pijètao/Pévac kukùriče	kukurikuu	A rooster crows	cocka-doodle-doo
Kòkoška kokòdače	kokodakaaa	A hen cackles	buck-buck-pkaw
Pàtka gáče	kva-kva	A duck quacks	quack-quack
Kòza bléji	meee-meee	A goat bleats	naa-aa

Male Šále

Мале Шале

Kod bara.

Rudi: Slušaj, Bobi, ja vidim sve dvostruko.

Profesor: Od vas nikada ništa! Aleksandar Veliki je u vašim godinama bio osvojio

*Doubling or tripling of letters in these expressions is the popular way of indicating the lengthening of a particular sound and not separate instances of the same sound.

Bobi: Budalo jedna, zatvori onda jedno oko.

—Molim vas lijepo, koliko je sati?
—Pola.
—Pola četiri ili pola pet?
—To ne znam, jer mi je neki dan otpala mala kazaljka.

Pred suca dovedena su dva poznata "sumnjivca."
—Gdje stanujete vi? — upita jednoga sudac.
—Nigdje.
—A vi? —upita drugoga.
—Ja sam mu susjed.

pola onda poznatog svijeta.
Student: E, ali mu je profesor bio Aristotel!

Један пролазник на улици пита дечка:
—Како се зовеш, мали?
—Урош, —одговори дечак.
—А колико имаш година?
—Седам.
—А колико има година твој отац?
—Тридесет и пет.
—А шта мислиш колико ја имам година?
—Не могу да кажем. Ја знам да бројим само до педесет.

Професор географије осећао је у последње време приличне болове у нози и обратио се специјалисти.
—Ѓде вас боли, господине професоре?
—Североисточно од пете.

DEVETNAESTA LEKCIJA

Jugoslavija

1. Jugoslavija je najveća država na Balkanu.
2. Njena zapadna granica je Jadransko more i, malim dijelom, Italija.
3. Sa sjeverne strane Jugoslavija graniči s Austrijom i Madžarskom.
4. S istočne strane Jugoslavija graniči s Rumunjskom i Bugarskom.
5. Na jugu Jugoslavije nalaze se Grčka i Albanija.
6. Po prostoru Jugoslavija je gotovo isto tako velika kao Oregon.
7. "Jugoslavija" doslovce znači "Zemlja Južnih Slavena."
8. Glavni slavenski narodi Jugoslavije su: Slovenci, Hrvati, Srbi, Crnogorci, Makedonci i Muslimanci.
9. Tamo ima i mnogo manjinskih grupa kao: Albanaca, Roma, Turaka, Rumunja, Slovaka, Ukrajinaca itd.
10. Prema popisu iz tisuću devetsto osamdeset prve, Jugoslavija ima 22.500.000 (dvadeset dva milijuna petsto tisuća) stanovnika.
11. Iako je Jugoslavija uglavnom planinska zemlja, ona na sjeveru ima i plodnih ravnica.

ДЕВЕТНАЕСТА ЛЕКЦИЈА

Југославија

1. Југославија је највећа држава на Балкану.
2. Њена западна граница је Јадранско море и, малим делом, Италија.
3. Са северне стране Југославије се граничи с Аустријом и Мађарском.
4. С источне стране Југославија се граничи с Румунијом и Бугарском.
5. На југу Југославије налазе се Грчка и Албанија.
6. По простору Југославија је готово исто тако велика као Орегон.
7. "Југославија" буквално значи "Земља Јужних Словена."
8. Главни словенски народи Југославије су: Словенци, Хрвати, Срби, Црногорци, Македонци и Муслиманци.
9. Тамо има и много мањинских група као: Албанаца, Рома, Турака, Румуна, Словака, Украјинаца итд.
10. Према попису из хиљаду деветсто осамдесет прве, Југославија има 22.500.000 (двадесет два милиона петсто хиљада) становника.
11. Иако је Југославија углавном планинска земља, она на северу има и плодних равница.

12. Najduža jugoslavenska rijeka jest Sava, koja izvire u Sloveniji i utječe u Dunav kod Beograda.
13. Njena dužina iznosi 940 (devetsto četrdeset) kilometara.
14. Dunav protječe kroz sjeveroistočni dio Jugoslavije u dužini od 591 (petsto devedeset jednog) kilometra.
15. Druge velike rijeke su: Drava, Drina, Morava i Vardar.

TKO RADI NE BOJI SE GLADI.

12. Најдужа југословенска река је Сава, која извире у Словенији и утиче у Дунав код Београда.
13. Њена дужина износи 940 (деветсто четрдесет) километара.
14. Дунав протиче кроз североисточни део Југославије у дужини од 591 (петсто деведесет једног) километра.
15. Друге велике реке су: Драва, Дрина, Морава и Вардар.

КО РАДИ НЕ БОЈИ СЕ ГЛАДИ.

YUGOSLAVIA—1. Yugoslavia is the largest country in the Balkans. 2. Its western boundary is the Adriatic Sea and, for a small part, Italy. 3. On the northern side Yugoslavia is bounded by Austria and Hungary. 4. On the eastern side Yugoslavia is bounded by Rumania and Bulgaria. 5. To the south of Yugoslavia lie Greece and Albania. 6. In area Yugoslavia is almost exactly as large as Oregon. 7. "Yugoslavia" literally means "Land of the South Slavs." 8. The principal Slavic peoples of Yugoslavia are: the Slovenes, the Croats, the Serbs, the Montenegrins, the Macedonians, and the Moslems. 9. There are also many minority groups there, such as the Albanians, Gypsies, Turks, Rumanians, Slovaks, and Ukrainians. 10. According to the census of 1981, Yugoslavia has 22,500,000 inhabitants. 11. Although Yugoslavia is mainly a mountainous country, there are some fertile plains in the north. 12. The longest Yugoslav river is the Sava, which rises in Slovenia and flows into the Danube at Belgrade. 13. Its length is 940 kilometers. 14. The Danube flows across the northeastern part of Yugoslavia for a distance of 591 kilometers. 15. Other large rivers are the Drava, Drina, Morava, and the Vardar.

vježba I

Odgovorite na slijedeća pitanja.

1. Koja je najveća država na Balkanu?
2. S kojim državama se graniči Jugoslavija?

vežba I

Odgovorite na sledeća pitanja.

1. Koja je najveća država na Balkanu?
2. S kojim državama se graniči Jugoslavija?

3. Kako se zove more s kojim se graniči Jugoslavija?
4. Što znači "Jugoslavija" doslovce?
5. Koji su glavni slavenski narodi Jugoslavije?
6. Koje su druge nacionalne grupe u Jugoslaviji?
7. Je li Jugoslavija ravna zemlja?
8. Koja je najduža jugoslavenska rijeka?
9. Gdje Sava utječe u Dunav?
10. Koje su druge velike rijeke?

3. Kako se zove more s kojim se graniči Jugoslavija?
4. Šta znači "Jugoslavija" bukvalno?
5. Koji su glavni slovenski narodi Jugoslavije?
6. Koje su druge nacionalne grupe u Jugoslaviji?
7. Da li je Jugoslavija ravna zemlja?
8. Koja je najduža jugoslovenska reka?
9. Gde Sava utiče u Dunav?
10. Koje su druge velike reke?

vježba/vežba II

Popunite slijedeće/sledeće rečenice odgovarajućim oblikom zamjenica koji, čiji, kakav, tko/ko.

_______ traži knjigu?
Tko/Ko traži knjigu?

1. To je momak _______ sam dala knjigu.
2. _______ je ova velika kuća?
3. _______ boje je tvoj auto?
4. Ne znam _______ ću odvesti na izlet.
5. Poslovica kaže: S _______ si, onakav si.
6. Pročitao sam knjigu _______ sam dobio na poklon.
7. To je klub _______ sam član bio prošle godine.
8. Imam prijatelja _______ se zove Ranko.
9. Da li znate poslovicu: _______ radi, ne boji se gladi.
10. Poznajem osobu _______ će vam pomoći.

vježba/vežba III

Popunite ove rečenice odgovarajućim glagolom.

Čitavu noć je _______ pivo. (piti I, popiti P)
Čitavu noć je pio pivo.

1. On je _______ čitav dan. (svirati I, odsvirati P)
2. Večeras ću _______ televiziju jedno dva sata. (gledati I, pogledati P)
3. Kad _______ knjigu, posudi je meni. (čitati I, pročitati P)
4. Čitavo jutro sam _______ pisma. (pisati I, napisati P)
5. Začas _______ kroz prozor da li pada kiša. (gledati I, pogledati P)

6. Kad sam se ________ iz Londona, otišao sam u Dubrovnik na odmor. (vraćati se I, vratiti se P)
7. Ona je ________ pred nekoliko minuta. (ići I, doći P)
8. ________ je s konja i slomio je nogu. (skakati I, skočiti P)
9. Pošto sam ________ sendvič, nisam više gladan. (jesti I, pojesti P)
10. Moraš ________ dok ne ________ . (učiti I, naučiti P)

ТКО ČЕКА, ТАЈ DOČEKA. КО ЧЕКА, ТАЈ ДОЧЕКА.

The Population of Yugoslavia. Few countries in the world have such a mixture of nationalities as has Yugoslavia. In this country, the size of Oregon, there are (in descending order of numbers) Serbs, Croats, Moslems, Slovenes, Albanians, Macedonians, Montenegrins, Hungarians, Turks, Slovaks, Bulgarians, Romanians, Ukrainians, Gypsies, Czechs, Italians, Germans, Russians, Vlachs, Poles, Jews, Greeks, and Austrians. It must be remembered that this "chef's salad" of nationalities is not readily comparable to the American mixture. America has received an even greater number of distinct nationality types, but the "melting pot" process tends to fuse them (at least the groups from Europe) into a generalized American type. In Yugoslavia the larger nationalities are geographically separate and have distinct territories and distinctive ways of life, including language differences.

The two largest nationalities are the Serbs and Croats; the Serbs are in Serbia, Bosnia, and Herzegovina, and there are small enclaves of Serbs in Croatia (e.g. in Lika). The Croats are in Croatia, and also in Bosnia and Herzegovina. The category of Moslem is a special one: it is the only census category other than that of Jew which uses the criterion of religion or religious tradition. The Moslems are located for the most part in Bosnia and Herzegovina. In Montenegro, physically the most rugged part of Yugoslavia, are the Montenegrins, famed for their large size, their heroic history, and their easygoing lethargy. Their mountainous republic is so poor that today one out of every five Montenegrins lives outside the republic. With the restructuring of the Yugoslav state after World War II, the Macedonians achieved a separate nationality identification, a separate language, and a separate republic. There are also Macedonian Slavs across the borders in Greece and Bulgaria, a fact that can be exploited in different ways by any one or all three of the countries concerned. In the northern part of the country, in Slovenia, are the Slovenes, a tightly knit and clannish nationality that also spills across its borders into Italy and Austria.

The Hungarians are located in the autonomous region of Vojvodina in northern Serbia, while the Albanian minority is in the autonomous region of Kosovo in southern Serbia. The Albanians are the fastest-growing minority in Yugoslavia, with a birthrate more than twice the national average; at present they number over a million in Kosovo, and there is a substantial number of them in the Macedonian republic. There are many more Albanians than Montenegrins; in fact, more than one-third of the whole Albanian people now lives within the borders of Yugoslavia.

Tolstoj i stražar

Tolstoj je jednoga dana šetao kroz jednu od glavnih moskovskih ulica. Skup ljudi svrati njegovu pažnju. Tolstoj priđe i ugleda kako stražar gura pred sobom nekog pijanicu. Tolstoj priđe stražaru i upita ga:

—Znaš li čitati?

—Znam! —odgovori stražar.

—Imaš li kod kuće bibliju?

—Da! —odgovori ponovo stražar.

—No, dobro . . . Idi kući i pročitaj zapovijed koja kaže: "Ljubi bližnjega svoga kao samog sebe."

—Stražar ga pogleda začuđeno, a onda upita:

—Znaš li ti čitati?

—Svakako! —odgovori Tolstoj.

—Imaš li kod kuće knjigu "Instrukcije za policajce?"'

—Ne! —odgovori opet Tolstoj.

—Onda je kupi i čitaj što piše u paragrafu osamnaestom o hapšenju lica u pijanom stanju! —reče stražar i nastavi svoj posao.

DVADESETA LEKCIJA

Posjeta Jugoslaviji

1. Prošlog ljeta bio sam u Jugoslaviji.
2. Tamo sam proveo tri mjeseca.
3. Pošao sam iz New Yorka šestog lipnja i stigao u Le Havre u Francuskoj četrnaestog lipnja.
4. Od Le Havrea do Pariza putovao sam vlakom.
5. U Parizu sam ostao nekoliko dana.
6. Onda sam jedne večeri sjeo na Simplon orijent ekspres.
7. Pošto sam otprilike dvadeset i četiri sata putovao kroz Francusku, Švicarsku i Italiju, prešao sam jugoslavensku granicu kod Sežane.
8. Bilo je kasno uvečer kad sam stigao u Zagreb.
9. Zagreb, glavni grad Hrvatske, star je i vrlo lijep grad.
10. Poslije toga posjetio sam Beograd.
11. Beograd je glavni grad Srbije, a ujedno i glavni grad Jugoslavije.
12. Za vrijeme ljeta imao sam prilike da putujem po Jugoslaviji.
13. Obišao sam sve važnije gradove.
14. Nedjelju dana proveo sam kod nekih srpskih seljaka u

ДВАДЕСЕТА ЛЕКЦИЈА

Посета Југославији

1. Прошлог лета био сам у Југославији.
2. Тамо сам провео три месеца.
3. Пошао сам из Њујорка шестог јуна и стигао у Лавр у Француској четрнаестог јуна.
4. Од Лавра до Париза путовао сам возом.
5. У Паризу сам остао неколико дана.
6. Онда сам једне вечери сео на Симплон оријент експрес.
7. Пошто сам отприлике двадесет и четири сата путовао кроз Француску, Швајцарску и Италију, прешао сам југословенску границу код Сежане.
8. Било је касно увече када сам стигао у Загреб.
9. Загреб, главни град Хрватске, стар је и врло леп град.
10. После тога посетио сам Београд.
11. Београд је главни град Србије, а уједно и главни град Југославије.
12. За време лета имао сам прилике да путујем по Југославији.
13. Обишао сам све важније градове.
14. Недељу дана провео сам код неких српских сељака

jednom malom mjestu u zapadnoj Srbiji.
15. Njihovo selo zove se Rasna i nalazi se između Titova Užica i Požege.

[nastavit će se]

BOLJE GROB NEGO ROB.

у једном малом месту у западној Србији.
15. Њихово село се зове Расна и налази се између Титова Ужица и Пожеге.

[наставиће се]

БОЉЕ ЃРОБ НЕЃО РОБ.

A VISIT TO YUGOSLAVIA—1. Last summer I was in Yugoslavia. 2. I spent three months there. 3. I set out from New York on the sixth of June and arrived in Le Havre in France on the fourteenth of June. 4. I traveled from Le Havre to Paris on the boat-train. 5. I stayed in Paris for a few days. 6. Then I boarded the Simplon Orient Express one evening. 7. After traveling about twenty-four hours across France, Switzerland, and Italy, I crossed the Yugoslav border at Sežana. 8. It was late at night when I arrived in Zagreb. 9. Zagreb, the capital city of Croatia, is an old and very beautiful city. 10. Afterwards I visited Belgrade. 11. Belgrade is the capital city of Serbia and is at the same time the capital city of Yugoslavia. 12. During the summer I was able (had the opportunities) to travel around Yugoslavia. 13. I visited all the main (more important) cities. 14. For a week I lived with some Serbian farmers in a small place in western Serbia. 15. Their village is called Rasna and is located between Titovo Užice and Požega.

vježba/vežba I

Postavite pitanja na slijedeće/sledeće odgovore.

1. Proveo sam tri mjeseca/meseca u Jugoslaviji.
2. Pošao sam iz New Yorka/Njujorka.
3. Do Pariza sam putovao vlakom/vozom.
4. Simplon orijent ekspresom.
5. Kod Sežane.
6. Zagreb.
7. Beograd je glavni grad Jugoslavije.
8. Putovao sam po Jugoslaviji.
9. Putovao sam ljeti/leti.
10. Selo se zove Rasna.

vježba/vežba II

Stavite rečenice najprije u prošlo vrijeme, a zatim u buduće.

Marko ide u školu.
Marko je išao u školu.
Marko će ići u školu.

1. On čita detektivske priče.
2. Idem na posao svako jutro.
3. Vrijeme/Vreme je prijatno za šetnju.
4. Putujem po Evropi.
5. Vraćam se kući sa tržnice.
6. Oni stanuju u kući do naše.
7. Mi večeramo u četvrt do osam.
8. Polazim iz Zagreba i idem za Pariz.
9. Zatvaram prozor jer pada snijeg/sneg.
10. Idem s njime na sastanak.

vježba/vežba III

Stavite riječi/reči u zagradama u odgovarajući padež.

1. Prošle godine smo bili u ________. (Jugoslavija)
2. Proveli smo dva ________ u Splitu. (mjesec/mesec)
3. Stanovali smo blizu ________. (plaža)
4. Ići ćemo ________ na otok/ostrvo ________. (brod, Brač)
5. Na Braču ima mnogo ________. (selo)
6. Naša kuća je u ________ ________. (velika šuma)
7. Šetamo se uz ________. (obala)
8. Javite ________ se kad stignete. (ja)
9. Tu ima mnogo ________ ________. (zanimljiva stvar)
10. Putovao sam kroz ________ ________ ________. (taj lijepi/lepi kraj)

vježba/vežba IV

Prevedite.

1. He usually puts his books on the table, but this time he put them in the drawer.
2. I am still eating. I've already eaten quite a lot.
3. Are you writing letters? I wrote two yesterday.
4. Put the pen there and leave me in peace.
5. My wife has gone out and I'm going out soon, too.

vježba V

Odgovorite na ova pitanja usmeno. (Answer these questions orally.)

1. Koje su mjere za težinu?

vežba V

Odgovorite na ova pitanja usmeno. (Answer these questions orally.)

1. Koje su mere za težinu?

2. Koliko metara ima kilometar?
3. Koja je najmanja mjera za dužinu?
4. Kako se zove jugoslavenski novac?
5. Koliko je dinara jedan dolar?

2. Koliko metara ima kilometar?
3. Koja je najmanja mera za dužinu?
4. Kako se zove jugoslovenski novac?
5. Koliko je dinara jedan dolar?

Težìne i mjère/mère	**Weights and Measures**
Mètarski Sìstem	Metric System
mjère/mère za težìnu	Weight Measures
gràm [g]	0.035 ounce
dèkagram, dèka [dkg]	0.35 ounce
kìlogram, kìlo, kìla [kg]	2.2 pounds
tòna [t]	2,200 pounds
mjère/mère za dužìnu	length, distance
mètar [m]	1.09 yards or 39 inches
kìlometar [km]	0.62 mile or 5/8 mile
cèntimetar [cm]	0.39 inch
mìlimetar [mm]	0.039 inch
mjère/mère za tekùćine/tèčnosti	liquid measures
lìtar [l], lìtra [l]	1.06 quarts
dècilitar [dl]	0.1 quart
hèktolitar [hl]	26.5 gallons

ČIST RAČUN, DUGA LJUBAV. ЧИСТ РАЧУН, ДУГА ЉУБАВ.

Yugoslav Currency. The basic unit of Yugoslav currency is the **dinar** (from Latin **denarius**). It is divided into 100 **para**'s. In the 1980s Yugoslavia suffered from severe inflation and so it is not feasible to cite the dinar's value in dollars since the rate will undoubtedly change. Look at the foreign-exchange column in your local newspaper or call the exchange specialist at your local bank for the latest rates.

Major Cities	**Glávni gràdovi**		
Amsterdam	Àmsterdam	Lisbon	Lìsabon
Athens	Aténa/Atína	London	Lòndon
Berlin	Bèrlin	Madrid	Màdrid
Bucharest	Bùkurešt	Marseilles	Màrselj
Budapest	Bùdimpešta	Munich	Mìnhen
Brussels	Brìsel	Moscow	Mòskva

Cairo	Kàiro
Chicago	Chicàgo/ Čikàgo*
Geneva	Žénéva
The Hague	Hág
Istanbul	Càrigrad
Jerusalem	Jerusàlim
Leningrad	Lènjingrad
Prague	Pràg
Rome	Rím
Salonika	Sòlun
Sofia	Sòfija
State College	State Còllege/ Stejt-Kòledž
Stockholm	Štòkholm

New York	Nèw York/ Njùjork*
Paris	Pàriz
Peking, Beijing	Pèking
Philadelphia	Philadèlphia/ Filadèlfija*
Pittsburgh	Pìttsburgh/ Pìtsburg*
Tokyo	Tòkio
Trieste	Tȑst
Venice	Vènecija
Vienna	Béč
Warsaw	Vàršava
Washington	Wàshington/ Vàšington

Male Šale

—Uh, kako me užasno tište nove cipele.
—A zašto si kupio tako tijesne cipele?
—Da zaboravim na druge brige.

Učiteljica: Kada kažem "Ja sam lijepa," koje je to glagolsko vrijeme?
Đak: To je prošlost.

Otac, pošto je izmlatio sinčića:
—Znaš, magare jedno, da mene boli više nego tebe kad te moram izmlatiti.
—Možda —plačući odgovori sinčić —ali ne na istom mjestu.

Susjeda: Susjede, vi ste učen čovjek. Liječnik je mome

Мале Шале

Професор: Одречни облик од глагола цртати гласи: ја не цртам, ти не црташ, он не црта, ми не цртамо, ви не цртате, они не цртају.
Петре, понови!
Петар: Нико не црта.

Келнер: Јесте ли имали чорбу од парадајза или од грашка?
Гост: Ђаво би га знао! Мирисала је на сапун.
Келнер: Значи да је била чорба од парадајза. Чорба од грашка мирише на бензин.

—Јао, мамице, —пожалила се

*Foreign names can be represented in one of two ways in Cr&S: phonetically, that is by respelling them with Cr&S letters in order to approximate the pronunciation (e.g. **Njujork**); or simply by using the spelling of the source language (e.g. **New York**). The phonetic method is, for obvious reasons, favored by users of Cyrillic; it also tends to be used by Serbs when they are writing in Latin letters. The original spellings (e.g. **New York**) are favored by Croats. However, some place names have a special and traditional representation in the language (e.g. **Beč** for **Vienna**).

mužu rekao da je hipohondar. A šta je to?

Susjed: To je čovjek koji se samo onda osjeća dobro, kad se osjeća loše.

тринаестогодишња девојчица мајци, —сваког дана кад се враћам из школе један неваљали дечко хоће да ме пољуби!

—Ништа, чим ти приђе, ти треба да потрчиш.

—Знам, али замисли ако он не потрчи за мном!

DVADESET PRVA LEKCIJA

Posjeta Jugoslaviji [nastavak]

16. Seljaci su tamo siromašni, ali veoma gostoljubivi.
17. Oni vole Amerikance i žele da što više saznaju o Americi.
18. Potkraj ljeta prisustvovao sam seljačkoj svadbi u jednom malom hrvatskom selu.
19. To selo se nalazi blizu Zagreba i zove se Šestine.
20. U Jugoslaviji je gostoprimstvo naroda ostavilo na mene dubok dojam.
21. Svako selo ima svoju posebnu nošnju.
22. Kad narod nedjeljom ide u crkvu u svojim lijepim nošnjama, čovjek uživa da ih gleda.
23. Jugoslavenski narodni plesovi, koji se zovu kola, veoma su zanimljivi.
24. Omladina pleše kolo uz harmoniku ili uz tamburicu.
25. Nedavno je jedna grupa plesača iz Pittsburgha išla u Jugoslaviju.
26. Jugoslaveni su bili iznenađeni kad su vidjeli kako američki mladići lijepo plešu jugoslavenske plesove.
27. Većina tih Amerikanaca bila je jugoslavenskog porijekla.

NIJE ZLATO SVE ŠTO SIJA.

ДВАДЕСЕТ ПРВА ЛЕКЦИЈА

Посета Југославији [наставак]

16. Сељаци су тамо сиромашни, али веома гостољубиви.
17. Они воле Американце и желе да што више сазнају о Америци.
18. Пред крај лета присуствовао сам сељачкој свадби у једном малом хрватском селу.
19. То село се налази близу Загреба и зове се Шестине.
20. У Југославији је гостопримство народа оставило на мене дубок утисак.
21. Свако село има своју посебну ношњу.
22. Кад народ недељом иде у цркву у својим лепим ношњама, човек ужива да их гледа.
23. Југословенске народне игре, које се зову кола, веома су занимљиве.
24. Омладина игра коло уз хармонику или уз тамбурицу.
25. Недавно је једна група играча из Питсбурга ишла у Југославију.
26. Југословени су били изненађени кад су видели како амерички младићи лепо играју југословенске игре.
27. Већина тих Американаца била је југословенског порекла.

НИЈЕ ЗЛАТО СВЕ ШТО СИЈА.

A VISIT TO YUGOSLAVIA (continued from Lesson XX)—16. The farmers there are poor, but they are very hospitable. 17. They like Americans and want to know more about America. 18. Later in the summer I attended a peasant wedding in a small Croatian village. 19. That village is located near Zagreb and is named Šestine. 20. The hospitality of the people in Yugoslavia made a strong (deep) impression on me. 21. Every village has a distinctive costume. 22. On Sundays, when the people go to church in their beautiful costumes, they present an inspiring sight (a person enjoys watching them). 23. Yugoslav folk dances, which are called *kolo*'s, are very interesting. 24. The young people dance the *kolo* to the accompaniment of an accordion or a tambura. 25. Not long ago a group of dancers from Pittsburgh went to Yugoslavia. 26. The Yugoslavs were surprised when they saw how well the American youngsters danced (dance) the Yugoslav dances. 27. The majority of those Americans were of Yugoslav descent.

vježba I

Odgovorite na slijedeća pitanja.

1. Jesu li seljaci u Jugoslaviji gostoljubivi?
2. Je li oni vole Amerikance?
3. Ima li svako selo svoju posebnu nošnju?
4. Kako se zovu jugoslavenski narodni plesovi?
5. Pleše li se kolo uz tamburicu?
6. Imate li vi narodne plesove?

vežba I

Odgovorite na sledeća pitanja.

1. Da li su seljaci u Jugoslaviji gostoljubivi?
2. Da li oni vole Amerikance?
3. Da li svako selo ima svoju posebnu nošnju?
4. Kako se zovu jugoslovenske narodne igre?
5. Da li se kolo igra uz tamburicu?
6. Imate li vi narodne igre?

vježba/vežba II

Stavite slijedeće/sledeće rečenice u množinu a zatim ih stavite u odrečni oblik.

> Ovaj student je Amerikanac.
> Ovi studenti su Amerikanci.
> Ovi studenti nisu Amerikanci.

1. Seljak je siromašan.
2. On vas je dugo čekao.
3. Taj gost je platio račun za sobu.
4. Ti si čekao tri puna sata.
5. Doći ću za deset minuta.
6. Kupila sam marke za pisma.
7. Novine ću čitati popodne.
8. On pleše/igra narodna kola.

9. Ona ga je pozvala na ručak.
10. Rekao sam im da sam u školi.

vježba/vežba III

Zamjenite/Zamenite podvučene imenice nenaglašenim oblikom zamjenice/zamenice. (Replace the underlined nouns with the unaccented form of the pronoun.)

Telefonirao sam Petru.
Telefonirao sam mu.

1. Kupit ću majci poklon.
2. Vidio/Video je prijatelje u gostionici.
3. Rekli su Ani da požuri.
4. Pomogla je Petru da napiše esej.
5. Nadi se sviđaju/dopadaju crne cipele.
6. Imam puno šešira.
7. Reći ću roditeljima da si otputovao.
8. Nadi ću vratiti knjigu sutra.
9. Želio/Želeo bih pročitati taj članak o jeziku.
10. Kaži Ivanu da kupi karte.

vježba/vežba IV

Prevedite slijedeće/sledeće rečenice.

1. What's the date today?
2. It's the second of February.
3. It means that I've been here for a month.
4. Do you like this place?
5. I like it very much and I hope to stay here for a year or two.

Yugoslav Customs and Manners It would probably astound a Yugoslav to be told that he and his fellow-countrymen (whether from Slovenia, Zagreb, Dalmatia, Bosnia, Bačka, or Belgrade) seem quite similar to a foreigner. Of course, there are regional differences in physical type and personality (Slovenians are supposed to be fair-complexioned, very industrious, very cautious, very musical; Dalmatians are generally dark, musical, and lively; Montenegrins have heroic physiques and a heroic distaste for work; Serbs are generally dark, fiery, and zestful). But all countries have regional differences (America has Texans, New Yorkers, New Englanders), but the differences are large and important only to a native.

The average Yugoslav is distinguished by an extended emotional range such that he can swing rapidly from wild excitement and happiness to moods of depression or apathy. It can be an exhausting experience for an American to spend much time with a lively Yugoslav group. To the Yugoslav, on the other hand, an American, talking calmly (with lifeless hands!), must sometimes seem like a "cold fish," because his emotional responses are made within a narrower range than the Yugoslav's.

Take voice volume, for example. Two Yugoslavs can work themselves into a shouting argument, then just as quickly break out into gusts of laughter and clap each other on the back. Americans cannot change that rapidly, since increased voice volume signifies to the American real anger or strong emotion.

A Yugoslav feels the need for physical contact in the communication process, so you can expect to be constantly tapped on the arm or knee when in conversation with him.

On the other hand, Yugoslavs do not use the smile as loosely as we do. In America you can go into some office for information or help, and you will be met by a barrage of polite smiles; you may not get any help, but you'll get a dental display. In Yugoslavia clerks and officials usually do not smile at all; you may or may not get help from them, but you won't get a string of smiles. Thus Americans feel that such Yugoslavs are cold, even boorish, when such is not the case at all. Yugoslavs in turn are misled by our easy smiles into expecting personal help and attention which they probably will not get. Watch an American stop somebody on the street and ask for directions or a match: he'll smile ingratiatingly while making his request; a Yugoslav will be just as polite, but he won't waste the smile, which he reserves for pleasant, friendly situations.

You will encounter one interesting custom if you visit a Yugoslav in his office. You'll be offered Turkish coffee and maybe a shot of shlivovitz [**šljivovica**.] Usually it's difficult for an American to relax during such an office visit, or he relaxes too much, depending on the shlivovitz. At home he's not used to this combination of work and hospitality.

Don't be offended if a Yugoslav doesn't meet his appointment on time. We Americans are such slaves to clock time that we'll be ready for a 2 P.M. appointment at 5 till 2, and we'll be offended if the other party is late. Yugoslavs are more reasonable about this, operating on clock time but with a Balkan correction factor that permits a person to show up twenty or so minutes after an appointment. On the other hand, a Yugoslav won't throw you out of the office just because he has another appointment; if your business takes more time, he'll stay with it until a conclusion has been reached.

About handshaking. I guess everybody knows that Europeans (not the British!) shake hands a lot more than we do; the Yugoslavs are right in there with them, pumping hands in all directions. In America a man shakes hands only when he is introduced to another man or when he is leaving on a trip. No one is quite sure when an American woman shakes hands; she does it even more rarely and when no one expects it. This ancient custom (which arose as a guarantee that two warriors would not slug each other) has so languished in America that to call an American a "handshaker" is to insult him, since the term connotes a servile, fawning person. Thus it seems to an American that Yugoslavs, men, women, and children, shake hands every time they turn around, but it's not really that often; and they all, even the women, shake with a firm grip. So, once you've decided to visit Yugoslavia, you had better start practicing the very pleasant Yugoslav custom of frequent handshaking.

Male Šale

Liječnik: Koliko spavate svakog dana?
Bobi: Dva sata.
Liječnik: To je premalo.
Bobi: Znam, ali osim toga spavam osam sati noću.

Učitelj: Jesu li "hlače" jednina ili množina?
Đak: Gore su jednina, a dolje množina.

Znanac: Oho! Vi vozite auto? Koliko ste trebali da naučite šofirati?
Bobi: Četiri . . .
Znanac: Mjeseca?
Bobi: Ne, automobila.

Profesor: Koje je najveće svjetsko more?
Đak: (šuti)
Profesor: Vrlo dobro, TIHI OCEAN.

Мале Шале

У аутобусу жена се окрене према човеку који је стајао поред ње и запита:
—Да ли сте ви члан партије?
—нисам, одговори човек.
—Да ли вам је неко у породици члан партије?
—Не, поново рече човек.
—Онда макни ногу с мога палца!

Два чиновника су седела у београдској кафани и пила турску кафу. Прелиставајући Борбу, један од њих рече:
—Овај чланак каже да се неки људи поново буне. Тврде да читав профит њиховог рада одлази на издржавање бирократа.
Други чиновник гуцне кафу, запали Вардар и лено испуштајући дим у ваздух рече:
—Бре, нек се буне колико хоће само нек не престану да раде.

DVADESET DRUGA LEKCIJA

U Jugoslaviji

1. Oprostite, gospodine, možete li mi kazati gdje je kolodvor.
2. Naravno. Idite ravno dolje ovom ulicom, prijeđite preko trga, onda okrenite nalijevo prema katedrali.
3. Kad dođete do tržnice, okrenite nadesno i produžite dok ne prijeđete još dvije ulice.
4. Na lijevoj strani ulice vidjet ćete kolodvor.
5. To je suviše komplicirano za mene.
6. Ja sam Amerikanac i ne govorim sasvim dobro hrvatski.
7. Amerikanac! Mislio sam da ste Nijemac ili Francuz.
8. Ovdje u gradu nema mnogo Amerikanaca.
9. Kako ste Amerikanac, ja ću vam sam pokazati.
10. O, hvala lijepo. To je vrlo ljubazno od vas.
11. Nema na čemu. Imam brata u Minnesoti.
12. Kakav slučaj! Ja sam iz Minnesote.
13. Zaista? Moj brat Ivo je rudar u sjevernoj Minnesoti. Grad u kojem živi zove se Hibbing.

ДВАДЕСЕТ ДРУГА ЛЕКЦИЈА

У Југославији

1. Извините, господине, можете ли да ми кажете где је железничка станица?
2. Наравно. Идите право доле овом улицом, пређите преко трга, онда окрените налево према катедрали.
3. Кад дођете до пијаце, окрените надесно и продужите док не пређете још две улице.
4. На левој страни улице видећете железничку станицу.
5. То је сувише компликовано за мене.
6. Ја сам Американац и не говорим сасвим добро српски.
7. Американац! Мислио сам да сте Немац или Француз.
8. Овде у граду нема много Американаца.
9. Пошто сте Американац, ја ћу вам сам показати.
10. О, хвала лепо. То је врло љубазно од вас.
11. Нема на чему. Имам брата у Минесоти.
12. Какав случај! Ја сам из Минесоте.
13. Стварно? Мој брат Јово је рудар у северној Минесоти. Град у коме живи зове се Хибинг.

14. Dobro poznajem Hibbing. Ja sam rođen u Duluthu, ali sada živim u Minneapolisu.

15. Svijet je malen. Dobro. Hajdemo na kolodvor.

OD JEDNOG UDARA DUB NE PADA.

14. Добро познајем Хибинг. Ја сам рођен у Дулуту, али сада живим у Минеаполису.

15. Свет је мали. Добро. Хајдемо на станицу.

ОД ЈЕДНОГ УДАРА ДУБ НЕ ПАДА.

IN YUGOSLAVIA—1. Excuse me, sir, can you tell me where the station is? 2. Of course. Go straight down this street, cross the square, then turn left at the cathedral. 3. When you come to the marketplace, turn to the right and continue for two blocks more. 4. You'll see the station on the left side of the street. 5. That's too complicated for me. 6. I'm an American and I don't speak Croatian/Serbian too well. 7. American! I thought that you were (are) a German or a Frenchman. 8. There are not many Americans in the city. 9. Since you're an American, I'll show you [the station] myself. 10. Oh, thank you very much. That's real nice of you. 11. Don't mention it. I have a brother in Minnesota. 12. What a coincidence! I'm from Minnesota. 13. Really? My brother, Ivo/Jovo, is a miner in northern Minnesota. The city in which he lives is called Hibbing. 14. I know Hibbing well. I was born in Duluth, but now I'm living in Minneapolis. 15. It's a small world. Well, let's go to the station.

vježba/vežba I

Stavite ove rečenice u upitni i odrečni oblik.

Ovo je veliki trg.
Je li ovo veliki trg? [or] Da li je ovo veliki trg? Ovo nije veliki trg.

1. Katedrala je blizu.
2. Treba prijeći/preći preko trga.
3. To je prilično jednostavno.
4. Ja sam stranac u ovom gradu.
5. Moj brat živi u Minnesoti/Minesoti.
6. Ivo/Jovo je rudar.
7. On živi u gradu Hibbingu/Hibingu.
8. Mogu vas dopratiti do kuće.
9. Moja kuća je na desnoj strani ulice.
10. U ovom gradu ima mnogo Amerikanaca.

vježba/vežba II

Stavite imperativ umjesto/umesto infinitiva.

(Zatvoriti) prozor. (vi)
Zatvorite prozor!

1. (Vratiti se) brzo. (vi)
2. (Ići) i (kupiti) tri litre vina. (ti)
3. (Ostati) i (čuti) što će kazati. (mi)
4. Ako ne znaju, (pitati). (oni)
5. (Reći) mu da mu ne mogu pomoći. (ti)
6. (Doći) poslije/posle sastanka. (ti)
7. (Priznati) da niste u pravu. (vi)
8. (Paziti) kad prelaziš preko ulice. (ti)
9. (Kazati) im neka (stići) na vrijeme/vreme. (vi, oni)
10. (Pisati) kako govoriš. (ti)

vježba/vežba III

Popunite slijedeće/sledeće rečenice odgovarajućim oblikom kondicionala.

Ja ________ mu ________ tu knjigu. (dati)
Ja bih mu dao tu knjigu.

1. Zašto vi ne ________ ________ večeras. (doći)
2. Ja ________ vam rado ________ u tom poslu. (pomoći)
3. Mi ________ ________ putovati. (željeti/želeti)
4. Ti ________ ________ da znaš. (odgovoriti)
5. Ja ________ ________ da ste Amerikanac. (reći)
6. ________ ________, ali moram učiti. (doći)
7. Rado ________ ________ u New York. (otići)
8. Najviše ________ ________ popiti čaj. (voljeti/voleti)
9. ________ ________ avionom, ali se bojim. (putovati)
10. Ako ________ ja to ________, ________ ________. (reći, lagati)

vježba/vežba IV

Napišite kratki sastav na temu "Moji praznici."

Po lojtrici gor i dol

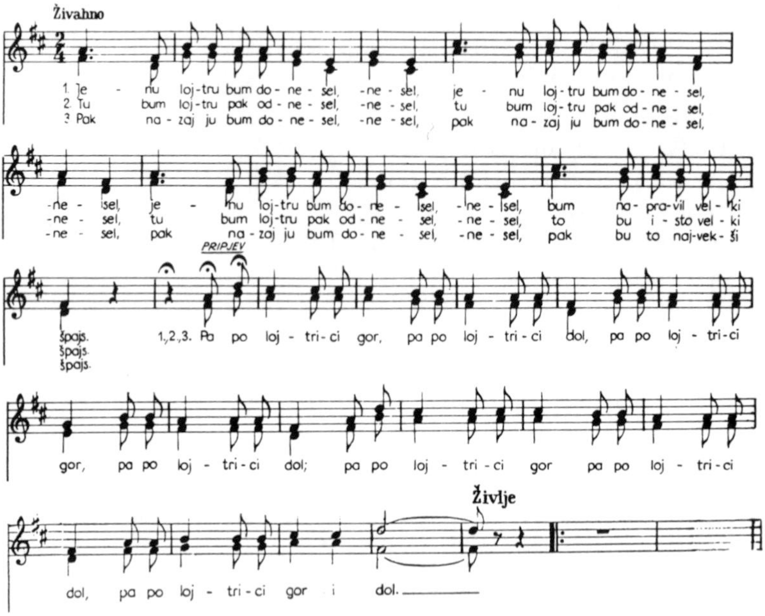

"Up and Down the Ladder" is a lively kajkavian song from Zagorje, the region north of Zagreb. Special kajkavian forms that appear in the song are presented below along with their Cr&S equivalents.

bùm [=bùdem] "I will"
bùm donèsel [=dònijet ću/dòneću] "I will bring"
bùm nàpravil [=nàpravit ću/nàpraviću] "I will make, will have"
bùm odnèsel [=òdnijet ću/òdneću] "I will take away"
dòl [=dòlje/dòle] "down"
gòr [=gòre] "up"
jèn [=jèdan] "one, a"
lójtra [=ljèstve/lèstve] "ladder"
nájvekši [=nájveći] "the biggest, the most, a lot of"
nàzaj [=nàzad] "back"
pàk "then"
prípjev/prípev "refrain"
špàjs "pantry, fun, a big time"
vèlki [=vèliki] "large, big"
žìvahno "sprightly, lively"
žìvlje "more lively, brisker"

Лукава ученица

Професор, објашњавајући архитектуру катедрале, запитао је:
—Шта мислите зашто је архитекта употребио овај бели лук, Наташа?

Изненађена питањем, пошто је читала роман под клупом, Наташа је одговорила:
—Не знам, друже професоре, али моја мама употребљава бели лук да побољша укус јела.*

*The point of this story turns on the difference between **béli lúk,** "white arch," and **béli lùk,** "white onion, garlic"; Nataša did not hear the difference in vowel length either because she was too preoccupied or because she comes from an area (e.g. southern Serbia) that lacks this distinction.

DVADESET TREĆA LEKCIJA

U gostionici

1. Molim vas, konobar,* mogu li sjesti za ovaj stol?
2. Želim večerati.
3. U redu, gospodine. Tu je tanjur, žlica, nož, vilica i ubrus.
4. Ne zaboravite sol, papar i šećer!
5. Izvolite jelovnik, gospodine.
6. Prije svega želio bih juhu.
7. Zatim mi donesite teleći odrezak s jajetom, miješanu salatu, crnog vina i kruha.
8. Molim. Kruh je već na stolu, gospodine.
9. Konobar, molim vas, kažite prodavaču novina da mi donese "Politiku."
10. Htio bih čitati dok čekam večeru.
11. [kasnije] Je li vam jelo prijalo, gospodine?
12. Da. Večera je bila vrlo dobra. Molim vas, donesite mi crnu kavu.
13. Gdje mogu platiti račun?
14. Možete platiti meni. Da vidimo što ste imali.
15. To bi bilo ________** dinara, gospodine.

ДВАДЕСЕТ ТРЕЋА ЛЕКЦИЈА

У гостиомици

1. Молим вас, келнер,* могу ли да седнем за овај сто?
2. Желим да вечерам.
3. У реду, господине. Ту је тањир, кашика, нож, виљушка и салвета.
4. Не заборавите со, бибер и шећер!
5. Изволите јеловник, господине.
6. Пре свега желео бих супу.
7. Затим ми донесите бифтек с јајетом, мешану салату, црног вина и хлеба.
8. Молим. Хлеб је већ на столу, господине.
9. Келнер, молим вас, кажите продавцу новина да ми донесе "Политику."
10. Хтео бих да читам док чекам вечеру.
11. [доцније] Је ли вам јело пријало, господине?
12. Да. Вечера је била врло добра. Молим вас, донесите ми црну кафу.
13. Где могу да платим рачун?
14. Можете да платите мени. Да видимо шта сте имали.
15. То би било ________** динара, господине.

*A vocative usage, but the nominative forms are usually used. V forms would be **konobaru** and келнеру.

**Because of severe inflation in Yugoslavia in recent years, it is impossible to present prices that would be realistic even for a few years. One can call the local bank and get the current exchange rate; then, with help from the Numbers section (see Index), appropriate figures can be used in the sentences above.

16. Izvolite ________ .* Ostatak zadržite!	16. Изволите ________ .* Остатак задржите!
17. Hvala. Najljepša hvala.	17. Хвала. Најлепша хвала.
KAKAV NA JELU, TAKAV NA DJELU.	КАКАВ НА ЈЕЛУ, ТАКАВ НА ДЕЛУ.

IN A RESTAURANT—1. Waiter, may I (please) sit down at this table? 2. I want to have dinner. 3. All right, sir. Here is a plate, spoon, knife, fork, and napkin. 4. Don't forget the salt, pepper, and sugar! 5. Here's the menu, sir. 6. First of all, I'd like some soup. 7. Then bring me beef steak with egg, a tossed salad (mixed salad), some red (black) wine and some bread. 8. Very good. The bread is already on the table. 9. Waiter, please tell the paper-boy to bring me a copy of "Politika." 10. I would like to read while I'm waiting for dinner. 11. [later] Did you enjoy your food (Was the food agreeable to you), sir? 12. Yes. The meal was very good. Please bring me (a) black coffee. 13. Where can I pay the bill? 14. You can pay me. Let's see, what did you have [to eat]? 15. That will be (would be) *dinars, sir. 16. Here's * . Keep the change (the remainder)! 17. Thanks. Thank you very much.

Names of Common Foods	**Imèna òbičnih jéla****
food—hrána, jèlo	
Vegetables	**pòvrće (neut. sg.)**
beans	gràh/pàsulj
beans (green)	màhune/borànija
beets	cìkla/cvèkla
cabbage	zélje, kùpus
carrot	mȑkva/šargarépa
cauliflower	cvjètača/karfìol
celery	cèler
corn	kukùruz
cucumber	kràstavac (pl. -vci)
garlic	bìjeli/béli luk, čèšnjak
kale	kèlj, G kèlja
lettuce	zèlena salàta
melon	dìnja
mushroom	pèčurka, gljìva

*Because of severe inflation in Yugoslavia in recent years, it is impossible to present prices that would be realistic even for a few years. One can call the local bank and get the current exchange rate; then, with help from the Numbers section (see Index), appropriate figures can be used in the sentences above.

**As noted before, the words on the left of the slash mark are Croatian, those on the right Serbian.

onion	lùk
parsley	péršin/péršun
peas	grášak
pepper	pàprika
potato	krùmpir/kròmpir
boiled	kùhan/kùvan
fried	pȑžen
mashed	krumpir-pìre/krompir-pìre
pumpkin	tìkva, tìkvica
radish	ròtkvica
rice	rȉža/pìrinač
sauerkraut	kìselo zélje, kìseli kùpus
spinach	špìnat/spànač
tomato	rájčica/paradàjz
watermelon	lubènica
Fruits	**vòće (neut. sg.)**
apple	jàbuka
apricot	kájsija
banana	banána
berry	jàgoda
cherry	trèšnja
cherry (sour)	vìšnja
fig	smòkva
orange	nàranča/pomòrandža
peach	brèskva
pear	krùška
pineapple	ànanas
plum	šljìva
strawberry	jàgoda
Soup	**júha/čórba, sùpa**
beef soup	gòveđa júha/gòveđa čórba
with noodles	sa rezáncima
chicken soup	pìleća júha/čórba
fish soup, chowder	rìblja júha/čórba
Eggs	**jája (neut. pl.)**
fried egg	pȑženo nà oko
hard-boiled egg	tvŕdo kùhano/kùvano jáje
omelette	òmlet
scrambled eggs	kájgana
soft-boiled egg	méko kùhano/kùvano jáje
Meats	**mésa (neut. pl.)**
bacon	slànina

beef	gòvedina/gòveđina
beef (adj.)	gòveđi
boiled meat	kuhano/kùvano méso
chicken	pìletina
chicken (adj.)	pìleći
roast chicken	pìleće pèčenje
cutlet	òdrezak, šnìcl/šnìcla
grilled meat	méso sa ròštilja
ground meat	fàširano méso, mljèveno/mlèveno méso
ham	šúnka
smoked ham	pr̀šut/pr̀šuta
lamb	jànjetina/jàgnjetina
lamb (adj.)	jànjeći/jàgnjeći
roast lamb	jànjeće/jàgnjeće pèčenje
mutton	òvčevina/òvčetina
mutton (adj.)	òvčji
pork	svìnjetina, pràsetina
pork (adj.)	svìnjski, svìnjeći
sausage	kobàsica
turkey	pùretina/ćùretina
turkey (adj.)	pùreći/čùreći
roast turkey	pùreće/ćùreće pèčenje
veal	tèletina
veal (adj.)	tèleći
roast veal	tèleće pèčenje
Wiener schnitzel	Béčki òdrezak/Béčka šnìcla
Fish and shellfish	**rìbe (fem. pl.) i ràkovi (masc. pl.)**
carp	šáran
catfish	sòm
eel	jègulja
fish (adj.)	rìblji
haddock	tòvar
herring	sléđ
lobster	jàstog
mackerel	skúša
octopus	hòbotnica
perch	gr̀geč, smúđ
sardine	sardína
shrimp	skàmp
squid	lìgnja
trout	pàstrva/pàstrmka

Beverages	**píća (neut. pl.)**
beer	pívo
brandy	ràkija
plum brandy	šljìvovica
coffee	kàva/kàfa
café au lait	bìjela/béla k.
Turkish coffee	tùrska k., cŕna k.
fruit juice	vòćni sók
lemonade	limunáda
milk	mlijèko/mléko
raspberry drink	màlina
tea	čàj
water	vòda
mineral water	kìsela vòda
wine	víno
red wine	cŕno víno, rùžica
white wine	bìjelo/bélo víno
yogurt	jògurt

[a Yugoslav soft-drink with a corn-flour base is **bóza**]

Various	**rázno**
bread	krùh/hlèb
butter	màslac/pùter, buter
candy	bònbon/bonbóna, slàtkiš
cheese	sìr
cookie	kòlač
flour	bràšno
horseradish	hrèn, rèn
ice cream	slàdoled
jam	džèm
lard	mást, G másti
marmalade	marmeláda
oil	úlje
pepper	pàpar/biber
pie	pìta
popcorn	kòkice (fem. pl.)
pudding	pùding
salt	sòl/só, G sòli
sandwich	sèndvič
spice	miròdija/záčin
sugar	šèćer
tart	pòslastica, kòlač
vinegar	òcat/sìrće

vježba I	**vežba I**
Stavite pitanja na slijedeće odgovore.	Stavite pitanja na sledeće odgovore.
1. Želim večerati.	1. Želim da večeram.
2. Na stolu se nalaze: tanjur, nož i čaša.	2. Na stolu se nalaze: tanjir, nož i čaša.
3. Najprije želim juhu.	3. Najpre želim supu.
4. Volim teleći odrezak sa jajetom i salatom.	4. Volim teleću šniclu sa jajetom i salatom.
5. Obično pijem crno vino.	5. Obično pijem crno vino.
6. Ne čitam novine kad jedem.	6. Ne čitam novine kad jedem.
7. Večera je bila vrlo dobra.	7. Večera je bila vrlo dobra.
8. Šalicu crne kave.	8. Šolju crne kafe.

vježba/vežba II

Popunite slijedeće/sledeće rečenice odgovarajućim oblikom priloga sadašnjeg ili priloga prošlog.

________ ________ sa nama, otišao je. (pozdraviti se) Pozdravivši se sa nama, otišao je.

1. ________ ga prešao sam na drugu stranu ulice. (ugledati)
2. ________ ________ po parku, sreo sam svog prijatelja. (šetati se)
3. Našao je veliku školjku, ________ ________ u pijesku/pesku. (igrati se)
4. ________ članak, izašao sam iz biblioteke. (pročitati)
5. Mnogo sam naučio ________ . (putovati)
6. ________ račun, izašao sam iz gostionice. (platiti)
7. ________ te, zakasnio sam na predavanje. (čekati)
8. ________ ________ iz Slovenije, ostao sam nekoliko dana u Zagrebu. (vraćati se)
9. ________ u dućan, ustanovio sam da nemam novaca. (ući)
10. Proveo sam čitav sat ________ čestitke za rođendan. (kupovati)

vježba/vežba III

Stavite priloge u komparativ ili superlativ.

(Cr.) Jučer je bilo ________ nego prekjučer. (hladno)
Jučer je bilo hladnije nego prekjučer.
(S.) Juče je bilo ________ nego prekjuče. (hladno)
Juče je bilo hladnije nego prekjuče.

1. Ovu lekciju sam naučio ________ od tebe. (dobro)
2. ________ volim jagode od jabuka. (mnogo)
3. ________ volim višnje. (mnogo)

4. Vidjet ćemo/Videćemo se ________ . (kasno)
5. Zadržao sam se ________ nego obično. (dugo)
6. Govorite ________ jer vas ne čujemo. (glasno)
7. On trči ________ od tebe. (brzo)
8. ________ je plivati u moru nego u rijeci/reci. (lako)
9. ________ pamtim brojeve. (teško)
10. U svibnju/maju će biti ________ i ________ . (ugodan, topao)

vježba/vežba IV

Prevedite.

1. I usually have a cup of milk and a fried egg for breakfast. 2. I like red wine best. 3. He prefers lemonade to fruit juice. 4. Today we had chicken with fried potatoes for dinner. 5. Waiter, please bring me some sugar for my coffee.

vježba/vežba V

Napišite kratki sastav na temu "Moji obroci."

GOVORITI JE LAKO, STVARATI JE TEŠKO

ЂОВОРИТИ ЈЕ ЛАКО, СТВАРАТИ ЈЕ ТЕШКО.

Yugoslav Eating Customs To get some understanding of Yugoslav culture, you literally have to eat your way into it. Food, its preparation and consumption, plays a large part in the everyday life and habits of the Yugoslav family. However, if you are a calorie-conscious American, you should be warned that your enthusiastic participation in Yugoslav eating rituals will be rewarded by an appreciable gain in weight, but it's worth it. For the Yugoslav family the pattern of meals is roughly this: a light continental breakfast (*café au lait*, rolls, marmalade or jam) early in the morning, a light snack about 10 A.M. (**gàblec** in Zagreb, **màrenda** in Split, **hàjdemo na bùrek i jògurt** ["Let's go for a meat pie and yogurt!"] in Belgrade), a heavy meal sometime after midday (about 2:30 or 3 P.M.), a light "pick-up" supper between 8 and 10 in the evening. After the midday meal Yugoslavs either take a nap or sink into a pleasant stupor.

If you want to get any sightseeing and visiting done while you are in Yugoslavia, you are advised to skip the heavy afternoon meal; if it slows down the Yugoslav, it will sink an American! During the day you can have a pleasant time just sitting at a sidewalk café (e.g. the **kavana** of the Hotel Dubrovnik in Zagreb, the **kafana** of Hotel Moskva in Belgrade; both are in the center of their cities.) Here you can drink numerous cups of **turska kava/kafa** or beer, read newspapers, or write postcards; meanwhile the natives are all around you, sitting at nearby tables, strolling past, hurrying to the market.

In the evening let your nose be your guide: wander through a Yugoslav city until you smell the delicious odors of barbecued meat and follow the odors to a garden restaurant (usually behind a wall or set back off the street). There you can have your choice of wine, Yugoslav salad of cucumbers (**salata od krastavaca**), bread, and **ćevapčići** or **ražnjići.** Ordering **čevapčići** will give you good practice in distinguishing the sounds ć and č; it will also give you some ten small sausage-like rolls of mixed pork, veal, and beef that have been cooked over an open grill. **Ražnjići** are small portions of veal or pork threaded on a skewer and also cooked over an open grill.

If your garden restaurant has a musical group, you will hear a fascinating mixture of American, European, and Balkan music. Stay late enough, though, and the foreign music will be abandoned. In Zagreb some customer will shout for **Po lojtrici gor i dol** ("Up and Down the Ladder"); in Belgrade you will appreciate how five centuries of Turkish rule have influenced Serbian music as the **pevačica** renders a song such as **Magla je padala** ("The Mist Has Fallen") with its wailing, repetitive Eastern strains.

By the way, don't be embarrassed if you see Yugoslavs picking their teeth at the table after a meal; it's quite all right as long as it is done in the correct fashion: the toothpick is in your right hand, probing away, while the left hand is cupped over your mouth as if you were playing a silent mouth organ; meanwhile your gaze is fixed on some distant object; you have to all appearances achieved nirvana.

If you have the opportunity to eat in a Yugoslav home, you will start out with a **dobar tek** (in Croatia), "Good Appetite," or **prijatno** (in Serbia). Then you must eat rather slowly, because Yugoslav hospitality can be overwhelming and your plate will be replenished beyond your imagined capacity. If you must refuse, you should say **hvala, ne,** but the **ne** must be said at least four times before it means "no"; this **ne** should not, of course, be abrupt, but should be accompanied by an apologetic smile, rolling head motions, and hands spread out in "I'm only a puny foreigner" gesture.

ГОСТ С УЖЕТОМ

Марк Твен стиже једном у познати њујоршки хотел с кофером у једној и дугачким ужетом у другој руци. Хотелијер се одмах заинтересовао за ову несвакидашњу опрему свога госта.

—Ово уже ми служи у случају да у хотелу изненада избије пожар, —објасни му Марк Твен. —Тада по ужету могу лако да се спустим с прозора.

—Врло добро, мистер Твен, —одговори хотелијер. —Но морам вас на нешто упозорити: код нас је обичај да гости с ужетом плаћају унапред.

MUZIKALNI OBITELJ

Jedna poznata zagrebačka dama dovede svoga sina skladatelju Ivanu Zajcu i ponosno mu reče:

—Maestro, moj mladić ima veliki dar za glazbu. Osim toga ima frizuru kao Beethoven. Budite strpljivi pa ga poslušajte kako udara po klaviru!

Zajc odmjeri momka koji je zbilja imao umjetničku frizuru preko ušiju, zamoli ga da za klavirom pokaže što zna. Kada mladić prestade svirati, sretna majka upita skladatelja, što da radi s momkom.

Zajc mirno i ravnodušno reče:

—Dajte ga ošišati!

DVADESET ČETVRTA LEKCIJA

Liječnički pregled

1. O, gospodine doktore, konačno ste stigli! Nisam htio umrijeti dok vas ne upoznam.
2. Šala, a? To je loš simptom. Što vam je?
3. O, gospodine doktore, glava me boli, oči mi gore, u ušima mi zuji, nos me svrbi, zub me boli, u ruci me žiga, leđa me bole, u želucu imam boli, lijeva noga mi je utrnula, gležanj mi se odrvenio, imam žulj na jednom stopalu i kurje oko na drugom.
4. Vi ste bolesni! Dajte da vam opipam bilo. A sada da izmjerimo temperaturu.
5. No, temperatura je normalna za nekoga tko je u vašem stanju, ali ne mogu vam naći bilo. Uostalom, to uopće nije važno. Vi imate samo balkanski "simulantis."
6. Je li to ozbiljno?
7. Ne. Svaki se stranac od toga razbolijeva. Evo moga recepta: dvije čaše vruće rakije svaki dan i ne jedite ništa dok ne ojačate.
8. O, hvala vam, gospodine doktore. Koliko vam dugujem?
9. Nemojte me vrijeđati nuđenjem novaca. Ja ću vam već poslati račun.

ДВАДЕСЕТ ЧЕТВРТА ЛЕКЦИЈА

Лекарски преглед

1. О, господине докторе, најзад сте стигли! Нисам хтео да умрем док вас не упознам.
2. Шала, а? То је рђав симптом. Шта вам је?
3. О, господине докторе, глава ме боли, очи ми горе, у ушима ми зуји, нос ме сврби, зуб ме боли, у руци ме жига, леђа ме боле, у стомаку имам болове, лева нога ми је утрнула, чланак ми се удрвенио, имам плик на једном стопалу и жуљ на другом.
4. Ви сте болесни! Дајте да вам опипам пулс. А сада да измеримо температуру.
5. Но, температура је нормална за некога ко је у вашем стању, али не могу да вам нађем пулс. Уосталом, то уопште није важно. Ви имате само балкански "симулантис."
6. Да ли је то озбиљно?
7. Не. Сваки се странац од тога разболева. Ево мога рецепта: две чаше вруће ракије сваки дан и не једите ништа док не ојачате.
8. О, хвала вам, господине докторе. Колико вам дугујем?
9. Немојте ме вређати нуђењем новаца. Ја ћу вам већ послати рачун.

SVRBI ME NOS, ČUVAJ SE! СВРБИ МЕ НОС, ЧУВАЈ СЕ!

THE DOCTOR'S EXAMINATION—1. Oh, doctor, at last you arrived! I didn't want to die until I had met you. 2. Humor, eh? That's a bad symptom. What's troubling you? 3. Oh, doctor, my head hurts, my eyes burn, I have a ringing in the ears, my nose itches, my tooth aches, my arm is sore, my back hurts, I have a stomachache, my left leg is numb, my ankle is stiff, I have a blister on one foot and a corn on the other. 4. You're sick! Let me feel your pulse. And now let me take your temperature. 5. Well, your temperature is normal for one in your condition, but I can't detect any pulse. Well, anyway, that's not important. You only have Balkan "fakeitis." 6. Is that serious? 7. No, every foreigner contracts it. Here's my prescription: two glasses of hot rakija every day and don't eat anything until you get stronger. 8. Oh, thank you, doctor. How much do I owe you? 9. Don't insult me by offering money. I'll send you a bill instead.

vježba/vežba I

Stavite slijedeće/sledeće rečenice u odrečni oblik.

1. Doktor je pregledao bolesnika.
2. Boli me glava i zuji mi u ušima.
3. To je vrlo važno i ozbiljno.
4. Svakog dana pijte vruću rakiju.
5. Imam dovoljno novaca da vam platim.
6. Poslala sam vam račun kući.
7. Odlučio je da primi novac.
8. Doktor mu je izmjerio/izmerio temperaturu.
9. Boli me glava.
10. Reci majci da ću otići kod zubara.

vježba/vežba II

Stavite slijedeće/sledeće rečenice u buduće vrijeme/vreme.

On se vraća u četvrtak.
On će se vratiti u četvrtak.

1. Večeras idem u kino/bioskop.
2. Telefonirao sam mu da dođe.
3. Idemo na izlet u subotu.
4. Da li idete tramvajem?
5. Oni stanuju u vrlo lijepom/lepom kraju.
6. Pomaže li vam Nada?

7. Odmarao sam se nekoliko dana.
8. Pokazao sam mu put do parka.
9. Nisam te zaboravio.
10. Pitao sam ga da li zna gdje/gde je katedrala.

vježba/vežba III

Stavite imenice i zamjenice/zamenice u zagradama u odgovarajući padež.

1. Na posao odlazim ________ i ________ . (autobus, tramvaj)
2. Što/Šta biste rado jeli za ________ . (večera)
3. Kupio sam dva ________ ________ (kilogram, voće) i dva ________ ________ ________. (veliki, komad, riba)
4. Oni će večerati kod ________ . (mi)
5. Večerali smo na ________ ________ ________ . (naša velika terasa)
6. Poslije/Posle ________ (večera) možemo otići kod ________ ________. (moj prijatelj)
7. To je interesantan film o ________ (život) u ________ ________. (naša država)
8. Autobus prolazi ispred ________ ________ . (moja kuća)
9. Silazimo kod ________ (trg) i moja kuća je u ________ ________ (prva ulica) desno.
10. Da li želite ________ ________ ________ . (knjiga, žuta boja)

vježba/vežba IV

Prepričajte dvadeset četvrtu lekciju svojim riječima/rečima. (Retell the twenty-fourth lesson in your own words.)

Children's Chant

Cimbuli-rambuli
Banda svira
Mene doktor vizitira
Pa me pita što mi fali
Meni fali trbuh mali.

НАПОЛЕОН И ЕНГЛЕЗ

Наполеон у једној љутитој расправи с енглеским послаником узвикну:

—Знате ли да ћу напасти Енглеску?

—То је ваша ствар. —одговори енглески посланик.

—А знате ли ви да ћу срушити Енглеску?

—То је наша ствар. —одговори Енглез.

Gaudeamus igitur!

Pacijent: Doktore, jako se loše osjećam. Recite mi što mi je ali, molim vas, nemojte mi reći na latinskom ili grčkom nego na čistom hrvatskom jer želim točno doznati koji je moj problem.

Doktor: Ako baš želite znati, kažem vam na čistom hrvatskom da ste pijanac a osim toga jedete kao prasac.

Pacijent: Mnogo hvala! A sad mi recite na latinskom ili na grčkom tako da mogu objasniti svojoj ženi.

DVADESET PETA LEKCIJA

Beogradski kolodvor

1. Joj! Koliko je ovdje na kolodvoru ljudi!
2. Uvečer na beogradskom kolodvoru ima uvijek mnogo svijeta.
3. Gdje možemo dobiti karte za Sarajevo?
4. Tamo na onom prozorčiću gdje se prodaju karte.
5. Nemoj zaboraviti da pokažeš svoj pasoš.
6. Turisti imaju popust na cijenama.
7. Kad polazi vlak za Sarajevo?
8. U osam sati s četvrtog kolosijeka.
9. Molim, dajte nam dvije karte!
10. Prvog razreda?
11. Ne, drugog razreda.
12. Kada vlak stiže u Sarajevo?
13. Vlak dolazi tamo u ponoć.
14. Hajdemo u kolodvorsku restauraciju popiti po jednu tursku kavu.
15. Ali zapamti, trebamo se požuriti na vlak jer je drugi razred uvijek natrpan između dva velika grada.
16. Nosač! Uzmite našu prtljagu i osigurajte nam dva mjesta na sarajevskom ekspresu.
17. Sad se možemo malo odmoriti. Ovi su nosači stručnjaci za osiguravanje mjesta.
18. To je besmisleno. Tvoja napojnica nosaču zapravo je razlika između mjesta u

ДВАДЕСЕТ ПЕТА ЛЕКЦИЈА

Београдска станица

1. Јао! Колико је овде на станици света.
2. Увече на београдској станици има увек много света.
3. Ѓде можемо добити карте за Сарајево?
4. Тамо на оном прозорчићу где се продају карте.
5. Немој да заборавиш да покажеш свој пасош.
6. Туристи имају попуст на ценама.
7. Кад полази воз за Сарајево?
8. У осам сати са четвртог колосека.
9. Молим, дајте нам две карте!
10. Прве класе?
11. Не, друге класе.
12. Када воз стиже у Сарајево?
13. Воз долази тамо у поноћ.
14. Хајдемо у станични ресторан да попијемо по једну турску кафу.
15. Али запамти, треба да пожуримо на воз јер је друга класа увек препуна између два велика града.
16. Носач! Узмите наш пртљаг и осигурајте нам два места на сарајевском експресу.
17. Сад можемо мало да се одморимо. Ови су носачи стручњаци за осигуравање места.
18. То је бесмислено. Твој бакшиш носачу у ствари је разлика између места у

prvom i mjesta u drugom razredu.

19. Nikad nisam bio dobar matematičar.

DA BISMO RADILI,
POTREBNO JE ZNATI,
A DA BISMO ZNALI,
POTREBNO JE UČITI.

првој и места у другој класи.

19. Никад нисам био добар математичар.

ДА БИСМО РАДИЛИ,
ПОТРЕБНО ЈЕ ЗНАТИ,
А ДА БИСМО ЗНАЛИ,
ПОТРЕБНО ЈЕ УЧИТИ.

THE BELGRADE STATION—1. Wow! What a crowd here in the station! 2. The Belgrade station is always crowded in the evening. 3. Where can we get tickets to Sarajevo? 4. Over there at that little window where tickets are sold. 5. Don't forget to show your passport. 6. Tourists receive a discount (have a discount in prices). 7. When does the train leave for Sarajevo? 8. At eight o'clock on (from) track four. 9. Give us two tickets, please. 10. First class? 11. No, second class. 12. When does the train arrive in Sarajevo? 13. The train gets there at midnight. 14. Let's go into the station restaurant and drink a cup of Turkish coffee. 15. But remember, we have to hurry to make the train, because second class is always crowded between two big cities. 16. Porter! Take our baggage and get us (ensure us) two seats on the Sarajevo express. 17. Now we can relax a bit. These porters are experts at getting seats. 18. That's silly! Your tip to the porter is actually the difference between a second-class and a first-class seat. 19. I never was good at mathematics (a good mathematician).

vježba I

Odgovorite na slijedeća pitanja.

1. Gdje se prodaju karte?
2. Imaju li turisti popust?
3. Kada vlak stiže u Sarajevo?
4. Pijete li tursku kavu?
5. Tko su stručnjaci za osiguravanje mjesta u vlaku?
6. Dajete li napojnicu nosaču?
7. Kome se još daje napojnica?
8. Kada polazi vlak za Sarajevo?

vežba I

Odgovorite na sledeća pitanja.

1. Gde se prodaju karte?
2. Da li turisti imaju popust?
3. Kada voz stiže u Sarajevo?
4. Da li pijete tursku kafu?
5. Ko su stručnjaci za osiguravanje mesta u vozu?
6. Da li dajete bakšiš nosaču?
7. Kome se još daje bakšiš?
8. Kada polazi voz za Sarajevo?

vježba/vežba II

Stavite slijedeće/sledeće rečenice u upitni i odrečni oblik.

Napisali smo pismo
Da li ste napisali pismo? [or] Jeste li napisali pismo?
Nismo napisali pismo.

1. Pokazao sam svoj pasoš.
2. Autobus polazi u pet i četrdeset.
3. Jutros sam učio dva sata.
4. Katedrala se nalazi na trgu.
5. Šetali smo se uz obalu.
6. Žurimo na vlak/voz.
7. On je vrlo dobar matematičar.
8. Treba mi samo nekoliko stotina dinara.
9. Poslije/Posle ručka se obično odmaram.
10. Sviđa/Dopada mi se to narodno kolo.

vježba/vežba III

Stavite slijedeće/sledeće rečenice u neupravni govor. [nèupravan, "indirect"]

Doći ću večeras.
Rekao je da će doći večeras.

1. Koliko je sati?
2. Ovdje/Ovde ima mnogo ljudi.
3. (Cr.) Želite li večerati? (S.) Da li želite večerati?
4. Da li je Ana kod kuće?
5. Kad polazi vlak/voz za Beograd?
6. Prija li vam večera?
7. Jeste li pročitali novine?
8. Ta priča mi se sviđa/dopada.
9. Hoćete li s nama na izlet?
10. Ne mogu.

vježba/vežba IV

Prevedite.

1. I wonder whether that restaurant is better than this one?
2. Do we have time for a cup of coffee?
3. Thank you, but I don't drink coffee.
4. I didn't understand him because he spoke too quickly.
5. We shall go out in the afternoon to see the town.

vježba/vežba V

Translate.

1. Obećao je da će doći.
2. Da sam znao, bio bih mu rekao.
3. Ako budem dobro raspoložen, ići ćemo u šetnju.
4. Nosač je odnio/odneo naše kofere iako nismo rekli da ih odnese.
5. Reći će vam da ih je kupio, ali mu nemojte vjerovati/verovati.

TKO LAŽE, TAJ I KRADE. КО ЛАЖЕ, ТАЈ И КРАДЕ.

Razumijemo li se?

Znam da vjeruješ da razumiješ ono što misliš da sam rekao, ali nisam siguran da shvaćaš da ono što čuješ nije ono što ja mislim.

СУПЕРБЕБА

КРЕСТЛАЈН: ДЕЧАК ЛЕТИ КАО СУПЕРМЕН.— Један малиша из калифорнијског града Крестлајна толико се одушевио Суперменом да се одмах после гледања филма попео на прозор на другом спрату родитељске куће и покушао да полети. На срећу, трогодишњи дечко је са собом понео и јастук који га је спасао повреда приликом скока са висине од готово осам метара.

DVADESET ŠESTA LEKCIJA

Život na selu u Jugoslaviji

1. Mile je mlad zemljoradnik.
2. On i njegova žena Dobrila imaju dva dječaka: Mišu i Rašu.
3. Milina majka Milesa živi s njima.
4. Njihovo gospodarstvo je maleno, ali zemlja je plodna.
5. Mile je vrijedan radnik.
6. Njegovi glavni usjevi su kukuruz i pšenica.
7. Ali on uzgaja i grah, mrkvu, rotkvice, krumpir i slično.
8. Na gospodarstvu ima mnogo voćaka.
9. Šljive su veoma korisne.
10. Mile peče šljivovicu—rakiju od šljiva.
11. On je prodaje, kad mu treba gotovih novaca.
12. Ljeti Mile ustaje u tri sata ujutro.
13. On cio dan mnogo radi.
14. Raša mu pomaže oko stoke.
15. Ali od Miše nema pomoći.
16. On ima samo šest godina.
17. On naganja piliće i prasad.
18. Njegov ga tata zove "mali mangup."
19. Dobrila radi u kuhinji.
20. Ona od mlijeka pravi kajmak i sir.
21. Milina majka Milesa također mnogo radi.
22. Ponekad ona tka lijepe vunene ćilime.

ДВАДЕСЕТ ШЕСТА ЛЕКЦИЈА

Живот на селу у Југославији

1. Миле је млад земљорадник.
2. Он и његова жена Добрила имају два дечака: Мишу и Рашу.
3. Милетова мајка Милеса живи с њима.
4. Њихово имање је мало, али земља је плодна.
5. Миле је вредан радник.
6. Његови главни усеви су кукуруз и пшеница.
7. Али он узгаја и пасуљ, шаргарепу, ротквице, кромпир и слично.
8. На имању има много воћака.
9. Шљиве су веома корисне.
10. Миле пече шљивовицу—ракију од шљива.
11. Он је продаје, кад му треба готових новаца.
12. Лети Миле устаје у три сата изјутра.
13. Он цео дан много ради.
14. Раша му помаже око стоке.
15. Али од Мише нема помоћи.
16. Он има само шест година.
17. Он јури пилиће и прасад.
18. Његов га тата зове "мали мангуп."
19. Добрила ради у кухињи.
20. Она од млека прави кајмак и сир.
21. Милетова мајка Милеса такође много ради.
22. Понекад она тка лепе вунене ћилиме.

23. Subotom je sajamski dan u obližnjem gradiću.
24. Mile, Raša i Miša idu na sajam da prodaju svinje i da ponekad kupe nove opanke.

25. Dobrila i Milesa ostaju kod kuće, jer na gospodarstvu uvijek ima posla.

OBITELJ, KOJA SE IGRA ZAJEDNO, OSTAJE ZAJEDNO.

23. Суботом је пазарни дан у оближњој варошици.
24. Миле, Раша и Миша иду на пазар да продају свиње и да понекад купе нове опанке.

25. Добрила и Милеса остају код куће, јер на имању увек има посла.

ПОРОДИЦА, КОЈА СЕ ИГРА ЗАЈЕДНО, ОСТАЈЕ ЗАЈЕДНО.

VILLAGE LIFE IN YUGOSLAVIA—1. Mile is a young farmer. 2. He and his wife, Dobrila, have two boys: Miša and Raša. 3. Mile's mother, Milesa, lives with them. 4. Their farm is small, but the soil is rich. 5. Mile is an industrious worker. 6. His chief crops are corn and wheat. 7. But he also raises beans, carrots, radishes, potatoes, and the like. 8. There are many fruit trees on the farm. 9. Plums are very useful. 10. Mile makes (cooks) "shlivovits"—a plum brandy (a brandy from plums). 11. He sells it when he needs ready cash. 12. In the summer Mile gets up at three in the morning. 13. He works hard the whole day. 14. Raša helps him by taking care of the stock (around the stock). 15. But he gets no (there is no) help from Miša. 16. He's only six years old. 17. He chases the chickens and the pigs. 18. His dad calls him a "little rascal." 19. Dobrila works in the kitchen. 20. She makes butter and cheese out of milk. 21. Mile's mother, Milesa, also works hard. 22. Sometimes she weaves beautiful woolen rugs. 23. Saturday (on Saturdays) is market day in the nearby town. 24. Mile, Raša, and Miša go to market to sell pigs and sometimes to buy new shoes [**opanci**, a type of leather moccasin]. 25. Dobrila and Milesa stay home, because there's always work on a farm.

vježba I

Odgovorite na slijedeća pitanja.
1. Koliko djece imaju Mile i Dobrila?
2. Što je Mile po zanimanju?
3. Je li njegovo gospodarstvo veliko?
4. Koji su njegovi glavni usjevi?
5. Kad Mile ustaje ljeti?

vežba I

Odgovorite na sledeća pitanja.
1. Koliko dece imaju Mile i Dobrila?
2. Šta je Mile po zanimanju?
3. Da li je njegovo imanje veliko?
4. Koji su njegovi glavni usevi?
5. Kad Mile ustaje leti?

6. Što pravi njegova žena?
7. Pomaže li Raša tati?
8. Gdje oni odlaze subotom?
9. Što Mile prodaje na sajmu?
10. Je li oni često kupuju nove opanke?

6. Šta pravi njegova žena?
7. Da li Raša pomaže tati?
8. Gde oni odlaze subotom?
9. Šta Mile prodaje na pazaru?
10. Da li oni često kupuju nove opanke?

vježba/vežba II

Stavite slijedeće/sledeće rečenice u negativni oblik prošlog vremena.

On je zemljoradnik.
On nije bio zemljoradnik.

1. Mile je vrijedan/vredan zemljoradnik.
2. Mi ustajemo u pet sati ujutro/izjutra.
3. Moja kćerka voli jabuke.
4. Raša se brine za stoku.
5. Ona radi u polju.
6. Tu se prave kajmak i sir.
7. Prodajemo kukuruz i pšenicu.
8. To je rakija od šljiva.
9. Kupili smo opanke na sajmu/pazaru.
10. Ja ostajem kod kuće.

vježba/vežba III

Stavite odgovarajući padež.

1. Mile je radio na ________ ________. (veliko gospodarstvo/imanje)
2. Ugledao sam ________ ________. (mladi zemljoradnik)
3. Kupili smo dva ________ ________ ________. (veliki vuneni ćilimi)
4. Dođite s ________! (mi)
5. Uzmite ________ ________! (ova stara torba)
6. Pili smo ________ ________ (vruća rakija) u ________ (restoran).
7. Oni će stanovati kod ________. (mi)
8. Susreo sam ga poslije/posle ________ ________. (zimski praznici)
9. Bili smo na ________ (sajam) u ________ ________. (obližnji gradić)
10. Možete putovati ________ (autobus) do ________ ________ ________. (to malo selo)

vježba/vežba IV

Prevedite slijedeće/sledeće rečenice.

1. We shall leave as soon as you are ready.
2. They lost their money because they were not careful enough.
3. I'll study until you come.
4. Although I saw that film, I could not remember the name of the main actor.
5. They began singing after you had left.

U VINU ISTINA. У ВИНУ ИСТИНА.

Vèza

If you plan to spend much time in Yugoslavia, it would be wise to have some understanding of this word and its concept. Literally, **vèza** means "connection," though a better English rendition would be "connections." The practice of exploiting connections (relatives, friends, acquaintances) to secure favors is not unknown in the United States or other countries, but in Yugoslavia the practice is widespread and almost an essential part of everyday functioning. **Vèza** can get your son or daughter into a university, it can help with examinations, it can get you a bed near a window if you go to a hospital, it can help you acquire scarce supplies, it can get your progeny into jobs with the diplomatic service, and so on. It is not a matter of who is best qualified for a job, it is a matter of who has stronger **vèza**. Getting favors **preko vèze,** "through **vèza**," may not be an ideal system for a modern state, but it is ingrained in Yugoslav life.

MALI OGLASI*

ŽENIDBA–UDAJA

Intelektualka, crnka, 25 godina, 168 cm, želi upoznati solidnog akademski obrazovanog samca od 28 do 35 godina. Alkoholičari i pušači isključeni. Brak moguć. Ponude poslati na adresu: Kleopatra Kismetović, Trg Slobode, br. 13.

Intelektualac, karakteran i iskren profesor fonetike, želi upoznati simpatičnu djevojku blage naravi i čiste prošlosti iz bolje obitelji, koja voli diskutirati o filologiji. Brak siguran. Ponude s kratkom biografijom i fotografijom poslati na adresu: Miodrag Glogotović, ul. Đure Salaja, br. 6.

Udovica sa nešto gotovine, inteligentna, ugodne vanjštine, traži

*__Máli òglasi__, "small advertisements," are want-ads that appear in Yugoslav newspapers. Names and some details have been changed. These ads are for marriage: **žènidba** for men, **ùdaja** for women.

slobodnog građanina sa dvosobnim stanom blizu centra. Brak moguć. Ponude poslati na adresu: Zagorka Barončck, ul. Kumičićeva 9.

DVADESET SEDMA LEKCIJA

Gradovi Jugoslavije

1. Najveći grad Jugoslavije je Beograd, koji je glavni grad Srbije, a istodobno i glavni grad Jugoslavije.
2. Beograd ima oko jednog i po milijuna stanovnika.
3. Nalazeći se na brijegu, gdje se sastaju Dunav i Sava, Beograd je danas, kao i u prošlosti, važna spona između Zapada i Istoka.
4. Povijest kaže da su Kelti u četvrtom stoljeću prije Krista na tom mjestu sazidali grad (Singidunum).
5. Kasnije su došli Rimljani, koji su tu, u Beogradu (Singidunumu), držali vojni garnizon.
6. Hunski vođa Atila razorio je grad u petom stoljeću poslije Krista.
7. Slavenski narodi naselili su se ovdje u početku devetog stoljeća.
8. Za one koji vole povijest, Beograd je jedan od najzanimljivijih gradova Evrope.
9. Zagreb, glavni grad Hrvatske, ima oko devetsto tisuća stanovnika.
10. Moderni je Zagreb zapravo sastavljen od dva grada, koji su se nalazili u neposrednoj blizini; jedan je bio Gradec, koji se danas zove Gornji

ДВАДЕСЕТ СЕДМА ЛЕКЦИЈА

Ѓрадови Југославије

1. Највећи град Југославије је Београд, који је главни град Србије, а истовремено и главни град Југославије.
2. Београд има око једног и по милиона становника.
3. Налазећи се на брегу, где се састају Дунав и Сава, Београд је данас, као и у прошлости, важна спона између Запада и Истока.
4. Историја каже да су Келти у четвртом веку пре Христа на том месту сазидали град (Сингидунум).
5. Доцније су дошли Римљани, који су ту, у Београду (Сингидунуму), држали војни гарнизон.
6. Хунски вођа Атила разорио је град у петом веку после Христа.
7. Словенски народи су се овде населили у почетку деветог века.
8. За оне који воле историју, Београд је један од најинтересантнијих градова Европе.
9. Загреб, главни град Хрватске, има око деветсто хиљада становника.
10. Модерни град Загреб је у ствари образован од два града, који су се налазили у непосредној близини; један је био Ѓрадец, који

grad, a drugi Kaptol, naseobina, koju su osnovali crkveni velikodostojnici.

се данас зове Горњи град, а други Каптол, насеобина, коју су основали црквени великодостојници.

11. Pogled na starodrevnu katoličku katedralu ostavlja na posjetioca Zagreba najljepši dojam.

11. Поглед на стародревну католичку катедралу оставља на посетиоца Загреба најлепши утисак.

12. U Zagrebu stranca najviše iznenađuje veliki broj knjižara.

12. У Загребу странца највише изненађује велики број књижара.

13. Zagrepčani su uvijek imali ljubavi za prosvjetu i kulturu.

13. Загрепчани су увек имали љубави за просвету и културу.

14. Ljubljana, glavni grad Slovenije, ima oko trista tisuća stanovnika.

14. Љубљана, главни град Словеније, има око триста хиљада становника.

15. Službeni jezik Slovenije je slovenski. To je slavenski jezik.

15. Званични језик Словеније је словеначки. То је словенски језик.

16. Slovenci upotrebljavaju kao svoje pismo latinicu, isto kao i Hrvati. [Nastavit će se]

16. Словенци употребљавају као своје писмо латиницу, исто као и Хрвати. [Наставиће се]

SVUGDJE JE LIJEPO POĆI, AL' JE NAJLJEPŠE KUĆI DOĆI.

СВУЃДЕ ЈЕ ЛЕПО ПОЋИ, АЛ' ЈЕ НАЈЛЕПШЕ КУЋИ ДОЋИ.

THE CITIES OF YUGOSLAVIA—1. The largest city in (of) Yugoslavia is Belgrade, the capital (main city) of Serbia and, at the same time, the capital of Yugoslavia. 2. Belgrade has about one and a half million residents. 3. Located on a bluff where the Danube and Sava meet, Belgrade is today, as also in the past, an important link between the West and the East. 4. History tells [us], that the Celts built a city (Singidunum) on this spot in the fourth century before Christ. 5. Later came the Romans and they maintained a garrison here, in Belgrade (Singidunum). 6. The leader of the Huns, Attila, destroyed the city in the fifth century after Christ. 7. Slavic peoples settled here at the beginning of the ninth century. 8. For those who like history Belgrade is one of the most interesting cities in (of) Europe. 9. Zagreb, the capital of Croatia, has about 900,000 inhabitants. 10. Modern Zagreb is really formed out of two cities, which were located right next to one another (in close proximity); one was Gradec, which today is called Upper City, and the other is Kaptol, a settlement founded by church dignitaries (which church dignitaries founded). 11. The sight of the ancient Catholic cathedral makes (leaves) a very beautiful impression on the visitor to (of) Zagreb. 12. The foreigner in Zagreb is astounded by the great number of bookstores (the great number . . . astounds the foreigner). 13. The inhabitants of Zagreb have always had a love of education and culture. 14. Ljubljana, the capital of Slovenia, has about 300,000 residents. 15. The official language of Slovenia is Slovenian. It's a Slavic language. 16. The Slovenians use the Latin writing system, as do the Croats. [To be continued]

vježba I

Odgovorite na slijedeća pitanja.

1. Koji je glavni grad Jugoslavije?
2. Gdje se nalazi Beograd?
3. Kako se zvao grad koji su sazidali Kelti?
4. Što je bio Beograd za vrijeme Rimljana?
5. U kojem su se stoljeću tu naselili slavenski narodi?
6. Od koliko gradova je sastavljen moderni Zagreb?
7. Što iznenađuje strance u Zagrebu?
8. Koji je glavni grad Slovenije?
9. Kako se zove službeni jezik Slovenije?
10. Kojim se pismom služe Slovenci?

vežba I

Odgovorite na sledeća pitanja.

1. Koji je glavni grad Jugoslavije?
2. Gde se nalazi Beograd?
3. Kako se zvao grad koji su sazidali Kelti?
4. Šta je bio Beograd za vreme Rimljana?
5. U kojem su se veku tu naselili slovenski narodi?
6. Od koliko gradova je sastavljen moderni Zagreb?
7. Šta iznenađuje strance u Zagrebu?
8. Koji je glavni grad Slovenije?
9. Kako se zove zvanični jezik Slovenije?
10. Kojim se pismom služe Slovenci?

vježba/vežba II

Stavite ove rečenice u imperativ.

Rekao sam mu da zatvori prozor.
Zatvori prozor!

1. Zvali smo ih da dođu ovamo.
2. Nada je kupila voće.
3. Rekao sam im da odu po njih u pet sati.
4. Oni putuju u subotu izjutra/ujutro.
5. Vi ste poslušni.
6. Dopratili smo ga do kolodvora/stanice.
7. Uzeo je moje knjige.
8. Oni dolaze k nama na selo.

9. Rekli smo mu da večeras ide kod tetke.
10. Oni putuju avionom.

vježba/vežba III

Stavite slijedeće/sledeće rečenice u buduće vrijeme/vreme, a zatim u upitni oblik budućeg vremena.

Idem kući. Ići ću kući.
Da li ćeš ići kući? [or] Hoćeš li ići kući?

1. Radim čitav dan.
2. Oni čitaju.
3. Rekli su mu istinu u oči.
4. Kupili smo novine.
5. Nemam vremena.
6. Ona živi na selu.
7. Predstava počinje u osam i trideset.
8. Marko i Maja se igraju u dvorištu.
9. Susreo sam svog učitelja.
10. On odlazi u inozemstvo/inostranstvo.

vježba/vežba IV

Prevedite.

1. Ispratila sam ga na kolodvor/stanicu.
2. Recite im da smo ih vidjeli/videli.
3. Da li ćete im ih kupiti?
4. Telefoniraj joj popodne.
5. Oni su nam govorili da nam se to neće svidjeti/svideti.
6. Kad ga vidim, reći ću mu da je dovede.
7. Otišao je po nju i rekao je da će se vratiti ako je ne nađe kod kuće.
8. Pisala mi je da će nam poslati knjigu.

ZDRAVLJE JE NAJVEĆE BOGATSTVO.

ЗДРАВЉЕ ЈЕ НАЈВЕЋЕ БОГАТСТВО.

МАЛИ ОГЛАСИ

ОБАВЕШТЕЊЕ

Инжењер Јесам Киселић, доцент Пољопривредног факултета у Београду, браниће своју докторску дисертацију под насловом: “Утицај хладних руку на млечност крава и квалитет млека,” у петак 16. јуна 1990 го-

ЗАМЕНА СТАНА

Трособан комфоран стан у Дубровнику у центру мењам за исти или сличан у ближем или у даљем центру Београда. Јавити или погледати на адресу: Мила Моруна, Дубровник, ул. Р. Бошковића, бр. 7.

дине у 17 часова. Приступ слободан.

СЛУЖБА

Млада певачица, свира виолину и пева, и певач са властитим џезом, слободни одмах. Дајна Зуза, Булевар Цара Лазара, бр. 5/6.

DVADESET OSMA LEKCIJA

Gradovi Jugoslavije [nastavak]

17. Glavni grad Bosne i Hercegovine je Sarajevo, koje ima oko petsto tisuća stanovnika.
18. Sarajevo predstavlja divnu mješavinu muslimanske i slavenske kulture.
19. Sarajevo je svijetu dobro poznato jer je tu godine 1914. (tisuću devetsto četrnaeste) izvršen atentat na austrijskog nadvojvodu Franju Ferdinanda.
20. Smatra se da je ovim atentatom u Sarajevu počeo prvi svjetski rat.
21. Skoplje (Makedonci kažu Skopje) je glavni grad Makedonije i ima oko petsto tisuća stanovnika.
22. Skoplje je bilo prijestolnica srednjovjekovne srpske države. Tu se srpski kralj Stefan Dušan u četrnaestom vijeku okrunio za cara.
23. Službeni jezik Makedonije je makedonski. To je slavenski jezik.
24. Makedonci upotrebljavaju kao svoje pismo ćirilicu, isto kao i Srbi i Crnogorci.
25. Rijeka Vardar dijeli grad u dva dijela: stari turski grad i moderni novi grad.

ДВАДЕСЕТ ОСМА ЛЕКЦИЈА

Ѓрадови Југославије [наставак]

17. Ѓлавни град Босне и Херцеговине је Сарајево, које има око петсто хиљада становника.
18. Сарајево представља дивну мешавину муслиманске и словенске културе.
19. Сарајево је свету добро познато јер је ту године 1914. (хиљаду деветсто четрнаесте) извршен атентат на аустријског надвојводу Франца Фердинанда.
20. Сматра се да је овим атентатом у Сарајеву почео први светски рат.
21. Скопље (Македонци кажу Скопје) је главни град Македоније и има око петсто хиљада становника.
22. Скопље је било престоница средњовековне српске државе. Ту се српски краљ Стефан Душан у четрнаестом веку крунисао за цара.
23. Службени језик Македоније је македонски. То је словенски језик.
24. Македонци употребљавају као своје писмо ћирилицу, исто као и Срби и Црногорци.
25. Река Вардар дели град у два дела: стари турски град и модерни нови град.

26. Utorkom je sajamski dan, koji pruža šarenu sliku raznovrsnih narodnih nošnja Makedonaca, Albanaca, Turaka i Cigana.
27. Glavni grad Crne Gore je Titograd koji ima oko sto četrdeset tisuća stanovnika.
28. Ali Cetinje, koje se nalazi u visokom planinskom predjelu, daleko je zanimljivije od Titograda.
29. Dubrovnik se nalazi na dalmatinskoj obali i jedan je od najljepših gradova Evrope.
30. U srednjem vijeku Dubrovnik (talijanski Ragusa) bio je nezavisna republika.
31. Sjevernije duž jadranske obale leži Split, gdje se još mogu vidjeti ostaci Dioklecijanove palače.
32. Rimski car Dioklecijan zidao je tu palaču 302. (trista druge) godine poslije Krista.
33. Ima još mnogo drugih mjesta u Jugoslaviji koja oduševljavaju putnika ili zbog lijepih samostana, kao što je Sveti Naum kod Ohrida u Makedoniji, ili zbog historijskih događaja (Duvanjsko polje, Kosovo polje itd.), ili čak zbog biranih vina, kao što je malo mjesto Lumbarda na otoku Korčuli na Jadranskom moru, koje je poznato po vinu nazvanom "grk."

26. Уторком је пазарни дан, који пружа шарену слику разноврсних народних ношња Македонаца, Албанаца, Турака и Цигана.
27. Ѓлавни град Црне Ѓоре је Титоград који има око сто четрдесет хиљада становника.
28. Али Цетиње, које се налази у високом планинском пределу, далеко је интересантније од Титограда.
29. Дубровник се налази на далматинској обали и један је од најлепших градова Европе.
30. У средњем веку Дубровник (талијански Рагуза) је био независна република.
31. Северније дуж јадранске обале лежи Сплит, где се још могу видети остаци Диоклецијанове палате.
32. Римски цар Диоклецијан је зидао ту палату 302. (триста друге) године после Христа.
33. Има још много других места у Југославији која одушевљавају путника или због лепих манастира, као што је Свети Наум код Охрида у Македонији, или због историјских догађаја (Дувањско поље, Косово поље итд.), или чак због бираних вина, као што је мало место Лумбарда на острву Корчули на Јадранском мору, које је познато по вину названом "грк."

TKO BRZO SUDI, BRZO SE KAJE. | КО БРЗО СУДИ, БРЗО СЕ КАЈЕ.

THE CITIES OF YUGOSLAVIA—(Continued from Lesson XXVII.) 17. The capital of Bosnia and Herzegovina is Sarajevo, which has about 500,000 inhabitants. 18. Sarajevo presents a fascinating combination of Moslem and Slavic culture. 19. Sarajevo is well known to the world, because here in the year 1914 the assassination of the Austrian Archduke Franz Ferdinand took place. 20. It is believed that World War I began with this assassination in Sarajevo. 21. Skoplje (the Macedonians say Skopje) is the capital of Macedonia and has about 500,000 inhabitants. 22. Skoplje was the capital (throne city) of the medieval Serbian state. Here the Serbian king Stefan Dušan was crowned emperor in the fourteenth century. 23. The official language of Macedonia is Macedonian. It's a Slavic tongue. 24. The Macedonians use Cyrillic as their writing system, as do the Serbs and the Montenegrins. 25. The river Vardar divides the city into two parts: the old Turkish city and the modern city. 26. On Tuesdays there is a fair (market day), which offers a colorful spectacle of the various costumes of Macedonians, Albanians, Turks, and Gypsies. 27. The capital of Montenegro is Titograd, which has about 140,000 inhabitants. 28. But Cetinje, which is high up in the mountains, is much more interesting than Titograd. 29. Dubrovnik is located on the Dalmatian coast and is one of the most beautiful cities in Europe. 30. In the Middle Ages Dubrovnik (in Italian, Ragusa) was an independent republic. 31. Further north along the Adriatic lies Split, where one may still see the remnants of Diocletian's palace. 32. The Roman emperor Diocletian built the palace here in A.D. 302. 33. There are many other places in Yugoslavia that will delight the traveler either because of beautiful monasteries, like Saint Naum at Ohrid in Macedonia, or because of historic events (Duvan Field [where Tomislav was crowned], Kosovo Field [historic battle between Serbs and Turks]), or even because of choice wines, like the small town of Lumbarda on the island of Korčula on the Adriatic, which is known for its wine, named "grk."

vježba/vežba I

Postavite pitanja na slijedeće/sledeće odgovore.

1. Sarajevo je glavni grad Bosne i Hercegovine.
2. 1914. u Sarajevu je izvršen atentat na nadvojvodu Ferdinanda.
3. (Cr.) Skoplje je bilo prijestolnica srednjovjekovne srpske države.
   (S.) Skoplje je bilo prestonica srednjovekovne srpske države.
4. Makedonski jezik je slavenski/slovenski jezik.
5. Stari turski grad i moderni novi grad.
6. Titograd se prije/pre zvao Podgorica.

7. Dubrovnik je bio nezavisna republika.
8. Split se nalazi na dalmatinskoj obali.
9. Car Dioklecijan.
10. Lumbarda na otoku/ostrvu Korčuli.

vježba/vežba II

Stavite u množinu a zatim u odrečni oblik množine.

Ovaj momak je učenik.
Ovi momci su učenici.
Ovi momci nisu učenici.

1. Kupila sam šareni vuneni kostim.
2. Moj prijatelj ima velik, udoban auto.
3. Ovaj seljak živi na velikom gospodarstvu/imanju.
4. Mladi pisac je napisao novu priču.
5. Učenik voli modernu poeziju.
6. Moja kćerka je nosila punu korpu jabuka.
7. Ova haljina je lijepa/lepa ali je prevelika za mene.
8. Vaš konj je mlađi i brži od moga.
9. Imam velikog psa.
10. Ovaj čovjek/čovek je sigurno gladan.

vježba/vežba III

Popunite rečenice odgovarajućim oblikom riječi/reči u zagradama.

On (raditi) u (tvornica).
On radi u tvornici.

1. Kako (zvati se) ovi učenici?
2. Jutros (ustati) vrlo rano i (otići) u ribolov.
3. Jezero (biti) duboko i tu (imati) ribe.
4. (Ručati) u (pristojan restoran).
5. Popodne (igrati) rukomet.
6. Blizu (naše selo) nalazi se šuma.
7. U (šuma) ima mnogo (životinje).
8. Bio sam u (lov) sa (drugovi).
9. On živi u (grad) od (prošla zima).
10. Slika je na (zid) u (velika soba).

vježba/vežba IV

Popunite rečenice pluskvamperfektom.

1. Maturant ________ ________ ________ praznike na moru. (provesti)
2. Studenti ________ ________ ________ u domovima. (stanovati)

3. One ________ ________ ________ iz raznih krajeva Jugoslavije. (dolaziti)
4. Gazdarica ________ ________ ________ studenta na ručak. (pozvati)

vježba/vežba V

Stavite slijedeće/sledeće rečenice u pluskvamperfekt.

1. Ja imam sreće.
2. Mi nismo kupili novi auto.
3. Sreo sam svoga prijatelja.
4. On je našao lijep/lep stan.

BIBLIJA—Stari Zavjet

Knjiga Postanka

I. Počeci svijeta i čovječanstva. Stvaranje svijeta. Prvi izvještaj o stvaranju.

1. U početku stvori Bog nebo i zemlju. 2. Zemlja bijaše pusta i prazna;
tama se prostirala nad bezdanima, i Duh Božji lebdio je nad vodama.
3. I reče Bog: "Neka bude svjetlost!" I bi svjetlost. 4. I vidje Bog da
je svjetlost dobra; i rastavi Bog svjetlost od tame. 5. Svjetlost prozva
Bog dan, a tamu prozva noć. Tako bude večer, pa jutro—dan prvi. 6.
I reče Bog: Neka bude svod posred voda da dijeli vode od voda!" I
bi tako. 7. Bog načini svod, i vode pod svodom odijeli od voda nad
svodom. 8. A svod prozva Bog nebo. Tako bude večer, pa jutro—dan
drugi.

The selection above comprises the first eight verses of the Book of Genesis in the Old Testament.

DVADESET DEVETA LEKCIJA

Jedan dan sa zagrebačkom obitelji

1. Obitelj Horvatić stanuje na drugom katu jedne stare trokatnice.
2. Ta kuća je u Kumičićevoj ulici, u blizini glavnog kolodvora.
3. Obitelj Horvatić ima tri člana: oca, majky i šestogodišnju kćerku.
4. Očevo ime je Vjekoslav, no žena i prijatelji ga zovu Vjeko.
5. Majčino ime je Mira, ali je njen muž često zove "zlato moje."
6. Djevojčica se zove Maja i ima nadimak "Bubica," jer je dražesna kao kakva mala buba.
7. Majka izjutra prva ustaje, u šest sati ljeti, a zimi nešto kasnije.
8. Ona se brzo opere i obuče, i ide ravno u kuhinju da pripremi doručak.
9. Vjeko obično doručkuje bijelu kavu, dvije kriške crnog kruha s maslacem i marmeladom.
10. Mira više voli čaj s limunom za doručak i bijeli kruh bez maslaca, ali s tankim slojem marmelade.
11. Vjekov doručak traje vrlo kratko, jer se on mora žuriti na posao.

ДВАДЕСЕТ ДЕВЕТА ЛЕКЦИЈА

Један дан са београдском породицом

1. Породица Србић станује на другом спрату једне старе троспратнице.
2. Та кућа је у Сарајевској улици, у близини главне железничке станице.
3. Породица Србић има три члана: оца, мајку и шестогодишњу кћерку.
4. Очево име је Војислав, но жена и пријатељи зову га Воја.
5. Мајчино име је Мира, али је њен муж често зове "злато моје."
6. Девојчица се зове Маја и има надимак "Бубица," јер је дражесна као каква мала буба.
7. Мајка ујутро прва устаје, у шест сати лети, а зими нешто доцније.
8. Она се брзо умије и обуче, и иде право у кухињу да припреми доручак.
9. Воја обично доручкује белу кафу, два парчета црног хлеба са путером и мармеладом.
10. Мира више воли чај са лимуном за доручак и бели хлеб без путера, али с танким слојем мармеладе.
11. Војин доручак траје врло кратко, јер се он мора да жури на посао.

12. On je arhitekt u jednom velikom građevnom poduzeću koje gradi stambene zgrade u predgrađima grada Zagreba.	12. Он је архитекта у једном великом грађевинском предузећу које гради стамбене зграде у предграђима града Београда.
13. Njegovo radno vrijeme je od sedam sati ujutro do tri poslije podne, šest dana u tjednu.	13. Његово радно време је од седам сати изјутра до три после подне, шест дана у недељи.
14. Bubica najkasnije ustaje. Dolazi u kuhinju s poluotvorenim očima i viče: "Mama, ja sam gladna."	14. Бубица најдоцније устаје. Долази у кухињу с полуотвореним очима и виче: "Мама, ја сам гладна."
15. A brižna majka je već pripremila njezin doručak koji se sastoji od kakaa, peciva s maslacem i jednog meko kuhanog jajeta. [nastavit će se]	15. А брижна мајка је већ припремила њен доручак који се састоји од какаа, пецива са путером и једног меко куваног јајета. [наставиће се]
ZDRAV DUH U ZDRAVOM TIJELU.	ЗДРАВ ДУХ У ЗДРАВОМ ТЕЛУ.

ONE DAY IN THE LIFE OF A ZAGREB/BELGRAD FAMILY—1. The Horvatić/Srbić family lives on the second floor of an old three-story building. 2. That building is located on Kumičićeva/Sarajevska street near the main railroad station. 3. The Horvatić/Srbić family has three members: father, mother, and a six-year-old daughter. 4. The father's name is Vjekoslav/Vojislav, but his wife and friends call him Vjeko/Voja. 5. The mother's name is Mira, but her husband often calls her "dearest one" ("my gold"). 6. The little girl. is called Maja and has the nickname "Bubica," because she is as cute as a little bug. 7. The mother is the first to get up in the morning—at six o'clock in the summer, somewhat later in the winter. 8. She quickly washes and dresses and then goes directly to the kitchen to prepare breakfast. 9. Usually for breakfast Vjeko/Voja has milk-coffee (*café au lait*), two slices of dark bread with butter and jam. 10. Mira prefers tea with lemon at breakfast and white bread without butter but with a thin layer of jam. 11. Vjeko/Voja does not spend much time at breakfast because he must hurry off to work. 12. He is an architect in a large construction enterprise that is erecting apartment dwellings in the suburbs of Zagreb/Belgrade. 13. He works from seven o'clock in the morning until three in the afternoon, six days a week. 14. Bubica is the last to get up. She comes into the kitchen with half-opened eyes and calls out: "Mama, I'm hungry." 15. But the thoughtful mother has already prepared her breakfast, which consists of cocoa, a buttered roll, and a soft-boiled egg. [to be continued]

vježba I

Odgovorite na slijedeća pitanja.
1. Gdje stanuje obitelj Horvatić?
2. Koliko članova ima obitelj Horvatić?
3. Zašto Maja ima nadimak "Bubica?"
4. Kada majka ustaje ujutro?
5. Što Mira ima za doručak?
6. Zašto Vjekov doručak traje vrlo kratko?
7. Što je Vjeko po zanimanju?
8. Gdje Vjeko radi?
9. Tko ustaje najkasnije?
10. Što Bubica doručkuje?

vežba I

Odgovorite na sledeća pitanja.
1. Gde stanuje porodica Srbić?
2. Koliko članova ima porodica Srbić?
3. Zašto Maja ima nadimak "Bubica?"
4. Kada majka ustaje izjutra?
5. Šta Mira ima za doručak?
6. Zašto Vojin doručak traje vrlo kratko?
7. Šta je Voja po zanimanju?
8. Gde Voja radi?
9. Ko ustaje najdocnije?
10. Šta Bubica doručkuje?

vježba/vežba II

Stavite ove rečenice u buduće vrijeme/vreme i u upitni oblik budućeg vremena.

Ana je došla.
Ana će doći.
Da li će Ana doći? [or] Hoće li Ana doći?

1. Vozim se po gradu.
2. Majka ustaje rano.
3. Mira priprema doručak.
4. Danas ja spremam ručak.
5. Oni su kupili moju novu sliku.
6. Ulovio sam ribu za večeru.
7. Ja sam kupila vino.
8. Vozili smo se lađom po mjesečini/mesečini.
9. Moj brat je svirao i pjevao/pevao.
10. Proveli smo po jedan dan u svakom gradiću.

vježba/vežba III

Stavite slijedeće/sledeće rečenice u množinu a zatim u odrečni oblik množine.

On radi za nju.
Oni rade za njih.
Oni ne rade za njih.

1. Dočekao sam ga na kolodvoru/stanici.

2. Kupio sam ti poklon.
3. Moj sin živi na selu.
4. Njegova kćerka studira u Beogradu.
5. Otišao je prema glavnom trgu.
6. Susreo sam prijatelja.
7. Kaži mi gdje/gde da parkiram auto.
8. On će doći ako bude slobodan.
9. Donesite mi sendvič i kavu/kafu.
10. Igrao sam karte sve do ponoći.

vježba/vežba IV

Stavite slijedeće/sledeće rečenice u upitni i upitno-negativni oblik.

Bit ću/Biću kod kuće u tri sata.
Da li ćete biti kod kuće u tri sata? [or] Hoćete li biti kod kuće u tri sata?
Zar nećete biti kod kuće u tri sata?

1. Svako jutro ustajem vrlo rano.
2. Idem na izlet u planinu.
3. Radim osam sati svakog dana.
4. Oni su bili jako gladni.
5. Otputovao je prije/pre nekoliko dana.

vježba/vežba V

Popunite slijedeće/sledeće rečenice futurom egzaktnim.

1. Ako ________ ________ pažljivo, znat ćete/znaćete. (slušati)
2. Čim ________ ________ , doći ću. (čuti)
3. Ako ________ ________ ________ , doći ćemo na vrijeme/vreme. (žuriti se)
4. Tko/Ko ________ ________ , on će napredovati. (raditi)
5. Bit će/Biće ugodno kad ________ ________ ________ u moru. (kupati se)
6. Kad ________ ________ loptu, igrat ćemo/igraćemo košarku. (kupiti)

vježba/vežba VI

Napišite sastav na temu "Moja obitelj/porodica."

The following children's story is useful in that it contains a variety of verb forms. After reading the story, select all the verb forms and label them as to aspect and tense.

—Ujače, molimo te, pričaj nam kakvu priču! Tako rekoše Zdravko i Zlata svom ujaku.

—Pa što da vam pričam? . . . No, dakle, slušajte.

—Jednoć, kad bijah dječak, zamolih mamu, neka me pusti, da se poigram sa svojim vjernim drugom kraj rijeke. Mama mi je dopustila. Krenusmo veseli i zadovoljni. Igrasmo razne igre. Najednoć mi pade na pamet, da bacim u vodu daščicu, da bi plivala kao lađa. Promatrao sam, kako se daščica udaljuje, tako da ju ne mogoh doseći palicom. Onda pozvah mog druga i rekoh mu, da ide po daščicu. On je činio sve, što sam mu rekao, ali ovaj put me ne posluša. Ja sam ga izgrdio, a on se okrene da ode kući. To me je jako razljutilo. Pograbim kamen i bacih za njim. U taj čas se moj drug okrene i kamen ga pogodi upravo u čelo.

—Za Boga miloga, ujače, što si učinio? —zaviče u isti glas oboje djece.

—Da, od jakog udarca mu se zamagli pred očima i on, siromah, padne na zemlju. No ja sam još uvijek bio srdit. Nisam htio ni misliti na njega. Svukoh cipele i čarape i zagazih u rijeku, da izvadim daščicu. No—počeo sam tonuti. Stadoh vikati u pomoć i najednom osjetih, da me neko vuče prema obali. Kad se okrenuh, vidio sam, da je to moj drug.

—Ah, ta to je krasan dječak! Je li ti bio u rodu, ujače? —upita Zdravko.

—Ne! —odgovori ujak.

—Ja sam zagrlio svog druga, lijevao suze i molio ga za oproštenje.

—Pa što ti reče on? —upita Zlata.

—Molimo te, ujače, reci nam, ko je bio taj tvoj drug?

—Moj pas bijaše moj spasitelj. Od onoga doba nisam više ni pomišljao, da bacam kamen na psa ili koju drugu životinju.

National and Regional Names Cr&S has specific names to indicate the nationality, the region, and the city of residence for every man or woman in Yugoslavia. The principal designations are given below in pairs; the first name in the pair denotes a male, the second a female. With few exceptions (e.g. **Nišlija, Sarajlija**), the noun for the male designation has a suffix in **-ac** or **-anin**; in the former type the **a** disappears in non-N cases (e.g. **Makedonac,** G **Makedonca**), while in the latter type the plural stem loses the **-in** syllable of the singular (e.g. **Ličanin,** N pl. **Ličani**).

Nationality Designations

Albánac, Àlbanka	an Albanian
Crnògorac, Crnògorka	a Montenegrin
Hȑvat, Hrvàtica	a Croat
Jugoslàven/Jugoslòven, Jugoslàvenka/Jugoslòvenka	a Yugoslav

Màđar *or* Màdžar, Màđarka *or* Màdžarka	a Hungarian
Makedónac, Makèdonka	a Macedonian
Muslìman, Muslìmanka	a Moslem
Róm, Ròmkinja	a Gypsy
Slovénac, Slòvenka	a Slovene
Srbijánac, Srbìjanka	a Serb, inhabitant of Serbia proper
Sȑbin [pl. Sȑbi], Sȑpkinja	a Serb
Tùrčin [pl. Túrci], Tùrkinja	a Turk

Some Regional Designations

Bosánac, Bòsanka	a Bosnian
Dalmatínac, Dalmàtinka	a Dalmatian
Hèrcegovac, Hèrcegovka	a Herzegovinian
Líčanin, Líčanka	a person from Lika
Slavónac, Slàvonka	a person from Slavonia
Vòjvođanin, Vòjvođanka	a person from Vojvodina
Zágorac, Zágorka	a person from Zagorje

Designations of Inhabitants of Various Cities

Beògrađanin, Beògrađanka	a resident of Belgrade
Ljubljánčanin, Ljubljánčanka	a resident of Ljubljana
Mostárac, Mòstarka	a resident of Mostar
Nìšlija, Nìšlijka	a resident of Niš
Novòsađanin, Novòsađanka	a resident of Novi Sad
Rijèčanin, Rijèčanka	a resident of Rijeka
Saràjlija, Sàrajka	a resident of Sarajevo
Skopljánac, Skòpljanka	a resident of Skopje
Splìćanin, Splìćanka	a resident of Split
Tìtograđanin, Tìtograđanka	a resident of Titograd
Zágrepčanin, Zágrepčanka	a resident of Zagreb

BOG DAO, BOG UZEO. БОГ ДАО, БОГ УЗЕО.

НОВИ ЗАВЕТ ГОСПОДА НАШЕГА ИСУСА ХРИСТА

Јеванђеље по Матеју

Глава осма. 5. А кад уђе у Капернаум, приступи к њему капетан молећи га, 6. И говорећи: Господе! слуга мој лежи дома узет, и мучи се врло. 7. А Исус рече му: ја ћу доћи и исцелићу га. 8. И капетан одговори и рече: Господе, нисам достојан да под кров мој уђеш; него само реци реч, и оздравиће слуга мој. 9. Јер и ја сам човек од власти, и имам под собом војнике, па речем једноме: иди, и иде, и другоме: дођи, и дође; и слузи својему: учини то, и учини. 10.

А кад чу Исус, удиви се и рече онима што иду за њим; заиста вам кажем: ни у Израиљу толико вере не нађох. 11. И то вам кажем да ће многи од истока и запада доћи и сешће за трпезу с Авраамом и Исаком и Јаковом у царству небескоме. 12. А синови царства изагнаће се у таму најкрању; онде ће бити плач и шкргут зуба. 13. А капетану рече Исус: иди, и како си веровао нека ти буде. И оздрави слуга његов у тај час.

The forms уђе and нађох have the infinitives ући and наћи, respectively; сешће results from the normal fusion of сести and ће.

TRIDESETA LEKCIJA

ТРИДЕСЕТА ЛЕКЦИЈА

Jedan dan sa zagrebačkom obitelji

[nastavak]

16. Dok Bubica doručkuje, Mira zrači posteljinu, namješta krevete, mete pod i briše prašinu na pokućstvu.
17. Kada je stan pospremljen, Mira uzima košaru za trg i zajedno s Bubicom odlazi u kupovinu.
18. Prvo idu na plac gdje traže svježu salatu, krastavce, rajčicu, luk i krumpir.
19. Da umiri nemirnu Bubicu, majka joj kupuje malog drvenog konja, koji nije veći od njenog palca.
20. Zatim idu u samoposlugu i kupuju bocu mlijeka, kilu kruha, paketić maslaca, pola kilograma sira, kilu šećera, litru ulja i dvije konzerve sardina u ulju.
21. Kod mesara na uglu ulice uzimaju kilogram teletine za ručak i pola kilograma kobasica za večeru.
22. Poslije ručka ide cijela obitelj malo spavati.
23. Kasnije Bubica ide s tatom u šetnju u obližnji perivoj.
24. Tamo se Bubica igra sa svojim prijateljicama, a njen

Један дан са београдском породицом

[наставак]

16. Док Бубица доручкује, Мира ветри постељину, намешта кревете, мете под и брише прашину са намештаја.
17. Када је стан спремљен, Мира узима корпу за пијацу и заједно са Бубицом одлази у куповину.
18. Прво иду на пијацу где траже свежу салату, краставце, парадајз, лук и кромпир.
19. Да умири немирну Бубицу, мајка јој купује малог дрвеног коња, који није већи од њеног палца.
20. Затим иду у самопослугу и купују флашу млека, кило хлеба, пакетић путера, пола килограма сира, кило шећера, литру зејтина и две конзерве сардина у уљу.
21. Код месара на углу улице узимају килограм телетине за ручак и пола килограма кобасица за вечеру.
22. После ручка иде цела породица да мало спава.
23. Доцније Бубица иде са татом у шетњу у оближњи парк.
24. Тамо се Бубица игра са својим пријатељицама, а њен

tata sjedi na klupi, puši cigaretu i čita večernje novine.
25. Navečer se cijela obitelj opet okupi kod kuće.
26. Oni često gledaju zabavni program na televiziji prije večere.
27. Katkada im dođe u posjetu Vjekoslavova majka i onda ostaje s njima na večeri.
28. Bubica ide u krevet oko devet sati, ali ona to čini vrlo nerado kada je na televiziji neki film s Indijancima.
29. Vjeko i Mira ostaju još neko vrijeme budni i razgovaraju o planovima za slijedeći dan.
30. Oko jedanaest sati oboje umorni i pospani zažele jedno drugome "laku noć" i odlaze na spavanje.

MI O VUKU, A VUK NA VRATA.

тата седи на клупи, пуши цигарету и чита вечерње новине.
25. Увече се цела породица опет окупи код куће.
26. Они често гледају забавни програм на телевизији пре вечере.
27. Понекад им дође у посету Војислављева мајка и онда остаје с њима на вечери.
28. Бубица иде у кревет око девет сати, али она то чини врло нерадо када је на телевизији филм са Индијанцима.
29. Воја и Мира остају још неко време будни и разговарају о плановима за следећи дан.
30. Око једанаест сати обоје уморни и поспани зажеле једно другоме "лаку ноћ" и одлазе на спавање.

МИ О ВУКУ, А ВУК НА ВРАТА.

ONE DAY IN THE LIFE OF A ZAGREB/BELGRADE FAMILY (Continued from Lesson XXIX.) 16. While Bubica is having breakfast, Mira airs the bedding, makes the beds, sweeps the floor, and dusts the furniture. 17. When the apartment is put in order, Mira takes a market basket and together with Bubica goes shopping. 18. First they go to the open-air market, where they look for fresh lettuce, cucumbers, tomatoes, onions, and potatoes. 19. In order to keep Bubica somewhat happy, the mother buys her a small wooden horse, which is no larger than her thumb. 20. Then they go to the self-service store and buy a bottle of milk, a kilo [2.2 lbs.] of bread, a package of butter, a pound of cheese, a kilo of sugar, a liter of olive oil, and two cans of sardines in oil. 21. At the butcher's on the corner they get a pound of veal for the afternoon meal [about 3 P.M.] and a pound of sausage for the evening meal [about 8:30 P.M.]. 22. After the afternoon meal they all lie down for a short nap. 23. Later Bubica and her dad take a walk to a nearby park. 24. There Bubica plays with her girlfriends while her dad sits on a bench, smokes a cigarette, and reads the evening newspaper. 25. In the evening the whole family is together at home once again. 26. Before the evening meal they often watch a variety program on television. 27. Sometimes Vjekoslav's/Vojislav's mother visits them and then stays for supper. 28. Bubica goes to bed about nine o'clock, but she does this unwillingly whenever there is any cowboy film on television (with Indians). 29. Vjeko/Voja and Mira stay up for awhile and discuss plans for the coming day. 30. About eleven o'clock both, tired and sleepy, exchange "good nights" and go to bed (go off to sleep).

vježba I

Odgovorite na pitanja.

1. Što radi Mira kad Bubica doručkuje?
2. Tko ide u kupovinu?
3. Što se može kupiti na tržnici?
4. Gdje Mira kupuje teletinu i kobasice?
5. Spava li čitava obitelj poslije ručka?
6. Spavate li obično poslije ručka?
7. Što radi tata dok se Bubica igra sa prijateljicama?
8. Tko ide najranije na spavanje?
9. Kada Bubica ide nerado na spavanje?
10. O čemu Vjeko i Mira razgovaraju poslije večere?

vežba I

Odgovorite na pitanja.

1. Šta radi Mira kad Bubica doručkuje?
2. Ko ide u kupovinu?
3. Šta se može kupiti na pijaci?
4. Gde Mira kupuje teletinu i kobasice?
5. Da li čitava porodica spava posle ručka?
6. Da li vi obično spavate posle ručka?
7. Šta radi tata dok se Bubica igra sa prijateljicama?
8. Ko ide najranije na spavanje?
9. Kada Bubica ide nerado na spavanje?
10. O čemu Voja i Mira razgovaraju posle večere?

vježba/vežba II

Stavite zamjenice/zamenice u odgovarajući padež.

Vidio/Video sam ________ . (on)
Vidio/Video sam ga.

1. Doći ću po ________ autom. (vi)
2. Putovao sam s ________ do Zagreba. (oni)
3. Zamolio sam ________ da odlože sastanak. (oni)
4. Je li Mira bila s ________ ? (ti)
5. Svidjela/Svidela ________ se predstava. (ja)
6. Da li će biti posla i za ________ ? (on)
7. Dao sam ________ nekoliko knjiga. (ona)
8. Da li ________ se sviđa/dopada poklon? (ti)

9. Kad sam ________ sreo, izgledali su sretni/srećni. (oni)
10. Radije ću reći ________ nego ________ . (vi, ona)

vježba/vežba III

Popunite rečenice odgovarajućim glagolskim vremenom.

Jučer/Juče ________ ________ rano. (ustati)
Jučer/Juče sam ustao rano.

1. Danas ________ ne ________ dobro. (osjećati se/osećati se)
2. Jučer/Juče ________ ________ meso za ručak. (kupiti)
3. Da li ________ ________ popodne? (doći)
4. ________ ________ dosta novaca, ali sam sve potrošio. (imati)
5. Gdje/Gde ________ ________ vaša kuća? (nalaziti se)
6. ________ ________ ________ satima jer je vrijeme/vreme bilo vrlo ugodno. (šetati se)
7. Kad ________ ________ ________ kući, večera ________ već ________na stolu. (vratiti se, biti)
8. Sinoć ________ mu ________ da ________ ranije. (reći, doći)
9. ________ dobre i zabavne filmove. (voljeti/voleti)
10. ________ ________ kuću a sada ________ auto. (kupiti)

vježba/vežba IV

Umetnite odgovarajuće veznike: ako, nego, iako, ali.

1. ________ ste obećali, trebalo je da dođete.
2. Ne sjećam/sećam ga se ________ sam ga vidio/video nekoliko puta.
3. (Cr.) Nemoj gledati televiziju ________ uči.
   (S.) Nemoj da gledaš televiziju ________ uči.
4. Mislio sam da joj je danas rođendan ________ sam se prevario.
5. ________ požurite, stići ćete na vrijeme/vreme.
6. Došao je ________ nije bio pozvan.
7. Više bih volio/voleo da mi telefonirate danas ________ sutra.
8. Reći ću ti tajnu ________ ti nemoj nikome kazati.
9. Neću jesti sada ________ sam gladan.
10. ________ vam treba pomoć, telefonirajte mi.

vježba/vežba V

Stavite slijedeće/sledeće rečenice u neupravni govor.

Putujemo večeras.
Rekli su da putuju večeras.

1. Kako se zove vaš brat?
2. Moja sestra dolazi prvim avionom.
3. Radio sam prekovremeno.

4. Govorite li francuski?
5. Molim vas, zatvorite vrata.
6. Što/Šta biste uradili da ste na mome mjestu/mestu?
7. Vrlo sam zauzeta. Imam mnogo posla.
8. Da li bi vam prijala čaša vina?
9. Tamo nema nikoga.
10. Pričekajte me ako možete.

vježba/vežba VI

Napišite sastav na temu "Hrvatski/Srpski jezik."

vježba/vežba VII

Prevedite.

1. I wonder whether that room is nicer than this.
2. She'll have to bring a glass if she wants to have some wine.
3. You ought to think it over before you make up your mind.
4. Nothing is ever good for her.
5. I think you've read these books. Will you return them to her?

The Slavic Languages of Yugoslavia Besides Cr&S there are two other major Slavic languages, Slovenian and Macedonian, spoken in Yugoslavia. An official text in these two languages and in the two variants of Cr&S will enable the reader to get an idea of their similarities and differences. The translation of the text is as follows:

Military Obligation

All mature citizens of Yugoslavia, whether they live in the country or abroad, are subject to the military obligation.

The legal regulations that affect Yugoslav citizens permanently residing abroad regulate the national defense obligation in Yugoslavia in a simple manner.

According to the regulations of the National Defense Law, emigrants, Yugoslav citizens, who live permanently abroad [and who are] between the ages of 17 and 27, must report to the appropriate Yugoslav diplomatic or consular office for the sake of arranging their military obligations.

Croatian

VOJNA OBAVEZA

Svi punoljetni državljani Jugoslavije podliježu vojnoj obavezi bez obzira da li prebivaju u zemlji ili u inozemstvu.

Zakonski propisi koji se odnose na jugoslavenske državljane stalno nastanjene u inozemstvu na jednostavan način reguliraju obavezu prema narodnoj obrani u Jugoslaviji.

Prema propisima Zakona o narodnoj obrani, iseljenici, jugoslavenski državljani, koji stalno žive u inozemstvu, dužni su da se, radi reguliranja svoje vojne obaveze, prijave nadležnom jugoslavenskom diplomatskom ili konzularnom predstavništvu u vremenu između navršene 17. i 27. godine života.

Serbian

ВОЈНА ОБАВЕЗА

Сви пунолетни држављани Југославије подлежу војној обавези без обзира да ли пребивају у земљи или у иностранству.

Законски прописи који се односе на југословенске држављане стално настањене у иностранству на једноставан начин регулишу обавезу према народној одбрани у Југославији.

Према прописима Закона о народној одбрани, исељеници, југословенски држављани, који стално живе у иностранству, дужни су да се, ради регулисања своје војне обавезе, пријаве надлежном југословенском дипломатском или конзуларном представништву у времену између навршене 17. и 27. године живота.

Slovenian

VOJAŠKA OBVEZNOST

Vsi polnoletni jugoslovanski državljani so pod vojaško obveznostjo, ne glede na to, ali živijo v domovini ali v inozemstvu.

Zakonski predpisi, ki se nanašajo na jugoslovanske državljane s stalnim prebivališčem v tujini, na enostaven način urejajo njihovo vojaško obveznost v Jugoslaviji.

Po predpisih zakona o narodni obrambi se morajo izseljenci — jugoslovanski državljani, ki stalno živijo v tujini, priglasiti pristojnemu jugoslovanskemu diplomatskemu ali konzularnemu predstavništvu v dobi med 17. in 27. letom svoje starosti in s tem urediti svojo vojaško obveznost.

Macedonian

ВОЕНА ОБВРСКА

Сите полнолетни државјани на Југославија подлежат на воена обврска без оглед дали живеат во земјава или во странство.

Законските прописи што се однесуваат на југословенските државјани постојано настанети во странство на едноставен начин ја регулираат обврската спрема народната одбрана во Југославија.

Според прописите на Законот за народната одбрана, иселениците, југословенски државјани, што постојано живеат во странство, се должни, заради регулирање на својата воена обврска, да му се пријават на надлежното југословенско дипломатско или конзуларно претставништво во времето помеѓу наполнетата 17 и 27 година возраст.

KONAC DJELO KRASI. КОНАЦ ДЕЛО КРАСИ.

ČITANKA ЧИТАНКА

Reader*

1. ZAPAŽEN NASTUP AMERIČKOG ZBORA

Studenti iz SAD oduševili publiku

Budući da plakat za nastup američkog zbora The Bemidji Choir nije sadržavao detaljnije informacije o ovom vokalnom tijelu niti o skladbama koje su na programu, odlazak na njihov koncert je donekle predstavljao i rizik. Na sreću, ono što smo čuli te večeri predstavljalo je vokalno majstorstvo na visokoj razini.

Zbor sačinjavaju studenti istoimenog univerziteta** koji njeguju a cappella glazbu (što znači bez instrumentalne pratnje), a svoj program su podijelili u tri tematske cjeline: pjesme vjere, pjesme ljubavi i pjesme nade. Izvedene skladbe datiraju od 16. stoljeća pa do suvremenih djela—

*The texts in this little reader are not in the category of belles-lettres. Rather they are practical little texts, each written by a native Croat or Serb; Nušić's hilarious story (#12) would be an exception.

Croats generally use **sveučilište for "university," while Serbs usually use **univerzitet**. Sometimes the selection of a member of a lexical pair is arbitrary or region-specific. Bemidji is a town in northern Minnesota.

posljednje izvedeno skladao je dirigent i umjetnički vođa ovog ansambla, Paul Brandvik.

Tijekom nastupa mnogi od članova ovog zbora su se pokazali i kao vrsni solisti, što je dokaz više njihovoj kvaliteti. Pjevajući na kraju crnačke duhovne pjesme još jednom su pokazali stilsku širinu repertoara.

Sanja Dražić
Dubrovački vjesnik
Subota 18. lipnja 1988.

2. PROGNOZA VREMENA*

МЕТЕОРОЛОЗИ ПРОГНОЗИРАЈУ ЗА ДАНАС

ХЛАДНО

Јутро ће бити хладно, местимично магловито, по појединим котлинама и речним долинама магла ће се задржати и у већем делу дана. Током дана у већем делу земље преовлађиваће сунчано. На југу ће пре подне бити облачно, а у поподневним часовима и у овим крајевима очекује се разведравање. Ветар слаб, променљивог правца. Јутарња температура од —8 до —2, на Јадрану 3 до 6 степени, највиша дневна од 5 до 10 а у приморским местима 12 до 15 степени.

БЕОГРАД И ОКОЛИНА. — Јутро ће бити хладно и у широј околини града магловито, током дана претежно ведро. Ветар слаб променљивог правца. Јутарња температура око —3, у околини града до —5 а максимална дневна око седам степени.

ИЗГЛЕДИ ЗА СУТРА. — Јутро ће бити хладно, местимично магловито. Током дана у већем делу земље претежно ведро. Температура без знатније промене.

vrijeme

RAZMJERNO TOPLO

SITUACIJA: Zbog jake i prostrane istočno-evropske anticiklone u utorak je u većini krajeva bilo suho, pretežno sunčano i tiho vrijeme. Magle ili niske naoblake bilo je jedino u zapadnim kopnenim predjelima, te na sjevernom i srednjem Jadranu.

PROGNOZA: U većini krajeva bit će suho i pretežno sunčano, jedino će u noći i ujutro u zapadnim i središnjim kopnenim predjelima prevladavati magla. Mjestimične jutarnje magle bit će i na sjevernom dijelu Jadrana. Više naoblake očekuje se u zapadnim krajevima gdje je u drugom dijelu dana moguća i slaba kiša. Prevladavat će tiho vrijeme a temperatura zraka bit će slična jučerašnjoj.

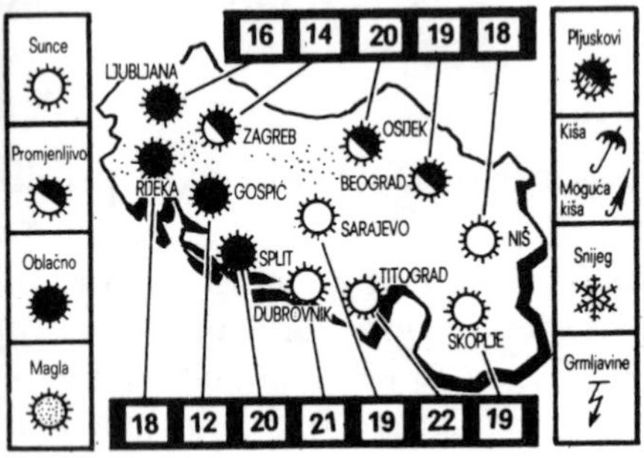

*The weather report in **latinica** was for an October 19th, that in **ćirilica** for a November 1st. Yugoslavia uses the Celsius or Centigrade scale for temperatures, while the United

3. ЦВЕЋЕ*

Традиционални људи још увек одржавају одређене обичаје укључујући и врсту цвећа за одређене прилике као што су: кућне посете, венчања, рођендани, разне прославе и сахране.

Руже се не користе само за свечане прилике, већ се могу користити и за било другу прилику. Пошто је ружа симбол љубави, даје се девојкама и вољеним људима. Мали букет који млада баца би требало да је направљен од свежих ружа, иако многи користе вештачко цвеће. Овај букетић је познат као "бидер мајер"—немачка реч. На великим венчањима, обичај да млада баца букет још је присутан. Све невенчане девојке се скупе, док млада баца букет, и девојка која га ухвати, по предању, би требало да се прва уда. Руже се такође користе за годишњицу венчања, рођендане, Дан жена, кућне посете или било коју другу прилику.

Пријатељима, познаницима или фамилији за мање формалне прилике као што су посете, рођендани итд. могу се поклонити и зумбул, мали букет љубичица или мимоза—које се могу наћи на Медитеранском подручју. Важно је нагласити да број цвећа који се даје мора бити *непаран*. Цвеће у *парном* броју се користи само за сахране и смртне случајеве.

4. ŽIVOT MLADIH U BEOGRADU

Vraćam se u Beograd posle više godina, po ne znam koji put. Na prvi pogled toliko privlačan i istinski nedokučiv. . . .

Centar grada je uvek prepun ljudi. Zapanjujuće. Ranije sam se pitala: Da li je ovo slučajnost? Odkud ovoliko ljudi pre podne, posle podne, u svako doba dana? Da li je u toku odmor za užinu? Od jutra do mraka

---

States uses the Fahrenheit scale. To convert C to F, multiply by 9, divide by 5, then add 32; thus, 20 C equals 68 F. To go from F to C, subtract 32, multiply by 5, then divide by 9: thus, 77 F would be 25 C.

Here are some equivalencies with the first figure being C, the second F: 0 = 32, 10 = 50, 20 = 68, 30 = 86, 40 = 104.

The weather terms above can be found either in Lesson V or in the glossary.

*This passage is an excerpt from a letter written by a young Serbian woman in Belgrade who had been asked by an American friend which flowers Serbs use for different occasions.

bujice ljudi se slivaju ulicama. Svi nekud žure, razgledaju izloge, guraju se, sudaraju. . . .

Glavni pravac vodi prema najprometnijem trgu—Terazije—i, naravno, svi moraju proći nezaobilaznu Knez Mihajlovu ulicu. Knez Mihajlova—glavno šetalište mladih. Ah! Taman posla da izađemo, a da ne prošetamo kroz Knez Mihajlovu i pokažemo svoje novo perje. Dok šetaju Knez Mihajlovom ulicom, mladi gledaju izloge, a najviše jedni druge. Gledaju tuđe perje, istina vrlo kritično. Često zastanu, okreću se, komentarišu, kada primete nešto interesantno. Bilo bi vrlo kritično obući nešto staromodno. Komentari bi pljuštali na sve strane. Interesantno je primetiti da kada određena stvar dođe u modu, bilo frizura ili odevni predmet, svi skoro bez izuzetka isto nose, bez obzira na to da li im lepo stoji. U obaveznoj šetnji ovom ulicom zastane se pored Fontane—radnje sa uvoznim čokoladama, nakitom, parfemima i ostalom kozmetikom. Usput se razgledaju svi izlozi i dosta se komentariše, kao i svuda.

Da pređemo sada na zabavu i život mladih. Kako naizlaze hladni dani, malo manje se šeta ulicom i ne sedi u baštama ili napolju kao u letnje doba. Više se ide u bioskope i pozorišta. Mnogo mladih gleda akcione filmove, uglavnom beznačajne. Gledaoce je osvojio najbolji film ovogodišnjeg Filmskog festivala—*Poslednji kineski car* koji je dobio veliki broj priznanja.

Kad sam već kod kafana, moram da napomenem da su one gotovo danonoćno pune. Vrlo je teško naći mesto u kafani, ako se izađe posle osam sati uveče. Kafana ima raznih. Variraju od tradicionalnih, zadimljenih sa paradoksalno tmurnom i veselom atmosferom do super modernih kafića zapadnoevropskog stila. S vremena na vreme pojedini kafići su isključivo u modi— više posećeni i opsedani nego ostali. Prošle zime i proleća, to je bio kafić *Galerija*, a ovog leta kafić *Knez*. Važno je napomenuti da su na ovakvim mestima cene tri puta veće nego na drugima, a još važnije da odeća posetioca mora biti srazmerno bar tri i više puta skuplja od prosečne. Na ovakvim mestima pojedini mladi ljudi se sastanu, "zauzmu pozu"—poziraju, gledaju druge i komentarišu. Niko nov ko uđe ne može da prođe nezapažen.

Relevantna ovome je klasifikacija mladih po stilu i oblačenju—superficijalni odraz društvenog statusa. Uglavnom se dele na izuzetno lepo i moderno obučene *šminkere*— kojima su mame i tate diplomate i direktori preduzeća i predstavništava i ostale normalno obučene ljude. Šminkeri, budući direktori i šefovi, voze strogo uvozna kola i nose ekstravagantnu odeću. Često sede u kafiću *Trozubac* na Terazijama i odmeravaju okolinu. Oni mogu i biti prirodno inteligentni, ali malo manje načitani, kulturno nadahnuti ili intelektualno nastrojeni. Mame, tate i rođaci ih preko veze upisuju na fakultet, i oni preko veze polažu ispite.

Oni nose lepo perje, opipavajući proveravaju kvalitet odeće svojih prijatelja i s ponosom pokažuju svoje nove kožne patike. Šminkera, ipak, ima malo. Ljudi su različiti. Mladi jako puno studiraju. U slobodno vreme puno izlaze i bave se sportovima. U letnje doba bazeni su prepuni, kao i veliko, poznato kupalište *Ada Ciganlija*.

I tako dok se guramo u našim standardnim trolejbusima i autobusima—sardinama, željno iščekujemo izgradnju Beogradskog metroa i naredni skup Nesvrstanih zemalja u Beogradu.

Jasmina Petrović

5. STUDENTSKI ŽIVOT U ZAGREBU

U Jugoslaviji uopće nije lako steći status studenta. S obzirom na to da je školovanje besplatno, mnogo ljudi se želi upisati na fakultet, a mjesta za sve, naravno, nema. Zbog toga postoje kvalifikacijski ispiti i tek kad ih mladi čovjek položi s izuzetnim rezultatima, može sebe smatrati studentom. Kada govorimo o studentskom životu u milijunskom gradu kao što je Zagreb, treba imati na umu da svi studenti nisu iz Zagreba. Za njih je život za studentskih dana znatno teži, no za one koji studiraju iz roditeljskog doma. Studenti iz drugih dijelova zemlje najčešće žive u studentskim domovima ili privatno iznajmljenim sobama.

Život u studentskim domovima odiše zajedništvom, a cijene sobe i hrane su subvencionirane. Međutim, sobu u studentskom domu mogu dobiti samo strani studenti i domaći studenti koji imaju roditelje s veoma niskim primanjima, a koji nisu iz Zagreba. Oni drugi snalaze se po iznajmljenim sobičcima koji su veoma skupo plaćeni.

Oni studenti koji su stalni građani Zagreba, u neusporedivo su boljoj situaciji, jer se roditelji u potpunosti brinu za njih i veoma ih često i materijalno potpomažu, dok ostali studenti često moraju za vrijeme studija raditi da bi se uzdržavali. Postoji razlika u životu studenata i prema vrstama fakulteta koje pohađaju. Ako je netko student tehničkog fakulteta, tada obično, ima jutro ispunjeno fakultetskim obavezama, no u poslijepodnevnim satima je slobodan za učenje, sport ili izlazak. Kod studenata društvenih znanosti, predavanja traju tokom čitavog dana s pauzama od nekoliko sati, pa oni često gube cijele dane trčeći s predavanja na predavanje. Odnosi studenata i profesora su nešto ležerniji, nego u srednjim školama, no to je još uvijek daleko od one ležernosti kojoj teže svi mladi ljudi, bez obzira na zemlju u kojoj žive.

Studenti ispite polažu u ljeto i jesen, pa je to vrijeme takozvanog "kampanjskog učenja". To bi značilo da za vrijeme trajanja semestra, studenti ne uče previše, te im se sve skupi za ispitni rok.

Noćni život studenata u Zagrebu ovisi o njihovim afinitetima i o dubini njihovih džepova. Studenti skromnijeg materijalnog stanja idu u posjete prijateljima, te provode slobodno vrijeme baveći se različitim sportovima ili, jednostavno, gledajući TV i slušajući radio. Oni studenti boljeg imovinskog stanja često odlaze u klubove koji su u modi u tom trenutku, na kućne zabave zatvorenog tipa ili na koncerte. Studente možete sresti na koncertima ozbiljne glazbe, na baletnoj ili kazališnoj predstavi, a i na koncertima rock-muzike.

Možda treba spomenuti da je veoma bitan činilac zabave studenata, pa i onih mlađih i starijih, Omladinski radio— radio stanica čiji program stvaraju učenici i studenti. To je veoma slušana i politizirana radiostanica s mnogo zabave i angažiranog humora.

Anica Medvešek

6. SPORT U JUGOSLAVIJI

Poput Amerikanaca, Finaca ili Mađara, i Jugoslaveni vole sport. Vole trčati i skakati, plivati i roniti, vole se penjati na Triglav i Velebit, vole voziti bicikl ili jedriti modrim valovima Jadranskog mora.

Moram vam odmah odati tajnu: Jugoslaveni se više vole igrati nego natjecati. Umjesto da naporno trči na 10 ili 20 kilometara ili baca kuglu i koplje, Jugoslaven će radije udarati loptu— rukom, glavom, ramenom, koljenom. Kao da se okretnost i vještina u loptanju više cijene nego snaga i izdržljivost.

Stoga su u Jugoslaviji tako popularne igre loptom, osobito nogomet, košarka, rukomet, odbojka i vaterpolo. Jugoslaveni se najradije igraju u grupi: međusobno se dogovaraju, nadvikuju i dijele radost i tugu što ih donose pobjede i porazi. Možda je to razlog da bolje igramo košarku ili vaterpolo nego, primjerice, tenis. U košarci, vaterpolu i rukometu jugoslavenski sportaši postižu i najveće uspjehe, osvajajući medalje na Olimpijskim igrama i prva i druga mjesta na svjetskim i evropskim prvenstvima.

Nogomet ima najviše pristalica. Kao i u američkom nogometu, u toj igri sudjeluje po 11 igrača sa svake strane. Igralište je dugačko preko 100 metara. Ne igra se jajolikom već okruglom loptom koja se udara nogom i glavom. Mnogi igrači odlično igraju glavom. Za razliku od američkih nogometaša, igrači ne nose kacige. Uostalom, jeste li ikada pokušali udariti loptu kacigom? Rukama smije igrati samo vratar (ili golman) koji loptu hvata ili je odbija, braneći svoja vrata (ili gol). Protivnika ne smijemo blokirati tijelom ili oboriti na tlo. Pobjednik je ona momčad koja više puta pogodi loptom mrežu protivničkog gola.

Gotovo svaki dječak, a i poneka djevojčica, imaju svoje miljenike među jugoslavenskim nogometnim klubovima, pa navijaju za "plave", "bijele", "crvene", "crno-bijele" ili "zelene". Klubovi nemaju tako slikovita imena kao američki; nema "Sokolova", "Lavova", "Poglavica", "Vikinga", niti "Orlova". U Jugoslaviji se navija za "Hajduk", "Partizan", "Dinamo", "Crvenu zvezdu" ili "Željezničar". Imamo nekoliko nogometnih stadiona koji primaju više od 50.000 gledalaca.

U posljednje je vrijeme sve popularniji tzv. mali nogomet u kojem, na znatno manjem igralištu, igra po sedam nogometaša sa svake strane. Ta je igra sasvim slična nogometu koji se igra u Sjedinjenim Državama, naročito u dvoranama na Istočnoj obali.

Košarka i rukomet najpopularniji su dvoranski sportovi u nas. Košarka se proširila iz svoje američke postojbine i osvojila svijet, a u Jugoslaviji se igra vrlo uspješno već četrdesetak godina. Naša publika uživa u košarkaškim nadmetanjima između naših i najboljih evropskih momčadi, a katkad kod nas gostuju i američke sveučilišne ekipe.

Rukomet samo imenom podsjeća na američki handball, igru u kojoj igrači pojedinačno ili u paru udaraju rukom tvrdu lopticu prema suprotnom zidu dvorane. U našem rukometu, koji je potekao iz skandinavskih zemalja, nastupa po sedam rukometaša sa svake strane (vratar i šest igrača u polju). Igra se na igralištu dugačkom 40 metara. Igrači vode loptu udarajući je o tlo, slično kao u košarci, dodaju je rukom jedan drugome i zatim pucaju na protivnički gol, pazeći da pritom ne prekorače kružnu crtu ispred gola. Kao i u nogometu, u rukometu se postiže pogodak ili gol, a u košarci koš.

Jugoslaveni se bave i atletikom i gimnastikom, kuglanjem i borilačkim vještinama: mačevanjem, boksom i rvanjem. Uživamo u plivanju, ali u međunarodnim plivačkim takmičenjima ne postižemo uspjehe. Bolji smo veslači i jedriličari, a naši vaterpolisti u samom su svjetskom vrhu.

Volimo se penjati na planine. Planinari su vesela bića koja se druže s prirodom i štite je od ljudske nebrige.

Naši se ljudi bave i zimskim sportovima, pa se skijaju i sanjkaju na padinama bregova, kližu na prirodnim i umjetnim klizalištima i igraju hokej na ledu. U jugoslavenskim hokejaškim ekipama nastupa sve više Kanađana, Amerikanaca, Rusa i Čeha, dakle hokejaša iz zemalja u kojima se igra vrhunski hokej.

Neki sportovi organizirani su profesionalno, pa igrači i igračice dobivaju u svojim klubovima novčanu naknadu za sportske uspjehe. Najbolji jugoslavenski nogometaši, košarkaši i košarkašice te rukometaši i rukometašice nastupaju kao profesionalci i za inozemne ekipe.

Školska i studentska omladina koja se ozbiljno bavi sportom nastupa za klubove, a ne za školu ili sveučilište, kao što je to slučaj u SAD. Premda za sveučilišni sport raste zanimanje, moji se susjedi čude kad im pričam da je Dabrov stadion u srcu Pennsylvanije ispunjen do posljednjeg mjesta svaki put kad na njemu zaigra Penn State u utakmici američkog sveučilišnog nogometa. A taj stadion prima preko 80.000 gledalaca!

Jugoslaveni su i vrlo dobri organizatori velikih međunarodnih sportskih natjecanja. U Sarajevu su održane Zimske olimpijske igre, u Splitu Mediteranske sportske igre, a u Zagrebu Univerzijada—Svjetske studentske sportske igre. *The family that plays together, stays together,* kaže engleska poslovica. Obitelj koja se igra zajedno, ostaje zajedno. Kad su moj sin Tomislav i kći Ana bili još nejaka dječica, slagali smo zajedno kule od kocaka, igrali se majušnim vojnicima i uspavljivali lutke. Kako su rasli, tako je i lopta postajala sve važnija u njihovu životu. Loptati se—kako je to zgodno! Lopta skače, udara o zid, pogodi te u glavu pa se odbije, možda sruši i vazu sa cvijećem . . . I kao što vi, dragi američki prijatelji, igrate s tatom, bratom i sestrom touch football na tratini pred kućom, tako i Ana, Tomislav i ja često igramo košarku u našem dvorištu. Postavili smo u njemu pravi-pravcati koš, pa se natječemo u tome tko će postići više koševa. A kad pada kiša, odemo k susjedu i u njegovu podrumu odigramo partiju stolnog tenisa; mama Nada i Tomislav prvaci su naše ulice u popularnom ping-pongu.

Trinaestogodišnja Ana igra košarku u pionirskoj ekipi "Dubrave". Ona to shvaća vrlo ozbiljno i trenira tri puta tjedno, a subotom i nedjeljom igra utakmice. Njena je ekipa ove godine osvojila pionirsko prvenstvo Zagreba u košarci.

Djevojke se u Jugoslaviji najčešće bave košarkom, rukometom i odbojkom, ali i plivanjem, skijanjem, klizanjem, tenisom i stolnim tenisom.

Šesnaestogodišnji Tomislav igra sa svojim prijateljima nogomet, rukomet, košarku i stolni tenis. On nije član nijednog kluba i kaže da je za njega sport čista razonoda. Možda je u pravu. On je i vatreni navijač. Odlazi redovito na nogometne, rukometne, košarkaške i hokejaške utakmice, maše ondje klupskim šalovima i zastavicama, gromoglasno navija, plješče, pjeva i zviždi sucima.

Kao i mnogi njegovi vršnjaci, Tomislav se zanima i za tipične američke sportove. Baseball se već i službeno igra u nas. Zahvaljujući filmu i televiziji, mladi sve češće razgovaraju i o američkom nogometu. Svijet kao da postaje sve manji. Naposljetku, svrha je sporta da smanjuje razdaljine i zbližava ljude sa svih meridijana i paralela. Zar ne?

Ivan Horvatin

7. СТО ПЕДЕСЕТ ЃОДИНА УНИВЕРЗИТЕТА У БЕОЃРАДУ

За време Турака, негде половином прошлог века, у Београду су постојале три основне школе. Прве две су имале по три разреда, а трећа четири. Ова последња називала се Велика школа, а касније је названа Доситејев лицеј из почасти према великом просветитељу Доситеју Обрадовићу. По опису савременика, на високим димњацима лепе зграде ове школе гнездиле су се роде. После часова деца су играла разне дечје игре: лопте, дугмића, војника са тророгим шеширима од хартије и пушкама од трске, а пуштала су и змајеве.

Из некадашњег старог Лицеја израсла је Велика школа у којој се изводила и средњошколска и високошколска настава. Ова школа је радила у условима непрекидног ратовања српских устаника против Турака. Ученик Велике школе био је и Вук Стефановић Караџић, будући реформатор српског језика и правописа. Истакнути професори Лицеја били су: Јован Стерија Поповић, Ђура Даничић и Јосиф Панчић. Лицеј није могао да подмири све потребе за школованим људима, па су се младићи редовно упућивали на најчувеније европске универзитете.

Ѓодине 1863. Лицеј је прерастао у Велику школу (или Академију) и њу су сачињавала три факултета: Филозофски, Правни и Технички. Факултети су се брзо развијали, па су морали да се деле на одсеке. Ниво наставе је био висок, а студенти су радили у семинарима, лабораторијама и библиотекама. Тада су дошли до изражаја даровити српски студенти школовани у земљи и Европи који су радили као наставници. До краја прошлог века диплому Велике школе добило је око 900 студената.

Велика школа је прерасла у Универзитет 1905. године. Предвиђена су, поред постојећих, још два нова факултета: Медицински и Богословски. Законом је проглашено да су наставници слободни у излагању своје науке, али су одредбе о студентима и даље остале строге. На челу Универзитета налазио се ректор, а на челу факултета декан. Кад је отворен Универзитет било је око 800 студената. Студенткиња је било знатно мање од студената, свега око стотину.

У новој држави, Краљевини Срба, Хрвата и Словенаца, Универзитет се морао брже развијати, па су основани факултети изван Србије и тиме је знатно унапређено високошколско образовање. Број наставника различитих звања и број студената нагло је порастао. Ѓодине 1926. подигнута је и зграда за Универзитетску библиотеку.

Окупацијом Југославије 1941. године престао је рад Универзитета у Београду да би био обновљен 1945., након ослобођења. Универзитет је дао 127 народних хероја, својих бивших студената.

После рата Универзитет се веома проширио. Под његовим окриљем образовала су се, а затим и осамосталила, четири нова универзитета. Данас Универзитет у Београду има 24 факултета, 55.000 студената и око 4.000 наставника. На Универзитету у Београду школовао се велики број странаца, нарочито из афричких земаља. Поред редовних студија, на Универзитету су организоване постдипломске студије, одбране докторских дисертација и разни видови специјализација. Скупштина Универзитета, ректор са проректорима и Наставно-научно веће јесу органи Универзитета у Београду. Студенте у факултетској управи заступа студент продекан, а у универзитетској управи студент проректор.

За век и по свога постојања Универзитет у Београду је дао Кнежевини и Краљевини Србији, Краљевини Југославији, Социјалистичкој Федеративној Републици Југославији, а и свету, многе истакнуте научнике, просветне и културне раднике и у том погледу је његов значај немерљив.

Ксенија Васић

8. ŠESTINSKA SVADBA

Jedne sam se nedjelje uputio u selo Šestine, nedaleko od Zagreba, gdje sam bio pozvan na svadbu seljaka Mirka Kosa. Kada sam došao tamo, vidio sam skupinu mladića pred kućom mladoženje, sina seljaka Kosa, te sam se i ja priključio tome društvu nestrpljivo čekajući što će se sve dogoditi.

Eto što je bilo: Svečanost je započela kada su došli berdaši i počeli svirati svadbenicu pred kućom. U međuvremenu se je sin Ivan oprostio od svoje majke i svog oca i zahvalio im na svemu što su mu pružili u njegovom životu. Majka mu je uručila vrč s vinom i komad kruha, pričvrstila mu trobojku i ružmarin na šešir, te se poslije tog obreda, plačući od sreće i žalosti, uputila prema kući nevjeste (mladojke). I mi smo se uputili s pjesmom i glazbom do kuće u kojoj živi nevjesta. Iza glazbe su išli kumovi i otac mladoženje, noseći zastavu, a iza kumova je mladoženja nosio svoj vrč i komad kruha. Svi su bili obučeni u šarene i kičene narodne nošnje. Nekoliko koraka iza mladoženje, slijedila je ostala rodbina, prijatelji, susjedi i još mnogi seljaci iz Šestina.

10.*

Сплит, 8. VII 1961 г.

Моја драга америчка пријатељице Мери,

Већ одавно дугујем одговор на твоје писмо, али ме је спремање за испите у јунском року спречило да то урадим. Чиним то сада, па верујем да ћу се најбоље одужити твом стрпљењу, ако ти опишем своје летовање на Јадранском мору.

Синоћ сам стигла возом из Београда у Дубровник, градић на јужном Јадрану, после путовања које је трајало један дан и једну ноћ. У возу је било много света, који је такође пошао на летовање, па је због гужве цео пут био веома заморан.

Сада седим на хотелској тераси, за доручком, преда мном се пружила блистајућа, плава морска пучина. Сунце дивно сија, а свежи морски ваздух као да односи собом сав мој замор.

*The letter was written by a young Serbian woman named Ljilja (short for Ljiljana, "Lily") almost thirty years ago, but it is used in the **čitanka** because it is a good example of cursive writing in Cyrillic and the contents are still interesting. Today it is no longer possible to reach Dubrovnik by train (**vozom** in second paragraph); one goes there by car (**autom**), by ship (**brodom**), or by airplane (**avionom**).

Дубровник је врло стари град, основан још у римско доба. Стога, он представља мешавину старог и новог. Ја много волим да шетам кроз његове старе, уске камените улице и да разгледавам споменике из прошлости: дивне катедрале, палате средњевековних племића, тргове. Премда га скоро сваке године посећујем, увек изнова уживам у његовим природним и уметничким лепотама.

Али, сад је већ и време да кренем на плажу. Она се налази право испред хотела. Видим већ једну веселу групу америчких туриста у купаћим костимима како улазе у море, опрезно газе и „испитују" морско жало. Весели узвици купача чују се на све стране, њихово прскање водом пресеца иначе као огледало глатку морску површину.

Остајем овде до сутра, а онда бродом крећем даље на север уз обалу.

Ово писмо настављам следећег дана. Пре пар сати стигли смо у град Сплит, на средњем Јадрану. На броду је било врло угодно, и могли су се чути разни страни језици, понајвише немачки и енглески, јер су енглеско-аме-

рички и немачки туристи увек били најбројнији на нашој „ривијери."

Обала је била пуна шетача кад је брод пристао уз обалу. Свет излази предвече да се освежи после великих врућина у току дана. Особито је бројна омладина, која тако има прилике да се сретне, и у шали и разговору пријатно проведе вече.

У луци је било пуно бродова, великих и малих, домаћих и страних. Између њих лагано клизе мале лађе, и кроз тиху ноћ одјекује сетна и блага песма веслача.

Интересоваће те да знаш да се Сплит, уствари, развио у зидинама палате римског цара Диоклецијана, у седмом веку, и одатле постепено ширио унаоколо. И зато, као и остали градови уздуж Јадрана, пун је историских споменика.

Сплит се особито поноси што је у њему рођен највећи југословенски уметник-вајар Иван Мештровић. Али,*

*Иван Мештровић (1883–1962). Ljilja is mistaken here: Meštrović was born in Vrpolje, but he did live and work in Split. One of the chief attractions for the visitor to Split is the Meštrović Gallery. This world-famous sculptor spent his last years as a professor of art at the University of Notre Dame; he died in South Bend, Indiana, a year after Ljilja wrote to her American friend.

он данас живи и ради код вас у Америци. Његово је дело и споменик Индијанцима у Чикагу.

Намеравам да останем недељу дана у Сплиту, а онда се враћам авионом у Београд.

Са нестрпљењем ћу очекивати твој одговор и опис са твог летовања. Ти знаш да ја нисам никада била у Америци, и зато сваки опис ваших крајева, обичаја и живота, су изванредно занимљиви за мене.

Поздрави срдачно твоје родитеље, а тебе увек много воли твоја

Миља

11. KAKO SE ŽIVI U DALMATINSKOM GRADIĆU

Na dalmatinskoj obali ima nekoliko desetaka malih gradova u kojima teče život već stoljećima. Takav gradić je i Korčula na istoimenom otoku. Evo kako u ovom gradiću protekne dan. Ovdje ljudi rano ustaju. Neki se primaju posla već u šest ili sedam sati u dućanima, radionicama, uredima ili brodogradilištu, drugi šetaju, promatraju dolazak i odlazak brodova ili jednostavno zure u more.

Kraj mora nikad nije dosadno. Satima se s obale može gledati život riba među algama i morskim biljem. Nekada se to i isplati jer se može jeftino doći do ručka. Evo kako. Kad neki šetač opazi u blizini obale hobotnicu ili sipu, otrči najbližoj kući po osti na dugom štapu, baci ih i ako je sretne ruke hobotnica ili sipa uskoro će se naći u loncu.

Oko osam ujutro gradić potpuno oživi. Mali motorni čamci dovode školsku djecu iz okolnih sela u gimnaziju. Ti isti čamci dovode seljake koji prodaju svoje proizvode na maloj gradskoj tržnici ili obavljaju svoje poslove na općini, na sudu ili kod advokata. U ovo doba dućani su puni domaćica koje kupuju hranu.

Prvi jutarnji val života slegne se oko devet sati. S ulice se izgubi dosta svijeta, naročito muškaraca. Sada oživi onih nekoliko malih gostionica u uskim ulicama. Prosječan zajutrak u tim krajevima je šalica kave ili čašica rakije. Zato oko devet ili deset sati odlično prija porcija tripica, gulaša, pečene ribe na žaru ili, u najgorem slučaju, nekoliko soljenih srdela i komad svježeg kruha. To se onda zalije čašom domaćeg crnog vina. Nekad se zalije s dvije čaše, a onda odjekne ulicama dalmatinska pjesma.

Slijedeća tačka na dnevnom redu gradskog života, kojoj svatko želi prisustvovati, je pristajanje dvaju parobroda "brze pruge" koji stižu iz dva suprotna pravca, iz Rijeke i iz Dubrovnika, otprilike u isto vrijeme. Ove linije saobraćaju valjda jedno stoljeće. Njima putuju stanovnici u veće centre na obali, a nekada i u svijet, "trbuhom za kruhom" da se onda dugo dugo ne vrate. Ljeti ovi brodovi dovoze tisuće turista iz svih zemalja svijeta da uživaju u suncu, moru, vinu i srednjovjekovnom ambijentu.

Prije je glas zvona sa stare katedrale u dvanaest sati označavao prekid rada, ručak i kratak popodnevni odmor. Rad bi uskoro ponovo započeo i trajao do mraka. Danas se radi do dva ili tri sata popodne. Tada se ruča, i obavezno malo odspava. Ostatak dana svatko provodi na svoj način. Netko popravlja čamac koji može biti lijep izvor prihoda za vrijeme turističke sezone a koristan je i za ribarenje, netko strpljivo čeka uz more da riba zagrize udicu, netko jednostavno šeta i priča s prijateljima.

Ljeti se poslije večere do kasno u noć sjedi pred kućom ili pred kavanom gdje ugodno propuhuje svježi lahor s mora. Zimi hladan vjetar potjera ljude rano u kuće.

Način života ovih ljudi mijenja se, ali nešto sporije nego drugdje. Čuvaju se običaji iz starih dana. Tako jednom godišnje mladi stanovnici igraju za svoje starije i za mnoštvo turista zanimljivu narodnu igru "Morešku" koja simbolizira borbu dvije vojske zbog djevojke.

Čuva se također i mjesni govor—filolozi ga zovu čakavski—sličan govoru ostalih dalmatinskih gradića, koji ima mnogo starih jezičnih crta. On se ponešto razlikuje od govora na radiju i u novinama. Ovdje je mlijeko "mliko," djevojka "divojka," ljeto "lito," čamac "barka."

Mnogi ljudi koji su se ovdje rodili, odselili su u druge gradove ili zemlje. I oni i ovi koji ovdje žive vole svoje rodno mjesto, stare zidine, ponosni su na povijest svoga grada i na legendu da se u njemu rodio Marko Polo.

Ante Pilić

12. СРПСКИ ЈЕЗИК

—Беше ли ти оно магаре што ни прошлога пута не знађаше лекцију?

—Јест, ја сам тај!—одговарам ја усхићен задовољством што ме се професор тако добро сећа.

—А нађох ли ја канда, на твоме писменоме задатку ону мастиљаву мрљу коју ви, ђаци, крмачом називате?

—Да, да!—тврдим ја, сав усхићен што ме се професор тако добро сећа.

—Ја тада рекох теби: ако будеш био и даље тако немарљив и небрижљив да ћу те казнити.

Ја и то потврђујем, али без усхићења, а он узима писаљку и мени "буде био" бележи јединицу и упућује ме, једном чисто граматичком реченицом, да клечим иза табле.

—Остаћеш клечећи до краја овога часа, учећи за то време склањање заменице *себе* или *се*. Будеш ли био кадар научити то склањање, јавићеш ми се и исправићу ти белешку, а даљу казну опростити.

Како ни до краја часа нисам "будем био" научио то проклето склањање, остао сам на коленима све док није закуцало звонце.

То склањање нам је задавало нарочите главобоље. Сећам се на пр. мојих мука да научим пети падеж од именице: *пас*. Сви остали падежи ишли су којекако, али пети падеж једнине (покојни звателни) никако ми није ишао у главу, нити сам умео да га погодим.

И не само мени, већ и свима у мојој околини задао је тај падеж главобољу. Мој најстарији брат, који је већ био у старијим разредима, изгледа да се провукао и није у животу имао посла са том именицом; мој млађи брат ми рече да је од именице пас пети падеж: куче. Отац ми није умео казати ништа, пошто граматика нема никакве везе са трговином, већ изгледа да ту чак важи правило: што мање граматике, то више зараде.

Питао сам и бакалина, нашега комшију, пошто сам му претходно објаснио да се петим падежом зове, и он ми рече:

—Ја кад вабим куче, ја му кажем: куц, куц, куц, а кад га терам, ја му кажем: шибе! А бог ће га свети знати који је то падеж!

Питао сам најзад и господина проту, једном приликом када је био на вечери код нас, верујући необично у његову ученост, па се и он збунио и није умео да ме научи.

—Пети падеж, пети падеж!—узе да замуцкује прота, бринући се да пред мојом породицом сачува ауторитет учена човека.—Па, колико падежа ви учите?

—Седам.

—Седам?—зграну се прота.—Е, то је много, то је баш много!

—Много!—уздишем и ја.

—Ја не знам само—окреће се прота мојим родитељима—што ће им толики падежи. То је просто професорски бес. Узмите само једна Немачка, колико је то пространа и силна царевина, па нема више него четири падежа; па онда Француска, па Енглеска, све велике и моћне државе, па немају више него четири падежа. А шта смо ми, једна тако рећи мала земља, тек неколико округа, па седам падежа. Па зар то није, молим вас, бес кад се не простиремо према своме губеру?

Те су протине мисли биле у ствари врло утешне за мене, али ми пред професором нису могле ништа помоћи. Он је одлучно тражио од мене да му кажем пети падеж од именице пас, чему сам се ја одлучно одупро једним бескрајним ћутањем, једном од оних мојих особина којом сам се врло често у школи одликовао.*

Бранислав Нушић

*According to the 1960 *Pravopis (Orthographical Dictionary)*, the vocative form of **pàs**, "dog," can be either **psù** or **psè**, though we do not know which one Nušić's teacher expected.

GRAMATIKA

HRVATSKOGA I SRPSKOGA JEZIKA

GRAMMAR OF THE CROATIAN AND SERBIAN LANGUAGE

The Croatian and Serbian language (Cr&S) is a South Slavic language spoken by some 16½ million of the population of 24 million (est. 1990) in Yugoslavia. The other two major languages of Yugoslavia, Slovenian and Macedonian, are Slavic languages related to Cr&S. Other relatives in this Slavic family are Russian, Ukrainian, and Belorussian in the Soviet Union, Polish in Poland, Czech and Slovak in Czechoslovakia, and Bulgarian in Bulgaria. English is distantly related to these Slavic tongues, as the following words indicate:

Croatian and Serbian	English
brat	brother
sestra	sister
matere	mothers
nos	nose
tri	three
sin	son

LETTERS AND SOUNDS

Alphabet **abecéda/àzbuka***

Cr&S has two alphabets: a Latin alphabet used mainly by Croats and a Cyrillic alphabet used mainly by Serbs. The student will have to master one of these alphabets and should be familiar with the other. Fortunately, each alphabet is a model of scientific simplicity and the letters of one can be exactly equated to the letters of the other.

*For ease of representation, Croatian and Serbian forms that differ will be separated by a slash, with the Croatian form coming first: **mlijeko/mleko,** "milk"; **abeceda/azbuka,** "alphabet." Variant forms, both of which can occur in either Croatian or Serbian, will be separated by a comma: **akcent, akcenat,** "accent."

The main difficulty for American students is that the English alphabet also uses Latin letters, but often inconsistently, and in some cases with different values than the Latin letters of the Croatian alphabet. In English, for example, *c* and *k* can be used to represent the same sound, as in the words *cat* and *kill*; or *c* can have the same sound as *s*, as in *race* and *base*. Further, in the words *sure* and *pleasure*, the *s* represents two sounds, both mutually distinct and both different from the sound represented by *s* in *base*. These spelling irregularities in English are well known to the reader, who will no doubt be relieved to learn that, in both the Latin alphabet and the Cyrillic alphabet, each letter represents one definite speech sound, and each sound normally corresponds to one definite letter.

Latin Alphabet **latìnica**

The order of the thirty letters in the Latin alphabet is as follows:

Aa	**Bb**	**Cc**	**Čč**	**Ćć**	**Dd**	**Dždž**	**Đđ**	**Ee**	**Ff**
1	2	3	4	5	6	7	8	9	10
Gg	**Hh**	**Ii**	**Jj**	**Kk**	**Ll**	**Ljlj**	**Mm**	**Nn**	**Njnj**
11	12	13	14	15	16	17	18	19	20
Oo	**Pp**	**Rr**	**Ss**	**Šš**	**Tt**	**Uu**	**Vv**	**Zz**	**Žž**
21	22	23	24	25	26	27	28	29	30

Cyrillic Alphabet **ћирилица**

Every letter (**slovo**) in the Cyrillic alphabet is the exact equivalent of one in the Latin alphabet, though the order of letters is different in each alphabet. In the chart of the thirty Cyrillic letters, the numbers in parentheses are the equivalent Latin letters.

Аа	Бб	Вв	Гг	Дд	Ђђ	Ее	Жж	Зз	Ии
1	2	3	4	5	6	7	8	9	10
(1)	(2)	(28)	(11)	(6)	(8)	(9)	(30)	(29)	(13)
Јј	Кк	Лл	Љљ	Мм	Нн	Њњ	Оо	Пп	Рр
11	12	13	14	15	16	17	18	19	20
(14)	(15)	(16)	(17)	(18)	(19)	(20)	(21)	(22)	(23)
Сс	Тт	Ћћ	Уу	Фф	Хх	Цц	Чч	Џџ	Шш
21	22	23	24	25	26	27	28	29	30
(24)	(26)	(5)	(27)	(10)	(12)	(3)	(4)	(7)	(25)

Variations in Cyrillic Print. For special purposes in printing (such as italicizing or letters to the editor), a slanting variety of the Cyrillic letters may be used. With the exception of three letters, all the slanted letters will be easily recognizable, since they vary only slightly from the familiar vertical letters. In the chart, which shows the slanted varieties under the appropriate vertical letters, arrows point to the three exceptions.

Aa	Бб	Вв	Гг	Дд	Ђђ	Ее	Жж	Зз	Ии
Аа	*Бб*	*Вв*	*Гг*	*Дд*	*Ђђ*	*Ее*	*Жж*	*Зз*	*Ии*
Jj	Кк	Лл	Љљ	Мм	Нн	Њњ	Оо	Пп	Рр
Jj	*Кк*	*Лл*	*Љљ*	*Мм*	*Нн*	*Њњ*	*Оо*	*Пп*	*Рр*
Сс	Тт	Ћћ	Уу	Фф	Хх	Цц	Чч	Џџ	Шш
Сс	*Тт*	*Ћћ*	*Уу*	*Фф*	*Хх*	*Цц*	*Чч*	*Џџ*	*Шш*

Књига и игра	Book and Play
Хајде, брацо, хајде амо,	Come, little brother, come here,
хватај књигу да читамо.	take a book so we can read.
А кад нама	And when mama
рекне мама,	tells us,
да све добро знамо,	that we know everything well,
онда ћемо мало	then we will
да се поиграмо.	play a while.

Cursive Cyrillic. The cursive or handwritten shapes of Latin letters are essentially the same as those used in writing English. The Cyrillic cursive letters have, for the most part, distinctive shapes and so must be imitated carefully. The first list below has thirty words printed in and alphabetized according to **latìnica**, the Latin alphabet. These same thirty words then serve as examples for the printed and handwritten forms of the Cyrillic letters.

ako	if	jaja	eggs
baba	old woman	kako	how
curica	little girl	lala	tulip
Čačak	[Serbian city]	Ljubljana	[Slovenian capital]
ćilim	rug	momak	youth
doba	time	nizina	lowlands
džamija	mosque	njen	her
đak	student	ognjen	fiery
evo	here!	pepeo	ashes
filozof	philosopher	ribar	fisherman
gaj	grove	srpski	Serbian
Hrvat	Croat	šašav	crazy
izaći	to go out	tetka	aunt

ukus	taste	zabadava	free
(vol/)vo	ox	žaba	frog

ако	низина
баба	њен
во	огњен
гај	пепео
доба	рибар
ђак	српски
ево	тетка
жаба	ћилим
забадава	укус
изаћи	филозоф
jaja	Хрват
како	цурица
лала	Чачак
Љубљана	џамија
момак	шашав

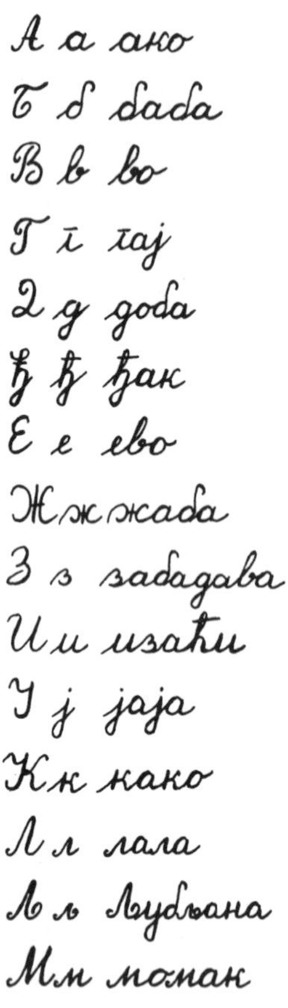

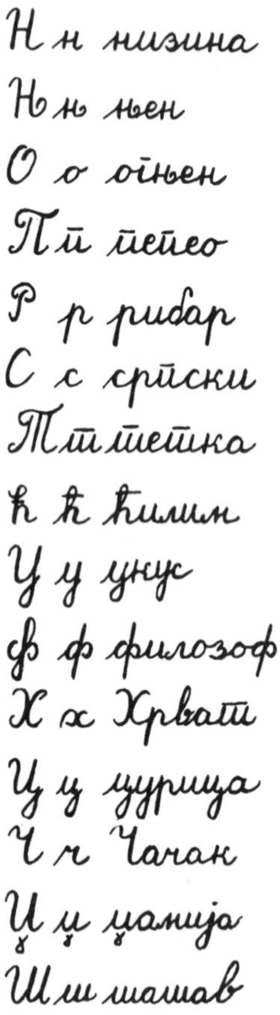

In Cyrillic handwriting (**rùkopisna ćìrilica**), three letters have a horizontal stroke at the top.

г [Latin g] **glagol** verb — глагол

п [Latin p] **pripisati**	to attribute	приписати	*приписати*
т [Latin t] **tupoglavost**	stupidity	тупоглавост	*тупоглавост*

Three Cyrillic letters are separated from preceding letters by a small upward stroke.

lula	pipe	лула	*лула*
ljuljati	to swing	љуљати	*љуљати*
mumljanje	mumbling	мумљање	*мумљање*

Pronunciation — ìzgovor

No written description of the pronunciation of Cr&S will be adequate for all readers of this book. It is recommended that the student either purchase the recordings made especially for this text or find a native speaker of Cr&S to pronounce the words used as examples.

The following Latin letters have the same appearance as English letters and represent similar consonant sounds (**sùglasnici**):

p,t,k are like English *p,t,k,* though the Cr&S sounds do not have the rush of air that follows the English sounds in initial position, as in *poor, tame, king*. In the production of Cr&S **t**, the tongue tip touches the back of the upper teeth and not, as in English, the upper gum ridge. Some examples: **paprika,** pepper; **pekar,** baker; **pop,** priest; **lopta,** ball; **tele,** calf; **tigar,** tiger; **tata,** dad; **potpis,** signature; **kako,** how; **kost,** bone; **kum,** godfather; **jak,** strong.

d,n represents sounds similar to English *d* and *n*. The Cr&S sounds are "dentalized," however, as in *t*. Do not lengthen final *n*, as is the practice in English, e.g. *nub,* but *bun* with the final *n* lengthened.
danas, today; **dim,** smoke; **kad,** when; **dom,** home; **nos,** nose; **nanovo,** again; **bon,** coupon; **neznan,** unknown.

s as in **sada,** now; **sir,** cheese; **kaos/haos,** chaos; **rasti,** to grow.

z as in **zbogom,** goodbye; **zima,** winter; **bez,** without; **mozak,** brain.

b as in **baba,** old woman; **torba,** bag; **Bog,** God; **zub,** tooth.

m as in **magla,** fog; **mek,** soft; **lom,** fracture; **musliman,** Moslem. The **m** in final position, as in **dom,** home, should be no longer than the **m** in any other position, e.g. **moda,** fashion. In English the final *m* is lengthened slightly, e.g. *may,* but *yam.*

f as in **fazan,** pheasant; **funta,** pound; **Krf,** Corfu; **oficir,** officer.

v as in **vatra,** fire; **vuna,** wool; **lav,** lion; **olovka,** pencil.

l as in **lako,** easily; **luk,** onion; **stol/sto,** table; **tabla,** board.

g is pronounced like English *g* in *get* and *gild,* but NOT like *g* in *gem* or *giant;* Cr&S **g** as in **gazda,** master; **godina,** year; **guska,** goose; **rog,** horn.

The remaining Latin letters and their sounds must be examined more carefully, because resemblances to English letters and sounds may be only partial and so misleading.

š is the letter *s* with a little *v* or "chevron" over it. This letter represents a sound similar to English *sh,* as in *shush.* In producing the Cr&S sound, the tip of the tongue is turned back slightly, so that *š* has a duller sound than English *sh.* Some examples:
šašav, crazy; **šuma,** woods; **šišmiš,** bat; **škola,** school

ž is pronounced like the *z* in our word *azure* or the *s* in *pleasure.* The Cr&S sound has a duller-sounding quality than the English (see **š**).
žaba, frog; **župa,** parish; **muž,** husband; **žena,** woman

c is pronounced like *ts* in the word *bats.* English does not have this combination of sounds initially, unless one cultivates it in *tsetse-fly.* To achieve this combination, take the English sentence: "That's all for now," say it in a more colloquial fashion: "'at's all for now," then clip it even shorter: "'tsall for now," and an initial *ts* or Cr&S **c** results.
car, tsar; **cigareta,** cigarette; **cement,** cement; **novac,** money

č is the letter *c* with a chevron and is pronounced like English *ch* in *church.* During the production of the Cr&S sound, the lips should be protruded and rounded, with the tip of the tongue turned back slightly.
čaša, glass; **čelo,** forehead; **čist,** clean; **čupa,** tuft of hair

ć is the letter *c* with an acute mark over it and has a sound similar to **č**, except that **ć** is produced with the tip of the tongue behind the lower teeth and with the lips spread and drawn back. Some speakers of Cr&S do not make this sound, using the sound **č** for both **č** and **ć**. One may approximate this sound (**ć**) by spreading the lips, bunching the tongue up in the front part of the mouth, and saying *cheese.* Some Cr&S examples are:
ćaća, papa; **ćevapčići,** roasted meat patties; **ćorda,** sword; **ćup,** jug

dž is a combination of the letters **d** and **ž** and calls for a pronunciation like *j* in the English *judge.* **dž** is the voiced equivalent of

č and, like č, is produced with the tongue tip turned back and the lips slightly rounded.
džak, sack; **džep,** pocket; **džungla,** jungle; **udžbenik,** textbook

đ is the letter *d* with a short horizontal stroke drawn through the upper part of the letter. **đ** represents a sound similar to **dž** but is produced with the tip of the tongue behind the lower teeth and with the lips spread and drawn back.
đak, student; **đuveč,** stew; **rđa,** rust; **smuđ**, perch (fish)

Many speakers of Cr&S do not distinguish between **č** and **ć** or between **dž** and **đ**. An American may pronounce **č** and **ć** in the same way as *ch* in English *cheer,* and the **dž** and **đ** just as with *j* in English *jingle.* There will be two reactions on the part of Yugoslav listeners: either they will notice nothing out of order, since they themselves do not distinguish the sounds, or they will note the lack of distinction and classify it mentally as a regional pronunciation, from some region other than their own. These distinctions, however, are observed quite regularly in Serbia.

j is pronounced like English *y* in *boy* and *year*. One should be careful not to confuse Cr&S **j** with the English *j* of *judge* and *jeep*.
boj, fight; **jun,** June; **kraj,** end; **jezik,** language

lj represents a "soft" *l*, one made by bunching the front part of the tongue up against the upper gum ridge and pronouncing *l*. If the speaker prepares to say the *y* in *year* and says *l* instead, an **lj** sound will be produced.
ljiljan, lily; **ljuljati,** to swing; **žulj,** blister; **prijatelj,** friend

nj indicates a "soft" *n*. As in the case of **lj**, one should first prepare to say the *y* in *year,* but say *n* instead; the result will be "soft" *n* or **nj**.
njen, her; **konj,** horse; **njuška,** snout; **panj,** tree-stump

r represents a trilled sound, produced by vibrating the tip of the tongue against the upper gum ridge. Many speakers of English make this sound after *th,* as in *through* or *three.*
rano, early; **ruka,** arm; **para,** small coin; **bor,** pine

h calls for a "scraping" sound, made in the same position as *k*. To make this sound, prepare to say the English word "kill" but, instead of making a closure in the back of the mouth for the *k,* let the air "scrape" over the back of the tongue. It will sound as if you are clearing your mouth. This sound, a voiceless velar fricative, is like the *h* sound in English *hill* or *have* but with more breath.
heroj, hero; **hitro,** cleverly; **hrabar,** brave; **duh,** spirit

[ŋ] There is another consonant sound that has no special letter but is indicated by the letter **n** before the letters **g** or **k**, as in **banka** "bank" or **rang** "rank." It has the same sound value as English *-ng* in *song* or *n* in *bank*. Unlike the English sound, the Cr&S sound does not occur independently of **-g** or **-k**; thus, the final **g** would be pronounced in the Cr&S word **rang [raŋg].**

There are six vowel sounds (**samòglasnici**) in Cr&S, indicated by the letters **a, e, i, o, u,** and **r:**

a is pronounced like the *a* in English *father*. Thus, **adresa,** address; **baš,** just; **kratak,** short; **papa,** pope.

e is pronounced like the *e* in English *bet,* **engleski,** English; **ne,** no; **repeticija,** repetition; **polje,** field.

i sounds like the *ee* of English *seen* or *tee*. In English, however, this *ee* sound has usually two parts, the second part sounding like the *y* sound in *boy*. To make the Cr&S **i**, start by producing the English *ee*, but do not allow the tongue to move during the production of this sound.
ići, to go; **vi,** you; **nizina,** lowlands; **piti,** to drink

o is similar in sound to English *o* in *for*. **odbor,** council; **oko,** eye; **odgovor,** answer; **nož,** knife

u sounds like English *oo* in *boot*. To avoid the tendency in English to add a *w* as the second part of this sound, do not move the lips once they have been rounded for the production of Cr&S **u**.
uši, ears; **put,** road; **duša,** soul; **Na dnu,** Lower Depths

r also serves to indicate a vowel sound in Cr&S. One can approximate its pronunciation by saying the English word *bird* with a trilled *r*.
brdo, hill; **prvi,** first; **vrt,** garden; **trg,** market

Cr&S vowels have consistently the same pronunciation regardless of their position in the word or their relationship to the accent. A native speaker of English must take care to give full value to all vowels and not slur them or replace them with other vowels. The importance of giving an accurate pronunciation to all vowels is demonstrated in the following two words, where the difference in meaning turns on the final vowels, which an English-speaker might tend to merge: **govòriti,** to speak; **govòrite,** (you) speak!

Long and Short Vowels — dùgi i kràtki samòglasnici

The vowel sounds described above may appear as short or long in duration, depending on the words in which they occur. A speaker pronounces a long vowel simply by prolonging a short vowel. English has differences in vowel length, but these variations are determined by the sounds following the vowels. Take, for example, the English words *pot* and *pod;* the vowel sound in *pod* is longer than that in *pot.* By comparing *bat* and *bad,* or *bet* and *bed,* we will conclude that English vowels are short when followed by *t* and longer when followed by *d.* This conclusion can then be enlarged by considering English words ending in *k* and *g, p* and *b, f* and *v,* and *s* and *z.*

The system in English of automatically lengthening vowel sounds before certain consonant sounds will obviously not suffice for Cr&S, where the word for "hail" is **grad** with a short *a* (like English *o* in *pot*) while the word for "city" is **grad** with a long *a* (slightly longer than the *o* in *pod*). Here are some examples of long and short vowels in Cr&S; a short bar (̄) over a vowel indicates length.

grad, hail; versus **grād,** city
žena, woman; versus **žēna,** of women
pitati, to feed; versus **pītati,** to ask
roda, of the species; versus **rōda,** stork
luk, onion; versus **lūk,** arch
Grk, a Greek; versus **gr̄k,** bitter

In the following two sentences the difference in meaning is indicated only by vowel length:

Tu nema konja. There is no horse here.
Tu nema kōnja. There are no horses here.

Accent* **àkcent, àkcenat**

English has a strong stress or loudness accent on words, that is, one syllable is pronounced louder than all the others, as in the word *eleMENtary* or *interNAtional.* Where the stress falls sometimes distinguishes meaning: *blackbird* versus *black bird,* or *perfect* (adjective) versus *perfect* (verb). Cr&S also has a stress accent, though not as strong as in English: **sunčanica(SUNčanica),** "sunbeam," versus **sunčanica(sunČAnica),** "sunstroke," or **pa da(paDA),** "of course," versus **pada(PAda),** "it falls." In Cr&S the stress can fall on any syllable except the last; there are a dozen or so exceptions, e.g. **asistent(asisTENT),** "assistant." This means that in a two-syllable word the stress will be regularly on the first syllable, e.g. **voda(VOda),** while in the three-syllable word the stress may be on the first or the second syllable, e.g. **godina(GOdina),** "year," **kultura (kulTUra),** "culture." Long vowels occur only under the stress.

*The accentual system described here is valid for the Cr&S spoken in the major cities. The traditional system, now used only in enclaves of Bosnia and Herzegovina, is described in Thomas F. Magner and Ladislav Matejka, *Word Accent in Modern Serbo-Croatian* (The Pennsylvania State University Press, 1971).

Accent Markings. Two accent marks suffice to indicate the place of stress and the shortness or length of the vowel in the syllable being stressed: a grave accent (`) for a short stressed syllabic, an acute accent (´) for a long stressed syllabic; thus **gràd,** "hail," and **grád,** "city"; **lùk,** "onion," and **lúk,** "arch"; **pàs,** "dog," and **pás,** "belt"; **kònja,** "of a horse," and **kónja,** "of horses"; **sùnčanica,** "sunbeam" and **sunčànica,** "sunstroke"; **kultúra,** "culture." In Zagreb, where the speakers do not use long vowels, one accent mark would suffice. Accent marks are not normally used in writing Cr&S, though they are employed in grammars and dictionaries. One orthographic sign (ˆ) is generally used to distinguish between genitive singular and genitive plural forms of masculine and neuter nouns, which would otherwise look exactly alike: G sg. **od profesora,** "from the professor" : G pl. **od profesorâ,** "from the professors."

Sound Changes and Writing "Rules." In Cr&S, as in English, certain consonants are voiced while others are voiceless, that is, sound from the vocal cords is either present or absent during the production of the consonant sound. To demonstrate the difference between a voiced and a voiceless sound, cover your ears with your hands and say *pa,* then *ba, ka,* then *ga, ta,* and then *da.* During the production of *b, g,* and *d,* you will sense the reverberation of vocal-cord sounds inside your head; thus, these sounds in Cr&S (and in English) are called voiced, while *p, k,* and *t* are called voiceless. On this basis Cr&S consonants may be paired as follows:

voiced:	**b**	**d**	**z**	–	**đ**	**ž**	**dž**	**v**	**g**	–
voiceless:	**p**	**t**	**s**	**c**	**ć**	**š**	**č**	**f**	**k**	**h**

There are, of course, other voiced sounds in Cr&S: **l, lj, m, n, nj, r, j,** and the vowels, but the table above shows pairs of sounds that are distinguished one from the other (**b-p, g-k,** etc.) by the presence or absence of voicing.

When two or more of the consonants in the table come together and form a group or cluster of consonants, the entire cluster assumes the "voiced" or "voiceless" characteristic of the last consonant.* Some examples are:

b> p	before **c**	vrabac	sparrow	:	vrapci N *pl.* [> means *becomes*]	
d> t	before **k**	sladak	sweet	:	slatki *def. adj.*	
z> s	before **k**	dolazak	arrival	:	dolaska G *sg.*	
g> k	before **c**	bogac	beggar	:	bokca G *sg.*	
p> b	before **dž**	top	gun	:	tobdžija	gunner
t> d	before **b**	svat	wedding guest	:	svadba	wedding

*v does not participate in these changes, e.g. **tvoj[tvoj],** your; **ovca[ovca],** sheep.

č> dž	before **b**	uč-iti	to study	:	udžbenik	textbook
k> g	before **d**	svak-i	everyone	:	svagda	always

As the examples indicate, the voicing or devoicing of a cluster of consonants is reflected in the spelling of the word. Actually, the same sound change occurs in consonant groups formed by the junction, in speech, of separate words, but this change is not noted in the writing, e.g. **bez posla,** "without work," but **besposlen,** "unemployed," **od prilike,** "approximately," but **otprilike** (adv.), "approximately."

There is one notable exception to the exact notation of voicing or devoicing within words. Cr&S maintains the letter **d** before the letters **s** and **š**, though the sound is **t.** This will be noted in words that have the prefixes **nad-, od-, pod-,** and **pred-** and the suffixes **-ski** and **-stvo.**

odskok	rebound [but]	otpadak	refuse
gradski	urban	ropski	slavish (**rob,** slave)
gospodstvo	authority	bjekstvo/bekstvo	flight (**bijeg/beg,** escape)
odšteta	indemnity	otkriće	discovery

Treatment of Double Consonants. As a general rule double consonants of the same type (*-tt-, -gg-*, etc.) do not occur in Cr&S. Where such a combination would occur through prefixation, or by the disappearance of the "movable" vowel *a* in inflection, or in word-compounding, one consonant is dropped. Thus,

odbaciti	to throw off	[but]	odati (< od-dati) to betray, to let out
raskidan	broken up		rasječen/rasečen (< ras-s-) chopped up [see sječen/sečen, chopped]

otac, G oca (< ot-ca = ot-tsa), father
sudac, G suca (< sut-ca = sut-tsa < sud-ca), judge
pedeset (< ped-deset < pet-deset), fifty
šezdeset (< šezd-deset < šest-deset), sixty

The major exception is the maintaining of the cluster **-jj-** in some superlative forms, e.g. **najjači,** "the strongest," **najjunačniji,** "the most courageous."

d *and* **dj, t** *and* **tj.** Ijekavian speech has in many words a **dj** or **tj** combination where the corresponding word in ekavian has simply **d** or **t**, e.g. **djed/ded(a)**, "grandfather," **tjerati/terati,** "to chase." The letter **j** in the position after **t** or **d** is pronounced like the *y*-glide in the English word *pure (pyure)*; pronounce *pure* and then *poor* and note the difference caused by the presence of or lack of the *y*-glide. In the speech of some Americans this *y*-glide may occur after a *t* or *d*, as in the words *dew (dyew*, but *do*) or *student (styudent)*.

đ *Written as* **dj.** When the Latin letters **Đ, đ** are not represented on a typewriter or in a type font, Yugoslavs often substitute the letters **dj.** Thus, **vođa** might be printed or written as **vodja** or **đak** as **djak.** This causes no difficulty for the native speaker of Cr&S, who is, of course, familiar with the words **vođa,** "leader," and **đak,** "student." It will probably not trouble students of the language if they encounter the digraph **dj** for the sound **đ** in an ekavian text, since the actual sound combination of **d** + **j** (e.g. **predjelo,** "appetizer") is rather infrequent; thus, when ekavian speech is represented by the Latin alphabet, the spelling **dj** will usually represent the sound **đ**.

Care must be exercised, however, when an ijekavian text follows this practice, since the actual sound combination **dj** (i.e. **d** + **j**) occurs fairly frequently and is to be distinguished from the sound **đ**. Thus, **vodje,** "of the leader," and **djeca,** "children," with the first **dj** representing **đ** (**vođe**), the second **dj** being **d** + **j (djeca).**

Sound Patterns. It soon becomes apparent to the student of Cr&S that the consonant changes in derived (or inflected) words are not haphazard but enter into definite patterns with the consonants of the original word (the shorter form) or of the word root; for example, **blag,** "mild"; **blaži,** "milder"; **drag,** "dear"; **draži,** "dearer." Sound changes that have taken place in the past have set up the following relationships:

1. Consonant plus **-j-.** The effect of **-j-** on a preceding consonant can be seen if we take our examples from one of the following situations:

a. Comparative formed with **-ji,** e.g. **tan-ak,** thin : **tanji,** thinner
b. The instrumental singular in **-ju** of feminine **i**-nouns, e.g. **stvar,** thing : **stvarju**
c. The past passive participle in **-jen,** e.g. **hvaliti,** to praise : **hvaljen,** praised
d. Nouns formed with a **-je** suffix (neuter nouns) or with a **-ja** suffix (feminine nouns), e.g. **vesel-i,** cheerful : **vesel-je,** joy : **vol-im,** I like : **volja,** will

j Changes

p : plj **tup,** dull : **tuplji,** duller; **grabiti,** to take hold of : **grablje,** rake
b : blj **grub,** coarse : **grublji,** coarser; **ljubiti,** to love : **ljubljen,** loved
v : vlj **kriv,** crooked : **krivlji,** more crooked; **krv,** blood : **krvlju[I]**
m : mlj **bezum-an,** mad : **bezumlje,** madness; **mamiti,** to lure : **mamljen,** lured

t : ć	**smrt,** death : **smrću[I]; vratiti,** to return : **vraćen,** returned
d : đ	**mlad,** young : **mlađi,** younger; **glad,** hunger : **glađu[I]**
s : š	**iznositi,** to wear out : **iznošen,** worn out; **visok,** high : **viši,** higher
z : ž	**brz,** fast : **brži,** faster; **gaziti,** to trample upon : **gažen,** trampled
k : č	**jak,** strong : **jači,** stronger; **peku,** they bake : **pečen,** baked
h : š	**duh,** spirit : **duša[< duh-ja],** soul; **tih,** quiet : **tiši,** quieter
g : ž	**blag,** mild : **blaži,** milder; **drag,** dear : **draži,** dearer
st : šć	**gust,** dense : **gušći,** denser; **radost,** happiness : **radošću[I]**
zd : žđ	**grozd,** bunch of grapes : **grožđe [< grozd-je]** grapes; **zabrazditi,** to plow a furrow : **zabražđen,** furrowed

The consonant **j** does, of course, occur without effecting changes in certain adjectives, e.g. **pasji,** "dog's, canine" (**pàs**, "dog"), and in ijekavian forms, e.g. **tjerati,** "to drive" (*ek.* **terati**).

2. The sounds **g, h,** and **k** are replaced by **ž, š,** and **č** before the vocative ending **-e** and before **e-**endings of the present tense.

Bog, God	:	**Bože! oni strigu,** they clip	:	**on striže,** he clips
Vlah, Vlach	:	**Vlaše! oni vrhu,** they place	:	**on vrše,** he places
junak, hero	:	**junače! oni peku,** they bake	:	**on peče,** he bakes

In the matter of these latter examples it should be noted that some speakers of Cr&S have re-formed the third plural on the model of the third singular and would say **peču** instead of **peku, strižu** instead of **strigu,** and **vršu** instead of **vrhu.**

3. The sounds **g, h, and k** are replaced by **z, s,** and **c** in the following situations:
   a. before the N pl. ending **-i** and the D/I pl. ending **-ima** of nouns:
      bubreg, kidney : **bubrezi,** (G *pl.* **bubrega**), **bubrezima**
      duh, spirit : **dusi, (duha), dusima**
      (also **duhovi, duhova, duhovima**)
      vojnik, soldier : **vojnici, (vojnika), vojnicima**
   b. before the D. sg. ending **-i** of nouns:
      noga, leg : **na nozi**
      epoha, epoch : **u eposi**
      ruka, arm : **u ruci**
   c. before the imperative ending **-i** of verbs:
      strigu, they clip : **strizi!** (also **striži;** see 2 above)
      vrhu, they place : **vrsi!** (also **vrši;** see 2 above)
      peku, they bake : **peci!**

Separation Vowel **a.** At one time only four consonant clusters commonly occurred at the end of Cr&S words. They are: **-st** as in **post,** "fast," **-zd** as in **grozd,** "bunch of grapes," **-št** as in **plašt,** "mantle," and **-žd** as in **dažd,** "rain." Other combinations of consonants that cluster in nonfinal position would usually appear in final position separated by the vowel **a.*** Some examples are:

-mk-, -mak	**momka**(G sg.), **momak,** lad
-rc-, -rac	**starca**(G sg.), **starac,** old man
-br-, -bar	**dobri** (definite masc. N sg.), **dobar** (indef.), good
-dn-, -dan	**hladni, hladan,** cold
-zm-, -zam	**liberalizma**(G sg.), **liberalizam**, liberalism

l *and* **o.** At one time in the history of the Cr&S language every **l**-sound, which stood at the end of a word or a syllable, turned into the sound **o.** Though final **l** has been reintroduced into Cr&S in loan words, there is still a striking correspondence between nonfinal **l** and final **o** in related forms.

a. **-l-** : **-o** (word final)

čitala je, čitao je	she read, he read
mi smo veseli, ja sam veseo	we're cheerful, I'm cheerful
misli (G sg.), **misao**[< **mis*a*l;** for **a** see above]	thought
posla (G sg.), **posao**	work
stola, sto[< **sto-o** < **stol**]	table (also **stola, stol**)

b. **-l-** : **-o** (syllable final)

vla-da-lac, ruler, **vla-dao-ca** (G sg.)	
Beograd[< **Bel-grad**]	Belgrade
gr-lo, throat, **gro-ce,**	little throat [< **grl-ce**]

Whispered Vowels. In normal rapid speech many speakers of Cr&S devoice or "whisper" final short vowels after a voiceless consonant:

na sveùčilištu/univerzitétu	at the university
plátiti	to pay

At first it sounds to the foreigner that the final vowel (the **-u** or the **-i** in the examples) is simply not there, but after some observation he or she will detect the "whispered" variant of the expected vowel.

*Modern loans have resulted in many other possible clusters, e.g. **akt, film, mart, student.** There are also doublets such as **fakt** and **fakat, parlamenat,** and **parlament.**

Dialects of the Croatian and Serbian Language

As in the United States, the various regions of Yugoslavia have distinctive dialects or regional features of pronunciation and word usage. Thus, after listening to a fellow countryman talk for a few minutes, a Yugoslav can say: "He's from Dalmatia," or "She's from Zagorje," or "That's the Leskovac dialect." Though it is impossible to detail all the varieties of Cr&S speech here, some broad groupings can be presented.

One criterion for distinguishing Cr&S dialects is the word for "what." A Yugoslav who uses **kaj** for "what" is said to speak **kajkavski** or a kajkavian dialect; one who uses **ča** speaks **čakavski** or a čakavian dialect. One whose normal word for "what" is **što** or **šta** belongs to the majority group, which speaks **štokavski** or a štokavian dialect. The standard Cr&S language is based on **štokavski** speech.

The **štokavski** dialects may then be grouped according to the one main criterion: the treatment of vowels in certain words.* Note in the following short lists some definite correspondences in the matter of vowel quality.

	Dialect A	Dialect B	Dialect C
place	mèsto	mjèsto	mìsto
faith	vèra	vjèra	vìra
girl	dèvojka	djèvojka	dìvojka
to run	bèžati	bjèžati	bìžati
village	sèlo	sèlo	sèlo

The last example, **selo,** was added to indicate that all three dialects have the simple **e**-vowel and that the correspondence noted above (**e** : **je** : **i**) occurs in certain specific words. This correspondence varies slightly if the **e** and **i** members are long vowels.

	Dialect A	Dialect B	Dialect C
flower	cvét	cvìjet	cvít
hay	séno	sìjeno	síno
milk	mléko	mlijèko	mlíko
time	vréme	vrijème	vríme
five	pét	pét	pét

*Words that in earlier Slavic times had the vowel referred to as **jat** [ě] in distinction from the vowel **e,** which continues as **e,** as in **selo.** The **e** in the word **pet** comes from an earlier nasal vowel [ę]. Thus, in Dialect A(ekavian) above, the vowel **e** in the words **mesto, pet, selo** has three different ancestors, i.e. **město, selo, pęt**.

On the basis of this criterion **štokavski** dialects may be classified as **ekavski (e, ē)**, or **ijekavski (je, ije)**, or **ikavski (i, ī)**. In general, **ekavski** is spoken in Serbia, while **ijekavski** (also referred to as **jekavski)** is spoken in Montenegro, Herzegovina, Bosnia, Croatia, Southern Dalmatia and Lika; ikavski dialects are spoken in western Bosnia, in Slavonia (Posavina), in northwestern Dalmatia, and in the archipelago north of Pelješac.

je : e. Ordinarily, the variant **je** appears only when the ekavian form has a short **e,** while **ije** corresponds to the long **e** of the ekavian form:

cvìjet/cvèt*	flower	—	**cvjètovi/cvètovi** N pl.
snìjeg/snég	snow	—	**snjègovi/snègovi** N pl.
dijète/déte	child	—	**djèteta/dèteta** G sg.

However, a correspondence of **jē : ē** sometimes occurs, e.g. **vjéra/véra, ljéta/léta;** these are G pl. forms of words that have **je : e** in the N sg.: **vjèra/vèra,** "faith," **ljèto/lèto,** "summer."

Loss of **j** *in Ijekavian Forms.* After a consonant cluster ending in **r,** the long reflex of ijekavian forms (i.e. **ije**) can appear, but the short reflex loses its **j,** becoming identical to the ekavian form:

vrijème/vréme, time [but] **vrèmena/vrèmena** G sg.
brijeg/brég, hill [but] **brègovi/brègovi** N pl.
sprijèčiti/sprééiti *P*, to prevent [but] **sprečávati/sprečávati** *I*
rješénje/rešénje, decision [but] **odrešénje/odrešénje,** absolution

As the Cr&S word for "decision" indicates, the normal alternation of **je/ije** does operate after a single **r.** Another example would be:

rìječ/réč, word [and] **rječnik/rèčnik,** dictionary

Replacement of **je** *by* **i.** Ijekavian forms have **i** instead of **je** before the vowel **o** or the consonant **j.** In these particular situations the **ijekavian** and **ikavian** forms are identical. Thus,

ekavski	*ijekavski*	*ikavski*
ón je žíveo, he lived	ón je žívio	ón je žívio
òna je žívela, she lived	òna je žívjela	òna je žívila
htèo je, he wanted	htìo je	htìo je
htèla je, she wanted	htjèla je	htìla je
vèjati, to blow	vìjati	vìjati
vètar, wind	vjètar	vìtar

*Forms after the slash are ekavian.

smèjati se, to laugh	smìjati se	smìjati se
sméh, laugh	smìjeh	smíh

Use of Capital Letters. Cr&S does not use capital letters as much as English. The chief differences are:

1. The Cr&S use of a small letter for nationality adjectives: **američki,** "American," **francuski,** "French," **dalmatinski,** "Dalmatian."
2. The use of small letters for points of the compass: **jug,** "South," **zapad,** "West," **istok,** "East," **sjever/sever,** "North." If these terms are used to indicate governmental concepts, they are capitalized: **Ako se Istok i Zapad slože, svjetski/svetski mir će biti osiguran,** "If East and West reach an agreement, world peace will be assured."
3. A capital letter is used only for the first word in geographical designations (except country and place names), names of holidays, names of organizations, and titles of books and articles.

	Jadransko more	Adriatic Sea
	Balkanski poluotok	Balkan Peninsula
	Crna gora	Black Mountain
[but]	Crna Gora	Montenegro [place name]
	Božić	Christmas
	Nova Godina	New Year's Day
	Hrvatsko narodno kazalište	Croatian National Theater
	Beogradsko dramsko pozorište	Belgrade Drama Theater
	Jugoslavenska akademija znanosti i umjetnosti	Yugoslav Academy of Sciences and Arts
	Gorski vijenac	"Mountain Wreath" [title of poem]
	Sloboda u našoj zemlji	*Freedom in Our Land* [book title]
	Razgovori s milicijom	*Conversations with the Police* [book title]

Differences Between Croatian and Serbian. There is no doubt that Croatian and Serbian are different. The difficulty arises when one attempts to answer the question, How different? Part of the problem results from the lack of up-to-date descriptions of the language usage of the various regions and the principal cities. Even if the differences could be detailed exactly, the next question—Are Croatian and Serbian related dialects, that is, variants of the same language, or are they closely related languages?—transcends simple language description and involves political and nationalistic considerations. Here we shall just list those differences cited by various Croatian and Serbian language specialists. In this sketch Serbian will be understood to be the representative speech of **Srbijánci,** that is, of Serbs living in Serbia.

1. Ijekavian pronunciation for the Croats, ekavian for the Serbs,* e.g. **dijète/déte,** "child," **djèvojka/dèvojka,**† "girl."
2. Other phonetic differences are difficult to systematize since some of the differences involve only a few forms:

-uh/-uv	dùhan/dùvan	tobacco
	mùha/mùva	fly
	súh/súv	dry
-ć/-št	òpći/òpšti	general (adj.)
	svèćenik/svèštenik	priest

3. Maintenance or loss of distinction of **č : ć** and **dž : đ**. Many Croats, particularly those around Zagreb, do not have these two distinctions, while Serbs (in Serbia) by and large maintain them:

já ču čùti/já ću čùti	I will hear
smèdža džámija/smèđa džámija	a brown mosque

4. Difference in place of accent:

ìdemo/idémo	we go
bòrimo se/borímo se	we fight

5. Differences in noun gender:

kvalitéta/kvalìtet	quality
pòsjet/pòseta	a visit
naslònjač/naslònjača	armchair

6. Difference in word formation:

súdac/sùdija	judge
sùradnik/sàradnik	co-worker
konkurírati/konkùrisati	to compete

7. Syntactic differences. Perhaps the most obvious difference is the tendency of the Serbs to use a **da-**clause with a verb in the present tense where the Croats would use an infinitive. Thus, the following statements can be either Croatian or Serbian:

já ću čìtati	I'll read
já hòću čìtati	I want to read
já móram čìtati	I ought to read
já se móram ùčiti čìtati	I must learn to read

A Serb, however, would tend to use the following constructions:
já ću da čìtam

*The Serbs in Croatia (i.e. **Lika**), those in Bosnia and Herzegovina, and the Montenegrins also use ijekavian.

†The form or forms to the left of the slash mark are Croatian (e.g. **dijete, djevojka**), those to the right are Serbian (e.g. **dete, devojka**).

já hòću da čìtam
já móram da čìtam
já móram da se ùčim da čìtam*

8. Lexical differences. In some cases only a minor phonetic change is involved (e.g. **plaća/plata**); in others the words are completely different (e.g. **kino/bioskop**). The doublets below are part of what could be an extensive list:

tìsuća/hìljada	thousand
jugoslàvenski/jugoslòvenski	Yugoslavian
kàt/spràt	building floor
kàzalište/pòzorište	theater
kèmija/hèmija	chemistry
kíno/bìoskop	movie theater
kòlodvor/stànica	train station
knjìžnica/bibliotéka	library
krùh/hlèb	bread
nògomet/fùdbal	football
pàpir/hàrtija	paper
pláća/pláta	pay
poduzéće/preduzéće	enterprise
pòvijest/ìstorija	history
rùčnik/pèškir	towel
slòvenski/slòvenački	Slovenian
slàvenski/slòvenski	Slavic
srètan/srèćan	happy
strój/mašína	machine
svèmir/vasìona	universe
sveùčilište/univerzìtet	university
tvórnica/fàbrika	factory
ùvjet/ùslov	condition

9. Differences in meaning:
   zrák = air in Cr., beam, ray, in S.
   ùbrus = napkin in Cr., towel in S.
   raspuštènica = wanton woman in Cr., divorcée in S.
10. Different alphabets. This is a secondary difference, a difference in writing and not one of speech. The Croats use the Latin alphabet (**latinica**) almost exclusively, while the Serbs use both Cyrillic (**ćirilica**) and Latin, with a preference for the Cyrillic.

*__dakanje__ is the name given to excessive use of this construction, e.g. **Rèkla mi je da dóđem da vìdim da stvár nàpreduje i da kážem štà jòš trèba da rádimo,** "She told me to come and see that the affair moves ahead and to say what more we should be doing."

Nouns and Gender — ìmenice i ród

If one points to various objects and asks a speaker of Cr&S, **Što/Šta je to?** "What's that?" or **Što/Šta je ovo?** "What's this?" or **Što/Šta je ono?** "What's that over there?" the replies might be:

Tő je pòd.	That's the floor.
Ȍvo je knjìga.	This is a book.
Ȍno je pèro.	That's a pen over there.

Forms like **pod, knjiga,** and **pero** are called nouns, just as "floor," "book," and "pen" are called nouns in English. As the speaker of Cr&S continued answering questions, the listener would soon notice that certain nouns had final sounds in common with others. Thus, in the utterances

Ȍvo je knjìga.	This is a book.
Tő je žèna.	That's a woman.
Ȍvo je škóla.	This is a school.
Tő je ùlica.	That's a street.
Ȍna je ùčenica.	She is a schoolgirl.

all the nouns end in the sound **a;** while in the utterances

Ȍvo je pèro.	This is a pen.
Tő je sèlo.	That's a village.
Ȍvo je kòlo.	This is a wheel.

the final sound and letter is **o.** Then he would find a third group that did not have final **a** or **o** and that, in fact, had no final vowel sound. Thus,

Ȍvo je pòd.	This is the floor.
Tő je grád.	That's a city.
Ȍvo je prózor.	This is a window.
Tő je kàput.	That's a coat.
Ón je muškárac.	He's a man.
Tàmo je ùčenik.	There's the schoolboy.

Since most nouns that refer to female beings have the final **a,** the nouns in the group **knjiga, žena, škola, ulica, učenica** are said to be of the *feminine gender*; they are usually called "feminine" nouns. Most nouns designating male beings fall into the last group such as **pod, grad,** and **muškarac,** and these are "masculine" nouns or nouns of the *masculine gender.* The other group, **pero, selo, kolo,** usually denotes nonanimate objects and so the nouns are referred to as "neuter."

Gender and Agreement — ród i sláganje

This classification of nouns into gender groupings has a wider meaning, since all words that describe or define nouns and are in direct association with these nouns have variant forms depending on the gender of the nouns. Thus, adjectives ("good," "bad") and possessive pronouns ("my," "his") are said to "agree" with their nouns, that is, to adopt the same gender. For example,

Màrija je mòja pŕva kćérka.	Mary is my first daughter.
Ìvan/Jòvan je mój pŕvi sin.	John is my first son.
Òvo je mòje pŕvo pèro.	This is my first pen.

Case — **pádež**

Cr&S nouns and adjectives undergo a variety of changes in different contexts. For the native speaker of English this is something new, since English has only a few basic variations for nouns. English does have special forms for the plural number,

singular	*plural*
book	books
child	children

but once a singular or plural has been selected, it would be used without further change in the following statements:

The book is here.
I see the book.
I tore a page from the book.
Dear little book!
The pencil is lying in front of the book.
What's he saying about the book?

In Cr&S, however, there would be a special form for "book" in each one of these statements: **knjiga-knjigu-knjige-knjigo-knjigom-knjizi.** These special forms belong to different categories, or "cases," which are determined by the particular situation, that is, what is being said at the time. English has only two cases: a possessive case and a nonpossessive case. For example,

singular	*plural*
The book is here.	The books are here.
The book's title is here.	The books' titles are here.

The words *book's* and *books'* (pronounced alike) represent the only case variation in English, and one can even avoid their use by saying: "The title of the book. . . ," "The titles of the books are here."

Nominative Case — **nòminativ**

If one asks the questions **Što/Šta je to?** or **Tko/Ko je on?** or **Tko/Ko je ona?** the answers might be:

Tó je mój šèšir.	That's my hat.
Tó je mòja knjìga.	That's my book.
Tó je mòje sèlo.	That's my village.

Ón je mój bràt.	He's my brother.
Òna je mòja sèstra.	She's my sister.

These nouns (**šešir,** etc.) and their possessive adjectives (**moj,** etc.) are said to be in the nominative case. Dictionaries classify nouns according to their nominative case form and, if a Yugoslav is asked for the Cr&S equivalent of an English noun, he or she will usually reply with a noun in its nominative case.

Accusative Case **àkuzativ**

Other case variations show up in response to questions such as these:

Štò/Štà vìdite?	What do you see?
Kóga vìdite?	Whom do you see?

The possible answers could be:

Vìdim šèšir.	Vidim knjìgu.	Vidim sèlo.
Vidim bràta.	Vidim sèstru.	Vidim pèro.

The feminine noun here substitutes **-u** for its nominative **-a,** the neuter noun (**selo, pero**) remains the same, and the masculine noun has a double treatment: **šešir,** but **brata.** A few more examples will show the basis for this change.

Vìdim šèšir.	I see the hat. [but]	Vidim bràta.	[N **bràt,** brother]
Vidim grád.	I see the city.	Vidim òca.	[**òtac,** father]
Vidim tràmvaj.	I see the streetcar.	Vidim vúka.	[**vúk,** wolf]
Vidim pàket.	I see the package.	Vidim kònja.	[**kònj,** horse]
Vidim pòd.	I see the floor.	Vidim vojníka.	[**vòjnik,** soldier]

If a masculine noun denotes an animate being (human or animal), it adds the ending **a** in the accusative case. This permits a very free word order in Cr&S with no danger of ambiguity. Thus,

Òtac vòli sína.
Sína vòli òtac.

Both sentences mean "The father loves the son," with stronger emphasis in the second sentence on *the son.*

Genitive Case **gènitiv**

A third case, the genitive, involves such questions and responses as the following:

Od čèga ón tó pràvi?	What's he making that out of?
Od kóga je tó písmo?	From whom is that letter?
Pràvi kùću od kàmena. [N kàmen]	He's building the house out of stone.
Tó je písmo od móga bràta. [bràt]	That's a letter from my brother.
Pràvi prózor od metála. [mètal]	He's making the window (frame) from metal.

Pràvi cìpele od kòže. [kòža]	He's making shoes out of leather.
Tő je písmo od mòje sèstre. [sèstra]	That's a letter from my sister.

Both masculine and neuter nouns have the ending **a** in the genitive case, the masculine nouns adding the **a** and the neuter nouns substituting **a** for N-A **o.** Actually, except for the nominative and accusative cases (singular and plural), the endings for neuter nouns in the various cases will be the same as those for masculine nouns; likewise, adjectives agreeing with neuter nouns in these cases will be the same as those agreeing with masculine nouns. The ending of a singular, feminine noun in the genitive case is, as above, **-e.** In a later section, Review of Case Usages, you will see several uses of the genitive case without prepositions. Here are a few examples of such usage:

Pòsjetio/Pòsetio je glàvni grád dȑžave. [dȑžava]	He visited the principal city of the country.
Pòpeo se nà vrh dȑveta. [dȑvo]	He climbed to the top of the tree.

Dative Case **dàtiv**

The dative case of nouns could be used in answer to questions such as these:

Kòmu [or] Kòme gòvorite?	To whom are you speaking?
O kòme govorite?	About whom are you talking?
O čèmu govorite?	What are you talking about?

Possible answers are:

Gòvorim bràtu i sèstri.	[bràt, sèstra]	I'm talking to the brother and sister.
Govorim o šešíru.	[šèšir]	I'm talking about the hat.
Govorim o stùdentu.	[stùdent]	I'm talking about the student.
Govorim o sèlu.	[sèlo]	I'm talking about the village.
Govorim o pòlju.	[pòlje]	I'm talking about the field.
Govorim o sòbi.	[sòba]	I'm talking about a room.
Govorim o sèstri.	[sèstra]	I'm talking about the sister.

Masculine and neuter nouns are alike in having the dative ending of **u,** while the ending for feminine nouns is **i.** Feminine nouns with stem-final **k, g,** or **h** replace these consonants with **c, z,** and **s** before this dative ending **-i.** Some examples:

Amèrika	America	o Amèrici
snága	power	o snázi
snàha	daughter-in-law	o snàsi

Instrumental Case **ìnstrumental**

Following the "what-who" method of examining the various noun cases, one may ask:

Číme píšete?	With what are you writing?
S kím ìdete/idéte?	With whom are you going?

Possible answers might be:

Píšem pèrom.	[pèro]	I'm writing with (by means of) a pen.
Ìdem s bràtom.	[bràt]	I'm going with (my) brother.
Šétam s prìjateljem.	[prìjatelj]	I'm strolling with a friend.
Pišem òlovkom.	[òlovka]	I write with a pencil.
Razgòvaram sa sèstrom.	[sèstra]	I'm chatting with (my) sister.

Considering also the statement: **Ja idem poljem.** [N **pòlje**], "I'm going through (by means of) the field," one can say that the instrumental ending for masculine and neuter nouns is usually **-om,** but **-em** after a preceding **j** (**poljem, prijateljem**). The **-em** ending occurs after other consonants, such as **ž,** e.g. **múž,** "husband," **s mužem.** The ending for feminine nouns is always **-om;** this ending is not affected by a preceding **j** (N **linija,** "line"; I **linijom**).

Instrumental of Means. The means or instrument by which some action is performed is usually indicated by a noun in the instrumental case. This usage is well demonstrated in the following short passage from a Yugoslav primer:

ČIME ŠTO RADIMO?	"WHAT DO WE DO WITH WHAT?"
Òčima glèdamo. Ùšima slùšamo. Nòsom mìrišemo. Jèzikom kùšamo. Pr̀stima pìpamo. Nògama ìdemo. Rúkama rádimo. Ìglom šìjemo. Čètkom čìstimo. Pèrom píšemo. . .	"We see with [i.e. by means of] our eyes. We hear with our ears. We smell with our nose. We taste with our tongue. We feel with our fingers. We walk with our legs. We work with our hands. We sew with a needle. We clean with a brush. We write with a pen. . ."

In colloquial language there is a tendency to use the preposition **s** with the instrumental of means. Thus, the expression "I'm going by train" would be, according to traditional grammar, **Ìdem vlákom** (Cr.) or **Ìdem vózom** (S.), but it is often expressed as **Idem s vlakom/Idem s vozom.**

Vocative Case — vòkativ

Cr&S has a special case for "calling" people or objects, that is, summoning their attention or addressing them. This is called the "vocative" case and applies especially to the names or titles of people to whom one wishes to talk.

Gdjè/Gdè je gospòdin Pòpović? [nominative case]

[but]

Gospòdine Pòpoviću! Kako ste?	Mr. Popović! How are you?

Although both the title and full name may be put into this vocative case,

Gospòdine Jòvane Pòpoviću!

some speakers make only one element specifically vocative.

Gospòdine Pòpović! [or] Gospòdin Pòpoviću!

The use of this case for objects or things would occur mostly in poetry or stylized language, e.g. **dràžesna knjìgo,** "dear little book!"

Forming the Vocative. For masculine nouns the ending is **e**

Bóg	God	**Bòže mój!**	My Lord!
gospòdin	mister	**gospòdine!**	Mister!
bràt	brother	**bràte!**	Brother!
òtac	father	**òče!**	Father!

or **u,** when the noun ends in **č, ć, đ, j, lj, nj, š,** or **ž.**

òrač	plowman	òraču!	O plowman!
mlàdić	youth	mlàdiću!	
smúđ	perch [fish]	smúđu!	
prìjatelj	friend	prìjatelju!	
kònj	horse	kònju!	
bój	battle	bòju!	
gàjdaš	bagpiper	gàjdašu!	
múž	husband	múžu!	

There is some vacillation for masculine nouns in **-ar** in that some speakers of Cr&S would form their vocative in **-u,** while others would use the ending **-e.**

pìsar	clerk	pìsaru, pìsare!	Clerk!
rìbar	fisherman	rìbaru, rìbare!	Fisherman!
rùdar	miner	rùdaru, rùdare!	Miner!

Feminine nouns appear in the vocative case with an ending **o** replacing the nominative ending **a.**

žèna	woman	žèno!	Woman!
májka	mother	májko!	Mother!
gòspođa	Mrs.	gòspođo!	Mrs.!

However, feminine nouns in **-ica,** such as **gòspođica,** "Miss," have a vocative ending **e.**

gòspođice! Miss!

More About the Vocative Case. The vocative forms of neuter nouns, like **selo** and **polje,** have the same shape as the nominative and accusative forms; thus, **selo!** and **polje!** Feminine nouns of the **i**-type (**stvár,** G **stvári**) have vocative forms exactly like the genitive forms (**stvári!**). An example:

O ràdosti mòja! [ràdost, G ràdosti]	Oh my joy! [a mother to her infant]

Usually only the definite forms of adjectives are used with nouns in the vocative case, e.g. **dragi oče!** "dear father!" There is, of course, no vocative category for adjectives. Another example of a vocative construction is:

Kȑšna Líko, pùna si brègova, jòš pùnija sívih sokòlova.	O rocky Lika, you are full of hills, but fuller yet of gray falcons (heroes)!

One of the chief characteristics of the vocative case is that it has distinctive forms only in the singular number; in the plural number there are a few vocative plural forms, distinguished by accent from the nominative plural forms, but, in general, the vocative plural forms are the same as the nominative plural forms, e.g. N pl. **stùdenti, "students**," and V pl. **stùdenti!,** "students!"

Names and Order of Cases. Yugoslav grammarians follow the old Greek-Latin tradition in the order of cases, while the individual cases have names based on the Latin terms or are indicated by an ordinal number. Here is the Cr&S word for "window" as it would be set forth in a Yugoslav textbook and as it is set forth in this textbook.

Traditional Order

	jednìna (sg.)	**množìna** (pl.)
nòminativ *ili* pȓvi pádež	prózor	prózori
gènitiv *ili* drùgi padež	prozora	prozora
dàtiv *ili* trèći padež	prozoru	prozorima
àkuzativ *ili* čètvrti padež	prozor	prozore
vòkativ *ili* péti padež	prozore	prozori
lòkativ *ili* šésti padež	prozoru	prozorima
ìnstrumental *ili* sédmi padež	prozorom	prozorima

Modern Order

		jednìna (sg.)	**množìna** (pl.)
Nominative	(N)	prózor	prózori
Vocative	(V)	prozore	prozori
Accusative	(A)	prozor	prozore
Genitive	(G)	prozora	prozora
Dative	(D)	prozoru	prozorima
Instrumental	(I)	prozorom	prozorima

Aside from a different order of cases, this textbook merges the traditionally distinct dative and locative cases into one case, the dative. There is no difference in the ending, e.g. Dative **prozoru** (=Dative **prozoru**/ Locative **prozoru**), Dative **ženi** (=Dative **ženi**/Locative **ženi**).

Noun Plurals. The plural formation of nouns is much simpler than the singular, because the vocative plural and the nominative plural have the same forms, as do the dative and instrumental plural. Simple sentences, employing noun plurals in all cases except the vocative, are presented below; the nominative singular forms of the nouns used as examples are **šèšir,** "hat," **stùdent,** "student," **sèlo,** "village," **pòlje,** "field," **knjìga,** "book," and **sèstra,** "sister."

	masculine	*neuter*	*feminine*
Nominative			
Tàmo su. . .	šešíri,	sèla,	knjìge,
	stùdenti	pòlja	sèstre
There are. . .			
Accusative			
Vìdim. . .	šešíre,	sèla,	knjìge,
	stùdente	pòlja	sèstre
I see. . .			
Genitive			
Tó je blízu. . .	šešíra,	séla,	knjíga,
	stùdenata	pólja	sestára
That's near the. . .			
Dative			
Tó prìpada. . .			
That belongs to. . .	šešírima,	sèlima,	knjìgama,
[or]	stùdentima	pòljima	sèstrama
Gòvorim o. . .			
I'm talking about. . .			
Instrumental			
To je pred. . .	šešírima,	sèlima,	knjìgama,
	stùdentima	pòljima	sèstrama
That's in front of. . .			

Feminine **i**-*nouns.* There is a large group of "feminine" nouns that may be called **i**-nouns, since the vowel **i** occurs in most of the case endings. Though these endings are somewhat different than those associated with "feminine" nouns of the type **žena, knjiga, tiranija,** etc., the modifying words (adjectives, demonstrative pronouns) still agree in the same way for both types:

Tkò/Kò je tá kràsna žèna? Who is that beautiful woman?
Štò/Štà je tá kràsna stvár? What is that beautiful thing?

The various case forms of **stvar** are as follows:

	singular		*plural*	
	(**i**-fem.)	(**a**-fem.)	(**i**-fem.)	(**a**-fem.)
N	stvár*	(žèna)	stvári	(žène)
V	stvari	(ženo)	stvari	(žène)

*In paradigms such as these the accent is not repeated if there is no change in the other forms; where there is a change (see the plural forms of **žena**), all the accent marks are provided.

A	stvar	(ženu)	stvari	(žène)
G	stvari	(žene)	stvari	(žéna)
D	stvari	(ženi)	stvarima	(žènama)
I	stvari, stvarju	(ženom)	stvarima	(žènama)

Since most of the **i**-nouns have a N sg. form that ends in a consonant and are in this case similar to "masculine" nouns, e.g. **smrt,** "death," and **vrt,** "garden," the distinction in gender will be indicated by a modifying word or by another case form: **čija smrt,** "whose death," and **čiji vrt,** "whose garden," or G sg. **smrti** and G sg. **vrta.**

Most nouns ending in **-ost** and having two or more syllables in the N sg. belong to this type of "feminine" **i**-nouns; e.g. **ràdost,** "joy," **budúćnost,** "the future."

Instrumental Singular. The instrumental endings **-ju** and **-i** are optional alternates, except where ambiguity (e.g. confusion of cases in **-i**) might result. Thus:

Jèdnom rìječju/réčju [or] jèdnom rìječi/réči	in a word
Òvom stvárju [or] Òvom stvári se zanímaju filòlozi	Philologists concern themselves with this matter.
[but only]	
rìječju i djèlom/réčju i dèlom	in word and deed
Kònji se mjère/mère péđu, a ljúdi pàmeću. [péđ. . .pàmet in N sg.]	Horses are measured by the span, but people by intelligence.

The two instrumental forms in the last example exemplify some of the sound changes brought about by combining **-j-** with a preceding consonant. Some other examples of this type of change are:

smȑt	death	I smȑti, smȑću
ràdost	joy	I ràdosti, ràdošću
ljúbav	love	I ljúbavi, ljúbavlju

Genitive Plural of Nouns. If the stress falls on the penultimate vowel (i.e. the second from the end) of a G pl. noun (not **i**- stems), the vowel is usually lengthened:

G sg.	kònja	horse	G pl.	kónja
	ìmena	name		iména
	prìjatelja	friend		prijatélja

Consonant clusters of the word stem (except **i**-stem words) are often broken up by the insertion of **-a-**:

N sg.	stùdent, student	sèdlo, saddle	djèvojka/dèvojka, girl
G sg.	studenta	sedla	djevojke/devojke
N pl.	studenti	sedla	djevojke/devojke
G pl.	studenata	sedála	djevojaka/devojaka

Some exceptions, a few nouns not of the **i**-declension, have their genitive plural forms in **-i**:

N sg.	čòvjek/čòvek, person	mjèsec/mèsec, month	cŕv, worm
G sg.	čovjeka/čoveka	mjeseca/meseca	crva
N pl.	ljúdi, people	mjèseci/mèseci	cŕvi
G pl.	ljudi	mjeséci/meséci	crvi

N sg.	mráv, ant	sát, hour
G sg.	mrava	sata
N pl.	mrávi	sáti, sátovi
G pl.	mravi	sati, satova

Several nouns have genitive plural forms in **-u** or **iju,** although variant "regular" forms in **-a** also occur:

N sg.	nòga, leg	rúka, hand	pȑst, finger	òko, eye	ùho, ear
G sg.	noge	ruke	prsta	oka	uha
N pl.	nòge	rúke	pȑsti	òči	ùši
G pl.	nògu, nóga	rùku, rúka	pȑstiju, pȑsta	očiju	ušiju

Plural Stems in **-ov-/-ev-.** A number of masculine nouns (whose N sg. forms are usually one syllable in length) have plural stems enlarged by **-ov-** or **-ev-: grad,** "city," and **panj,** "tree-stump," will be used as examples:

	singular		*plural*	
N	grád	pánj	gràdovi	pánjevi
V	grade	panju	gradovi	panjevi
A	grad	panj	gradove	panjeve
G	grada	panja	gradova	panjeva
D	gradu	panju	gradovima	panjevima
I	gradom	panjem	gradovima	panjevima

Other nouns like **grad** are: **bór,** pine; **brìjeg/brég,** hill; **cvìjet/cvét,** flower; **dvór,** court; **plód,** fruit; **plùg,** plow; **rád,** work; **sin,** son; **sòm,** sheath-fish; **stól/stó,** table; **vìjek/vék,** century; **vrát,** neck; and **zid,** wall.

Nouns like **panj** are these: **brój,** number; **gròš,** small coin; **kljúč,** key; **kòš,** creel; **kȑš,** rocky soil; **lèš,** corpse; **màč,** sword; **mìš,** mouse; **múž,** husband; **nóž,** knife; **púž,** snail; and **žúlj,** blister.

Some nouns may occur either with or without the **-ov-/-ev-** extension. A few examples of this type are: **gòlub,** pigeon: **gòlubi, gòlubovi; slùčaj,** incident : **slùčaji, slùčajevi; sòkol/sòko,** falcon : **sòkoli, sòkolovi; znák,** sign : **znáci, znákovi; zrák,** air (Cr.), ray (S.) : **zráci, zrákovi.**

Neuter Nouns in **-men-.** Several neuter nouns with stems in **-men-** have special forms with a shorter stem and the ending **-e** in the N and A singular. A familiar example is **ime,** "name":

	singular	*plural*
N	ìme	imèna
V	ime	imèna
A	ime	imèna
G	imena	iména
D	imenu	imènima
I	imenom	imènima

Other such neuter nouns are: **brème,** burden; **plème,** tribe; **prèzime,** family name (NA pl. **prèzimena**); **ràme,** shoulder; **sjème/sème,** seed; **sljème/slème,** peak; **tjème/tème,** top; **vìme,** udder; **vrijème/vréme,** time.

mati *and* **kći.** Two feminine nouns, **mati,** "mother," and **kći,** "daughter," have a stem in **-er-** in most of the case forms. The case endings of **mati** are like those of the noun **žena,** while those of **kći** are like those of **stvar:**

	singular	*plural*	*singular*	*plural*
N	màti	màtere	kćí	kćèri
V	mati	matere	kćèri	kćeri
A	mater	matere	kćér	kćeri
G	matere	matera	kćèri	kćeri
D	materi	materama	kćèri	kćerima
I	materom	materama	kćérju, kćèri	kćerima

čovjek/čovek : ljudi. The noun **čovjek/čovek,** "man, human being, person," has only singular forms; plural forms are provided by the stem **ljud-:**

	singular		*plural*
	ijek.	ek.	
N	čòvjek	čòvek	ljúdi
V	čovječe	čoveče	ljudi
A	čovjeka	čoveka	ljude
G	čovjeka	čoveka	ljudi
D	čovjeku	čoveku	ljudima
I	čovjekom	čovekom	ljudima

Masculine Nouns in **-in.** The category of masculine nouns indicating nationality or place of origin has a N sg. ending of **-in** (**-janin**). In the plural the **-in** element is dropped:

N sg.	Sȑbin, Serb	Beògrađanin, resident of Belgrade	Zágrepčanin, resident of Zagreb
G sg.	Srbina	Beograđanina	Zagrepčanina
N pl.	Srbi	Beograđani	Zagrepčani
G pl.	Srba	Beograđana	Zagrepčana

Plurals of **brat, gospodin, dijete/dete.** The plural forms of **bràt,** "brother," **gospòdin,** "mister, sir," and **dijète/déte,** "child," are provided by the feminine collective nouns **bràća, gospòda,** and **djèca/dèca.** These are singular nouns with plural (collective) meanings. Adjectives used with them have the appropriate feminine singular form, but associated verbs have a plural form:

Stàrija bràća dòlaze.	The older brothers are coming.
Bràća su dòšla.	The brothers have arrived.

Since these nouns are, in form, like the type **žena,** their vocatives would end in **-o** like **ženo;** thus, **bràćo,** "brothers!" **djèco/dèco,** "children!" **gòspodo,** "Gentlemen!"

oko; uho/uvo. The singular forms of **oko,** "eye," and **uho/uvo,** "ear," are those of a regular neuter noun (e.g. **selo**). However, the plural forms have different stems, **i**-endings, and a distinctive G pl. The gender of the plural is feminine, e.g. **crne oči,** "dark eyes":

		plural		*plural*
N	(òko)	òči	(ùho/ùvo)	ùši
V		oči		uši
A		oči		uši
G		očiju, oči		ušiju, uši
D		očima		ušima
I		očima		ušima

doba. A few Cr&S nouns are indeclinable, that is, they maintain the same form in all the cases. One of the most frequently used of these nouns is **dòba,** "time, times"; its gender, as exhibited by associated adjectives, is neuter:

u svàko dòba	at any time
od ònog dòba	ever since
u svà dòba gòdine	at all seasons of the year

Neuter Nouns with Stem Extension in **-et-:**

	singular	*plural*
N	dùgme button	dùgmeta
V	dugme	dugmeta
A	dugme	dugmeta
G	dugmeta	dugmeta
D	dugmetu	dugmetima
I	dugmetom	dugmetima

Similarly declined are **kùbe,** G **kùbeta,** "dome"; **tùce,** G **tùceta,** "dozen"; **táne,** G **táneta,** "bullet"; **úže,** G **úžeta,** "rope." **dȑvo,** "tree, wood," has a singular in **-et-** (G **dȑveta**), but it has a regular neuter plural (NA **dȑva,** G **dŕva,** . . .) for the meaning "wood, firewood" and a plural as above for the meaning "woods, trees," e.g. NA **drvèta.*** **jáje,** "egg," has a regular neuter singular (G **jája**) or one like **dugme** (G **jàjeta**), but its plural follows the regular neuter pattern, i.e. NA **jája,** G **jája.**

Feminine Collective Nouns in **-ad.** A number of the nouns with the neuter **-et-** formation in the singular (**pìle,** G **pìleta,** "chicken"; **práse,** G **pràseta,** "pig"; **tèle,** G **tèleta,** "calf"; **mòmče,** G **mòmčeta,** "men, crew") employ a feminine collective noun in **-ad** to express the plural (**pìlad, pràsad, tèlad, mòmčad**). This type of collective noun is declined like **stvar,** except that it has alternate instrumental forms in **-ma, -ima:**

NA	pìlad, chickens	pràsad, swine	tèlad, calves	mòmčad, men, team
GD	piladi	prasadi	teladi	momčadi
I	piladi, piladma, piladima	prasadi, prasadma, -dima	teladi, teladma, -dima	momčadi, momčadma, -dima

Some of these nouns have alternate plural formations that vary like masculine plural nouns (**pìlići, pràsci, tèlići**). The collectives in **-ad** are feminine singular, though associated verb forms are usually in the plural, with the exception of **momčad,** which is usually accompanied by singular forms:

Mláda mòmčad je dòšla.	The young people have come.
Mláda pràsad su stìgla.	The young pigs have arrived.

Masculine Words in **-a.** As pointed out above, nouns with a N sg. ending in **a** are feminine in gender, e.g. **žena,** "woman," **knjìga,** "book." There are, however, exceptions since a number of masculine nouns have a N sg. ending in **a** and indeed are declined exactly like **žena** and similar nouns. Such exceptions are nouns like **slúga,** "servant," **vòđa,** "leader," **prìstaša,** "follower," or **Vása** (a man's name). Adjectives and verbs in agreement with such nouns in the singular have the appropriate masculine endings:

Gáj je bìo nájbolji vòđa hr̀vatskog národa.	Gaj was the best leader of the Croatian people.
Já sam vàš vjèrni/vèrni slúga, izjávio je dìktator.	"I am your faithful servant," the dictator declared.
Trážimo mládog Vásu Pètrovića.	We're looking for young Vasa Petrović.

In the plural, associated forms have feminine endings:

	Nàš stári slúga je dòšao.	Our old servant has arrived.
[but]	Nàše stáre slúge su dòšle.	Our old servants have arrived.

Nouns of Variable Gender. Certain nouns in **-a** can be either masculine or feminine, depending on the speaker's intention. Such nouns are:

***dr̀veće,** "trees," is a collective noun, neuter singular.

muštèrija, "customer, clientele," **pròpalica,** "a dissolute person," **pìjanica,** "drunkard," **prìstalica,** "a follower." Thus:

Ón je vèliki pìjanica.	He's a big drunkard.
Òna je vèlika pìjanica.	She's a big drunkard.

Croatian and Serbian Names. Serbs and Croats normally use only two names: **ìme,** "name, first name," and **prèzime,** "last name, family name, surname." Thus, a brother and sister, or husband and wife, might have the following names:

Bòžidar Filìpović Dàrinka Filìpović

While the first names are distinctive for men and women, the last name is the same for both. This last or family name is declined only when it indicates a male:

Vìdim Bòžidara Filìpovića.	I see Božidar Filipović.
[but] Vìdim Dàrinku Filìpović.	I see Darinka Filipović.

The **prezime,** or family name, is similar in origin to that of many English names: some indicate an ancestral occupation, e.g. **Kòlar,** "Wheelwright, Cartwright," **Kòvač,** "Blacksmith, Smith"; others originated in nicknames, e.g. **Ćósić** from **ćóso,** "a beardless person"; others indicate nationality, e.g. **Sr̀bić, Hòrvatić, Bugàrski;** while the most characteristic type is that derived by means of the diminutive suffix **-ić, -ović** from first names of male ancestors. Thus:

Pètar	Peter	Pètrović [like Peterson]
Jòvan	John	Jovànović [like Johnson]
Fìlip	Philip	Filìpović [like Philips]

Adjectives — prídjevi/prídevi

The Cr&S adjective varies not only according to the case, number, and gender of an associated noun, but it has in addition a system of alternate endings for each category. Using one set of endings, the adjective has an "indefinite" meaning; using the other, it has a "definite" meaning.

indefinite		*definite*	
stàr sèljak	an old peasant	stári sèljak	the old peasant
stàra žèna	an old woman	stára žèna	the old woman
stàro sèlo	an old village	stáro sèlo	the old village

The distinction in use and meaning between the various definite and indefinite forms is becoming blurred and speakers of Cr&S mix them up, with a tendency, however, to prefer the definite type. The distinction is still clearly felt and observed in a few situations and these will be described below. The following forms will exemplify the categories of the indefinite adjective still in active use and all the categories of the definite adjective.

indefinite singular

	m	*n*	*f*
N	mlád	mládo	mláda
A	mlad, mlada*	mlado	mladu
G	mlada		mlade

As the following paradigm shows, the masculine and neuter definite forms are identical in the singular except for the N/A cases; in the plural all genders have the same form for cases other than the N/A.

definite singular

	m	*n*	*f*
N	mládi young	mládo	mláda
A	mladi, mladog(a)†	mlado	mladu
G	mladog(a)		mlade
D	mladom(e/u)‡		mladoj
I	mladim		mladom

indefinite and definite plural

	m	*n*	*f*
N	mládi	mláda	mláde
A	mlade	mlada	mlade
G	mladih		
D	mladim(a)		
I	mladim(a)		

The longer D/I pl. forms are usually used only when they occur without nouns, e.g. **s mládima,** "with the young ones."

Ending Variations for Definite Adjectives. If the base of an adjective ends in **š, ć, đ,** or **j** (e.g. **loš-i, vruć-i, tuđ-i, srednj-i, riblj-i, pasj-i, božj-i, ptičj-i**), the singular masculine and neuter forms of the definite adjective have the vowel **e** where other adjectives would have **o:**

singular (definite)

	m		*n*	
N	vrúći hot	mládi young	vrúće	mládo
A	vrući, vrućeg(a)*	mladi, mladog(a)*	vruće	mlado
G	vrućeg(a)	mladog(a)	vrućeg(a)	mladog(a)
D	vrućem(e, u)	mladom(e, u)	vrućem(e, u)	mladom(e, u)
I	vrućim	mladim	vrućim	mladim

*With animate masculine nouns.

†**mladog(a)** would be used with animate masculine nouns. Parentheses around final vowels indicate that such forms often occur without the final vowel, i.e. **mladog, mladoga; mladom, mladome; mladim, mladima.**

‡Dative sg. forms (masc. and neut.) infrequently occur with final **-u,** i.e. **mladomu,** though rarely in dative usage with the prepositions: **po, prema, pri, o, u,** and **na.**

		f
N	vrúća	mláda
A	vruću	mladu
G	vruće	mlade
D	vrućoj	mladoj
I	vrućom	mladom

From Nouns to Adjectives. Many nouns can be transformed into possessive or descriptive adjectives by the suffix **-ov/-ev** to masculine nouns ending in a consonant or **-in** to the stem of masculine and feminine nouns ending in **a:**

bràt	brother	:	bràtov kàput	brother's coat
bòb	bean	:	bòbovo zȑno	bean shoot
králj	king	:	králjev zámak	king's castle
òtac	father	:	òčev blàgoslov	father's blessing
sèstra	sister	:	sèstrina ljúbav	sister's love
bàba	old woman	:	bàbino ljeto/leto	Indian summer
slùga (masc.)	servant	:	slúgin žìvot	servant's life

Once formed, these adjectives are of the "indefinite" type.

Speakers of Cr&S tend to use adjectives such as those above (and other types, e.g. those in **-ski**) instead of a one-word genitive of possession or specification:

kàput móga bràta my brother's coat [or] bràtov kàput
[rather than] kàput bràta

Use of the Indefinite Adjective. There are two situations in which the use of the indefinite adjective is still required:

1. Predication:

Ón je dòbar.	He is good.
Žèna je mláda.	The woman is young.
Sèlo je stàro.	The village is old.

2. After the numbers 2, 3, and 4, e.g. **dvá dòbra psà,** "two good dogs," but:

Téško je lòviti bez dòbrog [definite] psà.	It's difficult to hunt without a good dog.

dobar-dobri. Though some indefinite and definite adjective forms are distinguished by vowel length, e.g. **stàra** [indefinite], **stára** [definite], the masculine forms in the nominative singular are clearly differentiated by the **i**-ending of the definite form (**mlád, mládi**). Thus, if you know the definite form, you can merely subtract the final **-i** and arrive at the indefinite form. But if you start with the definite form **dobri,** eliminating the **-i** would yield **dobr.** Since Cr&S only tolerates certain groupings of consonants at the end of words, other potential clusters are broken up by inserting the vowel **-a-.** This process results in **dòbar** alongside **dòbri, hládan** and **hládni,** "cold," **górak** and **górki,** "bitter," **mȑtav** and **mȑtvi,** "dead," etc.

Some Exceptions. Certain types of adjectives appear only with definite endings and others only with indefinite endings. The large group of adjectives ending in **-ski** is the principal representative of the "definite only" kind; e.g. **hȑvatski, sȑpski, èngleski, jùnački (junak + ski), ràtnički.** Also, comparative and superlative adjectives, e.g. **stàriji,** "older," **nájstariji,** "oldest," and number adjectives (ordinals), e.g. **pŕvi,** "first," **drùgi,** "second," etc., occur only with the definite endings.

The possessive adjectives in **-ov, -ev,** and **-in** appear only with the indefinite endings, at least in the nominative and accusative cases, e.g. **bràtov,** "brother's," **òčev,** "father's," **sèstrin,** "sister's," **njègov,** "his," **njén,** "her," **njìhov,** "their." In the other cases (including the accusative of animate masc. sg. nouns), there is a preference among many speakers of S-Cr. for the definite forms.

Pávle je čùo njègov glás.	Paul heard his [another's] voice.
Gústa šùma je bíla između njèga i njègovog [def.] progònitelja.	A dense forest was between him and his pursuer.

Comparison of Adjectives — komparácija prídjeva/prídeva

In comparing people or things, a speaker may say that one person is "bigger" than another, that a certain object is "more expensive" than another object. These words of comparison, "bigger," "more expensive," are called comparative adjectives, and in Cr&S they are derived from "positive" adjectives ("good," "expensive") in one of the following ways:

1. By adding **-iji (-ije** [neut.], **-ija** [fem.], etc.) to the masculine indefinite form:

stàr	old	:	stàriji, stàrije, stàrija	older
pȑljav	dirty	:	prljàviji, prljàvije, prljàvija	dirtier

2. By adding **-ji** to the masculine indefinite form. (The addition of **-j-** alters a preceding consonant or consonants, as detailed in the section on Sound Patterns, Consonant plus **-j-.)**

drág	dear	:	dràži	dearer
mlád	young	:	mlàđi	younger

3. Three adjectives form their comparatives by adding **-ši (-še, ša):**

lìjep/lèp	beautiful	:	ljèpši/lèpši	more beautiful
làk	easy, light	:	làkši	easier
mèk	soft	:	mèkši	softer

4. A few adjectives have comparatives based on other word stems:

dòbar	good	:	bòlji	better

zào	evil	:	gòri	worse
vèlik	big	:	vèći	bigger
máli	little	:	mànji	smaller

5. The analytic comparative (see below).

Use of Comparative Adjectives. Comparative adjectives may be used like other adjectives, e.g. **on je star, ali ona je starija,** or **to je dobro, ali ovo je bolje.** However, to make a comparison (in the same clause) between two or more persons or things, use:

1. Either **nego** or **no** (higher style) with both objects of comparison having the same case:

Vàši kònji su br̀ži nego mòji [kònji].	Your horses are faster than mine [horses].
I túžan žìvot je bòlji no smr̀t.	Even a sad life is better than death.

2. Or **od** with the second object of comparison in the genitive case:

Vàši kònji su br̀ži od mòjih [kónja].	
Mój bràt je vèći od mene. [or] Mòj bràt je vèći nego já.	My brother is bigger than I.

Superlative Adjectives **sùperlativ**

A superlative adjective (e.g. "the biggest," "the most expensive") is formed simply by prefixing **náj-** to a comparative adjective.

dòbar	good	:	bòlji	better	:	nájbolji	best
pòšten	honest	:	poštèniji	more honest	:	nájpoštèniji	most honest

Analytic Comparative. Speakers of Cr&S sometimes use the analytic comparative, particularly with indeclinable (nonchanging) adjectives, e.g. **fer,** "fair," those in **-čki** and **-ski,** e.g. **šovinistički,** "chauvinistic," **reakcionarski,** "reactionary," and certain others, such as **tuđ,** "foreign." This type of comparison maintains the basic adjective and effects the comparison by adding either the adverbial form **više,** "more," or **manje,** "less." With the latter form a comparison "downward" is possible, e.g. "less foreign," "less expensive."

U ìgri je Márko vìše fér od Mìlana.	In a game Marko is fairer than Milan.
Mìlan mi je mànje túđ nego prìje/prè.	Milan is (seems) less strange to me than before.
Àlbanija je vìše plàninska zèmlja nego Jugoslávija.	Albania is a more mountainous country than Yugoslavia.
Njègove nòvije knjìge su mànje šovinìstičke od rànijih.	His more recent books are less chauvinistic than his earlier ones.

An analytic superlative is also possible with such forms as **nájviše** or **nájvećma,** "most," and **nájmanje,** "least." Thus:

Tá zèmlja je nájmanje razvìjena na tóm kontìnentu.	That country is the least developed on that continent.

Adjectives in Common Use A list of frequently used adjectives and their comparative forms is presented below. After the English entry the first form is the masculine nominative singular of the indefinite adjective, then the definite form, and finally the comparative form or forms. Thus, "wet," **mòkar-mòkri, mòkriji.** Other forms of the "positive" adjective can be derived from the masculine definite form, e.g. **mokr-i, mokr-a, mokr-o.**

	positive form	*comparative form*
alive	žív-žívi	žìvlji
angry	ljút-ljúti	ljùći
bad	lòš-lòši, r̀đav-r̀đavi	gòri
beautiful	lìjep-lìjepi/lép-lépi	ljèpši/lèpši
big	vèlik-vèliki	vèći
bitter	górak-górki	gòrči
black	cŕn-cŕni	cr̀nji
blonde, blue	pláv-plávi	plàvlji
blue, blonde	pláv-plávi	plàvlji
blue (dark)	mòdar-mòdri	mòdriji
brave	hrábar-hrábri	hràbriji
brown	smèđ-smèđi	vìše smèđ
calm	míran-mírni	mìrniji
cheap	jèftin-jèftini	jeftìniji
clean	čìst-čìsti	čìšći, čìstiji
close	blìzak-blìski	blìži
cold	hládan-hládni	hlàdniji
crooked	krív-krívi	krìvlji
dark	táman-támni	tàmniji
dead	mr̀tav-mr̀tvi	mr̀tviji
deep	dùbok-dùboki	dùblji
dense, solid	gúst-gústi	gùšći
difficult	téžak-téški	tèži
dirty	pr̀ljav-pr̀ljavi	prljàviji
dry	súh-súhi/súv-súvi	sùši/sùvlji
dull	túp-túpi	tùplji
easy, light	làk-làki	làkši
empty	prázan-prázni	prázniji
expensive	skúp-skúpi	skùplji
far	dàlek-dàleki	dàlji
fast	bŕz-bŕzi	br̀ži

fat	dèbeo-dèbeli	dèblji
fearful	stràšljiv-stràšljivi	strašljìviji
full	pùn-pùni	pùniji
gay	vèseo-vèseli	vesèliji
gentle	blág-blági	blàži
good	dòbar-dòbri	bòlji
gray	sìv-sìvi	sìvlji
gray-haired	sìjed-sìjedi/séd-sédi	sjèđi/sèđi
green	zèlen-zèleni	zelèniji
guilty	krív-krívi	krìvlji
happy	srètan-srètni/srèćan-srèćni	srètniji/srèćniji
hard	tvŕd-tvŕdi	tvȑđi
high, tall	vìsok-vìsoki	vìši, visòčiji
hot	vrúć-vrúći	vrùći
humble	kròtak-kròtki	kròtkiji
hungry	gládan-gládni	glàdniji
innocent	pràv-právi	pràviji
intelligent	pàmetan-pàmetni	pamètniji
light	svijètao-svìjetli/svétao-svétli	svjètliji/svètliji
little	máli, màlen	mànji
long	dùg-dùgi	dùlji, dùži
low	nìzak-nìski	nìži
narrow	ùzak-ùski	ùži
old	stàr-stári	stàriji
poor	siròmašan-siròmašni	siromàšniji
proud	pònosan-pònosni	ponòsniji
red	cȑven-cȑveni	crvèniji
rich	bògat-bògati	bogàtiji
roomy	pròstran-pròstrani	prostràniji
rough	grúb-grúbi	grùblji
sad	túžan-túžni	tùžniji
salty	slán-sláni	slàniji, slànji
satiated	sìt-sìti	sìtiji
shallow	plítak-plítki	plìći
sharp	òštar-òštri	òštriji
short	kràtak-kràtki	kràći
slim	tànak-tànki	tànji
slow	spòr-spòri	spòriji
smart	pàmetan-pàmetni	pamètniji
smooth	glàdak-glàtki	glàđi
solid, dense	gúst-gústi	gùšći
sour	kìseo-kìseli	kisèliji
stern	sùrov-sùrovi	suròviji
straight, innocent	pràv-právi	pràviji

strong	ják-jáki	jàči
stupid	glúp-glúpi	glùplji
sweet	slàdak-slàtki	slàđi
tall, high	vìsok-vìsoki	vìši, visòčiji
thin	mr̀šav-mr̀šavi	mršàviji
thin [liquid]	žídak-žítki	žìtkiji
thirsty	žédan-žédni	žèdniji
tight	tijèsan-tìjesni/tésan-tésni	tjèšnji/tèšnji
ugly	òdvratan-òdvratni	odvràtniji
unhappy	jàdan-jàdni	jàdniji
weak	slàb-slàbi	slàbiji
wet	mòkar-mòkri	mòkriji
white	bìjel-bìjeli/bèo-béli	bjèlji/bèlji
wide	širok-široki	šìri
yellow	žút-žúti	žùći
young	mlád-mládi	mlàđi

Forming Adverbs — prílozi

Adverbs may be formed from adjectives in one of the following ways:
1. By using the neuter sg. (NA) form of the adjective:
   dòbar, *dòbro,* dòbra : Ón *dòbro* píše. He writes well.
2. By taking the masculine sg. nominative form of an adjective in **-ski:**
   hr̀vatski, hr̀vatsko, hr̀vatska : Ón gòvori *hr̀vatski.* He speaks Croatian.
   sr̀pski, sr̀psko, sr̀pska : Òni čìtaju *sr̀pski.* They read Serbian.

Possessive Adjectives. The following three phrases will provide a rapid survey of Cr&S possessive adjectives:

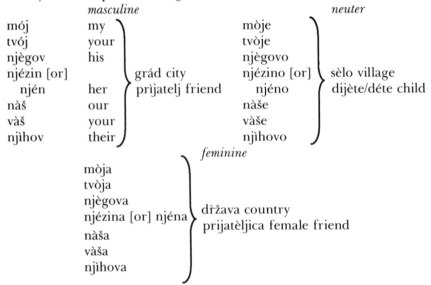

	masculine			*neuter*
mój	my	grád city	mòje	sèlo village
tvój	your	prìjatelj friend	tvòje	dijète/déte child
njègov	his		njègovo	
njézin [or] njén	her		njézino [or] njéno	
nàš	our		nàše	
vàš	your		vàše	
njìhov	their		njìhovo	

feminine

mòja
tvòja
njègova
njézina [or] njéna
nàša
vàša
njìhova
} dr̀žava country, prijatèljica female friend

Of the several possessive adjectives, only three need be selected as representative of the basic types. Thus, the forms of **moj** below will also represent those of **tvoj** and **svoj** "one's own," **naš** will also serve for **vaš,** while **njezin, njen,** and **njihov** will be represented by **njegov.**

mój, "my, mine" (so also **tvój,** "your," **svój,** "one's own")

	singular m	*n*	*f*	*plural m*	*n*	*f*
N	mój	mòje	mòja	mòji	mòja	mòje
A	mój, mòjeg(a),* móg(a)*	mòje	mòju	moje	moja	moje
G	mòjeg(a), móg(a)		mòje	mojih		
D	mòjem(u), móm(u/e)		mòjoj	mojim(a)		
I	mòjim		mòjom	mojim(a)		

nàš, "our" (so also **vàš,** "your"):

	singular m	*n*	*f*	*plural m*	*n*	*f*
N	nàš	nàše	nàša	nàši	nàša	nàše
A	naš, našeg(a)*	naše	našu	naše	naša	naše
G	našeg(a)		naše	naših		
D	našem(u)		našoj	našim(a)		
I	našim		našom	našim(a)		

njègov, "his, its" (so also **njézin** or **njén,** "her, its," and **njìhov,** "their"):

	singular m	*n*	*f*	*plural m*	*n*	*f*
N	njègov	njègovo	njègova	njègovi	njègova	njègove
A	njegov, njegova,* njegovog(a)*	njegovo	njegovu	njegove	njegova	njegove
G	njegova, njegovog(a)		njegove	njegovih		
D	njegovu, njegovom(e)		njegovoj	njegovim(a)		
I	njegovim		njegovom	njegovim(a)		

The Possessive Adjective **svoj. Svoj** and its related forms have the general meaning of possession, i.e., "one's own," with the possessor being specified by a nominative noun or pronoun in the same clause. Thus, "one's own" may be particularized as "my own, my," "your own, your," "our own, our," "his own, his," "her own, hers,""its own, its," and "their own, their." Cr&S always distinguishes between "his own" and "his" (i.e. another person's), "her own" and "her" (i.e. another person's), etc. This distinction is optional in English since "his" can mean "his own" or "his" (another person's).

Já trážim *svòju* knjìgu. Tí trážiš *mòju* knjìgu.

*With animate masculine nouns.

I'm looking for my (own) book.		You're looking for my book.	
Ti tražiš *svoju* knjigu.	your (own) book	Ja tražim *tvoju* knjigu.	your book
Ona traži *svoju* knjigu.	her (own) book	On traži *njenu* knjigu.	her book
Mi tražimo *svoje* knjige.	our (own) books	Vi tražite *naše* knjige.	our books
Vi tražite *svoje* knjige.	your (own) books	Mi tražimo *vaše* knjige.	your books
Oni traže *svoje* knjige.	their (own) books	Oni traže *njihove* knjige.	their books

Notice that **svoj** denotes possession in reference to the noun with which it agrees, e.g. **svoju knjigu, svoje knjige,** while the possessor is indicated by the pronoun or noun in the nominative case, e.g. **ja . . . svoju knjigu.** In the examples on the right-hand side of the page, the possessor or possessors are denoted as persons other than the subject-actor(s), e.g. **on . . . njenu knjigu.** The following examples will contrast **njegov,** "his," and **svoj,** "his own":

Pùkovnik Krìstijan Bárutanski, gospòdar Blìtve, mìslio je o sèbi, o *svóm* pòložaju . . .	Colonel Christian Barutanski, ruler of Blitva, thought about himself, about *his* (own) position . . . [Krleža]
Što je s *njègovom* žènom?	What about his wife?

kòji, "which, who" (similarly **čìji,** "whose"):

	singular			*plural*		
	m	*n*	*f*	*m*	*n*	*f*
N	kòji	kòje	kòja	kòji	kòja	kòje
A	kòji, kòjeg(a),* kóg(a)*	kòje	koju	koje	koja	koje
G	kòjeg(a), kóg(a)		koje	kojih		
D	kòjemu, kóm(u/e)		kojoj	kojim(a)		
I	kòjim, kìm		kojom	kojim(a)		

kàkav, "what kind of":

	singular			*plural*		
	m	*n*	*f*	*m*	*n*	*f*
N	kàkav	kàkvo	kàkva	kàkvi	kàkva	kàkve
A	kakav, kakva,* kakvog(a)*	kakvo	kakvu	kakve	kakva	kakve

*With animate masculine nouns.

G	kakva, kakvog(a)	kakve	kakvih
D	kakvu, kakvom(e)	kakvoj	kakvim(a)
I	kakvim	kakvom	kakvim(a)

The forms for **kakav** above are patterned after those of the "indefinite adjective," but forms with "definite" endings are often used, e.g. G sg. **kakvog(a),** D sg. **kakvom(e).**

ovaj; taj; onaj. The demonstrative adjectives **òvaj,** "this, this one," **táj,** "that, that one," and **ònaj,** "that one there," have similar form variations; **taj** and its forms will serve as models for all three:

	singular			*plural*		
	m	*n*	*f*	*m*	*n*	*f*
N	táj	tó	tá	tí	tá	té
A	táj, tòg(a)*	tó	tu	té	tá	té
G	tòg(a)		te	tíh		
D	tòm(u/e)		toj	tìma, tím		
I	tím(e)		tom	tìma, tím		

sàv, "all, entire":

	singular			*plural*		
	m	*n*	*f*	*m*	*n*	*f*
N	sàv	svè	svà	svì	svà	svè
A	sàv, svèga**	svè	svù	svè	svà	svè
G	svèga		své	svíh, svíju		
D	svèm(u)		svój	svím(a)		
I	svím(e)		svóm	svím(a)		

"who" and "what":

N	tkò (Cr.), **kò** (S.) who	štò, štà (S.) what
A	kòg(a)	štò, štà (S.)
G	kòg(a)	čèg(a)
D	kòm(u/e)	čèm(u)
I	kím(e)	čím(e)

In the Serbian variant **šta** is used in questions while **što** is used in relative clauses, e.g. **Štà rádiš?** "What are you doing? but **Primétila sam hàljinu štò si jùče kúpila,** "I noticed the dress that you bought yesterday." In both situations the Croatian variant uses **što.**

Personal Pronouns — lične zámjenice/zámenice

N	já I	tí you[sg.]	mí we	ví you[pl.]	— -self
A	mène, me	tèbe, te	nás, nas	vás, vas	sèbe, se

*With animate masculine nouns.

G	mène, me	tèbe, te	nás, nas	vás, vas	sèbe
D	mèni, mi	tèbi, ti	nàma, nam	vàma, vam	sèbi, si*
I	mnóm(e)	tòbom	náma	váma	sòbom

	m	*n*	*f*	*m*	*n*	*f*
N	**ón** he, it**	**òno** it	**òna** she, it**	**òni** they	**òna** they	**òne** they
A	njèga, ga, nj		njú, ju, je	njíh, ih		
G	njèga, ga		njé, je	njíh, ih		
D	njèmu, mu		njój, joj	njìma, im		
I	njím(e)		njóm(e)	njìma		

Using Personal Pronouns. As indicated above, there are alternate forms for the instrumental case of three of the personal pronouns, while all of the pronouns have at least two possible forms in three cases: the accusative, the genitive, and the dative.

The choice of the form for the alternation in the instrumental case is as follows: the shorter form (**mnom, njim, njom**) is usually selected for use after prepositions, while the longer form (**mnome, njime, njome**) usually appears in the instrumental usage without prepositions:

Dòšao je sa njóm.	He came with her.
Ožènio se njóme.	He married her.

In the three cases mentioned (A, G, D), the various forms are distinguished by the presence or absence of an accent. The accented forms are used in initial position, after prepositions, or when emphasis is desired:

Meni se svíđa/dòpada kòmad. [but]	I like the play [the play is pleasing to me].
Kòmad *mi* se svíđa/dòpada.	I like the play
Kòmad se svíđa/dòpada *mèni,* a ne Márku.	I like the play, but Marko doesn't.
Čujem *ga.*	I hear 'im.
Čujem *njega.*	I hear him.
Okrénuo se *k mèni.*	He turned around toward me.
Stànujemo *kod njíh.*	We're staying at their place.
Prímio sam písmo *od njé.*	I received a letter from her.

There are, however, four unaccented forms (**me, te, se, nj**), which may occur after prepositions in the accusative usage:

Ne sŕdi se *ná me!*	Don't be angry at me!

*This form, frowned upon by Yugoslav grammarians, occurs frequently in the speech of Croats in and around Zagreb.

"it" would usually be used in English when referring to inanimate nouns, which might be "masculine" or "feminine" in Cr&S; e.g. **grad, "city," **knjìga,** "book." **òno** could be translated as "he, she," when referring to an animate "neuter," e.g. **dijète/déte,** "child."

Ùzdaj se *ú se!*	Rely upon yourself!
Òna će stàviti hránu *prèda te.*	She'll place the food in front of you.
Rastvòrite kìšobran *nàda nj!*	Open the umbrella over him!

The accented forms (**mène, sèbe, tèbe, njèga**) could also be used in the above examples.

The pronoun **òna** has two unaccented forms in the accusative: **je** and **ju.** Use the form **je,** except where it might occur next to the verb form **je,** "is"; then select **ju** as the pronoun form to avoid any ambiguity:

Já sam je vìdio/vìdeo.	I saw her.
[but] Ón ju je vìdio/vìdeo.	He saw her.

Numbers **bròjevi**

Cardinal numbers (**òsnovi bròjevi**): Ordinal numbers (**rédni bròjevi**):

0	nùla		
1	jèdan (masc.), jèdno (neut.), jèdna (fem.)	pŕvi (masc.), pŕvo (neut.), pŕva (fem.)	1st
2	dvá (masc., neut.), dvìje/dvé (fem.)	drùgi, drùgo, drùga	2nd
3	trí	trèći	3rd
4	čètiri	čètvrti	4th
5	pét	péti	5th
6	šést	šésti	6th
7	sèdam	sédmi	7th
8	òsam	ósmi	8th
9	dèvet	dèveti	9th
10	dèset	dèseti	10th
11	jedànaest	jedànaesti	11th
12	dvánaest	dvánaesti	12th
13	trínaest	trínaesti	13th
14	četr̀naest	četr̀naesti	14th
15	pètnaest	pètnaesti	15th
16	šèsnaest	šèsnaesti	16th
17	sedàmnaest	sedàmnaesti	17th
18	osàmnaest	osàmnaesti	18th
19	devètnaest	devètnaesti	19th
20	dvádeset	dvádeseti	20th
21	dvádeset i jèdan/jèdno jèdna	dvádeset i pŕvi/pŕvo pŕva	21st
22	dvádeset i dvá, dvádeset i dvìje/dvé	dvádeset i drùgi/drùgo/drùga	22nd

23	dvádeset i trí	dvádeset i trèći/trèće/ trèća	23rd
30	trídeset	trídeseti	30th
37	trídeset i sèdam	trídeset i sédmi/ sédmo/sédma	37th
40	četrdèset	četrdèseti	40th
50	pedèset	pedèseti	50th
60	šezdèset	šezdèseti	60th
70	sedamdèset	sedamdèseti	70th
80	osamdèset	osamdèseti	80th
90	devedèset	devedèseti	90th
100	stó, stòtina	stóti, stótiniti	100th
200	dvjèsta/dvèsta, dvìje/ dvé stòtine	dvjèstoti/dvèstoti	200th
300	trìsta, trí stòtine	trístoti	300th
400	čètiri stòtine, čètiristo	čètiristóti	400th
500	pét stòtina, pétsto	pétstoti	500th
600	šést stòtina, šéststo	šéstoti	600th
700	sèdam stòtina, sèdamsto	sèdamstoti	700th
800	òsam stòtina, òsamsto	òsamstoti	800th
900	dèvet stòtina, dèvetsto	dèvetstóti	900th
1,000	tìsuća (Cr.) hìljada (S.)	tìsući, tìsućni (Cr.), hìljaditi (S.)	1,000th
3,000	trí tìsuće, trí hìljade	trítisući (Cr.) tríhiljaditi (S.)	3,000th
5,000	pét tìsuća, pét hìljada	pétisući/ péthiljaditi	5,000th
1,000,000	milìjun (Cr.), milìon (S.)	milìjunti (Cr.), milìoniti (S.)	millionth
1,000,000,000	milìjarda	milìjarditi	billionth

jèdan/jèdno/jèdna. The Cr&S word for *one* is an adjective and thus it agrees in number, case, and gender with the noun it defines:

Ùčenik je ìmao sàmo jèdnu knjìgu. The schoolboy had only one book.
Jèdan za svè, svì za jèdnoga. One [person] for all, all for one.

jedan is used commonly in the meaning of "a, an":

Vòlio/Vòleo bih kúpiti jèdan dòbar šèšir. I'd like to buy a good hat.

Plural forms of this adjective are used:

1. In the meaning of "one" with plural nouns that have a singular meaning:

   U sòbi su sàmo jèdna vráta. [neut. pl.] There's only one door in the room.

2. In the meaning of "some":

Jèdni spávaju, a jèdni čìtaju.	Some are sleeping, and some are reading.

3. In the meaning of "same, the same":

Ùčili su iz jèdnih knjíga.	They studied from the same books.

In certain coarse or affectionate expressions (facial expression and intonation indicate which), the word **jedan** has the meaning "you" and appears after a noun in the vocative case.

Práse jèdno!	You pig!
Màgarče jèdan!	You donkey!

dvá, trí, čètiri. The numbers "two, three, four" are unusual in that they are followed by the indefinite forms of the adjective and by a masculine noun in the genitive singular or a feminine noun in the nominative plural:

Dvá mláda stùdenta vas čèkaju.	Two young students are waiting for you.
Dvìje/Dvé mláde žène vas čèkaju.	Two young women are waiting for you.
Svàko ljùdsko bíće ìma dvìje/dvé rúke.	Every human being has two arms.
Pròšao sam čètiri sèla.	I passed four villages.
Trážim trí jáka rádnika.	I'm looking for three strong workers.

When these numbers serve as subject, the verb is usually in the plural and in the neuter plural in the past tense, e.g. **Dvá su mláda stùdenta čèkala,** "Two young students were waiting." **òba, òbje/òbe,** "both," and **òbadva, òbadvije/òbadve,** also meaning "both," function in the same manner as **dvá, dvìje/dvé:**

dvá prózora	two windows	òba prózora	both windows
dvá sèla	two villages	òbadva sèla	both villages
dvìje/dvé rúke	two arms	òbje/òbe rúke	both arms

The numbers **dva, dvije/dve, oba, obje/obe, tri,** and **četiri** have special forms for the various cases, but they are seldom used in speech. The complete paradigms are:

	m., n.	*m., n.*	*f.(ijek.)*	*f.(ijek.)*
N/A	dvá	òba	dvìje	òbje
G	dváju	obáju	dvíju	obíju
D/I	dvàma	obéma	dvjèma	objèma
	f.(ek.)	*f.(ek.)*	*m., n., f.*	*m., n., f*
N/A	dvé	òbe	trí	čètiri

G	dvéju	obéju	tríju	četiríju
D/I	dvèma	obéma	tríma	čètirma

Té trèšnje prìpadaju òvim dvjèma/dvèma sèljankama.	Those cherries belong to these two village women.

But normally the number forms **dva, tri, četiri** do not change, especially after prepositions.

Nèprijatelji su nas opkòlili sa trí stráne.	The enemies besieged us from three sides.

From 5 to 99. All the rest of the numbers, from 5 on up, are unchangeable and are followed by adjectives and nouns in the genitive plural. Exceptions would be those compound numbers that have 1, 2, 3, or 4 as their last component.

pét šìrokih prózora	five wide windows
dvádeset šìrokih prózora	twenty wide windows
[but]	
dvádeset dvá šìroka prózora	twenty-two wide windows
tìsuća/hìljada i jèdan prózor	a thousand and one windows

When the numbers 5 through 99 serve as subject, the verb is in the singular and neuter in the past tense, e.g. **Pét je mládih stùdenata čèkalo,** "Five young students were waiting."

stòtina, tìsuća/hìljada. These Cr&S words for 100 and 1,000 are feminine nouns and, when used separately, would vary like **kuća,** "house"; so also the word denoting a billion, **milìjarda.** The word for a million (**milìjun/milìon**) is a masculine noun, like **jèlen,** "deer."

Ón je jèdan od tìsuće/hìljade.	He's one in a thousand.

When used after other numbers, they appear in the nominative plural or genitive plural, depending on the number, that is N pl. after 2, 3, 4 and G pl. after 5 and above.

U strášnim bòrbama jugoslòvenski dobrovóljci izgùbili su sèdam stòtina šezdèset mr̀tvih i šést hìljada dvé stòtine pedèset rànjenih ljúdi.	In terrific battles [against the Bulgarians, 1916] the Yugoslav volunteers lost 760 dead and 6,250 wounded. [Ćorović]

Collective Number Nouns. There are two types of nouns, derived from the cardinal numbers, which express a collective meaning, that is, they indicate a group of two, or three, etc.

1. Nouns in **-òrica(-òjica** in two formations). These feminine nouns are declined like **žena** and are used only in counting *male humans,* e.g. **četvòrica momáka,** "four lads," **desetòrica stùdenata,** "ten stu-

dents." The nouns following (i.e. that being counted) are always in the G plural, as indicated in the preceding examples and in this example: **Ìmam sàstanak s petòricom písaca,** "I have a meeting with five writers." Pronouns with such collective nouns are in the G case and precede the number, e.g. **vás dvòjica,** "you two," **njíh šestòrica,** "the six of them," except in the D or I case, where the pronoun is in the same case as the noun, e.g. **o nàma tròjici,** "about the three of us." The more common cardinal numbers can, of course, be used instead of these collectives, e.g. **čètiri mòmka** or **četvòrica momáka,** "four lads."

The verb in agreement would be plural or neuter plural in the past tense, e.g. **četvòrica su stùdenata čèkala,** "Four students were waiting." Here are some of these collective numbers; in a compound number (see "twenty-eight" below), only the last element is a collective noun.

dvòjica	two (i.e. duo, twosome)	osmòrica	eight
		devetòrica	nine
tròjica	three	desetòrica	ten
četvòrica	four	dvadeset i osmòrica	twenty-eight
petòrica	five	pedesetòrica	fifty
šestòrica	six	devedesetòrica	ninety
sedmòrica	seven		

2. Number nouns in **-oro** or **-ero.** These neuter nouns, rarely declined, are collectives used for counting groups of mixed humans (men, women, children) or mixed (as to sex and age) animals; the suffix is optionally either **-oro** or **-ero**, with two exceptions. Some examples are: **Njíh je tròje òtišlo u Lòndon,** "The three of them [e.g. father, mother, and son] went to London." Note that the verb is neuter singular.* Some of these collective numbers for mixed groups are:

dvòje	two	sèdmoro, sèdmero	seven
òboje	both	òsmoro, ósmero	eight
tròje	three	dèvetoro, dèvetero	nine
čètvoro, čètvero	four	dèsetoro, dèsetero	ten
pètoro, pètero	five	pedèset i òsmoro (*or* òsmero)	fifty-eight
šèstoro, šèstero	six	devedèsetoro, devedèsetero	ninety

There are no special number forms for counting females. The examples below recapitulate the three types (cardinal numbers and the two types above) of forms used in counting.

pét stùdenata	five students (no specification about students: could be all male, or mixed, but usually not all

*There is also a variant with the verb in the masculine plural: **Njíh su tròje òtišli u Lòndon.**

	female, since then **stùdentica** (Cr.) or **stùdentkinja** (S.) would be used).
petòrica stùdenata	five students (five *male* students)
pètoro stùdenata	five students (male and female)

Fractions. In Cr&S fractions (**ràzlomak;** N pl. **ràzlomci**) are expressed by using a cardinal number (e.g. **tri**) and a derived noun in **-ina.** Since the **-ina** noun has feminine gender, the cardinal numbers would be **jedna** with N sg., **dvije/dve, tri, četiri** with N pl. but G pl. for **pet** and above. Thus:

jèdna polòvina	1/2, one-half
jèdna trèćina	1/3, one-third
trí četvr̀tine	3/4, three-fourths
pét šèstina	5/6, five-sixths
dèvet stotnína	9/100, nine-hundredths

For indicating fractions when the number symbols are used, Cr&S employs a comma where English has a period, e.g. Cr&S 5,75 equates to English 5.75, "5 57/100." The reverse is true in numbers entering the thousands, e.g. Cr&S 1.575 equals English 1,575, "one thousand five hundred and seventy-five." A period is also used after the figure for a year, e.g. **Kolùmbo je 1492. òtkrio Amèriku,** "In 1492 Columbus discovered America."

Ordinal Numbers and Dates. Ordinal numbers ("first," "second," etc.) are definite adjectives in form and function like other adjectives.

Mòja sòba je na pétom kàtu/spràtu.	My room is on the fifth floor.
Tó je njègova trèća žèna; ón móra bìti Muslìman.	That's his third wife; he must be a Moslem.

In Cr&S, as in English, ordinal numbers are used in specifying dates.

Kòji je dátum dànas?	What's the date today?
Dànas je dvádeset dèveti kòlovoz/àvgust.	Today's the 29th of August.

It should be noted that the number adjective is N sg. masc. (**dátum** is understood) and that the month is also in the nominative case. However, in answering the question: "On what date . . . ?" the number adjective and the month name appear in the G case.

Kóga ste dátuma ròđeni?	On what date were you born?
Ròđen sam dvádeset dèvetog kòlovoza/àvgusta.	I was born on the 29th of August.

To express the year 1972 in Cr&S, we say the equivalent of "the thousand nine hundred seventy-second year," i.e. **tìsuću/hìljadu dèvet stòtina sedamdèset drùga gòdina.** That is how it would appear in the sentence: **Ovo je** . . . , "This is the year 1972." Usually, however, the last element of the year term and the word for year will appear in the genitive singular (**druge godine**) as the year expression serves to specify a date on which something took place.

Ròđena sam jedànaestog òžujka/màrta, tìsuću/hìljadu dèvet stòtina trídeset sédme gòdine.	I was born on the 11th of March in the year 1937.
Ljùdevit Gáj ròdio se kao nájmlađi sín svòjih ròditelja ósmog sŕpnja/júla, tìsuću/hìljadu òsam stòtina dèvete gòdine.	Ljudevit Gaj was born the youngest son of his parents on the 8th of July in the year 1809.
Ùmro je od kápi dvádesetog trávnja/àprila, tìsuću/hìljadu òsam stòtina sedamdèset drùge gòdine.	He died of apoplexy on the 20th of April, 1972.

Note that the word for "thousand" in these time expressions has the accusative case form, i.e. **tisuću/hiljadu.**

Asking and Telling Age

Kòliko ìmaš gòdina, Pávle?	How old are you, Paul?
Ìmam dvádeset trí gòdine.	I'm twenty-three years old.
Kòliko ìmate gòdina, gospòdine?	How old are you, sir?
Ìmam trídeset sèdam gòdina.	I'm thirty-seven.

Summary of Prepositions and Their Uses. No mere listing of a preposition along with an example or two can suffice to show all the possibilities of its usage. This is particularly true of a frequently used preposition whose area of meaning may not equate to that of one English preposition. In the examples below one Cr&S preposition, **od,** has four possible equivalents in English.

písmo *od* májke	a letter *from* mother
ròđen *od* siròmašnih ròditelja	born *of* poor parents
ròman *od* Júrja Hàbdelića	a novel *by* Juraj Habdelić
záštita *od* pòplava	a protection *against* floods

Students of Cr&S would thus be well advised to add examples from their own reading and conversations to those listed below.

s/sa, k/ka, pod/poda . . . Several prepositions can occur with a final **a;** it may be used optionally in any situation, but it is required in certain situations:

1. **sa** appears instead of **s** when the following word begins with **s/š/z/ž/,** e.g. **sa sèla, sa šùme, sa zèmlje, sa žènom.**

2. **ka** replaces **k** before a following **g/h/k,** e.g. **ka glávi, ka hrástu, ka kònju.**

3. other prepositions have the longer form with **-a** when used with the short forms of pronouns, e.g. **uza me,** but **uz mene, nada nj,** but **nad njega;** and

4. when used with nouns whose initial sounds would be similar to the final consonant sound of the prepositions, e.g. **kroz pàrk,** but **kroza zíd, niz br̀do,** but **niza sèlo.**

Prepositions Followed by the Genitive Case

A. Simple prepositions:

bez without	Ȍna pȉje kàvu/kàfu bez šèćera.	She drinks coffee without sugar.
blízu* near	Àvala se nàlazi blízu Beògrada.	The Avala [memorial] is located near Belgrade.
do up to	Písao sam do òvog čàsa. Ìdi do kràja òve ùlice!	I've been writing up to this moment. Go up to the end of this street!
duž along	Duž ùlice ìma mnògo pàrkiranih automobíla.	There are a lot of parked cars along the street.
iz from, out of	Ìzvadio sam nòvac iz džèpa.	I took the money from my own pocket.
kod† at, at the home of	Ón stànuje kòd nas. Jùčer/Jùče sam bìo kod zubára.	He's staying at our home. Yesterday I was at the dentist.
kraj alongside	Tùmač sjèdi/sèdi kraj mène.	The interpreter sits alongside me.
mjesto/mesto instead of	Já ću písati mjesto/mesto svòje sèstre.	I'll write instead of my sister.
mimo by, past	Ùčenik je protr̀čao mimo gróblja.	The schoolboy raced past the graveyard. [see also A usage below]
nìže* below	Lìvada je niže kùće.	The meadow is below the house.
od from, of	Ón je dòbio pòklon od bràta.	He received a gift from his brother.

***blizu** and other prepositions so indicated (*) may also function as adverbs, that is, in association with verbs and without a following adjective or noun, e.g. **Ne ìdi blízu!** "Don't come near!"

†In colloquial speech **kod** is used frequently after verbs of motion, e.g. **Idem kod zubara,** "I'm going to the dentist," instead of **Idem k zubaru.**

	Njègova je kòšulja nàpravljena od pàmuka a ne od vùne.	His shirt is made of cotton and not of wool.
oko around	Oko òve zgràde ìma dòsta tráve.	There's plenty of grass around this building.
osim except	Đáci ìdu u škólu svàki dán osim sùbote i nèdjelje/nèdelje.	Students go to school every day except Saturday and Sunday.
pored beside, besides	Otac stòji pored mène.	My father is standing beside me.
	Pored pára ìma i ràzuma.	Besides money he has brains too.
pòslije/pòsle* after	Poslije/Posle òve lèkcije ùčit ćemo/ùčićemo drùgu.	After this lesson we'll study another.
prìje/pré* before	Òtišao je prije/pre móga dòlaska.	He left before my arrival.
preko over, across	Prèđite preko púta!	Come across the road!
	Òna je čìtala preko dvá sáta.	She's been reading for more than two hours.
protiv against	Protiv smȑti lijèka/léka néma.	There's no cure for death.
radi for the sake of	Ròditelji ráde i žíve radi srèće svòje djèce/dèce.	Parents work and live for the happiness of their children.
s from, off of	Povjetárac/Povetárac púše s jèzera. Skìni kàpu s gláve!	The breeze is blowing from the lake. Take your cap off your head!
sem(S.) except	Sem jèdnog prózora svì su òtvoreni.	Except for one window, all [the others] are open.
sred in the middle of	Sred pàrka ìma jèdan vòdoskok.	There's a fountain in the middle of the park.
u in the possession of	U nàšeg ùčitelja je nòvo odijèlo/odélo.	Our teacher has a new suit.

***blizu** and other prepositions so indicated (*) may also function as adverbs, that is, in association with verbs and without a following adjective or noun, e.g. **Ne ìdi blízu!** "Don't come near!"

vàn* outside	Sùbotu ćemo provèsti van gráda.	We'll spend Saturday outside the city.
vìše* above	Šùma je na bȑdu vìše sèla.	The woods are on a hill above the town.
za during the time of	Tó se dèsilo za ràta.	That happened during the war.
zbog because of	Ón nìje mògao ìći na rád zbog bòlesti.	He couldn't go to work because of illness.

B. Compound prepositions are those that represent a blend of two prepositions (**iznad** from **iz nad**) or a stereotyped prepositional phrase (**navrh** from **na vrh**). Prepositions of these two types, which require the use of the genitive case, are:

ispod under, from under	Ispod šùme je jèzero. Ìzvukao sam psà ispod stòla.	The lake is below the woods. I dragged the dog out from under the table.
ispred before, from before	Àutobusna/Àutobuska stànica je ispred mòje kùće.	The bus stop (station) is in front of my house.
iza behind, from behind	Iza cŕkve su dvá dȑveta.	There are two trees behind the church.
između between, among	Bolèsnik je između živòta i smȑti.	The patient is between life and death.
iznad above	Iznad òčiju je čèlo.	The forehead is above the eyes.
izvan outside	Izvan gráda vòzimo se brzìnom od šezdèset mílja nà sat.	Outside the city we drive at a speed of 60 miles an hour.
nakon after	Nakon téškog ráda čòvjek/čòvek zaslùžuje òdmor.	After hard work a person deserves a rest.
nasred in the middle of	Àuto se zaùstavio nasred Zágreba.	The auto stopped in the middle of Zagreb.
navrh on the top of	Gròmobran je pòstavljen navrh nebòdera/ Gròmobran je pòstavljen navrh oblakòdera.	A lightning rod is placed on top of the skyscraper.

*__blizu__ and other prepositions so indicated (*) may also function as adverbs, that is, in association with verbs and without a following adjective or noun, e.g. **Ne ìdi blízu!** Don't come near!"

pokraj alongside	Pokraj škóle vòzite poláko!	Drive slowly near the school.
poput like	Djèca/Dèca se čésto pònašaju poput svòjih ròditelja.	Children often act like their parents.
poradi for the sake of	Ne trèba se ljútiti poradi sìtnih stvári.	There's no need to get mad over trifles.
povrh over, above	Njègov stán je povrh móga.	His apartment is above mine.
uoči on the eve of	Što/Štà rádite uoči práznika?	What do you do on the eve of a holiday?
usred in the middle of	Lópov je òpljačkao bánku usred dána.	The bandit robbed the bank in the middle of the day.

Prepositions Followed by the Accusative Case.

Several prepositions are followed by the accusative case, but only when the idea of motion or transmission of motion (from the verb to the prepositional phrase) is involved. Otherwise, these prepositions have the connotation of "location" and are followed, in the case of some, by the dative case or, for others, by the instrumental case.

1. Prepositions with accusative of "motion" and dative of "location." Here the examples illustrate the accusative usage:

u to, into	Ljúdi ùlaze u cŕkvu.	People are entering the church.
na on, onto, to, in	Djèca/Dèca bàcaju lòptu na króv.	Children throw the ball on the roof.
	Ìdem na sàstanak.	I'm going to the meeting.

2. Prepositions with accusative of "motion" and instrumental of "location." The examples show the accusative usage:

među between, among	Lòpta je pàla ùpravo među igráče.	The ball fell right among the players.
	Stàvite òvu stòlicu među òstale!	Place this chair among the others!
nad over	Ùplašena kvòčka šíri svòja kríla nad mláde.	The frightened hen spreads her wings over her young.
	Òbjesite/Òbesite kàput nad vàtru da se òsuši.	Hang your coat over the fire so that it can dry out!
pod under	Sòkol/Sòko se dìže pod òblake.	The falcon soars up under the clouds.

	Màčka je pòbjegla/pòbegla pod krèvet.	The cat ran under the bed.
pred in front of	Jòvanka je izàšla pred kùću.	Jovanka came out in front of the house.
	Òna mu je bàcila pȑsten pred nòge.	She threw the ring at his feet.
za behind	Nètko/Nèko se za líst sàkrije a nètko/nèko ne mòže ni za dúb.	Some people could hide themselves behind a leaf, while others couldn't hide behind an oak.
	Súnce zàlazi za bŕdo.	The sun is setting behind the hill.

3. The preposition **o**, "against, on" (there is also a preposition **o**, "about, concerning," followed by the dative case.) Here the example is of **o** with the A:

Válovi ùdaraju o stijènu/sténu.	The waves are beating against the cliff.
Òbjesite/Òbesite slìku o zíd!	Hang the picture on the wall!

Other prepositions followed by the accusative case (with no specific implication of "motion") are:

kroz through, in [time]	Pòtok tèče kroz nàšu lìvadu. Bìt ću/Bìću tàmo kroz nèkoliko dána.	A stream flows through our meadow. I'll be there in a few days.
	Kroz òvo sèlo pròlazi mnògo tèretnih vòzila.	Many trucks pass through this village.
mimo contrary to, different from	Ón je ùvijek/ùvek mimo òstale ljúde.	He is always different from other people.
niz down	Jèdno dijète/déte tȑči niz ùlicu.	A child is running down the street.
	Sìlazili su bŕzim kòrakom niza stránu.	They were descending the slope at a rapid pace.
po for [purpose], at [manner]	Stùdent se mórao vrátiti po svòju knjìgu.	The student had to return for his book.
	Já ću mu tó učìniti po svàku cijènu/cénu.	I'll do that for him at any cost.
uz Up, with, to	Nìje se làko pènjati uz bȑdo.	It's not easy to climb up a hill.

	Òvo se kòlo ìgra uz búbanj.	This "kolo" is danced to a drum.
za for, by, to become	Tó je vážno za mène.	That's important for me.
	Za neznánje se kàje, za nèrad pláća.	For ignorance one has regrets, for idleness one must pay.
	Òna ga dȓži zà ruku.	She holds him by the hand.
	Sàda ùčim za lìječnika/lekára.	Now I'm studying to become a doctor.
	Náda ùči za učitèljicu.	Nada is studying to become a schoolteacher.

Prepositions Followed by the Dative Case.
In the event that you have the occasion to refer to a traditional grammar of Cr&S, you will find that the following two groups of prepositions are usually classified in two historically distinct cases.

1. Traditional Dative Case

k to, toward	Vòzimo se k Nòvom Sádu.	We're driving toward Novi Sad.
	Ìšao je ka glávnoj ùlici.	He was going toward the main street.
nasùprot* opposite	Nasùprot cŕkvi je gìmnazija.	Opposite the church is the secondary school.
unátoč, ùsprkos in spite of	Unàtoč svòjim ròditeljima prèkinuo je škòlovanje.	In spite of his parents he gave up his schooling.

2. Traditional Locative Case

po through, according to	Putòvao je po mnògim zèmljama.	He's traveled in many lands.
	Po móm mìšljenju ón je màngup.	In my opinion he's a rascal.
o about, concerning	Govòrili smo o vàšem ùspjehu/ùspehu na ùtakmici.	We were talking about your success in the match (game).
prema opposite, toward, according to	Đáci su ùčtivi prema pròfesoru.	The students are courteous toward their professor.
pri at	Pri pòlasku zabòravio sam kùfer na stànici.	At (on) my arrival I forgot my suitcase at the station.
	Prema nòvinama mnògo	According to the papers

*__nasuprot__ is used by some speakers with the G case also: **nasuprot cŕkve.**

	je svìjeta/svéta bílo pri otváranju mùzeja.	there was a large crowd at the opening of the museum.
u at, in [location]	Igráči su u dòbroj fórmi.	The players are in good form.
	Mój ùjak žívi u Amèrici.	My uncle (mother's brother) lives in America.
na on, at [location]	Na rúci ìma pét pȑstiju.	There are five fingers on the hand.
	Djèca/Dèca se ìgraju lòpte na ìgralištu.	The children are playing ball on the playground.

Special Uses of **na**. In the beginning of this section on prepositions it was pointed out that English and Cr&S prepositions are not always exact equivalents.. Thus, though Cr&S **u** with the A case after verbs of motion generally corresponds to English "to," while **u** with the D case in situations connoting location generally corresponds to English "at, in," and Cr&S **na** in the same two usages means "onto" (A usage) or "on" (D usage), there are certain words in Cr&S that use **na** in the English meaning of "to (A), in, at (D)." For example:

Ìdem u škólu.	I'm going to school.
Sàda sam u škóli.	Now I'm in school.
[but]	
Ìdem na sveùčilište/univerzìtet.	I'm going to the university.
Sàda sam na sveùčilištu/univerzitétu.	Now I'm at the university.

Fifty or so such words require **na**. Some of them can be put into categories, such as points of the compass, e.g. **na istok,** "to the East," **na istoku,** "in the East," or the names of meals, e.g. **na večeru,** "to supper," **na večeri,** "at supper," or the names of places or events where people assemble, e.g. **na igranku,** "to the dance," **na igranci,** "at the dance." However, this latter category is not very exact (e.g. **u kínu/bìoskopu,** "at the movies") and so it is probably easier to simply identify the words that take **na** without worrying about the logic of the situation. Here are those words used with **na:**

Bàlkan	Balkans
demonstrácija	demonstration
dópust	leave
dòručak (D na dòručku)	breakfast
ìgranka (S.) (D na ìgranci)	dance
ìspit	examination
ìzbori N pl. (na ìzborima)	elections

jùg	South
kòlodvor (Cr.)	railroad station
kòncert	concert
kráj	end
kȑštenje	baptism
ljètovanje/lètovanje	summer vacation
mír	peace
mìsa	Mass
mjèsečina/mèsečina	moonlight
móre	sea
nèbo	heaven, sky
òdmor	rest, vacation
òdsustvo	leave
pjèvanje/pèvanje	singing, singing group
plés (Cr.)	dance
počétak (D na počétku)	beginning
pògreb	funeral
pòsao (D na pòslu)	work
pòšta	post office
predávanje	lecture
prèdstava	performance
próba	rehearsal
rád	work
ràstanak (D na ràstanku)	parting
rèizbori N pl.	new elections
repetícija	repetition, renewal
rúčak (D na rúčku)	noon meal
sàstanak (D na sàstanku)	meeting
sjèdnica/sèdnica	meeting
sjèver/sèver	North
stànica	station
súd	court, trial
súnce	sun
svàdba	wedding
sveùčilište (Cr.)	university
univerzìtet (S.)	university
ùtakmica	match, game
vèčera	supper
vjenčánje/venčánje	wedding
vlást (D na vlásti)	power, authority
vráta N pl. (D na vrátima)	door, doorway
zábava	party, entertainment
západ	West
zimòvanje	winter vacation

Certain words can be used with either **u** or **na** with different nuances of meaning. For example:

Bìo sam na lèkciji iz matemàtike.	I was at the mathematics class.
U òvoj lèkciji ìma mnògo teškóća.	In this lesson there are many difficulties.
Òtišli smo na sèlo.	We went to the country.
Òtišli smo u sèlo Tršić.	We went to the village (of) Tršić.
Sàda gòvore na èngleskom jèziku.	Now they're speaking English (in the English language).
U èngleskom jèziku ìma mnògo nèpravilnih glàgola.	There are many irregular verbs in the English language.

Prepositions Followed by the Instrumental Case.

There are six prepositions associated with the instrumental case, and five of these have, in addition to their specific meaning, the general notion of "location" as contrasted with "motion." With the connotation of "motion" these prepositions (**među, nad, pod, pred, za**) would be followed by the accusative case. Examples of their use with the instrumental case are:

među between, among	Tó nèka je rečèno među nàma.	Let this be said between ourselves.
	Lòpta je među igráčima.	The ball is among the players.
nad over	Nad jèzerom lète ptìce.	The birds are flying over the lake.
	Slìka vìsi nad krèvetom.	The picture hangs over the bed.
pod under	Ljúdi stòje pod dȑvetom.	The people are standing under a tree.
	Pod njègovom kòmandom bílo je mnògo vojníka.	There were many soldiers under his command.
pred in front of	Àutobusna/Àutobuska stànica je pred nàšom kùćom.	The bus stop is in front of our house.
	Òvi ljúdi čèkaju pred vrátima vìše od sáta.	These people have been waiting in front of the door more than an hour.
za behind	Za cŕkvom je málo jèzero.	Behind the church there's a small lake.
	Tàta sjèdi/sèdi za stòlom.	Dad is sitting at the table.

The sixth and last preposition used with the instrumental case is **s/sa** in its meaning "with, along with, together with."* Some examples are:

Tȍ je u skládu sa nȁšim rezultátima.	It's in harmony with our results.
Ìdem u kíno/bìoskop s prìjateljem.	I'm going to the movies with my friend.

Review of Case Usages

Vocative Case. This is a special category for singular nouns (masculine and feminine only), in which a person or thing is addressed ("called"), referred to directly, or spoken to directly:

Pȍštovani *gospòdine pròfesore!*	Dear (Mr.) Professor: [in a letter]
Plòvi, plòvi, mòja láđo, [N sg. láđa]	Sail on, sail on, my ship, [Preradović]

Nominative Case. Nouns appear in this case when they are used in:

1. A one-word sentence:

Vatra!	Fire!

2. As subject of a sentence:

Óvdje/Óvde ljúdi ràno ùstaju.	People get up early here.

3. As either member of a verbal equation:

Òvaj stàrac je *mój ùjak.*	This old man is my uncle.
Vȁš će *mòmak* biti *dòbar ùčenik.*	Your lad will be a good student.
Králjević Márko je bìo *nájveći jùnak.*	Kraljević Marko was the greatest hero.

Accusative Case. This category is employed when nouns (and adjectives or pronouns) are used:

1. As the objects of most Cr&S verbs:

Já ìmam *nòvu tórbu/tȁšnu.*	I have a new briefcase.
Svàki cìganin hváli *svóga kònja.*	Every gypsy praises his own horse.
S òvog je prózora mòguće vìdjeti/vìdeti *planìnu.*	It's possible to see the mountain from this window.

2. In certain expressions of time:

Rádio je u tvórnici/fàbrici *gòdinu dána.*	He worked in the factory for a year.
Bòlje je bìti pijèvac/pévac *jèdan dán* nego kòkoš *mjèsec/mèsec.*	It's better to be a rooster for one day than a chicken for a month.

*Some speakers of Cr&S have extended the usage of **s** to denote "by means of," saying **Dóći cu sa vlákom/vózom.** "I'll come by train," instead of the textbook model **Doći ću vlakom//vozom.**

3. After the prepositions **u, na, o, pod, nad, pred, za, među,** when the prepositional phrase serves as a terminus for (i.e. receives) an act of motion:

Nástavnik je stàvio knjìgu na *stól/stó.*	The teacher placed the book on the table.
Péro je izàšao *pred kùću.*	Pero came out in front of the house.

4. After the prepositions **kroz, mimo, niz, uz, po,** "for," and **za,** "for":

Pút vòdi *uz rijèku/réku.*	The road leads up the river.
Òvo je vážno *za tébe.*	This is important for you.

Genitive Case. Nouns are put in the genitive case:

1. To indicate possession:

Tó je imánje *móga òca.*	That's the property of my father.

or specification,

Na lícu mu se pojávio ìzraz *dùboke zàmišljenosti.*	On his face there appeared an expression of deep thought.

2. With partitive meaning; this happens frequently after such verbs as **pìti,** "to drink," and **ùzimati** I (**ùzeti** P), "to take (some)":

Dájte mi sìra, mésa i vòde!	Give me some cheese, some meat, and some water!

[**Dájte mi sìr, méso i vòdu!** would mean "Give me the cheese, the meat, and the water," an order you might give when unloading a car.]

3. After certain reflexive verbs, such as:

bòjati se	to be afraid of	màšati se	to reach out for
čúvati se	to be wary of	opròstiti se	to part from
dr̀žati se	to catch hold of	plàšiti se	to be afraid of
hvàtati se	to have recourse to	prèpasti se	to shrink from
ìzbavljati se	to get rid of	prímati se	to adhere to
làćati se	to undertake	rješávati se/rešávati se	to get rid of
lišávati se	to deprive oneself of	srámiti se	to be ashamed of

Bòjimo se *ìspita.*	We're afraid of the examination.
Làćaj se *pòsla!*	Get some work!

4. In certain expressions of time; in this usage the noun cannot occur alone but must be accompanied by an adjective or pronominal modifier:

Pròšle gòdine putòvao sam po Evrópi.	Last year I traveled in Europe.
Písat ću/Písaću ti *òvih dána.*	I'll write you in a few days.
Kìša je pàdala *cìjelog pròljeća/célog pròleća.*	It rained all spring.

5. After the following words of general measurement:

dòsta	enough	mnògo	much of, many
kòliko	how much, how many	nèkoliko	some, any, several
màlo	little of, a few	tòliko	so much, so many
mànje	less, fewer	vìše	more

Ón ìma dòsta nòvaca za pút.	He has enough money for the trip.

6. After all numbers except "one" (**jedan/jedno/jedna**); masculine nouns after **dva, tri, četiri,** are in the G sg. and feminine nouns are in the N pl., while numbers from five and up are followed by the G pl.:

Trí *Mostárca*—čètiri *pjèsnika/pèsnika.*	Three men from Mostar—four poets. [Yugoslav saying]
U òvom rázredu ìma trídeset *stùdenata.*	There are thirty students in this class.

7. After certain adjectives, such as:

dòstojan	worthy (of)	svìjestan/svéstan	conscious (of)
gládan	hungry (for)	vrijèdan/vrédan	deserving (of)
pùn	full (of)	žédan	thirsty (for)
sìt	satiated	žèljan	desirous (of)

Kàradžić i Gáj su dòstojni *vjèčnog/vèčnog* spòmena u svóme národu.	Karadžić and Gaj deserve everlasting remembrance among their people.

8. After the exclamatory particles **evo, eto, eno:**

Èvo *mòje sùpruge!*	Here's my wife now!
Èto *móga sína!*	There's my son (coming)!
Èno *mòjih ćérki!*	There go my daughters over there!

9. After a large number of prepositions (for additional examples, see Prepositions Followed by Genitive Case):

Sa kùlturno-històrijskog glèdišta Dùbrovnik je . . . òrganski zaòkružena cijelìna/celìna.	From a cultural-historical point of view Dubrovnik is . . . an organic whole.

10. After a negated transitive verb, though the accusative usage is more common and colloquial:

Màrija nìje čìtala *romána*.	Marija didn't read the novel.
[but usually]	
Màrija nìje čìtala *ròman*.	

Dative Case. The principal uses of this case are:

1. To indicate the recipient of an object:

Òtac je dào písmo *sínu*.	The father gave the letter to the son.
Prùžite *mi* sol/so!	Pass me the salt!

2. To indicate possession:

Májka *mu* je ùmrla.	His mother died.
Djètetu/Dètetu su rúke pr̀ljave.	The child's hands are dirty.

3. To indicate the person (sometimes a thing) affected by some action or verbal situation:

Otvòri mi vráta!	Open the door for me!
Štò *mi* žèliš, nèk *ti* bùde!	May you get what you wish for me.

4. Certain verbs are usually followed by nouns or pronouns in the dative case. Some of these verbs are:

čìniti se	to seem	slúžiti	to be of service to
dòpadati se (S.)	to be pleasing to	smétati	to disturb
pomágati	to help	svíđati se (Cr.)	to be pleasing to
prìpadati	to belong to	vjèrovati/vèrovati	to believe

Kàko *vam* se svíđa/dòpada Jugoslávija?	How do you like Yugoslavia?

5. The impersonal construction of adverb plus **je** is completed by a noun or pronoun in the dative case:

Drágo *mi* je dà sam vas upòznao.	I'm happy to make your acquaintance.
Téško je *májci* kad djèca/dèca ne slùšaju.	It's difficult for a mother when the children don't obey.

6. The dative case is used after the prepositions **k, nasùprot,** and **unátoč** or **ùsprkos:**

Síne, ìdi *k tàti!*	Son, go to your dad!

7. After the prepositions **u** and **na** (in their connotation of "location"), and after **po, prema, pri,** and **o,** "about, concerning":

Svàka je ptìca *u svóm gnijèzdu/ gnézdu* jáka.	Every bird is powerful in his own nest. [proverb]

Instrumental Case. The uses of this case are the following:

1. Designation of instrument by which some action is accomplished:

Đak píše *pèrom* i *òlovkom.*	The student writes with [by means of] a pen and a pencil.
Ìdem u škólu *àutobusom* ili *tramvá-jem.*	I go to school by bus or streetcar.

2. It answers the question **kùda,** "where to, which way":

Šétamo se *pòljem (ùlicom, grádom).*	We're strolling through the field (street, city).

3. It may designate points in time:

kràjem	at the end	svršétkom	at the conclusion
počétkom	at the beginning	tókom	in the course (of)
sredìnom	in the middle	zòrom	at dawn

Vòjnik je bìo rànjen *tókom* ràta.	The soldier was wounded in the course of the war.

or it [I case] may specify recurring units of time:

jùtrom	in the morning, on mornings, every morning
nòću	at night, nights, every night
sùbotom	on Saturday, Saturdays, every Saturday
vèčerom	in the evening, evenings, every evening

Nòvine se pròdaju jùtrom.	Newspapers are sold in the morning (i.e. every morning).

4. After certain verbs, some of which are:

bàviti se	to engage in	ùpravljati	to govern, to manage
gospodòvati	to be master over	vládati	to rule
òbilovati	to abound in	zanímati se	to occupy oneself with
trgòvati	to trade, to deal in	zapovijèdati/ zapovédati	to order, to command

U Amèrici národ ùpravlja *svòjom sudbìnom.*	In America the people manage their own destiny.

5. Specification after certain adjectives:

Zàdovoljni smo *tvòjim ùspjehom/ ùspehom.*	We're satisfied with your progress.
Jugoslávija je bògata *rúdnim blágom.*	Yugoslavia is rich in mineral wealth.

6. With the prepositions **među, nad, pod, pred, za** in their connotation of "location" and also with the prepositions **s**, "with, along with." For additional examples, see pages 256–57.

Iznad kùće dìzao se dìm kao *nad svím òstalim kùćama.*	Smoke was rising over [their] house just as it was over all the other houses too. [Kranjec]

The Verb

Present Tense — sàdašnje vrijème/vréme

The Cr&S verb has many more variations than in English. In English the present tense is quite simple in that one can say: I/ you/we/they work, he/she/it works, which requires only two verb forms, *work* and *works*. The equivalent expressions in Cr&S demand six distinct forms. However, to compensate for this complexity, Cr&S has only one present type, since the present tense form **radim** may mean either "I work" or "I am working."

já rádim	I work, I am working
tí rádiš	You [familiar form] work, you are working
ón/òna/òno* rádi	He/ she/it works, he/she/it is working
rádimo	We work, we are working
rádite	You work, you are working
òni/òne/òna* ráde	They work, they are working

The Cr&S verb forms are usually used without the personal pronouns. Use of the pronouns adds emphasis; thus, **Što radite?** would be the normal way to ask "What are you doing?" while **Što vi radite?** would mean "What are *you* doing?"

Inspection of present tense forms of some other verbs will show that there is a definite and regular system for expressing verbal situations in the present time.

rádi-m**	stòji-m	I stand, I'm standing	ìde-m	I go, I'm going

*__Ono radi,__ "it works," could be used when referring to a neuter noun such as **zvòno,** "bell," or **pèro,** "pen." More specific situations for the third person plural form could be **Ljúdi (/òni) ràde,** "The people are working," **Žène (/òne) ráde,** "The women are working," and **Zvòna (/òna) ráde,** "The bells are working."

**As noted before, in a paradigm such as this, the accent mark will just be used once if the other forms have the same accent; where a change occurs within the paradigm, all the forms will be accented.

radi-š	stoji-š	ide-š
radi	stoji	ide
radi-mo	stoji-mo	ide-mo
radi-te	stoji-te	ide-te
rad-e	stoj-e	id-u

čìta-m	I read, I'm reading	pùtuje-m	I travel, I'm traveling
čita-š		putuje-š	
čita		putuje	
čita-mo		putuje-mo	
čita-te		putuje-te	
čita-j-u		putuj-u	

Using the third person singular form (the "he/she/it form") as a base, simply add the specific endings **-m, -š, -mo, -te** to produce four other present tense forms; thus, **(on) ide: ide-m, ide-š, ide-mo, ide-te.** And similarly for the other verbs above and, in fact, for the majority of verbs in Cr&S!

The third person plural form is different from the others in its pre-ending shape; that is, while **idem** and **ideš** can be considered as **ide-** plus ending **-m** or **-š,** third person **idu** is **id-** plus ending **-u.** And **rade** is **rad-** plus ending **-e.** But these third person plural forms are completely predictable (1) if at least one other present form is known, and (2) if you remember the three basic types of correspondences that appear in these examples:

i : e	rádim-radiš-radi-radimo-radite : rade
	stòjim-stojiš-stoji-stojimo-stojite : stoje
e : u	ìdem-ideš-ide-idemo-idete : idu
	pùtujem-putuješ-putuje-putujemo-putujete : putuju
a : aju	čìtam-čitaš-čita-čitamo-čitate : čitaju
	pítam-pitaš-pita-pitamo-pitate : pitaju [pítati, to ask]

Present Tense of Special Verbs. Two verbs have a first singular in **-u** instead of the typical **-m;** they are **mòći,** "to be able" and **htjèti/htèti,** "to want"; the latter has both emphatic and unemphatic (unaccented) forms.

				emphatic		*unemphatic*	
1st sg.	(ja)	mògu	I can	hòću	I want, I will, I'll	ću	I will, I'll
2nd sg.	(ti)	možeš		hoćeš		ćeš	
3rd sg.	(on)	može		hoće		će	
1st pl.	(mi)	možemo		hoćemo		ćemo	
2nd pl.	(vi)	možete		hoćete		ćete	
3rd pl.	(oni)	mogu		hoće		će	

The emphatic forms are required in initial position, which makes for a certain ambiguity of meaning between "want" and "will." For example:

Márko će dóći.	Marko will come.
Márko hòće dóći.	Marko wants to come.
Hòće li Márko dóći?	Does Marko want to come? [or] Will Marko come?

This ambiguity does not occur in the **da li** question:

Dà li će Márko dóći?	Will Marko come?
Dà li hòće Márko dóći?	Does Marko want to come?

The present tense of **bìti** also has emphatic (or initial) and unemphatic (unaccented) forms:

		emphatic	*unemphatic*	*negated*
1st sg.	(ja)	jèsam I am	sam I'm	nísam I'm not
2nd sg.	(ti)	jesi	si	nísi
3rd sg.	(on)	jest, jeste (S.)	je	nìje
1st pl.	(mi)	jesmo	smo	nísmo
2nd pl.	(vi)	jeste	ste	níste
3rd pl.	(oni)	jesu	su	nísu

Dà li ste iz Jugoslávije?	Are you from Yugoslavia?
Jèsam.	I am.
Jèste li iz Amèrike?	Are you from America?
Nísam. Já sam iz Èngleske.	No (literally, I'm not). I'm from England.

You and you. Cr&S has two words to express English "you": **tí** and **ví.** In speaking to more than one person, one would use **vi.** However, in speaking to one person, one could use either **vi** or **ti,** depending upon the speaker's relationship to that person. If he is addressing a member of his family, a friend, a child, an animal, or a colleague, he would use the "familiar form" **ti.** In other situations, where his relationship is more formal or he might wish to show respect, he would use **vi.** It is important to observe this distinction since his listener could be offended by being addressed as **ti** when he expects a **vi.** If in some cases it is not clear which form should be used, it is wise to rely on the more formal **vi.**

The possessive adjectives **tvój-tvòje-tvòja** (familiar) and **vàš-vàše-vàša** (formal), "your," also reflect this distinction. Often in writing letters the forms "you" and "your" are capitalized; this is especially the case for the **vi** and **vaš** along with their variations:

Kako ste Vi?	How are you?
Primio sam Vaše pismo.	I received your letter.

To have. One of the most frequently used verbs in Cr&S is **imati,** "to have," and its negated form **nemati (<ne imati).** The present tense is:

	sg.			*pl.*	
(ja)	ìmam	némam	(mi)	ìmamo*	némamo
(ti)	imaš	nemaš	(vi)	imate*	nemate
(on)	ima	nema	(oni)	imaju	nemaju

Some speakers use the present forms **imádem-imadeš-imademo-imadete-imadu. znàti,** "to know," has, similarly, two possible sets of present forms: **znám-znaš-zna-znamo-znate-znaju** and **znádem-znadeš-znade-znademo-znadete-znadu.**

Imati is mainly used to denote possession:

Ìmamo vȑt.	We have a garden.
Ìmam pèro.	I have a pen.
Ìmate li bràta?	Do you have a brother?

Ima li is a good equivalent for the English expression: "Is there. . . ?"

Ìma li katedrála u òvom grádu?	Is there a cathedral in this city?
Jèst/Jèste, ìma.	Yes, there is.

Forms of **nemati** are usually followed by the genitive case. This is especially so for **nema,** "there is not, there are not":

Néma vrèmena.	There is no time.
Néma ga kòd kuće**	He's not at home.
Néma kónja.	There are no horses.

Imperative — ìmperativ

When you want to give orders to others or even to yourself, use a special form of verb called the "imperative." The most common situation of ordering is that of a command from the speaker to a listener, actual or potential: "(You) do this!" "(You) read that!" Since Cr&S distinguishes between the familiar and the formal "you," there are thus two imperative forms for such commands to a listener:

2nd sg.	ìdi	Go!	govòri	Speak!	pítaj	Ask!	ne bój se	Don't fear!
2nd pl.	idi-te		govori-te		pitaj-te		ne bojte se	

As shown, some verbs take the imperative ending **(i-te)** and the imperative accent is that of the infinitive: **govòriti, govòri** (but **ón gòvori**). Other verbs have the imperative ending **(j-te)** and the preceding vowel is lengthened: **bòjati se, ón se bòji,** but **bój se.**

To determine which imperative ending to use for a particular verb, apply this rule of thumb: if a **-j-** appears in the ending of the third person plural of the present tense, select the imperative ending **-j;** otherwise, select **-i:**

*Also **imámo, imáte.**

The accentuation **kod kùće is becoming increasingly common in the cities.

(3rd pl.	òni ìdu	gòvore	pítaju	bòje se	čùju)
2nd sg. imperative	ìdi!	govòri!	pítaj!	bój se!	čúj! Hear!

There are occasions when one wishes to say: "Let's do such and such!" Cr&S has an imperative form for this type of situation, a form that consists of the imperative base (the 2nd sg. form) plus the "we" ending: **-mo.**

ìdi-mo Let's go! govòri-mo Let's talk! pítaj-mo Let's ask!

In sum, then, the three imperative forms of similar construction are:

2nd sg.	ìdi	govòri	pítaj	čúj	bój se
1st pl.	idimo	govorimo	pitajmo	čujmo	bojmo se
2nd pl.	idite	govorite	pitajte	čujte	bojte se

Third Person Imperative. In order to express a command to a third person or persons or to give permission to him or her (/them) to do something, use the word **nèka** in conjunction with the third person (singular or plural) form of the present tense:

(on ide)	: nèka ìde	Let him go!	nèka gòvori	nèka píta
(oni idu)	: nèka ìdu	Let them go!	nèka gòvore	nèka pítaju

Nemoj. Very often a negated imperative is expressed by using **nèmoj** or **nèmojte,** "Don't," plus an infinitive or a **da-** clause:

Nèmojte písati!	Don't write!
Nèmoj da me gnjáviš!	Stop harassing me!

The Infinitive — ìnfinitiv

The infinitive is a verbal form that appears in sentences such as these:

Tő trèba *učìniti.*	That must be done.
Já ću *písati.*	I'll write.
Já hòću *písati.*	I want to write.

The infinitives used above all end in **-ti.** This is also the situation for the majority of Cr&S infinitives. However, a small number of infinitives end in **-ći;** for example:

Já ću ìći. — I'll be going, I'll go.

The infinitive is the form used by Cr&S dictionaries to serve as the first entry for groupings of closely related verb forms, e.g. **čìtati,** "to read," **já čìtam, já sam čìtao,** etc. And if one asks a Yugoslav for the Cr&S equivalent of an English verb, he or she will usually respond with the infinitive form.

Future Tense — bùdućе vrijème/vréme

To express actions or situations that will occur in future time, take the present, unaccented forms of the verb **htjeti/hteti** and add an infinitive form:

já ću	čìtati	I'll read.
tí ćeš		You'll [familiar] read, etc.
ón/òna/òno će		
mí ćemo		
ví ćete		
òni/òne/òna će		

If the accented forms of this verb are used with the infinitive, the meaning will be changed and the time of the verbal action or situation will be in the present:

(ja)	hòću	čitati	I want to read.
(ti)	hoćeš		You [familiar] want to read, etc.
(on)	hoće		
(mi)	hoćemo		
(vi)	hoćete		
(oni)	hoće		

However, as pointed out above, the accented forms of **htjeti/hteti** are used in expressing a question involving future time, if the helping verb has to come first in the sentence:

	Ón će tó čìtati.	He'll read that.
[but]	Hòće li ón tó čìtati?	Will he read that?

The answer to the latter question could be simply **Hòće,** meaning "he will (read that)."

More About the Future. Future time may be expressed by using the unaccented, present forms of the verb **htjeti/hteti** together with an infinitive:

Mí ćemo putòvati. We'll travel.

Since the arrangement of words in a phrase is much freer in Cr&S than in English, the infinitive can appear before the helping verb: ***putovati ćemo.** An asterisk is used with this example to show that the writing of the forms is artificial, because speakers of Cr&S pronounce these two forms together and eliminate the **-ti,** saying **putovaćemo.** Though Croats and Serbs both have this pronunciation habit, they have slightly different ways of expressing it in writing.

Croatian	*Serbian*
putòvat ću	putòvaću
putovat ćeš	putovaćeš
putovat će	putovaće
putovat ćemo	putovaćemo

putovat ćete	putovaćete
putovat će	putovaće

In the Croatian system the final **i** of the infinitive is eliminated and the two words are written separately, while in the Serbian system the final **ti** of the infinitive is eliminated and the two forms are then written together. Infinitives in **-ći,** however, are not shortened, nor are they written together with the helping verb:

	Já ću ìći.	I'll go.
[or]	Ìći ću.	

The personal pronoun cannot be used when the future is expressed in this latter fashion.

Já ću putòvati.	I'll travel.	[but] Putòvat ću/putòvaću.	[without **ja**]
Mí ćemo stìći.	We'll arrive.	[but] Stìći ćemo.	[without **mi**]

Reinforced Negation. In standard English only one negative is tolerated in a simple sentence, e.g. "I never gave him anything." If you reinforce or double the negation, e.g. "I never gave him nothing," your speech will be labeled "substandard." In Cr&S, however, negation may be emphasized by adding more negative words; in fact, the "I never gave him nothing" type would be standard Cr&S, while a Cr&S parallel of "I never gave him anything" would be unacceptable.

Ón *nìkad nìgdje/nìgde ne* rádi.	He *never* works anyplace.
Nìkad više *néću nìkome nìkakvu* stvár dàti.	I'll *never* give anything to anybody anymore.

Past Tense **pròšlo vrijème/vréme**

To describe an action or situation that occurred in the past, select the appropriate "to be" form, **ja sam, ti si,** etc., and add a short form adjective based on an infinitive. Thus, just as you might say:

Já sam vèseo. I am cheerful. Òna je vèsela. She is cheerful.

so also you can take an infinitive adjective like **čitao, čitala, čitalo** [inf. **čitati,** "to read"] and say:

Já sam čìtao.	I was reading, I read [literally, I am a male person who was reading].
Òna je čìtala.	She was reading, she read.

The full set of forms would be:

masculine		*feminine*	
(emphatic)	(usual)	(emphatic)	(usual)
já sam čìtao	čìtao sam	já sam čìtala	čìtala sam
ti si čitao	čitao si	ti si čitala	čitala si

on je čitao	čitao je	ona je čitala	čitala je
mi smo čitali	čitali smo	mi smo čitale	čitale smo
vi ste čitali	čitali ste	vi ste čitale	čitale ste
oni su čitali	čitali su	one su čitale	čitale su

neuter

(emphatic)	(usual)
________	________
________	________
òno je čìtalo	čìtalo je
________	________
________	________
òna su čìtala	čìtala su

The plural feminine forms (those with **čitale**) are used when referring to two or more female beings or two objects in the feminine category (**knjiga, kuća,** etc.); references to mixed groups (masculine and feminine nouns) require the masculine plural form.

Kàd sam bìo u gìmnaziji, *knjìge* su se mnògo *čìtale.*	When I was in secondary school, books were read a lot.
Májka i òtac dùgo su *čìtali* písmo od sína.	The mother and father were a long time reading their son's letter.

To illustrate the use of the neuter form **čitalo,** one could say: **Dijète/Déte je čìtalo,** "The child was reading." The neuter plural form **čìtala** would rarely, if ever, be used because of the limitation imposed by the meaning of this particular verb. However, an example of this category could be:

Zvòna su ìmala prìjatan zvúk.	The bells had a pleasant sound.

If the helping verb (am/is/are) occurs as the first word in the sentence, use the longer, accented forms:

Áno! Jèsi li čìtala òvu knjìgu?	Ann! Have you read this book?
Jèste li glèdali táj fràncuski fìlm, gospòdine Bràon?	Have you seen that French film, Mr. Brown?
Jèsu li vàše sùpruge vèčerale?	Have your wives eaten supper?

Forming the Past Tense. Take an infinitive, such as **čitati,** subtract the final **-ti** and add **-o** for the masculine singular forms, **-li** for the masculine plural; **-la** for the feminine singular, **-le** for the feminine plural; **-lo** for the neuter singular, **-la** for the neuter plural. These infinitive adjectives, together with the appropriate forms of the helping verb (am/is/are), constitute the past tense of Cr&S.

Though this process of forming the past tense holds true for the majority of Cr&S verbs, in a small group of frequently used verbs the transition from infinitive to infinitive adjective is not readily obvious, e.g. **mòći** "to be able," **já sam mògao, òna je mògla.** The best way to deal with these verbs is simply to learn the individual forms.

Verb Stems. For many verbs the stem used to make present tense forms is essentially no different from the stem used to make past tense forms. For such verbs the basic stem is contained in the infinitive and can be abstracted to make past tense forms and also, though sometimes with accentual changes, present tense forms. Thus,

infinitive	*past tense*	*present tense*
znàti[=zna-ti] to know	znào[=zna-o],	znám[=zna-m]
	znàla[=zna-la]	znáš[=zna-š]

Another verbal type with similar stem for past and present tense forms has a characteristic stem vowel **i,** e.g. **govòri-ti,** "to speak," past tense: **govòri-o, govòri-la;** present tense: **gòvori-m, gòvori-š.** The two verbal types represented by **znati** and **govoriti** include many Cr&S verbs. Thus, the verbs **spávati,** "to sleep," **smátrati,** "to consider," **ìgrati,** "to play, dance," **kòpati,** "to dig," and many others are conjugated like **znàti,** while the verbs **bròjiti,** "to count," **mòliti,** "to request," **nòsiti,** "to carry, wear," **gùbiti,** "to lose," and many others are conjugated like **govòriti.**

Most of the other verbal types have a present stem that is distinctively different from the infinitive or past tense stem. Here are the major types:

	infinitive	*past tense*	*present tense*
1.	**put-òva-ti** to travel	**put-òva-o, put-òva-la**	**pùt-uje-m**
	dokaz-íva-ti to prove	**dokaz-íva-o, dokaz-íva-la**	**dokàz-uje-m**

Like **putòvati** are **dugòvati [dùgujem],** "to owe," **kupòvati [kùpujem],** "to buy," **kraljèvati [kràljujem],** "to rule," **ràtovati [ràtujem],** "to make war," **vjèrovati/vèrovati [vjèrujem/vèrujem],** "to believe". Like **dokazívati** are **darívati [dàrujem],** "to contribute," **objavljívati [objàvljujem],** "to announce, publish," **pobjeđívati/pobeđívati [pobjèđujem/pobèđujem],** "to win," **približívati [priblìžujem],** "to approach," **zabranjívati [zabrànjujem],** "to forbid."

2.	**pì-ti** to drink	**pì-o, pì-la**	**pìje-m**

Like **bìti [bìjem],** "to beat," **krìti [krìjem],** "to conceal," **lìti [lìjem],** "to pour," **šìti [šìjem],** "to sew."

3.	**làja-ti** to bark	**làja-o, làja-la**	**làje-m**

Similarly, **brìjati [brìjem],** "to shave," **pljùvati [pljùjem],** "to spit," **sìjati [sìjem],** "to sow," **tràjati [tràjem],** "to last."

4.	**písa-ti** to write	**písa-o, písa-la**	**píše-m**

Similarly, **kázati [kážem],** "to say," **dísati [díšem],** "to breathe," **skákati [skáčem],** "to jump," **víkati [víčem],** "to scream."

5.	**tònu-ti** to drown	**tònu-o, tònu-la**	**tòne-m**

Similarly, **dìgnuti [dìgnem],** "to raise," **stìsnuti [stìsnem],** "to squeeze out," **skìnuti [skìnem],** "to take off," **pòginuti [pòginem],** "to perish."

6. **brà-ti** to pick **brào, brála** **bère-m**
Similarly, **pràti [pèrem],** "to wash," **sràti [sèrem],** "to defecate," **òrati [òrem],** "to plough," **zvàti [zòvem],** "to call."

7. **vìdje-ti/vìde-ti** to see **vìdi-o/vìde-o, vìdje-la/vìde-la** **vìdi-m**
Similarly, **žívjeti/žíveti [žívim],** "to live," **vòljeti/vòleti [vòlim],** "to like, love," **gòrjeti/gòreti [gòrim],** "to burn," **vìsjeti/vìseti [vìsim],** "to hang."

8. **dȑža-ti** to hold **dȑža-o, dȑža-la** **dȑži-m**
Similarly, **réžati [réžim],** "to cut," **stàjati [stòjim],** "to stand," **bòjati se [bòjim se],** "to be afraid," **kríčati [kríčim],** "to cry, shout."

The infinitive stem of all the verbal types shown above ends in a vowel, e.g. **pisa-ti, govori-ti, vidje-ti/vide-ti.** Some verbs have a consonantal stem in the infinitive and past forms, but the original consonant is usually obscured because of sound changes occurring when certain consonants came into contact, e.g. **plèsti** [<**plet-ti],** "to knit," past tense forms: **plèo** [<**plel** <**pletl**], **plèla** [<**pletla**]. The present stem usually preserves the original consonant, e.g. **plètem.** Some verbs of this type are:

infinitive		*past tense*	*present tense*
grèpsti	to scratch	grèbao, grèbla	grèbem
grìsti	to bite	grìzao, grìzla	grízem
ìći	to go	ìšao, ìšla	ìdem
jèsti	to eat	jèo, jèla	jèdem
mòći	to be able	mògao, mògla	mògu (2nd sg. mòžeš)
rèći	to say	rèkao, rèkla	rèčem (3rd pl. rèku)
srèsti	to meet	srèo, srèla	srètem

Negative Particle **ne.** When used alone, the particle **ne** is accented (**nè**) and means "no"; when used with verbs, it usually has no accent and means "not," as in the sentences below:

Zár ne čìtaš mòja ljùbavna písma?	You aren't reading my love letters, are you?
Nè, nè. Ne čìtam tvòja písma.	No, no. I'm not reading your letters.
Òvo su sàmo mòji škòlski sástavi.	These are only my school compositions.

Negation and the Present Tense of **biti** *"to be"*

When **ne** is used with the "am-is-are" forms, it has the shape **ni-** and combines with the unaccented forms of **biti** (**sam, si** . . .):

(ja)	nísam	I am not

(ti)	nísi
(on)	nìje
(mi)	nísmo
(vi)	níste
(oni)	nísu

Negation and the Future. When combined with the future helping verb, the particle **ne** carries the accent. These two elements are then written together:

(ja)	néću písati	I will not write.
(ti)	nećeš pisati	
(on)	neće pisati	
(mi)	nećemo pisati	
(vi)	nećete pisati	
(oni)	neće pisati	

Negation and the Past. Since the "am-is-are" forms are used in forming the past tense, the negated forms of **biti** would appear in a past construction involving the negative:

(ja)	nisam čitao.	I wasn't reading, I didn't read.
(ti)	nisi čitao, itd.	You weren't reading, etc.

Reflexive Verbs **pòvratni glàgoli**

Transitive verbs (those that can be followed by the accusative case without a preposition) may reflect the action back on the doer by the use of the reflexive particle **se,** "oneself":

Brìjač/Bèrberin brìje vojníka.	The barber is shaving the soldier.
Brijač/Berberin brije sèbe.	The barber is shaving *himself.*
Brijač/Berberin se brije.	The barber is shaving himself.
Vòjnik se brije.	The soldier is shaving (i.e. himself).

In the second example **sebe** is used for special emphasis; ordinarily, a transitive verb, such as **brijati,** would be used either with an object, as in the first example, or reflexively, as in the third example. Another example of reflexive usage is:

vrátiti	to return	Vrátio sam mu knjìgu.	I returned the book to him.
vratiti se	to return (oneself)	Vrátio sam se kùći.	I returned home.

When two or more agents are involved in the verbal action, a reciprocal meaning (one to the other) may result:

Tàkmičimo se za bòlju òcjenu/òcenu.	We're competing for a better mark.

Ljùbili su se.	They kissed each other.
Na pàši se kràve bòdu.	The cows are butting each other in the pasture.

With Passive Meaning. Some reflexive verbs may be translated into English with a passive meaning, a meaning such as that indicated in the sentences: "The letter is being written, . . . was being written, . . . has been written, . . . had been written," etc.

Kàko se tó káže hȑvatski/sȑpski?	How is that said in Croatian/Serbian?
Stán se čìsti ùjutro.	The apartment is cleaned in the morning.
Tá se pjèsma pjèva po čìtavoj Jugosláviji./ Tá se pèsma pèva po čìtavoj Jugosláviji.	That song is sung all over Yugoslavia.

Special Reflexive Verbs. A small number of verbs occur only with the reflexive particle **se,** although their meaning does not seem to be either reflexive or passive:

bòjati se	to fear	Bòjim se ìspita.	I'm afraid of the exam.
čùditi se	to wonder	Òna se čùdi zàšto joj òtac nìje vèć dòšao.	She wonders why her father hasn't come yet.
dèsiti se	to happen	Tá se nèsreća dèsila pròšle gòdine.	That accident happened last year.
dogòditi se	to happen	Sìnoć se tó dogòdilo.	That happened last night.
nádati se	to hope	Nádamo se dà će sùtra bìti tòplo.	We hope that it'll be warm tomorrow.
smìjati se/smèjati se	to laugh	Svàtko se smìje duhòvitom čòvjeku. /Svàko se smèje duhòvitom čòveku.	Everyone laughs at a witty fellow.

Conditional — kòndicional

Many of the "should-would" expressions in English are represented in Cr&S by the conditional construction. Like the past tense formation with its helping verb (**sam-si-je-smo-ste-su**) and infinitive adjective (**pisao, pisala,** etc.), the conditional is composed of a helping verb (the unaccented aorist forms of **biti: bih-bi-bi-bismo-biste-bi**) and the infinitive adjective:

já bih písao, písala ti bi pisao, pisala on bi pisao, ona bi pisala	I would write, I'd write, I would have written, I'd have written
mi bismo pisali, pisale vi biste pisali, pisale oni bi pisali, one bi pisale	

In everyday speech **bi** is used for all persons, e.g. **já bi rèkao,** "I'd say," **mí bi rèkli, ví bi rèkli.**

Conditional forms are to be used if one action in the future is conditioned upon the performance of another action:

Òna bi pjèvala/pèvala za nás, àko biste umírili gòste.	She would sing for us, if you would quiet the guests.
Já bih ti ga dào kàd bi ga tí prímila.	I'd give it to you, if you'd take it.

A reference to action that might have happened in the past is also expressed by the conditional; the simple past tense, however, is usually employed in a **da-** clause:

Sìnoć bi òna pjèvala/pèvala za nás, dà ste umírili gòste.	She would have sung for us yesterday evening, if you had quieted the guests.

Just as in English, an expression such as "I'd like to have. . ." seems politer than "I want. . . ," so also in Cr&S expressions using the conditional are preferred to direct statements and questions:

Htjèli/Htèli bismo kúpiti òve dòpisnice.	We'd like to buy these postcards.
Dà li biste mi mògli rèći gdjè/gdè bih mògao rúčati?	Could you tell me where I could eat?

The following imaginary exchange between **Marko Kraljević** and a Serbian farmer provides several examples of conditional usage:

—Kàko bi bílo kad bi sàd ùstao Márko Králjević, pa da dóđe k tèbi?	How would it be if Marko Kraljević were to rise up now and come to you?
—Tó vèć nè može da bùde, —vèli sèljak.	That's really impossible, says the farmer.
—Al' bàš kàd bi dòšao, štà bi tí rádio?	But supposing he did come, what would you do?
—Zvào bih ga dà mi pòmogne da òkopam òvaj kukùruz! —nàšali se sèljak.	I'd call him over to help me pile dirt around the corn! joked the farmer.
—Al' kàd bi te ón pòzvao na Kòsovo?	But what if he summoned you to Kosovo [to fight the Turks]?

[R. Domanović]

Verbal Aspect **glàgolski víd**

If you look up the Cr&S equivalent of the verb "to write" in the dictionary, you will find two infinitives: **písati** and **napísati.** That these two forms are not merely synonyms will become apparent when you discover that "to throw" is **bàcati** or **báciti,** that "to read" is **čìtati** or **pročìtati,** etc. This situation holds true for the rest of the Cr&S verbal system in that there are usually two possible verbs for each English verb.

The reason for the existence of these verbal doublets is the Cr&S *aspect* or way of considering verbal meanings: the Cr&S speaker expects a verb form not only to denote verbal action or verbal status (like the English verb) but also to indicate whether the action is in process or whether it has been completed.

Dòk sam čìtao nòvine, mòja je sùpruga *písala* písmo.	While I read the paper, my wife *wrote* a letter.
Dòk sam čìtao nòvine, mòja je sùpruga *napísala* písmo.	While I read the paper, my wife *wrote* a letter.

The distinction between **písala** and **napísala** can be shown by adding more words to the English translation:

Òna je písala.	She was writing [in the process of writing].
Òna je napísala.	She wrote, she got (it) written [completion of act of writing].

Some more examples:

žèniti se	to marry [process]
Kàd se Mìloš žènio, mí smo pìli i ìgrali.	While Miloš was getting married, we drank and danced.
ožèniti se	to marry [completion]
Pòšto se Mìloš ožènio, òtišao je u àrmiju.	After Miloš got married, he went into the army.
vràćati se	to return [process]
Kàd se stùdent vràćao iz Jugoslávije, srèo je na bròdu svóga škòlskog drúga.	When the student was returning from Yugoslavia, he met a school friend on the ship.
vrátiti se	to return [completion]
Kàd se vrátio iz Jugoslávije, upísao se na sveùčilište/univerzìtet.	When he returned from Yugoslavia, he enrolled in the university.

In the two examples above (**vraćati se : vratiti se**) the verb forms **sreo (srèsti)** and **upisao se (upísati se)** were also employed; these are themselves verbs of completed action, and their "partner" verbs of process would appear in such utterances as:

Kàd je srètao svòje prìjatelje, ón se ùvijek/ùvek sr̀dačno rùkovao.	When(ever) he met his friends, he always shook hands warmly.
Kàd se upisívao na sveùčilište/ univerzìtet, ón je srèo svóga stárog pròfesora.	While he was enrolling in the university, he met his old professor.

Practically every Cr&S verb is a member of an aspectual pair. Either it is a verb of process, of uncompleted action, of repetitive action, or it is a verb whose action is instantaneous or of limited duration. The first type is commonly called *durative* or *imperfective* (I), while the second is called *perfective* (P).

The *P* verb has the implication of completeness, either instantaneously (**báciti,** "to throw once") or within a limited time (**napísati,** "to complete the writing of. . ."). If the general meaning of both *I* and *P* members of an aspectual pair is "the beginning of a certain action or condition," then the specific meaning of the *P* verb is "the completion of the beginning":

pjèvati/pèvati *I*, òtpjevati/òtpevati *P*	to sing
zapijèvati/zapèvati *I*, zàpjevati/ zàpevati *P*	to begin singing
Na pútu kùći seljáci su čésto zapijèvali/zapèvali.	On the way home the peasants would often begin singing.
Kàd je bìo blizu kùće, ón je zàpjevao/zàpevao iz svèg glása.	When he was near the house, he began singing with full voice.

Aspect and Tense. Each member of the aspectual pair can be used in the past and future tenses:

já ću písati I'll be writing : já ću napísati I'll complete the writing [of something]

já sam písao : já sam napísao (see examples on page 275)

But the present tense imposes some limitations on the use of the perfective verb. Present forms of a *P* verb may ordinarily appear only after the clause connectives: **ako,** "if," **kad,** "when," **da,** "that," **dok,** "while, until," **čim,** "as soon as," and **pošto,** "because, after." In this usage the *P* form has a future meaning:

Kàd pročìtaš òvu knjìgu, dàt ću/ dàću ti i drùgu.	When you read this book, I'll give you another.
Àko dóđe ùjak, kážite mu da me čèka.	If my uncle comes, tell him to wait for me.

The future meaning of **kad pročitaš** . . . could be rendered more explicit by translating it: "When you will have finished reading . . ." Imperfective verbs may also be used after these connectives, but without the connotation of future action:

Kàd čìtas òvu knjìgu, obráti pážnju na stíl.	When you read this book, pay attention to the style.
Àko tó dòlazi ùjak, otvòri mu vráta.	If that's our uncle coming, open the door for him.

Aspect and the Imperative. The same consideration of continuing action as against completed action will guide the choice of verb in the imperative:

Čìtajte dòbre knjìge!	Read (as a general rule) good books!
Pročìtajte òvu knjìgu!	Read (and finish the reading of) this book!

Usually the imperfective verb is selected for the negated imperative, since this involves an order not to complete some action:

	Ne čìtajte òvo písmo!	Don't read this letter!
[or]	Nèmojte čìtati òvo písmo!	

Determining Aspect. One restriction on aspectual usage will enable you to determine whether a verb is of imperfective or perfective aspect: only *I* verbs can be used after the perfective verb **početi,** "to begin," and **prestati,** "to stop." Thus:

	Pòčeo sam gráditi [*I*] kùću.	I began building a house.
[but not]	Pòčeo sam sagráditi [*P*] kùću.	
	Màrija je prèstala govòriti.	Marija stopped speaking.
[but not]	Màrija je prèstala rèći [*P*].	

Double Aspect. There are some verbs with double aspect, that is, they can be either *I* or *P*. Such verbs are **čuti,** "to hear," **vìdjeti/vìdeti,** "to see," **òbrazovati,** "to educate," **ìmenovati,** "to name," **rúčati,** "to dine, have lunch," **vèčerati,** "to have supper." In addition, an ever-growing number of verbs based on loan words falls into this double aspectual category, e.g. **telefonírati,** "to telephone," **financírati/finansírati,** "to finance," **konstatírati/konstàtovati,** "to state":

Pètar je pòčeo telefonírati [*I*].	Peter began telephoning.
Čím je Pètar telefonírao [*P*], bŕzo je òtišao iz sòbe.	As soon as Peter had telephoned, he quickly left the room.

Sequence of Tenses. In reported speech in English there is a strong tendency to put the verb of the dependent clause in the past tense if the principal verb is in the past tense. Thus, "He said that he was sick" could mean that the person speaking *was* sick at some time in the past or is sick now. It is possible to say: "He said that he is sick," but generally the usage would be *was*. So also one might say "I told him that I was studying French," even though the studying is going on now. Cr&S, however, uses the same tense in the dependent clause that would be used in direct speech. Thus:

Bòlestan je.	He is sick.
Rèkao je da je bòlestan.	He said that he was (is) sick.
Ùčim fràncuski.	I'm studying French.
Rèkao sam mu da ùčim fràncuski.	I told him that I was (am) studying French.

Historical Present — **històrijski/istòrijski prèzent**

The one situation in which present forms of perfective verbs may be used without the connectives (**ako, da,** etc.) is the "historical present." This is the device, particularly appropriate for storytelling, of describing past events as though they were taking place at the time of the telling. In the example the perfective present forms are italicized.

Pròšle gòdine sredìnom ljèta/lèta *dòbijem* òdsustvo i *krénem* za Splìt. Tàmo *srètnem* prìjatelja, sa njím *sjèdnem/sèdnem* u àuto i *pròdužim* za Dùbrovnik gdjè/gdè smo òstali trí dána.	Last year in the middle of the summer I get myself a leave and take off for Split. There I meet a friend, climb into (sit in) a car with him, and continue on to Dubrovnik, where we stayed three days.

To describe ongoing action, use *I* equivalents of the above *P* verbs, that is, **dòbijam, kréćem, srètam, sjèdim/sèdim,** and **prodùžavam.**

Exact Future — **fùtur ègzaktni**

When two statements about the future are associated, a priority in time can be indicated for one by using the "exact future." The verbal action of the "exact future" will thus take place before the action expressed by the regular future. The "exact future" involves the use of the perfective forms of **biti** "to be" (**budem-budeš-bude-budemo-budete-budu**) along with a verbal adjective (e.g. **pročitao**) in a clause introduced by **da, čim, kada, pošto, ako,** or **dok.***

Àko ne *bùdeš* dòbro *ùčio,* tí ćeš kòpati.	If you don't study well, you'll dig [i.e. end up doing manual labor].

*These are the usual clause connectives employed here; others are **kako, tko/ko** (see example), etc. The connective may even be lacking, as in the example **Bùdem li ga vìdio/vìdeo, rèći ću mu,** "Should I see him, I'll tell him."

Kàd *bùdete pročìtali* òvu knjìgu, dàt ću/dàću vam i drùgu. — When you finish reading (will have finished reading) this book, I'll give you another.

Tkò/Kò *bùde* přvi *dòšao,* nèka pòdloži vàtru. — Whoever arrives first will start the fire.

The same time sequence may be expressed by using a present form of a perfective verb in the dependent clause and the regular future in the main clause. This construction is more frequently used than that employing the "exact future":

Kàd pročìtaš òvu knjìgu, dàt ću/dàću ti i drùgu.* — When you finish reading this book, I'll give you another.

More About Verbs.

You have already met three tenses of the Cr&S verb: the present (**ja pišem**), the future (**ja ću pisati**), and the past tense (**ja sam pisao**). You are also familiar with the part that verbal aspect plays in the selection of a verb for these tenses, e.g. **ja pišem : (ako) ja napišem, ja ću pisati : ja ću napisati, ja sam pisao : ja sam napisao.**

There are three more tenses of past time in Cr&S. They are, in order of the frequency of their use, the aorist, the imperfect, and the pluperfect. The aorist is sometimes used in speech, but its usage is usually limited to storytelling. Forms from all three tenses, and especially the aorist, do appear in written Cr&S, and thus they must be recognized and interpreted correctly.

The Aorist **àorist**

Aorist forms of a verb indicate that the verbal action or situation took place in the past and that this verbal action or situation was terminated, though perhaps not completed, at a definite time in the past. Usually verbs of perfective aspect are selected for the aorist tense, though verbs of imperfective aspect may be used in the aorist and have often been so used in the folk literature.

Kàd *učìniše* štò im gospòdar *zàpovjedi/zàpovedi, prímiše* pláću/plátu svòju.† — When they had done what the owner had instructed them [to do], they received their wages.

Já *ùzeh* knjìgu, a ón mi je *òte.* — I took the book, but he grabbed it from me.

*A common mistake for beginners is to use **kad ćete pročitati** instead of **kad budete pročitali** or **kad pročitate** in the dependent clause.

†**učìniti,** "to do," **zapòvjediti/zapòvediti,** "to command," **prímiti,** "to receive," **ùzeti,** "to take," and **òteti,** "to grab," are perfective verbs, while **mùčiti se,** "to strive hard," and **jèsti,** "to eat," are imperfective.

Tàko se *mùčismo* dvìje/dvé ràtne gòdine bez sòli i *jèdosmo* nèslanu i nèukusnu hránu.	That's the way we struggled along without salt for two years of the war, eating (and we were eating) unsalted and tasteless food.

Forming the Aorist. The aorist is formed from the infinitive stem and, if this stem ends in a vowel (**napisa-ti**), the characteristic aorist endings are **-h-, -, -smo, -ste, -še.** The following perfective verbs will be used as examples: **napisati,** "to write," **pròkleti,** "to curse," **odgovòriti,** "to answer," **dòčuti,** "to be informed," and **potònuti,** "to sink":

(ja)	napísah	pròkleh	odgovòrih	dòčuh	potònuh
(ti)	napisa	prokle	òdgovori	doču	pòtonu
(on)	napisa	prokle	òdgovori	doču	pòtonu
(mi)	napisasmo	proklesmo	odgovòrismo	dočusmo	potònusmo
(vi)	napisaste	prokleste	odgovòriste	dočuste	potònuste
(oni)	napisaše	prokleše	odgovòriše	dočuše	potònuše

In general, the accent of aorist forms is that of the infinitive, though, as indicated above, the second and third singular forms of some verbs have a distinctive accent on the first syllable.

Verbs that have infinitive stems ending in consonants add the aorist endings **-oh, -e, -e, -osmo, -oste, -oše.** In the case of certain verbs, sound changes in the infinitive form have obscured the nature of the stem, but other forms of these verbs indicate the basic stem; e.g. **rèći** [from **rek-ti**], present **ja rèčem** or **ja rèknem,** past **rèkao, rèkla,** etc. Aorist forms of the following perfective verbs will be used as examples: **rèći,** "to say," **istrésti (istrésem),** "to shake out," **lèći (lèžem, lègnem),** "to lie down," **ovŕći (ovŕšem),** "to thresh out," and **zaplèsti (zaplètem),** "to entangle":

(ja)	rèkoh, rèknuh	istrésoh	zaplètoh	lègoh	ovŕhoh
(ti)	reče, reknu	ìstrese	zàplete	leže	òvrše
(on)	reče, reknu	ìstrese	zàplete	leže	òvrše
(mi)	rekosmo, reknusmo	istrésosmo	zaplètosmo	legosmo	ovŕhosmo
(vi)	rekoste, reknuste	istrésoste	zaplètoste	legoste	ovŕhoste
(oni)	rekoše, reknuše	istrésoše	zaplètoše	legoše	ovŕhoše

In the examples above and in similar verbs **k, g,** and **h** become **č, ž,** and **š,** respectively, before the ending **-e** of the second and third singular aorist. Other examples of this change would be: **mògoh, mòže** (**mòći,** "to be able"), **pèkoh, pèče** (**pèći,** "to bake") and **dìgoh, dìže** (**dìći,** "to lift").

The aorist forms of **biti** "to be" are:

(ja)	bìh	(mi)	bìsmo
(ti)	bí	(vi)	bìste
(on)	bí	(oni)	bìše

The Imperfect — ìmperfekt/ìmperfekat

The imperfect tense specifies the continuing process of verbal action in the past or the repetition of verbal action in the past. As expected, only verbs of imperfective aspect can appear in this tense.

Dòsad *písah* jèdno písmo, a pòslije/pòsle rúčka ću ga završiti.	I was writing a letter up to now, and I'll finish it after lunch.
Zvòna bez prèstanka *zvònjahu* za mrtvàca. [inf. **zvòniti** I]	The bells were tolling without cessation for the deceased.

Forming the Imperfect. The imperfect stem is usually derived from the present stem, though some verbs use the infinitive stem as a basis. The endings are **-ah, -aše, -aše, -asmo, -aste, -ahu,** and these are added to the verb stem, which, in the case of certain verbs, is enlarged by **-j-** or by **-ij-.** The imperfect forms of the following verbs will serve as examples: **písati (píšem),** "to write," **govòriti (gòvorim),** "to speak," **kléti (kùnem),** "to curse," **tònuti (tònem),** "to sink," **trésti (trésem),** "to shake," and **čùti (čùjem),** "to hear" [**čuti** is exceptional in being both imperfective and perfective in aspect]:

(ja)	písah	gòvorah	kùnjah	tònjah	trésijah	čùjah
(ti)	pisaše	govoraše	kunjaše	tonjaše	tresijaše	čujaše
(on)	pisaše	govoraše	kunjaše	tonjaše	tresijaše	čujaše
(mi)	pisasmo	govorasmo	kunjasmo	tonjasmo	tresijasmo	čujasmo
(vi)	pisaste	govoraste	kunjaste	tonjaste	tresijaste	čujaste
(oni)	pisahu	govorahu	kunjahu	tonjahu	tresijahu	čujahu

The imperfect forms of **biti**, "to be," are the following:

	ijekavian	*ekavian*
(ja)	bìjah, bjèh	bèjah, bèh
(ti)	bijaše, bješe	bejaše, beše
(on)	bijaše, bješe	bejaše, beše
(mi)	bijasmo, bjesmo	bejasmo, besmo
(vi)	bijaste, bjeste	bejaste, beste
(oni)	bijahu, bjehu	bejahu, behu

The Pluperfect — plùskvamperfekt/plùskvamperfekat

The pluperfect, a little-used compound tense, is composed of the imperfect tense forms of **biti** (see above) plus the infinitive adjective (e.g. **pisao, pisala**) or the regular past of **biti** (**ja sam bio, ja sam bila,** etc.) plus the infinitive adjective, e.g. **ja bjeh/beh pisao** or **ja sam bio pisao,** "I had been writing." The pluperfect specifies verbal action or a verbal situation that took place or existed prior to some other verbal action or situation. (For a summary of all verb tenses, see diagram on page 285).

Ìako *su* mu *bíli obèćali* pòklone, ón se ne obàziraše na sve to.	Although they had promised him gifts, he paid (was paying) no attention to all that.
Prèvrtahu ga i òbrtahu, ali ón vèć *bjèše/bèše izdàhnuo.*	They were turning him over and around, but he had already breathed his last.

Past Passive Participle — prídjev/prídev tŕpni

Adjectival forms derived from verbs fall into two types: the **l-** adjectives (e.g. **čitao, čitala**), which are active in meaning, and the **n-/t-** adjectives, which are passive in meaning.

Verbal adjectives in **-n/-t** (traditionally called "past passive participles") have a meaning of "something having been done." They are formed only from transitive verbs, that is, verbs that may be followed by the accusative case without a preposition, e.g. **ja pišem pismo,** "I write a letter," but not **ja idem u grad,** "I go into the city." The verbs used as a base may be either of imperfective or perfective aspect, though the latter type is more frequently selected.

Once formed, these verbal adjectives function in all ways as regular adjectives, appearing either as a noun modifier: **pòtpisano písmo,** "a signed letter," or as the terminus of a "to be" equation: **písmo je pòtpisano,** "the letter is signed." And like other adjectives, they may have both indefinite and definite endings, e.g. **zàtvoren kìšobran,** "a closed umbrella," and **zàtvoreni kìšobran,** "the closed umbrella."

Here are some examples using **zatvoren,** a verbal adjective based on the perfective verb **zatvòriti,** "to close"; the form **vráta** is a neuter plural with a singular meaning "door":

Vráta su zàtvorena.	The door is closed.
Vráta će bìti zàtvorena.	The door will be closed.
Vráta su bíla zàtvorena.	The door was/has been closed.
Zàtvorena vráta štíte od pása.	A closed door keeps away dogs.
Pàs je làjao pred zàtvorenim vrátima.	The dog was howling in front of the closed door.

Forming Past Passive Participles. Verbal adjectives of passive meaning are formed from the infinitive stems of transitive verbs (either aspect) in the following four ways:

1. **-n** is added to infinitive stems that end in **a:**

písa-ti *I*	to write	:	písan	written
napísa-ti *P*	to write	:	nàpisan	written
píta-ti *I*	to ask	:	pítan	asked
upíta-ti *P*	to ask	:	ùpitan	asked

2. **-en** is added to infinitive stems that end in a consonant. In cases where the consonant has disappeared or has been changed in the infinitive form, the consonant of the infinitive stem may be seen in the forms of the present tense:

dovèsti [òni dovèdu] *P*	to conduct	:	dovèden	conducted
plèsti [òni plètu] *I*	to knit	:	plèten	knitted
rèći [ón rèče] *P*	to say	:	rèčen	said
dònijeti/dòneti [já donèsem] *P*	to bring	:	donèsen	brought

3. **-jen** is added to the bare infinitive root of infinitives in **-iti** and **-jeti, -ijeti/-eti.** These are the verbs whose present forms have the **i-**endings, e.g. **nòsiti,** "to carry," **ón nòsi,** "he carries," and **tŕpjeti/tŕpeti,** "to endure," **ón tŕpi,** "he endures":

brán-iti *I*	to defend	:	bránjen	defended
hvál-iti *I*	to praise	:	hváljen	praised
nòs-iti *I*	to carry	:	nòšen	carried
tŕp-jeti/tŕp-eti *I*	to endure	:	tȑpljen	endured

For the various consonantal changes brought about by the addition of **-j-**, see pages 208–9.

4. **-t** is added to infinitive stems in **nu (dignu-ti)** and to a small number of monosyllabic verbal stems (**kle-ti**) along with their derivatives:

dìgnu-ti *P*	to elevate	:	dìgnut	elevated
màknu-ti *P*	to move	:	màknut	moved
klé-ti *I*	to curse	:	klét	cursed
pròkle-ti *P*	to curse	:	pròklet	accursed

A few verbal types do not fit exactly into the classification above, e.g. **ùbiti,** "to kill" : **ubìjen, šìti,** "to sew" : **šìven.**

Verbal Adverbs — glàgolski prílozi

Cr&S has two adverbial forms that are derived from verbs. One is a verbal of present or *contemporaneous* time, the other of past or *prior* time. These verbals are sometimes referred to as indeclinable participles, present and past. Their usage is usually limited to the written language.

1. Present or contemporaneous verbal adverb (**prílog sàdašnji**). This can be formed by taking the third person plural form of the present tense (**ìgraju,** "they dance," **bèru,** "they pick," **gòvore,** "they talk," **pùtuju,** "they travel") and adding the suffix **-ći.** Thus **ìgrajući,** "dancing," **bèrući,** "picking," **gòvoreći,** "speaking" and **pùtujući,** "traveling." Once formed, these verbals do not change,* that is, they have

*Some exceptions are **bùdući** (**mòja bùduća žèna,** "my future wife") and **ìdući** (**ìduće gòdine,** "in the coming year"), which can function as adjectives.

THE CATEGORIES OF THE CROATIAN AND SERBIAN VERB IN DIAGRAM FORM

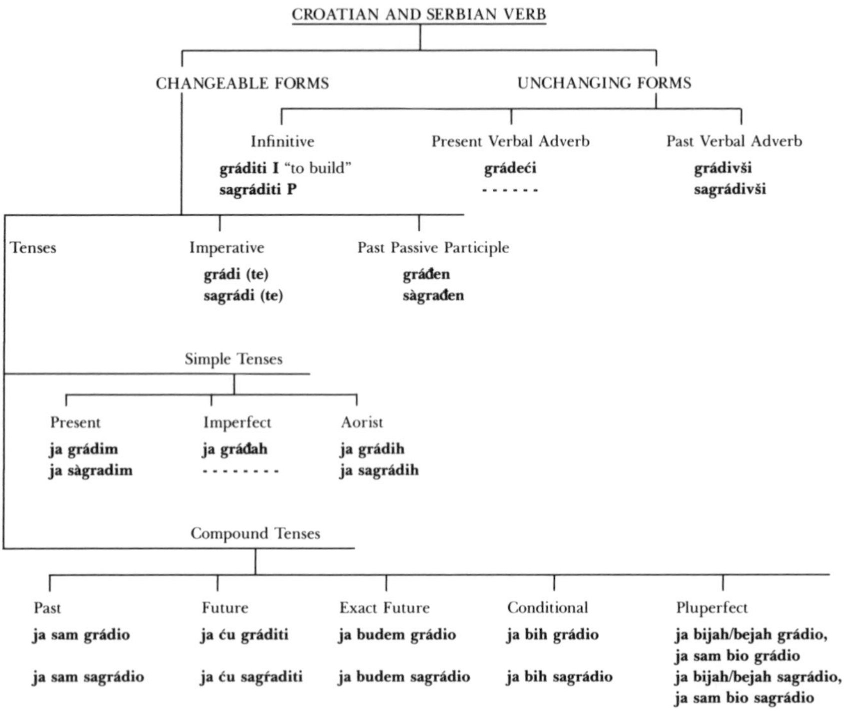

only one ending: **-ći.** They are formed only from verbs of imperfective aspect. The verbal meaning of this form supplements that of the main verb; the actor (person or thing) would be the same for both forms. The action expressed by the verbal goes on at the same time (i.e. is contemporaneous) as that of the main verb:

Čèkajući àutobus, čìtam knjìgu. [or] Dòk čèkam àutobus, čìtam knjìgu.	While waiting for the bus, I read a book.
Čèkajući àutobus, já ću čìtati knjìgu.	While waiting for the bus, I'll read a book.
Čèkajući àutobus, pročìtao sam knjìgu.	While waiting for the bus, I read the book.
Ùlazeći u grád, Pètar je srèo stárog seljáka.	Entering the city, Peter met an old farmer.

2. Past or prior time verbal adverb (**prílog pròšli**). This may be formed by adding **-vši** (/**-v** appears in a few stereotypes) to the infinitive stem of verbs of either aspect, e.g. **čìtavši, pročìtavši.** The verbal action or status denoted by this verbal is prior in time to that of the main verb:

Čèkavši àutobus ùzalud, òtišao sam kùći.	Having waited for the bus in vain, I set off for home.
Ùšavši u grád, Pètar je srèo stárog seljáka.	After he had entered the city, Peter met an old farmer.

In spoken Cr&S, clauses with **kada,** "when," **dok,** "while," **čim,** "as soon as," and **pošto,** "after," would usually be used in place of these verbal adverbs, e.g. **Pòšto je ùšao u grád, Pètar** . . . , "After he had entered the city, Peter . . ."

Enclitics and Proclitics

Unaccented Words. A number of Cr&S words have no independent accent of their own. Although written separately, these short forms (all either of one or two syllables) are joined in pronunciation with a neighboring accented word. If these forms are joined to a following word, we call them *proclitic*; the forms *a* and *in* in the English phrase "a friend in need," would thus be called proclitic. If they are attached to a preceding word, like *'d* in "I'd go" or *'m* in "tell'm (tell him)," they are called *enclitic.*

Enclitic and proclitic forms are further distinguished in Cr&S by two main differences: (1) proclitic forms may receive an accent under certain conditions, while enclitic forms never carry an accent; and (2) two or more enclitic forms may occur together, in a rigidly determined sequence, while usually only one proclitic form is associated with an accented word.

Enclitic Forms. The following forms would be classified as enclitic:

1. The question particle **li**:
2. Present form of the "helping" verbs:

ću, ćeš, će, ćemo, ćete, će	I'll, you'll, etc.
sam, si, ____, smo, ste, su	I'm, you're, etc.
bih, bi, bi, bismo, biste, bi	I'd, you'd, etc.

3. The unemphatic forms of personal pronouns in the dative case (emphatic forms are in parentheses):

mi	(mèni)	to me	nam	(nàma)	to us
ti	(tèbi)	to you	vam	(vàma)	to you
mu	(njèmu)	to him, to it	im	(njìma)	to them
joj	(njój)	to her, to it			

4. The unemphatic forms of personal pronouns in the accusative case:

me	(mène)	me	nas	(nás)	us
te	(tèbe)	you	vas	(vás)	you
ga	(njèga)	him, it	ih	(njíh)	them
ju, je	(njú)	her, it			

5. The reflexive form **se** (A case), "oneself":

6. The third singular present form of **biti,** i.e. **je:**

The six groupings above reflect the actual sequence of enclitic forms when they occur in association with the same accented word.

Arrangement of Enclitic Forms. In the sentence **Já sam dào knjìgu bràtu,** "I've given the book to the brother," there are four accented words and one enclitic form (**sam**), which will be pronounced as though it were an unaccented syllable in a word **Jàsam,** like English "I'm" or "I've." If you do not wish to specify "book" in this sentence, you can say:

	Já sam je dào bràtu.	[Jásamje dào. . .]	I've given it to the brother.
[or]	Dào sam je bràtu.	[Dàosamje . . . bràtu]	I've given it to the brother.

The enclitic form **je,** "her, it," is the accusative of **ona,** "she, it," and was selected because it stands for **knjigu,** a feminine noun in the A case. If it is obvious to the listener that the brother is the recipient of the book, you may then simply use the pronoun form meaning "to him":

	Já sam mu je dào.	[Jásamuje dào]	I've given it to him.
[or]	Dào sam mu je.	[Dàosamuje]	I've given it to him.

With future and conditional meanings, you can say:

	Já ću mu je dàti.	[Jáćumuje dàti]	I'll give it to him.
[or]	Já bih mu je dào.	[Jábihmuje dào]	I'd have given it to him.

Changing the sentences slightly, you could ask:

Dà li joj ju je dào [Dàlijojuje dào] Did he give it to her?

In this last sentence the form **ju** is the enclitic "her" while **je** is the third singular form that appears in **On je,** "He is," and **On je dao,** "He gave, he has given." Whenever this verb form **je** occurs, then the pronoun **je** meaning "her" is replaced by the enclitic form **ju.** Thus:

	Primijètio/Primétio sam je.	I noticed her.
[but]	Primijètio/Primétio ju je.	He noticed her.

Or, referring to "the book" (**knjigu**), you could say: **Dào sam je,** "I gave it," but **Dào ju je,** "He gave it." When the reflexive form **se** occurs with the verb form **je,** the order can be **se je,** though the **je** is usually omitted entirely:

	Vrátio sam se.	I returned.
	Vrátio se je.	He returned.
[but usually]	Vrátio se.	He returned.

The examples above indicate that when the enclitic forms occur together the question particle **li** has priority of position, with second place reserved for the helping verbs (**sam, ću, bih**), third place for the dative forms of pronouns, fourth place for the accusative forms of pronouns, fifth position for **se,** and sixth position for the verb form **je.** Fortunately for students of Cr&S, normally only four of these "positions" can be filled:

Dà li ćeš mu ga ______ ______dàti?	Will you give it [e.g. **med,** "honey"] to him?
Dà li su joj ga ______ ______dáli?	Did they give it to her?
Dà li biste im ______se ______po-kòrili?	Would you have yielded to them?
Dà li ______vam ga ______je dála?	Did she give it to you?
Dà li ______joj ______se (je) obèć-ao?	Did he pledge himself to her?

Usually the student will be concerned with the proper ordering of only two to three of these enclitic forms in any one clause.

Position of the Enclitic Forms in the Sentence. The previous section has considered the positions of enclitic forms when they occur together. Now it is necessary to relate the single enclitic form or the grouping of enclitic forms to the larger environment of the sentence or clause. There are only two possible positions for the enclitics within the sentence:

1. The enclitic form or forms appear immediately after the first accented word in the sentence or clause:

Živòtinje *su* jèdnog dána ràspravljale o vr̀lo vážnim stvárima.	The animals were discussing important things one day. [folktale]
Mògao *bi ga* jòš ùhvatiti.	You could still catch him.
Kàd *ga* vìdim, rèći *ću mu.*	When I see him, I'll tell him.
Pávle *bi* žèlio/žèleo vìše zíme, dà *bi se* mògao klìzati po lèdu.	Paul would like a longer winter, so he could skate on the ice.
Òva *se* stvár zòve novčànik.	This thing is called a purse.
U grádu *se* o tòme gòvori.	That's being talked about in the city.
U òvoj *se* knjìzi objàvljuju predávanja . . .	In this book are published the lectures . . .

Cr&S speakers tend not to separate parts of a subject. For example, the following sentences adhere to the textbook prescriptions:

Mòja je sòba malèna.	My room is small.
Mládi će pomòćnik kúpiti knjìge.	The young assistant will buy the books.

But usually a Cr&S speaker would say:

Mòja sòba je malèna.
Mládi pomòćnik će kúpiti knjìge.
[or] Mládi pomòćnik kúpit će/kúpiće knjìge.

2. The enclitic forms may appear in any part of the sentence immediately after an accented verb form:

Òva stvár *zòve se* novčànik.	This thing is called a purse.
Hrábri vojníci pod kòmandom generála Grànta *vrátili su se* preko rijèke/réke.	The brave soldiers under the command of General Grant returned across the river.
Slàvenska plemèna na Balkánu *bíla su* dòista mijèšana. /Slòvenska plemèna na Balkánu *bíla su* dòista méšana.	The Slavic tribes in the Balkans were indeed mixed.

Proclitics. Phrase and clause connectives (e.g. **i,** "and," **ako,** "if") and prepositions (e.g. **bez,** "without") are in the category of proclitics, that is, they usually have no accent and are pronounced together with the following accented word. In the older language and still in the language of rural speakers in Bosnia and Herzegovina, the proclitics can bear the accent under certain accentual conditions. Thus:

ì dan ì noć	both day and night
kòd kuće	at home
ù grad	into the city
nè vidim	I don't see

In modern Cr&S proclitics seldom carry the accent, and then usually only in stereotyped expressions such as **kòd kuće;** however, **kod kùće** can now be heard in the cities. The examples above now tend to be pronounced:

i dán i nóć
u grád
ne vìdim

Forming Questions. In Cr&S there are several ways of forming questions that expect an answer of "yes" or "no":

1. Òna píše písmo?	"Is she writing a letter?" Statement word order but with rising intonation on the element being questioned, that is, **ona** or **piše** or **pismo.**
2. Píše li òna písmo?	Here the word order is reversed and the question particle **li** is used; **li** must follow the first accented word in

	a sentence. Rising intonation characterizes the element questioned (see 1 above).
3. Dà li òna píše písmo?	Here the particles **da li** are used with normal statement word order. The intonation is that of a statement, with **da li** indicating that a question is involved.
4. Jè li òna píše písmo?	Rising intonation on initial **je li** with statement order and intonation for the rest of the sentence.
5. Òna píše písmo, zar nè?	As in 4 above; **zar ne** is stronger than **je li** and would mean something like "Isn't that right?"
6. Zár òna píše písmo?	As in 5 above. **Zar** has connotation of surprise: "Is she really writing a letter?"
7. Òna píše písmo, jè li?	Again statement word order with statement intonation but rising intonation on **je li,** which is similar in meaning to English "Isn't that so?"

The first three methods are those most commonly used. Both Croats and Serbs use 1 (statement order with question intonation), but then Croats favor 2 (**li** and inverted word order), while Serbs prefer 3 (**da li** with statement order and statement intonation).

Question Words. Certain words, like **zar** above, have an interrogative or questioning meaning and so automatically introduce questions.

1. Question pronouns: **tkò/kò,** "who," and **štò/štà,** "what":

Kóga vìdite?	Whom do you see?
O *čèmu* gòvorite?	What are you talking about?

2. Question adjectives: **kòji,** "which," **čìji,** "whose," and **kàkav,** "what kind of":

Kòja je vàša kùća?	Which is your house?
Čìje je òvo pèro?	Whose pen is that?
Kàkav je ón stùdent?	What kind of student is he?

3. Question adverbs: **kàda, kàd,** "when," **kàko,** "how," **kòliko,** "how much," **gdjè/gdè,** "where," **kùda, kùd, kàmo,** "where to, in which direction":

Kàda ćemo stìći u Beògrad?	When will we arrive in Belgrade?
Kàko pùtujete po Jugosláviji?	How are you traveling through Yugoslavia?
Kòliko knjíga ìmate?	How many books do you have?

Gdjè/Gdè stànuješ?	Where are you rooming?
Kùda ìdeš?	Where are you going?

The last two examples illustrate the distinction between "where" in the meaning "where at" (**gdje/gde**) and "where" in the meaning "where to" (**kuda**); many speakers of Cr&S ignore this distinction and would say **Gdjè/Gdè ìdeš?** as well as **Gdjè/Gdè stànuješ.**

From Questions to Answers. In Cr&S question words may be altered into general responses in much the same way that the English word "where" can be changed into "anywhere," "nowhere," "somewhere," or "wherever." This process will be illustrated below using three prefixes: **i-,** "any-," **ni-,** "no," and **ne-,** "some," one suffix: **-god,** "some-," and one separate word: **god,** "ever":

gdjè/gdè	where	ìgdje/ìgde	anywhere
kàda*	when	ìkada	anytime
kàko	how	ìkako	anyhow
štò/štà	what	ìšta	anything
tkò/kò	who	ìtko/ìko	anybody
nìgdje/nìgde	nowhere	nègdje/nègde	somewhere
nìkada	never	nèkada	sometime
nìkako	in no way	nèkako	somehow
nìšta	nothing	nèšto	something
nìtko/nìko	nobody	nètko/nèko	somebody
gdjègod/gdègod	somewhere	gdjè gòd/gdè gòd	wherever
kàdagod	sometime	kàda gòd	whenever
kàkogod	somehow	kàko gòd	however
štògod/štàgod	something	štò gòd/štà gòd	whatever
tkògod/kògod	somebody	tkò gòd/kò gòd	whoever

Here are some examples showing the use of **tko/ko** and its related forms:

Tkò/Kò je dòšao?	Who came?
Àko ìtko/ìko dóđe, bìt će/bìće dòbro.	If anybody comes, it'll be good.
Nìtko/Nìko nìje dòšao.	Nobody came.
Nètko/Nèko je dòšao.	Somebody came.
Àko tkògod/kògod dóđe, prímite ga.	If somebody comes, receive him.
Tkò gòd/Kò gòd dóđe, mòže me čèkati.	Whoever comes can wait for me.

Although the combinations with **-god** and **god** seem very similar, there are two distinguishing factors: (1) **-god,** "some-," has no accent of its own and so becomes part of the preceding word, while **god,** "ever," has its own accent and maintains itself as a separate word; and (2) this

*Forms without final **a** are common: **kad, ikad, nikad, nekad, kadgod,** and **kad god.**

independent word **god,** "ever," may be separated from the question word by an enclitic (unaccented) form. Some examples:

Urádite *štògod*; nèmojte stàjati stálno!	Do something; don't keep on standing around!
Štò gòd zàradite, já ću vam plátiti.	Whatever you earn, I'll pay you.
Štò ste gòd urádili, kážite mi!	Whatever you did, tell me about it!

Clause Connectives. It is not difficult to make short Cr&S statements such as "I went home" and "She came" and "It was raining," etc. The next step in learning Cr&S will be to learn to link these small units together in a larger speech unit, e.g. "I went home, because she came," or "I went home, although it was raining." These small units are clauses and the linking elements (*because, although, when,* etc.) are clause connectives or conjunctions. The more common clause connectives are exemplified below, but additional examples from one's own reading and speech experience will be necessary for an adequate understanding of the many possibilities of meaning of these small, unchanging forms.

a* and, but	Já sam vèliki a mój bràt je jòš máli.	I'm big, but my brother is still small.
ako if	Dàt ću/Dàću ti svè òvo, ako pògodiš.	I'll give you all this if you guess correctly.
ali but	Dùgo sam ga čèkao, ali ón nìje dòšao.	I waited for him a long time, but he didn't come.
čím when, as soon as	Čím ùstanete, pozòvite me telefónom.	As soon as you get up, call me on the telephone.
gdje/gde where	Pítao je òtac gdjè/gdè sam bìo.	My father asked where I had been.
i and	Ùzmite nòvine i čìtajte!	Take the paper and read it!
da [uses listed in following section]		
dok while	Dòk ja stùdiram, bùdite mírni!	Be quiet while I'm studying.
dok (ne)† until	Čèkajte nas óvdje/óvde, dòk se (ne) vrátimo.	Wait for us here until we return.
iako although	Ìako kìša pàda, já móram ìći u škólu.	Although it's raining, I must go to school.
ili or	Pošàlji nam pòmoć ili ćemo svì ìzginuti.	Send us help or we'll all perish.

*Clause connectives are proclitics and sometimes take the accent; when this occurs, the accent will be short, e.g. **à, àko, àli;** a few connectives have a long accent, e.g. **čím.**

†The parentheses around the **ne** in **dok (ne)** indicates that its use is optional.

jer because	Ne mògu ìći, jèr sam bòlestan.	I can't go because I'm sick.
kad, kada when, while	Kàda màčka nìje u kùći, mìševi se vesèle.	When the cat's away, the mice will play.
kako how, as	Kàko sìješ/sèješ, tàko ćeš i žèti.	As you sow, so shall you reap.
	Promátrali/Posmátrali su seljáka kàko bère gróžđe.	They watched the peasant gathering grapes.
mada although	Màda zná da ne pìjem àlkohol, ón mi je dònio/dòneo vína.	Although he knows I don't drink, he brought me some wine.
nego but	Nèmoj se razgovárati nego ùči!	Don't talk but study!
no but	Néću ìći na sjèdnicu/sèdnicu, nò ću se vrátiti kùći.	I'll not go to the meeting, but I'll go home.
pa and also	Mìlica je tó rèkla mèni, pà će rèći i tèbi.	Milica told that to me, and she'll tell it to you also.
pa ipak and yet	Ón mi je tòliko neprìjatnosti učìnio, pa ìpak ga vòlim.	He's caused me so much unpleasantness, and yet I like him.
pošto after, because	Pòšto se svè svŕšilo, mi smo òtišli.	After everything was finished, we left.
	Ne mògu putòvati, pošto nèmam ni nóvca ni vrèmena.	I can't travel because I have neither the money nor the time.
premda although	Prèmda je bílo tòplo, ón nìje ìšao na kúpanje.	Although it was warm, he didn't go for a swim.
prìje/pré nego štò before	Zaključao sam vráta, prìje/pré nego štò sam òtišao.	I locked the door before I left.
što/šta what, that which, the fact that, that (for)	Káži mi štò/štà mìsliš.	Tell me what you're thinking.
	Što kìša pàda, nàma ne sméta.	The fact that it's raining doesn't bother us.
	Opròsti/Izvíni me, što dòlazim tàko ràno.	Excuse me for coming so early.

te and so	Ón će prímiti pláću/plátu sùtra, tè se ne brìni za dùg.	He'll get his pay tomorrow, and so don't worry about the debt.
tek što hardly, no sooner. . .	Tèk što sam dòšao kùći, prìjatelj mi je telefonírao.	No sooner had I arrived home than a friend of mine called on the phone.
zato therefore, so	Tàko ste sámi htjèli/htèli, zàto se nèmojte žàliti.	You wanted it that way yourself, so don't complain.
zato što because	Pròšle nòći nísam dòbro spávao zàto što sam pìo sùviše kàve/kàfe.	I didn't sleep well last night because I drank too much coffee.

Uses of **da**

dà that

The use of **da** in "indirect discourse" is perhaps its most common use. Usually one can take any statement in "direct discourse" and link it up by means of **da** to someone who thinks, or hears, or makes the statement. For example,

Direct Discourse:

	Ón će sùtra dóći.	He'll come tomorrow.

Indirect Discourse:

	Rèkao je dà će sùtra dóći.	He said that he'll come tomorrow.
	Čùo sam dà . . .	I heard that . . .
	Mìslimo dà . . .	We think that . . .
	Làku noć, i nádam se dà se nòćas néće nìšta dèsiti.	Goodnight, and I hope that nothing will happen tonight.
da in order	Nòsimo nàočale/nàočare da bòlje vìdimo.	We wear glasses in order to see better.
da that (as a result)	Mràz je bìo tàko ják dà su se prózori zalèdili.	The frost was so heavy that the windows were iced over.
da let's, may one	Da pòpijemo po šàlicu/šólju kàve/kàfe.	Let's have a cup of coffee.

da . . .

[The English sentence type: "We heard them talking," or "I see him playing," is usually rendered by a **da-** clause (see also **kako**) in Cr&S.]

	Čùli smo da òni gòvore o škóli.	We heard them talking about school.

da . . . [**da** with a present verb form often replaces the infinitive in Serbian usage.]

Cr. and S.	Já ću ìći.	I'll go.
S.	Já ću da ìdem.	I'll go.
da li Does/Do . . . ?	Dà li Pávle stànuje kod Pètrovića?	Does Paul live at Petrović's place?
kao da as if, as though	Èmil gòvori hȑvatski kào da je ròđen u Hȑvatskoj.	Emil speaks Croatian as though he were born in Croatia.

Uses of **kòji.** An important connective is **kòji,** "who, which," whose forms vary according to the antecedent nouns or pronouns and to the function (e.g. subject, object) required in the dependent clause. Thus,

Gdjè/Gdè je tá žèna *kòju* sam srèo sìnoć?	Where is that woman I met last night?
Òdluke *kòje* je vláda dònijela/dònela òdmah pòsle ràta bíle su bòlje od njénih kàsnijih òdluka.	The decisions which the government took immediately after the war were better than its later decisions.
Svȉjet/Svét nȉje nȉšta drùgo nego jèdna vèlika knjìga od *kòje* sa svàkim kòrakom prèvrnemo po jèdan líst.	Life is nothing but a big book in which we turn one page with each stride.

Uses of **što.** As shown above, **što/šta** can be used in the meaning of "what" in a sentence such as the following:

Káži mi štò/štà mìsliš? — Tell me what you are thinking.

If **da** were used, the meaning would be different:

Káži mi dà mìsliš. — Tell me that you are thinking.

But **što** (not **šta**) can also be used in place of **kòji:**

Òvaj ùdžbenik prìpada stùdentu štò sjèdi/sèdi kraj mène. — This textbook belongs to the student who sits next to me.

In the sentence above, **kòji** could be used, e.g. **kòji sjedi/sedi** . . . In clauses where **što** does not function as the subject, a pronoun can be added to specify the syntactic relationship:

Òvo je stránac štò ste mu dàli màpu.	Here is the foreigner to whom you gave the map.
[or]	
Òvo je stránac kòjemu/kòme ste dàli màpu.	
U òvoj se knjìzi objàvljaju predávanja štò ih je Stjèpan Ívšić sprémio.	In this book are published the lectures that Stjepan Ivšić prepared.
[or]	
. . . predávanja kòja je Stjèpan Ívšić sprémio.	

Review of Adjective and Noun Case Forms

Masculine singular

N	òvaj	stári	ìspit	kònj
V	———	stari	ispite	konju
A	ovaj, ovoga*	stari, staroga*	ispit	konja
G	ovoga*	staroga*	ispita	konja
D	ovome*	starome*	ispitu	konju
I	ovim	starim	ispitom	konjem

Masculine plural

N	òvi	stári	ìspiti	kònji
V	———	stari	ispiti	konji
A	ove	stare	ispite	konje
G	ovih	starih	ispita	kónja
D	ovima*	starima*	ispitima	kònjima
I	ovima*	starima*	ispitima	konjima

Neuter singular

N	òvo	stáro	sèlo	pòlje
V	———	staro	selo	polje
A	ovo	staro	selo	polje
G	ovoga*	staroga*	sela	polja
D	ovome*	starome*	selu	polju
I	ovim	starim	selom	poljem

Neuter plural

N	òva	stára	sèla	pòlja
V	———	stara	sela	polja
A	ova	stara	sela	polja
G	ovih	starih	séla	pólja
D	ovima*	starima*	sèlima	pòljima
I	ovima*	starima*	selima	poljima

Feminine singular (**a**-nouns)

N	òva	stára	žèna	zèmlja
V	———	stara	ženo	zemljo
A	ovu	staru	ženu	zemlju
G	ove	stare	žene	zemlje
D	ovoj	staroj	ženi	zemlji
I	ovom	starom	ženom	zemljom

*There are variant forms without the final vowel, e.g. **ovog** for **ovoga** or **starom** for **starome.** The adjective forms in the above paradigms are the "definite" forms.

Feminine plural (**a**-nouns)

N	òve	stáre	žène	zèmlje
V	_____	stare	žene	zemlje
A	ove	stare	žene	zemlje
G	ovih	starih	žéna	zemálja
D	ovima*	starima*	žènama	zèmljama
I	ovima*	starima*	ženama	zemljama

	Feminine singular (**i**-nouns)			*Feminine plural* (**i**-nouns)		
N	òva	stára	stvár	òve	stáre	stvári
V	_____	stara	stvari	_____	stare	stvari
A	ovu	staru	stvar	ove	stare	stvari
G	ove	stare	stvari	ovih	starih	stvari
D	ovoj	staroj	stvari	ovima*	starima*	stvarima
I	ovom	starom	stvarju, stvari	ovima*	starima*	stvarima

Review of Verb Forms

A survey of the various forms and formations of the Cr&S verb may be effected by a close examination of three representative verbs: **pítati** "to ask," **trésti,** "to shake," and **govòriti,** "to speak."

	Present Tense			*Imperfect Tense*		
(ja)	pítam	trésem	gòvorim	pítah	trésijah	gòvorah
(ti)	pitaš	treseš	govoriš	pitaše	tresijaše	govoraše
(on)	pita	trese	govori	pitaše	tresijaše	govoraše
(mi)	pitamo	tresemo	govorimo	pitasmo	tresijasmo	govorasmo
(vi)	pitate	tresete	govorite	pitaste	tresijaste	govoraste
(oni)	pitaju	tresu	govore	pitahu	tresijahu	govorahu

Present Verbal Adverb

pítajući trésući gòvoreći

Imperative

(ti)	pítaj	trési	govòri
(mi)	pitajmo	tresimo	govorimo
(vi)	pitajte	tresite	govorite

Infinitive

pítati trésti govòriti

Future

ja	ću	pítati, trésti, govòriti
ti	ćeš	
on	će	
mi	ćemo	
vi	ćete	
oni	će	

*See preceding footnote.

Past Verbal Adverb

pítavši	trésavši	govòrivši

Past Passive Participle

pítan	trésen	gòvoren

Past Tense

ja	sam	pítao, trésao, govòrio
ti	si	
on	je	
mi	smo	pítali, trésli, govòrili
vi	ste	
oni	su	

Conditional

ja	bih	pítao, trésao, govòrio
ti	bi	
on	bi	
mi	bismo	pítali, trésli, govòrili
vi	biste	
oni	bi	

Exact Future

ja	bùdem	pítao, trésao, govòrio
ti	budeš	
on	bude	
mi	budemo	pítali, trésli, govòrili
vi	budete	
oni	budu	

Aorist

ja	pítah	trésoh	govòrih
ti	pita	trese	gòvori
on	pita	trese	gòvori
mi	pitasmo	tresosmo	govòrismo
vi	pitaste	tresoste	govòriste
oni	pitaše	tresoše	govòriše

The verb biti "to be"

Present Tense (Imperfective aspect)

ja	jèsam, sam	mi	jèsmo, smo
ti	jèsi, si	vi	jèste, ste
on	jèst/jèste, je	oni	jèsu, su

Present Tense (Perfective aspect)

ja	bùdem	mi	bùdemo
ti	budeš	vi	budete
on	bude	oni	budu

Imperfect Tense (ijekavski)	*Imperfect Tense (ekavski)*
ja bìjah *or* bjèh	ja bèjah *or* bèh
ti bijaše, bješe	ti bejaše, beše
on bijaše, bješe	on bejaše, beše
mi bijasmo, bjesmo	mi bejasmo, besmo
vi bijaste, bjeste	vi bejaste, beste
oni bijahu, bjehu	oni bejahu, behu

Present Verbal Adverb bùdući

Imperative

(ti)	bùdi
(mi)	budimo
(vi)	budimo

Infinitive bìti

Past Verbal Adverb bívši

Future ja ću bìti itd

Past Tense ja sam bìo (bìla)

Aorist

ja	bìh	mi	bìsmo
ti	bí	vi	bìste
on	bí	oni	bíše

Conditional ja bih bìo (bìla)

The verb ići "to go"

Present

(ja)	ìdem	(mi)	ìdemo/idémo
(ti)	ìdeš	(vi)	ìdete/idète
(on)	ìde	(oni)	ìdu

Imperfect

ìđah	ìđasmo
iđaše	iđaste
iđaše	iđahu

Present Verbal Adverb ìdući

Imperative

(ti)	ìdi
(mi)	idimo
(vi)	idite

Infinitive ìći

Past Verbal Adverb ìšavši

Aorist

ìdoh	ìdosmo
ide	idoste
ide	idoše

Past Tense ja sam ìšao (ìšla)

Exact Future
ja bùdem ìšao (ìšla)

Conditional ja bih ìšao (ìšla)

Abbreviations **Skraćènice**

br.	broj	number
č.	čitaj	read, confer
d.	drug	comrade
dca	drugarica	comrade (female)
dr	doktor	doctor

MÁLI RJÈČNIK/RÈČNIK GLOSSARY

This glossary, or small dictionary, is divided into two parts: (1) a Cr&S-to-English section, and (2) an English-to-Cr&S section. The first section contains all the words used in the conversations and reading texts, while the second section has a listing of frequently used words that a student can employ in creating Cr&S conversations or in writing compositions. At the end of each section are blank pages a student can use to enter words suggested by a teacher or found in other Cr&S texts. This is not a reference dictionary (you will not find, for example, an entry for English "aardvark"); a large library will usually have more complete dictionaries of the Cr&S language.

In addition to this glossary, there are specialized vocabularies in various parts of this textbook. They are:

- adjectives in common use (pages 234–36)
- clothing and footwear (pages 101–2)
- countries and continents (pages 75–77)
- names of common foods (pages 131–34)
- national and regional names (pages 166–67)
- numbers (pages 241–42)
- occupations and professions (pages 54–57)
- parts of the body (pages 81–83)
- weather terms (pages 26–27)

SECTION 1. EXPLANATION OF CR&S-TO-ENGLISH ENTRIES

Croatian or Serbian. A user of a glossary such as this must distinguish between the Croatian and Serbian variants of the standard Cr&S language. The Croatian variants uses ijekavian forms and a number of specifically Croatian words, e.g. **kruh,** "bread." The Serbian variant uses ekavian (in Serbia proper) and a number of specifically Serbian words, e.g. **hleb,** "bread." Regardless of nationality (Croatian, Montenegrin, Moslem, Serbian), speakers in Bosnia-Herzegovina and Montenegro use ijekavian. Thus, one can say that all Croats use ijekavian, but not all speakers of ijekavian are Croats. On the other hand, it can be said that all ekavian speakers (dialects aside) are Serbs, but not all Serbs speak ekavian. This situation is **kompliciràno,** as a Croat might say, or

kòmplikovano, as a Serb might affirm. Where ijekavian (/jekavian) and ekavian forms occur in this section, they will be so identified.

Accents. Two accent marks, the grave (̀) and the acute (́), are used. The grave accent indicates a stress (i.e. loudness) accent on a short vowel, e.g. **pàs,** "dog," **kùpiti,** "to gather"; the acute accent indicates a stress accent on a long (i.e. in duration) vowel, e.g. **pás [pās],** "belt," **kúpiti [kūpiti],** "to buy." Thus, an accented vowel can be short in duration or long in duration, depending on the particular word. The accent can fall on any syllable, though it occurs on the last syllable *only* in about a score of words, e.g. **paradàjz,** "tomato," **assistènt,** "assistant." Changes in the place of accent within noun and verb paradigms will be specified as much as possible, e.g. **vòjnik,** "soldier," G **vojníka, govòriti,** "to speak" [3rd sg. pres. **gòvori**]. In some places in Yugoslavia (e.g. Zagreb) the accentual situation is less complicated and in other places (e.g. Sarajevo) more complicated.

Nouns. The gender of each noun will be indicated by the letters *m* for masculine, *n* for neuter, and *f* for feminine, e.g. **sáveznik** *m,* "ally," **sèlo** *n,* "village," **kćérka** *f,* "daughter." Genitive (G) forms will be added where necessary to show accent or stem changes, e.g. **advòkat** *m,* G **advokáta,** "lawyer"; **Bosánac** *m,* G **Bosánca,** "a Bosnian." Other case forms will be added to indicate changes not easily predictable for a beginning student, e.g. k**ak** *m;* N plural k**aci,** "student, pupil"; **smr̀t** *f,* G **smr̀ti, I smr̀ću,** "death." Ijekavian or jekavian forms will be indicated by *ijek,* while *ek.* will signal the ekavian variants, e.g. **smìjeh** *m ijek.,* "laughter"; **sméh** *m ek.,* "laughter." Words specifically Croatian or Serbian will be so indicated, e.g. **krùh** *m* (Cr.), "bread"; **hlèb** *m* (S.), "bread," though it is often difficult to be positive in such assignments. The situation is such that for some English words there is a specifically Croatian equivalent and a specifically Serbian equivalent, as in the preceding example of "bread," but quite often there is a general Cr&S word, used by both Croats and Serbs, with a specific word used on occasions by one group. For example, both Croats and Serbs use the word **hìljada,** "thousand," while Croats also use **tìsuća;** in such a case **hìljada** is given with no specification, while **tìsuća** is labeled as Croatian. Likewise, since both Croats and Serbs use the word **ùho** for "ear," it is considered to be the general Cr&S word, while the special Serbian variant **ùvo** is specified as Serbian. Some masculine nouns have alternate forms with *a*-ending in the N case, e.g. **tùrist** *m* and **tùrista** *m,* "tourist"; nouns like **turista** are declined like feminine nouns of the **žena** type. The forms without *a* (e.g. **turist**) are considered to be general Cr&S, while the *a*-forms are labeled as Serbian; this identification may not be exact in all cases, but it does seem that Serbs are generally more inclined to use the *a*-forms. For Cr&S entries that have particular meanings valid for one or the other variant, the specification Cr. or S. will be placed after the relevant English meaning, e.g. **kùcati [kùca]** I "to type (S.), knock"; here the meaning "to knock" is a general Cr&S meaning for **kucati** while "to type" is specifically Serbian for this verb. Some entries have meanings for both variants, but the meanings differ, e.g. **ùbrus** *m* "napkin (Cr.), towel (S.)."

Adjectives. All adjectives will be so identified by use of the abbreviation *adj.* Where a stem change is involved, both the indefinite and definite forms will be shown in the nominative masculine singular, e.g. **čùdan-čùdni,** "wondrous, unusual"; here one sees that the stem is **čudn-** for all forms except for *one,* namely, the indefinite nominative masculine singular. An entry like **ják** *adj.,* "strong," shows the indefinite form and also indicates that **jak-** is the stem; the definite nominative masculine form would be **jáki.** Some adjectives (e.g., those in **-ski**) have no indefinite forms and thus appear with the *i*-ending, e.g. **gràdski,** "urban." Ijekavian and ekavian variants are distinguished by the notation *ijek.* or *ek.,* e.g. **lép** *ek. adj.,* "beautiful"; **lìjep** *ijek. adj.,* "beautiful." Adjectives specifically Croatian or Serbian will be so noted, e.g. **srètan-srètni** *adj.* (Cr.), "happy"; **srèćan-srèćni** *adj.* (S.), "happy."

Adjective Nouns. Certain Cr&S words are adjectives in form but function as nouns; many country names are of this type, e.g. **Ȅngleska,** "England," **u Ȅngleskoj,** "in England." Such words will be identified by the abbreviation *adj. noun.*

Pronouns. Pronouns, identified by *pron.,* are given in the nominative case form. Other forms will be found in the Grammar section.

Pronominal Adjectives: This special type of adjective will not be specifically identified but will be indicated by the presentation of the nominative singular form in the three genders, e.g. **mój** *m,* **mòje** *n,* **mòja** *f,* "my, mine." Complete forms will be found in the Grammar section.

Adverbs. Adverbs will be indicated by the abbreviation *adv.,* e.g. **dòbro** *adv.,* "good, well, o.k."; **nájpre** *ek. adv.,* "firstly, above all"; **nájprije** *ijek. adv.,* "firstly, above all." It should be remembered that many adverbs not included in this section can easily be derived from adjectives listed; thus, **bŕzo,** "quickly," can be derived from the listed **bŕz,** "quick, fast." The **-ski** adjectives and adverbs are largely interchangeable and the listing of one will suggest the other.

Prepositions. The case required after a particular preposition will be specified in parentheses, e.g. **kod** (prep. with G), "at, at home of." Prepositions do not usually have an accent.

Verbs. The basic entry form for the verb is the infinitive; the third person singular form of the present tense is then given in brackets, followed by specification of the aspect: *I* for imperfective aspect, *P* for perfective aspect. For example, **prímati [príma]** *I*, "to take, receive, accept"; **prímiti [prími]** *P*, "to take, receive, accept." Ekavian and ijekavian variants will be noted by means of *ek.* and *ijek.*, e.g. **bèležiti [bèleži]** *ek. I*, "to note, write down"; **bìlježiti [bìlježi]** *ijek. I*, "to note, write down." Croatian and Serbian variants will be so distinguished, e.g. **shvàćati [shvàća]** *I* (Cr.), "to grasp. comprehend"; **shvàtati [shvàta]** *I* (S.), "to grasp, comprehend." If the past tense forms are not easily predictable, the masculine and feminine singular forms will be cited, e.g. **mòći [mòže; mògao, mògla]** *I*, "to be able." Other unusual forms that occur in the text will also be cited.

ABBREVIATIONS	SKRAĆÈNICE
A	accusative case
adj.	adjective
adj. noun	adjective noun
adv.	adverb
aor.	aorist
coll.	collective noun
conj.	conjunction
Cr.	Croatian
Cr&S	Croatian and Serbian language
dial.	dialectal
D	dative case [=traditional dative and locative cases]
ek.	ekavian
excl.	exclamation
f	feminine gender
G	genitive case
gram.	grammatical
I [for nouns]	instrumental case
I [for verbs]	imperfective aspect
ijek.	ijekavian
imp.	imperative
impf.	imperfect tense
indecl.	indeclinable
m	masculine gender
n	neuter gender
N	nominative case
num.	numeral
P	perfective aspect
pert.	pertaining
pl.	plural
prep.	preposition
pres.	present tense
pron.	pronoun
S.	Serbian
sg.	singular
V	vocative case
v.	verbal

A a

a *conj.* and, but
á *excl.* ah!
abecéda *f* (Cr.) alphabet
adrèsa *f* address
advòkat *m*, **G advokáta** lawyer
aeròdrom *m* airport
afinìtet *m* affinity, preference
àfrički *adj.* African
Ãfrika *f*, **D Ãfrici** Africa
agrònom *m* agronomist
àh *excl.* oh!
àjde *ili* **hàjde** *excl.* come now!, let's
àjkula *f* (S.) shark
àjvar *m* (S.) pepper salad
akadèmija *f* academy
akadèmik *m*; **N** *pl.* **akadèmici** academician
akàdemski *adv.* university (-trained)
àkcenat *m*, **G àkcenta** accent
àkcent *m* accent
àkcioni *adj.* action (adj.)
ako *conj.* if
akròbatski *adv.* acrobatically
àktivan–àktivni *adj.* active
àktovka *f*, **D àktovci** briefcase
alarmírati [**alàrmira**] **I/P** to alarm
àlat *m* tools
Albánac *m*, **G Albánca** male Albanian
Ãlbanija *f* Albania
Ãlbanka *f* female Albanian
àlbanski *adj.* Albanian
Alèksandar Vèliki *m* Alexander the Great
alfàbet *m* alphabet
álga *f* algae, seaweed
àli *conj.* but
alkohòličar *m* alcoholic, drunk
ambasáda *f* embassy
ambàsador *m* ambassador
ambìjent *m* atmosphere, environment
amèrički *adj.* American (adj.)
Amèrika *f*, **D Amèrici** America
Amerikánac *m*, **G -kánca** male American
Amerìkanka *f* female American
amerìkanski *adj.* American (adj.)
anèmičan–anèmični *adj.* anemic
angàžiran *adj.* involved, committed
ankèta *f* questionnaire
ansàmbl *m* ensemble
anticiklóna *f* high-pressure area
antikvarìjat *m*, **G -játa** second-hand bookstore
apotéka *f*, **D apotéci** drugstore
apotèkar *m*, **G apotekára** druggist
àpril *m* April
àpsolutan–àpsolutni *adj.* absolute
àrapski *adj.* Arabic
argùmenat *m*, **G -menta** argument, point
argùment *m* argument, point
arhìtekt *m* architect
arhìtekta m (S.) architect
arhitektúra *f* architecture
Aristòtel *m* Aristotle
aritmètičar *m* arithmetician
aritmètika *f*, **D -tici** arithmetic
arìvati [**arìva**] **P** *dial.* to arrive
àrmija *f* army
asistènt *m* assistant
asistírati [**asìstira**] **I** to assist
àstronaut *m* astronaut
astrònom *m* astronomer
astronòmija *f* astronomy
atèlje *m*, **G ateljéa** studio, atelier
atèntat *m*, **G atentáta** assassination
atlètika *f* athletics, track and field
àtletski *adj.* athletic
atmosféra *f* atmosphere, ambiance
àtom *m*, **G atóma** atom
àtomski *adj.* atomic
àugust *ili* **àvgust** *m* August (month)
Austrálac *m*, **G -rálca** male Australian
Ãustralija *f* Australia
àustralski *adj.* Australian
Ãustrija *f* Austria
Austrijánac *m*, **G -jánca** male Austrian
Austrìjanka *f* female Austrian
àustrijski *adj.* Austrian
Ãustro-Ũgarska *f adj. noun* Austro-Hungarian Empire
àuto *m*, **G àuta** automobile
àutobus *m* bus
àuto-cèsta *f* highway
automòbil *m*, **G -bíla** automobile, car
àuto-pút *m* highway
autorìtet *m*, **G -téta** authority
Ãvala *f* a hill near Belgrade
avantúra *f* adventure
avijàtičar *m* aviator, pilot
avìon *m*, **G avióna** airplane
aviónom *adv.* by air, airmail
avìonski *adj.* air (adj.), airplane (adj.)
àzbuka *f*, **D àzbuci** (S.) alphabet
Ãzija *f* Asia
azìjatski *adj.* Asiatic
àzijski *adj.* Asiatic
àždaja *f* dragon

B b

bàba *f* grandmother, old woman
bàcati [**bàca**] **I** to throw
bàcati se I to be thrown
báciti [**báci**] **P** to throw
báčen *adj.* thrown
badàva *adv.* free, gratis
bàgaž *m*, **G bagáža** (S.) baggage
bagáža *f* (Cr.) baggage
bájka *f*, **D bájci** fable, legend
báka *f*, grandmother, old woman
bàkalin *m* (S.) grocer
bàkšiš *m* (S.) tip, gratuity
balerína *f* ballerina
bàlet *m* ballet
bàletni *adj.* ballet (adj.)
Bàlkan *m*, **G Balkána** the Balkans
Balkánac *m*, **G Balkánca** male inhabitant of Balkans
Bàlkanka *f* female inhabitant of Balkans
bàlkanski *adj.* Balkan (adj.)
bàlkon *m*, **G balkóna** balcony
banána *f* banana
bánda *f* band
banknóta *f* banknote, paper money
bár *m* bar
bàr *adv.* at least, if only
bàra *f* puddle, pool
bàrem *adv.* at least, if only
bàrica *f* puddle
barikáda *f* barricade
bárka *f* boat
bàš *adv.* just, exactly
bášča *f* garden, truck farm
bášta *f* (S.) garden
bàviti se [**bàvi se**] **I** to be occupied with, do, study
báza *f* base, foundation
bàzen *m*, **G bazéna** swimming pool
béba *f* baby, doll
Béč m Vienna
béčki *adj.* Viennese
bèdem *m* wall, rampart
bédan–bédni *ek. adj.* poor, miserable
bèdeker *m* guidebook
bég *m*; **N** *pl.* **bézi** *ili* **bègovi** *ek.* flight, escape
bèleg *m*; **N** *pl.* **bèlezi** *ek.* stamp, mark, characteristic
bèlega *f*, **D bèlezi** *ek.* stamp, mark, characteristic
bèleška *f*, **D bèlešci** *ek.* note, mark, grade
bèležiti [**bèleži**] *ek.* **I** to note, write down
bèležnica *f ek.* notebook
Bèlgija *f* Belgium
Belgijánac *m*, **G -jánca** male Belgian
Belgìjanka *f* female Belgian
bèlgijski *adj.* Belgian (adj.)
bènzin *m*, **G benzína** gasoline
bènzinski *adj.* gas (adj.)
bèo–béli *ek.* white
Beògrad *m* Belgrade
beògradski *adj.* Belgrade (adj.)
Beògrađanin *m*; **N** *pl.* **-đani** male native of Belgrade
Beògrađanka *f* female native of Belgrade
bérba *f* grape-gathering
bèrberin *m*; **N** *pl.* **-beri** (S.) barber
bèrbernica *f* (S.) barbershop
bèrdaš *m* musician
bèrlinski *adj.* Berlin (adj.)
bés *m*; **N** *pl.* **bési** *ili* **bèsovi** *ek.* rage, fury, madness
bésan–bésni *ek. adj.* wild, furious
beskònačan–beskònačni *adj.* endless
bèskrajan–bèskrajni *adj.* endless
bèskrajnost *f*, **G -nosti** endlessness, infinity
bèsmislen *adj.* senseless
bèsmrtan–bèsmrtni *adj.* immortal
bèsplatan–bèsplatni *adj.* gratis, free
bèsposlen *adj.* unemployed, idle
bèsposlenost *f*, **G -nosti** idleness, unemployment
bèsvestan–bèsvesni *ek. adj.* unconscious
bèsvjestan–bèsvjesni *ijek. adj.* unconscious
bèton *m*, **G betóna** pavement, concrete
bez (prep. with G) without
bèzbolan–bèzbolni *adj.* painless
bèzbrižan–bèzbrižni *adj.* carefree
bèzdan *m* abyss, deep, depth
bezgràničan–bezgrànični *adj.* boundless
bèzličan–bèzlični *adj.* impersonal, faceless
bèznačajan–bèznačajni *adj.* insignificant, unprincipled
bèzopasan–bèzopasni *adj.* safe, harmless
bèzosećajan–bèzosećajni *ek. adj.* insensitive
bèzosećajan–bèzosećajni *ijek. adj.* insensitive
bèžati [**bèži**] *ek.* **I** to run
bìber *m* (S.) pepper
bìblija *f* bible

bibliotéka *f*, **D -téci** library
bicìkl *m* bicycle
bìč *m;* N *pl.* **bìči** *ili* **bìčevi** whip
bíće *n* being, creature
bíće [= će bìti] (S.) will be, will
bìder màjer *m* bridal bouquet
bìftek *m* beefsteak, steak
bìjedan–bìjedni *ijek. adj.* poor
bìjeg *m;* N *pl.* **bìjezi** *ili* **bjègovi** *ijek.* flight, escape
bìjel *ijek. adj.* white
bìjes *m;* N *pl.* **bìjesi** *ili* **bjèsovi** *ijek.* rage, fury, madness
bìk *m;* N *pl.* **bìkovi** bull
bìkini *m*, **G bìkinija** bikini
bìkini-kòstim *m* bikini
bìlo *n* pulse
bílo *conj.* either
bílo kòji *conj.* any
bílje *n* (coll.) plants
bìljeg *m;* N *pl.* **bìljezi** *ijek.* stamp, mark, characteristic
bìljega *f*, **D bìljezi** *ijek.* stamp, mark, characteristic
bìlješka *f*, **D bìlješci** *ijek.* note
bìlježiti [**bìlježi**] *ijek.* **I** to note, write down
bìlježnica *f ijek.* notebook
bíljka *f* plant
bíljni *adj.* plant (adj.)
bìo *ili* **bìjel–bìjeli** *ijek. adj.* white
biogràfija *f* biography
biològija *f* biology
bìoskop *m* (S.) movie theater
bìrač *m*, **G biráča** voter
bíran *adj.* selected, choice
bìro *m*, **G biròa** office
birokràcija *f* bureaucracy
bìser *m* pearl, bead
bìskup *m* bishop
bìstar-bìstri *adj.* clear, pure, clever
bít *m* essence, substance
bìt će [= će biti] (Cr.) will be, will
bìtan–bìtni *adj.* essential
bìti [**bìje**] **I** to beat
bìti [**jèst/jèste, je I; bùde P**] to be
bìti pri rúci to be at hand, help
bìtka *f*, **D bìci** *ili* **bìtki** battle
bívši *adj.* former
Bìzant *m* (Cr.) Byzantine Empire
Bizàntija *f* (Cr.) Byzantine Empire
bizàntijski *adj.* (Cr.) Byzantine
bjèžati [**bjèži**] *ijek.* **I** to run
blág *adj.* gentle, sweet, meek
blàgajna *f* safe, treasure, ticket office
blàgajnik *m;* N *pl.* **-nici** treasurer
blágdan *m* holiday
blágo *n* riches, cattle
blagodáriti [**blagòdari**] **I** to thank
blàtan–blàtni *adj.* dirty, muddy
blàto *n* mud, dirt, filth
bléd *ek. adj.* pale
blènuti [**blène**] **I** to gaze stupidly, gape
blìjed *ijek. adj.* pale
blìstajući *adj.* dazzling, brilliant
blìzak–blìski *adj.* close, near
blizànac *m*, **G blizànca** twin
blizìna *f* nearness, vicinity
blízu (prep. with G; adv.) near, near by, close to
blìže *adv.* closer
blìži *adj.* closer
blìžnji *adj. noun* neighbor, fellow man
blokírati I/P to block, blockade
blúza *f* blouse
bljùtav *adj.* insipid, tasteless
bljùvati [**bljùje**] **I** to belch, spout
bòca *f* bottle
bòčan–bòčni *adj.* lateral, side (adj.)
bód *m;* N *pl.* **bòdovi** point, score
Bòg *m*, **G Bòga, V Bòže** God
bògami *excl.* by God!
bògat *adj.* rich
bogàtaš *m*, **G -táša** rich man
bògati *excl.* by God! my God!
bògatstvo *n* riches, wealth
bòginja *f* goddess
bogòslovski *adj.* theological
bogùmilski *adj.* pert. to Bogomils, medieval religious sect in B-H
bòja *f* color
bojàdisati [**bojàdiše**] **I** (Cr.) to color, dye
bòjati se [**bòji se**] **I** to fear
bòjiti [**bòji**] **I** (S.) to color, dye
bójni *adj.* war (adj.), battle (adj.)
bók *m*, **G bòka; N** *pl.* **bòkovi** side, hip
bòks *m* boxing
bòksač *m*, **G boksáča** (Cr.) boxer
bòkser *m* (S.) boxer
ból *f*, **G bóli** pain, ache
ból *m*, **G bóla; N** *pl.* **bólovi** pain, ache
bolèsnik *m*, **G -níka; N** *pl.* **-níci** patient
bòlest *f*, **G bòlesti** sickness
bòlestan–bòlesni *adj.* sick
bòleti [**bòli**] *ek.* **I** to pain, ache
bòliti (see **bòljeti**) to pain, ache
bólnica *f* hospital
bólničar *m* male nurse
bólničarka *f* nurse
bòlje *adv.* better
bòljeti [**bòli**] *ijek.* **I** to pain, ache
bòlji *adj.* better
bòmba *f* bomb
bombardíranje *n* bombardment
bòmbon *m*, **G bombóna** candy
bór *m*, **G bòra; N** *pl.* **bòrovi** pine tree
bòrac *m*, **G bòrca** fighter
borànija *f* (S.) green beans
bòraviti [**bòravi**] **I** to stay at, reside
bòrba *f* struggle, fight, match
Bòrba *f* communist party newspaper in Belgrade
bòrilački *adj.* fighting (adj.), martial
bòriti se [**bòri se**] **I** to fight
bós *adj.* barefoot
Bosánac *m*, **G Bosánca** male Bosnian
Bòsanka *f* female Bosnian
bòsanski *adj.* Bosnian
Bòsna *f* Bosnia
bosònog *adj.* barefoot
botànički *adj.* botanical
botànika *f*, **D -nici** botany
botulìzam *m*, **G -ìzma** botulism, food poisoning
Bòžić *m* Christmas
bòžji *adj.* God's
Bráč *m* an island near Split
bráčni *adj.* nuptial, marriage (adj.)
bràća *f* (coll.) brothers
bráda *f* chin, beard
bràdavica *f* wart, mole
bràdva *f* axe
brák *m;* N *pl.* **bràkovi** matrimony, wedding
brániti [**bráni**] **I** to defend
brániti se I to resist, defend oneself
bràon *adj.* (indecl.) (S.) brown
bràšno *n* flour
bràt *m* brother
bràtski *adj.* brotherly, fraternal
bràtstvo *n* brotherhood
br̀bljanje *n* chattering, gossip
br̀bljati [**br̀blja**] **I** to chatter, gossip
br̀do *n* hill, mountain
brè *excl.* (S.) well now!
brég *m;* N *pl.* **brègovi** *ek.* hill
brème *n*, **G brèmena** burden
brèskva *f* peach
brìga *f*, **D brìzi** care, worry
brigáda *f* brigade
brìjač *m*, **G brijáča** (Cr.) barber
brìjačnica *f* (Cr.) barbershop
brìjati se [**brìje se**] **I** to shave oneself
brìjeg; N *pl.* **brègovi** *ijek.* hill
briljàntan–briljàntni *adj.* brilliant
brìnuti se [**brìne se**] **I** to care for, worry about
brìsati [**brìše**] **I** to wipe, remove
brìtanski *adj.* British
brìžan–brìžni *adj.* thoughtful, careful
bŕk *m;* N *pl.* **bŕci** *ili* **br̀kovi** moustache
bród *m*, **G bròda;** N *pl.* **bròdovi** ship, boat
bròdar *m*, **G brodára** sailor
brodogràdilište *n* shipyard
bròdolom *m* shipwreck
bròdski *adj.* ship's
brój *m*, **G bròja;** N *pl.* **bròjevi** number
brójan–brójni *adj.* numerous
bròjiti [**bròji**] **I** to count
brójka *f* (Cr.) number, figure
bròjniji *adj.* more numerous
brúcoš *m* freshman
brúcoški *adj.* freshman's
bŕz *adj.* fast, quick
brzìna *f* speed
br̀zojav *m* (Cr.) telegram
bùba *f* bug, insect
búbanj *m*, **G búbnja** drum
bùbreg *m;* N *pl.* **bùbrezi** kidney
bubùljica *f* pimple, blister
búčan–búčni *adj.* loud, noisy
búčno *adv.* loudly, noisily
budàla *m/f* fool
búdan–búdni *adj.* awake
bùdem . . . bùdu (*see* **biti**) is, will be
bùdilnik *m;* N *pl.* **-nici** alarm clock
búditi [**búdi**] **I** to wake
bùdući *adj.* coming, future (adj.)
bùdući da *conj.* since, for, because
budúćnost *f*, **G -nosti** future
Bùgarin *m;* N *pl.* **Bùgari** male Bulgarian
Bùgarka *f* female Bulgarian
Bùgarska *f adj. noun* Bulgaria
bùgarski *adj.* Bulgarian
bùjica *f* flood, swift current
bùket *m* bouquet
bùketić *m* little bouquet
bùkva *f* beech tree
bùkvalno *adv.* literally
bulèvar *m*, **G bulevára** boulevard
búljiti [**búlji**] **I** to stare, gaze, gape
búna *f* rebellion
búniti se [**búni se**] **I** to revolt, agitate
bùntovnik *m;* N *pl.* **-nici** rebel, militant
bùra *f* storm, gale
bùre *n*, **G bùreta** barrel

C c

càr *m;* N *pl.* **càrevi** emperor, czar
càrevina *f* empire
càrica *f* empress

Càrigrad *m* Istanbul
càrina *f* border customs
càrinarnica *f* customhouse
cárstvo *n* empire, kingdom
cèdulja *f* slip of paper, note
cèh *m*; N *pl.* **cèhovi** shop, guild, restaurant bill
celìna *f ek.* totality, entirety, whole, unit
céna *f ek.* price, value
céniti [**céni**] *ek.* **I** to value, rate
cèntar *m,* **G cèntra** center
cèntimetar *m,* **G -metra** centimeter
cèntralan–cèntralni *adj.* central
centralìstički *adj.* centralized
cèo–céli *ek. adj.* whole, entire
cépanje *n ek.* split, splitting, dissension
cerèmonija *f* ceremony
cèsta *f* highway
Cètinje *n* city in Montenegro
cìfra *f* (S.) number, figure
Cìganin *m*; N *pl.* **Cìgani** male Gypsy
Cìganka *f* female Gypsy
cìganski *adj.* Gypsy (adj.)
cigarèta *f* cigarette
cígla *f* brick
cijèna *f ijek.* price, value
cijèniti [**cìjeni**] *ijek.* **I** to value, rate
cijèpanje *n ijek.* splitting, dissension
cìjev *f* **G cìjevi** *ijek.* tube, pipe
cíl–cíli *adj. dial.* whole, entire
cìlj *m;* N *pl.* **cìljevi** aim, goal
cìničan–cìnični *adj.* cynical
cìo *ili* **cìjel–cìjeli** *ijek. adj.* whole, entire
cìpela *f* shoe
citírati [**cìtira**] **I/P** to cite
cìvilni *adj.* civic, civilian
cjelìna *f ijek.* totality, entirety, whole, unit
cm (*for* **cèntimetar**) centimeter
crép *m*; N *pl.* **crèpovi** *ek.* roofing tile
crìjep *m*; N *pl.* **crèpovi** *ijek.* roofing tile
cŕkva *f* church
crkvèni *adj.* church
cŕn *adj.* black
Cŕna Gòra *f* Montenegro
Cŕnac *m,* **G Cŕnca** Negro, black man
cr̀nački *adj.* negroid, black, Negro
cr̀nilo *n* ink
cŕnka *f* a brunette (woman)
Cr̀nkinja *f* Negress, black woman
Cŕno móre *n* Black Sea
cŕno-béli *adj. ek.* black and white
cŕno-bìjeli *adj. ijek.* black and white
Crnògorac *m,* **G Crnògorca** male Montenegrin
Crnògorka *f* female Montenegrin
crnògorski *adj.* Montenegrin
cr̀ta *f* line
cr̀tati [**cr̀ta**] **I** to draw
cŕv *m* worm
cr̀ven *adj.* red
crvenòkožac *m,* **G -košca** redskin, Indian
cùra *f* young girl
cùrica *f* little girl
cvàsti [**cvàte**] **I** to blossom
cvéće *n* (coll.) *ek.* flowers
cvèćnjak *m;* N *pl.* **-njaci** *ek.* flower garden
cvètati [**cvèta**] *ek.* **I** to blossom, flourish
cvìjeće *n* (coll.) *ijek.* flowers
cvjètati [**cvjèta**] *ijek.* **I** to blossom, flourish
cvjètnjak *m*; N *pl.* **-njaci** *ijek.* flower garden
cvr̀kut *m* warble, chirping
cvrkùtati [**cvr̀kuće**] **I** to warble, chirp

Č č

čà *dial.* what
čàčkalica *f* toothpick
čàj *m,* **G čàja;** N *pl.* **čàjevi** tea
čàk *adv.* even, as far as
čàk ni *adv.* not even
čákavski *adj.* pert. to chakavian dialects
čámac *m,* **G čámca** boat, canoe
čár *m/f* charm
čàrapa *f* sock, stocking
čàroban–čàrobni *adj.* charming, enchanting
čàršav *m* (S.) sheet
čàs *m;* N *pl.* **čàsi** *ili* **čàsovi** moment, lesson (S.); o'clock, hour (S.)
čàs . . . čàs . . . *adv.* now . . . now, by turns
čáskom *adv.* momentarily, for a second
čàsopis *m* journal, magazine
čàsovnik *m;* N *pl.* **-nici** clock, watch
část *f,* **G části** honor
čàstan–čàsni *adj.* honorable, sacred
čàša *f* glass
čàšica *f* small glass
čàvao *m,* **G čávla** (Cr.) nail, spike
čavr̀ljati [**čavr̀lja**] **I** to chat
Čèh *m* a Czech
čèhan *adj.* plucked
Čehoslòvačka *f adj. noun* Czechoslovakia
čèk *m*; N *pl.* **čèkovi** check
čèkaonica *f* waiting room
čèkati [**čèka**] **I** to wait
čèkić *m* hammer
čèkinjav *adj.* edgy, irritable
čèlik *m*; N *pl.* **čèlici** steel
čèlo *n* forehead, brow
čèp *m;* N *pl.* **čèpovi** cork
čèsma *f* well
čèstit *adj.* honest
čestítati [**čèstita**] **I** to congratulate
čèstitka *f* greeting card
čèstito *adv.* properly
čèsto *adv.* often, frequently
čèšalj *m,* **G čèšlja** comb
čèšati [**čèše**] **I** to scratch
čèšati se I to scratch oneself
čèšće *adv.* more often
čèšljati [**čèšlja**] **I** to comb
čèšnjak *m,* **G češnjáka** garlic
čètiri *num.* four
čètnik *m;* N *pl.* **čètnici** guerrilla fighter
četrdèset *num.* forty
četrdesétak *m,* **G -tka** group of about forty
četrdèseti *adj.* fortieth
četr̀naest *num.* fourteen
četr̀naesti *adj.* fourteenth
čètverokut *m* (Cr.) square
četvoròugaonik *m*; N *pl.* **-nici** (S.) square
čètvrt *f,* **G čètvrti** quarter, district
četvŕtak *m,* **G četvŕtka** Thursday
čètvrti *adj.* fourth
četvr̀tina *f* fourth part, quarter
čìji *m,* **čìje** *n,* **čìja** *f* whose
čìk *m;* N *pl.* **čìkovi** butt (cigarette)
čìka *m* old man, "uncle"
čìm *conj.* as soon as
čìn *m;* N *pl.* **čìni** *ili* **čìnovi** deed, act
čìnilac *m,* **G čìnioca** source, cause, factor
čìniti [**čìni**] **I** to do, make, accomplish
čìniti se I to seem, appear
činòvnica *f* female official, clerk
činòvnik *m;* N *pl.* **-nici** official, clerk
čìnovništvo *n* officialdom, civil service
čìnjenica *f* fact, reality
čír *m;* N *pl.* **čìrovi** ulcer
čìst *adj.* clean
čìstiti [**čìsti**] **I** to clean
čìsto *adv.* completely, absolutely
čistòća *f* cleanliness
čìtalac *m,* **G čìtaoca** reader, person reading
čìtanka *f,* **D -anci** reader, anthology
čìtanje *n* reading
čìtaonica *f* reading room
čìtati [**čìta**] **I** to read
čìtav *adj.* whole
čìzma *f* boot
člán *m;* N *pl.* **člànovi** member
člának *m,* **G člànka;** N *pl.* **článcì** news article, ankle
čokoláda *f* chocolate
čórba *f* thick soup
čovečànstvo *n ek.* humanity
čòvečji *ek. adj.* human (adj.)
čòvek *m* **V čòveče** *ek.* man, human being
čovječànstvo *n ijek.* humanity
čòvječji *ijek. adj.* human (adj.)
čòvjek *m,* **V čòvječe** *ijek.* man, human being
čúčati [**čúči**] **I** to perch, sit, crouch
čùdan–čùdni *adj.* wondrous, unusual
čùdesan–čùdesni *adj.* marvelous, amazing
čùditi se [**čùdi se**] **I** to wonder, be amazed
čùdo *n*; N *pl.* **čùda** *ili* **čudèsa** wonder, marvel
čúlo *n* (S.) sense, sensory faculty
čùpav *adj.* untidy, shaggy
čùpavac *m,* **G -pavca** hippie, slob
čùti [**čùje**] **I/P** to hear
čùti se I/P to be heard
čùvar *m,* **G čuvára** keeper, guard
čúvati [**čúva**] **I** to keep, save
čúvati se I to be kept, be saved
čùven *adj.* famous
čvŕst *adj.* strong, tough, solid

Ć ć

ćakùlati [**ćakùla**] **I** *dial.* to talk, chat
ćèlav *adj.* bald
ćérka (*see* **kćérka**) daughter
ćevàpčić *m* barbecued ground meat
ćìlim *m* (S.) rug
Ćìril *ili* **Ćìrilo** *m* Cyril (Slavic apostle)
ćìrilica *f* Cyrillic alphabet
ćòšak *m,* **G ćòška;** N *pl.* **ćòškovi** (S.) corner
ćúd *f,* **G ćúdi** temper, nature
ćùlbastija *f* sweetbread, tripe
ćùprija *f* bridge
ćútanje *n* (S.) silence
ćútati [**ćúti**] **I** (S.) to be silent, be quiet

D d

dà *adv.* yes
da *conj.* in order to, that, let . . .
Dàbrov *adj.* Beaver (adj.)
dàdilja *f* nurse, governess

dáh *m*; N *pl.* **dàhovi** breath
dakàko *adv.* of course
dàkle *adv.* consequently, so now
daktilògraf *m* typist
daktilògrafkinja *f* typist
dàlek *adj.* far, distant
dalèko *adv.* far away, by far
Dàlmacija *f* Dalmatia
Dalmatínac *m*, **G -tínca** male Dalmatian
Dalmàtinka *f* female Dalmatian
dalmàtinski *adj.* Dalmatian
dàlje *adv.* further, forth
dàlji *adj.* farther
daljìna *f* distance
dáljnji *adj.* further
dáma *f* lady
dán *m* day
Dánac *m*, **G Dánca** Dane
dànas *adv.* today
dànašnji *adj.* present-day, today's
danònoćno *adv.* day and night
Dánska *f adj. noun* Denmark
dánski *adj.* Danish
dàpače *adv.* even, on the contrary
dár *m*; N *pl.* **dàrovi** gift, present
darèžljiv *adj.* generous
daròvit *adj.* gifted, talented
dàska *f*; G *pl.* **dasáka** board
dàšćica *f* small board
dàti [**dá** *ili* **dáde**] **P** to give
dáj [**imper.**]
datírati I/P to date (from)
dátum *m* date
dávati [**dáje**] **I** to give
dáviti [**dávi**] **I** to strangle, choke
dávno *adv.* long time, years ago
dèbeo–dèbeli *adj.* fat
debljìna *f* obesity, stoutness
dèca *f* (coll.) *ek.* children
dèčak *m*, **G dečáka; N** *pl.* **dečáci** *ek.* lad, youth, boy
dècembar *m*, **G dècembra** December
dèčica *f* (coll.) *ek.* small children
dèčji *ek. adj.* childish, child's
dèčko *m*; N *pl.* **dèčki**, G *pl.* **dèčki** lad, youth, boy
dèd *m*; N *pl.* **dèdovi** *ek.* grandfather
dèda *m ek.* (S.) grandfather
dèdovina *f ek.* ancestral land
dèjstvo *n* (S.) influence, impact
dèjstvovati [**-vuje**] **I** (S.) to work, influence
dèkan *m* dean
dèlatnost *f*, **G -nosti** *ek.* activity
dèlfin *m*, **G delfína** dolphin
dèlikatan–dèlikatni *adj.* delicate, fine
dèlimično *ek. adv.* partly
déliti [**déli**] *ek.* **I** to divide, separate
dèliti se I to be divided, separated
dèlo *n ek.* deed, product, work
dèlovati [**dèluje**] *ek.* **I** to work, influence
demòkrat *m* democrat
demòkrata *m* (S.) democrat
demòkrátski *adj.* democratic
dèo *m*, **G déla; N** *pl.* **délovi** *ek.* part, portion, branch
dèrati [**dère**] **I** to tear, rip
dèrati se I to bawl, blubber
dèpeša *f* (S.) telegram
dèset *num.* ten
desétak *m*, **G desétka** ten, about ten
dèseti *adj.* tenth
dèsetleće *n ek.* decade
dèsetljeće *n ijek.* decade
dèsiti se [**dèsi se**] **P** to happen, take place
dèsni *adj.* right (hand)
désni *f pl.* gums
dèsno *adv.* right, on the right
dešávati se [**dèšava se**] **I** to happen, take place
dètaljniji *adj.* more detailed
déte *n*, **G dèteta** *ek.* child
detèktivski *adj.* detective (adj.)
dètinjast *ek. adj.* childish
dètinjstvo *n ek.* childhood
dèva *f* (Cr.) camel
devedèset *num.* ninety
devedèseti *adj.* ninetieth
dèvet *num.* nine
dèveti *adj.* ninth
devètnaest *num.* nineteen
devètnaesti *adj.* nineteenth
dèvica *f ek.* virgin
devíza *f* foreign currency
dèvizni *adj.* pert. to foreign currency
devòjčica *f ek.* little girl
dèvojka *f*, **D dèvojci; G** *pl.* **dèvoja** *ek.* girl, young woman
dežúrstvo *n* guarding, guard duty, shift
dìći *ili* **dìgnuti** [**dìgne; dìgao, dìgla**] **P** to raise, elevate
dijagnóza *f* diagnosis
dijàlekat *m*, **G dijàlekta** dialect
dijàlekt *m* dialect
dijèliti [**dìjeli**] *ijek.* **I** to divide, share
dijèliti se I to be divided, separated
dijéta *f* diet
dijète *n*, **G djèteta** *ijek.* child
dìm *m* smoke
dìmiti se [**dìmi se**] **I** to emit smoke
dìmničar *m* (S.) chimney-sweep
dìmnjačar *m* (Cr.) chimney-sweep
dìmnjak *m*; N *pl.* **dìmnjaci** chimney
Dìnamo *m* Dynamo (name of soccer team)
dìnar *m* dinar (currency unit)
dinàstija *f* dynasty
dìo *ili* **dìjel** *m*, **G dìjela; N** *pl.* **dijèlovi** *ijek.* part, portion, branch
Dioklecìjan *m*, **G -jána** Roman emperor (284–305)
Dioklecijánov *adj.* Diocletian's
diplóma *f* diploma
diplòmat *m* diplomat
diplòmata *m* (S.) diplomat
diplomírati [**diplòmira**] **I/P** to graduate
dírati [**díra**] **I** to touch, feel
dìrektor *m* director
dìrektorov *adj.* director's
dirigènt *m* conductor (of music)
dìrljiv *adj.* touching, moving
dìrnut *adj.* touched, moved
dísati [**díše**] **I** to breathe
disertácija *f* dissertation
diskùsija *f* discussion
diskutírati [**diskùtira**] **I** (Cr.) to discuss
dìskutovati [**dìskutuje**] **I** (S.) to discuss
dìv *m*; N *pl.* **dìvi** *ili* **dìvovi** giant
dìvan *m*, **G divána** couch
dìvan–dìvni *adj.* wonderful
dìviti se [**dìvi se**] **I** to admire
dìvljač *f*, **G dìvljači** wild game
dìvljak *m*, **G divljáka** savage, barbarian
dìvlji *adj.* wild
divljìna *f* wilderness
divòta *f* splendor, glory
dìzalo *n* (Cr.) elevator
dìzati [**dìže**] **I** to lift up, raise
djèca *f* (coll.) *ijek.* children
djèčak *m*, **G dječáka; N** *pl.* **dječáci** *ijek.* lad, youth, boy
djèčica *f* (coll.) *ijek.* small children
djèčji *ijek.* childish, child's
djèd *m*; N *pl.* **djèdovi** *ijek.* grandfather
djèdovina *f ijek.* ancestral land
djèlatnost *f*, **G -nosti** *ijek.* activity
djèlimično *ijek. adv.* partly
djèlo *n ijek.* deed, product, work
djèlovati [**djèluje**] *ijek.* **I** to work, influence
djètinjast *ijek. adj.* childish
djètinjstvo *n ijek.* childhood
djèvica *f ijek.* virgin
djevòjčica *f ijek.* little girl
djèvojka *f*, **D djèvojci; G** *pl.* **djèvojaka** *ijek.* girl, young woman
dlàka *f*, **D dlàci** (a single) hair
dlàkav *adj.* hairy
dlàn *m*; N *pl.* **dlànovi** palm (of hand)
dnévni *adj.* daily
dnévni réd *m* agenda
dnévnica *f* daily wages
dnévnik *m*; N *pl.* **dnévnici** diary, journal
dnò *n*, **G dnà** bottom
do (prep. with G) up to, until, next to
do viđénja goodbye, au revoir
dòba *n* (indecl.) time, season, times
dòbar–dòbri *adj.* good
dobíjati [**dòbija**] **I** to get, obtain
dobítak *m*, **G dobítka; N** *pl.* **dobíci** profit
dòbiti [**dòbije**] **P** to get, obtain
dobívati I to receive, get
dòbro *n* goods, possessions, property
dòbro *adv.* good, well, o.k.
dòbro dòšao *excl.* welcome!
dòbro dòšli *excl.* welcome!
dobrodòšlica *f* a welcome, welcoming
dobròdušno *adv.* good-naturedly
dobròta *f* goodness, kindness
dòbrotvor *m* benefactor
docènt *m* instructor, assistant professor
dòckan *adv.* (S.) late, lately
dócni *adj.* (S.) late
dòcnije *adv.* (S.) later
dòcniti [**dòcni**] **I** (S.) to be late
dòček *m*; N *pl.* **dòčeci** welcome
dòčekati [**dòčeka**] **P** to meet, welcome
dočèpati se [**dočèpa se**] **P** to lay hold of, seize upon
dòći [**dóđe; dòšao, dòšla**] **P** to come, arrive
dodátak *m*, **G dodátka; N** *pl.* **dodáci** addition
dòdati [**dòda**] **P** to add to, pass (in sports)
dodéliti [**dòdeli**] *ek.* **P** to assign, allot
dòdijati [**dòdije**] **P** to annoy, pester
dodijèliti [**dòdijeli**] *ijek.* **P** to assign, allot
dodírnuti [**dòdirne**] **P** to touch
dodúše *adv.* in truth, indeed, certainly
dògađaj *m* event
dògled *m* field of vision, view
dògledan–dògledni *adj.* visible, foreseeable
dogòditi se [**dògodi se**] **P** to happen
dogovárati se [**dogòvara se**] **I** to confer, deliberate

dògovor *m* agreement
dogovòriti se [dogòvori se] P to agree upon
dòhodak *m*, **G -hotka; N** *pl*. **-hoci** income
dòhvatiti [dòhvati] P to reach, take hold
dòista *adv*. certainly
dójam *m*, **G dójma; N** *pl*. **dójmovi** (Cr.) impression
dòjenče *n*, **G dòjenčeta** (Cr.) nursing baby
dòjiti [dòji] I to nurse, suckle
dójka *f*, **D dójci; G** *pl*. **dòjaka** *ili* **dòjci** breast
dok *conj*. until, while
dòkaz *m* proof
dokazívanje *n* reasoning, arguing, disputing
dòkolica *f* leisure, spare time
dòktor *m* doctor
dòktorski *adj*. doctoral
dokùmenat *m*, **G -menta** document
dokùment *m* document
dòlazak *m*, **G dòlaska; N** *pl*. **dòlasci** arrival
dòlaziti [dòlazi] I to come, arrive
dòle *ek. adv*. below, lower, down, downstairs
dolìna *f* valley
dòlje *ijek. adv*. below, lower, down, downstairs
dóm *m*, **G dòma; N** *pl*. **dòmovi** home, house
dòma *adv*. at home
dòmaći *adj*. native, local, home (adj.)
domàćica *f* housewife
dòmovina *f* homeland
dònekle *adv*. to a degree, partly
dòneti [donèse; dòneo, dònela] *ek*. **P** to bring
dònijeti [donèse; dònio, dònijela] *ijek*. **P** to bring
donòsiti [dònosi] I to bring
dónji *adj*. lower
dòpadati se [dòpada se] I to be pleasing to
dopisívanje *n* correspondence
dopisívati se [-pìsuje se] I to correspond
dòpisnica *f* postcard
dòplivati [dòpliva] P to swim up to
dòpratiti [dòprati] P to go along with, accompany
dòpreti [dòpre; dòpro, dòprla] *ek*. **P** to penetrate
dòprijeti [dòpre; dòpro, dòprla] *ijek*. **P** to penetrate
doprínos *m* contribution
doprinòsiti [-prìnosi] I to contribute
dópust *m* leave, vacation
dopùstiti [dòpusti] P to allow, permit
dopúštati [dòpušta] I to allow, permit
dopušténje *n* permission
doputòvati [-pùtuje] P to arrive
dòručak *m*, **G dòručka** breakfast
dòručkovati [-kuje] I/P to breakfast
dòsad *adv*. up to now
dòsada *f* boredom
dòsadan–dòsadni *adj*. boring, dull, annoying
dòsadno *adv*. boring
doséći [dòsegne; dòsegao, dòsegla] P to reach, arrive, attain to, equal
dosèliti se [dòseli se] P to move to, settle
doseljènik *m*, **G -níka; N** *pl*. **-níci** immigrant, settler
dòsetka *f ek*. joke, witticism
Dòsitejev *adj*. Dositej's
dòsjetka *f ijek*. joke, witticism
dòsledan–dòsledni *ek. adj*. consistent
doslòvce *adv*. literally
dòsljedan–dòsljedni *ijek. adj*. consistent
dòspeti [dòspe] *ek*. **P** to arrive at, mature
dòspjeti [dòspije; dòspio, dòspjela] *ijek*. **P** to arrive at, mature
dòsta *adv*. enough of, rather
dòstići *ili* **dòstignuti [-stigne; -stigao, -stigla] P** to reach, achieve
dóstojan–dóstojni *adj*. worthy
dostojànstven *adj*. dignified, stately
dòšljak *m*, **G -ljáka; N** *pl*. **-ljáci** newcomer
dòtada *adv*. up to that time
dòtle *adv*. thus far, up to that time
dotr̀čati [dotr̀či] P to run up to
dovèden *adj*. brought, led up
dovèsti [dovède; dòveo, dòvela] P to conduct, lead to, bring
dovòditi [dòvodi] I to bring, lead
dòvoljno *adv*. enough
dovòziti [dòvozi] I to bring, cart
dòznati [dòzna] P to find out
dòzvola *f* permission
dozvòliti [dòzvoli] P to allow, permit
dozvoljávati [dozvòljava] I to allow, permit
dòživljaj *m* experience, adventure
doživeti [doživi] *ek*. **P** to experience, live to see
doživjeti [doživi] *ijek*. **P** to experience, live to see
dòživotan–dòživotni *adj*. lifelong
drág *adj*. dear, cherished
drágo *adv*. pleasantly, glad
dragòcen *ek. adj*. precious
dragòcjen *ijek. adj*. precious
dràgulj *m* jewel
dráma *f* drama
dramàtičan–dramàtični *adj*. dramatic
Dráva *f* river in northern Yugoslavia
dràžestan–dràžesni *adj*. cute, dear
drémati [dréma] *ek*. **I** to doze, nap
dr̀htati [dr̀šće] I to tremble, shiver
drijémati [drìjema] *ijek*. **I** to doze, nap
Drína *f* river in central Yugoslavia
dr̀mati [dr̀ma] I to shake
dróga *f* drug
dr̀skost *f*, **G dr̀skosti** impudence, audacity
dr̀sko *adv*. insolently
drúg *m*, **V drúže; N** *pl*. **drùgovi** comrade
drugàčiji *adj*. different, unlike
drugàrica *f* female comrade
drùgarski *adj*. comradely
drugárstvo *n* companionship
drùgde *ek. adv*. elsewhere, some other place
drùgdje *ijek. adv*. elsewhere, some other place
drùgi *adj*. other, second, following
drùkčiji *adj*. different, unlike
drùm *m*; **N** *pl*. **drùmovi** highway
drùštven *adj*. social, friendly
drúštvo *n* society, group, association
drùžina *f* company, party
drúžiti se I to be friendly with
dr̀veće *n* (coll.) trees
dr̀ven *adj*. wooden
dr̀vo *n*, **G dr̀veta; N** *pl*. **dr̀va** *ili* **drvèta** tree, wood, firewood
dr̀vored *m* avenue
drvòseča *m ek*. woodcutter
drvòsječa *m ijek*. woodcutter
dr̀zak–dr̀ski *adj*. insolent, bold
dr̀žati [dr̀ži] I to keep, hold, grasp
dr̀žava *f* state, country
dr̀žavljanin *m*; **N** *pl*. **-ljani** citizen, subject
dr̀žavljanstvo *n* citizenship
dr̀žavni *adj*. state's, governmental
dúb *m*; **N** *pl*. **dùbovi** oak tree
dubìna *f* depth
dùbok *adj*. deep
Dùbrava *f* grove, name of soccer team
dùbrovački *adj*. relating to Dubrovnik
Dùbrovčanin *m*; **N** *pl*. **-čani** inhabitant of Dubrovnik
Dùbrovnik *m* historic city on Adriatic
dùćan *m*, **G dućána** store, shop
dùg *adj*. long
dúg *m*; **N** *pl*. **dùgovi** debt
dúga *f* rainbow
dùgačak–dùgački *adj*. long
dùgme *n*, **G dùgmeta** button
dùgmić *m* little button, children's game
dùgo *adv*. long, for a long time
dugosìlazni *adj*. long falling (accent)
dugoùzlazni *adj*. long rising (accent)
dugòvati [dùguje] I to owe, be indebted to
dugùljast *adj*. oblong
dùh *m*; **N** *pl*. **dùsi** *ili* **dùhovi** spirit, mind
dùhan *m*, **G duhána** (Cr.) tobacco
dùhati [dúše/dúha] I (Cr.) to blow, puff
duhòvit *adj*. witty
dùhovni *adj*. spiritual
duljìna *f* length
Dùnav *m* the Danube River
dúša *f*, **V dúšo** soul, mind, spirit, love, darling
Dùšan, Stèvan Serbian ruler (1348–1355)
dùšek *m*; **N** *pl*. **dùšeci** (S.) mattress
dùševan–dùševni *adj*. spiritual
dùvan *m*, **G duvána** (S.) tobacco
Dùvanjsko pòlje *n* site of famous battle in Croatian history
dúvati [dúva] I (S.) to blow, puff
duž (prep. with G) along
dúžan–dúžni *adj*. obliged
dùže *adv*. longer
dùži *adj*. longer
dužìna *f* length
dúžnost *f*, **G -nosti** duty, obligation
dvá *num*. two
dvádeset *num*. twenty
dvadesétak *m*, **G -tka** group of about twenty
dvádeseti *adj*. twentieth
dvánaest *num*. twelve
dvánaesti *adj*. twelfth
dváput *adv*. twice
dvé *ek. num*. two
dvìje *ijek. num*. two
dvòjba *f* (Cr.) doubt
dvójnik *m*; **N** *pl*. **dvójnici** twin
dvopàrtijski *adj*. two-party (adj.)
dvór *m*; **N** *pl*. **dvóri** *ili* **dvórovi** court, yard

dvórac *m*, G **dvórca** castle
dvòrana *f* hall, sports auditorium
dvòrišni *adj.* yard (adj.)
dvòrište *n* yard
dvòsobni *adj.* two room (adj.)
dvòstruko *adv.* double

Dž dž

džák *m*; N *pl.* **džákovi** sack
džámija *f* mosque
džèm *m* jam
džèp *m*; N *pl.* **džèpovi** pocket
džepárac *m*, G **-párca** pocket money
džèpni *adj.* pocket (adj.)
džèz *m* jazz, jazz band
džìgerica *f* liver
džìn *m* giant
džìp *m*; N *pl.* **džìpovi** jeep
Džòrdž, Lòjd Lloyd George, English statesman (1863–1945)
džùngla *f* jungle

Đ đ

đáčki *adj.* pert. to student, pupil's
đák *m*; N *pl.* **đáci** student, pupil
đàvao *m*, G **đávla** devil
đàvo *m*, G **đàvola** devil
đùbre *n*, G **đùbreta** manure, fertilizer, muck, trash
đùbrivo *n* manure, fertilizer
đùl *m* rose
đùveč *m* meat and vegetable stew
đùveče *n*, G **đùveča** *ili* **đùvečeta** meat and vegetable stew

E e

é *excl.* well now!
èfikasan–èfikasni *adj.* effective, efficacious
Ègipat *m*, G **Ègipta** Egypt
ègipatski *adj.* Egyptian (adj.)
Ègipćanin *m*; N *pl.* **-ćani** male Egyptian
egzistèncija *f* existence
ekípa *f* team, squad
ekonòmist *m* economist
ekonòmista *m* (S.) economist
ekònomski *adj.* economic
ekskùrzija *f* excursion, trip
ekspedícija *f* expedition
eksperìmenat *m*, G **-menta** experiment
ekperìment *m* experiment
èkspres *m* express train
èkspres bár *m* snack bar
ekstravagàntan-tni *adj.* extravagant
elektroinžènjer *m*, G **-njéra** electrical engineer
elektromòtor *m* generator, dynamo
emìsija *f* program
enèrgija *f* energy
Èngleska *f adj. noun* England
èngleski *adj.* English (adj.)
Èngleskinja *f* Englishwoman
ènglesko-amèrički *adj.* English and American
Ènglez *m*, G **Engléza** Englishman
èno *excl.* there! behold!
èsej *m*, G **eséja** essay
ètički *adj.* ethical
èto *excl.* there, see there, here is
èvo *excl.* here is, here comes
Èufrat *m* Euphrates River (SW Asia)
evakuácija *f* evacuation
evànđelje *n* gospel
Evrópa *f* Europe
Evrópljanin *m*; N *pl.* **-ani** male European
Evrópljanka *f* female European
èvropski *adj.* European (adj.)

F f

fàbrika *f*, D **fàbrici** (S.) factory
fàh *m*; N *pl.* **fàhovi** occupation, work
fàktor *m* factor
fakùltet *m*, G **fakultéta** university division, college
fakùltetski *adj.* belonging to college
fála (*see* **hvála**) *f* thanks
fàliti [**fàli**] **I** to ail, be lacking
fàmilija *f* family
faràonski *adj.* Pharaoh's
fárma *f* farm
fèbruar *m* (S.) February
fèderativan–fèderativni *adj.* federal
fèljton *m*, G **feljtóna** dispatch, essay
fèrije *f pl.* holidays, vacation
fèstival *m* festival
feudalìzam *m*, G **-ìzma** feudalism
fijàker *m* coach (vehicle)
fijàkerski *adj.* cab (adj.) coach (adj.)
fijóka *f* (S.) drawer
fìlm *m*; N *pl.* **fìlmovi** film, movie
filòlog *m*; N *pl.* **filòlozi** philologist
filològija *f* philology
filòzof *m* philosopher
filozòfija *f* philosophy
filòzofski *adj.* pert. to philosophy or to "liberal arts"
fìn *adj.* fine, exquisite
Fínac *m*, G **Fínca** male Finn
fíno *adv.* fine, nicely
Fínska *f adj. noun* Finland
fínski *adj.* Finnish
fìzički *adj.* physical
fìzika *f*, D **fìzici** physics
fjàka *f dial.* Dalmatian summer languor
flàša *f* bottle
fòlklor *m*, G **folklóra** folklore
fonètika *f*, D **fonètici** phonetics
fontána *f* fountain
fòrmalan-lni *adj.* formal
fòtelj *m*, G **fotélja** (Cr.) easy chair
fotélja *f* (S.) easy chair
fotogràfija *f* photograph
Fràncuska *f adj. noun* France
fràncuski *adj.* French
Fràncuskinja *f* Frenchwoman
Fràncuz *m*, G **Francúza** Frenchman
frèska *f*; G *pl.* **frèsaka** fresco
frìzer *m*, G **frizéra** hairdresser (male)
frìzerka *f* hairdresser (female)
frizúra *f* hairdo
frìžider *m*, G **-déra** refrigerator
fùdbal *m* (S.) soccer
fudbàler *m*, G **-léra** (S.) soccer player
fùdbalski *adj.* soccer (adj.)

G g

gàćice *f pl.* panties
gàdan–gàdni *adj.* disgusting, hateful
gáj *m*; N *pl.* **gáji** *ili* **gájevi** grove
Gáj, Ljùdevit leader of Illyrian movement (1809–1872)
gájiti [**gáji**] **I** to raise, breed
galáma *f* uproar, noise
galámiti [**gàlami**] **I** to make a loud noise, cause disturbance
gàleb *m* seagull
garàncija *f* guarantee
garantírati [**garàntira**] **I/P** (Cr.) to guarantee
gàrantovati [**-tuje**] **I/P** (S.) to guarantee
garáža *f* garage
garderóba *f* checkroom
gàrniran *adj.* garnished
gásiti [**gási**] **I** to extinguish
gátati [**gáta**] **I** to foretell, predict
gàvran *m* raven
gàzda *m* boss
gàzdarica *f* housekeeper, hostess, landlady
gàzdaričin *adj* pert. to landlady
gàziti [**gàzi**] **I** to walk on, wade, touch
gdè *ek. adv.* where
gdèkad *ek. adv.* somewhere
gdjè *ijek. adv.* where
gdjèkad *ijek. adv.* somewhere
genèral *m*, G **generála** general
geogràfija *f* geography
gìbanica *f* cheese cake
gíbati se [**gíba se**] **I** to move, stir
gimnàstika *f*, D **-tici** sitting-up exercises, gymnastics
gìmnazija *f* secondary school
gìnuti [**gìne**] **I** to perish, wither, long for
glàčalo *n* (Cr.) flat-iron
glàčati [**glàča**] **I** (Cr.) to iron
glád *m*, G **gláda** hunger
glád *f*, G **gládi** hunger
glàdak–glàtki *adj.* smooth
gládan–gládni *adj.* hungry
glàgol *m* verb
glàgolski *adj.* verb (adj.), verbal
glás *m*; N *pl.* **glàsovi** sound, voice, vote
glàsač *m*, G **glasáča** voter
glàsić *m*, G **glasíća** little voice, thin voice
glàsilo *n* organ, publication
glásiti [**glási**] **I** to read, sound
glàsno *adv.* loudly
glasòvit *adj.* famous
gláva *f* head, chapter
glàvat *adj.* big-headed
glávni *adj.* main, chief
glavòbolja *f* headache
glàvurda *f* big head, heavy head
glàzba *f* (Cr.) music, ensemble
glè *excl.* look! see!
glèdalac *m*, G **glèdaoca** spectator
glèdanje *n* watching
glèdati [**glèda**] **I** to look at, watch
glèdište *n* standpoint, attitude, view
glèžanj *m*, G **glèžnja** ankle
glìser *m* hydrofoil (boat)
glòba *f* fine, penalty
glóbus *m* globe
glòmazan–glòmazni *adj.* unwieldy
glúh *adj.* (Cr.) deaf
glùhonijem *adj.* (Cr.) deaf and dumb
glúma *f* acting
glúmac *m*, G **glúmca** actor
glùmica *f* actress
glúp *adj.* stupid
glúv *adj.* (S.) deaf
glùvonem *adj.* (S.) deaf and dumb
gljìva *f* mushroom
gnév *m ek.* anger
gnézditi I *ek.* to nest
gnézdo *n ek.* nest

gnijèzditi I *ijek.* to nest
gnijèzdo *n ijek.* nest
gnjàvator *m* bore
gnjáviti [gnjávi] I to bore, annoy
gnjév *m ijek.* anger
gó–gòli *adj.* (S.) naked, bare
gòd *adv.* ever
gód *m*, **G gòda** year, anniversary
gòdina *f* year
gòdišnje *adv.* yearly, a year
gòdišnji *adj.* yearly
gòdišnjica *f* anniversary
gòjiti [gòji] I to nourish, cherish
gòjiti se I to be nourished, cherished
gól *m*; N *pl.* **gólovi** goal (sports)
gól–gòli (Cr.) naked, bare
gòlem *adj.* vast, huge, enormous
golìcati [golìca] I to tickle
gòlub *m* pigeon
gòmila *f* mass, pile, heap
górak–górki *adj.* bitter
górd *adj.* proud
gòre *adv.* above, higher up
gòre *adv.* worse
gòreti [gòri] *ek.* **I** to burn
gòri *adj.* worse
gòrivo *n* fuel
gòrjeti [gòri; gòrio, gòrjela] *ijek.* **I** to burn
górko *adv.* bitterly, painfully
górnji *adj.* upper
goròstas *m* giant, monster
gòrski *adj.* mountain (adj.)
góspa *f* lady, Virgin
Gòspod *m* Lord
gospòda *f* (coll.) gentlemen, Messrs.
gospòdar *m*, **G -dára** master, owner, farmer
gospòdarski *adj.* ruling, agricultural
gospodárstvo *n* economy, farm
gospòdin *m* Mister, sir
gòspođa *f* married woman, Mrs., lady
gòspođica *f* Miss, young lady
góst *m*, **G gòsta** guest
gòstinski *adj.* guest (adj.)
gòstiona *f* inn, tavern
gòstionica *f* inn, tavern
gostoljùbiv *adj.* hospitable
gostoprímstvo *n* hospitality
gostòvati [gòstuje] I to be a guest
gòšća *f* woman guest
gòtov *adj.* ready, complete
gotovìna *f* ready money
gòtovo *adv.* nearly, almost, practically
gòvedina *f* (Cr.) beef
gòvedo *n* ox, head of cattle
gòveđi *adj.* beef (adj.)
gòveđina *f* (S.) beef
gòvor *m* language, idiom, speech, dialect
govòriti [gòvori] I to speak, talk, say
govòrnik *m*, **G -níka**; N *pl.* **-níci** speaker, orator
gòzba *f* feast, banquet
gràba *f* ditch, drain
gràblje *n* rake
grád *m*; N *pl.* **gràdovi** city
gràd *m* hail
Grádec *m* upper city, part of Zagreb
gràdić *m*, **G gradíća** small town
gráditi [grádi] I to build
gradonáčelnik *m*; N *pl.* **-nici** mayor
gràdski *adj.* city (adj.), urban
gràđanin *m*; N *pl.* **gràđani** citizen, city dweller
gràđanski *adj.* civil, civic, civilian
gràđanstvo *n* citizens, community
gráđen *adj.* built, formed
gràđevina *f* edifice, building
gràđevinski *adj.* building (adj.), construction (adj.)
gràđevni *adj.* construction (adj.)
gràh *m* (Cr.) beans
gramàtički *adj.* grammatical
gramàtika *f*, **D-tici** grammar
gramòfon *m*, **G -fóna** record player
gramòfonska plòča *f* record, disk
grána *f* branch, limb
grànica *f* boundary, frontier
grànìčan–grànični *adj.* border (adj.)
grànìčiti [grànìči] I to border upon
grànìčiti se I to border upon
grášak *m*, **G gráška** (Cr.) peas
gravitácija *f* gravitation
gȑbavac *m*, **G gȑbavca** hunchback
gȑčenje *n* spasm
Gȑčka *f adj. noun* Greece
gȑčki *adj.* Greek (adj.)
grèben *m* ridge
gréda *f* beam
gréh *m*; N *pl.* **grési** *ili* **gréhovi** *ek.* sin, fault
grèjati [grèje] *ek.* **I** to warm
grèjati se *ek.* **I** to warm oneself
grèpsti [grèbe; grèbao, grèbla] I to scratch, irritate
grèšan–grèšni *adj.* guilty, sinful
gréšiti [gréši] *ek.* **I** to make a mistake, sin
grèška *f*, **D grèšci; G** *pl.* **grèšaka** error, mistake
grèšnik *m*; N *pl.* **grèšnici** sinner
gȑgljanje *n* gargling
grìjati [grìje] *ijek.* **I** to warm
grìjati se *ijek.* **I** to warm oneself
grìjeh *m*, **G grijèha**; N *pl.* **grijèsi** *ili* **grijèhovi** *ijek.* sin, fault
grijèšiti [grìješi] *ijek.* **I** to make a mistake, sin
grìp *m* (S.) flu
grìpa *f* (Cr.) flu
grìsti [gríze] I to bite, gnaw
gȑk *m* Lumbarda wine
Gȑk *m*; N *pl.* **Gȑci** male Greek
Gȑkinja *f* female Greek
gȑlat *adj.* loud-voiced
gȑliti [gȑli] I to embrace
gȑlo *n* throat
gȑm *m*; N *pl.* **gȑmovi** bush
gȑmljavina *f* thunderstorm, thunder
gròb *m*; N pl. **gròbovi** grave, tomb
gròban–gròbni *adj.* burial (adj.)
gròbnica *f* grave, mausoleum
gròhot *m* loud laughter
gróm *m*, **G gròma**; N *pl.* **gròmovi** thunder, lightning
gromòglasno *adv.* loudly
grót (= **gròhot**) loud laughter
grózan–grózni *adj.* terrible, dreadful
gróžđe *n* grapes
grúb *adj.* rude, crude, coarse
grúdi *f pl.* bosom, breast(s)
grúdni *adj.* breast (adj.)
grúdnjak *m*; N *pl.* **grúdnjaci** brassiere
grùpa *f* group
Gúbec, Màtija Cr. peasant leader (16th cent.)
gùber blanket
gubítak *m*, **G -bítka**; N *pl.* **-bíci** loss
gùbiti [gùbi] I to lose, waste
gùbiti se I to be lost
gùcnuti [gùcne] P to sip, have a sip, gulp
gùlaš *m* goulash
gúliti [gúli] I to peel, scale, rub
gùma *f* rubber, tire
gùnđati [gùnđa] I to grumble, mutter
gúrati [gúra] I to push, shove
gúrati se I to push, shove one another
gùska *f*, **D gùsci** goose
gùslar *m* fiddler, ballad-singer
gùsle *f pl.* one-stringed mus. instrument
gúst *adj.* thick, dense
gúšiti [gúši] I to choke, suffocate
gùtanje *n* swallowing
gùtati [gùta] I to swallow, slur over
gùtljaj *m* sip, gulp, swig, swallow
gùtnuti [gùtne] P to sip, have a sip, gulp
gúžva *f* crowd, jam
gvòzden *adj.* iron (adj.)
gvóžđe *n* iron (metal)

H h

hàjde *excl.* come on!
hàjdemo *excl.* let's go!
Hàjduk *m*; N *pl.* **Hajdúci** highwayman, name of soccer team
hàljina *f* dress
hàpsiti [hàpsi] I to arrest
hàpšenje *n* arrest
harmònika *f*, **D -nici** accordion
hàrtija *f* (S.) paper
Hèlena *f* (Cr.) Helen
helikòpter *m* helicopter
Hèrcegovina *f* Herzegovina
hèroj *m* hero
hìljada *f* thousand
Himaláji *m pl.* Himalayas
hìpijevac *m*, **G hìpijevca** hippie
hìpijevka *f* female hippie
hipohòndar *m*, **G -dra** hypochondriac, chronic worrier
històričar *m* historian
hìstorija *f* (Cr.) history
històrijski *adj.* (Cr.) historical
hìtan–hìtni *adj.* urgent
hlàče *f pl.* (Cr.) trousers
hlád *m* shade, coolness
hládan–hládni *adj.* cold (adj.)
hladnòća *f* cold, chill
hlèb *m ek.* (S.) bread
hlèbac *m*, **G hlèpca** *ek.* roll, loaf
hljèb *m ijek.* (S.) bread, loaf
hljèbac *m*, **G hljèpca** *ijek.* roll, loaf
hòbotnica *f* octopus
hòću (*see* **hteti**) I will, I want
hód *m*, **G hòda** walk, pace
hódati [hóda] I to walk
hòdnik *m*; N *pl.* **-nici** corridor
hòdža *m* Moslem priest
hòkej *m* hockey
hokèjaš *m* hockey player
hokèjaški *adj.* hockey (adj.)
Holàndez *m*, **G -déza** Dutchman
Holàndija *f* Holland
holàndski *adj.* Dutch
hór *m*; N *pl.* **hórovi** (S.) choir
hòtel *m* hotel
hotelìjer *m*, **G -jéra** hotel clerk
hòtelski *adj.* hotel (adj.)
hòtimice *adv.* on purpose, intentionally

jedìnstven *adj.* unique, united
jedínstvo *n* unity, agreement, harmony
jèdnak *adj.* equal, similar, same
jèdnako *adv.* equally, likewise
jèdni drùgi *adj.* **N** *pl.* one another, each other
jednìna *f* singular number (gram.)
jèdnoć *adv.* once upon a time
jednòdnevan–jednòdnevni *adj.* lasting one day
jednòglasno *adv.* in unison, unanimously
jednòličan–jednòlični *adj.* uniform
jèdnom *adv.* once, once more
jednòsoban–jednòsobni *adj.* having one room
jèdnostavno *adv.* simply, easy
jèdrilica *f* sailing boat, glider
jèdriličar *m* sailor, yachtsman
jèdriti I to sail, glide
jèdro *n* sail
jèdva *adv.* scarcely, hardly
jèftin *adj.* cheap
jèftino cheaply
jék *m* full force, full power
jèka *f*, **D jèci** echo
jéla *f* fir tree
jèlen *m* deer, stag
Jèlena *f* (S.) Helen
jèlo *n* food, meal
jèlovnik *m*; **N** *pl.* **-nici** menu
jèmčiti [jèmči] I to guarantee
jèr *conj.* because, for
jèsen *f* **G jèseni** autumn, fall (season)
jèsenski *adj.* autumn (adj.), autumnal
jèsenji *adj.* autumn (adj.), autumnal
jèst (Cr.) is, yes
jèste (S.) is, yes
jèsti [jède; jèo, jèla] I to eat
jèsti se I to be eaten, be worried
jevànđelje *n* gospel
Jèvrej *m* (S.) Jew
Jèvrejin *m*; **N** *pl.* **Jèvreji** (S.) Jew
jèvtin *adj.* cheap
jèzero *n* lake
jèzičan–jèzični *adj.* talkative, linguistic
jèzik *m*; **N** *pl.* **jèzici** tongue, language
jezikoslóvac *m*, **G -óvca** linguist
jèziv *adj.* horrible, frightful
jèž *m*; **N** *pl.* **jèževi** porcupine
JNA (= **Jugoslàvenska národna àrmija**) Yugoslav army
jój *excl.* wow!
jòš *adv.* still, yet
jòš jèdnom *adv.* one more time
jùče *adv.* (S.) yesterday
jùčer *adv.* (Cr.) yesterday
jučèrašnji *adj.* yesterday's
jùg *m* south
jugoìstok *m* southeast
Jugoslàven *m*, **G -véna** (Cr.) Yugoslav
Jugoslàvenka *f* (Cr.) female Yugoslav
jugoslàvenski *adj.* (Cr.) Yugoslav (adj.)
Jugoslávija *f* Yugoslavia
Jugoslòven *m*, **G -véna** (S.) Yugoslav
Jugoslòvenka *f* (S.) female Yugoslav
jugoslòvenski *adj.* (S.) Yugoslav (adj.)
jugozápad *m* southwest
jugozápadno *adv.* southwesterly
júha *f* (Cr.) soup, broth
júl *ili* **júli** *m*, **G júla** July
jún *ili* **júni** *m*, **G júna** June
jùnački *adj.* heroic
jùnak *m*, **G junáka; N** *pl.* **junáci** hero
junáštvo *n* heroism, courage, prowess
júnski *adj.* June (adj.)
júriti [júri] I to hurry, speed
jùtarnji *adj.* morning (adj.)
jùtro *n* morning
jùtros *adv.* this morning
jùžni *adj.* southern

K k

k *ili* **ka** (prep. with D) toward, to
kabína *f* cabin, cab (of truck)
kàciga *f* helmet
kàd *ili* **kàda** *adv.* when
káda *f* bathtub
kádar–kádri *adj.* able (to), competent
kàfa *f* (S.) coffee
kafàna *f* (S.) coffeehouse, café
kàfić *f* café
kàj *pron. dial.* what
kàjkavski *adj.* pert. to kaykavian dialects
kàjati se [kàje se] I to regret, be sorry
kàjgana *f* scrambled eggs
kàjmak *m* Serbian butter
kàkao *m*, **G kàkaa** cocoa
kàkav *m*, **kàkvo** *n*, **kàkva** *f* what kind of
kàko *adv.* how
kál *m* dirt, mud, filth
Kalemègdan *m* Belgrade park at confluence of Danube and Sava rivers
kálan–kálni *adj.* dirty, troubled
kàluđer *m* (S.) monk
kàljača *f* boot, rubber(s)
kàmata *f* rate of interest
kàmen *m* stone
kàmen *adj.* made of stone
kàmenit *adj.* stony, rocky
kàmila *f* (S.) camel
kamìon *m*, **G kamióna** truck
kàmo *adv.* where to
kampànjski *adj.* crash (adj.), intensive
Kanáđanin *m* a Canadian
kànal *m*, **G kanála** canal
kancelàrija *f* office
kánda *adv.* perhaps
kániti [káni] I to intend, aim at
kánta *f* can
kánta za òtpatke garbage can
kànuti [kàne] P to drop (a tear)
kào *adv.* like, as
kào da *conj.* as though
kào što *conj.* as, like
káp *f*, **G kápi** drop, bead (of sweat)
kàpa *f* cap
kàpak *m*, **G kàpka; N** *pl.* **kàpci** eyelid, shutter
kapètan *m* captain, centurion
kàpija *f* (S.) gate
kàplja *f* drop, bead (of sweat)
kàpljica *f* droplet
Kàptol *m* the lower city, a section of Zagreb
kàput *m*, **G kapúta** coat
Kàradžić, Vúk Stefánović *m* Serbian linguist and lexicographer (1787–1864)
Kàrađorđe *m* "Black George" (leader of first Serbian uprising)
karàkter *m*, **G -téra** character
kàrakteran–kàrakterni *adj.* upright, honest
karakterìstičan–karakterìstični *adj.* characteristic (adj.)
karakterìstika *f*, **D -tici** characteristic
karijéra *f* career
karikatúra *f* cartoon, caricature
karikatùrist *m* cartoonist
Karpáti *m pl.* Carpathian Mountains
kárta *f*; **G** *pl.* **kàrata** card, map
kàsan–kàsni *adj.* (Cr.) late
kàsapin *m* (S.) butcher
kàsnije *adv.* (Cr.) later
kàsniji *adj.* (Cr.) later
kàsniti [kàsni] I (Cr.) to be late
kàsno *adv.* (Cr.) late, lately
kàša *f* porridge
kàšalj *m*, **G kàšlja** cough
kàšika *f*, **D kàšici** (S.) spoon
kàšljati [kàšlje] I to cough
kàt *m*; **N** *pl.* **kàtovi** (Cr.) floor, story
kàtarka *f*, **D kàtarci** mast
katastròfalan–katastròfalni *adj.* catastrophic
katedrála *f* cathedral
kàtkada *ili* **kàtkad** *adv.* sometimes
katòlički *adj.* Catholic (adj.)
katòlik *m*; **N** *pl.* **katòlici** a Catholic
kàtran *m* tar
kàuč *m* sofa, couch
kàva *f* (Cr.) coffee
kavàna *f* (Cr.) coffeehouse, café
kàvez *m* cage
kàzališni *adj.* (Cr.) theatrical, theater (adj.)
kàzalište *n* theater
kàzaljka *f*, **D kàzaljci** pointer, watch hand
kàzan *m* big kettle
kázati [káže] I/P to say, tell
kázna *f* punishment
kàzniti [kàzni] P to punish
kàžiprst *m* index finger
kćérca *f* little daughter
kćérka *f* daughter
kćí *f*, **G kćèri** daughter
kéc *m*; **N** *pl.* **kéčevi** ace (in cards)
kèks *m* cookie
kèlner *m* (S.) waiter
Kèlt *m* Celt
kèlj *m*, **G kèlja** kale
kìćen *adj.* ornate, decorated
kíhati [kíše] I (Cr.) to sneeze
kíjati [kíja] I (S.) to sneeze
kikirìki *m*, **G kikirìkija** peanut
kìla *f* kilogram
kìlo *n* kilogram
kìlogram *m* kilogram (2.2 pounds)
kilometar *m* **G -tra** kilometer
Kína *f* China
kìneski *adj.* Chinese (adj.)
Kìnez *m*, **Kinéza** male Chinese
kíno *n*, **G kína** (Cr.) movie theater
kíp *m*; **N** *pl*, **kípovi** statue, effigy
kìpar *m*, **G kipára** (Cr.) sculptor
kipárstvo *n* (Cr.) sculpture
kípeti [kípi] *ek.* **I** to boil
kípjeti [kípi] *ijek.* **I** to boil
kìrija *f* (S.) rent
kìša *f* rain
kìšan–kìšni *adj.* rainy
kìseo–kìseli *adj.* sour
kìsnuti I to get wet
kìšobran *m* umbrella
kìt *m*; **N** *pl.* **kìtovi** whale
kìtiti [kìti] I to decorate
klàsa *f* class
klàsičan–klàsični *adj.* classic
klasifikácija *f* classification
klàti [kòlje] I to slaughter, kill

klàvir *m*, **G klavíra** piano
kléčati [kléči] I to kneel down
klèsar *m*, **G klesára** stonecutter
klèsati [klèše] I to carve, chisel, cut
kléti [kùne; klèo, kléla] I to curse, swear
klétva *f* curse, oath
klìcati [klìče] I to shout (for joy)
klíma *f* climate
klìmati [klìma] I to sway, nod
klìsura *f* cliff, crag
klìzalište *n* skating rink
klízanje *n* skating, sliding
klìzati se [klìza se] I to skate
klíziti [klízi] I to glide, slide
klúb *m*; N *pl*. **klùbovi** club, organization
klúpa *f* bench
ključ *m*; N *pl*. **klúči** *ili* **ključevi** key
ključan–ključni *adj*. essential
kljún *m* bill, beak
knéz *m*; N *pl*. **knèzovi** *ili* **knèževi** prince, headman
kneževina *f* kingdom, principality
knjìga *f*, **D knjìzi** book
knjìžara *f* bookstore
knjìževan–knjìževni *adj*. literary
knjìževnik *m*; N *pl*. **-nici** author, writer
knjìževnost *f*, **G -nosti** literature
knjìžnica *f* library
kò *pron*. (S.) who
kóban–kóbni *adj*. fatal, ominous
kobàsica *f* sausage
kòcka *f*; G *pl*. **kòcaka** die (pl. dice), cube, block
kòckar *m* gambler
kòckarnica *f* gambling house
kòckati se [kòcka se] I to gamble
kóčiti [kóči] I to check, brake
kóčnica *f* brake
kod (prep. with G) with, at home of, at
kòd kuće home, at home
kòfer *m* suitcase
kojekàko *adv*. haphazardly, superficially
kòji *m*, **kòje** *n*, **kòja** *f* which, who
kòkoš *f*, **G kòkoši** chicken
kòla *n pl*. vehicle, cart, car
kòlač *m*, **G koláča** cookie, pastry
Kolàrčev univerzìtet *m* Belgrade institute of foreign languages, concert hall
kolèbanje *n* indecision, fluctuation
kolèbati se [kolèba se] I to vacillate, waver, sway
kòledž *m* college
koléga *m* colleague, companion
kòleno *n ek*. knee, generation
kòlevka *f*, **D kòlevci** *ek*. cradle
kòliba *f* hut, cottage
količina *f* quantity
kòlijevka *f*, **D kòlijevci** *ijek*. cradle
kòliko *adv*. how much, how
koliko gòd *adv*. no matter how much
kòlo *n* wheel, dance
kòlodvor *m* (Cr.) railroad station
kòlodvorski *adj*. pert. to RR station
kòlokvijum *m* colloquium
kòlosek *m*; N *pl*. **-seci** *ek*. RR track, gauge
kòlosijek *m*; N *pl*. **-sijeci** *ijek*. RR track, gauge
kòlovođa *m* kolo dance leader
kòlovoz *m* (Cr.) August (month)
kòljeno *n ijek*. knee, generation
kòmad *m*, **G komáda** piece, chunk, bit
komàdić *m* small piece
kòmanda *f* command
komàndant *m* commander
komárac *m*, **G komárca** mosquito
kombinácija *f* combination
kombìne *m*, **G kombinèa** slip, petticoat
komèntar *m* remark, commentary
komentarírati I/P (Cr.) to comment, remark
komentàrisati I/P (S.) to comment, remark
kòmforan–kòmforni *adj*. comfortable
komplìcirano *adv*. (Cr.) complicated
kòmplikovano *adv*. (S.) complicated
komplìmenat *m*, **G -menta** compliment
komplìment *m* compliment
kòmšija *m* (S.) neighbor
komùnist *m* a Communist
komùnista *m* (S.) a Communist
kònac *m*, **G kónca** end, thread
kònačan–kònačni *adj*. final
kònačno *adv*. finally
kònak *m*; N *pl*. **kònaci** shelter
kòncerat *m*, **G kòncerta** concert
kòncert *m* concert
konfèkcija *f* ready-made clothes
konferèncija *f* conference
kòngres *m* congress
kònobar *m* (Cr.) waiter
kònopac *m*, **G kònopca** string, rope
kontróla *f* control
konverzácija *f* conversation
kònzerva *f* tin, can
kònj *m*, **G kònja** horse
kònjica *f* cavalry, squadron
kònjić *m* little horse
kòpati [kòpa] I to dig
kòplje *n* javelin
kòpneni *adj*. land (adj.), terrestrial
kòpno *n* land, shore
kòra *f* peel, bark
kòrak *m*; N *pl*. **kòraci** step, pace
Kórčula *f* an island in Adriatic
kòren *m ek*. root
kòrenje *n ek*. root(s)
kòrienski (= **kòrijenski** *ijek*.) *adj*. basic (former Croatian spelling)
kòrijen *m ijek*. root
kòrijenje *n ijek*. root(s)
kòrisno *adv*. usefully, effectively
kòrist *f*, **G kòristi** profit, usefulness
kòristan–kòrisni *adj*. useful
kòristiti I to use
kòristiti se [kòristi se] I to take advantage of, use, be useful
kòrito *n* river channel, bed, trough
kórpa *f* basket
korpulèntniji *adj*. bigger, heavier
kòsa *f* hair
kòsidba *f* mowing
Kòsovo pòlje *n* "Field of the Blackbirds," scene of Turkish victory over Serbs (1389)
kóst *f*, **G kòsti** bone
kòstim *m*, **G kostíma** costume, suit
kòš *m*; N *pl*. **kòševi** basket
kòšara *f* basket, hamper
kòšarka *f* basketball
košàrkaš *m* basketball player
košàrkašica *f* basketball player (fem.)
košàrkaški *adj*. basketball (adj.)
kòšava *f* cold northern wind
kóštati [kòšta] I to cost
kòšulja *f* shirt
Kòšutnjak *m* a part of Belgrade
kòtač *m*, **G kotáča** (Cr.) wheel
kòtar *m*, **G kotára** (Cr.) district, county
kòtlina *f* valley, ravine
kòvač *m*, **G kováča** blacksmith, smith
kòvčeg *m*; N *pl*. **kòvčezi** trunk, chest
kòza *f* goat
kozmètika *f* cosmetics
kòža *f* skin
kòžan–kòžni *adj*. skin (adj.), leather (adj.)
kràdljivac *m*, **G -ivca** thief
kràđa *f* theft
kraj (prep. with G) besides, at the side of, next to
kráj *m*, **G kràja**; N *pl*. **kràjevi** end, border, region
kràjem (prep. with G) at the end of
králj *m*; N *pl*. **králjevi** king
králjević *m* prince
Králjević Márko *m* Prince Marko, Serbian epic hero
králjevina *f* kingdom
králjevstvo *n* kingdom
kràljica *f* queen
kràńjski *adj*. pert. to Carniola (Slovenia)
krásan–krásni *adj*. beautiful, grand
krásiti [krási] I to adorn, crown
kràstavac *m*, **G kràstavca** cucumber
kràsti [kráde; krào, kràla] I to steal
krátak–krátki *adj*. short, brief
kràtica *f* abbreviation
kratkosìlazni *adj*. short falling (accent)
kratkoùzlazni *adj*. short rising (accent)
kratkòvidan–kratkòvidni *adj*. shortsighted
kràva *f* cow
kravàta *f* tie
kr̀čma *f* tavern
kr̀čmar *m*, **G krčmára** tavern-keeper
krčmàrica *f* tavern-keeper (female)
kréda *f* chalk
krèdenac *m*, **G krèdenca** cupboard
krèdenc *m* cupboard
krénuti [kréne] P to move, set out, set off
krénuti se P to move, set out
Krèstlajn *m* California town (Crestline)
krétanje *n* movement, rotation
krétati [kréće] I to move, go, leave, drive
krétati se I to move, stir
krétnja *f* movement, gesture
krèvet *m* bed
krijumčáriti [krijùmčari] I to smuggle
krílo *n* wing, lap
kríška *f*, **D kríšci** slice
kríšom *adv*. stealthily, secretly
krìtičan–krìtični *adj*. critical
krìtički *adv*. critically
krív *adj*. wrong, guilty
krivìca *f* guilt, fault
kríviti [krívi] I to twist, distort, accuse, blame
krivotvòriti [krivòtvori] I (Cr.) to falsify, forge
krivùdati [krivùda] I to meander, wind
kríž *m*; N *pl*. **krìževi** (Cr.) cross
kríža *n pl*. (Cr.) small of the back
kr̀letka *f* cage
kr̀mača *f* sow, ink-spot
kŕmak *m*, **G kŕmka**; N *pl*. **kŕmci** hog
krmenádla *f* pork chop
kr̀ntija *f* wreck, ruin

kròjač *m*, **G krojáča** tailor
kròmpir *m*, **G krompíra** (S.) potato
krompírov *adj.* potato (adj.)
króv *m*, **G kròva; N** *pl.* **kròvovi** roof
kroz (prep. with A) through
kr̀pa *f* rag
kr̀st *m*; **N** *pl.* **kr̀stovi** (S.) cross
kr̀sta *n pl.* (S.) small of back
krstáriti [kr̀stari] I to cruise
kr̀š *m* karst, rocky terrain
kr̀šćanin *m*; **N** *pl.* **kr̀šćani** (Cr.) Christian
kr̀šćanski *adj.* (Cr.) Christian (adj.)
krúg *m*; **N** *pl.* **krùgovi** circle
krùh *m*; **N** *pl.* **krùhovi** (Cr.) bread
krùmpir *m*, **G krumpíra** (Cr.) potato
krumpírov *adj.* (Cr.) potato (adj.)
krùna *f* crown
krùnisati [krùniše] I/P (S.) to crown
krùniti [krùni] I/P (Cr.) to crown
krúniti [krúni] I to shred (corn), shell
krúpan–krúpni *adj.* large, bulky
krùška *f*, **D krùšci** pear
krúžan-krúžni *adj.* circle (adj.), circular
kŕv *f*, **G kr̀vi** blood
kŕzno *n* fur
kùbe *n*, **kùbeta** dome, cupola
kùbik *m*, **G -bíka; N** *pl.* **-bíci** meter, cube
kùc *excl.* here boy! (calling dog)
kùcati [kùca] I to type (S.), knock
kùče *n*, **G kùčeta** small dog
kùća *f* house
kùća, ròbna department store
kùćni *adj.* home (adj.)
kùd *ili* **kùda** *adv.* where to
kud gòd *adv.* wherever
kùga *f* plague
kúgla *f* ball, sphere, bowling ball, shot
kùglanje *n* bowling
kùhan *adj.* (Cr.) cooked, boiled
kùhar *m* cook, chef
kùhati [kùha] I (Cr.) to cook
kùhati se I (Cr.) to cook, be cooked
kùhinja *f* kitchen
kùhinjski *adj.* kitchen (adj.)
kùk *m*; **N** *pl.* **kùkovi** hip
kùkavica *f* cuckoo, coward
kukavìčluk *m* cowardly behavior
kukùruz *m* corn
kúla *f* tower
kultúra *f* culture
kùlturan–kùlturni *adj.* cultural
kùlturno-polìtički *adj.* cultural and political
kúm *m*; **N** *pl.* **kùmovi** godfather, sponsor
kúma *f* godmother, sponsor
kùnić *m* rabbit
kúpac *m*, **G kúpca** buyer, purchaser, customer
kùpač *m*, **G kupáča** bather, swimmer
kùpaći *adj.* bathing (adj.)
kùpaći kòstim *m* bathing suit
kùpalište *n* swimming pool, bathing beach
kúpanje *n* swimming, bathing
kùpaonica *f* (Cr.) bathroom
kúpati (se) [kúpa (se)] I to bathe, swim
kupàtilo *n* (S.) bathroom
kúpiti [kúpi] P to buy
kùpiti [kùpi] I to gather
kupòvati [kùpuje] I to buy
kùpovina *f* shopping
kùpus *m* cabbage
kùrje òko *n* (Cr.) callous ("chicken eye"), corns (on feet)
kùšati [kùša] I to taste
kút *m*; **N** *pl.* **kútovi** (Cr.) corner, angle
kútak *m*, **G kútka; N** *pl.* **kúci** corner, nook
kùtija *f* box
kùvan *adj.* (S.) cooked, boiled
kùvar *m* (S.) cook, chef
kùvati [kùva] I (S.) to cook
kùvati se I (S.) to cook, be cooked
kvàdrat *m*, **G -dráta** square
kvàlifikacijski *adj.* qualifying (i.e. exam)
kvalìtet *m*, **G -téta** quality
kvalitéta *f* (Cr.) quality
kvàlitetan–kvàlitetni *adj.* of good quality
kváriti [kvári] I to spoil, ruin
kvásac *m*, **G kvásca** yeast
kvr̂cnuti [kvr̂cne] P to tap, rap

L l

laboràtorija *f* laboratory
làbud *m* swan
làdica *f* (Cr.) drawer
láđa *f* ship, boat, craft
láđin *adj.* ship (adj.)
làgano *adv.* slowly, leisurely
làgati [làže] I to lie, fib
làgvić *m* barrel, keg
làhor *m* breeze
làik *m*; **N** *pl.* **làici** layman
làjati [làje] I to bark
làk *adj.* light, easy
làku nóć goodnight
lákat *m*, **G lákta** elbow
lakirati [làkira] I to polish
làko *adv.* easily, easy
làkom *adj.* greedy, keen on
lakòmislen *adj.* light-minded, reckless
làkše *adv.* more easily
lála *f* (S.) tulip
lámpa *f* lamp
lánac *m*, **G lánca** chain
láne *adv.* (S.) last year
láni *adv.* (Cr.) last year
lànjski *adj.* last year's
làskati [làska] I to flatter
lásta *f* swallow (bird)
làstavica *f* swallow (bird)
latìnica *f* Latin alphabet
làtinski *adj.* Latin (adj.)
làv *m*; **N** *pl.* **làvovi** lion
làvor *m*, **G lavóra** basin, sink
làž *f*, **G làži** lie
làžac *m*, **G làšca** liar
lèbdeti I *ek.* to soar, float, move above
lèbdjeti I *ijek.* to soar, float, move above
léčiti [léči] *ek.* **I** to treat (medically)
lèći [lèže *ili* **lègne; lègao, lègla] P** to lie down
léd *m*, **G lèda** ice
lèden *adj.* icy
lèdina *f* lawn, grass
lèditi se [lèdi se] I to freeze, congeal
léđa *n pl.* back, shoulders
lègenda *f* legend
legitimácija *f* identity card
lék *m*; **N** *pl.* **lékovi** *ek.* medicine
lèkar *m* **G, lekára** *ek.* (S.) doctor
lèkarski *ek. adj.* medical, doctor's
lèkcija *f* lesson
lenčáriti [lènčari] *ek.* **I** to loaf
léno *adv.* (S.) lazily
lénj *adj.* (S.) lazy
lép–lépi *ek.* beautiful, fine
lèpilo *n ek.* glue, paste
lèpljiv *ek. adj.* sticky
lépo *ek. adv.* nicely, very much
lepòta *f ek.* beauty
lepòtica *f ek.* a beauty
lèpše *ek. adv.* more beautiful
lèpši *ek. adj.* more beautiful
lèptir *m* butterfly
lèstve *f pl.*, **G** *pl.* **lèstava** *ek.* ladder
lèšnjak *m*; **N** *pl.* **lèšnjaci** *ek.* hazelnut
lét *m*; **N** *pl.* **létovi** flight
lèteti [lèti] *ek.* **I** to fly
lèti *ek. adv.* in summer
lètjeti [lèti] *ijek.* **I** to fly
lètnji *ek. adj.* summer (adj.)
lèto *n ek.* summer
lètovalište *n ek.* summer resort
lètovanje *n ek.* summer vacation
lètovati [lètuje] *ek.* **I** to spend the summer
lévati [léva] *ek.* **I** to pour out
lévi *ek. adj.* left (side)
lèžati [lèži] I to lie down, recline
lèžerniji *adj.* more relaxed
lèžernost *f* relaxation
li *conj.* (indicates question), if, whether
líce *n*, **G líca** face, person
lìcej *m* lycée, secondary school
licèmer *m ek.* hypocrite
licèmjer *m ijek.* hypocrite
lìčan–lìčni *adj.* personal
líčiti [líči] I to resemble
lìčno *adv.* personally, in person
lìčnost *m*, **G lìčnosti** personage, person
lìft *m*; **N** *pl.* **lìftovi** elevator
lijèčenje *n ijek.* medical treatment
lijèčiti [lìječi] *ijek.* **I** to treat medically
lìječnički *ijek. adj.* medical
lìječnik *m*; **N** *pl.* **-nici** *ijek.* (Cr.) physician
lìjek *m*, **G lijèka; N** *pl.* **lijèkovi** *ijek.* medicine
lìjen *adj.* (Cr.) lazy
lìjeno *adv.* (Cr.) lazily
lìjep *ijek. adj.* beautiful
lijèpiti [lìjepi] *ijek.* **I** to glue, paste
lìjepo *ijek. adv.* nicely, very much
lijèvati [lìjeva] *ijek.* **I** to pour out
lìjevi *ijek. adj.* left (side)
Líka *f*, **D Líci** region in Croatia
lìker *m*, **G likéra** liqueur
lìmenka *f* tin, canister
lìmun *m*, **G limúna** lemon
lìngvist *m* linguist
lìngvista *m* (S.) linguist
línija *f* line, (human) figure
lìpa *f* lime tree
lípanj *m*, **G lípnja** (Cr.) June (month)
lìsica *f* fox
lìsnica *f* (Cr.) wallet, pocketbook
líst *m*; **N** *pl.* **lìstovi** leaf, page, letter
lìstopad *m* (Cr.) October
líšće *n* (coll.) leaves, foliage
lìtar *m*, **G lìtra** liter (1.06 quarts)
lìti [lìje] I to pour
lìtra *f* liter (1.06 quarts)
lìvada *f* meadow
lízati [líže] I to lick
lògika *f*, **D lògici** logic
lógor *m* camp
lòjalan–lòjalni *adj.* loyal
lòmiti [lòmi] I to break
lòmiti se I to break against, toil

lòmljiv *adj.* breakable, fragile
lònac *m*, G **lónca**; G *pl*. **lònaca** pot, saucepan
lópov *m* thief
lòpta *f* ball
lòptanje *n* ball playing
lòptati se I to play ball
lòptica *f* small ball, ping-pong ball
lòš *adj*. bad, poor
lóv *m*, G **lòva** hunting, pursuit
lòvac *m*, G **lóvca**; G *pl*. **lòvaca** hunter, sportsman
Lóvćen *m* highest mountain in Montenegro
lòviti [**lòvi**] **I** to pursue, hunt
lòza *f* vine, pedigree, line
Lòznica small city in western Serbia
lòžiti [**lòži**] **I** to stoke (a fire), lay (a fire)
lòžiti se I to be stoked, tended
lùbanja *f* skull
lubènica *f* watermelon
lúd *adj*. mad, crazy
lùda *f* fool, clown
lúdnica *f* insane asylum
lùđak *m*, G **luđáka**; N *pl*. **luđáci** madman
lùk *m*; N *pl*. **lùkovi** onion
lúka *f*, D **lúci** harbor, port
lùkav *adj*. shrewd, sly
lùla *f* pipe (smoking)
Lùmbarda *f* village on Korčula
lúpati [**lúpa**] **I** to strike, beat, knock
lútati [**lúta**] **I** to roam, stray
lùtka *f*; G *pl*. **lùtaka** toy, doll
lùtrija *f* lottery

Lj lj

ljèkarna *f ijek*. (Cr.) drugstore
ljèkarnik *m*; N *pl*. **-nici** *ijek*. (Cr.) druggist
ljèkarski *ijek. adj*. medical, doctor's
ljenčáriti [**ljènčari**] *ijek*. **I** to loaf
ljèpilo *n ijek*. glue, paste
ljèpljiv *ijek. adj*. sticky
ljepòta *f ijek*. beauty
ljepòtica *f ijek*. a beauty
ljèpše *ijek. adv*. more beautiful
ljèpši *ijek. adj*. more beautiful
ljèstve *f pl*., G *pl*. **ljèstava** *ijek*. ladder
ljèšnak *m ijek*. hazelnut
ljèti *ijek. adv*. in summer
ljèto *n ijek*. summer
ljètovalište *n ijek*. summer resort
ljètovanje *n ijek*. summer vacation
ljètovati [**ljètuje**] *ijek*. **I** to spend the summer
ljúbav *f*, G **ljúbavi** love
ljùbavnik *m*; N *pl*. **-nici** lover
ljùbazan–ljùbazni *adj*. kind, friendly, thoughtful
ljùbičica *f* violet
ljùbimac *m*, G **ljùbimca** pet, favorite
ljúbiti [**ljúbi**] **I** to love, kiss
ljùbitelj *m* fan, lover
ljubòmora *f* jealousy
ljùbomoran–ljùbomorni *adj*. jealous
ljubopìtljiv *adj*. curious
ljúdi *m pl*. people
ljùdski *adj*. human (adj.)
ljùdsko *adv*. humanely
ljúljati [**ljúlja**] **I** to rock, swing, vacillate
ljút *adj*. angry
ljùtit *adj*. angry, annoyed

M m

mà *conj*. but
máca *f* kitty, kitten
màč *m*; N *pl*. **màči** *ili* **màčevi** sword
máčak *m*, G **máčka**; N *pl*. **máčci** male cat
màčevanje *n* fencing
màčka *f*; G *pl*. **màčaka** cat
màćeha *f* step-mother
màda *conj*. although
màdrac *m*, G **madràca** mattress
Màdžar *m*, G **Madžára** (Cr.) male Hungarian
Màdžarska *f adj. noun* (Cr.) Hungary
màdžarski *adj*. (Cr.) Hungarian
maèstro *m* maestro
Màđar *m*, G **Mađára** (S.) male Hungarian
Màđarska *f adj. noun* (S.) Hungary
màđarski *adj*. (S.) Hungarian
màgarac *m*, G **màgarca** donkey
màgare *n*, G **màgareta** little donkey
magàzin *m*, G **magazína** storehouse, warehouse
màgla *f* mist, fog
maglòvit *adj*. foggy, misty
máh *m*, G **màha**; N *pl*. **màhovi** movement, swoop
máhati [**máše**] **I** to wave, shake (+ **I** case)
máj *m*, G **màja** month of May
májčin *adj*. mother's
màjica *f* undershirt, T-shirt
májka *f*, D **májci** mother
màjmun *m* monkey
májstor *m* skilled workman
májstorstvo *n* mastery, skill
majúšan-šni *adj*. tiny
màkar *conj*. although, even
màkaze *f pl*. (S.) scissors
Makedónac *m*, G **-dónca** male Macedonian
Makèdonija *f* Macedonia
Makèdonka *f* female Macedonian
makèdonski *adj*. Macedonian (adj.)
màknuti [**màkne**] **P** to move, set in motion
màknuti se P to stir, move
màksimalan-lni *adj*. maximum (adj.), maximal
màla *f adj*. little girl
màlen *adj*. small, little
malénkost *f*, G **-kosti** trifle
máli *adj*. little, small, small boy
màlina *f* raspberry
màliša *m* little man
màlo *adv*. a little, somewhat
malòletnik *m*; N *pl*. **-nici** *ek*. a minor
malòljetnik *m*; N *pl*. **-nici** *ijek*. a minor
màlo-pòmalo *adv*. little by little
màma *f* mama, mom
mámac *m*, G **mámca** lure, bait, decoy
màmica *f* mommy
mána *f* fault, flaw, defect
mànastir *m* (S.) monastery
màngup *m* rascal
mànje *adv*. less
mànji *adj*. smaller, less
manjìna *f* minority
manjìnski *adj*. minority (adj.)
mànjkanje *n* lack, deficiency
mànjkati [**mànjka**] **I** to be lacking, need
màrama *f* shawl, kerchief
màramica *f* handkerchief
márka *f*; G *pl*. **màraka** stamp
màrkiran *adj*. marked
màrljiv *adj*. hard-working
marmeláda *f* marmalade, jam
màrt *m* month of March
márva *f* (coll.) cattle
màsa *f* mass
másan-másni *adj*. greasy
màslac *m* butter
mást *f*, G **másti** lard, fat
mástan-másni *adj*. greasy
màstilo *n* (S.) ink
mastìljav *adj*. (S.) ink (adj.), inky
mašína *f* machine, motor
mašìnist *m* mechanic, engineer
mašìnista *f* (S.) mechanic, engineer
màšna *f* (S.) tie
màšta *f* imagination
màštati [**màšta**] **I** to imagine, dream
matemàtičar *m* mathematician
matemàtika *f*, D **-tici** mathematics
màterijalan-lni *adj*. material, financial
màterinski *adj*. (Cr.) maternal, mother (adj.)
màternji *adj*. (S.) maternal, mother (adj.)
màti *f*, G **màtere** mother
matúra *f* graduation from high school
matùrant *m* high school senior
maturírati [**matùrira**] **I/P** to graduate from high school
màturski *adj*. senior (adj.)
mèćava *f* blizzard
méd *m*, G **mèda** honey
mèdalja *f* medal
mèdan–mèdni *adj*. honey-sweet
mèden *adj*. honey (adj.)
mèdeni mèsec *m ek*. honeymoon
mèdeni mjèsec *m ijek*. honeymoon
medicína *f* medicine
medìcinski *adj*. medical
Medìteranski *adj*. Mediterranean
mèdved *m ek*. bear
mèdvjed *m ijek*. bear
među (prep. with A/D) between, among
međunárodni *adj*. international
međùsobno *adv*. mutually, reciprocally
međùtim *adv*. meanwhile, by the way
međuvréme *n*, G **međùvremena** *ek*. interval
međuvrijème *n*, G **međùvremena** *ijek*. interval
mèhur *m ek*. bubble, blister
mèkan *adj*. soft, tender
mèko *adv*. soft, softly
mèko kùhano jáje *n* (Cr.) soft-boiled egg
mèko kùvano jáje *n* (S.) soft-boiled egg
mèksički *adj*. Mexican (adj.)
Meksikánac *m*, G **-kánca** male Mexican
Mèksiko *m* Mexico
ménjati [**ménja**] *ek*. **I** to change
ménjati se *ek*. **I** to change, alter
mènza *f* student cafeteria
mèra *f ek*. measure
meridìjan *m* meridian
mèrilo *n ek*. measure, rule
mèriti [**mèri**] *ek*. **I** to measure
mèrmer *m* (S.) marble
mèsar *m*, G **mesára** butcher
mèsec *m ek*. month, moon

njézin *m*, **njézino** *n*, **njézina** *f* her, its
njèžan–nježni *ijek. adj.* gentle, tender
njìhov *m*, **njìhovo** *n*, **njìhova** *f* their, theirs
njiva *f* field, meadow
njùh *m* (Cr.) sense of smell
njùjorški *adj.* New York (adj.)
njúška *f* snout

O o

o (prep. with D) about, concerning
o (prep. with A) against
òba *m/n num.* both
òbadva *m/n num.* both
òbadve *f ek. num.* both
òbadvije *f ijek. num.* both
òbala *f* shore, coast
obàmreti [**òbamre; òbamro, òbamrla**] *ek.* **P** to become numb
obàmrijeti [**òbamre; òbamro, òbamrla**] *ijek.* **P** to become numb
obàsjati [**obàsja**] **P** to illuminate, light up
obasjávati [**obàsjava**] **I** to illuminate, light up
òbavest *f*, **G òbavesti** *ek.* information, notice
obavéstiti [**obàvesti**] *ek.* **P** to inform, notify
obaveštávati [**obavèštava**] *ek.* **I** to inform, notify
obavešténje *n ek.* announcement
òbaveza *f* duty, obligation
òbavezan–òbavezni *adj.* compulsory, obligatory
òbavezno *adv.* obligatory
obavíjati [**obàvija**] **I** to wind, wrap around
òbavijest *f*, **G òbavijesti** *ijek.* information, notice
obavijèstiti [**obàvijesti**] *ijek.* **P** to inform, notify
obavještávati [**-vjèštava**] *ijek.* **I** to inform, notify
obavješténje *n ijek.* announcement
òbdanište *n* nursery school
òbe *f ek. num.* both
obećánje *n* promise
obèćati [**obèća**] **P** to promise
òbed *m ek.* dinner (midday)
òbedovati [**òbeduje**] *ek.* **I** to dine
òbesiti [**òbesi**] *ek.* **P** to hang
obezbéditi [**obèzbedi**] *ek.* **P** to provide for
obezbijèditi [**obèzbijedi**] *ijek.* **P** to provide for
òbičaj *m* custom, practice
òbičan–òbični *adj.* usual, customary
òbično *adv.* customarily, usually
obíći [**òbiđe; òbišao, òbišla**] **P** to go around, circle
òbilan–òbilni *adj.* plentiful, lavish
òbilje *n* abundance
obítelj *f*, **G obítelji** (Cr.) family
objásniti [**òbjasni**] **P** to explain
objašnjávati [**objàšnjava**] **I** to explain
objašnjénje *n* explaining, explanation
òbjava *f* proclamation
objáviti [**òbjavi**] **P** to announce, inform, declare
òbjavljen *adj.* announced, published
objavljívati [**objàvljuje**] **I** to announce, declare
òbje *f ijek. num.* both
òbjed *m ijek.* dinner (midday)
òbjedovati [**òbjeduje**] *ijek.* **I** to dine
òbjesiti [**òbjesi**] *ijek.* **P** to hang
obláčiti [**òblači**] **I** to put on, clothe, dress
obláčiti se I to dress oneself
òblačno *adv.* cloudy
òblak *m*; **N** *pl.* **òblaci** cloud
oblakòder *m* (S.) skyscraper
òblast *f*, **G òblasti** region
òblik *m*; **N** *pl.* **òblici** shape, form
òbližnji *adj.* neighboring, near
òbnova *f* renewal, restoration
obnòviti [**òbnovi**] **P** to restore
òbnovljen *adj.* renewed, restored
òbod *m* brim, flap
òboje *n*, **G obóga** *ili* **òbojega** both of them
òbojen *adj.* colored
obòjica *f* both of them
obòriti P to overturn, penetrate
obožàvalac *m*, **G -vaoca** fan, follower
obožávati [**obòžava**] **I** to adore, admire
òbradovati se [**òbraduje se**] **P** to be glad, rejoice
Obrádović, Dosìtej Serbian traveler, writer and educator (1742/43–1811)
òbrana *f* (Cr.) defense
obrániti [**òbrani**] **P** (Cr.) to defend, beat off
òbrati [**òbere**] **P** to pick
obrátiti se [**òbrati se**] **P** to turn to, consult, address oneself to
òbratno *adv.* vice-versa, on the contrary
òbraz *m* cheek, countenance
obrazlágati [**obràzlaže**] **I** to explain in detail, expound
obrazlòžiti [**obràzloži**] **P** to explain in detail, expound
òbrazovan *adj.* educated
òbrazovanje *n* education
òbrazovati se I/P to be formed, be educated
òbred *m* ritual, ceremony
Obrénović Serbian royal family
òbrisati [**òbriše**] **P** to wipe off, dry
òbrnuto *adv.* conversely, opposite
òbrok *m*; **N** *pl.* **òbroci** meal, share, portion
òbrt *m* trade, craft, skill
òbrtnik *m*; **N** *pl.* **òbrtnici** craftsman, artisan, tradesman
obúčen *adj.* dressed
òbučen *adj.* trained
òbuća *f* footwear
obúći [**obúče; òbukao, obúkla**] **P** to put on, clothe, dress
obúći se P to dress oneself, get dressed
obùhvaćati [**obùhvaća**] **I** (Cr.) to encircle, embrace
obùhvatati [**obùhvata**] **I** (S.) to encircle, embrace
òbzir *m* regard, reference
òcat *m*, **G òcta** (Cr.) vinegar
ocèan *m*, **G oceána** (Cr.) ocean
ocèanski *adj.* (Cr.) ocean (adj.)
òcena *f ek.* evaluation, mark, judgment
océniti [**òceni**] *ek.* **P** to evaluate, assess, review
ocijèniti [**òcijeni**] *ijek.* **P** to evaluate, assess, review
òcjena *f ijek.* evaluation, mark, judgment
òčaj *m* despair
òčajan–òčajni *adj.* desperate
očekívanje *n* expectation
očekívati [**očèkuje**] **I** to expect, wait for
očekívati se I to be expected
òčev *adj.* father's
òči (N/A *pl. of* oko) eyes
očìgledan–očìgledni *adj.* evident, visual
očìgledno *adv.* obviously
òčit *adj.* obvious, clear
òčito *adv.* evidently, obviously
òčni *adj.* eye (adj.), ocular
òčuh *m*; **N** *pl.* **òčusi** step-father
od (prep. with G) from, away from, of
odabírati [**odàbira**] **I** to select, choose
odàbrati [**odàbere**] **P** to select, choose
òdakle *adv.* from where
òdan *adj.* devoted
òdati P to disclose, reveal
òdatle *adv.* from here, from there, therefore
òdavno *adv.* long ago, a long time
odbáciti [**òdbaci**] **P** to reject, discard
odbacívati [**odbàcuje**] **I** to reject, discard
odbíjati [**òdbija**] **I** to refuse, deny, subtract
òdbiti [**òdbije**] **P** to refuse, deny, subtract
òdbiti se P to return (the ball)
òdbojka *f*, **D òdbojci** volleyball
òdbrana *f* (S.) defense
odbrániti [**òdbrani**] **P** (S.) to defend
òdeća *f ek.* clothing
odéliti P *ek.* to separate, part
odélo *n ek.* clothes, suit
òdeljen *ek. adj.* separated
odèven *ek. adj.* dressed
òdevni *adj.* clothing (adj.)
odgòditi [**òdgodi**] **P** to postpone
òdgoj *m* (Cr.) education, upbringing
odgòjiti [**òdgoji**] **P** (Cr.) to raise, educate
odgovárajući *adj.* corresponding
odgovárati [**odgòvara**] **I** to answer
òdgovor *m* answer
òdgovoran–òdgovorni *adj.* responsible
odgovòriti [**odgòvori**] **P** to answer
odgovórnost *f*, **G -nosti** responsibility
odíći P [**òde**] to go off to, leave
odìgrati [**òdigra**] **P** (S.) to dance, finish dancing, play, finish playing
odijèliti P *ijek.* to separate, part
odijèlo *n ijek.* clothes, suit
òdijeljen *ijek. adj.* separated
òdisati I [**òdiše**] to smell, emanate, breathe of
òdista *adv.* really, truly
odìstinski *adj.* true, real
òdjeća *f ijek.* clothing
odjèdnom *adv.* suddenly, all at once
òdjek *m*; **N** *pl.* **òdjeci** echo, repercussion
odjekívati [**odjèkuje**] **I** to echo, resound
odjèven *ijek. adj.* dressed
òdlazak *m*, **G -laska**; **N** *pl.* **-lasci** departure
òdlaziti [**òdlazi**] **I** to depart, go away
òdličan–òdlični *adj.* excellent
òdlično *adv.* excellently
òdlika *f*, **D òdlici** distinctive feature
òdlikovati se [**òdlikuje se**] **I** to distinguish

òdlomak *m*, G **-lomka;** N *pl.* **-lomci** fragment
odlòžiti [**òdloži**] **P** to postpone, put aside
odlúčiti [**òdluči**] **P** to decide
odlučívati [**odlùčuje**] **I** to decide
òdlučno *adv.* decisively
òdluka *f*, D **òdluci** decision
odmàći *ili* **odmàknuti** [**òdmakne; òdmakao, odmàkla**] **P** to move off, go off
òdmah *adv.* at once, immediately
odmáralište *n* vacation resort
odmárati se [**òdmara se**] **I** to rest, relax
odmerávati I *ek.* to measure, weigh out
òdmeriti P *ek.* to measure, weigh out
odmjerávati I *ijek.* to measure, weigh out
òdmjeriti P *ijek.* to measure, weigh out
òdmor *m* rest, vacation
odmòriti se [**òdmori se**] **P** to rest, repose
òdneti [**odnèse; òdneo, òdnela**] *ek.* **P** to carry away
òdnijeti (**odnèse; òdnio, òdnijela**] *ijek.* **P** to carry away
òdnos *m* relationship
odnòsiti [**òdnosi**] **I** to carry away
odnòsiti se I to relate to, concern
òdnosno *adv.* or, respectively
òdnošaj *m* relationship, intercourse
odobrénje *n* approval
òdojak *m*, **G òdojka** suckling-pig
òdojče *n*, **G òdojčeta** suckling baby, infant
odòleti [**òdoli**] *ek.* **P** to resist, overcome
odòljeti [**òdoli**] *ijek.* **P** to resist, overcome
odòzdo *adv.* from below
odòzgo *adv.* from above
òdrastao–òdrasli *adj.* grown-up, mature
òdraz *m* expression, reflection
òdrečan–òdrečni *adj.* negative
òdredba *f*; G *pl.* **-daba** rule, regulation
òdredište *n* destination
odréditi [**òdredi**] **P** to order, direct, appoint, decree
òdređen *adj.* determined, definite, specific, certain
òdrezak *m*, **G -reska;** N *pl.* **-resci** steak, chop
òdrveniti se [**òdrveni se**] **P** to become like wood
održávati [**odřžava**] **I** to hold, maintain, keep (house)
òdsada *adv.* from now on
òdsek *m ek.* division, department, section
odsèliti se [**òdseli se**] **P** to move away, emigrate
òdsjek *m ijek.* division, department, section
odspávati [**òdspava**] **P** to get some sleep
òdsto *adv.* percent
odstrániti [**òdstrani**] **P** to remove
odstranjívati [**odstrànjuje**] **I** to remove
odstúpanje *n* withdrawal
òdsutan–òdsutni *adj.* absent
odsvírati [**òdsvira**] **P** to play (music)
òdšteta *f* compensation, amends
odùpreti [**òdupre; òdupro, òduprla**] *ek.* **P** to resist
odùprijeti [**òdupre; òdupro, òduprla**] *ijek.* **P** to resist
odùstati [**odùstane**] **P** to give up, withdraw
odušèviti [**odùševi**] **P** to inspire, excite
odušèviti [**odùševi**] **P** to inspire, excite, charm
odušèviti se P to be inspired, charmed
oduševljávati [**odušèvljava**] **I** to inspire, excite
odùševljen *adj.* enraptured, pleased
oduševljénje *n* enthusiasm, rapture
odúžiti [**òduži**] **P** to repay
òdvažan–òdvažni *adj.* brave, daring
odvèsti [**odvède; òdveo, òdvela**] **P** to lead away, conduct
òdvjetnik *m*; N *pl.* **-nici** (Cr.) lawyer
òdvojen *adj.* separated from
òdvratan–òdvratni *adj.* disgusting, repulsive
odvrátiti [**òdvrati**] **P** to reply, turn aside
òglas *m* announcement, ad
oglásiti se [**òglasi se**] **P** to utter a sound, announce
oglèdalo *n* (S.) mirror
ògnjen *adj.* fiery
ògnjište *n* fireplace
ògorčen *adj.* bitter, embittered
ogovárati [**ogòvara**] **I** to defame, slander, backbite
ògrada *f* fence
ogràničen *adj.* limited
ògrejati [**ògreje**] *ek.* **P** to warm
ògrejati se *ek.* **P** to warm oneself
ògrev *m ek. and ijek.* fuel, firewood
ògrijati [**ògrije**] *ijek.* **P** to warm
ògrijati se *ijek.* **P** to warm oneself
ògrjev *m ijek.* fuel, firewood
ògrlica *f* necklace
ògroman–ògromni *adj.* huge, enormous
ogřtač *m*, **G ogrtáča** overcoat
ohò *excl.* oho!
òhol *adj.* arrogant
Ȍhrid *m* city and lake in Macedonia
ojàčati [**ojàča**] **P** to strengthen
okèan *m*, **G okeána** (S.) ocean
okèanski *adj.* (S.) ocean (adj.)
òklada *f* bet, wager
òkladiti se [**òkladi se**] **P** to bet, wager
oklijèvati [**òklijeva**] **I** to hesitate
òko *n*; N *pl.* **òči** *f* eye
oko (prep. with G) around
òkolina *f* surroundings
òkolni *adj.* roundabout, circuitous
okólnost *f*, **G -nosti** situation, fact, circumstance
okolo (prep. with G) around
òkomit *adj.* vertical, sheer
okrénuti [**òkrene**] **P** to turn
okrénuti se P to turn, turn back
òkretanje *n* revolution, rotation, gyration
òkretati [**òkreće**] **I** to turn, rotate
òkretati se I to revolve, turn around
òkretnost *f* agility
òkrilje *n* wing, guidance
òkrugao–òkrugli *adj.* round
okruglìna *f* curvature
òkruniti [**òkruni**] **P** (Cr.) to crown
òkruniti se P (Cr.) to be crowned
òkrutan–òkrutni *adj.* cruel
òkrutnost *f*, **G -nosti** cruelty
òkružen *adj.* surrounded
òktobar *m*, **G òktobra** October
òkuka *f*, **D òkuci** curve, bend
okùlist *m* eye doctor, oculist
okùlista *m* (S.) eye doctor, oculist
okulìstika *f*, **D -tici** optics
òkup *m* gathering, assembly
okupácija *f* occupation (of country)
okúpati se [**òkupa se**] **P** to bathe, take a bath
okùpator *m* occupier
okupírati [**okùpira**] **I** to occupy
òkupiti se [**òkupi se**] **P** to assemble
òkus *m* (Cr.) sense of taste
òkvir *m*, **G okvíra** framework
olakšánje *n* relief, easing
olàkšati [**olàkša**] **P** to relieve, ease
òlimpijski *adj.* Olympic (adj.)
òloš *m* rabble
òlovka *f*, **D òlovci** pencil
òltar *m*, **G oltára** altar
olúja *f* storm, gale
òmiljen *adj.* favorite, popular
òmladina *f* youth(s), young people
òmladinski *adj.* youth (adj.)
omlátiti [**òmlati**] **P** to beat off, repel, shake, pick off
òmlet *m* omelette
omògućen *adj.* made possible
omogúćiti [**omògući**] **P** to make possible
ón *m*, **òno** *n*, **òna** *f* he/it, it, she/it
ònaj *m*, **òno** *n*, **òna** *f* that, that one
onàkav *m*, **onàkvo** *n*, **onàkva** *f* such a person, that kind
onàko *adv.* in that way, so-so
ònamo *adv.* there, in that direction
ònda *adv.* then, thereupon
ónde *adv. ek.* there
óndje *adv. ijek.* there
onemogúćiti [**-mògući**] **P** to make impossible
onesvéstiti se [**onèsvesti se**] *ek.* **P** to faint
onèsvešćen *ek. adj.* fainted
onesvijèstiti se [**onèsvijesti se**] *ijek.* **P** to faint
onèsviješćen *ijek. adj.* fainted
òpadati [**òpada**] **I** to decrease, decline, fall away
òpanak *m*, **G òpanka;** N *pl.* **òpanci** leather sandal, moccasin
òpasan–òpasni *adj.* dangerous
opásnost *f*, **G -nosti** danger, peril
òpasti [**òpadne; òpao, òpala**] **P** to decrease, decline, fall away
òpaziti [**òpazi**] **P** to notice, perceive
òpćečovječànski *ijek. adj.* (Cr.) humanity's, humanitarian
općènito *adv.* (Cr.) generally
òpći *adj.* (Cr.) general, public
òpćina *f* (Cr.) community, township
òpeka *f*, **D òpeci** brick
operácija *f* operation
òpet *adv.* again
opìjen *adj.* enraptured, drunk, intoxicated
òpip *m* (Cr.) sense of touch
òpipati [**òpipa**] **P** to feel, touch
opìpavajući *v. adj.* feeling, fingering
opipávati [**opìpava**] **I** to feel, touch
opípljiv *adj.* tangible, obvious
òpis *m* description
opisati [**òpiše**] **P** to describe
opisívati [**opìsuje**] **I** to describe
òpiti se [**òpije se**] **P** to get drunk

òpkoljen *adj.* surrounded
òpomena *f* warning
opoménuti [**opòmene**] **P** to warn
opòravilište *n* nursinghome
òporuka *f*, **D òporuci** will, testament
opráštati se [**òprašta se**] **I** to say goodbye, take leave
òprati [**òpere**] **P** to wash
òprati se P to wash (oneself)
opravdánje *n* apology, defense
opravdávati se [**opràvdava se**] **I** to apologize, justify oneself
òpreka *f*, **D òpreci** opposition, contrast
òprema *f* equipment
òprez *m* caution
òprezan–òprezni *adj.* cautious
opròstite *imp.* (Cr.) excuse me
opròstiti [**òprosti**] **P** to excuse, forgive, pardon
opròstiti se P to say farewell
òproštaj *m* leave-taking, parting
oproštěnje *n* pardon
òpsada *f* siege
òpsedan *adj.* besieged, obsessed
òpseg *m*; **N** *pl.* **òpsezi** volume
òpsežan–òpsežni *adj.* extended, voluminous
opsòvati [**òpsuje**] **P** to curse, swear
òpstanak *m*, **G -anka**; **N** *pl.* **-anci** subsistence, existence, life
òpširan–òpširni *adj.* extensive
òpštečovečànski *ek. adj.* (S.) humanity's, humanitarian
òpšti *adj.* (S.) general, public
òpština *f* (S.) community, township
optrčávati [**optr̀čava**] **I** to run around
òptužba *f* accusation
òptužen *adj.* accused
opùstošen *adj.* plundered, devastated
òrah *m*; **N** *pl.* **òrasi** walnut
òrao *m*, **G órla**; **N** *pl.* **órli** *ili* **òrlovi** eagle
òrati [**òre**] **I** to plow
ordinácija *f* doctor's office
ordinírati [**ordìnira**] **I/P** to receive patients, take care of patients
òrgan *m* organ
organizácija *f* organization
organìzator *m* organizer
organìziran *adj.* organized
organizírati [**-nìzira**] **I/P** (Cr.) to organize
orgànizovan *adj.* organized
orgànizovati [**-zuje**] **I/P** (S.) to organize
òriti se [**òri se**] **I** to resound
òrlov *adj.* eagle's
òrman *m*, **G ormána** (S.) cabinet, clothes closet
òrmar *m*, **G ormára** (Cr.) cabinet, clothes closet
òruđe *n* tools
òružje *n* arms
ós *f*, **G ósi** axis
òsa *f* wasp
òsam *num.* eight
osamdèset *num.* eighty
osamdèseti *adj.* eightieth
òsamljen *adj.* solitary
osàmnaest *num.* eighteen
osàmnaesti *adj.* eighteenth
osamostáliti P to make independent
òsećajan–òsećajni *ek. adj.* sensitive, sentimental
òsećati [**òseća**] *ek.* **I** to feel, sense
òsećati se *ek.* **I** to feel, sense, be aware of
òseka *f*, **D òseci** low tide
osètilo *n ek.* sense, sensory faculty
òsetiti [**òseti**] *ek.* **P** to feel, sense
osètljiv *ek. adj.* sensitive
òsiguran *adj.* assured, secure
osiguránje *n* insurance, (social) security
osigùrati [**osigùra**] **P** to insure, protect
osiguráνanje *n* assurance, protection
osim (prep. with G) except, besides
osim tòga in addition
osiròmašiti [**osiròmaši**] **P** to become impoverished, make poor
òsjećajan–òsjećajni *ijek. adj.* sensitive, sentimental
òsjećati [**òsjeća**] *ijek.* **I** to feel, sense
òsjećati se *ijek.* **I** to feel, sense, be aware of
osjètilo *n ijek.* (Cr.) sense, sensory faculty
òsjetiti [**òsjeti**] *ijek.* **P** to feel, sense
osjètljiv *ijek. adj.* sensitive
òskudica *f* poverty, want, penury
oslabljénje *n* weakening
oslobòditi [**oslòbodi**] **P** to free
oslobòditi se P to free oneself, get rid of
oslobođénje *n* freedom
òsmeh *m*; **N** *pl.* **òsmesi** *ek.* smile, grin
osmehívati se [**osmèhuje se**] *ek.* **I** to smile, grin
òsmi *adj.* eighth
òsmijeh *m*; **N** *pl.* **òsmijesi** *ijek.* smile, grin
osmjehívati se [**osmjèhuje se**] *ijek.* **I** to smile, grin
osnìvač *m*, **G osniváča** founder
osnívanje *n* establishing
osnívati [**òsniva**] **I** to found, establish
òsnov *m* fundamental, element, base
òsnova *f* foundation, basis
òsnovan *adj.* founded
òsnovan–òsnovni *adj.* basic, elementary, cardinal
osnòvati [**òsnuje**] **P** to found, establish
òsnovna škóla *f* primary school
òsoba *f* person
òsobina *f* characteristic
òsobit *adj.* remarkable, special
òsobito *adv.* particularly, specially
osòvina *f* axis, shaft, pivot
ospsòbiti [**ospòsobi**] **P** to enable, qualify
osramòtiti [**osràmoti**] **P** to disgrace
òstajati [**òstaje**] **I** to stay, remain
òstali *adj.* the rest, remaining
òstareti [**òstari**] *ek.* **P** to grow old
òstarjeti [**òstari**] *ijek.* **P** to grow old
ostátak *m*, **G ostátka**; **N** *pl.* **ostáci** remainder, residue
òstati [**òstane**] **P** to stay, remain
òstaviti [**òstavi**] **P** to leave, quit, abandon
òstavljati [**òstavlja**] **I** to leave, quit, abandon
òsti *f pl.* harpoon, trident
òstrvo *n* (S.) island
ostváriti [**òstvari**] **P** to realize, achieve
òsuda *f* sentence, verdict
osúditi [**òsudi**] **P** to sentence
òsuđen *adj.* condemned, sentenced
osvàjač *m*, **G osvajáča** conqueror, victor
òsvajajući *v. adj.* winning, conquering
osvájanje *n* conquest
osvájati [**òsvaja**] **I** to conquer
osvànuti [**òsvane**] **P** to appear, arrive, dawn
òsveta *f* revenge, retaliation
osvétiti se [**òsveti se**] **P** to revenge
osvétliti [**òsvetli**] *ek.* **P** to illuminate
osvetljávati [**osvètljava**] *ek.* **I** to illuminate
òsvetljen *ek. adj.* illuminated
òsvežiti se [**òsveži se**] *ek.* **P** to refresh oneself, freshen up
osvijètliti [**òsvijetli**] *ijek.* **P** to illuminate
òsvijetljen *ijek. adj.* illuminated
osvjetljávati [**osvjètljava**] *ijek.* **I** to illuminate
òsvježiti se [**òsvježi se**] *ijek.* **P** to refresh oneself, freshen up
osvòjiti [**òsvoji**] **P** to conquer, charm
osvŕnuti se [**òsvrne se**] **P** to look back, consider, refer to
òsvrt *m* review, analysis
ošàmariti [**ošàmari**] **P** to slap
ošíšati [**òšiša**] **P** to cut (hair), clip
òštar–òštri *adj.* sharp
òštećen *adj.* damaged
oštećívati [**oštèćuje**] **I** to damage, harm
òštriji *adj.* more severe
òtac *m*, **G òca**; **N** *pl.* **òčevi** father
òtadžbina *f* homeland, fatherland
otàrasiti se [**otàrasi se**] **P** to get rid of
òteti [**òtme**] **P** to snatch away
òticanje *n* outflow, run off
otíći [**òde/òtiđe/òtide; òtišao, òtišla**] **P** to go away, depart
òtimati [**òtima** *ili* **òtimlje**] **I** to snatch away
òtisak *m*, **G òtiska** reprint, copy
òtkaz *m* notice, cancellation
otkrívati [**òtkriva**] **I** to discover
otkríće *n* discovery, invention
òtkucati [**òtkuca**] **P** to type (S.), sound out
òtkuda *ili* **òtkud** *adv.* from where
òtmen *ek. adj.* noble, fine
òtmjen *ijek. adj.* noble, fine
òtok *m*; **N** *pl.* **òtoci** (Cr.) island
otòpiti [**òtopi**] **P** to melt, thaw
òtpadak *m*, **G -patka**; **N** *pl.* **-paci** waste, garbage, trash, rubbish
òtpasti [**òtpadne; òtpao, òtpala**] **P** to fall off
otplésati [**òtpleše**] **P** (Cr.) to dance, finish dancing
otpòčeti [**òtpočne**] **P** to begin
òtpor *m* resistance
òtporan–òtporni *adj.* resistant, tough
otprílike *adv.* approximately
otpùstiti [**òtpusti**] **P** to dismiss, discharge, fire
otpúštati [**òtpušta**] **I** to dismiss, discharge, fire
otputòvati [**otpùtuje**] **P** to depart, leave
otrága *adv.* behind, in the rear
otr̀čati [**otr̀či**] **P** to run off
otrésti [**otrése; òtresao, òtresla**] **P** to shake off
òtrov *m* poison
otrovánje *n* poisoning
otròvati [**òtruje**] **P** to poison
òtužno *adv.* disgustedly, disagreeably
otvárati [**òtvara**] **I** to open
òtvoren *adj.* open, opened

otvòriti [**òtvori**] **P** to open
òvaj *m*, **òvo** *n*, **òva** *f* this, this one
ovàko *adv*. in this way, like this
òvamo *adv*. in this direction, here
óvca *f*; **G** *pl*. **ováca** sheep
óvde *ek*. *adv*. here
óvdje *ijek*. *adv*. here
òveći *adj*. rather large
òvisiti [**òvisi**] **I** to depend
òvo *pron*. this, it
ovogòdišnji *adj*. this year's
ovòliko *adv*. so many, this many
òvuda *adv*. this way, here
òzbiljan–òzbiljni *adj*. serious
òzbiljno *adv*. seriously
ozbíljnost *f*, **G -nosti** seriousness
òzdraviti [**òzdravi**] **P** to recover, get well
ozépsti [**ozébe; òzebao, òzebla**] **P** to be cold, catch cold
označávati [**oznàčava**] **I** to indicate, designate, define
òznačen *adj*. indicated, marked
oznáčiti [**òznači**] **P** to indicate, designate, define
òznaka *f*, **D òznaci** mark, label, license plate
oznòjiti se [**òznoji se**] **P** to sweat
ožèniti se [**òženi se**] **P** to marry (for a man)
òženjen *adj*. married (of a man)
oživeti [**òživi**] *ek*. **P** to come to life, animate, inspire
ožívjeti [**òživi**] *ijek*. **P** to come to life, animate, inspire
òžujak *m*, **G òžujka** (Cr.) March

P p

pa *conj*. and, and also
pacìjent *m* a patient
pácov *m* (S.) rat
pád *m*; **N** *pl*. **pádovi** fall, decline, crash, breakdown
pàdati [**pàda**] **I** to fall, drop
pádež *m* case (gram.)
pàdina *f* slope
pàdobran *m* parachute
padobránac *m*, **G- bránca** parachutist
pahùljica *f* flake, fluff
pàkao *m*, **G pàkla** hell
pàket *m*, **G pakéta** package
pakètić *m* package, small parcel
pàlac *m*, **G pálca** thumb, finger, toe
pàlača *f* (Cr.) palace
palačínka *f* pancake
pàlata *f* (S.) palace
pàlenta *f* corn mush
pàlica *f* stick, staff
páliti [**páli**] **I** to light, start a motor
pàluba *f* deck
pámćenje *n* memory
pàmet *f*, **G pàmeti** intelligence, mind
pàmetan–pàmetni *adj*. intelligent, smart
pàmetno *adv*. sensible, sensibly, wisely
pámtiti [**pámti**] **I** to remember
pàmuk *m* cotton
pànika *f*, **D pànici** panic
pantalóne *f pl*. (S.) trousers, pants
papàgaj *m*, **G papagája** parrot
pàpar *m*, **G pàpra** (Cr.) pepper
pàpir *m*, **G papíra** paper
pàpren *adj*. hot, spicy
pàprika *f*, **D pàprici** pepper (vegetable)
pàprikaš *m* veal stew with red pepper and potatoes
pàpuča *f* slipper
pàpučar *m* slipper maker, "henpecked" husband
pàr *m*; **N** *pl*. **pàrovi** pair, a few
pàra *f* coin, money
pàra *f* steam, vapor
paradàjz *m* (S.) tomato
pàradoksalno *adv*. paradoxically
paràgraf *m* paragraph, article
paralèla *f* parallel
páran-párni *adj*. equal, even
párče *n*, **G párčeta** (S.) piece, bit, slice
pàrfem *m* perfume
pàriski *adj*. Parisian
Pàriz *m*, **G Paríza** Paris
pàrk *m*; N pl. **pàrkovi** park
parkíranje *n* parking
parkírati [**pàrkira**] **I/P** to park
parlàmenat *m*, **G- menta** parliament
parlàment *m* parliament
párnica *f* lawsuit
pàrobrod *m* steamship
pàrtija *f* communist party, game (chess, cards)
partíjac *m*, **G partíjca** communist-party member
pàrtijka *f* female communist-party member
pàrtijski *adj*. pert. to communist party
partìzan *m*, **G partizána** partisan, guerrilla
pàs *m*, **G psà** dog
pás *m*, **G pása** belt
pásoš *m* passport
pàsti [**pàdne; pào, pàla**] **P** to fall, drop, fail (exam)
pàstir *m*, **G pastíra** shepherd
pàsulj *m*, **G pasúlja** (S.) beans
pàtika *f* slipper, sport shoe, sneaker
pàtiti [**pàti**] **I** to suffer
pàtka *f*; **G** *pl*. **pàtaka** duck
pàtnja *f* suffering
patrìjarh *m*, **G-járha** patriarch
patrìotski *adj*. patriotic
patúljak *m*, **G -úljka**; **N** *pl*. **-úljci** dwarf
pàučina *f* cobweb
pàuk *m*; **N** *pl*. **pàuci** spider
pàuza *f* pause, break, intermission
pàzar *m*, **G pazára** bazaar, fair
pazáriti [**pàzari**] **I/P** to trade, bargain, buy
pàzikuća *m* / *f* janitor
pàziti [**pàzi**] **I** to watch, be mindful of, be careful
pàžljiv *adj*. careful, attentive
pàžnja *f* attention
pčèla *f* bee
pècanje *n* fishing
pècivo *n* soft roll
pèčat *m* mark, stamp, seal
pèčen *adj*. baked, roasted
pèčenje *n* roasting, baking
pečénje *n* roast meat
péć *f*, **G pèći** stove, oven
pèći [**pèče; pèkao, pèkla**] **I pèku** (3rd pl. pres.) to roast, bake
pèćina *f* cave, crag
pedèset *num*. fifty
pedesétak *m*, **G-sétka** around fifty
pedèseti *adj*. fiftieth
pèga *f ek*. spot, speck
pégla *f* flat-iron
péglati [**pégla**] **I** to iron
pèkar *m* baker
pèkara *f* bakery
pèkmez *m* jam, marmalade
pèna *f ek*. foam
pènzija *f* pension, retirement
penziòner *m*, **G-néra** pensioner, retired person
pènjanje *n* climbing
pènjati se [**pènje se**] **I** to climb
pepèljara *f* ashtray
pèpeo *m*, **G pèpela** ash
pèrčin *m*, **G perčína** pigtail
pèrika *f*, **D pèrici** wig
pèrivoj *m* (Cr.) park
pérje *n* (*coll*.) feathers, fancy clothes
pèro *n* pen, feather
pèron *m*, **G peróna** platform
persóna *f* personage
pèrsonalan–pèrsonalni *adj*. personal
péršin *m* (Cr.) parsley
péršun *m* (S.) parsley
pésak *m*, **G péska** *ek*. sand
pèsma *f*; **G** *pl*. **pèsama** *ek*. song, poem
pésnica *f* fist
pèsnik *m*.; **N** *pl*. **pèsnici** *ek*. poet
pèšački *ek*. pedestrian (adj)
pešàdija *f ek*. infantry
pèšak *m*, **G pešáka** *ek*. pedestrian
pèške *ek*. *adv*. on foot
pèškir *m*, **G peškíra** (S.) towel
Pèšta *f* Budapest
pét *num*. five
péta *f* heel
pétak *m*, **G pétka**; **N** *pl*. **péci** Friday
pétao *m*, **G pétla** *ek*. rooster
Pètar *m*, **G Pètra** Peter
péti *adj*. fifth
pètnaest *num*. fifteen
pètnaesti *adj*. fifteenth
petròlej *m* petroleum
pévac *m*, **G pévca** *ek*. singer, rooster
pèvač m, **G peváča** *ek*. singer
pevàčica *f ek*. female singer
pèvajući *v*. *adj*. *ek*. singing
pèvanje *n ek*. singing
pèvati [**pèva**] *ek*. **I** to sing
pèvati se I to be sung
píće *n* drink
pidžáma *f* pajamas
pijaca *f* (S.) marketplace
pijan *adj*. drunk, intoxicated
pijánac *m*, **G -nca** drunkard
pìjanica *m* / *f* drunkard
pijèsak *m*, **G pijèska** *ijek*. sand
pijètao *m*, **G pijètla** *ijek*. rooster
pijèvac *m*, **G pijèvca** *ijek*. singer, rooster
pijùckati [**pijùcka**] **I** to sip slowly
pila *f* saw
pìlad *f* (*coll*.), **G pìladi** chickens, children (slang)
pìle *n*, **G pìleta** chicken, chick
pìleći *adj*. chicken (adj.)
pìlići *m pl*. chickens
pìlula *f* pill
píljiti [**pílji**] **I** to gaze, peer, stare
piònir *m*, **G pionira** pioneer, elem. school child
piònirski *adj*. pioneer (adj.), youth camp (adj.)
pípa *f* faucet, spigot
pìpanje *n* (S.) sense of touch
pìpati [**pìpa**] **I** to touch
pír *m* banquet, wedding feast
pìrinač *m*, **G pìrinča** (S.) rice

rázmer *m ek.* scale, proportion
rázmerno *adv. ek.* relatively
razmijèniti [**ràzmijene**] *ijek.* **P** to exchange
ràzmisliti [**ràzmisli**] **P** to consider
razmíšljanje *n* consideration, deliberation
razmíšljati [**ràzmišlja**] **I** to consider
razmjenjívati [**razmjènjuje**] *ijek.* **I** to exchange
rázmjer *m ijek.* scale, proportion
rázmjerno *adv. ijek.* relatively
razmlatàrati se [**-mlatàra se**] **P** to gesture, gesticulate
ràzmnožen *adj.* reproduced, multiplied
rázno *adv.* miscellany, etc., odds and ends
raznòvrstan–raznòvrsni *adj.* of different kinds
razòčaran *adj.* disappointed
ràzonoda *f* leisure, fun, hobby
razòriti [**ràzori**] **P** to wreck, destroy
rázred *m* class, grade
ràzum *m* reason, sense
razùmeti [**razùme**] *ek.* **I** to understand
razùmeti se *ek.* **I** to understand one another, be understood
razumévanje *n ek.* understanding
razumijèvanje *n ijek.* understanding
razùmjeti [**razùmije**] *ijek.* **I** to understand
razùmjeti se *ijek.* **I** to understand one another, be understood
razvâljati [**ràzvalja**] **P** to spread, flatten
razvèden *adj.* divorced
razvedrávanje *n* clearing up, freshening
razvesèliti [**razvèseli**] **P** to gladden
razvíjati se [**ràzvija se**] **I** to develop, arise, grow
razvìjen *adj.* well-formed, developed
ràzviti se [**ràzvije se**] **P** to develop, arise, grow
rázvoj *m* development
rážanj *m*, **G rážnja** roasting-spit
ràžnjić *m* roasted meat slice
rđav *adj.* bad, evil
rèalan–rèalni *adj.* real
rèbro *n* rib
rècept *m* recipe, prescription
recìtal *m* recital
réč *f*, **G rèči** *ek.* word
réčca *f ek.* particle (gram.)
rečènica *f* sentence, phrase
rèčni *adj. ek.* river (adj.)
rèčnik *m*; **N** *pl.* **-nici** *ek.* dictionary
rèći [**rèče** *ili* **rèkne**; **rèkao**, **rèkla**] **P** **rèci** *imp.*; **rèkoh** (1st. sg. aor.), **rèče** (3rd. sg. aor.) to say, tell
réd *m*, **D u rédu**; **N** *pl.* **rédovi** order, arrangement, schedule, o.k. (D)
réd vòžnje timetable
rédak–rétki *ek. adj.* scarce, sparse, rare
rédni *adj.* ordinal
rèdovan–rèdovni *adj.* regular
redòvito *adv.* regularly
rèdovno *adv.* regularly
refèrat *m*, **G -ráta** conference paper
refòrmator *m* reformer
réka *f ek.*, **D réci** river
rekreácija *f* recreation
rèktor *m* rector, president
rèlevantan-tni *adj.* relevant
rèligija *f* religion
renòviran *adj.* restored
rèpa *f* turnip
repertòar *m* repertoire
repòrter *m*, **G -téra** reporter
repùblički *adj.* republic (adj.)
repùblika *f*, **D -lici** republic
restaurácija *f* restaurant, restoration
restòran *m*, **G -rána** restaurant
rešénje *n ek.* solution, judgment
rèuma *f* rheumatism
révnosno *adv.* enthusiastically
révnost *f*, **G -nosti** zeal, eagerness
revolúcija *f* revolution
rezánac *m*, **G rezánca** noodle
rèzati [**rèže**] **I** to cùt
rezervòar *m*, **G -voára** tank, gas tank
rezùltat *m*, **G -táta** result
réžati [**réži**] **I** to murmer against, snarl at
rìba *f* fish
ríban *adj.* scraped, grated
rìbar *m* fisherman
ribárenje *n* fishing
ríbati [**ríba**] **I** to rub, scrub, grate, shred
rìbič *m* fisherman
rìblji *adj.* fish (adj.)
rìbolov *m* fishing
rìječ *f*, **G riječi** *ijek.* word
Rijèčanin *m*; **N** *pl.* **Rijèčani** inhabitant of Rijeka
rijèdak–rìjetki *ijek. adj.* scarce, sparse, rare
rijèka *f*, **D rijèci** *ijek.* river
Rijèka *f*, **D Rijèci** city on Adriatic, formerly Fiume
Rím *m* Rome
Rímljanin *m*; **N** *pl.* **Rímljani** Roman, inhabitant of Rome
rimokàtolički *adj.* Roman Catholic (adj.)
rímski *adj.* Roman (adj.)
rivijéra *f* Riviera
rìzik *m* risk
rjèčca *f ijek.* particle (gram.)
rjèčni *adj. ijek.* river (adj.)
rjèčnik *m*; **N** *pl.* **-nici** *ijek.* dictionary
rješénje *n ijek.* solution, judgment
ròb *m*; **N** *pl.* **ròbovi** slave
ròba *f* goods
róblje *n* (coll.) slaves
ròbna kùća *f* department store
ròbni prómet *m* trade
rock-mùzika *f* rock music
ród *m*, **G ròda**; **N** *pl.* **ròdovi** gender, race, family
róda *f* stork
ròdbina *f* (coll.) relatives
ròditelj *m* parent
ròditeljski *adj.* parent's, parental
ròditi [**ròdi**] **P** to give birth to
ròditi se P to be born
ròdni *adj.* native
ròdoljuban–ròdoljubni *adj.* patriotic
rodoljùbiv *adj.* patriotic
ròđak *m*; **N** *pl.* **ròđaci** relation, relative
ròđen *adj.* born
ròđendan *m* birthday
rođénje *n* birth
rók *m*, **G ròka**; **N** *pl.* **ròkovi** date, term
Róm *m* a Gypsy, Gypsies (coll.)
ròman *m*, **G romána** novel
romìnjati [**romìnja**] **I** to drizzle
Ròmkinja *f* a Gypsy woman
ròniti I to dive, swim underwater
ròpstvo *n* slavery
ròštilj *m*, **G roštílja** barbecue grill
ròtkvica *f* radish
rúbac *m*, **G rúpca** kerchief
rúblje *n* linen
rúčak *m*, **G rúčka**; **N** *pl.* **rúčci** *ili* **rúčkovi** mid-day meal
rùčnik *m*, **G -níka**; **N** *pl.* **-níci** (Cr.) towel
rùdar *m*, **G rudára** miner
rúdnik *m*; **N** *pl.* **rúdnici** mine
rújan *m*, **G rújna** (Cr.) September
rúka *f* arm, hand
rùkav *m*, **G rukáva** sleeve
rukàvica *f* glove
rùkomet *m* handball
rukomètaš *m* team-handball player
rukometàšica *f* team-handball player (fem.)
rùkometni *adj.* team-handball (adj.)
rùkopis *m* handwriting, manuscript
Rùmun *m*, **G Rumúna** (S.) male Rumanian
Rùmunija *f* (S.) Rumania
rùmunski *adj.* (S.) Rumanian (adj.)
Rùmunj *m*, **G Rumúnja** (Cr.) male Rumanian
Rùmunjska *f adj. noun* (Cr.) Rumania
rùmunjski *adj.* (Cr.) Rumanian (adj.)
rùpa *f* hole
Rùs *m* male Russian
Rùsija *f* Russia
rùski *adj.* Russian
Rùskinja *f* female Russian
rùšiti [**ruši**] **I** to demolish
rúža *f* rose
rúžan–rúžni *adj.* ugly, bad
rúžno *adv.* badly, meanly
r̀vanje *n* wrestling
r̀vati se [**r̀ve se**] **I** to wrestle
R̀vatska *f dial.* Croatia

S s

s *ili* **sa** (prep. with G) from, off of
s *ili* **sa** (prep. with I) with, along with
sàbat *m* Sabbath
sábor *m* assembly
Sáborna cŕkva *f* cathedral
sačinjávati [**sačìnjava**] **I** to form part of, include
sàčuvan *adj.* preserved
sačúvati [**sàčuva**] **P** to preserve
sačúvati se P to be preserved
sád *m*; **N** *pl.* **sádovi** garden, plant
sàd *ili* **sàda** *adv.* now
SAD = N *pl.* **Sjèdinjene Amèričke Dr̀žave** SAD for U.S.A (lit., United American States)
sàdašnji *adj* present-day
sáditi [**sádi**] **I** to plant
sàdržaj *m* contents, subject matter
sadržávati I to contain, hold
ság *m*; **N** *pl.* **ságovi** (Cr.) carpet, rug
sàgledati [**sàgleda**] **P** to perceive
sagráditi [**sàgradi**] **P** to build, construct
sàgrađen *adj.* built, constructed
sàhrana *f* funeral, burial
sàhranjen *adj.* buried
sájam *m*, **G sájma** fair, market
sájamski *adj.* market (adj.), of the fair
sàjmeni *adj.* market (adj.), of the fair
sàko *m*, **G sakòa** jacket (of man's suit)
sàkriti se [**sàkrije se**] **P** to hide, take shelter

sàkupiti [**sàkupi**] **P** to gather, assemble
sàkupiti se P to gather together, assemble
sakúpljati [**sàkuplja**] **I** to gather, assemble
sakúpljati se I to gather together, assemble
salàta *f* lettuce, salad
sàlvet *m*, **G salvéta** napkin
salvéta *f* napkin
sám *m*, **sámo** *n*, **sáma** *f* alone, only, sole, oneself
sámac *m*, **G sámca** male of species
sàmo *adv.* only
samòća *f* solitude
samòglasnik *m*; **N** *pl.* **-nici** vowel
samopòsluga *f*, **D -sluzi** self-service store
samoposluživanje *n* self-service store
samopòuzdano *adv.* self-confidently
sàmostalan–sàmostalni *adj.* independent
sàmostalno *adv.* independently
sàmostan *m* (Cr.) monastery
samòuk *m*; **N** *pl.* **samòuci** self-taught man
samoùpravan–samoùpravni *adj.* pert. to self-government
samoùpravljanje *n* self-government
sàn *m*, **G snà**; **N** *pl.* **snì** *ili* **snòvi** dream, sleep
sandolína *f* canoe
sànduk *m*; **N** *pl.* **-duci** box, trunk
sánjalica *m/f*, dreamer
sànjar *m*, **G sanjára** dreamer
sànjati I to sled, sleigh
sàobraćaj *m* communication, traffic
saòbraćati [**saòbraća**] **I** to communicate, connect, go between
saònice *f pl.* sled
saòpćiti [**sàopći**] **P** (Cr.) to inform, communicate
saòpštiti [**sàopšti**] **P** (S.) to inform, communicate
sàpun *m*, **G sapúna** soap
sàputnik *m*; **N** *pl.* **-nici** (S.) traveling companion
sàradnik *m*; **N** *pl.* **-nici** (S.) co-worker
sarádnja *f* (S.) collaboration
sarađívati [**saràđuje**] **I** (S.) to cooperate, work with
Sàrajevo *n* capital of Bosnia-Herzegovina
sàrajevski *adj.* pert. to Sarajevo
sardína *f* sardine
sárma *f* stuffed cabbage
sàstajalište *n* meeting place
sàstajati se [**sàstaje se**] **I** to convene, meet
sàstanak *m*, **G -anka**; **N** *pl.* **-anci** meeting, date
sàstati se P [**sàstane se**] to meet
sástav *m* composition, structure
sàstavljen *adj.* composed of
sastòjati se [**sastòji se**] **I** to consist of
sàsvim *adv.* completely, quite
sàvremen *adj.* (S.) contemporary
sàšiti [**sàšije**] **P** to sew
sát *m*; **N** *pl.* **sàtovi**, **G** *pl.* **sátova** *ili* **sáti** hour, clock, lesson (Cr.), class (Cr.)
sàv *m*, **svè** *n*, **svà** *f* all, whole
Sáva *f* major river in northern Yugoslavia
sávest *f*, **G sávesti** *ek.* conscience
sávestan–sávesni *ek. adj.* conscientious
sávet *m ek.* advice
sávetovati [**sávetuje**] *ek.* **I** to advise
sávez *m* union, alliance
sáveznik *m*; **N** *pl.* **-nici** ally
sàviti [**sàvije**] **P** to fold
sávjest *f*, **G sávjesti** *ijek.* conscience
sávjestan–sávjesni *ijek. adj.* conscientious
sávjet *m ijek.* advice
sávjetovati [**sávjetuje**] *ijek.* **I** to advise
savládati [**sàvlada**] **P** to conquer, master
sàvremenik *m*; **N** *pl.* **-nici** (S.) contemporary
sàvršen *adj.* perfect
sávski *adj.* pert. to Sava River
sazídati [**sàzida**] **P** to build, erect
sàznati [**sàzna**] **P** to learn, find out
sàzreti [**sàzri**] **P** to ripen, mature
sàzvati [**sazòve**] **P** to summon, convene
sàžet *adj.* condensed, succinct
sèbičan–sèbični *adj.* selfish, egotistic
sèćanje *n ek.* remembrance
sèćati se [**sèća se**] *ek.* **I** to remember
séd *ek. adj.* gray, gray-haired
sèdam *num.* seven
sedamdèset *num.* seventy
sedamdèseti *adj.* seventieth
sedàmnaest *num.* seventeen
sedàmnaesti *adj.* seventeenth
sèdati [**sèda**] *ek.* **I** to sit
sèdeti [**sèdi**] *ek.* **I** to sit, be sitting
sèdlo *n* saddle
sédmi *adj.* seventh
sèdmica *f* week
sèdmično *adv.* weekly
sèdnica *f ek.* session, meeting
sèjati [**sèje**] *ek.* **I** to sow
sèkira *f ek.* axe, hatchet
sekrètar *m*, **G -tára** secretary
sèlo *n* village
sèljački *adj.* rural, farm (adj.) village (adj.)
sèljak *m*, **G seljáka**; **N** *pl.* **seljáci** farmer, peasant
sèljanin *m*; **N** *pl.* **sèljani** farmer, peasant
sèljanka *f* country woman
sème *n*, **G sèmena** *ek.* seed
sèmestar *m*, **G sèmestra** semester
sèminar *m* seminar
semìnarski *adj.* seminar (adj.)
semìnarski rád *m* term paper
sèna *f ek.* shadow
sèndvič *m* sandwich
séno *n ek.* hay
Sénta *f* city in NW Yugoslavia
seòba *f* migration
sèoski *adj.* village (adj.), rural
sepàrat *m*, **G -ráta** offprint, copy
sèptembar *m*, **G -tembra** September
sèptembarski *adj.* September (adj.)
sérum *m* serum
servijéta *f* napkin
sèsti [**sède** *ili* **sèdne**; **sèo**, **sèla**] *ek.* **P** to sit down
sèstra *f* sister, nurse
sètan–sètni *ek. adj.* melancholy, dejected
sètiti se [**sèti se**] *ek.* **P** to remember
sèver *m ek.* north
sèverni *ek. adj.* northern
sevèrniji *ek. adj.* more northerly
sevérnjača *f ek.* North Star
severoìstočno *ek. adv.* northeasterly
sezóna *f* season
Sèžana *f* Slovenian border city
shvàćanje *n* (Cr.) concept, opinion
shvàćati [**shvàća**] **I** (Cr.) to grasp, comprehend
shvàtanje *n* (S.) concept, opinion
shvàtati [**shvàta**] **I** (S.) to grasp, comprehend
síći [**síđe**; **sìšao**, **sìšla**] **P** to descend, dismount
sìguran–sìgurni *adj.* sure, sound, certain
sìgurno *adv.* surely, certainly
sigúrnost *f*, **G -nosti** certainty
sìjalica *f* (S.) light-bulb
sìjati [**sìje**] *ijek.* **I** to sow
sìjati [**sìja**] **I** to shine
sìječanj *m*, **G sìječnja** (Cr.) January
sìjed *ijek. adj.* gray, gray-haired
sìjeno *n ijek.* hay
sìla *f* might, strength
sìlan–sìlni *adj.* strong, powerful
sìlaziti [**sìlazi**] **I** to descend, dismount
sílno *adv.* violently
sìmbol *m* symbol
simbolizírati [**-lìzira**] **I/P** (Cr.) to symbolize
simbòlizovati [**-lizuje**] **I/P** (S.) to symbolize
simpàtičan–simpàtični *adj.* likable, engaging
simpàtija *f* liking, sympathy
sìmptom *m*, **G -tóma** symptom
simulàntis *m* pretended illness
sín *m*; **N** *pl.* **sìnovi** son
sìnak *m*, **G sínka** little son, sonny
sìnčić *m* little son, sonny
Singidúnum *m* ancient Celtic settlement at site of present-day Belgrade
sìnoć *adv.* last night, yesterday evening
sínuti [**síne**] **P** to shine, burst forth
sínji *adj.* grayish, gray-blue
sìpa *f* cuttle-fish, squid
sìpati [**sìpa**] **I** to pour down (rain)
sípiti [**sípi**] **I** to drizzle
sìr *m*; **N** *pl.* **sìrevi** cheese
siròmah *m*; **N** *pl.* **siròmasi** poor man
siròmašan–siròmašni *adj.* poor, needy
sìstem *m*, **G sistéma** system
sistéma *f* (S.) system
sistèmatski *adj.* systematic
sìt *adj.* satiated, fed
sìtan–sìtni *adj.* tiny, minute, trifling
sitnìca *f* trifle
situácija *f* situation
sìv *adj.* gray
sjáj *m* radiance, brightness
sjájan–sjájni *adj.* shining, splendid
sjàti [**sjá**] **I** to shine
sjèćanje *n ijek.* remembrance
sjèćati se [**sjèća se**] *ijek.* **I** to remember
sjedíniti [**sjèdini**] **P** to unite
Sjèdinjene Amèričke Dr̀žave (**SAD**) United States of America (USA)
sjèditi *ili* **sjèdjeti** [**sjèdi**] *ijek.* **I** to be sitting, sit
sjèdnica *f ijek.* session, meeting
sjèkira *f ijek.* axe, hatchet
sjème *n*, **G sjèmena** *ijek.* seed
sjèna *f ijek.* shadow
sjèsti [**sjède** *ili* **sjèdne**; **sjèo** *ili* **sìo**, **sjèla**] *ijek.* **P** to sit down
sjètan–sjètni *ijek. adj.* melancholy, dejected

tjème *n.* **G tjèmena** *ijek.* top of head
tjèrati [tjèra] *ijek.* **I** to drive, chase
tjèšiti [tjèši] *ijek.* **I** to comfort
tkàti [tká] I to weave
tkò *pron.* (Cr.) who
tlák *m*; **N** *pl.* **tlàkovi** (Cr.) pressure
tmúran-tmúrni *adj.* somber
tó *pron.* this, it, that
toàletni *adj.* toilet (adj.)
tòčak *m*, **G tòčka**; **N** *pl.* **tòčkovi** (S.) wheel
tók *m*, **G tòka**; **N** *pl.* **tòkovi** flow, development, course
tokom (prep. with G) during
tolìki *adj.* so high, so many, such
tolìko *adv.* so much, so many
Tòlstoj *m* Leo Tolstoy, famous Russian writer (1828–1910)
Tòmislav *m* Croatian king (913–928)
tònuti [tòne] I to sink, drown
tòp *m*; **N** *pl.* **tòpovi** gun, cannon, (sleep like a) log
tòpao–tòpli *adj.* warm
Tòpčiderov *adj.* pert. to Topčider park or hill in Belgrade
tòplo *adv.* warmly, warm
tóranj *m*, **G tórnja**; **N** *pl.* **tórnjevi** tower
tórba *f* bag, kit
tràćiti [tràći] I (S.) to waste
tràdicionalan-lni *adj.* traditional
trág *m*; **N** *pl.* **tràgovi** track, vestige
trájan–trájni *adj.* lasting, imperfective (aspect)
tràjanje *n* duration
tràjati [tràje] I to last, endure
trájno *adv.* continuously
tràmvaj *m* streetcar, trolley
tràtina *f* lawn, meadow
tràtiti [tràti] I (Cr.) to waste
tráva *f* grass
trávanj *m*, **G trávnja** (Cr.) April
trážin (= **trážim**) *dial.* I am seeking
trážiti [tráži] I to seek, ask for, require, look for
tr̀buh *m* belly
tr̀čanje *n* running, race
tr̀čati [tr̀či] I to run
trèbati [trèba] I to be necessary, require
trèći *adj.* third
trém *m ek.* porch
trenírati I to train
trenútak *m*, **G -nútka**; **N** *pl.* **-núci** second, moment
trènutan–trènutni momentary, perfective (aspect)
trèpavica *f* eyelash
trésti [trése; trésao, trésla] I to shake
trésti se I to shake oneself
trèšnja *f* cherry
trézan–trézni *ek. adj.* sober
tŕg *m*; **N** *pl.* **tŕgovi** square, marketplace
tr̀govac *m*, **G tr̀govca** merchant
tr̀govina *f* business, trade, shop
trí *num.* three
tribína *f* platform for speakers
trídeset *num.* thirty
trídeseti *adj.* thirtieth
trìjem *m*, **G trijèma** *ijek.* porch
trijèzan–trìjezni *ijek. adj.* sober
trínaest *num.* thirteen
trínaesti *adj.* thirteenth
trinaestogòdišnji *adj.* 13-year-old (adj.)
trìpice *f pl.* tripe
tròbojka *f*, **D tròbojci** tricolored flag
trogòdišnji *adj.* three-year-old (adj.)
tròje *num.* trio, threesome
tròjica *f* three, trio
tròkatnica *f* (Cr.) three-story building
tròlejbus *m* street-car
tròrog *adj.* three-cornered, three-horned
tròsobni *adj.* three-room (adj.)
tròspratnica *f* (S.) three-story building
tròšak *m*, **G tròška**; **N** *pl.* **tròškovi** expense, cost
tròšiti [tròši] I to spend money on, use
trotòar *m*, **G trotoára** (S.) sidewalk
tròzubac *m*, **G -pca** trident
tŕpeti [tŕpi] *ek.* **I** to suffer, tolerate
tr̀peza *f* table [now obsolete]
tŕpjeti [tŕpi] *ijek.* **I** to suffer, tolerate
tŕpni *adj.* passive (gram.)
tr̀ska *f*; **G** *pl.* **tr̀saka** reed
trúd *m*; **N** *pl.* **trúdovi** pains, effort, labor
trúdan–trúdni *adj.* pregnant, tired
trúditi se I to labor, take pains
trúp *m*; **N** *pl.* **trúpovi** trunk, body, corpse, hull
tr̀žište *n* marketplace
tŕžnica *f* marketplace
tú *adv.* here
tùce *n*, **G tùceta** dozen
tùča *f* hail
túći [túče; túkao, túkla] I to beat, thrash
túđ *adj.* strange, foreign, someone's
tuđìna *f* foreign land
tuđìnac *m*, **G tuđínca** alien, stranger
túga *f*, **D túzi** sorrow
tulìpan *m*, **G -pána** (Cr.) tulip
tùmač *m*, **G tumáča** interpreter
túr *m*; **N** *pl.* **tùrovi** bottom, buttocks
Tùrčin *m*; **N** *pl.* **Túrci**, **G** *pl.* **Tùraka** Turk
tùrist *m* tourist
tùrista *m* (S.) tourist
turìstički *adj.* tourist
tùristkinja *f* tourist (female)
turìzam *m*, **G turìzma** tourist trade
Tùrska *f adj. noun* Turkey
tùrski *adj.* Turkish
tùš *m*; **N** *pl.* **tùševi** shower
tušírati se [tùšira se] I to take a shower
túžan–túžni *adj.* sad, sorrowful
túžiti [túži] I to accuse, complain
túžiti se I to grieve, complain, report an illness
Tvèn, Màrk Mark Twain, American writer (1835–1910)
tvój *m*, **tvòje** *n*, **tvòja** *f* your
tvórnica *f* (Cr.) factory
tvŕd *adj.* hard, solid
tvr̀dica *m/f* miser
tvŕditi [tvŕdi] I to assert, declare, affirm, claim
tvŕdnja *f* assertion, claim
tvrdòglav *adj.* opinionated, obstinate
tvr̀đava *f* fortress
tvr̀đi *adj.* harder, more solid
tzv. *for* **takòzvani** *adj.* so-called

U u

u (prep. with G) belonging to, near
u (prep. with A/D) into, in, at
u rédu o.k., all right
u stvári actually
ubéditi [ùbedi] *ek.* **P** to convince
ùbeđen *ek. adj.* convinced
ubeđénje *n ek.* conviction
ubeđívati [ubèđuje] *ek.* **I** to persuade
ubíca *m* (S.) murderer
ubíjati [ùbija] I to kill
ubijèditi [ùbijedi] *ijek.* **P** to convince
ùbijeđen *ijek. adj.* convinced
ubìjen *adj.* killed
ùbiti [ùbije] P to kill
ubjeđénje *n ijek.* conviction
ubjeđívati [ubjèđuje] *ijek.* **I** to persuade
ublážiti [ùblaži] P to soothe, alleviate
ùblažen *adj.* alleviated
ùbojica *m* murderer (Cr.), experienced soldier (S.)
ùbrus *m* napkin (Cr.), towel (S.)
ùbrzo *adv.* quickly
ubùduće *adv.* in the future
ùčen *adj.* learned, educated
ùčenica *f* female student
ùčenik *m*; **N** *pl.* **ùčenici** male student, apprentice
učènjak *m*, **G-áka**; **N** *pl.***-áci** scholar
ùčenje *n* study, learning
ùčenost f, **G ùčenosti** learning
ùčesnik *m*; **N** *pl.* **ùčesnici** participant
ùčestao–ùčestali *adj.* frequent, iteritive
učèstati [učèsta] P to become more frequent
ùčestvovati [-stvuje] I (S.) to participate
učíniti [ùčini] P to make, do
ùčionica *f* classroom
ùčitelj *m* teacher
učitèljica *f* woman teacher
ùčiti [ùči] I to teach, study
ùčiti se I to learn
úći [úđe; ùšao, ùšla] P to enter
ùdaja *f* marriage (of a woman)
ùdaljen *adj.* distant, removed
ùdaljenost *f*, **G-nosti** distance
udaljívati [udàljuje] I to remove, send off
udaljívati se I to move off, move away
ùdar *m* stroke, blow
ùdarac *m*, **G ùdarca** blow, hit
ùdarati [ùdara] I to strike, beat, beat against, play
ùdariti [ùdari] P to strike, lay (foundation)
ùdata *f adj.* married (woman)
ùdati se P to get married (for woman)
udávati se [ùdaje se] I to get married (for woman)
ùdeo *m*, **G ùdela** *ek.* portion, share
ùdešen *adj.* arranged, adapted
ùdica *f* fish-hook
ùdio *ili* **ùdjel** *m*, **G ùdjela** *ijek.* portion, share
udíviti se P to be astonished
ùdoban–ùdobni *adj.* comfortable, convenient
udostòjiti se [udòstoji se] P to condescend
udòvac *m*, **G udóvca** widower
udòvica *f* widow
udružénje n association, society
udrúžiti se [ùdruži se] P to join, associate with
ùdrveniti se [ùdrveni se] P to become like wood
ùdžbenik *m*; **N** *pl.* **-nici** textbook
ùgalj *m*, **G ùglja** coal
ùgao *m*, **G ùgla**; **N** *pl.* **ùglovi** corner

ugásiti (se) [**ùgasi** (se)] **P** to go out, stop, extinguish
uglàvnom *adv.* mainly, in general, chiefly
ùgled *m* reputation
ùgledan–ùgledni *adj.* distinguished, respected
ùgledati [**ùgleda**] **P** to notice, catch sight of
ùgodan–ùgodni *adj.* pleasing, agreeable
ugovárati [**ugòvara**] **I** to negotiate, agree
ùgovor *m* agreement, treaty
ùgristi [**ugríze; ùgrizao, ùgrizla**] **P** to bite
ugròziti [**ùgrozi**] **P** to threaten, menace, peril
ugrožávati [**ugròžava**] **I** to threaten, menace, peril
ùgrožen *adj.* threatened, endangered
ùgušen *adj.* suffocated, smothered
ugúšiti [**ùguši**] **P** to suppress, smother
ùh *excl.* ugh!
ùho *n*; **N** *pl.* **ùši** *f* ear
ùhvatiti [**ùhvati**] **P** to catch
ùjak *m*; **V ùjače; N** *pl.* **ùjaci** maternal uncle
ùjed *m* bite, sting
ujedíniti se [**ujèdini se**] **P** to combine, unite
Ujèdinjeni národi *m pl.* United Nations
ujedinjénje *n* union, federation
ùjedno *adv.* simultaneously, together
ùjutro *adv.* in the morning
ùjutru *adv.* in the morning
ukázati [**ùkaže**] **P** to point at, show
ukázati se P to appear, turn up
ukazívati [**ukàzuje**] **I** to point at, show
uključíti se [**ùključi se**] **P** to become part of, join
uključujući *v. adj.* including
ukòliko *adv.* as far as
ùkor *m* reprimand, blame
ùkraden *adj.* stolen
Ùkrajina Ukraine
Ùkrajinac *m*, **G Ùkrajinca** male Ukrainian
ùkras *m* decoration, ornament
ùkrasti [**ukráde; ùkrao, ùkrala**] **P** to steal
ukr̀cati se [**ukr̀ca se**] **P** to load up, climb into
ukròtitelj *m* tamer, keeper
ùkupno *adv.* all together, *in toto*
ùkus *m* taste, sense of taste
ùkusan–ùkusni *adj.* tasty
ùkvaren *adj.* spoiled
ulágati [**ùlaže**] **I** to deposit, invest
ùlaz *m* entrance, entry
ùlaziti [**ùlazi**] **I** to enter, go in
ùlaznica *f* ticket, pass
ùlica *f* street
ùličan–ùlični *adj.* street (adj.)
ùloga *f*, **D ùlozi** role, part
ulòviti [**ùlovi**] **P** to catch
úlje *n* (Cr.) oil
úm *m*; **N** *pl.* **úmovi** mind, intelligence
ùmereno *ek. adv.* moderately
umesto *ek.* (prep. with G) instead of
ùmeti [**ùme**] *ek.* **I** to know (how to)
ùmetnički *ek. adj.* artistic
ùmetnik *m*; **N** *pl.* **ùmetnici** *ek.* artist
ùmiranje *n* dying
umíriti [**ùmiri**] **P** to quiet, pacify
ùmišljen *adj.* conceited, vain
ùmiti se [**ùmije se**] **P** to wash oneself
umívati se [**ùmiva se**] **I** to wash oneself
ùmjereno *ijek. adv.* moderately
umjesto *ijek.* (prep. with G) instead of
ùmjetan–ùmjetni *adj.* (Cr.) artificial
ùmjeti [**ùmije; ùmio, ùmjela**] *ijek.* **I** to know (how to)
ùmjetnički *adj. ijek.* artistic
ùmjetnik *m*; **N** *pl.* **ùmjetnici** *ijek.* artist
ùmor *m* weariness, fatigue
ùmoran–ùmorni *adj.* tired
ùmoren *adj.* tired, exhausted
umòvanje *n* reasoning, reflection
ùmreti [**ùmre; ùmro, ùmrla**] *ek.* **P** to die
ùmrijeti [**ùmre; ùmro, ùmrla**] *ijek.* **P** to die
ùnaokolo *adv.* around
unàpred *ek. adv.* in advance
unàpređen *ek. adj.* advanced
unàprijed *ijek. adv.* in advance
unàprijeđen *ijek. adj.* advanced
unátoč (prep. with D) in spite of
ùnija *f* union
ùništen *adj.* ruined, destroyed
ùništiti [**ùništi**] **P** to destroy, ruin
Ùniverzida *f* university games
univerzìtet *m*, **G-téta** (S.) university
univerzìtetski *adj.* (S.) university (adj.)
ùnuk *m*; **N** pl. **ùnuci** grandson
ùnuka *f*, **D ùnuci** granddaughter
unútra *adv.* inside
ùnutrašnjost *f*, **G -osti** interior, inner part
uobìčajen *adj.* accustomed, usual, customary
uoči (prep. with G) on the eve of
uòčiti [**ùoči**] **P** to notice, catch sight of
ùopće *adv.* (Cr.) in general
ùopšte *adv.* (S.) in general
uòstalom *adv.* for the rest, after all
upáliti [**ùpali**] **P** to ignite, start (motor)
upáliti se P to ignite, start (motor), be interested in
upísati [**ùpiše**] **P** to register, enroll
upisívati I [**upìsuje**] to enroll in, register
upisívati se [**upìsuje se**] **I** to enroll oneself
upítati [**ùpita**] **P** to ask, inquire
ùplašen *adj.* frightened
ùplašiti [**ùplaši**] **P** to frighten, alarm
ùplašiti se P to become frightened, be alarmed
ùpliv *m* influence
ùporaba *f* (Cr.) use, usage, application
ùporedo, *adv.* paralleled, along with
ùporno *adv.* stubbornly, persistently
ùpotreba *f* use, usage, application
upotrébiti [**upòtrebi**] *ek.* **P** to use, employ
upotrebljávati [**upotrèbljava**] **I** to use, employ
upotrijèbiti [**upòtrijebi**] *ijek.* **P** to use, employ
upòznati [**upòzna**] **P** to acquaint, learn
upòznati se P to become acquainted
upoznávanje *n* introduction
upozorávati [**-zòrava**] **I** to warn, caution
upozòriti [**upòzori**] **P** to warn, caution
ùprava *f* administration, government
ùpravljanje *n* management, directing
ùpravljati [**ùpravlja**] **I** to direct, manage
ùpravo *adv.* just, exactly, really
ùpreti [**ùpre; ùpro, ùprla**] *ek.* **P** to fix one's eyes, direct one's gaze
ùprijeti [**ùpre; ùpro, ùprla**] *ijek.* **P** to fix one's eyes, direct one's gaze
ùprkos (prep. with D) despite, in spite of
upućivač *m*, **G upućiváča** starter (on vehicle)
upućívati [**upùćuje**] **I** to instruct, direct, order, send
upućívati se I to set off, direct oneself
upútiti [**ùputi**] **P** to instruct, direct, refer, send
upútiti se P to set out for a place
ùputstvo *n* instructions, directions
uráditi [**ùradi**] **P** to do, perform, effect
ùred *m* (Cr.) office
ùredan–ùredni *adj.* ordered, arranged
uréditi [**ùredi**] **P** to put in order, arrange
ùrednik *m*; **N** *pl.* **ùrednici** editor
ùredništvo *n* editorial staff
ùređaj *m* apparatus, arrangement
uređívati [**urèđuje**] **I** to put in order, edit
urúčiti [**ùruči**] **P** to hand, present, deliver
ùsev *m ek.* crops
ùshićen *adj.* overjoyed
ushićénje *n* enthusiasm
usisàvač m, **G -váča** vacuum cleaner
ùsjev *m ijek.* crops
usklàdišten adj. stored
ùskoro *adv.* soon
Ùskrs *m* Easter
usled *ek.* (prep. with G) as a consequence of
uslijed *ijek.* (prep. with G) as a consequence of
úslov *m* (S.) condition
ùsluga *f*, **D ùsluzi** favor, service
usluživanje *n* service, servicing
ùsna *f* lip
uspavljívati I to lull to sleep
ùspeh *m*; **N** *pl.* **ùspesi** *ek.* success
ùspešno *ek. adv.* successfully
ùspeti [**ùspe**] *ek.* **P** to succeed
ùspjeh *m*; **N** *pl.* **ùspjesi** *ijek.* success
ùspješno *ijek. adv.* successfully
ùspjeti [**ùspije; ùspio, ùspjela**] *ijek.* **P** to succeed
ùspomena *f* remembrance, memory
ùsprkos (prep. with D) despite, in spite of
ùsput *adv.* along the way
usred (prep. with G) in the middle of
ústa *n pl.* mouth
ùstajanje *n* getting up
ùstajati [**ùstaje**] **I** to get up, arise
ùstanak *m*, **G -anka**; **N** *pl.* **-anci** rebellion, uprising
ùstanički *adj.* rebel (adj.)
ùstanova *f* rule, institution
ustanòviti [**ustànovi**] **P** to establish, to find out
ùstaša *m* an insurgent, rebel
ùstati [**ùstane**] **P** to arise, get up
ùstav *m* constitution
ùstrajan–ùstrajni *adj.* persevering
ùstrajati [**ùstraje**] **I** to persevere
ùstupak *m*, **G -upka**; **N** *pl.* **-upci** yielding, surrender
ustúpati [**ùstupa**] **I** to give up, cede
ustúpiti [**ùstupi**] **P** to give up, cede
ustvári *adv.* really, indeed, actually

úš *f*, G **ùši** (Cr.) louse
ùšće *n* mouth of river
ùši (*pl. of* **uho/uvo**) *f* ears
ùtakmica *f* competition, match
ùtecaj *m ek.* influence
utèći [**utèče** *ili* **ùtekne**; **ùtekao, ùtekla**] **P** to escape, run away
ùtešan–ùtešni *ek. adj.* comforting
ùtešiti [**ùteši**] *ek.* **P** to comfort, console
ùticaj *m* (S.) influence
ùticati [**ùtiče**] **I** to flow into, influence
ùtisak *m*, G **-iska**; N *pl.* **-isci** (S). impression
ùtjecaj *m ijek.* influence
ùtjecati [**ùtječe**] *ijek.* **I** to flow into, influence
ùtješiti [**ùtješi**] *ijek.* **P** to comfort, console
ùtok *m*; N *pl.* **ùtoci** mouth of river, intake
utòpiti se [**ùtopi se**] **P** to drown
ùtorak *m*, G **ùtorka** Tuesday
utŕnuti P to become numb
ùtroba *f* bowels
utvŕditi [**ùtvrdi**] **P** to confirm, establish
ùtvrđen *adj.* established
ùveče *adv.* (S.) in the evening
ùvečer *adv.* (Cr.) in the evening
ùvek *ek. adv.* always
ùvenuti [**ùvene**] **P** to fade, wither
ùveriti [**ùveri**] *ek.* **P** to convince
ùveriti se *ek.* **P** to convince oneself
uvèsti [**uvède**; **ùveo, ùvela**] **P** to lead into, introduce
ùvijek *ijek. adv.* always
ùvjeriti [**ùvjeri**] *ijek.* **P** to convince
ùvjeriti se *ijek.* **P** to convince oneself
ùvjet *m* (Cr.) condition
ùvo *n*, G **ùva** *ili* **ùveta**; N *pl.* **ùši** (S.) ear
úvod *m* introduction, preface
uvòditi [**ùvodi**] **I** to lead into, introduce
ùvodnik *m*; N *pl.* **-nici** editorial
úvoz *m* import
ùvozni *adj.* imported
ùvreda *f* insult
uvréditi [**ùvredi**] *ek.* **P** to insult
ùvređen *ek. adj.* offended, insulted
uvrijèditi [**ùvrijedi**] *ijek.* **P** to insult
ùvrijeđen *ijek. adj.* offended, insulted
uz *ili* **uza** (prep. with A) along, next to, near by, along with, in spite of
ùzak–ùski *adj.* narrow
ùzalud *adv.* in vain
ùzaludan–ùzaludni *adj.* futile, useless
uzastòpce *adv.* constantly
ùzbuđen *adj.* excited
uzbuđénje *n* excitement
ùzdići *ili* **ùzdignuti** [**ùzdigne**; **ùzdigao, ùzdigla**] **P** to lift, raise, glorify
ùzdignut *adj.* lifted, raised
ùzdisaj *m* sigh
ùzdisati [**ùzdiše**] **I** to sigh
ùzdizati [**ùzdiže**] **I** to lift, raise, glorify
ùzdrmati se [**ùzdrma se**] **P** to shake, totter
uzdržávanje *n* keeping, maintenance, support
uzdržávati se I to subsist
uzduž (prep. with G) along, all along
ùzet *adj.* taken, described, paralyzed, palsied
ùzeti [**ùzme**; **ùzeo, ùzela**]**P** to take, begin
uzgájati [**ùzgaja**] **I** to grow, rear
ùzgredan–ùzgredni *adj.* incidental
ùzimati [**ùzimlje** *ili* **ùzima**] **I** to take
uznèmiren *adj.* alarmed, restless
ùzor *m* model, ideal
ùzoran *adj.* plowed up
ùzoran–ùzorni *adj.* ideal, exemplary, model
ùzrečica *f* proverb, saying
ùzrok m; N *pl.* **ùzroci** reason, cause, motive
ùzrokovan *adj.* caused by
ùzrujan *adj.* excited, nervous
ùzvik *m*; N *pl.* **ùzvici** shout, cry
uzvíknuti [**ùzvikne**] **P** to exclaim, shout
ùzvrat *m* return, retaliation
ùžas *m* horror
ùžasan–ùžasni *adj.* horrible, terrible
úže *n*, G **úžeta** rope
ùžina *f* snack
užítak *m*, G **užítka** pleasure, delight
užívanje *n* pleasure
užívati [**ùživa**] **I** to enjoy

V v

vábiti [**vábi**] **I** to allure, attract, call
vàdičep *m* corkscrew
vàditi [**vàdi**]**I** to take out
vága *f* balance, scales
vágati [**váže**] **I** to weigh
vàjar *m*, G **vajára** (S.) sculptor
vajárstvo *n* (S.) sculpture
vál *m*; N *pl.* **válovi** (Cr.) wave
valúta *f* currency
váljak *m*, G **váljka**; N *pl.* **váljci** roller, rolling pin
vàljati [**vàlja**] **I** to be valid, proper, necessary
vàljda *adv.* perhaps, probably
van (prep. with G) outside of
vàn *ili* **vàni** *adv.* (Cr.) out, outside
vanpartíjac *m*, G **-tíjca** a Yugoslav not member of Communist party
vànjski *adj.* (Cr.) outside, exterior (adj.)
vanjština *f* (Cr.) exterior, appearance
vàrati [**vàra**] **I** to cheat
Vàrdar *m*, G **Vardára** river in Macedonia, brand of cigarette
varijànta *f* variant, separate speech, dialect
varírati I to vary
vàrivo *n* (coll.) cooked vegetables
város *f*, G **városi** city
vasiona *f* (S.) universe
vaspitač, *m*, G **-táča** (S.) teacher, educator
vaspítanje n (S.) education, upbringing
vaš *m*, **vàše** *n*, **vàša** *f* your
váš *f*, G **vàši** (S.) louse
vàška *f*, D **vàšci** (S.) louse
vaterpòlist *m* water-polo player
vàterpolo *m* water-polo
vàtra *f* fire
vàtren *adj.* fiery, ardent
vatrogásac *m*, G **-gásca** fireman
vàtromet *m* fireworks
váza *f* vase
vàzda *adv.* always
vàzduh *m* (S.) air
vážan–vážni *adj.* important
váziti [**váži**] **I** to be valid, be important
vàžniji *adj.* more important
vážno *adv.* important, importantly
vážnost *f*, G **-nosti** importance
vèče *n*, G **vèčera** (S,) evening
vèčer *f*, G **vèčeri** (Cr.) evening
vèčera *f* supper
večèras *adv.* this evening
vèčerati [**vèčera**] **I/P** to eat supper
vèčernji *adj.* evening (adj.)
Vèčernji líst *m* Evening News (Zagreb newspaper)
vèčit *ek. adj.* eternal
vèć *adv.* already, but
véće *n ek.* council
vèći *adj.* bigger, greater
većìna *f* majority
vèdar–vèdri *adj.* clear, placid
vék *n*; N *pl.* **vékovi** *ek.* century
vèkna *f* (S.) loaf
vèkovan–vèkovni *ek. adj.* centuries-old
Velèbit *m* mountain in Croatia
velesájam *m*, G **-sájma** fair, exposition
vèleti [**vèli**; **no past tense**] *ek.* **I** to say
veličànstven *adj.* majestic, splendid
veličina *f* magnitude, size
vèlik *adj.* large, great, big
velikaš *m*, G **velikáša** nobleman
velikodóstonjik *m*; N *pl.* **-nici** dignitary
vèljača *f* (Cr.) February
vèljeti [**vèli**; no past tense] *ijek.* **I** to say
vénac *m*, G **vénca** *ek* crown, wreath
venčánje *n ek.* wedding-ceremony
Vènecija *f* Venice
veòma *adv.* very
vèra *f ek.* faith, religion
véran–vérni *ek. adj.* true, faithful
vèridba *f ek.* engagement, betrothal
Vèrn, Žil Jules Verne
vèrovati [**vèruje**] *ek.* **I** to believe
verovàtnije *ek. adv.* more probably
vèrovatno *ek. adv.* probably
vesèliti [**vesèli**] **I** to gladden
vesèliti se I to rejoice
vesélje *n* gaiety, joy
vèseo–vèseli *adj.* merry, gay
vèslač *m*, G **vesláča** rower, oarsman
vèslo *n*; G *pl.* **vesála** oar
vèsnik *m ek.* messenger, herald
vést *f*, G **vésti** *ek.* news, report
vèšalica *f ek.* hanger
vèšt *ek. adj.* skilled
vèštački *adj. ek.* artificial
vèštica *f ek.* witch
veština *f ek.* skill
vètar *m*, G **vètra**; N *pl.* **vètri** *ili* **vètrovi** *ek.* wind
veterína *f* veterinary college
veterìnar *m*, G **-nára** veterinarian
vètriti [**vètri**] *ek.* **I** to air
vèza *f* connection
vézan *adj.* connected, tied
vézati [**véže**] **I** to fasten, tie
véža *f* doorway, vestibule
vèžba *f ek.* exercise
ví *pron.* you
víd *m*; N *pl.* **vídovi** sight, view, aspect, mind
vìdeti [**vìdi**] *ek.* **I/P** to see
vìdeti se *ek.* **I/P** to see (one another), be seen
vìdjeti [**vìdi**; **vìdio, vìdjela**] *ijek.* **I/P** to see
vìdjeti se *ijek.* **I/P** to see (one another), be seen
Vìdovdan *ili* **Vìdov dán** *m* St. Vitus's day, June 28
viđénje *n*, G **do viđénja** seeing, meeting, goodbye (G)
vìhor *m* gale, storm

vijèće *n ijek.* council
vìjek *m*; N *pl.* **vijèkovi** *ijek.* century
vijènac *m*, G **vijènca** *ijek.* crown, wreath
vijest *f*, G **vijesti** *ijek.* news, report
vijùgati [**vijùga**] **I** to wind, twist, meander
vìka *f*, D **vìci** shouts, cries
víkati [**víče**] **I** to shout, cry out
vìkend *m* weekend
vìkendica *f* summer cottage
Vìking *m* a Viking
víknuti [**víkne**] **P** to shout, cry out
vìla *f* fairy, sprite
vìlica *f* (Cr.) fork
vìljuška *f* (S.) fork
víno *n* wine
vìnograd *m* vineyard
violína *f* violin
víriti [**víri**] **I** to stick out, peer out
visìna *f* height
vìsiti [**vìsi**] **I** to hang, hang down
vìsok *adj.* tall, high
visokòškolski *adj.* upper-level school (adj.)
víšak *m*, G **víška**; N *pl.* **víšci** surplus
vìše *adv.* above, more, many
vìše ne no longer
vìše púta repeatedly, many times
vìšeput *adv.* repeatedly, many times
višèstruk *adj.* multiple, various, manifold
vìšnja *f* sour cherry
vìtak–vìtki *adj.* slim, thin
víza *f* visa
Vìzant *m* (S.) Byzantine Empire
Vizàntija *f* (S.) Byzantine Empire
vizàntijski *adj.* (S.) Byzantine
vizitírati [**vizìtira**] **I** to visit
vjèčit *ijek. adj.* eternal
vjèkovan–vjèkovni *ijek. adj.* centuries-old
vjenčánje **n.** *ijek.* wedding-ceremony
vjèra *f ijek.* faith, religion
vjéran–vjérni *ijek. adj.* true, faithful
vjèridba *f ijek.* engagement, betrothal
vjèrojatno *ijek. adv.* probably
vjèrovati [**vjèruje**] *ijek.* **I** to believe
vjerovàtnije *ijek. adv.* more probably
vjèrovatno *ijek. adv.* probably
vjèsnik *m ijek.* messenger, herald
Vjèsnik *m*, G **-níka**; N *pl.* **-níci** "Messenger" (Zagreb newspaper)
vjèšalica *f ijek.* hanger
vjèšt *ijek. adj.* skilled
vjèštački *adj. ijek.* artificial
vjèštica *f ijek.* witch
vještìna *f ijek.* skill
vjètar *m*, G **vjètra**; N *pl.* **vjètri** *ili* **vjètrovi** *ijek.* wind
vjètriti [**vjètri**] *ijek.* **I** to air
vjèžba *f ijek.* exercise
vláda *f* rule, government
vlàdar *m*, G **vladára** ruler
vládati [**vláda**] **I** to rule
vlàdika *m*, D **vlàdíci** bishop
vlák *m*; N *pl.* **vlàkovi** (Cr.) train
vlás *f*, G **vlási** hair
vlás *m*, G **vlása** hair
vlàsnik *m*; N *pl.* **vlàsnici** owner
vlást *f*, G **vlásti**, I **vlášću** power, authority
vlàstit *adj.* (Cr.) one's own, personal
vlàžan–vlàžni *adj.* wet, damp
vó *m*, G **vòla**; N *pl.* **vòlovi** (S.) ox
vòće *n* fruit
vòćka *f*; G *pl.* **vòćaka** fruit tree
vód *m*, G **vòda**; N *pl.* **vòdovi** procession, wire, conduit, squad
vòda *f* water
vòden *adj.* water (adj.)
vodènica *f* watermill, coffeemill (S.)
vòdič *m*, G **vodíča** guide, guidebook
vòditi [**vòdi**] **I** to lead, guide, carry on, conduct
vòđa *m* leader
vojèvati [**vòjuje**] **I** to fight, wage war
vójni *adj.* military, war (adj.)
vòjnički *adj.* military, soldier (adj.)
vòjnik *m*, G **-níka**; N *pl.* **-níci** soldier
vójska *f*, D **vójsci** army, troops
vòkalan–vòkalni *adj.* vocal
vól *m*, G **vòla**; N *pl.* **vòlovi** (Cr.) ox
vòlan *m*, G **volána** wheel (of car)
vòleti [**vòli**] *ek.* **I** to like, love
vòlja *f* will, choice
vòljan–vòljni *adj.* willing
vòljen *adj.* in love, beloved
vòljeti [**vòli**; **vòlio**, **vòljela**] *ijek.* **I** to like, love
vòsak *m*, G **vòska** wax
vóz *m*; N *pl.* **vòzovi** (S.) train
vòzač *m*, G **vozáča** driver, rider
vòzilo *n* vehicle
vòziti [**vòzi**] **I** to drive, ride
vòziti se **I** to ride
vòžnja *f* ride, drive, trip
vràćati [**vràća**] **I** to return (something)
vràćati se **I** to return, come back
vrág *m*; N *pl.* **vrázi** *ili*. **vràgovi** devil
vrát *m*; N *pl.* **vràtovi** neck
vráta *n pl.* door, gate, goal (in soccer)
vràtar *m*, goalkeeper, doorman
vrátiti [**vráti**] **P** to return (something)
vrátiti se **P** to return, come back
vȑč *m*; N *pl.* **vȑčevi** pitcher, jug
vrèća *f* sack, bag
vrédan–vrédni *ek. adj.* worthy, diligent
vrédeti [**vrédi**] *ek.* **I** to be worth, be valuable
vrédnost *f*, G **-nosti** worth, value
vréđati [**vréđa**] *ek.* **I** to offend, insult
vréme *n*, G **vrèmena** *ek.* time, weather, tense
vrèo–vrèli *adj.* boiling hot
vȑh *m*, G **vȑha**; N *pl.* **vȑhovi** top, height
vrhúnac *m*, G **vrhúnca** culmination, pinnacle
vȑhunski *adj.* top-notch, first-class
vrijèdan–vrijedni *ijek. adj.* worthy, diligent
vrijèditi [**vrijèdi**] *ijek.* **I** to be worth, be valuable
vrijèdnost *f*, G **-nosti** *ijek.* value, worth
vrijèđati [**vrijeđa**] *ijek.* **I** to offend, insult
vrijème *n*, G **vrèmena** *ijek.* time, weather, tense
vríme (=**vrijème**/**vréme**) *dial.* time, weather
vrlìna *f* virtue
vȑlo *adv.* very
vŕsta *f* kind, sort
vŕstan–vŕsni *adj.* accomplished, excellent
vȑstati [**vȑsta**] **I** to arrange, sort
vŕšen *adj.* carried out, accomplished
vŕšiti [**vŕši**] **I** to perform, act
vȑšnjak *m*, G **vršnjáka** a contemporary
vȑt *m*; N *pl.* **vȑtovi** garden
vȑteti se [**vȑti se**] *ek.* **I** to revolve, gyrate
vȑtjeti se [**vȑti se**] *ijek.* **I** to revolve, gyrate
vrtòglavica *f* dizziness
vrúć *adj.* hot, torrid
vrućìna *f* heat, hot weather
vúći [**vúče**; **vúkao**, **vúkla**] **I** **vúku** (3rd. pl. pres.) to drag, pull
vúći se **I** to drag in, be pulled
vúk *m*; N *pl.* **vúci** *ili* **vùkovi** wolf
Vúk (*see* **Karadžić**)
vùlkan *m*, G **vulkána** volcano
vùnen *adj.* woolen, wool (*adj.*)

Z z

za (prep. with G) during
za (prep. with A/I) behind, for, during
zabadàva *adv.* in vain, gratis
zábava *f* amusement
zábavan–zábavni *adj.* amusing, funny
zàbavljati se [**zàbavlja se**] **I** to amuse oneself
zabòleti [**zabòli**] *ek.* **P** to begin aching, ache
zabòljeti [**zabòli**] *ijek.* **P** to begin aching, ache
zabòraviti [**zabòravi**] **P** to forget
zaborávljati [**zabòravlja**] **I** to keep forgetting, forget
zàbrana *f* prohibition, ban
zabrániti [**zàbrani**] **P** to forbid
zàbrinut *adj.* uneasy, troubled
zacélo *ek. adv.* indeed, certainly
zacijèlo *ijek. adv.* indeed, certainly
zacvètati [**zacvèta**] *ek.* **P** to bloom, begin to blossom
zacvjètati [**zacvjèta**] *ijek.* **P** to bloom, begin to blossom
zàčas *adv.* for a moment
začéće *n* conception
zàčuditi se [**zàčudi se**] **P** to be amazed, wonder
zàčuđen *adj.* amazed, astonished, surprised
zàdaća *f* task, assignment, exercise
Zàdar *m*, G **Zàdra** city on Adriatic, formerly Zara
zadátak *m*, G **-átka**; N *pl.* **-áci** task, assignment
zàdati [**zàda**] **P** to give, assign
zadávati [**zàdaje**] **I** to give, present
zàdimljen *adj.* smoke-filled
zadirkívati [**zadìrkuje**] **I** to tease
zádno *n* bottom
zàdnji *adj.* last
zadòcniti [**zàdocni**] **P** (S.) to delay, be late
zadocnjávati [**zadòcnjava**] **I** (S.) to delay, be late
zàdovoljan–zàdovoljni *adj.* satisfied
zàdovoljno *adv.* contentedly
zadovóljstvo *n* pleasure, happiness
Zàdranin *m*; N *pl.* **Zàdrani** inhabitant of Zadar
zadȑžati [**zadȑži**] **P** to keep back, retain
zadȑžati se **P** to be delayed, linger
zadúhati se [**zàduha se**] **P** (Cr.) to start blowing, breathe hard
zadúvati se [**zàduva se**] **P** (S.) to start blowing, breathe hard
zàdužbina *f* endowment, bequest

zàgaziti [**zàgazi**] **P** to tread down, wade out
zàgledati [**zàgleda**] **P** to catch sight of
zaglédati [**zàgleda**] **I** to gaze at
zaglédati se I to look into
zàgledati se P to take a look
zágorski *adj.* behind mountains
Zágreb *m* capital of Croatia
zágrebački *adj.* Zagreb (adj.)
zàgrejan *ek. adj.* warmed up
zàgrejati se [**zàgreje se**] *ek.* **P** to warm up
Zágrepčanin *m*; **N** *pl.* **-čani** inhabitant of Zagreb
Zágrepčanka *f* female inhabitant of Zagreb
zàgrijan *ijek. adj.* warmed up
zàgrijati se [**zàgrije se**] *ijek.* **P** to warm up
zàgristi [**zagríze; zàgrizao, zàgrizla**] **P** to bite in
zàgrliti [**zàgrli**] **P** to embrace
zahtévati [**zàhteva**] *ek.* **I** to demand
zahtijèvati [**zàhtijeva**] *ijek.* **I** to demand
zahváliti [**zàhvali**] **P** to thank
zahvaljívati [**zahvàljuje**] **I** to thank
zàhvatiti [**zàhvati**] **P** to grip, grasp
zaìgrati P to begin to play, begin to dance
zainterèsiran *adj.* (Cr.) interested in
zainteresírati se [**-rèsira se**] **P** (Cr.) to become interested in
zàinteresovan *adj.* (S.) interested in
zàinteresovati se [**-resuje se**] **P** (S.) to become interested in
zàista *adv.* indeed, of course
zájam *m*, **G zájma**; **N** *pl.* **zájmovi** loan
Zàjc, Ìvan *m* Croatian composer and musician (1832–1914)
zàjednica *f* union, community, cooperative
zàjedničar *m* member of cooperative or union
Zàjedničar *m* Croatian newspaper in Pittsburgh
zàjednički *adj.* common, joint, mutual
zàjedno *adv.* together, jointly
zàjutrak *m*, **G -tarka**; **N** *pl.* **-tarci** (Cr.) breakfast
zàkasniti [**zàkasni**] **P** (Cr.) to delay, be late
zakašnjávati [**zakàšnjava**] **I** (Cr.) to delay, be late
zaklòniti [**zàkloni**] **P** to protect, shelter, screen
zàključak *m*, **G zàključka** conclusion
zàkon *m* law
zàkržljao–zàkržljali *adj.* stunted
zàkucati [**zàkuca**] **P** to knock, begin to knock
zalágati se [**zàlaže se**] **I** to intervene, intercede for
zálaz *m* setting (of sun)
zàlaziti [**zàlazi**] **I** to visit often, set (of sun)
zàlet *m* run, sprint
záliha *f* supply, resource, provisions
zàliti [**zàlije**] **P** to fill up, pour in
zàljubljen *adj.* in love, enamored
zamàgliti se [**zàmagli se**] **P** to be misty, feel dizzy
zàmena *f ek.* exchange, substitution
zàmenica *f ek.* pronoun
zaméniti [**zàmeni**] *ek.* **P** to replace, exchange
zamerávati [**zamèrava**] *ek.* **I** to resent, bear a grudge
zàmeriti [**zàmeri**] *ek.* **P** to resent, bear a grudge
zàmeriti se *ek.* **P** to be in disgrace, in trouble
zamijèniti [**zàmijeni**] *ijek.* **P** to replace, exchange
zàmisao *f*, **G zàmisli** conception, idea
zàmisliti [**zàmisli**] **P** to imagine, conceive
zamíšljati [**zàmišlja**] **I** to imagine, conceive
zàmišljen *adj.* absorbed, thoughtful, designed
zàmjena *f ijek.* exchange, substitution
zàmjenica *f ijek.* pronoun
zamjerávati [**zamjèrava**] *ijek.* **I** to resent, bear a grudge
zàmjeriti [**zàmjeri**] *ijek.* **P** to resent, bear a grudge
zàmjeriti se *ijek.* **P** to be in disgrace, in trouble
zamòliti [**zàmoli**] **P** to request, ask
zámor *m* fatigue
zámoran–zámorni *adj.* tiring, fatiguing
zamuckívati [**zamùckuje**] **I** to stutter
zànat *m*, **G zanáta** trade, craft, shop
zanàtlija *m* tradesman, artisan, mechanic
zanátstvo *n* handicraft, skill
zanímanje *n* occupation, profession
zanímati se [**zànima se**] **I** to be engaged in, do, be attracted to
zanìmljiv *adj.* interesting
zanimljìviji *adj.* more interesting
zános *m* enthusiasm
zào–zlì *adj.* bad, evil, wicked
zaòstajati [**zaòstaje**] **I** to fall behind, lag, be backward
zaòstao–zaòstali *adj.* backward, retarded, reactionary
západ *m* West
západni *adj.* western
zapadnoèvropski *adj.* Western European
zapáliti [**zàpali**] **P** to light, set on fire, ignite
zàpamtiti [**zàpamti**] **P** to remember
zapànjujući *v. adj.* remarkable, astounding
zàpaziti [**zàpazi**] **P** to observe, catch sight of
zàpažen *adj.* noted, observed
zapìsati [**zàpiše**] **P** to copy down
zapisívati [**zapìsuje**] **I** to copy down
zápisnik *m*; **N** *pl.* **-nici** record, minutes, protocol
zapítati [**zàpita**] **P** to question, inquire
zàplakati [**zàplače**] **P** to start crying
zapòčeti [**zàpočne**] **P** to begin
zàposlen *adj.* employed
zàposlenost *f*, **G -nosti** employment
zapòsliti se [**zàposli se**] **P** to be hired
zàpoved *f*, **G -vedi** *ek.* command, injunction
zàpovijed *f*, **G -vijedi** *ijek.* command, injunction
zaprášiti [**zàpraši**] **P** to make dusty, powder
zaprášiti se P to get dusty, be sprinkled
zàpravo *adv.* really
zápreka *f*, **D zápreci** obstacle, hurdle
zaprèpašten *adj.* frightened, appalled
zapùstiti [**zàpusti**] **P** to neglect, forsake
zár *adv.* really?
zár ne *adv.* isn't that so?
zàrada *f* profit
zaráditi [**zàradi**] **P** to earn, gain
zarađívati [**zaràđuje**] **I** to earn, gain
zàrazan–zàrazni *adj.* infectious
zàručen *adj.* engaged
zàručnica *f* fiancée (woman)
zàručnik *m*; **N** *pl.* **-nici** fiancé (man)
záruke *f pl.* engagement
záseban–zásebni *adj.* separate, one's own
zàseda *f ek.* ambush
zàsipati [**zàsipa**] **I** to pour, pour over
zàsjeda *f ijek.* ambush
zásluga *f*, **D zásluzi** merit, credit
zaslúžiti [**zàsluži**] **P** to earn, deserve
zaslužívati [**zaslùžuje**] **I** to earn, deserve
zàspati [**zàspi**] **P** to fall asleep
zàstati [**zàstane**] **P** to halt
zàstati se P to stop
zástava *f* flag, standard
zàstavica *f* small banner, small flag
zàstrašiti [**zàstraši**] **P** to frighten, scare
zastúpati [**zàstupa**] **I** to represent
zàstupnik *m*; **N** *pl.* **-nici** representative
zàštita *f* protection
zàšto *adv.* why, for what reason
zatèći [**zatèče** *ili* **zàtekne; zàtekao, zàtekla**] **P** to come upon, surprise
zàtiljak *m*, **G -tiljka** (Cr.) back of neck
zàtim *adv.* then, thereafter
zàto *conj.* therefore, for this reason
zatvárati [**zàtvara**] **I** to close
zatvárati se I to be closed
zàtvoren *adj.* closed, exclusive
zatvòriti [**zàtvori**] **P** to close
zatvòriti se P to be closed
zaùstaviti [**zaùstavi**] **P** to stop, halt
zaùstavljanje *n* stopping, damming up
zaùstavljati [**zaùstavlja**] **I** to stop, halt
zàuvek *ek. adv.* for good, forever
zàuvijek *ijek. adv.* for good, forever
zàuzet *adj.* occupied, taken
zaùzeti [**zàuzme**] **P** to capture, take
zaùzimati [**zaùzima**] **I** to capture, take
zavèden *adj.* introduced, seduced, registered
závesa *f ek.* curtain
zàvesti [**zavède; zàveo, zàvela**] **P** to seduce, misdirect, register
závet *m ek.* vow, testament
zàvičaj *m* homeland
závideti [**závidi**] *ek.* **I** to envy
závidjeti [**závidi**] *ijek.* **I** to envy
zavíkati [**zàviče**] **P** to shout, cry out
závisiti [**závisi**] **I** to depend on
závjesa *f ijek.* curtain
závjet *m ijek.* vow, testament
závod *m* establishment, shop, department
závoj *m* bend, curve
zavòleti [**zàvoli**] *ek.* **P** to fall in love
zavòljeti [**zàvoli**] *ijek.* **P** to fall in love
završávati [**zavřšava**] **I** to finish
završétak *m*, **G -šétka**; **N** *pl.* **-šéci** end, finish
zavŕšiti [**zàvrši**] **P** to end, terminate
zavŕšiti se P to end, be ended
zazvòniti [**zàzvoni**] **P** to ring a bell
zažèleti [**zažèli**] *ek.* **P** to wish
zažèljeti [**zažèli**] *ijek.* **P** to wish

zbìlja *adv.* really, in fact
zbírka *f*, **D zbírci** collection
zbližávati se I to draw closer, come together
zbog (prep. with G) because of
zbògom *excl.* goodbye
zbór *m*, **G zbòra; N** *pl.* **zbòrovi** assembly, choir (Cr.)
zbȑka *f*, **D zbȑci** confusion, disorder
zbúniti se [zbúni se] P to become confused
zbúnjen *adj.* disconcerted, confused
zbunjívati [zbùnjuje] I to confuse
zdèla *f ek.* bowl, dish
zdjèla *f ijek.* bowl, dish
zdràv *adj.* healthy
zdràv ràzum *m* common sense
zdràvica *f* toast (to one's health)
zdrávlje *n* health
zdràvo *adv.* healthy
zdràvo *excl.* hello, goodbye, greetings
zdràvstvo *n* health, hygiene
zébnja *f* anxiety, fear
zéc *m*; **N** *pl.* **zèčevi** hare, rabbit
zéjtin *m* (S.) oil
zèlen *adj.* green
zèlenje *n* (coll.) vegetables, greens
zemàljski *adj.* earth (adj.), country (adj.)
zèmlja *f*; **G** *pl.* **zemálja** earth, land
Zèmlja *f* Earth
zèmljak *m*, **G -áka; N** *pl.* **-áci** fellow countryman
zamljàkinja *f* fellow countrywoman
zèmljica *f* earth
zèmljin *adj.* earth's
zèmljina kúgla *f* terrestrial sphere, globe
zèmljopis *m* geography
zemljòradnik *m*; **N** *pl.* **-nici** farmer
zèt *m*; **N** *pl.* **zètovi** son-in-law
zévati [zéva] *ek.* **I** to yawn
zévnuti [zévne] *ek.* **P** to yawn
zglòb *m*; **N** *pl.* **zglòbovi** joint, wrist
zgòda *f* opportunity
zgòdan–zgòdni *adj.* attractive
zgràbiti [zgràbi] P to seize, hold
zgràda *f* building, structure
zgránuti se [zgráne se] P to be shocked
zíd *m*; **N** *pl.* **zìdovi** wall
zìdar *m*, **G zidára** bricklayer, mason
zídati [zída] I to build
zìdina *f* thick wall
zijèvati [zìjeva] *ijek.* **I** to yawn
zijèvnuti [zìjevne] *ijek.* **P** to yawn
zíma *f* winter
zími *adv.* in the winter
zímski *adj.* winter (adj.)
zlátan–zlátni *adj.* golden
zláto *n* gold
zlò *n*; **G** *pl.* **zála** evil
zmáj *m*; **N** *pl.* **zmàjevi** dragon
zmìja *f* snake
zmìjin *adj.* snake's
zmíjski *adj.* snake (adj.)
znàčaj *m* meaning, character
znàčajan–znàčajni *adj.* distinctive, significant
znàčajka *f*, **D -čajci** characteristic, trait, badge
značàjniji *adj.* more significant
znàčajno *adv.* significantly
znáčiti [znáči] I to mean, signify
znák *m*; **N** *pl.* **znáci** *ili* **znàkovi** sign, mark
znàmenit *adj.* famous
znànac *m*, **G znánca** acquaintance
znànost *f*, **G znànosti** (Cr.) science, learning
znànstven *adj.* scientific, learned
znánje *n* knowledge, data
znàtan-znàtni *adj.* appreciable, considerable
znàti [zná *ili* **znáde] I** to know (something)
znàti se I to be known
znàtiželjan–znàtiželjni *adj.* (Cr.) inquisitive
znàtno *adv.* considerably
znój *m*, **G znòja** sweat, perspiration
znòjan–znójni *adj.* sweaty
znòjiti se [znòji se] I to sweat, perspire
zoòloški vȑt *m* zoo
zòra *f* dawn, daybreak
zóv *m*, **G zòva; N** *pl.* **zòvovi** call
zráčiti [zráči] I to air
zrák *m*; **N** *pl.* **zráci** *ili* **zràkovi** air (Cr.), beam, ray
zȑcalo *n* (Cr.) mirror
zrèlost *f*, **G zrèlosti** ripeness, maturity
Zrínjevac *m*, **G Zrínjevca** street in Zagreb
Zrinjski *adj. noun* famous family in Cr. history
zȑno *n* grain
zúb *m* tooth
zùbar *m*, **G zubára** dentist
zújati [zúji] I to hum, buzz, ring
zùmbul *m* hyacinth
zúriti [zúri] I to stare
zvàničan–zvànični *adj.* official
zvánje *n* profession, calling
zvàtelni *adj.* vocative (case)
zvàti [zòve] I to call, name
zvàti se I to be named, called
zvér *m*, **G zvéra; N** *pl.* **zvèrovi** *ek.* wild beast
zvér *f*, **G zvéri; N** *pl.* **zvéri** *ek.* wild beast
zvézda *f ek.* star
zvijer *m*, **G zvìjera; N** *pl.* **zvjèrovi** *ijek.* wild beast
zvìjer *f*, **G zvìjeri; N** *pl.* **zvìjeri** *ijek.* wild beast
zvijèzda *f ijek.* star
zvíznuti [zvízne] P to whistle
zvížđanje *n* whistling
zvížđati I [zvížđi] to whistle, hiss, boo
zvìžduk *m*; **N** *pl.* **zvìžduci** whistle
zvònar *m*, **G zvonára** bell-ringer
zvònara *f* bell-tower
zvónce *n*, **G zvónceta** *ili* **zvónca** small bell, class bell
zvònik *m*; **G -níka; N** *pl.* **-níci** belfrey
zvòniti [zvòni] I to ring
zvòno *n* bell
zvúk *m*; **N** *pl.* **zvùkovi** sound

Ž ž

žàba *f* frog
žàbar *m* "frog-catcher" (pejorative term for inland Yugoslavs)
žàlba *f* complaint
žálo *n* beach
žàlost *f*, **G žàlosti** sorrow, grief
žàlostan–žàlosni *adj.* sad
žào *adv.* sorry
žào mi je I'm sorry
žár *m*; **N** *pl.* **žárovi** live coals
žàrulja *f* (Cr.) electric bulb
ždrélo *n ek.* abyss, gorge, pharynx
ždrijèlo *n* abyss, gorge, pharynx
žédan–žédni *adj.* thirsty
žéđ *f*, **G žéđi** thirst
žéđa *f* thirst
žèleti [žèli] *ek.* **I** to wish, desire
žèlezan–žèlezni *ek. adj.* iron (adj.)
žèleznica *f ek.* railroad
žèlezničar *m ek.* railroad worker
žèleznički *ek. adj.* railroad (adj.)
žèludac *m*, **G žèluca** stomach
žèlja *f* wish, desire
žèljeti [žèli; žèlio, žèljela] *ijek.* **I** to wish, desire
žèljezan–žèljezni *ijek. adj.* iron (adj.)
žèljeznica *f ijek.* railroad
žèljezničar *m ijek.* railroad worker, name of soccer team
željeznički *ijek. adj.* railroad (adj.)
žèljezo *n* iron
žèljno *adv.* eagerly, anxiously
žèna *f*, **V žèno** woman, wife
žènidba *f* marriage, wedding
žèniti se [žèni se] I to get married (of man)
žénka *f* female
žènski *adj.* woman's, female (adj.)
žèstoko *adv.* violently, savagely
žètva *f* harvest
žgánci *m pl.*, **G** *pl.* **žgánaca** (Cr.) hominy, corn mush
žìca *f* wire, string (musical)
Žìdov *m* (Cr.) Jew
žìg *m*; **N** *pl.* **žìgovi** mark, stamp, seal
žìgati [žìga] I to pain, twinge
žìgica *f* (Cr.) match
Žìl Vèrn Jules Verne
žìla *f* vein, artery
žìlet *m* razor blade
žìto *n* cereals, grain
žív *adj.* living, alive
žívac *m*, **G žívca** nerve
žíveo *ek. excl.* long live!, hail!
žíveti [žívi] *ek.* **I** to live
žívežne námirnice *fl pl.* food supply, provisions
žívio *ijek. excl.* long live!, hail!
žívjeti [žívi; žívio, žívjela] *ijek.* **I** to live
Žívkov *adj.* Živko's
žìvnuti [žìvne] P to become lively
žìvot *m*, **G živòta** life
živòtinja *f* animal
žlìca *f* (Cr.) spoon
žmìrkati [žmìrka] I to blink
žmúriti [žmúri] I to squint, half-close one's eyes
žȑtva *f* sacrifice
žúč *f*, **G žùči** gall, bitterness
žùčan–žùčni *adj.* bitter, virulent
žúdeti [žúdi] *ek.* **I** to yearn for, long for
žúdjeti [žúdi] *ijek.* **I** to yearn for, long for
žúlj *m*; **N** *pl.* **žúljevi** blister, callous, corns (on feet)
žùpan *m*, **G župána** district-head, local leader
žùrba *f* haste
žúriti se [žúri se] I to hurry
žùrnal *m*, **G žurnála** newsreel
žút *adj.* yellow

For additional CR&S-to-English entries

SECTION 2. EXPLANATION OF ENGLISH-TO-CR&S ENTRIES

This section of the glossary contains a large selection of frequently used English words and their Cr&S equivalents. In this section the ijekavian and ekavian forms are not identified as such but are indicated by a slash mark, the ijekavian form appearing first, the ekavian second, e.g. **milk** mlijèko/mléko *n*; **advice** sávjet/sávet *m*; **like, to** vòljeti/vòleti [vòli] **I.** Where an English noun is rendered by a Cr&S phrase, the gender indicated will be that of the head noun in the phrase, e.g. **applicant** podnòsilac mòlbe *m*; here the *m* would refer to *podnòsilac*. Both verbal aspects, where relevant, are given after the appropriate verbs, e.g. **prove, to** dokazívati [dokàzuje] **I** : dokázati [dòkaže] **P.** Parts of speech are identified in this section only where there might be ambiguity; thus, one entry *gold* would be identified as *adj.* to distinguish it from the noun *gold,* while *golden,* an obvious adjective, would not need to be identified. It is to be understood that the Cr&S equivalent of the English entry is the same part of speech unless otherwise specified.

bunch svèžanj *m*, G svèžnja
bunch (of people) drùžina *f*
bundle svèžanj *m*, G svèžnja
burden brème *n*, G brèmena; tèret *m*
bureaucrat biròkrat *m*, biròkrata *m* (S.)
burial pogreb *m*
buried sàhranjen
burn, to páliti I : zapáliti P
bury, to sahranjívati [-hrànjuje] I : sahrániti P
bus àutobus *m*
bush gȓm *m*
business pòsao *m*, G pòsla; bìznis *m*
bust (breasts) grúdi *f pl.*
busy zàposlen
but a, àli, màda
butcher mèsar *m*, kàsapin *m* (S.)
butter màslac *m* (Cr.), pùter *m* (S.)
butterfly lèptir *m*
buttocks stràžnjica *f*, zàdnjica *f*
button dùgme *n*, G dùgmeta
buy, to kupòvati [kùpuje] I : kúpiti P
buyer kúpac *m*, G kúpca
buzz zújanje *n*
buzz, to zújati [zúji] I : zazúiati P
by *prep.* pokraj (+G), pòmoću (+G)
by no means nìkako
bye-bye do viđénja

C c

cab tàksi *m*, G tàksija
cabbage kùpus *m*
cabin kòliba *f*, kabína *f*
cabinet òrmar *m* (Cr.), òrman *m* (S.)
cable kábel *m*
cafe kavàna *f* (Cr.), kafàna *f* (S.)
cake kòlač *m*
calendar kalèndar *m*
calf tèle *n*, G tèleta
call póziv *m*
call, to zvàti [zòve] I : nàzvati [nazòve] P
call the roll, to prozívati I : pròzvati [prozòve] P
calm mír *m*, tišìna *f*
calm *adj.* tìh
calmly mírno, tìho
calorie kàlorija *f*
camel dèva *f* (Cr.), kàmila *f* (S.)
camera fòto-apàrat *m*, fotògrafski apàrat *m*
camp lógor *m*
camp, to lógorovati [-ruje] I
campaign kampànja *f*
camping lógorovanje *n*, kàmping *m*
campus kàmpus *m*
can kònzerva *f*, lìmenka *f*
can (be able) mòći [mòže; mògao mògla] I
can opener otvàrač za kònzerve *m*
Canada Kanàda *f*
Canadian Kanáđanin *m*, Kanáđanka *f*
Canadian *adj.* kànadski
canal kànal *m*
canary kanarínac *m*, G -rínca
cancer ràk *m*
candidate kandìdat *m*
candle svìjeća/svéća *f*
candy slàtkiš *m*, bòmbon *m* (Cr.), bombóna *f* (S.)
cannon tòp *m*
canoe làk čámac *m*, sandolína *f*
canvas plátno *n*
cap kàpa *f*
capable spòsoban-spòsobni
capacity sposóbnost *f*, kapacìtet *m*
capital (city) glàvni grád *m*
capital (letter) vèliko slòvo *n*
capitalism kapitalìzam *m*, G -ìzma
capitalist kapitàlist *m*, kapitàlista *m* (S.)
captain kapètan *m*
captive zarobljènik *m*
captivity zarobljeníštvo *n*
capture, to zarobljávati I : zaròbiti P
car àuto *m*, kòla *n pl.*
card kárta *f*
cardboard ljèpenka/lèpenka *f*, kàrton *m*
care brìga *f*
care, to (worry) brìnuti se [brìne se] I
care for, to máriti I
career karijéra *f*
careful pàžljiv
careless nepàžljiv
caress mìlovanje *n*
caress, to mìlovati [mìluje] I : pòmilovati P
cargo bròdski tèret *m*
carnation karànfil *m*
carp (fish) šàran *m*
carpenter tèsar *m*, tèsač *m*
carpet tàpet *m* (Cr.), tèpih *m* (S.)
carriage vàgon *m*, kòla *n pl.*
carrier nòsač *m*
carrot mȑkva *f* (Cr.), šargarépa *f* (S.)
carry, to nòsiti I : dònijeti/dòneti [donèse] P
carve, to rèzati [rèže] I : ìzrezati P
case slùčaj *m*
case (gram.) pàdež *m*
cash gotovìna *f*, nòvac *m*
cashier blàgajnik *m*, blàgajnica *f*
cast, to bàcati I : báciti P
castle zámak *m*, G zámka
casual svakòdnevni
cat màčka *f*
catalogue katàlog *m*
catch, to hvàtati I : ùhvatiti P
catfish sòm *m*
cathedral katedrála *f*, stólna cȑkva *f*
Catholic kàtolik *m*, kàtolikinja *f*
Catholic *adj.* kàtolički
cattle stòka *f*
caught ùhvaćen
cauliflower cvjètača *f* (Cr.), karfìol *m* (S.)
cause ùzrok *m*
caused ùzrokovan
caution obàzrivost *f*, opréznost *f*
cautious pàžljiv, òprezan-òprezni
cave pèćina *f*, jàma *f*, špìlja *f* (Cr.)
cease, to prèstajati [prèstaje] I : prèstati [prèstane] P
ceiling stròp *m* (Cr.), tavànica *f* (S.)
celebrate, to slàviti I : pròslaviti P
celebration pròslava *f*
celery cèler *m*
cell (biol.) ćèlija *f*
cell (prison) tàmnica *f*
cellar pòdrum *m*
cement cèment *m*
cemetery gróblje *n*
censure krìtika *f*
censure, to osuđívati [osùđuje] I : osúditi P
census pòpis *m*
cent cènt *m*
center sredìna *f*; cèntar *m*, G cèntra
centimeter cèntimetar *m* (Cr.), G -metra; sàntimetar *m* (S.), G -metra
central glàvni, cèntralan-cèntralni
century stòljeće/stòleće *n*, vìjek/vék *m*
ceramic keràmički, lònčarski
ceramics keràmika *f*
ceremony òbred *m*, svèčanost *f*
certain (sure) sìguran-sìgurni
certain, a nèkakav-nèkakvi, òdređen, stanòvit (Cr.)
certainly svàkako, sìgurno
certificate pòtvrda *f*
chain lánac *m*, G lánca
chair stòlica *f*
chairman prèdsjednik/prèdsednik *m*
chalk kréda *f*
champion pȑvak *m*, šampìon *m*
chance prílika *f*, rìzik *m*
change pròmjena/pròmena *f*
change (money) sìtan nòvac *m*
change, to mijènjati/ménjati (se) I : promijèniti/proméniti (se) P
changeable promjènljiv/promènljiv
channel kànal *m*
chaos zbȑka *f*, kàos *m* (Cr.), hàos *m* (S.)
chap mòmak *m*, G mòmka
chapter gláva *f*, pòglavlje *n*
character karàkter *m*
characteristic znàčajka *f*, karakterìstika *f*
charity milòsrđe *n*, dobrotvórnost *f*
charm čár *m*/*f*, šàrm *m*
charming dràžestan-dràžesni
chart kárta *f*
charter ìsprava *f*, pòvelja *f*
chase gònjenje *n*, lóv *m*
chase, to gòniti I
chat bȑbljanje *n*, ràzgovor *m*
chatter bȑbljanje *n*
chatter, to bȑbljati I
chatty bȑbljiv
chauffeur šòfer *m*
cheap jèftin
cheat, to vàrati I : prèvariti P
check čèk *m*
checkbook čèkovna knjìžica *f*
cheek òbraz *m*
cheer, to bòdriti I : obòdriti P
cheerful vèseo-vèseli, ràdostan-ràdosni
cheese sìr *m*
chemical *adj.* kèmijski (Cr.), hèmijski (S.)
chemist kèmičar *m* (Cr.), hèmičar *m* (S.)
chemistry kèmija *f* (Cr.), hèmija *f* (S.)
cherry trèšnja *f*
cherry (sour) vìšnja *f*
chess šàh *m*
chest (body) pȑsni kòš *m*, grúdi *f pl.*
chest (furniture) škrìnja *f*, sànduk *m*
Chetnik čètnik *m*
chick pilénce *n*, G -ceta
chicken pìle *n*, G pìleta; pìletina *f*
chief šèf *m*
chief *adj.* glàvni
chiefly ùglavnom
chieftain pòglavica *m*
child dijète/déte *n*, G djèteta/dèteta
childhood djètinjstvo/dètinjstvo *n*
childish djèčji/dèčji, djètinjast/dètinjast

children djèca/dèca *f*
chill hladnòća *f*
chilly hládan-hládni
chimney dìmnjak *m*, òdžak *m* (S.)
chin bráda *f*
china porcùlan *m*
China Kína *f*
Chinese Kìnez *m*, Kìneskinja *f*
Chinese *adj.* kìneski
chocolate čokoláda *f*
choice ìzbor *m*
choir zbór *m* (Cr.), hór *m* (S.)
choke, to gúšiti (se) I : ugúšiti (se) P
choose, to izàbirati I : izàbrati [izàbere] P
chop òdrezak *m*, G òdreska; šnìcla *f*
Christ Krìst *m* (Cr.), Hrìstos *m* (S.), Hrìst *m* (S.)
Christian kr̀šćanin *m* (Cr.), hrìšćanin *m* (S.)
Christian *adj.* kr̀šćanski (Cr.), hrìšćanski (S.)
Christianity kršćánstvo *n* (Cr.), hrišćánstvo *n* (S.)
Christmas Bòžić *m*
chuckle smijúljenje/smejúljenje *n*
church cŕkva *f*
cigar cigára *f*
cigarette cigarèta *f*
cinema kíno *n* (Cr.), bìoskop *m* (S.)
circle krúg *m*
circle, to obìlaziti I : obíći [òbiđe] P
circulation kòlanje *n*, cirkulácija *f*
circumstance okólnost *f*
circus cìrkus *m*
citizen gràđanin *m*, dr̀žavljanin *m*
city grád *m*
city *adj.* gràdski
civil gràđanski
civilization civilizácija *f*
claim záhtjev/záhtev *m*
claim (assert), **to** tvŕditi I : potvŕditi P
claim (demand), **to** zahtijèvati/zahtévati I
clap, to pljèskati rùkama [pljèšće] I : zàpljeskati rùkama P
clash sùdar *m*
class (school) rázred *m*
class (social) klàsa *f*, stálež *m*
classic klàsik *m*, klàsičar *m*
classical klàsičan-klàsični
classics klàsične nàuke *f pl.*
classroom rázred *m*, ùčionica *f*
clause rečènica *f*
clean čìst
cleanliness čistòća *f*
clear jàsan-jàsni, vèdar-vèdri
clergy svećénstvo *n* (Cr.), svešténstvo *n* (S.)
clergyman svèćenik *m* (Cr.), svèštenik *m* (S.)
clerk slùžbenik *m*, čìnovnik *m*, čìnovnica *f*
clever pàmetan-pàmetni
cliff stijèna/sténa *f*
climate klíma *f*
climb, to pènjati se [pènje se] I : pòpeti se [pòpne se] P
clinic klìnika *f*
clock zídni sát *m*, zídni čàsovnik *m*
close *prep.* kraj (+G)
close *adv.* blízu
close, to zatvárati I : zatvòriti P
close by *prep.* blízu (+G)
close by *adv.* blízu
closed zàtvoren
closet sòbica *f*, mànji próstor *m*
clothes òdjeća/òdeća *f*
clothing òdjeća/òdeća *f*
cloud òblak *m*
cloudy òblačan-òblačni
clover djètelina/dètelina *f*
clown komedìjaš *m*, lùda *f*
club (card) trèf *m*
club (organiz.) klùb *m*
club (stick) bàtina *f*
coach (sport) trèner *m*
coach (vehicle) kòla *n pl.*, kòčija *f*, fijàker *m* (S.)
coal ùgljen *m* (Cr.); ćùmur *m* (S.); ùgalj *m* (S.), G ùglja
coast òbala *f*
coat kàput *m*
cock (rooster) pijètao/pétao *m*, G pijètla/pétla
cocktail kòktel *m*
cocoa kàkao *m*, G kàkaa
coconut kòkosov òrah *m*
coffee kàva *f* (Cr.), kàfa *f* (S.)
coffeemill mlìnac *m* (Cr.), G mlínca; vodènica *f* (S.)
coin kòvani nòvac *m*
coincide, to podùdarati se I : podùdariti se P
coincidence podùdaranje *n*, slùčaj *m*
cold hladnòća *f*
cold (illness) prèhlada *f*
cold *adj.* hládan-hládni
colleague drúg *m*, koléga *m*
collect, to skúpljati I : skùpiti P; sakúpljati I : sàkupiti P
collection zbírka *f*
college kòledž *m*, fakùltet *m*
collision sùdar *m*
colonial kòlonijalan-kòlonijalni
colonize, to naseljávati I : nasèliti P
colony kòlonija *f*, nàseobina *f*
color bòja *f*
colored òbojen
column stúp *m* (Cr.), stúb *m* (S.)
column (newspaper) stùpac *m* (Cr.), G stùpca; stùbac *m* (S.), G stùpca
comb čèšalj *m*, G čèšlja
comb, to čèšljati (se) I : počèšljati (se) P
combination kombinácija *f*
come, to dòlaziti I : dóći [dóđe] P
come on! hàjde
come out, to ìzlaziti I : izáći [ìzađe] P, izíći [ìziđe] P
comedy kòmedija *f*
comfort ùdobnost *f*
comfortable ùdoban-ùdobni
comforting ùtješan/ùtešan-ùtješni/ùtešni
coming dòlaženje *n*, dòlazeći, bùdući
command zàpovijest/zàpovest *f*
comment òpaska *f*, komèntar *m*
comment, to komentírati I/P (Cr.), komentàrisati [-riše] I/P (S.)
commerce tr̀govina *f*
commercial tr̀govački
committee òdbor *m*, komìtet *m*
common zàjednički
common (simple) pròst
communicate, to saopćávati I : saòpćiti P (Cr.); saopštávati I : saòpštiti P (S.)
communication vèza *f*, komunikácija *f*
communism komunìzam *m*, G -ìzma
communist komùnist *m*, komùnista *m* (S.)
community zàjednica *f*, drúštvo *n*
companion drúg *m*, drugàrica *f*
company drúštvo *n*
comparative kòmparativ *m*
compare, to upoređívati [-rèđuje] I : uporéditi P
comparison upoređénje *n*, komparácija *f*
compassion sàmilost *f*
compatriot zèmljak *m*
compete, to tàkmičiti se I; nàtjecati se [nàtječe se] I (Cr.)
competition tàkmičenje *n*, kònkurs *m*, nàtjecanje *n* (Cr.)
complain, to žàliti se I : pòžaliti se P
complaint žàlba *f*
complete pòtpun
complete, to završávati I : zavŕšiti P
completely pòtpuno
complex cjelìna/celìna *f*, kòmpleks *m*
complex *adj.* slòžen
complexion pùt *f*, bòja líca *f*, tén *m*
complicate, to komplicírati I/P (Cr.), kòmplikovati [-kuje] I/P (S.)
complicated komplìciran (Cr.), kòmplikovan (S.)
complication komplikácija *f*
compliment komplìment *m*
compose, to sàstavljati I : sàstaviti P
composed of sàstavljen
composition sástav *m*
composition (mus.) sklàdba *f* (Cr.), kompozícija *f*
comprehend, to shvàćati I (Cr.), shvàtati I (S.) : shvàtiti P
comprehensible shvàtljiv
comprehension razumijèvanje/razumévanje *n*
compress, to stískati [stíšće] I : stìsnuti P
compressed stìsnut
compromise kompròmis *m*
computation račùnanje *n*, izračunávanje *n*
computer elèktronski mòzak *m*
comrade drúg *m*, drugàrica *f*
conceal, to sakrívati I : sàkriti [sàkrije] P
concealment tájna *f*, skròvište *n*
conceited sùjetan-sùjetni
conceive, to pójmiti I; izmíšljati I : ìzmisliti P
concentrate, to koncentrírati I/P (Cr.), koncèntrisati [-triše] I/P (S.)
concentration koncentrácija *f*, skúpljanje *n*
concept pòjam, *m*, G pójma
conception (biol.) začéće *n*
conception (idea) zàmisao *f*, G zàmisli
concern ìnteres *m*, brìga *f*
concern, to tícati se [tíče se] I
concerning štò se tíče (+G), u vèzi s (+I)
concert kòncert *m*; kòncerat *m*, G kòncerta
conclude, to zaključívati [-kljùčuje] I : zakljúčiti P
conclusion zàključak *m*, G zàključka
concrete bèton *m*
concrete *adj.* kònkretan-kònkretni
concrete (material) *adj.* bètonski
condemn, to osuđívati [osùđuje] I : osúditi P

condition (situation) pòložaj *m*
condition (proviso) ùvjet *m* (Cr.), ùslov *m* (S.)
conduct, to (lead) vòditi I
conductor kondùkter *m*
conductor (music) dirigènt *m*
confederacy sávez dȑžava *m*
conference konferèncija *f*
confess, to priznávati [prìznaje] I : prìznati P
confession priznánje *n*, ispovijest / ìspovest *f*
confident pòuzdan
confidential povjèrljiv / povèrljiv
confidently pòuzdano
confirm, to potvrđívati [-tvȓđuje] I : potvŕditi P
confirmation pòtvrda *f*
conflict súkob *m*, bòrba *f*
confrontation suočávanje *n*
confuse, to zbunjívati [zbùnjuje] I : zbúniti P
confused zbúnjen
confusion zbȑka *f*, nèred *m*
congratulate, to čestítati I/P
congratulation čestítanje *n*, čèstitka *f*
congress kòngres *m*
congressman člán kòngresa *m*
conjugate, to sprézati [spréže] I
conjugation sprézanje *n*
conjunction véznik *m*, svèza *f*
connect, to spájati I : spòjiti P
connected spòjen
connection vèza *f*
conquer, to osvájati I : osvòjiti P
conquered òsvojen
conquerer osvàjač *m*
conscience sávjest/sávest *f*
conscious svjèstan / svèstan - svjèsni / svèsni
consciousness svjèsnost/svèsnost *f*
consent, to prìstajati [prìstaje] I : prìstati [prìstane] P
consequence pòsljedica/pòsledica *f*
consequently stòga, dàkle
conservation održávanje *n*, čúvanje *n*
conservative kònzervativan - kònzervativni
consider, to razmíšljati I : ràzmisliti P
considerable prílìčan-prílični
consideration razmátranje *n*
consist, to sàstojati se [sàstoji se] I
consistent dòsljedan / dòsledan-dòsljedni/dòsledni
consolation ùtjeha/ùteha *f*
console, to tjèšiti/tèšiti I : ùtješiti / ùtešiti P
consonant sùglasnik *m*, konsònant *m*
conspiracy závjera/závera *f*
conspirator zavjerènik/zaverènik *m*
constancy pòstojanost *f*
constant pòstojan
constantly stálno, neprèstano
constipation tvŕda stòlica *f*
constitution (charter) ùstav *m*
construct, to gráditi I : sagráditi P
constructed sàgrađen
construction gráđenje *n*, konstrùkcija *f*
consul kónzul *m*
consulate konzùlat *m*
consult, to sávjetovati/sávetovati (se) [-tuje] I : posávjetovati/posávetovati (se) P
consume, to tròšiti I : potròšiti P
consumer potròšač *m*
contact dòdir *m*, vèza *f*
contact, to dòlaziti u vèzu I : dóći [dóđe] u vèzu P
contain, to sadržávati I : sadȓžati [sadȓži] P
container pòsuda *f*
contemplate, to razmíšljati I : ràzmisliti P
contemplation razmíšljanje *n*
contemporary sùvremenik *m* (Cr.), sàvremenik *m* (S.)
contemporary *adj.* sùvremen (Cr.), sàvremen (S.)
contempt prèzir *m*
content zàdovoljan-zàdovoljni
contentedly zàdovoljno
contest tàkmičenje *n*, mèč *m*
continent kòpno *n*, kòntinent *m*
continental kòntinentalan-kòntinentalni
continuation nástavak *m*, G nástavka
continue, to nastávljati I : nàstaviti P
continuous neprékidan-neprékidni
contract ùgovor *m*
contradict, to protìvrječiti/protìvrečiti I
contradiction protùslovlje *n*, kontradìkcija *f*
contradictory nedòsljedan/nedòsledan -nedòsljedni/nedòsledni, kòntradiktoran-kòntradiktorni
contrary sùprotan-sùprotni
contrary, on the nàsuprot, nàprotiv
contrast kòntrast *m*, rázlika *f*
contribute, to doprinòsiti I : doprìnijeti/doprìneti [-nèse] P
contribution doprínos *m*
control kontróla *f*
control, to krontrolírati I/P (Cr.), kontròlisati [-liše] I/P (S.)
controversy nesùglasica *f*
convenience ùdobnost *f*, pogódnost *f*
convenient pògodan-pògodni
convention skùp *m*, zasjédanje/zasédanje *n*
conversation ràzgovor *m*
converse, to razgovárati (se) I
conviction ubjeđénje/ubeđénje *n*
convince, to ubjeđívati/ubeđívati [-đuje] I : ubijèditi/ubéditi P
convinced ùbijeđen/ùbeđen
cook kùhar *m* (Cr.), kùharica *f* (Cr.); kùvar *m* (S.), kùvarica *f* (S.)
cook, to kùhati I : skùhati P (Cr.); kùvati I : skùvati P (S.)
cooked kùhan (Cr.), kùvan (S.)
cookie kòlač *m*
cool hládan-hládni
cooperate, to surađívati [suràđuje] I (Cr.), sarađívati [saràđuje] I (S.)
cooperation surádnja *f* (Cr.), sarádnja *f* (S.), kooperácija *f*
cooperative *adj.* kòoperativan-kòoperativni
copy kópija *f*
cord kònopac *m*, G kònopca
cordial sȓdačan-sȓdačni
cork čèp *m*, zapùšač *m*
corn kukùruz *m*
corner ùgao *m*, G ùgla; kút *m* (Cr.); ćòšak *m* (S.), G ćòška
corporation poduzéće *n* (Cr.), preduzéće *n* (S.)
corpse lèš *m*
correct, to ìspravljati I : ìspraviti P
correction ìspravka *f*
correspond, to dopisívati se [dopìsuje se] I
correspondence dopisívanje *n*
correspondent dópisnik *m*
corresponding *adj.* odgovárajući
corridor hòdnik *m*
corrupt pòkvaren, rázvratan-rázvratni
corruption pòkvarenost *f*, rázvrat *m*
cost cijèna/céna *f*; tròšak *m*, G tròška
costly skúp
costume kòstim *m*, nòšnja *f*
cottage kùćica *f*, kòliba *f*, vìkendica *f*
cotton pàmuk *m*
cotton *adj.* pàmučan-pàmučni
couch kàuč *m*; dìvan *m*; kanàbe *n* (S.), G -beta
cough kàšalj *m*, G kàšlja
cough, to kàšljati [kàšlje] I : zakàšljati P
council vijèće/véće *n*
counsel sávjet/sávet *m*
counselor sávjetnik/sávetnik *m*
count ràčun *m*
count, to računati I : izračùnati P; bròjiti I : izbròjiti P; bròjati [bròji] I : izbròjati P (S.)
countenance líce *n*, ìzgled *m*
countless bèzbrojan-bèzbrojni
country zèmlja *f*, dȑžava *f*, kráj *m*
countryman zèmljak *m*
countryman (peasant) sèljak *m*
countrywoman zemljàkinja *f*
countrywoman (peasant) sèljanka *f*
county òkrug *m*
couple pár *m*, dvòje *n*
courage hrábrost *f*
courageous hrábar-hrábri
course pràvac *m*, G pràvca
court súd *m*, súdnica *f*
courteous ljùbazan-ljùbazni, ùljudan-ùljudni
courtyard dvór *m*, dvòrište *n*
cousin ròđak *m*, ròđaka *f*, rođàkinja *f*
cover (blanket) pokrìvač *m*
cover (lid) pòklopac *m*, G pòklopca
cover (refuge) záklon *m*
cover, to pokrívati I : pòkriti [pòkrije] P
covered pokrìven
cow kràva *f*
coward kùkavica *f*
crab mòrski ràk *m*
cracker hȑskav kèks *m*
cradle kòlijevka/kòlevka *f*, zìpka *f* (Cr.)
craft (skill) vještìna/veštìna *f*
craftsman zanàtlija *m*, ùmjetnik/ùmetnik *m*
crafty lùkav
cram, to nabíjati I : nàbiti [nàbije] P
crammed nàtrpan
crash sùdar *m*
crash, to razbíjati I : ràzbiti [ràzbije] P
crawl, to pùzati [pùže] I : òtpuzati P
crazy lúd
cream krèma *f* (Cr.), krèm *m* (S.)
create, to stvárati I : stvòriti P
created stvòren
creation stváranje *n*
credit (financial) krèdit *m*
credit (recognition) zàsluga *f*, priznánje *n*
crew mòmčad *f*, grùpa *f*

crime zlòčin *m*
criminal kriminálac *m*, G -nálca; prèstupnik *m*
criminal *adj.* zlòčinački
cripple bògalj *m*
crisis kríza *f*
critic krìtičar *m*
critical krìtičan-krìtični
critically krìtički
criticism krìtika *f*
Croat Hȑvat *m*, Hrvàtica *f*
Croatia Hȑvatska *f adj. noun*
Croatian *adj.* hȑvatski
Croatian *adv.* hȑvatski
crooked svínut, krív
crooked (dishonest) nèpošten-nèpošteni
crop žètva *f*, ùsjev/ùsev *m*
cross kríž *m* (Cr.), kȓst *m* (S.)
cross, to prèlaziti I: préći [préđe] P
crossing prélaz *m*
crossroad ràskrsnica *f*, ráskršće *n*
crow vràna *f*
crowd gòmila *f*, gùžva *f*
crowded kȑcat
crown krùna *f*
crude pròst, sìrov
cruel òkrutan-òkrutni
cruelly òkrutno
cruelty sùrovost *f*, òkrutnost *f*
crumb mȑvica *f*
crusade krìžarski ràt *m* (Cr.), kȑstaški ràt *m* (S.)
crush, to gnjéčiti I: zgnjéčiti P
crust kòra *f*
crutch štàka *f*
cry krík *m*, plàč *m*
cry, to plàkati [plàče] I: zàplakati P
Cuba Kúba *f*
Cuban Kubánac *m*, G Kubánca; Kùbanka *f*
Cuban *adj.* kùbanski
cuckoo kùkavica *f*
cucumber kràstavac *m*, G kràstavca
cult kùlt *m*, obožávanje *n*
cultivate, to obrađívati [obràđuje] I: obráditi P
cultural kùlturan-kùlturni
culture kultúra *f*
cultured kùlturan-kùlturni
cunning lùkav, prèpreden
cup šàlica *f* (Cr.), šólja *f* (S.)
cupboard òrmar za pòsuđe *m* (Cr.), òrman za súdove *m* (S.)
curb kàmeni rúb *m* (plòčnika [Cr.], trotoára [S.])
cure lijèčenje/léčenje *n*
cure, to lijèčiti/léčiti I: izlijèčiti/izléčiti P
curiosity radòznalost *f*, znatižéljnost *f* (Cr.)
curious radòznao-radòznali, znàtiželjan-znàtiželjni (Cr.)
curl ùvojak *m*, G ùvojka
currency nòvac *m*, G nóvca; valúta *f*
current tók *m*, strúja *f*
current *adj.* tèkući
curse psóvka *f*
curse, to pròklinjati [-klinje] I: pròkleti [-kùne] P
cursed pròklet
curtain závjesa/závesa *f*
curve krivìna *f*
curve, to savíjati I: sàviti [sàvije] P
cushion jàstuk *m*

custom òbičaj *m*
customer kúpac *m*, G kúpca; muštèrija *f*
custom-house càrinarnica *f*
customs càrina *f*
cut, to rèzati [rèže] I: òdrezati P
cut hair, to šíšati I: ošíšati P
cute mìo-mìli
cutlet òdrezak *m*, G òdreska; šnìcla *f*
cynic cìnik *m*
cynical cìničan-cìnični
cypress čèmpres *m*, kìparis (S.)
czar càr *m*

D d

dad tàta *m*
daddy tàta *m*
daddy's tàtin
daily dnévni
dairy mljèkara/mlèkara *f*
dairy *adj.* mliječan/mléčan-mliječni/mléčni
Dalmatia Dàlmacija
Dalmatian Dalmatínac *m*, G -tínca; Dalmàtinka *f*
Dalmatian *adj.* dalmàtinski
dam násip *m*, brána *f*
damage štèta *f*
damage, to oštećívati [oštèćuje] I, oštećávati [oštèćava] I: òštetiti P
dance plés *m* (Cr.), ìgra *f* (S.)
dance, to plésati [pléše] I: otplésati P (Cr.); ìgrati I: odìgrati P (S.)
dancer plèsač *m* (Cr.), ìgrač *m* (S.)
dandy (dude) dèndi *m*, G dèndija
danger opásnost *f*
dangerous òpasan-òpasni
Danish dánski
dare, to smjèti/smèti [smìje/smé] I
daring smìon
dark mrák *m*, táma *f*
dark *adj.* mráčan-mráčni, táman-támni
darkness mrák *m*, táma *f*
darling dràgan *m*, dràgana *f*
data podáci *m pl.*
date (fruit) dàtula *f* (Cr.), ùrma *f* (S.)
date (meeting) sàstanak *m*, G sàstanka
date (time) dátum *m*
dative dàtiv *m*
daughter kćí *f*, G kćèri
daughter-in-law snàha *f*
dawn zòra *f*
day dân *m*
daybreak zòra *f*
daylight dnévno svjètlo/svètlo *n*
daytime dân *m*, dòba dána *n*
dead mȑtav-mȑtvi
deadly smrtònosan-smrtònosni
deaf glûh (Cr.), glûv (S.)
dealer (merchant) tȑgovac *m*, G tȓgovca
dean dèkan *m*
dean's office dekànat *m*
dear drág
death smȓt *f*, G smȑti
debate ràsprava *f*
debate, to ràspravljati I: ràspraviti P
debt dûg *m*
decade dèset gòdina, dekáda *f*
decay trûlež *m*
decay, to trùnuti [trùne] I: ìstrunuti P
deceit prèvara *f*, prijèvara/prévara *f*
deceive, to vàrati I: prèvariti P
December dècembar *m*, G dècembra; pròsinac *m* (Cr.), G pròsinca

decide, to odlučívati [-lùčuje] I: odlúčiti P
decided òdlučen
decidedly òdlučno
decision òdluka *f*
decisive òdlučan-òdlučni
deck pàluba *f*
declaration òbjava *f*
declare, to objavljívati [-jàvljuje] I: objáviti P
declension deklinácija *f*, sklànjanje *n*
decline, to òtklanjati I: otklòniti P
decline (nouns), **to** deklinírati I: izdeklinírati P; sklànjati I
decorate, to ukrašávati I: ukrásiti P
decoration ùkras *m*
decrease, to smanjívati [smànjuje] I: smánjiti P
decree òdluka *f*
dedicate, to posvećívati [-svèćuje] I: posvétiti P
dedicated prèdan, pòsvećen
dedication pòsveta *f*
deed djèlo/dèlo *n*
deep dubìna *f*
deep *adj.* dùbok
deer jèlen *m*
defeat pòraz *m*
defeat, to poražávati I: poráziti P
defecate, to vȓšiti vèliku nùždu I: izvȓšiti vèliku nùždu P; ìmati stòlicu I/P
defect nedostátak *m*, G -státka
defend, to bràniti I: obrániti P (Cr.), odbràniti P (S.)
defendant optužènik *m*
defense òbrana *f* (Cr.), òdbrana *f* (S.)
deficiency nedostátak *m*, G -státka
deficient nèdovoljan-nèdovoljni
definite òdređen, dèfinitivan-dèfinitivni
definition òdredba *f*, definícija *f*
degree stèpen *m*
delay, to odgáđati I: odgòditi P; odlágati [òdlaže] I: odložiti P
delegate delègat *m*
delegation delegácija *f*
delicate prèfinjen
delicious ìzvrstan-ìzvrsni
delight oduševljénje *n*
delighted odùševljen
delightful zánosan-zánosni
deliver, to uručívati [urùčuje] I: urúčiti P
delivery ìsporuka *f*
delivery (of child) pòrod *m*
delusion zàbluda *f*
demand záhtjev/záhtev *m*
demand, to zahtijèvati/zahtévati I
democracy demokràcija *f* (Cr.), demokràtija *f* (S.)
democrat demòkrat *m*, demòkrata *m* (S.)
democratic demòkratski
demolish, to rùšiti I: srùšiti P
demon dèmon *m*
demonstrate, to pokazívati [pokàzuje] I: pokázati [pòkaže] P; demonstrírati I/P
demonstration demonstrácija *f*
denial porícanje *n*
Denmark Dánska *f adj. noun*
denounce, to denuncírati I/P
dense gúst

density gustìna *f*
dental zûbni
dentist zúbar *m*, zubàrica *f*, zùbarka *f*
deny, to porícati [pòriče] I : pòreći [pòreče] P
depart, to òdlaziti I : otíći [òde] P
department odjeljénje/odeljénje *n*, òdsjek/òdsek *m*
departure òdlazak *m*, G òdlaska
depend, to závisiti I
dependence závisnost *f*
dependent *adj.* závisan–závisni
deposit depòzit *m*
depot kòlodvor *m* (Cr.), stànica *f* (S.)
depress, to pritiskívati [-tìskuje] I : prìtisnuti P
deprive, to lišávati I : líšiti P
depth dubìna *f*
descend, to spúštati se I : spùstiti se P
descendant pòtomak *m*, G pòtomka
descent sìlazak *m*, G sìlaska
describe, to opisívati [opìsuje] I : opísati [òpiše] P
description ópis *m*
desegregation desegregácija *f*
desert pústinja *f*
deserve, to zaslužívati [-slùžuje] I : zaslúžiti P
design nácrt *m*
design, to cŕtati I : nàcrtati P
desirable pòželjan–pòželjni
desire žèlja *f*
desire, to žèljeti/žèleti [žèli] I : zažèljeti/zažèleti P
desk pìsaći stól *m* (Cr.), pìsaći stó *m* (S.)
despair òčaj *m*
despair, to očajávati I
desperate òčajan–òčajni
despise, to prèzirati [prèzire] I : prèzreti [prèzre] P
despite *prep.* uspŕkos *ili* ùprkos (+D)
dessert dèsert *m*, slàtko *n adj. noun*
destination cílj *m*, òdredište *n*
destiny sudbìna *f*
destroy, to uništávati I : ùništiti P
destruction uništénje *n*
detail pojedínost *f*, dètalj *m*
determination òdlučnost *f*
determine, to određívati [-rèđuje] I : odréditi P
detour obìlaženje *n*, zaobìlazni pút *m*
develop, to razvíjati I : ràzviti [-vije] P
developed razvìjen
development rázvoj *m*
devil vrág *m*; đàvo *m*, G đàvola; đàvao *m*, G đàvla
devilish đavòlski, vràški
devise, to izmíšljati I : ìzmisliti P
devotion òdanost *f*
devour, to ždèrati [ždère] I : poždèrati P
dew ròsa *f*
dial brojčànik *m*
dial, to nazívati telèfonski brój I : nàzvati [nazòve] telèfonski brój P
dialect dijàlekt *m*; dijàlekat *m*, G dijàlekta; nárječje/nárečje *n*
dialogue ràzgovor *m*, dijàlog *m*
diamond dijàmant *m*
diamond (card) kàro *m*
diamond (sport) ìgralište *n*
diarrhea pròljev *m* (Cr.), pròliv *m* (S.)
diary dnévnik *m*
dice kòcke *f pl.*
dictate, to diktírati I/P
dictation dìktat *m*
dictator dìktator *m*
dictatorship diktatúra *f*
dictionary rjèčnik/rèčnik *m*
die (dice) kòcka *f*
die, to ùmirati [ùmire] I : ùmrijeti/ùmreti [ùmre] P
diet dijéta *f*, hrána *f*
differ, to rázlikovati se [-kuje se] I/P
difference rázlika *f*
different drugàčiji, rázan–rázni
difficult téžak–téški
difficulty teškòća *f*
dig, to kòpati I : iskòpati P
digest, to pròbavljati I : pròbaviti P
digestion pròbava *f*
digger kòpač *m*
dignity dostojánstvo *n*
diligence màrljivost *f*
diligent màrljiv
dim táman–támni, mûtan–mûtni
dime kòvanih dèset cénti
diminish, to umanjívati [umànjuje] I : umánjiti P
dine, to ručávati I; rúčati I/P
dining-room trpezàrija *f*
dinner rúčak *m*, G rúčka; glàvni òbrok *m*
dinner (evening) vèčera *f*
diploma diplóma *f*
diplomat diplòmat *m*, diplòmata *m* (S.)
diplomatic diplòmatski
direct dìrektan–dìrektni, nepòsredan–nepòsredni, ìzravan–ìzravni (Cr.)
direct, to upućívati [upùćuje] I : upútiti P
direction pràvac *m*, G pràvca
directly pràvo, rávno
director dìrektor *m*
dirt blàto *n*
dirty nèčist, pr̀ljav
disadvantage nèzgoda *f*
disagree, to ne slágati se [nè slaže se] I : ne slòžiti se P
disagreement nesláganje *n*
disappear, to nèstajati [nèstaje] I : nèstati [nèstane] P
disappearance nèstanak *m*, G nèstanka
disappoint, to razočarávati I : razočárati P
disappointed razòčaran
disappointment razočáranje *n*
disarm, to razoružávati I : razorùžati P
disarmament razoružánje *n*
disaster vèlika nèsreća *f*
disastrous pòguban–pògubni, kàtastrofalan–kàtastrofalni
disbelief nèvjerovanje/nèverovanje *n*
discharge, to rasterećívati [-rèćuje] I : rastèretiti P
disciple ùčenik *m*
discipline disciplína *f*
disclose, to otkrívati I : òtkriti [òtkrije] P
discomfort neùgodnost *f*
disconcert,to uznemirívati [-mìruje] I : uznemíriti P
disconcerted zbúnjen
discontent nèzadovoljan–nèzadovoljni
discord nèsloga *f*
discourage, to obeshrabrívati [-hràbruje] I : obeshrábriti P
discouragement obeshrabrénje *n*
discover, to otkrívati I : òtkriti [òtkrije] P
discovery otkríće *n*
discuss, to razmátrati I : razmòtriti P
discussion ràspravljanje *n*, dìskusija *f*
disease bòlest *f*
disfavor nèmilost *f*
disgrace sramòta *f*
disgrace, to sramòtiti I : osramòtiti P
disgust òdvratnost *f*
disgusting òdvratan–òdvratni
dish (course, food) jèlo *n*
dish (plate) zdjèla/zdèla *f*, tànjur *m* (Cr.), tànjir *m* (S.)
dishes pòsuđe *n*
dishonest nèpošten
dishonesty nepošténje *n*
dishonor sramòta *f*
disillusionment razočáranje *n*
disinterested nesèbičan–nesèbični
dislike, to ne vòljeti/vòleti [ne vòli] I
dismay ùžas *m*
dismiss, to otpúštati I : otpùstiti P
disobedience neposlúšnost *f*
disobedient nèposlušan–nèposlušni
disorder nèred *m*
displace, to premjéštati/preméštati I : prèmjestiti/prèmestiti P
display ìzložba *f*, ìzlog *m*
displease, to ne svíđati se I : ne svìdjeti/svìdeti se [ne svìdi] P
displeasure nezadovóljstvo *n*
disposition (nature) nárav *f*, ćúd *f*
disposition (tendency) sklònost *f*
dispute spòr *m*, prèpirka *f*
disrespect nèpoštovanje *n*
dissertation disertácija *f*
dissolution otápanje *n*, rástvor *m*
dissolve, to rastvárati (se) I : rastvòriti (se) P
distance ràzdaljina *f*, daljìna *f*
distant dàlek, ùdaljen
distinct jàsan–jàsni
distinction rázlika *f*
distinctive òsobit
distinguish, to rázlikovati (se) [-kuje (se)] I/P
distinguished òdličan–òdlični
distress jàd *m*, nèvolja *f*
distribute, to dijèliti/déliti I : razdijèliti/razdéliti P
distribution pòdjela/pòdela *f*
district pòdručje *n*, kòtar *m* (Cr.), srèz *m* (S.)
distrust nepovjerénje/nepoverénje *n*
disturb, to uznemirávati I : uznemíriti P
disturbance uznemirávanje *n*
ditch járak *m*, G járka
dive, to ròniti I : zaròniti P
diverse rázličit
diversity rázličnost *f*
divide, to dijèliti/déliti I : razdijèliti/razdéliti P
division dijèljenje/déljenje *n*
divorce rázvod bráka *m*
divorce, to ràstavljati (se) I : ràstaviti (se) P
dizziness vrtòglavica *f*
dizzy ošàmućen
do, to čìniti I : učìniti P
dock dòk *m*
dock, to prìstajati [-taje] I : prístati [-stane] P
doctor dòktor *m*
doctor (medical) lìječnik *m* (Cr.), lékar *m* (S.)

doctoral dòktorski
doctorate doktòrat *m*
doctrine ùčenje *n*, doktrína *f*
document dokùment *m*; dokùmenat *m*, G -menta; spìs *m*
dog pàs *m*, G psà
dog *adj.* pàsji
doings djèla/dèla *n pl.*
doll lùtka *f*, béba *f*
dollar dòlar *m*
dome kùpola *f*; kùbe *n*, G kùbeta
domestic *adj.* dòmaći
domination prèvlast *f*, dominácija *f*
done ùčinjen
donkey màgarac *m*, G màgarca
doom sudbìna *f*
doomsday súdnji dán *m*
door vráta *n pl.*
dope òpojno srèdstvo *n*, narkòtik *m*
dot tàčka *f*, tàčkica *f*
double *adj.* dvòstruk
doubt súmnja *f*, dvòjba *f* (Cr.)
doubtful sùmnjiv, dvòjben (Cr.)
doubtless bez súmnje, bez dvòjbe (Cr.)
dough tijèsto/tésto *n*
dove gòlub *m*, golùbica *f*
down dòlje/dòle
down *prep.* niz (+ A)
draft (breeze) pròpuh *m* (Cr.), pròmaja *f* (S.)
draft (military) vójna òbaveza *f*
drag, to vúći [vúče] I : povúći P
dragon zmáj *m*, G zmàja
drama dráma *f*
dramatist drámski písac *m*
draw (design), **to** cr̀tati I : nàcrtati P
draw (pull), **to** vúći [vúče] I : povúći P
drawer làdica *f* (Cr.), fijóka *f* (S.)
drawing cŕtež *m*
drawing-room sòba za prímanje *f*
dread stráh *m*
dreadful grózan–grózni
dream sàn *m*, G snà
dream, to sánjati I
dreamer sànjar *m*, sánjalica *m* / *f*
dress hàljina *f*
dress, to obláčiti (se) I : obúći (se) [obúče (se)] P
dressed obúčen
dresser òrmar *m* (Cr.), òrman *m* (S.)
drill obučávanje *n*
drill (tool) svr̀dlo *n*
drink píće *n*
drink, to pìti [pìje] I : pòpiti P
drip, to kàpati [kàplje] I : ìskapati P
drive vóžnja *f*
drive, to vòziti (se) I
driver šòfer *m*, vòzač *m*
driver's šòferski
drizzle sìtna kiša *f*
drizzle, to romìnjati I
drop káp *f*, kàpljica *f*
drop, to pàdati I : pàsti [pàdne] P
drop-out pròpali stùdent *m*
drought súša *f*
drown, to utápljati (se) I : utòpiti (se) P
drowsy pòspan, drèmljiv
drug òpojno srèdstvo *n*
druggist apotèkar *m*, apotèkarka *f*
drugstore apotéka *f*, ljèkarna *f* (Cr.)
drum búbanj *m*, G búbnja
drunk *adj.* pìjan
drunkard pìjanica *m* / *f*
dry súh (Cr.), súv (S.)
dry, to súšiti I : osúšiti P
duck pàtka *f*
duckling pàče *n*, G pàčeta
dues članàrina *f*
dull (blunt) túp
dull (boring) dòsadan–dòsadni
dumb (mute) nìjem/ném
dumb (stupid) glúp, tupòglav
dung gnój *m*; đùbre *n*, G đùbreta
durable trájan–trájni
duration tràjanje *n*
during za vrijème/vréme (+ G)
dusk sùmrak *m*
dust pràšina *f*
dusty pràšnjav
Dutch *adj.* nizòzemski, hòlandski
Dutchman Holànđanin *m*
Dutchwoman Holànđanka *f*
duty (obligation) dúžnost *f*
duty (tariff) càrina *f*
dwell, to stanòvati [stànuje] I
dwelling stán *m*, dóm *m*, kùća *f*
dye bòja *f*
dying ùmiranje *n*
dynamic dinàmičan–dinàmični
dynasty dinàstija *f*

E e

each svàki, svàki pojèdini
eager nestr̀pljiv, žéljan–žéljni
eagerly nestr̀pljivo, žéljno
eagerness žúdnja *f*
eagle òrao *m*, G órla
ear ùho *n*, ùvo *n* (S.); N *pl.* ùši *f*
early *adj.* ràn–ráni
early *adv.* ràno
earn, to zarađívati [-ràđuje] I : zaráditi P
earth zèmlja *f*
earth *adj.* zemàljski
earthquake zèmljotres *m*
earth's zèmljin
ease lakòća *f*
easily làko
east ìstok *m*
Easter Ȕskrs *m*
eastern ìstočni
easy làk
easy-chair fòtelj *m* (Cr.), fotélja *f* (S.)
eat, to jèsti [jède; jèo, jèla] I : pòjesti P
echo òdjek *m*, jèka *f*
echo, to odjekívati [-jèkuje] I : odjéknuti P
eclipse pomračénje *n*
economical ekònomski, štèdljiv
economics ekonòmija *f*
economy (financial) prìvreda *f*
economy (saving) štédnja *f*
edge ìvica *f*, rúb *m*
edible jèstiv
edit, to izdávati [ìzdaje] I : ìzdati P
edition izdánje *n*, náklada *f* (Cr.)
editor izdàvač *m*, ùrednik *m*, rèdaktor *m*
editorial *adj.* ùrednički
educate, to poučávati I : poùčiti P
educated òbrazovan
educating (rearing) òdgoj *m* (Cr.), vaspítanje *n* (S.)
education òbrazovanje *n*
educational òdgojan–òdgojni (Cr.), vàspitan–vàspitni (S.)
eel jègulja *f*
effect pòsljedica/pòsledica *f*
effective djèlotvoran/dèlotvoran–djèlotvorni/dèlotvorni
effort nápor *m*
egg jáje *n*, G jàjeta; N *pl.* jája
egoism egoìzam *m*, G egoìzma
Egypt Ȅgipat *m*, G Ȅgipta
Egyptian Egípćanin *m*, Egípćanka *f*
Egyptian *adj.* ègipatski
eight òsam
eighteen osàmnaest
eighteenth osàmnaesti
eighth ósmi
eightieth osamdèseti
eighty osamdèset
either . . . or ili . . . ili
elastic elàstičan–elàstični
elbow làkat *m*, G làkta
elder stàriji, starjèšina/starèšina *m*
elderly pòstariji
elect, to bírati I : izàbrati [izàbere] P
election ìzbori *m pl.*
elector bìrač *m*
electric elèktričan–elèktrični
electrical engineer elektroinžènjer *m*
electrician elèktričar *m*
electricity elèktrika *f*
elegance elegàntnost *f*
elegant elegàntan–elegàntni
element sástojak *m*, G sástojka; elèment *m*; elèmenat *m*, G elèmenta
elementary òsnovan–òsnovni
elephant slòn *m*
elevate, to pòdizati [pòdiže] I : pòdignuti P
elevation dìzanje *n*, visìna *f*
elevator lìft *m*, dìzalo *n*
elevator-operator lìftboj *m*
eleven jedànaest
eleventh jedànaesti
eliminate, to ùklanjati I : uklòniti P
eloquence rječìtost/rèčitost *f*
eloquent rjèčit/rèčit
else drùgi
elsewhere drùgdje/drùgde
embarrass, to zbunjívati [zbùnjuje] I : zbúniti P
embarrassed zbúnjen
embarrassment zbúnjenost *f*
embassy ambasáda *f*
embrace zàgrljaj *m*
embrace, to gr̀liti I : zàgrliti P
emerge, to pojavljívati se [-jàvljuje se] I : pojáviti se P
emergency hìtna pòtreba *f*
emigrant iseljènik *m*
emigration emigrácija *f*
eminent ùgledan–ùgledni
emotion òsjećaj/òsećaj *m*
emotional òsjećajan/òsećajan–òsjećajni/òsećajni
emperor càr *m*
emphasis naglašávanje *n*, ìsticanje *n*
emphasize, to ìsticati [ìstiče] I : istàknuti P
empire càrevina *f*, ìmperija *f*
employ, to zapošljávati I : zapòsliti P
employee slùžbenik *m*
employer poslodávac *m*, G -dávca
employment slùžba *f*, zaposlénje *n*
empty prázan–prázni
empty, to prázniti I : isprázniti P
enable, to omogućávati I : omogúćiti P
enclose, to (circle) okruživati [okrùžuje] I : okrúžiti P
enclose, to (insert) prilágati [prìlaže] I : prilòžiti P
encounter sùsret *m*

hasten, to žúriti (se) I : požúriti (se) P
hat šèšir *m*
hatchet sjèkira/sèkira *f*
hate mȑžnja *f*
hate, to mȑziti I : zamȑziti P; mȑzjeti/mȑzeti [mȑzi] I : zamȑzjeti/zamȑzeti P
hateful pùn mȑžnje
hatred mȑžnja *f*
have, to ìmati I
have to, to mórati I
haven lúka *f*, sklònište *n*, ùtočište *n*
hay sìjeno/séno *n*
haze màgla *f*
hazy maglòvit
he ón
head gláva *f*, poglàvar *m*
headache glavòbolja *f*
headquarters štáb *m*
heal, to lijèčiti/léčiti I : izlijèčiti/izléčiti P
health zdrávlje *n*
healthy zdràv
heap gòmila *f*, hȑpa *f*
heap, to gomìlati I : nagomìlati P
hear, to čùti [čùje] I/P
hearing slùh *m*
heart sȑce *n*
heart (card) hèrc *m*
heart attack sȑčani nápad *m*
hearth ògnjište *n*
heartless nèmilosrdan-nèmilosrdni
hearty sȑdačan-sȑdačni
heat vrućìna *f*, toplìna *f*
heaven nèbo *n*
heavenly nèbeski
heavens nebèsa *n pl.* (nèbo *n sg.*)
heavy téžak-téški
Hebrew *adj.* hèbrejski
heel péta *f*, nòga *f*
height visìna *f*
heir nàsljednik/nàslednik *m*
helicopter helikòpter *m*
hell pàkao *m*, G pàkla
hello zdràvo
help pòmoć *f*, G pòmoći
help, to pomágati [pòmaže] I : pomòći [pòmogne] P
helper pomàgač *m*, pomòćnik *m*
helpful kòristan-kòrisni
helpless bèspomoćan-bèspomoćni
hem rúb *m*
hemisphere pòlutka *f*, hemisféra *f*
hen kòkoš *f*, G kòkoši
hence òdavde, òdsada
her *adj.* njézin *ili* njén *m* (njézino *ili* njéno *n*, njézina *ili* njéna *f*)
herd stàdo *n*
here óvdje/óvde
here is èvo, èto
here comes èvo, èto
heredity nàsljednost/nàslednost *f*
heresy hèreza *f* (Cr.), jères *f* (S.)
heretic herètik *m* (Cr.), jerètik *m* (S.)
hero hèroj *m*, jùnak *m*
heroic jùnački, hèrojski
heroine junàkinja *f*, heroìna *f*
heroism junáštvo *n*; heroìzam *m*, G -ìzma
herself òna sáma, òna líčno
hesitate, to oklijèvati/oklévati I
hesitation oklijèvanje/oklévanje *n*
hidden skrìven
hide, to sakrívati I : sàkriti [sàkrije] P
high *adj.* vìsok
high *adv.* visòko
high jump skòk u vís *m*
high school gìmnazija *f*
highway glàvna cèsta *f*, àuto-pút *m*
highwayman hàjduk *m*
hill brežúljak *m*, G brežúljka
himself ón sám, ón lìčno
hinder, to smétati I : zasmétati P
hindrance smétnja *f*
hip bòk *m*, kùk *m*
hippie hìpijevac *m*, G hìpijevca; hìpijevka *f*
hippopotamus vòdeni kònj *m*, nílski kònj *m*
hire (employ), **to** zapošljávati I : zapòsliti P
his njègov *m* (njègovo *n*, njègova *f*)
hiss sìktanje *n*
historian pòvjesničar/pòvesničar *m*, hist`òričar *m* (Cr.), istòričar *m* (S.)
historical pòvijesni (Cr.), ìstorijski (S.)
history pòvijest *f* (Cr.), ìstorija *f* (S.)
hit, to ùdarati I : ùdariti P
hoarse pròmukao-pròmukli, hràpav
hobby hòbi *m*, G hòbija
hold, to dȑžati [dȑži] I : zadȑžati P
hole rùpa *f*, šupljìna *f*
holiday práznik *m*
holiness svétost *f*
hollow *adj.* šúpalj-šúplji
holy svét
homage iskazívanje òdanosti *n*
home kùća *f*, dóm *m*
home, at dòma, kòd kuće
homeland dòmovina *f*, zàvičaj *m*
homely prìprost
honest pòšten
honestly ìskreno, pòšteno
honey méd *m*, G mèda
honey *adj.* mèden
honor část *f*, G části
honorable čàstan-čàsni
hood kapùljača *f*
hook kùka *f*
hop, to skákati [skáče] I : skòčiti P
hope náda *f*
hope, to nádati se I : ponádati se P
hopeful pùn náde
hopeless bèznadan-bèznadni
horizon horìzont *m*
horn rôg *m*, G ròga
horrible ùžasan-ùžasni
horror ùžas *m*
horse kònj *m*
horseback, on jàšući na kònju
hose gùmena cìjev/cév *f*
hose (stockings) dùge čàrape *f pl.*
hospitable gostoprìmljiv
hospital bólnica *f*
hospitality gostoprímstvo *n*
host domàćin *m*
hostess domàćica *f*
hostile neprijatèljski
hostility neprijatéljstvo *n*
hot vrúć
hotel hòtel *m*
hotel clerk pòrtir *m*
hotplate rèšo *m*, G rešòa
hound lòvački pàs *m*
hour sát *m*, čàs *m* (S.)
house kùća *f*, dóm *m*
household kućánstvo *n*, domaćínstvo *n*
housekeeper domàćica *f*
housewife domàćica *f*
housing stanòvanje *n*
how kàko
how much kòliko
however međùtim
howl ùrlanje *n*
howl, to ùrlati I : zaùrlati P
hug zàgrljaj *m*
hug, to gȑliti I : zàgrliti P
huge ògroman-ògromni
human ljùdski
human being ljùdsko bíće *n*, čòvjek/čòvek *m*
humane čòvječan/čòvečan-čòvječni/čòvečni
humanist humànist *m*, humànista *m* (S.)
humanistic humanìstički
humanities humanìstičke nàuke *f pl.*
humanity ljùdski ród *m*
humble skròman-skròmni
humiliation poniženje *n*
humility pòniznost *f*
humor hùmor *m*
humorist humòrist *m*, humòrista *m* (S.)
hundred stó, stòtina
hundred-percent stopòstotni, stopròcentni
hundredth stóti
Hungarian Màdžar *m* (Cr.), Madžàrica *f* (Cr.), Màđar *m* (S.), Mađàrica *f* (S.)
Hungarian *adj.* màdžarski (Cr.), màđarski (S.)
Hungary Màdžarska *f* (Cr.), Màđarska *f* (S.)
hunger glád *f*, G gládi; glád *m*, G gláda
hungry gládan-gládni
hunt lóv *m*, G lòva
hunt, to lòviti I : ulòviti P
hunter lòvac *m*, G lóvca
hunting lóv *m*, G lòva
hurrah hùra!
hurricane uràgan *m*
hurry žùrba *f*
hurry, to žúriti (se) I : požúriti (se) P
hurt, to ranjávati I : ràniti P
hurt, to (offend) vrijèđati/vréđati I : uvrijèditi/uvréditi P
husband sùprug *m*, múž *m*
hut kòliba *f*
hygiene higijéna *f*
hymn hìmna *f*
hypocrisy licèmjerje/licèmerje *n*
hypocrite licèmjer/licèmer *m*
hypothesis hipotéza *f*
hysterical histèričan-histèrični

I i

I já
ice léd *m*, G lèda
ice cream slàdoled *m*
icon ìkona *f*
icy lèden
idea idéja *f*; mísao *f*, G mísli
ideal idèal *m*, ùzor *m*
ideal *adj.* ùzoran-ùzorni, ìdealan-ìdealni
idealism idealìzam *m*, G -ìzma
idealist ideàlist *m*, ideàlista *m* (S.)
identical ìsti, idèntičan-idèntični

identification identifikácija *f*
identity identìtet *m*
identity card legitimácija *f*
ideology ideològija *f*
idiom idìom *m*
idiot idìot *m*
idle bèsposlen
idle, to dàngubiti I : izdàngubiti P
idleness bèsposlenost *f*
idol ìdol *m*
if ako, kàda
ignite, to páliti I : zapáliti P
ignition páljenje *n*
ignorance neznánje *n*
ignorant nèuk
ill zlò *n*, nèsreća *f*
ill *adj.* bòlestan-bòlesni
illiterate nèpismen
illness bòlest *f*
illusion ìluzija *f*
illusory ìluzoran-ìluzorni
illustrate, to ilustrírati I/P (Cr.), ìlustrovati [-truje] I/P (S.)
illustration ilustrácija *f*, tumáčenje *n*
illustrious ùgledan-ùgledni
image slìka *f*, lík *m*
imaginary zàmišljen
imagination màšta *f*
imaginative domìšljat, màštovit
imagine, to zamíšljati I : zàmisliti P
imitate, to podražávati I
imitation podražávanje *n*, imitácija *f*
immature nèzreo-nèzreli
immediate nepòsredan-nepòsredni
immediately òdmah
immense ògroman-ògromni
immigrant doseljènik *m*
immigration doseljénje *n*
immobility nèpokretnost *f*
immoral nèmoralan-nèmoralni
immorality nèmoral *m*
immortal bèsmrtan-bèsmrtni
immortality bèsmrtnost *f*
impartial neprìstran
impatience nestrpljénje *n*
impatient nestȑpljiv
imperfect (tense) ìmperfekt *m*
imperfect *adj.* nesàvršen
imperfective trájan-trájni, nèsvršen
impersonal bèzličan-bèzlični
impertinence bezòbraznost *f*
impetuous nágao-nágli
implore, to prèklinjati [prèklinje] I
impolite neprístojan-neprístojni
import úvoz *m*
import, to uvòziti I : ùvesti [uvède] P
importance vážnost *f*
important vážan-vážni
impose, to namètati [nàmeće] I: nàmetnuti P
impossibility nemogúćnost *f*
impossible nèmoguć
impotence nèmoć *f*, G nèmoći
impracticable nepràktičan-nepràktični
impress, to impresionírati I/P
impression ùtisak *m*, G ùtiska; dójam *m* (Cr.), G dójma
impressive upečàtljiv
imprison, to utàmničiti P
imprisonment zátvor *m*, utamničénje *n*
improbable neočèkivan
improper neprìkladan-neprìkladni
improve, to poboljšávati I: pobòljšati P
improvement poboljšánje *n*
improvise, to improvizírati I/P (Cr.), impròvizovati [-zuje] I/P (S.)
impulse pòticaj *m*, pòbuda *f*
in *prep.* u (+A/D), na (+A/D)
in advance unàprijed/unàpred
in love zàljubljen
in order to dà
inability nesposóbnost *f*
inaccuracy nètačnost *f*
inaccurate nètačan-nètačni
inane glúp
inappropriate neprìkladan-neprìkladni
inattention nepážnja *f*
inattentive nepàžljiv
inborn ùrođen
incapable nèsposoban-nèsposobni
incessant neprèstan
incessantly neprèstano
inch ìnč *m*
incident slùčaj *m*
include, to uključívati [uključùje] I : uključìti P
income príhod *m*
incomparable neuporèdiv
incomplete nepòtpun
incomprehensible neshvàtljiv
inconstant nèpostojan
inconvenience neugódnost *f*
inconvenient nèpogodan-nèpogodni
incorrect nèpravilan-nèpravilni
increase pòrast *m*
increase, to povećávati I : povèćati P
incredible nevjeròjatan-nevjeròjatni (Cr.), neveròvatan-neveròvatni (S.)
incurable neizljèčiv/neizlèčiv
indebted zàdužen
indecent neprístojan-neprístojni
indecision nèodlučnost *f*
indecisive nèodlučan-nèodlučni
indeed zàista
indefinite neòdređen
independence nezávisnost *f*, samostálnost *f*
independent nezávisan-nezávisni, sàmostalan-sàmostalni
indescribable neopìsiv
index ìndeks *m*
index finger kàžiprst *m*
Indian (India) Indíjac *m*, G Indíjca
Indian (USA) Indijánac *m*, G Indijánca
Indian *adj.* ìndijski (India), indìjanski (USA)
indicate, to ukazívati [ukàzuje] I: ukázati [ùkaže] P
indication ukazívanje *n*, znák *m*
indicative ìndikativ *m*
indifference ravnòdušnost *f*
indifferent ravnòdušan-ravnòdušni
indignant ògorčen
indignation ogorčénje *n*, sȑdžba *f*
indirect nepòsredan-nepòsredni
indiscreet ìndiskretan-ìndiskretni
indiscretion neràzborit gòvor *m*, odávanje (tájne) *n*
individual lìčnost *f*, òsoba *f*
individual *adj.* lìčan-lìčni, ìndividualan-ìndividualni
indoor ùnutrašnji
indoors *adv.* unútra
indulgence popúštanje *n*, podávanje *n*
indulgent popùstljiv
industrial indùstrijski
industrious màrljiv
industry indùstrija *f*
inequality nejednákost *f*
inertia inèrcija *f*, tròmost *f*
inessential nèbitan-nèbitni
inevitable neìzbježan/neìzbežan-neìzbježni/neìzbežni
inexhaustible neiscȑpljiv
inexpensive jèftin
inexperienced neìskusan-neìskusni
infallible nepogrèšiv
infamous ozlòglašen
infant dijète/déte *n*, G djèteta/dèteta
infantry pješàdija/pešàdija *f*
infer, to zaključívati [zaključùje] I: zaključìti P
inferior nìži
infinite beskònačan-beskònačni
infinity beskònačnost *f*
inflame, to raspaljívati [-pàljuje] I: raspáliti P
inflation nàdutost *f*, inflácija *f*
influence ùtjecaj *m* (Cr.), ùticaj *m* (S.)
influential ùtjecajan-ùtjecajni (Cr.), ùticajan-ùticajni (S.)
inform, to obavještávati/obaveštávati I : obavijèstiti/obavéstiti P
information obavješténje/obavešténje *n*
ingenious dosjètljiv/dosètljiv
ingratitude nezahválnost *f*
ingredient sàstojina *f*, sástav *m*
inhabit, to stanòvati [stànuje] I
inhabitant stanòvnik *m*, žìtelj *m*
inherit, to nasljeđívati/nasleđívati [-đuje] I : naslijèditi/naslédíti P
inheritance nàsljedstvo/nàsledstvo *n*
inhuman nèljudski
initial pòčetni
initiative pòduzetost *f*
injure, to ozljeđívati/ozleđívati [-đuje] I : ozlijèditi/ozléditi P
injured òzlijeđen/òzleđen
injurious štètan-štètni
injury òzljeda/òzleda *f*
injustice nèpravda *f*
ink cȑnilo *n* (Cr.), màstilo *n* (S.)
inkwell tìntarnica *f* (Cr.), màstionica *f* (S.)
inland ùnutrašnjost *f*
inn gostiònica *f*, kȑčma *f*
innate ùrođen
inner nùtarnji, ùnutarnji
innocence nèvinost *f*
innocent nèvin
innumerable bèzbrojan-bèzbrojni
inquire, to ispitívati [-pìtuje] I: ispítati P
inquiry ìstraga *f*
insane lúd
inscription nàtpis *m*
insect kúkac *m*, G kúkca; ìnsekt *m*
insecure nèsiguran-nèsigurni
inseparable nèrazdvojan-nèrazdvojni
insert, to umètati [ùmeće] I: ùmetnuti P
inside ùnutrašnjost *f*
inside *adv.* unútra
insignificant bèznačajan-bèznačajni
insincere nèiskren
insist, to insistírati I
insistence insistíranje *n*, navaljívanje *n*
insolence dȑskost *f*
inspect, to nadgledávati I, nàdzirati I

inspection nadglédanje *n*
inspector ìnspektor *m*
inspiration nadahnúće *n*, inspirácija *f*
inspire, to nadahnjívati [-dàhnjuje] I : nadàhnuti P
install, to uvádati I, uvòditi I : ùvesti [uvède] P
installation ùvođenje *n*
installation (tech.) ùređaj *m*
instance slùčaj *m*
instance, for na prímjer/prímer
instant trenútak *m*, G trenútka
instant *adj.* trènutan–trènutni
instead of *prep.* umjesto/umesto (+G)
instinct ìnstinkt *m*, nágon *m*
instinctive nágonski, ìnstinktivan–ìnstinktivni
institute ùstanova *f*, závod *m*
institution ùstanova *f*, ustanovljénje *n*
instruct, to podučávati I : podùčiti P
instruction nástava *f*, podučávanje *n*
instructional pòučan–pòučni
instructive pòučan–pòučni
instructor ìnstruktor *m*, ùčitelj *m*, docènt *m*
instrument srèdstvo *n*, instrùment *m*
instrumental (case) instrumèntal *m*
insufficient nèdovoljan–nèdovoljni
insult ùvreda *f*
insult, to vrijèđati/vrèđati I : uvrijèditi/uvréditi P
insurance osigurānje *n*
insure, to osigurávati I : osigùrati P
intact nètaknut
intellect úm *m*, ràzum *m*
intellectual intelektuálac *m*, G -tuálka; intelektùalka *f*
intellectual *adj.* ìntelektualan–ìntelektualni
intelligence úm *m*, ràzum *m*
intelligent pàmetan–pàmetni, inteligèntan–inteligèntni
intend, to namjerávati/namerávati I
intense nàpet
intensity nàpetost *f*, jàkost *f*
intent ùporan–ùporni
intention námjera/námera *f*
interchange ràzmjena/ràzmena *f*
interest pážnja *f*, ìnteres *m*, interesíranje *n* (Cr.), interesovanje *n* (S.)
interested zainterèsiran–zainterèsirani (Cr.), zàinteresovan–zàinteresovani (S.)
interesting zanìmljiv, interèsantan–interèsantni
interfere, to miješàti/méšati se I : umiješàti/umésati se P
interior ùnutarnji
intermission prèkid *m*, pàuza *f*
internal ùnutarnji
international međunárodan–međunárodni
interpret, to tumáčiti I : rastumáčiti P
interpretation tumáčenje *n*, interpretácija *f*
interpreter tùmač *m*; prevòdilac *m*, G -dioca
interrogation ispitívanje *n*
interrupt, to prekídati I : prèkinuti P
interruption prekídanje *n*, smétnja *f*
intersection ráskršće *n*
interval rázmak *m*
intervention pòsredovanje *n*, intervèncija *f*
interview intèrvju *m*, G intervjùa
intimacy intímnost *f*, prísnost *f*
intimate prísan–prísni, ìntiman–ìntimni
intimidate, to zastrašívati [-stràšuje] I : zàstrašiti P
into *prep.* u (+A), na (+A)
intolerable nèsnosan–nèsnosni
intonation intonácija *f*
introduce, to upoznávati [upòznaje] I : upòznati P
introduction prèdstavljanje *n*
introduction (preface) prèdgovor *m*
intruder ùljez *m*
intuition intuícija *f*
invade, to provaljívati [-vàljuje] I : prováliti P
invalid invàlid *m*
invasion pròvala *f*, ùpad *m*
invent, to izmíšljati I : ìzmisliti P
invention pronàlazak *m*, G -laska
inventor izùmitelj *m*, pronalàzač *m*
investigate, to istražívati [-tràžuje] I : istrážiti P
investigation ispitívanje *n*, istražívanje *n*
investment ulágānje *n*, investíranje *n*, investícija *f*
invisible nevìdljiv
invitation pòziv *m*
invite, to pozívati I : pòzvati [pozòve] P
invited pòzvan
involuntary nèhotičan–nèhotični
inward ùnutrašnji, ùnutarnji
Ireland Írska *f adj. noun*
Irish *adj.* írski
Irishman Írac *m*, G Írca; Írkinja *f*
iron žèljezo/žèlezo *n*
iron (flat-) pégla *f*, glàčalo *n* (Cr.)
iron *adj.* žèljezan/žèlezan–žèljezni/žèlezni
iron, to péglati I : ispéglati P; glàčati I : izglàčati P (Cr.)
ironical iròničan–irònični
irony irònija *f*
irregular nèredovan–nèredovni
irreparable nepopràvljiv
irresistible neodòljiv
irresolute neòdlučan–neòdlučni
irrigation navodnjávanje *n*
island òtok *m* (Cr.), òstrvo *n* (S.)
islander òtočanin *m* (Cr.), òstrvljanin *m* (S.)
isolate, to izolírati I/P (Cr.), ìzolovati I/P [-luje] (S.)
isolation izolíranje *n* (Cr.), ìzolovanje *n* (S.)
issue (publication) izdánje *n*, brój *m*
issue (subject) glàvni prédmet ràsprave *m*
it òno, tó
Italian Italìjan *m*, Italìjanka *f*; Talìjan *m*, Talìjanka *f*
Italian *adj.* italìjanski, talìjanski
Italy Ìtalija *f*
itch, to svřbjeti/svřbeti [svřbi] I : zasvřbjeti/zasřvbeti P
item stávka *f*, malénkost *f*, kòmad *m*
its njègov (njègovo *n*, njègova *f*)
itself òno sámo
ivory slònovača *f*
ivy bršljan *m*
Izrael Ìzrael *m*
Izrael *adj.* ìzraelski

J j

jacket krátak kàput *m*, jàkna *f*, žàket *m*
jail tàmnica *f*, zátvor *m*
jam pèkmez *m*
jam, to stískati I : stìsnuti P
January jànuar *m*; sìječanj *m* (Cr.), G sìječnja
Japan Jàpan *m*
Japanese Japánac *m*, G Japánca; Jàpanka *f*
Japanese *adj.* jàpanski
jar vřč *m*
jargon žàrgon *m*
jaw čèljust *f*, G čèljusti
jazz džèz *m*
jealous závidan–závidni
jealousy ljubòmora *f*
jeans tràperice *f pl.* (Cr.), fàrmerke *f pl.* (S.)
jeep džìp *m*
jelly žèle *n*, G želèa
jerk třzaj *m*
jerk (person) màngup *m*
jest šála *f*, dòskočica *f*
Jesus `Isus *m*
Jesus Christ `Isus Krìst *m* (Cr), `Isus Hrìst *m* (S.)
jet (plane) mlàžnjak *m*
Jew Žìdov *m* (Cr.), Jèvrejin *m* (S.)
jewel dràgulj *m*, drági kàmen *m*
jewelry nákit *m*
job pòsao *m*, G pòsla
join (associate), **to** pridružívati se [-drùžuje se] I : pridrúžiti se P
join (connect), **to** spájati I : spòjiti P
joined spòjen
joint zglòb *m*
joke šála *f*
joke, to šàliti se I : nàšaliti se P
jolly vèseo–vèseli
journal čàsopis *m*
journalism nòvinarstvo *n*; žurnalìstika *f*; žurnalìzam *m*, G -ìzma
journalist nòvinar *m*
journalistic nòvinarski
journey putòvanje *n*
joy ràdost *f*
joyful ràdostan–ràdosni
joyous vèseo–vèseli, ràdostan–ràdosni
jubilee jubìlej *m*
judge súdac *m*, G súca
judge, to súditi I : dosúditi P
judgment (opinion) mìšljenje *n*
judgment (verdict) òsuda *f*
judicial právni
judiciary sùdstvo *n*
jug vřč *m*
juice sók *m*, G sòka
juicy sòčan–sòčni
July júl *ili* júli *m*, G júla; sŕpanj *m* (Cr.), G sŕpnja
jump skòk *m*
jump, to skákati [skáče] I : skòčiti P
June jún *ili* júni *m*, G júna; lípanj *m* (Cr.), G lípnja
jungle pràšuma *f*, džùngla *f*
junior mlàđi, júnior *m*
jury pòrota *f*; žìri *m*, G žirìja
just *adj.* pràvedan–pràvedni
just *adv.* ùpravo

justice právda *f*
justification opravdánje *n*
justify, to opravdávati I : òpravdati P

K k

karst kr̂š *m*
keen òštar–òštri, pronìcljiv
keep, to čúvati I : sačúvati P; dr̂žati [dr̂ži] I : zadr̂žati P
kerchief màrama *f*
kernel kòštica *f*, jèzgra *f*
kerosene keròzin *m*
kettle lònac *m*, G lónca
key kljûč *m*
kick ùdarac nògom *m*
kick, to ùdarati nògom I : ùdariti nògom P
kicks, for za zábavu
kid (child) dijète/déte *n*, G djèteta/dèteta
kid (goat) jàre *n*, G jàreta
kidney bùbreg *m*
kill, to ubíjati I : ùbiti [ùbije] P
killed ubìjen
kilogram kìlogram *m*, kìlo *n*, kìla *f*
kilometer kìlometar *m*, G -metra
kin ród *m*, G ròda; ròdbina *f*
kind vŕsta *f*
kind *adj.* ljùbazan–ljùbazni
kindle, to potpaljívati [-pàljuje] I : potpáliti P
kindly ljùbazno
kindness ljùbaznost *f*
king králjm
kingdom králjevstvo *n*
kinship sròdstvo *n*
kiss pòljubac *m*, G pòljupca
kiss, to ljúbiti I : poljúbiti P
kitchen kùhinja *f*
kitchen range štédnjak *m*
kitten máca *f*
knee kòljeno/kòleno *n*
kneel, to kléčati [kléči] I : klèknuti P
knife nôž *m*
knight vìtez *m*
knit, to plèsti [plète] I : ìsplesti P
knitting plètenje *n*
knock ùdarac *m*, G ùdarca
knock, to ùdarati I : ùdariti P; kùcati I : pòkucati P
knot ùzao *m*, G ùzla; čvór *m*
know, to znàti I
knowledge znánje *n*
known pòznat
knuckle zglòb pr̂sta *m*
kolo (dance) plés *m* (Cr.), kòlo *n* (S.)

L l

label nàljepnica/nàlepnica *f*, etikéta *f*
labor rád *m*
laboratory laboràtorij *m* (Cr.), laboràtorija *f* (S.)
laborer mànuelni rádnik *m*
lace vèzica *f*, vr̂pca *f*, čìpka *f*
lack nedostátak *m*, G -státka
lack, to ne dòstajati [-staje] I : ne dòstati [-stane] P
lad mòmak *m*, G mòmka
ladder stepènice *f pl.*, ljèstve/lèstve *f pl.*
lady dáma *f*, gòspođa *f*
lag, to zaòstajati [zaòstaje] I : zaòstati [zaòstane] P
lake jèzero *n*
lamb jànje *n*, jàgnje *n*
lamb (meat) jànjetina *f*, jàgnjetina *f*
lame hròm, šèpav
lament tùžaljka *f*, narícaljka *f*
lamp svjètiljka/svètiljka *f*
land zèmlja *f*, kòpno *n*
land (dock), **to** prìstajati [-staje] I : prìstati [-stane] P
land (on airplane), **to** spúštati se I : spùstiti se P
landlady gàzdarica *f*
landlord gàzda *m*
landscape pèjsaž *m*
lane ùličica *f*, pròlaz *m*
language jèzik *m*
lard mást *f*, G másti
large krúpan–krúpni, vèlik
lass djèvojka/dèvojka *f*
last pòsljednji/pòslednji, pròšli
last night sìnoć
lasting trájan–trájni
late kàsan–kàsni (Cr.), dócni (S.)
late *adv.* kàsno (Cr.), dòckan (S.)
lately nèdavno
later kàsnije (Cr.), dòcnije (S.)
lateral bòčan–bòčni
Latin *adj.* làtinski
latter pòtonji, drùgi
laugh smìjeh/sméh *m*
laugh, to smìjati/smèjati se [smìje/smèje] I; nasmìjati/nasmèjati se P
laughter smìjeh/sméh *m*
launch, to lansírati I/P
laundry (clothes) rúblje *n*
laundry (place) pràonica *f*, pèrionica *f*
lava láva *f*
lavatory umivaònica *f*
law zákon *m*
lawful zákonit
lawless bezákonit
lawn zèlena tráva *f*, trávnjak *m*
lawyer advòkat *m*, právnik *m*, òdvjetnik *m* (Cr.)
lay, to polágati [pòlaže] I : polòžiti P; stávljati I : stàviti P
layer slój *m*, G slòja
lazy lìjen (Cr.), lénj (S.)
lead, to vòditi I : dovèsti [dovède] P
leader vòđa *m*
leadership vòđstvo *n*
leaf líst *m*
league sávez *m*, líga *f*
leak pùkotina *f*, nàpuklina *f*
lean, to naslánjati se I : naslòniti se P
leap skòk *m*
leap, to skákati [skáče] I : skòčiti P
leap year préstupna gòdina *f*
learn, to ùčiti I : naùčiti P
learning ùčenost *f*
least nájmanji
least, at bàr, bàrem
leather kòža *f*
leave (depart), **to** òdlaziti I : otíći [òtiđe *ili* òde] P
leave (something), **to** òstavljati I : òstaviti P
leaves líšće *n*
lecture predávanje *n*
lecture, to predávati [prèdaje] I
left *adj.* lìjev/lév
left, to the nàlijevo/nàlevo
left-handed ljevòruk/levòruk
leg nòga *f*
legal zákonit, zákonski
legend lègenda *f*
legislation zakonodávstvo *n*
legislator zakonodávac *m*, G -dávca
legislature zàkonodavno tìjelo/télo *n*
legitimate zákonit
leisure dòkolica *f*
leisurely làgano, bez žùrbe
lemon lìmun *m*
lemonade limunáda *f*
lend, to posuđívati [-sùđuje] I : posúditi P; pozajmljívati [-zàjmljuje] I : pozájmiti P
length dužína *f*
lengthen, to produljívati [-dùljuje] I : prodúljiti P
less mànje
lesson lèkcija *f*
let (permit), **to** dopúštati I : dopùstiti P; dozvoljávati I : dozvòliti P
let's go hàjdemo!
letter slòvo *n*
letter (missive) písmo *n*
lettuce salàta *f*
level ràzina *f*; nìvo *m*, G nìvoa
liable òdgovoran–òdgovorni, òbavezan–òbavezni
liar làžac *m*, G làšca
liberal libèral *m*
liberal *adj.* lìberalan–lìberalni, slòbodouman–slòbodoumni
liberation oslobođénje *n*
liberator oslobòditelj *m*
liberty slobòda *f*
librarian bibliotèkar *m*, bibliotèkarka *f*
library knjìžnica *f*, biblioléka *f*
license dòzvola *f*
lick, to lízati [líže] I : polízati P
lid pòklopac *m*, G pòklopca
lid (eye) kàpak *m*, G kàpka
lie láž *f*, G làži
lie (prevaricate), **to** làgati [làže] I : izlàgati P
lie (recline), **to** lèžati [lèži] I : lèći [lègne] P
lieutenant pòručnik *m*
life žìvot *m*
lift, to dìzati [dìže] I : dìći [dìgne] P
light svjètlost/svètlost *f*
light (bright) *adj.* svìjetao/svétao–svìjetli/svétli
light (not heavy) *adj.* làk
light, to páliti I : upáliti P
lighten, to olakšávati I : olàkšati P
lightning múnja *f*
likable simpàtičan–simpàtični
like kào
like, to vòljeti/vòleti [vòli] I : zavòljeti/zavòleti P
likely vjeròjatan–vjeròjatni (Cr.), veròvatan–veròvatni (S.)
likeness slìčnost *f*
likewise jèdnako, ìsto tàko
liking simpàtija *f*
lilac jorgòvan *m*
lily ljìljan *m*
limb úd *m*
limit grànica *f*
limit, to ograničávati I : ogrànìčiti P
limitation ograničénje *n*
limp, to šèpati I : òdšepati P
linden lìpa *f*
line cr̂ta *f*, línija *f*
lineage ród *m*, G ròda; lòza *f*
linen rúblje *n*, plátno *n*

otherwise ìnače
our nàš (nàše *n*, nàša *f*)
ourselves mí sámi
out ìzvan, ván
outdoors *adv.* váni (Cr.), nàpolju (S.)
outer vànjski (Cr.), spòljašnji (S.)
outfit òprema *f*
outfit (dress) òdjeća/òdeća *f*
outlet òdušak *m*, G òduška
outline òbris *m*, kontúra *f*, òpći prègled *m* (Cr.), òpšti prègled *m* (S.)
output prodùkcija *f*, rezùltat *m*
outrage násilje *n*
outrageous prètjeran / prèteran
outside *adv.* váni (Cr.), nàpolju (S.)
outsider àutsajder *m*
oven péć *f*, G pèći; pèćnica *f*
over *prep.* preko (+G), iznad (+G)
overcast naoblačénje *n*
overcast *adj.* naòblačen
overcoat ogr̀tač *m*, kàput *m*
overcome, to nadvlađívati [-vlàđuje] I : nadvládati P
overflow pòplava *f*, òbilje *n*
overflow, to poplavljívati [-plàvljuje] I : pòplaviti P
overhead iznad gláve
overnight prèkonoć
overpopulation prenàseljenost *f*
overseas preko móra
overseas *adj.* prekòmorski
oversight pròpust *m*
overtake, to prèstizati [prèstiže] I : prèstići [prèstigne] P
overthrow, to obárati I : obòriti P
overturn, to prèvrtati [prèvrće] I : prevŕnuti P
overwhelm, to nadjačávati I : nadjàčati P
owe, to dugòvati [dùguje] I
owl sóva *f*
own, to pòsjedovati / pòsedovati [-duje] I
owner vlàsnik *m*
ox vól *m* (Cr.), G vòla; vó *m* (S.), G vòla
oxygen kìsik *m* (Cr.), kiseònik *m* (S.)
oyster òstriga *f*

P p

pace kòrak *m*; hód *m*, G hòda
Pacific Ocean Tìhi ocèan *m* (Cr.), Tìhi okèan *m* (S.)
pacific *adj.* miroljùbiv
pack (bundle) zàvežljaj *m*
pack (hiking) rùksak *m*
package pàket *m*
pad (cushion) jàstučić *m*
pad (of paper) blòk *m*
page strànica *f*
paid pláćen
pail kàbao *m*, G kàbla; vèdro *n*
pain ból *m*, G bóla; ból *f*, G bóli
painful bólan–bólni
paint bòja *f*
paint, to bojàdisati [-diše] I : obojàdisati P (Cr.); bòjiti I : obòjiti P (S.)
painter (art.) slìkar *m*, slìkarka *f*
painter (house) lìčilac *m* (Cr.), G lìčioca; mòler *m* (S.)
painting slikarstvo *n*
pair pár *m*
pajamas pidžáma *f*
palace dvórac *m*, G dvórca; pàlača *f* (Cr.), pàlata *f* (S.)
palate nèpce *n*
pale blìjed/bléd
Palestine Palestína *f*
palm pálma *f*
palm (of hand) dlàn *m*
pamphlet pàmflet *m*
pan tàva *f*; lònac *m*, G lónca
pancake palačínka *f*
pang ják ból *m*, jáka ból *f*
panic pànika *f*
panic *adj.* pàničan–pànični
panther pànter *m*, pantéra *f*
panties gàćice *f pl.*
pantry òstava *f*
pants hlàče *f pl.* (Cr.), pantalóne *f pl.* (S.)
paper pàpir *m*, hàrtija *f* (S.)
parade paráda *f*, svèčana smòtra *f*
paradise ráj *m*, G ràja; nèbo *n*
paragraph paràgraf *m*; òdlomak *m*, G òdlomka; pàsus *m*
parallel ùporedan–ùporedni, paralèlan–paralèlni
paralyze, to paralizírati I/P (Cr.), paràlizovati [-zuje] I/P (S.)
parcel pàket *m*, pòšiljka *f*
pardon oprošténje *n*
pardon, to izvinjávati (se) I : izvíniti (se) P; opráštati I : opròstiti P
pardon me opròstite *imp.* (Cr.), izvínite *imp.* (S.)
parent ròditelj *m*
parish žúpa *f*, paròhija *f*
park pàrk *m*, pèrivoj *m* (Cr.)
park, to parkírati I/P
parking parkíralište *n*
parliament parlàment *m*
parliamentary pàrlamentaran–pàrlamentarni
parrot papàgaj *m*
parsley péršin *m* (Cr.), péršun *m* (S.)
parson pòp *m*, pàstor *m*
part dìo/dèo *m*, G dijèla/déla
part, to (divide) dijèliti/déliti (se) I : podijèliti/podéliti (se) P
partial djèlimičan/dèlimičan–djèlimični/dèlimični
partially djèlimično/dèlimično
participant ùčesnik *m*
participate, to ùčestvovati [ùčestvuje] I
participation ùčestvovanje *n*
participle partìcip *m*
particle čèstica *f*
particular òsobit
particularly nàročito, òsobito
parting ràstanak *m*, G ràstanka
partisan prìstalica *m/f*, partìzan *m*
partly dijèlom/délom, dònekle
partner pàrtner *m*
part-time hònorarni
party (entertainment) zábava *f*
party (political) strànka *f*
party member partíjac *m*, G partíjca; pàrtijka *f*
pass (permit) pròpusnica *f*
pass, to pròlaziti I : próći [próđe] P
passage pròlaz *m*
passenger pútnik *m*
passerby pròlaznik *m*
passion strást *f*, G strásti
passionate stràstven
passive pàsivan–pàsivni, tr̀pni (gram.)
passport pásoš *m*
past pròšlost *f*, G pròšlosti
past *adj.* pròšao–pròšli
past *prep.* kraj (+G)
paste (glue) ljèpilo/lèpilo *n*
paste, to lijèpiti/lépiti I : zalijèpiti/zalépiti P
pastime zábava *f*
pastor pàstor *m*, žúpnik *m*
pastry koláči *m pl.*, tìjesto/tésto *n*
pasture pàšnjak *m*
patch kr̀pica *f*, komàdić tkànine *m*
patent pàtent *m*
paternal òčinski
paternal uncle stríc *m*
path stàza *f*, pút *m*, pùtanja *f*
pathetic patètičan–patètični
patience strpljénje *n*
patient bolèsnik *m*; pacìjent *m*; pacìjenat *m*, G pacìjenta
patient *adj.* str̀pljiv
patriarch patrìjarh *m*
patriot ròdoljub *m*
patriotic ròdoljuban–ròdoljubni, patrìotski
patron zàštitnik *m*, pàtron *m*
pattern ùzorak *m*, G ùzorka; òbrazac *m*, G òbrasca; šablóna *f*
pause pàuza *f*
pavement bèton *m*
pay pláća *f* (Cr.), pláta *f* (S.)
pay, to pláćati I : plátiti P
payment pláćanje *n*
peace mír *m*
peaceful míran–mírni, tìh
peach brèskva *f*
peacock pàun *m*
peak vr̀h *m*; vrhúnac *m*, G vrhúnca
peanut kikirìki *m*, G kikirìkija
pear krùška *f*
pearl bìser *m*
peas grášak *m*, G gráška
peasant sèljak *m*, seljàkinja *f*, sèljanka *f*
peasant *adj.* sèoski, sèljački
pebble šljúnak *m*, G šljúnka
peculiar čùdan–čùdni
pedagogical pedàgoški
pedagogue pedàgog *m*
pedant cjepìdlaka/cepìdlaka *m/f*
pedestrian pjèšak/pèšak *m*
pedestrian *adj.* pjèšački/pèšački
peel kòra *f*
peel, to gúliti I : ogúliti P
pen pèro *n*
penalize, to kažnjávati I : kàzniti P
penalty kàzna *f*
penance pòkora *f*
pencil òlovka *f*
penetrate, to pròdirati [pròdire] I : pròdrijeti/pròdreti [pròdre] P
penetration pròdiranje *n*
peninsula pòluotok *m* (Cr.), pòluostrvo *n* (S.)
penknife pèrorez *m*
pen-name pseudònim *m*
penny pèni *m*, G pènija
pension pènzija *f*, miròvina *f* (Cr.)
people národ *m*, ljúdi *m pl.*
pepper pàpar *m* (Cr.), G pàpra; bìber *m* (S.)
per *prep.* prema (+D)
perceive, to opážati I : òpaziti P
percent pòsto, òdsto

percentage pòstotak *m*, G pòstotka; pròcenat *m*, G pròcenta
perception opážanje *n*
perfect sàvršen
perfect, to usavršávati I : usavŕšiti P
perfection savršénstvo *n*
perfective (gram.) svŕšen, pèrfektivan-pèrfektivni
perfectly òdlično
perform, to vŕšiti I : izvŕšiti P; izvòditi I : izvèsti [izvèdē] P
performance prèdstava *f*
perfume mìris *m*, pàrfem *m*
perhaps mòžda
peril opásnost *f*
perilous òpasan-òpasni
period (of time) perìod *m*, dòba *n* (indecl.)
period (point) tàčka *f*
periodical čàsopis *m*
periodical *adj.* periòdičan-periòdični
perish, to gìnuti [gìne] I : pòginuti P
permanence trájnost *f*
permanent trájan-trájni
permission dòzvola *f*, dopušténje *n*
permit, to dozvoljávati I : dozvòliti P; dopúštati I : dopùstiti P
perpetual vjèčan/vèčan-vjèčni/vèčni
persecute, to progòniti I
persecution progánjanje *n*
perseverance pòstojanost *f*, stálnost *f*
persist, to bìti ùporan I
persistent ùporan-ùporni
persistently ùporno
person òsoba *f*, líce *n*
personage lìčnost *f*
personal lìčan-lìčni
personality lìčnost *f*
personally lìčno
personnel òsoblje *n*
perspiration znój *m*, G znòja; znòjenje *n*
perspire, to znòjiti se I : oznòjiti se P
persuade, to nagovárati I : nagovòriti P
pertain, to odnòsiti se I, tícati se [tíče se] I
pessimistic pesimìstičan-pesimìstični
pestilence kùga *f*
pet ljùbimac *m*, G ljùbimca
petal làtica *f*
petition mòlba *f*, záhtjev/záhtev *m*
petroleum petròlej *m*
petticoat pòdsuknja *f*
petty nèznatan-nèznatni
pharmacist apotèkar *m*, apotèkarka *f*, apotèkarica *f*
phase fáza *f*
phenomenon fenòmen *m*, pòjava *f*
philological filòloški
philologist filòlog *m*
philology filològija *f*
philosopher filòzof *m*
philosophical filòzofski
philosophy filozòfija *f*
phone telèfon *m*
phone, to telefonírati I/P
phoneme fònem *m* (Cr.), fonéma *f* (S.)
photograph fotogràfija *f*, slìka *f*
photograph, to fotografírati I/P (Cr.), fotogràfisati [-fiše] I/P (S.)
photographer fotògraf *m*
phrase fráza *f*
physical fìzički
physician dòktor *m*, lijèčnik *m* (Cr.), lèkar *m* (S.)
physicist fìzičar *m*
physics fìzika *f*
pianist klavìrist *m*, klavìrista *m* (S.), pijànist *m*, pijànista *m* (S.)
piano klàvir *m*
pickpocket džèpar *m* (Cr.), džèparoš *m* (S.)
picnic ìzlet *m*
picture slìka *f*
picturesque slikòvit
pie pìta *f*, pìroška *f*
piece kòmad *m*
pierce, to probíjati I : pròbiti [pròbije] P
pig svínja *f*
pigeon gòlub *m*
pigsty svínjac *m*, G svínjca
pigtail kìka *f*, pletènica *f*
pile gòmila *f*, hŕpa *f*
pile, to gomìlati I : nagomìlati P
pilgrim hodòčasnik *m*
pill pìlula *f*
pillow jàstuk *m*
pillow-case jàstučnica *f*
pilot pìlot *m*
pin (safety) pribàdača *f*, zìherica *f* (Cr.), zìhernadla *f* (S.)
pin (straight) čìoda *f*
pinch, to štípati I : štìpnuti P
pine bór *m*, G bòra
pineapple ànanas *m*
ping-pong pìng-pòng *m*
pink rùmen, rùžičast
pioneer piònir *m*
pious pòbožan-pòbožni
pipe cìjev/cév *f*
pipe (smoking) lùla *f*
pistol pìštolj *m*, revòlver *m*
pit (hole) jàma *f*
pit (seed) kòščica *f*
pitcher (jug) vȑč *m*
pitiful jàdan-jàdni
pitiless nèmilosrdan-nèmilosrdni
pity sažaljénje *n*, štèta *f*
place mjèsto/mèsto *n*
place, to stàvljati I : stàviti P
plague kùga *f*
plain ravnìca *f*
plain *adj.* rávan-rávni, pròst
plan plán *m*
plan, to planírati I : isplanírati P
plane (airplane) avìon *m*, G avióna
planet plànet *m* (Cr.), planéta *f* (S.)
plank dàska *f*
planning planíranje *n*
plant bìljka *f*
plant, to sáditi I : posáditi P
plantation plantáža *f*
plaster flàster *m*, žbùka *f*
plastic plàstika *f*
plastic *adj.* plàstičan-plàstični
plate tànjur *m* (Cr.), tànjir *m* (S.)
platform plàtforma *f*, pèron *m*
play ìgra *f*
play, to ìgrati (se) I : poìgrati (se) P
player ìgrač *m*
playful nèstašan-nèstašni
playground ìgralište *n*
playmate sùigrač *m*
plaything ìgračka *f*
plea mòlba *f*, ìsprika *f*
pleasant ùgodan-ùgodni, prìjatan-prìjatni
please izvòlite, mòlim vas
please, to svíđati se I : svìdjeti/svìdeti se P
pleased zàdovoljan-zàdovoljni
pleasure užítak *m*, G užítka
pledge zálog *m*, obećánje *n*
plentiful òbilan-òbilni
plenty òbilje *n*, bògatstvo *n*
plenty *adv.* mnògo
plot zàvjera/zàvera *f*
plow plùg *m*
plow, to òrati [òre] I: uzòrati P
plowed ùzoran
plowman òrač *m*
plum šljìva *f*
plum brandy šljìvovica *f*
plumber vodoinstalàter *m*
plump dèbeo-dèbeli, zdèpast
plunder pljàčkanje *n*
plural množìna *f*
pluralistic mnogòstruk
plus plùs
pneumonia ùpala plúća *f* (Cr.), zapaljénje plúća *n* (S.)
pocket džèp *m*
pocket-money džepárac *m*, G džepárca
poem pjèsma/pèsma *f*
poet pjèsnik/pèsnik *m*
poetic pjèsnički/pèsnički
point (dot) tàčka *f*
point (tip) šíljak *m*, G šíljka
point, to pokazívati [-kàzuje] I : pokázati [pòkaže] P
point of view glèdište *n*
pointed šìljast
poison òtrov *m*
poison, to tròvati [trùje] I : otròvati P
poisonous òtrovan-òtrovni
polar pòlarni
pole kòlac *m*, G kólca *ili* kóca
Pole Pòljak *m*, Poljàkinja *f*, Pòljkinja *f*
police polìcija *f*, mìlicija *f*
policeman milicájac *m*, G -cájca; policájac *m*, G -cájca
policy polìtika *f*
polio djèčja/dèčja paralíza *f*
polish làštilo *n*
Polish *adj.* pòljski
polite prístojan-prístojni
politeness prístojnost *f*, ùljudnost *f*
political polìtički
political party polìtička strànka *f*
politician polìtičar *m*
politics polìtika *f*
poll ìzbor *m*, glàsanje *n*
pollution káljanje *n*, zàgađenost *f*
pond rìbnjak *m*
ponder, to razmíšljati I : ràzmisliti P
pony pòni *m*, G pònija
pool bàra *f*
pool (swimming) bàzen *m*
poor siròmašan-siròmašni
Pope pápa *m*
poplar jàblan *m*
popular pòpularan-pòpularni
popularity populárnost *f*
population stanovníštvo *n*
populous nàpučen, nàseljen
porch trìjem/trém *m*
pork svìnjetina *f*
port lúka *f*
porter vràtar *m*, nòsač *m*
portion dìo/dèo *m*, G dijèla/déla; pórcija *f*

portrait pòrtret *m*
Portuguese *adj.* portùgalski
position pòložaj *m*
positive pòzitivan-pòzitivni
possess, to pòsjedovati/pòsedovati [-duje] I
possession pòsjedovanje/pòsedovanje *n*
possessor vlàsnik *m*, pòsjednik/pòsednik *m*
possibility mogúćnost *f*
possible mòguć
possibly vjèrojatno (Cr.), vèrovatno (S.), mòžda
post (pillar) stúp *m* (Cr.), stúb *m* (S.)
post (position) slùžba *f*
post office pòšta *f*
postage poštàrina *f*
postal pòštanski
postcard dòpisnica *f*
postcard (picture) ràzglednica *f*
poster plàkat *m*
posterior zàdnjica *f*, stràžnjica *f*
posterity potómstvo *n*
postman pòštar *m*
postpone, to odlágati [òdlaže] I : odlòžiti P odgáđati I : odgòditi P
postscript postskrìptum *m*
pot lònac *m*, G lònca
potato krùmpir *m* (Cr.), kròmpir *m* (S.)
potent mòćan-mòćni, ják
poultry žìvad *f*, pèrad *f*, živìna *f*
pound fúnta *f*
pour, to lìti [lìje] I : ìzliti P
poverty siròmaštvo *n*
powder práh *m*, púder *m*, bárut *m*
power móć *f*, vlást *f*
powerful mòćan-mòćni
power-station elektràna *f*
practical pràktičan-pràktični
practice pràksa *f*
practice, to vjèžbati/vèžbati I : ìzvježbati/ìzvežbati P
prairie prèrija *f*
praise pòhvala *f*
praise, to hváliti I : pohváliti P
prank òbijesna/òbesna šála *f*
pray, to mòliti I : zamòliti P
prayer mòlitva *f*
preach, to propovijèdati/propovédati I
preacher propovjèdnik/propovèdnik *m*
precaution opréznost *f*
precede, to prethòditi I
precious dragòcjen/dragòcen
precise tàčan-tàčni, prècizan-prècizni
precisely tàčno
precision tàčnost *f*
precocious prèrano razvìjen
predecessor prèthodnik *m*; prèdak *m*, G prètka
predict, to prorícati [pròriče] I : prorèći [prorèče] P
prediction prorícanje *n*
preface prèdgovor *m*
prefer, to vìše vòljeti/vòleti [vòli] I
preference prèdnost *f*, sklònost *f*
pregnant trúdna (žèna), u drùgom stánju
prejudice prèdrasuda *f*
preliminary úvodni
premature prèran
preparation priprémanje *n*, sprémanje *n*
prepare, to sprémati (se) I : sprémiti (se) P
preposition prijèdlog/prédlog *m*
prescribe, to propisívati [propìsuje] I : propísati [pròpiše] P
prescription rècept *m*
presence prìsutnost *f*
present pòklon *m*, dár *n*
present *adj.* prìsutan-prìsutni
present (current) *adj.* sàdašnji
present, to prèdstavljati I : prèdstaviti P
presentation prèdstavljanje *n*
presently skòro
preserve, to čúvati I : sačúvati P
preside, to prèdsjedati/prèdsedati I
president prèdsjednik/prèdsednik *m*
press (printing) štámpa *f*
press, to pritískati I : prìtisnuti P
pressure prìtisak *m*, G prìtiska
prestige ùgled *m*, prèstiž *m*
presume, to pretpòstavljati I : pretpòstaviti P
presumptuous dȑzak-dȑski
presuppose, to pretpòstavljati I : pretpòstaviti P
presupposition prètpostavka *f*
pretend, to pretvárati se I
pretense ìzgovor *m*, ìzlika *f*
pretty lìjep/lép, mìo-mìli
pretty *adv.* príliĉno, dòsta
prevail, to prevlađívati [-vlàđuje] I : prevládati P
prevent, to sprečávati I : sprijèčiti/spréčiti P
prevention sprečávanje *n*
previous pròšli
previously rànije, prèthodno
prey žȑtva *f*
price cijèna/céna *f*
priceless neocjènjiv/neocènjiv
prick, to ubádati I : ubòsti [ubòde] P
pride pònos *m*
priest svèćenik *m* (Cr.), svèštenik *m* (S.)
primary school òsnovna škóla *f*
prime minister premìjer *m*
primitive prìmitivan-prìmitivni
prince prìnc *m*, knéz *m*
princess princéza *f*
principal *adj.* glàvni
principle načélo *n*, prìncip *m*
print òtisak *m*, G òtiska
print, to štàmpati I : odštàmpati P; tìskati I : òtiskati P (Cr.)
printed štàmpan, tìskan (Cr.)
printer štàmpar *m*, tìskar *m* (Cr.)
printing press štampàrija *f*, tìskara *f* (Cr.)
priority prèdnost *f*
prison zátvor *m*
prisoner zarobljènik *m*
private prìvatan-prìvatni
privilege pòvlastica *f*, privìlegij *m* (Cr.), privìlegija *f* (S.)
prize nàgrada *f*
probability vjèrojatnost *f* (Cr.), vèrovatnost *f* (S.)
probable vjèrojatan-vjèrojatni (Cr.), vèrovatan-vèrovatni (S.)
probably vàljda, po svój prílici
problem pròblem *m*, zàgonetka *f*
procedure procedúra *f*; pòstupak *m*, G pòstupka
proceed, to nàstavljati I : nàstaviti P
process tók *m*, pròces *m*
procession pòvorka *f*
proclaim, to proglašávati I : proglásiti P
proclamation proklamácija *f*
procure, to pribávljati I : prìbaviti P
produce proìzvod *m*
produce, to proizvòditi I : proizvèsti [-vède] P
product proìzvod *m*
production ìzrada *f*, proizvòdnja *f*
productive plòdan-plòdni, pròduktivan-pròduktivni
profess, to iskazívati [iskàzuje] I : iskázati [ìskaže] P
profession zvánje *n*, profèsija *f*, strùka *f*
professional strùčan-strùčni, pròfesionalan-pròfesionalni
professor pròfesor *m*
profile pròfil *m*, òbris *m*
profit kòrist *f*, zàrada *f*
profit, to kòristiti I : iskòristiti P
profitable ùnosan-ùnosni
profound dùbok
program prògram *m*, plán *m*
progress nàpredak *m*, G nàpretka
progress, to nàpredovati [-duje] I : uznàpredovati P
progressive nàpredan-nàpredni
prohibit, to zabranjívati [-brànjuje] I : zabrániti P
prohibition zàbrana *f*, prohibícija *f*
project plán *m*; pròjekt *m*; pròjekat *m*, G pròjekta
proletarian prolèterski
proletariat proleterìjat *m*
prolong, to produžávati I : prodúžiti P
prominent ìstaknut
promise obećánje *n*
promise, to obećávati I : obèćati P
promotion unapređénje *n*
prompt bȓz, hìtar-hìtri
pronoun zámjenica/zámenica *f*
pronounce, to izgovárati I : izgovòriti P
pronounce (proclaim), **to** proglašávati I : proglásiti P
pronunciation ìzgovor *m*
proof dòkaz *m*
propaganda propàganda *f*
propagate, to raznòsiti I : ràznijeti/ràzneti [raznèse] P
proper prístojan-prístojni
properly tàčno, ìspravno
property vlàsništvo *n*, svojìna *f*
prophecy proročánstvo *n*
prophet prórok *m*
proportion rázmjer/rázmer *m*, količìna *f*
propose, to predlágati [prèdlaže] I : predlòžiti P
proposition prijèdlog/prédlog *m*
prosaic prozàičan-prozàični, svakìdašnji
prose próza *f*
prospect ìzgled *m*, očekívanje *n*
prosper, to obogaćívati se I : obògatiti se P
prosperity nàpredak *m*, G nàpretka; blagostánje *n*
prosperous ùspješan/ùspešan-ùspješni/ùspešni
prostitute prostìtutka *f*

protect, to štítiti I : zaštítiti P
protection òbrana *f* (Cr.), òdbrana *f* (S.)
protector záštitnik *m*
protest pròtest *m*
Protestant protèstant *m*
Protestant *adj.* protèstanski
Protestantism protestantìzam *m*, G -ìzma
proud pònosan-pònosni
proudly pònosno, pònosito
prove, to dokazívati [dokàzuje] I : dokázati [dòkaže] P
proverb pòslovica *f*
provide, to pribávljati I : prìbaviti P
providence provídnost *f*
province pòkrajina *f*
provincial pòkrajinski, sèoski
provision nàbava *f*, prìbavljanje *n*
provoke, to izazívati I : izàzvati [izazòve] P
proximity nájveća blizìna *f*
prudence ràzboritost *f*
prudent ràzborit, òprezan-òprezni
prune súha šljìva *f* (Cr.), súva šljìva *f* (S.)
psalm psàlam *m*, G psàlma
psychic psìhički
psychoanalysis psihoanalíza *f*
psycholinguistics psiholingvìstika *f*
psychological psihòloški
psychologist psihòlog *m*
psychology psihològija *f*
public pùblika *f*
public *adj.* jávan-jávni
publication òbjava *f*, izdánje *n*, publikácija *f*
publicity publicìtet *m*
publish, to objavljívati [-jàvljuje] I : objáviti P
publisher izdàvač *m*
pudding pùding *m*
pull, to vúći [vúče] I : povúći P
pulpit propovjèdaonica / propovèdaonica *f*
pulse bìlo *n*, pùls *m*
pump púmpa *f*
pump, to púmpati I : ìspumpati P
pumpkin tìkva *f*, bùndeva *f*
pun ìgra rijèči/réči *f*
punch, to ùdarati I : ùdariti P
punctual tàčan-tàčni
punctuation interpùnkcija *f*
punish, to kažnjávati I : kàzniti P
punishment kàzna *f*
pupil ùčenik *m*, đák *m*
pupil (of eye) zjènica/zènica *f*
puppy štène *n*, G štèneta
purchase, to kupòvati [kùpuje] I : kúpiti P
pure čìst
purge čìšćenje *n*, čìstka *f*
purge, to čìstiti I : òčistiti P
purify, to čìstiti I : òčistiti P
purity čistòća *f*, čèdnost *f*
purple grìmizan-grìmizni, tamnoljùbičast
purpose svȑha *f*
purposeful svȑsihodan-svȑsihodni
purse novčànik *m*
pursue, to progòniti I : prògnati P
pursuit gònjenje *n*, pòtraga *f*
push gúranje *n*
push, to gúrati I : izgúrati P
puss màčkica *f*
put, to stávljati I : stàviti P
put off, to odgáđati I : odgòditi P; odlágati [òdlaže] I : odlòžiti P
put on, to obláčiti I : obúći [obúče] P
put out, to gásiti I : ugásiti P
puzzle zàbuna *f*, zàgonetka *f*
pyjamas pidžáma *f*
pyramid piramída *f*

Q q

quaint neòbičan-neòbični, čùdan-čùdni
quake pòtres *m*
quake, to trésti se [trése se] I : potrésti se P
qualification kvalifikácija *f*, sposóbnost *f*
qualify, to osposobljávati (se) I : osposòbiti (se) P
qualitative kvàlitetan-kvàlitetni
quality kvalìtet *m*, kvalitéta *f* (Cr.)
quantitative kvàntitativan-kvàntitativni, kolìčinski
quantity kolìčina *f*
quarrel svàđa *f*
quarrel, to svàđati se I : svàditi se P
quarrelsome svàdljiv
quarry kamenòlom *m*
quarter četvȑtina *f*, čètvrt *f*
quaver dȑhtanje *n*
quaver, to dȑhtati [dȑšće] I : zadȑhtati P
quay kéj *m*, òbala *f*
queen kràljica *f*
queer čùdan-čùdni
quell, to ugušívati [ugùšuje] I : ugúšiti P
quench, to gásiti I : ugásiti P
question pítanje *n*
question, to pítati I : upítati P
questionable sùmnjiv
queue rép *m*, réd *m*
quick bȑz
quickly bȑzo
quiet mír *m*, tišìna *f*
quiet *adj.* tìh, míran-mírni
quilt prekrìvač *m*
quit, to òstavljati I : òstaviti P
quite sàsvim, pòtpuno
quiver dȑhtanje *n*
quiver, to dȑhtati [dȑšće] I : zadȑhtati P
quotation cìtat *m*
quote cìtat *m*
quote, to citírati I/P, iscitírati P

R r

rabbi ràbin *m*
rabbit kùnić *m*, zéc *m*
race ràsa *f*
race (running) tȑka *f*
race, to tȑčati [tȑči] I : istȑčati P
racial ràsan-ràsni
racism rasìzam *m*, G rasìzma
racist ràsist *m*, ràsista *m* (S.)
radiance sjáj *m*, bljèštavost / blèštavost *f*
radiant sjájan-sjájni, blìstav
radical radìkal *m*
radical *adj.* ràdikalan-ràdikalni
radio rádio *m*, G rádija
radish ròtkva *f*, ròtkvica *f*
rag kȑpa *f*
rage bìjes/bés *m*
rage, to bjèsnjeti/bèsneti [bjèsni/bèsni] I : pobjèsnjeti/pobèsneti P
ragged òdrpan, òtrcan
rail ògrada *f*, tráčnica *f*
railroad žèljeznica/žèleznica *f*
railroad station kòlodvor *m* (Cr.), stànica *f* (S.)
railroad worker žèljezničar / žèlezničar *m*
railway žèljeznica/žèleznica *f*
rain kìša *f*
rain, to pàda kìša; kìša je pàdala
rainbow dúga *f*
raincoat kìšna kabànica *f*, kìšni kàput *m*, kìšni màntl *m*
rainfall kìša *f*, kolìčina kìše *f*
rainy kišòvit
raise, to dìzati [dìže] I: dìći [dìgne] P
raised pòdignut
raisin sùhvica *f* (Cr.), súvo gróžđe *n* (S.)
rake (tool) gràblje *n*
rally skùp *m*, skùpina *f*
ranch stòčarska fárma *f*, rànč *m*
random slùčajan-slùčajni
rank réd *m*, čín *m*
ransom òtkup *m*
rape òtmica *f*, sìlovanje *n*
rape, to sìlovati [sìluje] I/P
rapid bȑz, hìtar-hìtri
rapture zános *m*
rare rijèdak/rédak-rìjetki/rétki
rarely rìjetko/rétko
rascal màngup *m*
rash ósip *m*
raspberry màlina *f*
rat štàkor *m* (Cr.), pácov *m* (S.)
rate ràta *f*, mjèra/mèra *f*
rather ràdije, prílično
ration dòpuštena kolìčina *f*
rational ràzuman-ràzumni
rationality ràzumnost *f*, racionálnost *f*
rattle, to zvèckati I : zàzveckati P
rattlesnake čegȑtuša *f* (Cr.), zvèčarka *f* (S.)
raven gàvran *m*
raw sìrov
ray zràka *f* (Cr.), zrák *m* (S.)
razor brìtva *f*
reach dòhvat *m*, dòseg *m*
reach, to dosézati [dòseže] I : doséći [dòsegne] P; stìzati [stìže] I : stìći [stìgne] P
react, to reagírati I/P (Cr.), rèagovati [rèaguje] I/P (S.)
reaction reàkcija *f*
reactionary nàzadan-nàzadni
read, to čìtati I : pročìtati P
reader (anthology) čìtanka *f*
reader (person) čìtalac *m*, G čìtaoca
readily sprèmno
readiness sprèmnost *f*
reading čìtanje *n*
reading room čìtaonica *f*
ready sprèman-sprèmni
real stváran-stvárni
realist reàlist *m*, reàlista *m* (S.)
reality reálnost *f*, stvárnost *f*
realization ostvarénje *n*, realizácija *f*
realize (learn), **to** spoznávati [spòznaje] I : spòznati P
realize (fulfill), **to** ostvarívati [ostvàruje] I : ostváriti P
really zàista
realm králjevstvo *n*
reap, to žèti [žànje] I : pòžeti P

sleeve rùkav *m*
sleigh saònice *f pl.*
slender vìtak-vìtki, tànahan-tànahni
slice krìška *f*
slide, to klìzati [klìže] (se) I : naklìzati (se) P
slight nèznatan-nèznatni
slim vìtak-vìtki
slip(clothing) kombìne *m*, G kombinèa
slip (paper) òmaška *f*, cèdulja *f*
slip, to sklízati [sklíže] se I : sklìznuti se P
slipper pàpuča *f*
slippery klìzav
slogan lòzinka *f*
slope nìzbrdica *f*
sloppy neùredan-neùredni
sloth lijènost/lénost f
Slovene Slovénac *m*, G Slovénca; Slòvenka *f*
Slovenia Slòvenija *f*
Slovenian slòvenski (Cr.), slòvenački (S.)
slow spòr
slow, to usporávati I : uspòriti P
slowness spòrost *f*
slumber dremùckanje *n*
slut blúdnica *f*
sly lùkav, prèpreden
smack (kiss) pòljubac *m*, G pòljupca
small màlen, máli
smallpox kòzice *f pl.* (Cr.), mále bòginje *f pl.* (S.)
smart pàmetan-pàmetni, bìstar-bìstri
smash, to razbíjati I : ràzbiti [ràzbije] P
smashed razbìjen
smell mìris *m*
smell, to mirìsati [mìriše] I : pomirìsati P
smile smijèšak/smèšak *m*, G smijèška/smèška
smile, to smìjati/smèjati se [smìje/smèje se] I : nasmìjati/nasmèjati se P
smith kòvač *m*
smithy kòvačnica *f*
smoke dìm *m*
smoke, to dìmiti I : zàdimiti P
smoke (cigarette), **to** pùšiti I : pòpušiti P
smoking pùšenje *n*
smoky zàdimljen
smooth glàdak-glàtki
snack zákuska *f*
snail púž *m*
snake zmíja *f*
snap, to škljòcati I : škljòcnuti P
snare zámka *f*
snatch, to gràbiti I : zgràbiti P
sneeze, to kíhati [kíše] I : kíhnuti P (Cr.); kíjati I : kínuti P (S.)
snob snòb *m*
snobbery snobìzam *m*, G snobìzma
snore hr̀kanje *n*
snore, to hr̀kati [hr̀če] I : zahr̀kati P
snout njùška *f*, gùbica *f*
snow snìjeg/snég *m*
snow, to pàda snìjeg/snég, snijèži/snéži; snìjeg/snég je padao, snijèžilo/snéžilo je
snowy snijèžan/snèžan-snìježni/snèžni
snuff bùrmut *m*
snug ùdoban-ùdobni
so tàko
so long do viđénja
so that tàko da
so-called takòzvani
soak, to mòčiti I : namòčiti P
soap sàpun *m*
sob jècanje *n*
sob, to jècati I : zàjecati P
sober trijèzan/trézan-trìjezni/trézni
soccer nògomet *m* (Cr.), fùdbal *m* (S.)
sociable drùštven
social drùštven
social science nàuka o drúštvu *f*
socialism socijalìzam *m*, G -ìzma
socialist socijàlist *m*, socijàlista *m* (S.)
society drúštvo *n*
sociolinguistics sociolìngvistika *f*
sociologist sociòlog *m*
sociology sociològija *f*
sock čàrapa *f*
socket utìkač *m*
socket (of eye) òčna dùplja *f*
soda sóda *f*
sofa divan *m*; sòfa *f*; kanàbe *n* (S.), G kanàbeta
soft mèkan
soft drink bezàlkoholno píće *n*
soft roll pècivo *n*
soften, to umekšávati I : umèkšati P
softly tìho, mèkano
soil tlò *n*, zèmlja *f*
sojourn prìvremeno bòravište *n*
solace ùtjeha/ùteha *f*
solar súnčev
sold pròdan
soldier vòjnik *m*
sole đòn *m*
sole jèdini, sám *m* (sámo *n*, sáma *f*)
solemn svèčan
solemnity svèčano dr̀žanje *n*
solicit, to mòliti I : zamòliti P
solid čvr̀st, màsivan-màsivni
solidity čvrstòća *f*, solídnost *f*
solitary ùsamljen
solitude samòća *f*
soluble rješìv/rèšiv
soluble (liquid) tòpiv
solution rješénje/rešénje *n*
solution (liquid) òtopina *f*
solve, to rješávati/rešávati I : rijèšiti/réšiti P
some nèki *m* (nèko *n*, nèka *f*), nèkoliko, màlo
somebody nètko (Cr.), nèko (S.)
somehow nèkako
someone nètko (Cr.), nèko (S.)
something nèšto
sometimes pònekad, kàtkada *ili* kàtkad
somewhat pònešto
somewhere nègdje/nègde
son sín *m*
son-in-law zèt *m*
song pjèsma/pèsma *f*
soon ùskoro
soothe, to ublažávati I : ublážiti P
sophomore stùdent drùge gòdine *m*
sore ràna *f*
sore *adj.* bólan-bólni
sorrow túga *f*, žàlost *f*
sorrowful žàlostan-žàlosni, túžan-túžni
sorry, I am žào mi je
sorry, to be kàjati se I : pòkajati se P
sort vŕsta *f*
soul dúša *f*
sound zvúk *m*
sound *adj.* zdràv, ìspravan-ìspravni
soup júha *f* (Cr.), sùpa *f* (S.)
sour kìseo-kìseli
source ìzvor *m*
south jùg *m*
southern jùžni
southwest jugozápad *m*
souvenir ùspomena *f*, suvènir *m*
sovereign vlàdar *m*
sovereign *adj.* vr̀hovan-vr̀hovni, vládajući
sovereignty nezávisnost *f*, suverenìtet *f*
Soviet Union Sòvjetski Sávez *m*
sow svínja *f*
sow, to sìjati/sèjati [sìje/sèje] I : zàsijati/zàsejati P
space próstor *m*, prostránstvo *n*
spacious pròstran
spade (cards) pìk *m*
spade (tool) lòpata *f*
Spain Špànjolska *f adj. noun* (Cr.), Špánija *f* (S.)
span rázmak *m*, ráspon *m*
Spaniard Španjólac *m* (Cr.), G -njólca; Špánac *m* (S.), G Špánca
Spanish špànjolski (Cr.), špánski (S.)
spare preòstao-preòstali
spare, to štédjeti/štédeti [štédi] I : uštédjeti/uštéditi P
spare time dòkolica *f*
spark ìskra *f*, várnica *f*
sparkle, to blìstati I : zablìstati P
sparrow vrábac *m*, G vrápca
speak, to govòriti I : rèći [rèče] P
speaker govòrnik *m*, spìker *m*, spìkerica *f* (Cr.), spìkerka *f* (S.)
special nàročit, òsobit
specialist strùčnjak *m*
specialty òsobitost *f*, specijálnost *f*
species vŕsta *f*
specific nàročit
specify, to određívati [-rèđuje] I : odréditi P
specimen ùzorak *m*, G ùzorka
speck (dot) tàčka *f*
speck (stain) mr̀lja *f*, pjèga/pèga *f*
spectacle prízor *m*, spektàkl *m*
spectator glèdalac *m*, G glèdaoca
speculation nagáđanje *n*
speech gòvor *m*
speed brzìna *f*
speedy žùstar-žùstri, br̀z
spell čár *f*, G čári; čár *m*, G čára
spell, to spèlovati [-luje] I/P
spend, to tròšiti I : potròšiti P
sphere sféra *f*
spice miròdija *f* (Cr.), miròđija *f* (S.)
spicy zàčinjen, pikàntan-pikàntni
spider pàuk *m*
spill, to pròsipati [pròsiplje] I : pròsuti P
spill (liquid), **to** prolijèvati/prolévati I : pròliti [pròlije] P
spilled *adj.* prolìven, pròsut
spin, to vr̀tjeti/vr̀teti [vr̀ti] (se) I : zavr̀tjeti/zavr̀teti (se) P
spinach špìnat *m* (Cr.), spànać *m* (S.)
spine kìčma *f*, hrptènjača *f*
spiral závojit, spìralan-spìralni
spirit dùh *m*, dúša *f*
spirit (apparition) privíđénje *n*
spirits àlkohol *m*
spiritual dùhovan-dùhovni
spit, to pljùvati [pljùje] I : pljùnuti P
spite pr̀kos *m*, ìnat *m*

splash, to štr̀cati I : pòštrcati P; pr̀skati I : pòprskati P
splashing štr̀canje *n*, pr̀skanje *n*
spleen zlòvolja *f*
splendid sjájan–sjájni
splendor sjáj *m*
split ráskid *m*, ràspuklina *f*
split, to razdvájati I : razdvòjiti P
spoil, to kváriti I : pokváriti P
spoiled pòkvaren, ràzmažen
sponge spùžva *f* (Cr.), sùnđer *m* (S.)
spontaneity prírodnost *f*, spòntanost *f*
spontaneous prírodan–prírodni, spòntan
spool špùla *f*, vìtlić *m*
spoon žlìca *f* (Cr.), kàšika *f* (S.)
sport spòrt *m*, zábava *f*
sport *adj.* spòrtski
spot (place) mjèsto/mèsto *n*
spot (stain) mr̀lja *f*, pjèga/pèga *f*
spouse sùprug *m*, sùpruga *f*, bráčni drúg *m*
spread, to šíriti I : proširiti P
spring (season) pròljeće/pròleće *n*
spring (water) ìzvor *m*
spring, to skákati [skáče] I : skòčiti P
springtime pròljeće/pròleće *n*
sprinkle, to škròpiti I : poškròpiti P
spy ùhoda *m*, špìjun *m*
spy, to uhòditi I
squadron eskàdron *m*, eskadrìla *f*
square tȑg *m*
square (geom.) kvàdrat *m*
square *adj.* kvàdratan–kvàdratni
squeak cíčanje *n*
squeak, to cíčati [cíči] I : cíknuti P
squeeze prìtisak *m*, G prìtiska; gùžva *f*
squeeze, to stískati [stíšće] I : stìsnuti P
squirrel vjèverica/vèverica *f*
stab, to bòsti [bòde] I : ubòsti P
stability pòstojanost *f*
stable *adj.* stálan–stálni, pòstojan
stack (pile) hȑpa *f*
stadium stádion *m*
staff òsoblje *n*
stage pòzornica *f*
stagger, to pòsrtati [pòsrće] I : posŕnuti P
stain mr̀lja *f*, pjèga/pèga *f*
stair stepènica *f*
stake stúp *m* (Cr.), stúb *m* (S.)
stale ùstajao–ùstajali, bàjat (S.)
stammer mùcanje *n*, zamuckívanje *n*
stammer, to mùcati I : pròmucati P
stamp márka *f*
stamp, to ùdarati pèčat I : ùdariti pèčat P
stand (news) kìosk *m*
stand, to stàjati [stòji] I : postàjati P
standard stàndard *m*
standard *adj.* stàndardan–stàndardni
standing pòložaj *m*
standing *adj.* stòjeći
star zvijèzda/zvézda *f*
stare ùkočen pògled *m*
stare, to búljiti I : zabúljiti se P
starry zvjèzdan/zvèzdan
start počétak *m*, G počétka
start, to pòčinjati [pòčinje] I : pòčeti [pòčne] P
starter stàrter *m*
startle, to plàšiti I : prèplašiti P
starve, to gladòvati [glàduje] I : izglàdnjeti/izglàdneti [-glàdni] P
state (condition) stánje *n*
state (country) dr̀žava *f*
state *adj.* dr̀žavan–dr̀žavni
statement ìzjava *f*
statesman dr̀žavnik *m*
station stànica *f*
statistics statìstika *f*
statue kíp *m*, státua *f*
stature stás *m*
statute stàtut *m*
stay, to òstajati [òstaje] I : òstati [òstane] P
steadfast pòstojan, nepokolèbljiv
steady čvȓst
steak òdrezak *m*, G òdreska; bìftek *m*
steal, to kràsti [kráde] I : ùkrasti P
steam pàra *f*
steamer pàrobrod *m*
steed bójni kònj *m*
steel čèlik *m*
steep *adj.* stȑm
steer (animal) júnac *m*, G júnca
steer, to ùpravljati I : ùpraviti P
stem pèteljka *f*
step kòrak *m*
step-brother polùbrat *m*
step-father òčuh *m*
step-mother màćeha *f*
step-sister polusèstra *f*
stern stròg, òzbiljan–òzbiljni
stick pàlica *f*, prût *m*
stick, to lijèpiti/lépiti I : zalijèpiti/zalépiti P
sticky ljèpljiv/lèpljiv
stiff ùkočen, krût
stiffness ùkočenost *f*, krûtost *f*
stifle, to gúšiti I : ugúšiti P
still tìh, míran–mírni
still *adv.* jòš
stillness tišina *f*
stimulus pòbuda *f*, pòticaj *m*
sting žálac *m*, G žálca
stipend pláća *f* (Cr.), pláta *f* (S.), stipèndija *f*
stir, to (move) mìcati [mìče] se I : màknuti [màkne] se P
stitch šàv *m*, òbod *m*
stock (cattle) stòka *f*
stocking žènska čàrapa *f*
stolen ùkraden
stomach stòmak *m*; žèludac *m*, G žèluca
stone kàmen *m*
stony kamènit
stool stòlica *f*
stoop, to sagíbati se I : sàgnuti se P
stop zaùstavljanje *n*, prèkid *m*, stòp *m*
stop, to zaùstavljati (se) I : zaùstaviti (se) P
stop (interrupt), **to** prekídati I : prèkinuti P
store dùćan *m*, rádnja *f*, ròbna kùća *f*
stork róda *f*
storm olúja *f*
stormy òlujan–òlujni
story príča *f*
story (building) kàt *m* (Cr.), spràt *m* (S.)
stout krúpan–krúpni, dèbeo–dèbeli
stove péć *f*, G pèći
straight pràv–právi
straight *adv.* rávno
straighten, to izravnávati I : izràvnati P
strain nápor *m*
strange stràn, nèpoznat
stranger stránac *m*, G stránca; tuđínac *m*, G tuđínca
strangle, to dáviti I : zadáviti P
strap kàiš *m*
strategic stràteški
strategy stratègija *f*
straw slàma *f*
strawberry jàgoda *f*
stray, to lútati I : zalútati P
streak prúga *f*, cȑta *f*
stream pòtok *m*
street ùlica *f*
streetcar tràmvaj *m*
strength snága *f*; móć *f*, G mòći
strengthen, to ojačávati I : ojàčati P
stretch, to rastézati [ràsteže] I : rastégnuti P
stretcher nòsiljka *f*, nòsila *n pl.*
stricken ùdaren, pògođen
strict tàčan–tàčni, stròg
stride dùg kòrak *m*
strife svàđa *f*, rázdor *m*
strike (blow) ùdarac *m*, G ùdarca
strike (labor) búna *f*, štràjk *m*
strike, to štràjkovati [-kuje] I/P
string kònopac *m*, G kònopca
strip, to svláčiti (se) I : svúći [svúče] (se) P
stripe prúga *f*
strive, to téžiti I
stroke ùdarac *m*, G ùdarca
stroke (apoplexy) káp *f*, G kápi
stroll, to šétati (se) I : prošétati (se) P
stroller šètač *m*
strong ják
structure sástav *m*, struktúra *f*
struggle bòrba *f*
struggle, to bòriti se I : izbòriti se P
stubborn ùporan–ùporni, tvrdòglav
stubbornly tvrdòglavo, ùporno
student stùdent *m*, stùdentica *f* (Cr.), stùdentkinja *f* (S.)
student *adj.* stùdentski
studious màrljiv
study, to ùčiti I : naùčiti P, studírati I
stuff stvár *f*
stuffed *adj.* pùnjen
stumble, to pòsrtati [pòsrće] I : posŕnuti P
stump pánj *m*
stupid glúp
stupidity glúpost *f*
stupor mȑtvilo *n*, túpost *f*
sturdy krúpan–krúpni, snážan–snážni
stutter mùcanje *n*
stutter, to mùcati I : pròmucati P
style stíl *m*
subdue, to prigušívati [-gùšuje] I : prigúšiti P
subject prédmet *m*
subject (citizen) pòdanik *m*
subject, to podvrgávati I : pòdvrgnuti P
submarine pòdmornica *f*
submission pòdložnost *f*
submit, to podvrgávati (se) I : pòdvrgnuti se P
subordinate pòdređen, závisan–závisni
subscribe, to pretplaćívati [-plàćuje] se I : pretplátiti se P
subscriber prètplatnik *m*
subscription prètplata *f*
subsequent slijèdeći/slédeći, ìdući
subsidy nòvčana prìpomoć *f*
subsist, to postòjati [postòji] I
substance suštìna *f*, sàdržina *f*

substantial bìtan-bìtni, stváran-stvárni
substitute zàmjenik/zàmenik *m*; nadòmjestak/nadòmestak *m*, G -estka
substitution zàmjena/zàmena *f*
subtle fîn, sùptilan-sùptilni
subtract, to odùzimati I : odùzeti [òduzme] P
subtraction odùzimanje *n*
suburb prèdgrađe *n*
subway pòdzemna žèljeznica/žèleznica *f*
succeed, to uspijèvati/uspévati I : ùspjeti/ùspeti [ùspije/ùspe] P
succeed (a person), **to** nasljeđívati/nasleđívati [-đuje] I : naslijèditi/naslèditi P
success ùspjeh/ùspeh *m*
successful ùspješan/ùspešan-ùspješni/ùspešni
succession slìjed/sléd *m*
succession (series) níz *m*
successive uzástopan-uzástopni
successor sljèdbenik/slèdbenik *m*
such tàkav-tàkvi
suck, to sìsati [sìše] I : pòsisati P
sudden ìznenadan-ìznenadni
suddenly najèdnom, ìznenada
suffer, to pàtiti I : pròpatiti P
suffering pàtnja *f*
suffice, to dòstajati [dòstaje] I : dòstati [-stane] P
sufficient dòstatan-dòstatni, dòvoljan-dòvoljni
suffix nástavak *m*, G nástavka; sùfiks *m*
suffrage právo glása *n*
sugar šèćer *m*
suggest, to predlágati [prèdlaže] I : predlòžiti P
suggestion prijèdlog/prédlog *m*, sugèstija *f*
suicide samoubójstvo *n* (Cr.), samoubístvo *n* (S.)
suit odijèlo/odélo *n*
suitable pòdesan-pòdesni
suitcase kùfer *m*, kòfer *m*
sulk, to dúriti se I
sullen zlòvoljan-zlòvoljni
sullenly zlòvoljno, mřko
sulphur súmpor *m*
sum sùma *f*, ìznos *m*
summer ljèto/lèto *n*
summer *adj.* ljètnji/lètnji
summit vřh *m*; vrhúnac *m*, G vrhúnca
summon, to sazívati I : sàzvati [sazòve] P
summons pòziv na súd *m*
sumptuous ráskošan-ráskošni
sun súnce *n*
sun *adj.* súnčev
sunbath súnčanje *n*
sunburned preplànuo od súnca-preplànuli od súnca
Sunday nèdjelja/nèdelja *f*
sunlight sùnčano svjètlo/svètlo *n*
sunny sùnčan
sunrise ìzlazak súnca *m*, G ìzlaska súnca
sunset zàlazak súnca *m*, G zàlaska súnca
sunshine sùnčano vrijème/vréme *n*
sunstroke sùnčanica *f*

superb prèdivan-prèdivini, sjájan-sjájni
superficial pòvršan-pòvršni
superfluous sùvišan-sùvišni
superhuman nàdljudski
superintendent nádzornik *m*, ùpravnik *m*
superior (boss) šèf *m*
superior *adj.* vìši
superiority nàdmoćnost *f*, prèvlast *f*
supermarket sùpermarket *m*
supernatural nadnáravan-nadnáravni (Cr.), natprírodan-natprírodni (S.)
superstition praznòvjerje/praznòverje *n*
superstitious praznòvjeran/praznòveran-praznòvjerni/praznòverni
supper vèčera *f*
supply snabdjèvanje/snabdèvanje *n*
supply, to snabdijèvati/snabdévati I : snàbdjeti/snàbdeti [snàbdi] P
support pòtpora *f*, pòmoć *f*
support, to podùpirati [podùpire] I : podùprijeti/podùpreti [pòdupre] P
suppose, to pretpòstavljati I : pretpòstaviti P
supposition prètpostavka *f*
suppress, to ugušívati [ugùšuje] I : ugúšiti P
suppression ugušénje *n*, zàbrana *f*
supreme vřhovan-vřhovni, nàjviši
supreme court vřhovni súd *m*
sure sìguran-sìgurni
sure *adv.* sìgurno
surely náravno, sìgurno.
surface pòvršina *f*
surgeon kìrurg *m* (Cr.), hìrurg *m* (S.)
surpass, to nadmašívati [-màšuje] I : nadmášiti P
surprise iznenađénje *n*
surprise, to iznenađívati [-nàđuje] I : iznenáditi P
surprising iznenàđujući
surrender, to predávati [prèdaje] se I : prèdati se P
surround, to okružívati [okrùžuje] I : okrúžiti P
surroundings òkolina *f*
survey nádzor *m*, prégled *m*
survive, to preživjeti/prežíveti [-žívi] P
suspect sùmnjiva òsoba *f*
suspect, to súmnjati I : posúmnjati P
suspend, to odgáđati I : odgòditi P; odlágati [òdlaže] I : odlòžiti P
suspense neìzvjesnost/neìzvesnost *f*
suspension prìvremena òdgoda *f*
suspicion súmnja *f*
suspicious sùmnjiv
sustain, to održávati se I : odřžati [odřži] se P
swallow gùtljaj *m*
swallow (bird) làstavica *f*
swallow, to gùtati I : progùtati P
swallowing gùtanje *n*
swamp mòčvara *f*
swan làbud *m*
swarm (of bees) rój *m*, G ròja
sway, to ljúljati I : zaljúljati P
swear (curse), **to** psòvati [psùje] I : opsòvati P
swear (take oath), **to** zàklinjati [zàklinje] se I : zàkleti [zakùne] se P
sweat znój *m*, G znòja
sweat, to znòjiti se I : oznòjiti se P
sweater pulóver *m*
sweaty znòjan-znòjni

Swede Švéđanin *m*, Švéđanka *f*
Sweden Švèdska *f adj. noun*
Swedish švèdski
sweep, to mèsti [mète] I : pòmesti P
sweet slàdak-slàtki
sweetheart dràgan *m*, dràgana *f*
sweetness slatkòća *f*
swell *excl.* ìzvrsno!
swell, to bùjati I : nabùjati P
swelling òteklina *f*
swift bŕz
swim, to plìvati I : zàplivati P
swimmer plìvač *m*, plivàčica *f*
swimming-pool bàzen *m*
swine svínja *f*
swing ljúljanje *n*
swing, to ljûljati se I : zaljúljati se P
Swiss Švìcarac *m* (Cr.), G -carca; Švàjcarac *m* (S.), G -carca
Swiss *adj.* švìcarski (Cr.), švàjcarski (S.)
switch prekìdač *m*
Switzerland Švìcarska *f* (Cr.), Švàjcarska *f* (S.)
swollen otèčen
sword màč *m*
symbol sìmbol *m*
symbolic simbòličan-simbòlični
syllable slòg *m*
sympathy sklònost *f*, simpàtija *f*
symphony simfònija *f*
symptom prèdznak *m*, sìmptom *m*
syndicate sindìkat *m*, udružénje *n*
syntax sìntaksa *f*
synthetic sintètičan-sintètični
syrup sìrup *m*
system sìstem *m*, sistéma *f*
systematic sistemàtičan-sistemàtični, sistèmatski

T t

table stól *m* (Cr.), G stòla; stó *m* (S.), G stòla
table *adj.* stólni (Cr.), stóni (S.)
tablecloth stólnjak *m*
tablet plòča *f*, plòčica *f*
tacit tìh, šùtljiv (Cr.), ćùtljiv (S.)
tact tàkt *m*
tactful tàktičan-tàktični
tactics tàktika *f*
tag prìvjesak/prìvesak *m*, G -eska; etikéta *f*
tail rép *m*
tailor kròjač *m*, šnàjder *m*
take, to ùzimati I : ùzeti [ùzme] P
take care, to pàziti (se) I : prìpaziti (se) P
take care of, to brìnuti se I : pòbrinuti se P
take off, to svláčiti I : svúći [svúče] P
take over, to preùzimati I : preùzeti [prèuzme] P
take place, to događati se I : dogòditi se P; dešávati se I : dèsiti se P
tale príča *f*
talent dár *m*; tàlent *m*; tàlenat *m*, G tàlenta
talented òbdaren
talk ràzgovor *m*
talk, to razgovárati I
talkative bŕbljiv
tall vìsok
tame pìtom, pripìtomljen
tame, to pripitomljávati I : pripitòmiti P

tang ùkus *m*
tangible opìpljiv
tangle záplet *m*, zbȑka *f*
tank tènk *m*, rezervòar *m*
tap kùcaj *m*
tap, to kùcati I : kùcnuti P
tape tràka *f*
tape-recorder màgnetofon *m*
tar kàtran *m*
tardy kàsan–kàsni (Cr.), dòcni (S.)
target méta *f*, cílj *m*, svȑha *f*
tart tórta *f*
task zadátak *m*, G zadátka; zàdaća *f*
taste ùkus *m*, òkus *m* (Cr.)
taste, to kùšati I : òkusiti P
tasty ùkusan–ùkusni
tatter drónjak *m*, G drónjka; kȑpa *f*
tavern gòstionica *f*
tax pòrez *m*, tàksa *f*
tax, to namètati pòrez I : nàmetnuti pòrez P; taksírati I/P
taxicab tàksi *m*, G tàksija
tea čàj *m*, G čàja
teach, to poučávati I : poùčiti P
teacher ùčitelj *m*, nástavnik *m*, učitèljica *f*, nástavnica *f*
teaching poučávanje *n*
teacup šàlica za čàj *f* (Cr.), šòljica za čàj *f* (S.)
team mòmčad *f*, G mòmčadi
teapot čàjnik *m*
tear sùza *f*
tear, to kìdati I : pòkidati P
tease, to zadirkívati [zadìrkuje] I
teaspoon čájna žlìčica *f* (Cr.), kàšičica *f* (S.)
technical tèhnički
technician tèhničar *m*
technique tèhnika *f*
technology tehnològija *f*
tedious dòsadan–dòsadni
teens gòdine od trínaeste do devètnaeste *f pl.*
telegram telègram *m*, bȑzojav *m* (Cr.)
telegraph telègraf *m*
telephone telèfon *m*
telescope telèskop *m*
television televízija *f*
tell, to govòriti I : rèći [rèče] P
temper (mood) raspoložénje *n*
temperature temperatúra *f*
temperment nárav *f*, ćúd *f*
tempest olúja *f*, bùra *f*
tempestuous búran–búrni, žèstok
temple (church) hrám *m*
temple (forehead) sljepòočnica/slepòočnica *f*
tempo tèmpo *m*
temporal vrèmenski
temporary prìvremen
tempt, to mámiti I : namámiti P, iskušávati I : ìskušati P
temptation iskušénje *n*
ten dèset
tenacious ùporan–ùporni, tvrdòglav
tenant stànar *m*; zákupac *m*, G zákupca
tend, to smjérati/smérati I, téžiti I
tendency sklònost *f*
tender njèžan/nèžan–njèžni/nèžni
tender (soft) mèkan
tenderness njèžnost/nèžnost *f*
tennis tènis *m*
tenor (voice) tènor *m*
tense *adj.* nàpet
tense, future bùduće vrijème/vréme *n*
tense, past pròšlo vrijème/vréme *n*
tense, present sàdašnje vrijème/vréme *n*
tension nàpetost *f*
tent šàtor *m*
tenth dèseti
term rók *m*, G ròka; škòlski rók *m*
terrace teràsa *f*
terrible stràšan–stràšni
terrific strahòvit
terrify, to stràšiti I : prèstrašiti P
territory pòdručje *n*, terìtorij *m*, terìtorija *f*
terror ùžas *m*
test próba *f*, tèst *m*
test, to iskušávati I : ìskušati P; testírati I : istestírati P
testament òporuka *f*, testàment *m*
Testament (bible) závjet/závet *m*
testify, to svjedòčiti/svedòčiti I : posvjedòčiti/posvedòčiti P
testimony svjedočànstvo/svedočànstvo *n*
text tèkst *m*
textbook ùdžbenik *m*
than od (+G), nègo, nó
thank, to zahvaljívati [-hvàljuje] (se) I : zahváliti (se) P
thankful zàhvalan–zàhvalni
thanks hvála *f*
that (one) ònaj *m* (òno *n*, òna *f*), táj *m* (tó *n*, tá *f*)
that *conj.* da, da bi
that is tj. (=tó jèst), òdnosno
thaw, to tòpiti se I : otòpiti se P
theater kàzalište *n* (Cr.), pòzorište *n* (S.)
theatrical kàzališni (Cr.), pòzorišni (S.)
theft kràđa *f*
their, theirs njìhov *m* (njìhovo *n*, njìhova *f*)
theme téma *f*, prédmet *m*
themselves òni sámi
then tàda, ònda
theological teòloški, bogòslovni
theology teològija *f*, bogòslovlje *n*
theoretical teòretski
theory tèorija *f*
there tàmo
there! èno!
thereby tíme, o tòme, dàkle
therefore stòga, zàto, zbog tòga
therein u tòme, u tòm pògledu
thereupon nàto, zàtim
thermometer tèrmometar *m*, G -metra; tòplomjer/tòplomer *m*
thesis téza *f*, téma *f*
they òni *m*, òna *n*, òne *f*
thick dèbeo–dèbeli, gúst
thickness debljìna *f*, gustòća *f*
thief lópov *m*, tát *m*
thigh bèdro *n*, stègno *n*
thimble nàprstak *m*, G nàprstka
thin tànak–tànki
thing stvár *f*, G stvári
think, to mìsliti I : pòmisliti P
thinker mìslilac *m*, G mìslioca
thinking razmíšljanje *n*
thinking *adj.* razmíšljajući
third trèći
thirst žéđ *f*, G žéđi
thirsty žédan–žédni
thirteen trínaest
thirteenth trínaesti
thirtieth trídeseti
thirty trídeset
this òvaj *m* (òvo *n*, òva *f*)
thorn tȓn *m*, bódlja *f*
thorough temèljit
though ìako, màkar
thought mísao *f*, G mísli
thoughtful zàmišljen
thoughtless lakòmislen
thousand hìljada *f*, tìsuća *f* (Cr.)
thousandth hìljaditi, tìsući (Cr.)
thrash, to mlátiti I : izmlátiti P
thread kònac *m*, G kónca; nít *f*, G níti
threat prijètnja/prétnja *f*
threaten, to prijètiti/prétiti (se) I : zaprijètiti/zaprétiti (se) P
three trí
threshold pràg *m*
thrift štédnja *f*
thrifty štèdljiv
thrill uzbuđénje *n*
throat gȑlo *n*
throne prijèstolje/préstolje *n*
throng gùžva *f*, vrèva *f*
through kroz (+A), preko (+G)
throughout kroz (+A)
throughout (during) za vrijème/vréme (+G), za (+G)
throw, to bàcati I : báciti P
thumb pàlac *m*, G pálca
thunder gróm *m*, G gròma; gȑmljavina *f*
thunderstorm olúja s gȑmljavinom *f*
Thursday četvŕtak *m*, G četvŕtka
thus stòga, ovàko
thus far do sàda, dòtle
ticket kárta *f*, ùlaznica *f*
tickle, to škàkljati I : poškàkljati P; golìcati I : zagolìcati P
tide, high plìma *f*
tide, low òseka *f*
tides plìma i òseka *f*
tidy ùredan–ùredni
tidy, to posprémati I : pospréмiti P
tie kravàta *f*, mášna *f* (S.)
tie, to vezívati [vèzuje] I, vézati [véže] I : svézati P
tiger tìgar *m*, G tìgra
tight čvȓst, tijèsan/tésan–tìjesni/tésni
tile òpeka *f*, cígla *f*
till dòk, dòk ne
till *prep.* do (+G)
timber dȑvo *n*, dȑvena gráđa *f*
time vrijème/vréme *n*
timely pravòvremen
timetable réd vòžnje *m*
timid plàšljiv, plàh
timidity plàšljivost *f*, plàhost *f*
tin kàlaj *m*
tiny sìtan–sìtni
tip (money) nápojnica *f* (Cr.), bàkšiš *f* (S.)
tip (peak) vȓh *m*, G vȓha
tire gùma *f*, gùma na àutu, gùma na kotáču (Cr.), gùma na tòčku (S.)
tired ùmoran–ùmorni
tiresome zámoran–zámorni
title náslov *m*, tìtula *f*
Titograd Tìtograd *m*
to k *ili* ka (+D), prema (+D)
toast pȑženi krùh *m* (Cr.), pȑženi hlèb *m* (S.)

toast (tribute) zdràvica *f*
tobacco dùhan *m* (Cr.), dùvan *m* (S.)
today dànas
toe nòžni pȑst *m*
together zàjedno, skùpa
toil mùka *f*, trúd *m*
toilet toalèta *f*, umìvaonica *f*
toilet *adj.* toalètan–toalètni
token znák *m*, znàmen *m*
tolerable podnòšljiv
tolerate, to podnòsiti I : pòdnijeti/pòdneti [podnèse] P
toleration trpèljivost *f*, toleràncija *f*
tomato rájčica *f* (Cr.), paradàjz *m* (S.)
tomb gròb *m*
tomorrow sùtra
ton tóna *f*
tone tón *m*, zvúk *m*
tongue jèzik *m*
tonight nòćas
too takóđer (Cr.), takóđe (S.)
tools àlat *m*
tooth zúb *m*
toothache zubòbolja *f*
toothbrush čètkica za zúbe *f*
toothpaste pàsta za zúbe *f*
toothpick čàčkalica *f*
top (peak) vȓh *m*, G vȓha
top *adj.* nàjviši
topic prédmet ràzgovora *m*
torch bàklja *f*, zùblja *f*
torment mùčenje *n*, mùka *f*
torment, to mùčiti I : nàmučiti P
torn pòderan
torture mùčenje *n*, tortúra *f*
torture, to mùčiti I : nàmučiti P
total ùkupan–ùkupni
touch dòdir *m*
touch, to dírati I : dírnuti P
touching *adj.* dìrljiv
tough žìlav
tour krúžno putòvanje *n*, vòžnja *f*
tourist tùrist *m*, tùrista *m* (S.), tùristkinja *f*
tournament tùrnir *m*, nàtjecanje *n* (Cr.), mèč *m*
tow, to vúći [vúče] I : povúći P
toward(s) prema (+D), k *ili* ka (+D)
towel rùčnik *m* (Cr.), pèškir *m* (S.)
tower kúla *f*
town grád *m*
townsman gràđanin *m*
toy ìgračka *f*
trace trág *m*
track trág *m*, stàza *f*
track and field làka atlètika *f*
tractor tràktor *m*
trade tȑgovina *f*
trade, to trgòvati [tȑguje] I
trader tȑgovac *m*, G tȑgovca
tradition tràdicija *f*
traditional tràdicionalan–tràdicionalni
traffic pròmet *m*, sàobraćaj *m*
traffic light pròmetno svjètlo/svètlo *n*, sèmafor *m*
traffic signal sàobraćajni znák *m*, sèmafor *m*
tragedy tràgedija *f*
tragic tràgičan–tràgični, pòtresan–pòtresni
trail trág *m*, stàza *f*
train vlák *m* (Cr.), vóz *m* (S.)
training škòlovanje *n*, treníranje *n*
traitor ìzdajica *m*
tramp skítnica *m/f*
trample, to gàziti I : pògaziti P
tranquil míran–mírni, spòkojan–spòkojni
tranquility mirnòća *f*, tišìna *f*, spokójstvo *n*
tranquilizer srèdstvo za umirénje *n*
transfer prijènos/prénos *m*
transfer, to prenòsiti I : prènijeti/prèneti [prenèse] P
transform, to pretvárati I : pretvòriti P
transformation preòbraženje *n*
transient pròlazan–pròlazni
transit pròlaz *m*, trànzit *m*
transition prijèlaz/prélaz *m*
transitory pròlazan–pròlazni
translate, to prevòditi I : prevèsti [prevède] P
translation prijèvod/prévod *m*
translator prevòdilac *m*, G prevòdioca
transparent pròziran–pròzirni
transport prijèvoz/prévoz *m*
transport, to prevòziti I : prèvesti [prevèze] P
transportation trànsport *m*, prijèvoz/prévoz *m*
trap zámka *f*, klòpka *f*
trash smèće *n*
travel putòvanje *n*
travel, to putòvati [pùtuje] I : proputòvati P
traveler pútnik *m*
traveling putòvanje *n*
tray poslùžavnik *m*
treacherous ìzdajnički, nèvjeran/nèveran–nèvjerni/nèverni
treachery ìzdaja *f*, nèvjera/nèvera *f*
tread, to stúpati I : stúpiti P
treason ìzdaja *f*
treasure blágo *n*
treasurer blàgajnik *m*, blàgajnica *f*
treasury rìznica *f*, blàgajna *f*
treat čàšćenje *n*
treat (deal with), **to** postúpati I : postúpiti P
treatment pòstupak *m*, G pòstupka
treatment (medical) lijèčenje/léčenje *n*
treaty ùgovor *m*
tree dȑvo *n*, G dȑveta; stáblo *n*
tremble, to dȑhtati [dȑšće] I : zadȑhtati P
tremendous strahòvit
trench járak *m*, G járka; róv *m*, G ròva
trend smjèr/smèr *m*
trespass prèstupak *m*, G prèstupka
trespass, to prestúpati I : prestúpiti P
tress pletènica *f*
trial sùđenje *n*
triangle tròkut *m* (Cr.); tròugao *m* (S.), G tròugla
tribe plème *n*, G plèmena
tribute (honor) priznánje
tribute (tax) pòrez *m*, pòreza *f* (S.)
trick, to vàrati I : prèvariti P
trifle sitnìca *f*
trifling nèznatan–nèznatni
trim ùredan–ùredni
trip ìzlet *m*, pút *m*
triple tròstruk
triumph trìjumf *m*, pòbjeda/pòbeda *f*
triumphant pòbjednički/pòbednički
trivial nèznatan–nèznatni, trìvijalan–trìvijalni
troop čèta *f*
trophy tròfej *m*
tropical tròpski, žárki
tropics trópi *m pl.*
trouble mùka *f*, brìga *f*
trouble, to uznemirívati [-mìruje] I : uznemíriti P; smétati I : zasmétati P
troublemaker mùtivoda *m/f*, izazìvač neprílika *m*
troublesome nèzgodan–nèzgodni, mùčan–mùčni
trousers hlàče *f pl.* (Cr.), pantalóne *f pl.* (S.)
trout pàstrva *f*, pàstrmka *f*
truck kamìon *m*
true ìstinit, vjèran/vèran–vjèrni/vèrni
truly zàista, ìskreno
trumpet trúba *f*
trunk (chest) vèliki sànduk *m*
trunk (tree) déblo *n*, stáblo *n*
trust, to vjèrovati/vèrovati [-ruje] I : pòvjerovati/pòverovati P
truth ìstina *f*
truthful ìstinit
try pòkušaj *m*
try, to pokušávati I : pòkušati P
tub (bath) káda *f*
tub (cask) bùre *n*, G bùreta
tube cìjev/cév *f*, G cìjevi/cévi
Tuesday ùtorak *m*, G ùtorka
tug, to vúći [vúče] I : povúći P
tulip tulìpan *m* (Cr.), lála *f* (S.)
tumor túmor *m*, ìzraslina *f*
tumult vrèva *f*, stȑka *f*
tune melòdija *f*
tunnel tùnel *m*
turkey pùran *m* (Cr.), pùra *f* (Cr.), ćùran *m* (S.), ćúrka *f* (S.)
Turkish tùrski
turn òkret *m*
turn, to òkretati [òkreće] I : okrénuti P
turning zàokret *m*
turnip rèpa *f*
turtle kòrnjača *f*
tutor tútor *m*, skȑbnik *m*
twelfth dvánaesti
twelve dvánaest
twentieth dvádeseti
twenty dvádeset
twice dváput
twig grànčica *f*
twilight súton *m*
twin blizànac *m*, G blizànca
twist, to vȑtjeti/vȑteti [vȑti] I : zavȑtjeti/zavȑteti P
two dvá m/n, dvìje/dvé *f*, dvòjica *f*, dvòje *n*
type típ *m*, vȓsta *f*
type, to tìpkati I : òtipkati P (Cr.); kùcati I : òtkucati P (S.)
typewriter pìsaća mašína *f*, pìsaći strój *m* (Cr.)
typical tìpičan–tìpični
typing tìpkanje *n* (Cr.), kùcanje *n* (S.)
typist daktilògraf *m*, daktilògrafkinja *f*
tyranny tirànija *f*
tyrant tìranin *m*

U u

udder vìme *n*, G vìmena
ugliness ružnòća *f*
ugly rúžan–rúžni
Ukraine Ùkrajina *f*

Ukrainian Ùkrajinac *m*, G Ùkrajinca; Ùkrajinka *f*
Ukrainian *adj.* ùkrajinski
umbrella kìšobran *m*
unable nèsposoban-nèsposobni
unacceptable neprihvàtljiv
unaccustomed nenàviknut
unanimity jednòglasnost *f*
unanimous jednòglasan-jednòglasni
unasked nèpitan, nètražen
unattainable nedòstižan-nedòstižni
unattended nèpraćen
unaware nèsvjestan / nèsvestan - nèsvjesni/nèsvesni
unbearable nèsnosan-nèsnosni
unbelievable nèvjerojatan-nèvjerojatni (Cr.), nèverovatan-nèverovatni (S.)
unbounded bezgràničan-bezgrànični
unbroken nèslomljen
unbutton, to otkopčávati I: otkòpčati P
unceasing neprèkidan-neprèkidni
uncertain nèsiguran-nèsigurni
uncertainty neìzvjesnost/neìzvesnost *f*
unchangeable nepromjènljiv / nepromènljiv
uncle (father's brother) stríc *m*
uncle (mother's brother) ùjak *m*
uncomfortable neùdoban-neùdobni
uncommon neòbičan-neòbični
unconscious nèsvjestan / nèsvestan - nèsvjesni/nèsvesni
uncover, to otkrívati I: òtkriti [òtkrije] P
undecided nèodlučen
under ispod (+G)
under *adv.* dòlje/dòle
undergo, to podnòsiti I: pòdnijeti/pòdneti [-nèse] P
undergraduate stùdent *m*, stùdentica *f* (Cr.), stùdentkinja *f* (S.)
underground pòdzemni
underline, to potcrtávati I: pòtcrtati P
underneath nìže, dòlje/dòle
undershirt màjica *f*
understand, to razumijèvati / razumévati I: razùmjeti/razùmeti P
understanding razumijèvanje / razumévanje *n*, spòrazum *m*
undertake, to predùzimati I: predùzeti [prèduzme] P
undertaker vlàsnik pògrebnog závoda *m*
underwear rúblje *n*, dónji vèš *m* (S.)
undesirable nèželjen
undisturbed nèsmetan
undo, to razvezívati [-vèzuje] I: razvézati [ràzveže] P
undo (open), **to** otvárati I: otvòriti P
undress, to svláčiti I: svúći [svúče] P
unearth, to iskopávati I: iskòpati P
uneasiness nèlagodnost *f*
uneasy nèlagodan-nèlagodni
unemployed nezàposlen
unequal nèjednak
unessential nèbitan-nèbitni
uneven nèravan-nèravni, nèjednak
unexpected neočèkivan
unfair nèpošten, nèpravedan-nèpravedni
unfavorable nèpovoljan - nèpovoljni, nèsklon
unfinished nèsvršen
unfit neprìkladan - neprìkladni, nèsposoban-nèsposobni
unfold, to šíriti I: raširiti P; otvárati I: otvòriti P
unforgettable nèzaboravan - nèzaboravni
unforgivable neopròstiv
unfortunate nèuspješan/nèuspešan - nèuspješni/nèuspešni, nèsretan - nèsretni (Cr.), nèsrećan-nèsrećni (S.)
unfortunately nà žalost
ungrateful nèzahvalan-nèzahvalni
unhappiness nèsreća *f*, jàd *m*
unhappy nèsretan-nèsretni (Cr.), nèsrećan-nèsrećni (S.)
unhealthy nèzdrav
unheard of nečùven, nèpoznat
uniform ùniforma *f*
uniform *adj.* jednòličan-jednòlični
unify, to ujedinjávati I: ujedíniti P
union sávez *m*
unique jedìnstven
unit jedìnica *f*, jèdinka *f*
unite, to ujedinjávati I: ujedíniti P
united ujèdinjen
United Nations Ujèdinjene Nácije *f pl.*
United States of America Sjèdinjene Amèričke Dřžave *f pl.*
unity jedínstvo *n*
universal òpći (Cr.), òpšti (S.), ùniverzalan-ùniverzalni
universe svèmir *m* (Cr.), vasìona *f* (S.), svìjet/svét *m*
university sveùčilište *n* (Cr.), univerzìtet *m* (S.)
unjust nèpravedan-nèpravedni
unkind nèljubazan-nèljubazni
unknown nèpoznat
unless àko ne, osim àko
unlike drùkčiji, drugàčiji
unlikely nèvjerojatno (Cr.), nèverovatno (S.)
unload, to iskrcávati I: iskr̀cati P
unlock, to otključávati I: otkljùčati P
unlucky nèsretan-nèsretni (Cr.), nèsrećan-nèsrećni (S.)
unmarried (man) nèoženjen
unmarried (woman) nèudata
unmistakable očèvidan-očèvidni
unmoved nèganut
unnecessary nèpotreban-nèpotrebni
unpaid nèplaćen
unpleasant nèprijatan-nèprijatni
unpopular nèpopularan-nèpopularni
unprejudiced bez prèdrasuda
unpublished neòbjavljen
unquestionable nèosporan-nèosporni
unreal nèstvaran-nèstvarni
unreasonable nèrazuman-nèrazumni
unrest nèmir *m*
unruly nèpokoran-nèpokorni, sàmovoljan-sàmovoljni
unsafe nèsiguran-nèsigurni
unsatisfactory nezadovoljávajući
unscrupulous bèzobziran-bèzobzirni
unseen nèviđen
unselfish nesèbičan-nesèbični
unsound nèzdrav
unspeakable neizrèciv
untidy nèuredan-nèuredni
until dòk (ne)
until *prep.* do (+ G)
untiring nèumoran-nèumorni
untrue nèistinit, làžan-làžni
unusual neòbičan-neòbični
unwanted nèželjen
unwilling neraspòložen
unwillingly nèrado
unworthy nedóstojan-nedóstojni
up gòre, nàviše
up to now dòsada *ili* dòsad
uphill ùzbrdo
uphold, to podùpirati [-pire] I: podùprijeti/podùpreti [pòdupre] P
upon na (+ A/D)
upper górnji, vìši
upright ùspravan-ùspravni
uproar vìka *f*, bùka *f*, métež *m*
upset uznèmiren
upset, to uznemirívati [-mìruje] (se) I: uznemíriti (se) P
upstairs na górnjem kàtu (Cr.), na górnjem spràtu (S.), gòre
upstart skoròjević *m*
uptight nàpet
up-to-date mòderan-mòderni, sùvremen (Cr.), sàvremen (S.)
upward(s) ùvis, prema gòre
urban gràdski
urge pòtreba *f*, hìtnost *f*, žèlja *f*
urge, to požurívati [-žùruje] I: požúriti P
urgency hìtnost *f*
urgent hìtan-hìtni
urinate, to mòkriti I: izmòkriti P
urine mòkraća *f*
us, all of mí svì
usage ùpotreba *f*, òbičaj *m*
use, to upotrebljávati I: upotrijèbiti/upotrébiti P
used upòtrijebljen/upòtrebljen
used to nàviknut
useful kòristan-kòrisni
usefully kòrisno
useless beskòristan-beskòrisni
usher vràtar *m*
usual òbičan-òbični
usually òbično
utensils príbor *m*
utility kòrist *f*, G kòristi
utilize, to kòristiti I: iskòristiti P
utmost krájnji
utter, to izúStiti P
utterance ìzreka *f*, rìječ/réč *f*

V v

vacancy praznìna *f*, ùpražnjeno mjèsto/mèsto *n*
vacant prázan-prázni, slòbodan-slòbodni
vacation práznici *m pl.* (Cr.), ráspust *m* (S.)
vaccinate, to vakcinírati I/P (Cr.), vakcìnisati [-niše] I/P (S.)
vaccination vakcinácija *f*
vacuum cleaner usisàvač za pràšinu *m*
vague neòdređen
vain (conceited) sùjetan-sùjetni
vain (useless) ùzaludan-ùzaludni
valentine ljùbavna čèstitka *f*
valiant hrábar-hrábri
valid vàžeći
validity vážnost *f*
valley dolìna *f*
valuable dragòcjen/dragòcen
value vrijèdnost/vrédnost *f*
vanish, to iščezávati I: iščeznuti P
vanity sùjeta *f*, taštìna *f*
vapor pàra *f*

variant varìjanta *f*
varied raznòlik
variety raznòlikost *f*, mnòštvo *n*
various rázličit
varnish làk *m*
vary, to mijènjati/ménjati I: izmijèniti/izméniti P
vase váza *f*
vast gòlem, ògroman-ògromni
vault svòd *m*
vault (safe) sèf *m*
veal tèletina *f*
veal *adj.* tèleći
vegetable pòvrće *n*
vegetarian vegeterijánac *m*, G -jánca
vegetation vegetácija *f*
vehement vàtren, žèstok
vehicle kòla *n pl.*, vòzilo *n*, àuto *m*
veil vèo *m*, G vèla; kòprena *f*
vein véna *f*, žìla *f*
velvet bàršun *m*, sàmt *m* (Cr.), sòmot *m* (S.)
venerable pòštovan
vengeance òsveta *f*
venison dìvljač *f*, sȑnetina *f*
venture rìzik *m*
venture, to usuđívati [usùđuje] se I: usúditi se P
verb glàgol *m*
verbal ùsmen
verdict prèsuda *f*
verse stìh *m*
versus protiv (+ G)
vertical òkomit
very veòma, mnògo, jáko
vessel (boat) láđa *f*; bród *m*, G bròda
vessel (container) pòsuda *f*, súd *m*
vest pȑsluk *m*, màja *f*, pòtkošulja *f*
veterinarian veterìnar *m*
veterinary veterìnarski
vex, to uznemirívati [-mìruje] I: uznemíriti P
vexation uznemirénje *n*, mùka *f*, neprijátnost *f*
via pútem (+ G)
vibrate, to tìtrati I: zàtitrati P
vibration tìtranje *n*, vibrácija *f*
vice pòrok *m*, mána *f*
vice president potprèdsjednik/potprèdsednik *m*
vice versa òbratno, òbrnuto
vicinity sùsjedstvo/sùsedstvo *n*
vicious òpak, zào-zlì
victim žȑtva *f*
victorious pòbjednički/pòbednički
victory pòbjeda/pòbeda *f*
Vienna Béč *m*
view pògled *m*, víd *m*, vìdokrug *m*
view, to promátrati I: promòtriti P
viewpoint stànovište *n*, glèdište *n*
vigor snága *f*, enèrgija *f*
vigorous snážan-snážni, enèrgičan-enèrgični
vile pòdao-pòdli
village sèlo *n*
village *adj.* sèljački
villain nìtkov *m*, hùlja *f*
vine lòza *f*, vìnova lòza *f*
vinegar òcat *m* (Cr.), G òcta; sìrće *n* (S.), G sìrćeta
vineyard vìnograd *m*
vintage lòza *f*
violate, to prekršávati I: prekȑšiti P
violation prèkršaj *m*
violence násilje *n*
violent nàsilan-nàsilni, žèstok
violently nàsilno, žèstoko
violet ljùbičica *f*
violet *adj.* ljùbičast
violin violína *f*
virgin djèvica/dèvica *f*
virtue vrlìna *f*
virtuous krèpostan-krèposni, čèstit
visa víza *f*
visibility vìdljivost *f*
visible vìdljiv
vision víd *m*
vision (apparition) priviđénje *n*, vízija *f*
visit pòsjeta/pòseta *f*, pòsjet/pòset *m*
visit, to posjećívati/posećívati [-ćuje] I: posjètiti/posètiti P
visitation posjećívanje/posećívanje *n*
visitor posjètilac/posètilac *m*, G -tioca
vital vìtalan-vìtalni, bìtan-bìtni
vitality vitálnost *f*, žìvotna snága *f*
vitamin vitàmin *m*
vivid žív, jàsan-jàsni
vocabulary rječnik/rèčnik *m*
vocation pòziv *m*, zanímanje *n*, sklònost *f*
vocational school strùčna škòla *f*
vocative (case) vòkativ *m*
vogue móda *f*
voice glás *m*
volcanic vùlkanski
volcano vùlkan *m*
volleyball òdbojka *f*
volt vòlt *m*
volume (book) tòm *m*
volume (size) obújam *m*, G obújma (Cr.); òbim *m* (S.)
voluntary dòbrovoljan-dòbrovoljni
voluptuous pòhotan-pòhotni, ràzbludan-ràzbludni
vomit, to pòvraćati I: povrátiti P
vomiting pòvraćanje *n*
vote glás *m*, glàsanje *n*
vote, to glàsati I: izglàsati P
voter glàsač *m*, bìrač *m*
voting glàsanje *n*, ìzbori *m pl.*
vow zákletva *f*, závjet/závet *m*
vow, to zàkljinjati [-klinje] se I: zàkleti [zakùne] se P
voyage putòvanje *n*, plòvidba *f*
(Bon) **voyage!** srètan pút! (Cr.), srèćan pút (S.)
vulgar vùlgaran-vùlgarni

W w

wag, to máhati [máše] I: máhnuti P
wage pláća *f* (Cr.), pláta *f* (S.)
wagon kòla *n pl.*
wail jàdikovka *f*
wail, to jàdikovati [-kuje] I
waist strúk *m*, pás *m*
wait, to čèkati I: pòčekati P
waiter kònobar *m* (Cr.), kèlner *m* (S.)
waitress kònobarica *f* (Cr.), kèlnerica *f* (S.)
wake, to búditi (se) I: probúditi (se) P
walk hódanje *n*, šétnja *f*
walk, to hódati I, šétati (se) I: prošétati (se) P
walker šètač *m*
wall zíd *m*
wallet lìsnica *f* (Cr.), novčànik *m*
walnut òrah *m*
wander, to lútati I, skítati (se) I: proskítati (se) P
want (desire) žèlja *f*
want (privation) òskudica *f*
want (desire), **to** žèljeti/žèleti [žèli] I: zažèljeti/zažèleti P
want (lack), **to** némati I
wanton òbijestan/òbestan-òbijesni/òbesni
war ràt *m*
war *adj.* ràtni, vòjnički
wardrobe (clothes) òdjeća/òdeća *f*
wares ròba *f*
warfare vojèvanje *n*, ràtovanje *n*
warlike ràtnički
warm tòpao-tòpli
warm, to grìjati/grèjati [grìje/grèje] I: zàgrijati/zàgrejati P
warmly sȑdačno, tòplo
warmth toplìna *f*, sȑdačnost *f*
warn, to opòminjati [-minje] I: opoménuti P
warning òpomena *f*
warrior ràtnik *m*; bórac *m*, G bórca
wash, to pràti [père] I: òprati P
washroom kùpaonica *f* (Cr.), kupàtilo *n* (S.)
washstand umìvaonik *m*
wasp òsa *f*
waste òtpadak *m*, G òtpatka
waste (land) pùstoš *f*, G pùstoši
waste, to ràsipati [ràsiplje] I: ràsuti [ràspe] P
watch sát *m*, čàsovnik *m*
watch (guard) stražárenje *n*
watch, to promátrati I: promòtriti P; pàziti I: prìpaziti P
watchful pàžljiv, òprezan-òprezni
watchman stràžar *m*, čùvar *m*
water vòda *f*
water (mineral) kìsela vòda *f*
water skiing skìjanje na vòdi *n*
watercolor vòdena bòja *f*, akvàrel *m*
waterfall sláp *m*, vòdopad *m*
watermelon lubènica *f*
waterproof nepromòčiv
watery vòden
wave vál *m* (Cr.), tàlas *m* (S.)
wave, to máhati [máše] I: máhnuti P
wax vòsak *m*, G vòska
way pút *m*, náčin *m*
way-out (*adj.*) bìzaran-bìzarni
we mí
weak slàb
weaken, to slàbiti I: òslabiti P
weakness slàbost *f*
wealth bògatstvo *n*
wealthy bògat
weapon òružje *n*
wear, to nòsiti I: iznòsiti P
weariness ùmor *m*, klònulost *f*
weary ìscrpljen
weather vrijème/vréme *n*
weave, to tkàti I: òtkati P
weaver tkálac *m*, G tkálca; tkálja *f*
web pàučina *f*, mrèža *f*
wed, to vjenčávati/venčávati (se) I: vjènčati/vènčati (se) P
wedding svàdba *f*, vjenčánje/venčánje *n*
wedding *adj.* svàdben
wedge klìn *m*
Wednesday srijèda/sréda *f*
wee màlen, sìćušan-sìćušni
weed kòrov *m*
week sèdmica *f*; tjèdan *m* (Cr.), G tjèdna; nèdelja *f* (S.)

weekly tjèdni (Cr.), nèdeljni (S.)
weep, to plàkati [plàče] I: ìsplakati se P
weigh, to mjèriti/mèriti I: ìzmjeriti/ ìzmeriti P
weight težìna *f*, tèret *m*
welcome dobrodòšlica *f*
welcome, to sr̀dačno dočekívati [-čèkuje] I: sr̀dačno dòčekati P
welfare dòbrobit *f*
well bùnar *m*, ìzvor *m*
well *adv*. dòbro
west západ *m*
western západni
wet mòkar–mòkri
whale kìt *m*
what štò (Cr.), štà (S.)
whatever što gòd, bílo štò
whatsoever bílo štò, štò mu drágo
wheat pšènica *f*
wheel kòlo *f*; kòtač *m* (Cr.); tòčak *m* (S.), G tòčka
wheel (steering) vòlan *m*
when kàda *ili* kàd
whenever kad gòd, bílo kàda
where gdjè/gdè
where to kàmo, kùda
whereby pòmoću čèga
whereupon nàšto, zàtim
wherever bílo gdjè/bílo gdè
whether li, dà li, bílo da
which kòji *m* (kòje *n*, kòja *f*)
while dòk
whip bìč *m*
whip, to bičèvati [bìčuje] I: izbičèvati P
whiskey vìski *m*, G vìskija
whisper šàpat *m*
whisper, to šàptati [šàpće] I: šàpnuti P
whistle zvìždukm
whistle, to zvízdati [zvížđi] I: zazvíždati P
white bìo *ili* bìjel/bèo–bìjeli/béli
whiten, to bijèliti/béliti I: pobijèliti/ pobéliti P
who tkò (Cr.), kò (S.)
whoever tko gòd (Cr.), ko gòd (S.)
whole cjelìna/celìna *f*
whole *adj*. pòtpun, čìtav
wholesome zdràv
wholly pòtpuno, sàsvim
whose čiji *m* (čìje *n*, čìja *f*)
why zàšto
wicked zào–zlì, zlòčest
wickedness zlòća *f*, zlòba *f*
wide šìrok
widen, to šíriti I: prošíriti P
widow udòvica *f*
widower udòvac *m*, G udóvca
width širìna *f*
wife sùpruga *f*, žèna *f*
wig vlàsulja *f*, pèrika *f*
wild dìvlji
wild beast zvijer/zvér *f*, zvìjer/zvér *m*
wilderness divljìna *f*, pùstoš *f*
will vòlja *f*, žèlja *f*
will (document) testàment *m*; testàmenat *m*, G -menta
willful svojèglav
willing vòljan–vòljni, sklòn
willow vŕba *f*
win, to pobjeđívati/pobeđívati [-đuje] I: pobijèditi/pobéditi P
wind vjètar/vètar *m*, G vjètra/vètra
window prózor *m*
windshield vjètrobran/vètrobran *m*
windshield wiper brìsač *m*
windy vjetròvit/vetròvit
wing krílo *n*
wink, to trèptati [trèpće] I: zatrèptati P
winner pòbjednik/pòbednik *m*
winter zíma *f*
winter *adj*. zímski
wipe, to brìsati [brìše] I: ìzbrisati P
wire žìca *f*
wisdom mùdrost *f*
wise múdar–múdri
wish žèlja *f*
wish, to žèljeti/žèleti I: zažèljeti/ zažèleti P
wit duhòvitost *f*, oštròumnost *f*
witch vjèštica/vèštica *f*
with s *ili* sa (+ I)
withdraw, to povláčiti (se) I: povúći [povúče] (se) P
withdrawal odstúpanje *n*, povláčenje *n*
withhold, to zadržávati I: zadr̀žati [zadr̀ži] P
within *adv*. ùnutra
without *prep*. bez (+ G)
withstand, to odùpirati [odùpire] se I: odùprijeti/odùpreti [òdupre] se P
witness svjèdok/svèdok *m*
witness, to svjedòčiti/svedòčiti I: posvjedòčiti/posvedòčiti P
witty duhòvit
wizard čaròbnjak *m*
woe jàd *m*, túga *f*
wolf vúk *m*, N *pl*. vúci *ili* vùkovi
woman žèna *f*
wonder čùđenje *n*, čùdo *n*
wonder (ask oneself), **to** pítati se I: zapítati se P
wonder (marvel), **to** čùditi se I: začùditi se P
wonderful prèkrasan–prèkrasni
wondrous čùdesan–čùdesni
wood dȑvo *n*, G dȑveta
wooded pòšumljen
wooden dȑven
woodpecker žúna *f*
woods šùma *f*
wool vùna *f*
woolen vùnen
word rìječ/réč *f*, G rìječi/réči
work rád *m*; pòsao *n*, G pòsla
work, to ráditi I: odráditi P
worker rádnik *m*, rádnica *f*
workman rádnik *m*, rádnica *f*
workmanship rád *m*, izradba *f* (Cr.)
workshop ràdionica *f*
world svìjet/svét *m*
worldly svjètski/svètski, svjètovan/ svètovan–svjètovni/svètovni
worm cȑv *m*
worn out ìznošen
worry brìga *f*
worry, to brìnuti [brìne] se I: zàbrinuti se P
worse gòri, lòšiji
worship obožávanje *n*, bogoslúženje *n*
worship, to obožávati I
worst nájgori, nájlòšiji
worth vrijèdnost/vrédnost *f*
worth *adj*. záslužan–záslužni
worthless bèzvrijedan/bèzvredan–bèzvrijedni/bèzvredni
worthy zásluzan–zásluzni, pòštovan
wound ràna *f*
wound, to ranjávati I: ràniti P
wounded rànjen
woven tkán
wow *excl*. jòj, jào
wrap, to umotávati I: umòtati P
wreath vijènac/vénac *m*, G vijènca/ vénca
wreck (person) pròpao čòvjek/čòvek *m*
wreck (ship) bròdolom *m*
wreck, to rùšiti I, srùšiti I
wrestle, to r̀vati se I: por̀vati se P
wrestler r̀vač *m*
wrestling r̀vanje *n*
wretch jàdnik *m*, bìjednik/bédnik *m*
wretched jàdan–jàdni
wrinkle bóra *f*, nábor *m*
wrist zglòb *m*, člának na rúci *m*
write, to písati [píše] I: napísati P
writer písac *m*, G písca
writing písanje *n*
writing *adj*. pìsaći
written nàpisan
wrong nèpravda *f*
wrong *adj*. pògrešan–pògrešni
wrong, to čìniti nèpravdu I: učìniti nèpravdu P
wrongly pògrešno

Y y

yacht jàhta *f*
yard dvòrište *n*
yard *adj*. dvòrišni
yawn, to zijèvati/zévati I: zijèvnuti/ zévnuti P
year gòdina *f*
yearly gòdišnji
yeast kvásac *m*, G kvásca
yell vrísak *m*, G vríska; krík *m*
yell, to víkati [více] I: víknuti P
yellow žút
yes dà, jè (Cr.), jèste (S.)
yesterday jùčer (Cr.), jùče (S.)
yesterday evening sìnoć
yet jòš, ìpak
yield plód *m*, G plòda; ljètina/lètina *f*
yield, to popúštati I: popùstiti P
yield, to (give) dávati [dáje] I: dàti [dáde] P
yoke járam *m*, G járma
yolk žumánce *n*, G žumánceta
you tí (sg.), ví (pl.)
young mlád
young man mlàdić *m*
your tvòj, vàš
yourself tí sám, ví sámi
yourselves ví sámi
youth mlàdost *f*, òmladina *f*, mlađàrija *f*
youthful mlád, mlàdenački
Yugoslav Jugoslàven *m* (Cr.), Jugoslòven *m* (S.), Jugoslàvenka *f* (Cr.), Jugoslòvenka *f* (S.)
Yugoslav *adj*. jugoslàvenski (Cr.), jugoslòvenski (S.)
Yugoslavia Jugoslávija *f*

Z z

Zagreb Zágreb *m*
Zagreb *adj*. zágrebački
Zagreb native Zágrepčanin *m*, Zágrepčanka *f*
zeal žár *m*, prèdanost *f*
zealous vàtren, odùševljen
zebra zèbra *f*
zero nùla *f*
zest oduševljénje *n*
zigzag cìkcak *m*
zipper pàtent *m* (Cr.), ràjsferšlus *m* (S.)
zone zóna *f*, pòjas *m*
zoo zoòloški vȑt *m*
zoology zoològija *f*

For additional English-to-CR&S entries

Index

Note: Information about purchasing tape recordings for this book may be obtained by calling 800–770–2111 or by writing to this address: Penn State Media Sales, 118 Wagner Building, University Park, PA 16802.